INTERNATIONAL DIMENSION
OF
POST-COMMUNIST
TRANSITIONS
IN
RUSSIA
AND THE
NEW STATES
OF EURASIA

THE INTERNATIONAL POLITICS OF EURASIA

Editors:
Karen Dawisha and Bruce Parrott

Volume 1
The Legacy of History in Russia and the New States of Eurasia
Edited by S. Frederick Starr

Volume 2
National Identity and Ethnicity in Russia and the New States of Eurasia
Edited by Roman Szporluk

Volume 3
The Politics of Religion in Russia and the New States of Eurasia
Edited by Michael Bourdeaux

Volume 4
The Making of Foreign Policy in Russia and the New States of Eurasia
Edited by Adeed Dawisha and Karen Dawisha

Volume 5
State Building and Military Power in Russia and the New States of Eurasia
Edited by Bruce Parrott

Volume 6
The Nuclear Challenge in Russia and the New States of Eurasia
Edited by George Quester

Volume 7
Political Culture and Civil Society in Russia and the New States of Eurasia
Edited by Vladimir Tismaneanu

Volume 8
Economic Transition in Russia and the New States of Eurasia
Edited by Bartlomiej Kaminski

Volume 9
**The End of Empire? The Transformation of the USSR
in Comparative Perspective**
Edited by Karen Dawisha and Bruce Parrott

Volume 10
**The International Dimension of Post-Communist Transitions
in Russia and the New States of Eurasia**
Edited by Karen Dawisha

THE INTERNATIONAL POLITICS OF EURASIA
Volume 10

THE INTERNATIONAL DIMENSION OF POST-COMMUNIST TRANSITIONS IN RUSSIA AND THE NEW STATES OF EURASIA

Editor:
Karen Dawisha

M.E. Sharpe
Armonk, New York
London, England

Library of Congress Cataloging-in-Publication Data

The international dimension of post-Communist transitions in Russia and the new states of Eurasia / edited by Karen Dawisha.
    p.   cm. — (The International politics of Eurasia : v. 10)
    Includes bibliographical references and index.
    ISBN 1-56324-370-9 (cloth : alk. paper).
    ISBN 1-56324-371-7 (pbk. : alk. paper)
    1. Former Soviet republics—foreign relations. 2. World politics—1989–   .   3. Former Soviet republics—Politics and government. 4. Former Soviet republics—Economic conditions. 5. Economic assistance—Former Soviet republics. 6. National security—Former Soviet republics. I. Dawisha, Karen. II. Series.
            DK293.I57   1997
        327.47—dc21   6-36919
                CIP
    Printed in the United States of America

The paper used in this publication meets the minimum requirements of American National Standard for Information Sciences— Permanence of Paper for Printed Library Materials, ANSI Z 39.48-1984.

BM (c)   10   9   8   7   6   5   4   3   2   1
BM (p)   10   9   8   7   6   5   4   3   2   1

Contents

About the Editors and Contributors

Karen Dawisha is professor of government and director of the Center for the Study of Post-Communist Societies at the University of Maryland, College Park. She graduated with degrees in Russian and politics from the University of Lancaster in England and received her Ph.D. from the London School of Economics. She has served as an advisor to the British House of Commons Foreign Affairs Committee and was a member of the policy planning staff of the U.S. State Department. Her publications include *Russia and the New States of Eurasia: The Politics of Upheaval* (coauthored with Bruce Parrott, 1994), *Eastern Europe, Gorbachev, and Reform: The Great Challenge* (1989, 2d ed., 1990), *The Kremlin and the Prague Spring* (1984), *The Soviet Union in the Middle East: Politics and Perspectives* (1982), *Soviet-East European Dilemmas: Coercion, Competition, and Consent* (1981), and *Soviet Foreign Policy Toward Egypt* (1979).

Bruce Parrott is professor and director of Russian Area and East European Studies at the Johns Hopkins University School of Advanced International Studies, where he has taught for twenty years. He received his B.A. in religious studies from Pomona College in 1966, and his Ph.D. in political science in 1976 from Columbia University, where he was assistant director of the Russian Institute. His publications include *Russia and the New States of Eurasia: The Politics of Upheaval* (coauthored with Karen Dawisha, 1994), *The Dynamics of Soviet Defense Policy* (1990), *The Soviet Union and Ballistic Missile Defense* (1987), *Trade, Technology and Soviet-American Relations* (1985), and *Politics and Technology in the Soviet Union* (1983).

George W. Breslauer is professor of political science and chair of the Program in Soviet and Post-Soviet Studies at the University of California at Berkeley, where he has taught since 1971. He is the author or editor of ten books, as well as dozens of scholarly articles on Soviet and post-Soviet politics and foreign policy. He is a member of the Council on Foreign Relations and the World

Affairs Council of Northern California, and is currently editor in chief of the quarterly journal *Post-Soviet Affairs*.

Yitzhak M. Brudny is assistant professor of political science at Yale University. He received his Ph.D. from Princeton University in 1992. He is the author of *Reinventing Russia: Russian Nationalism in Soviet and Post-Soviet Politics* (forthcoming, 1997). His published works deal with political leaders, intellectuals, social movements, parties, and elections in late Soviet and post-Soviet Russia.

Peter Dombrowski is assistant professor of political science at Iowa State University. He was recently a Federal Chancellor's Scholar of the Alexander von Humboldt Foundation in Bonn, Germany. His latest book is *Policy Responses to the Globalization of American Banking* (1996).

Murray Feshbach is a research professor at Georgetown University. He has served as chief of the USSR Population, Employment, and Research and Development branch of the Foreign Demographic Analysis Division of the U.S. Bureau of the Census, a Fellow of the Kennan Institute of the Woodrow Wilson International Center for Scholars, and a consultant to the World Bank on health problems in the former Soviet Union. Dr. Feshbach has published over one hundred articles and books, including *Ecocide in the USSR: Health and Nature Under Siege* (coauthored with Alfred Friendly Jr., 1992) and *Ecological Disaster: Cleaning Up the Hidden Legacy of the Soviet Regime* (1995).

Raymond L. Garthoff is a retired diplomat and diplomatic historian at the Brookings Institution, Washington, DC. He is the author of many works, including *Detente and Confrontation: American-Soviet Relations from Nixon to Reagan* (rev. ed., 1994) and *The Great Transition: American-Soviet Relations and the End of the Cold War* (1994).

Bartlomiej Kaminski is associate professor of government at the University of Maryland at College Park. He received his Ph.D. from the University of Warsaw in 1972. Dr. Kaminski has previously taught at the Johns Hopkins University, the University of Beijing, and the University of Warsaw. He was the director of the Center for the Study of Post-Communist Societies at the University of Maryland. Dr. Kaminski has also been a consultant to the World Bank since 1991. He has written numerous journal articles and book chapters. He is the editor of *Economic Transition in Russia and the New States of Eurasia* (volume 8 of *The International Politics of Eurasia*, 1996). His latest book is *The Collapse of State Socialism: The Case of Poland* (1991).

Kemal H. Karpat is distinguished professor of history and professor of Middle-East studies in the Department of History at the University of Wisconsin. He is the editor of the *International Journal of Turkish Studies* and president of the Association of Central Asian Studies, founded in 1985. He is the author of numerous books and articles on Turkey and Central Asia. He was most recently the editor of, and a contributor to, the 1994 volume of *Central Asian Survey*. He is also a contributor to *The Making of Foreign Policy in Russia and the New States of Eurasia* (volume 4 of *The International Politics of Eurasia* series, 1995).

Nancy Lubin is president of JNA Associates, Inc., and adjunct professor at Carnegie Mellon University. She received her B.A. from Harvard University and her Ph.D. from Oxford University. Dr. Lubin has served as associate professor at Carnegie Mellon University, a fellow at the U.S. Institute of Peace, a fellow at the Woodrow Wilson International Center for Scholars, and a project director and Sovietologist for the Congressional Office of Technology Assessment. She is the author of many books, congressional reports, and articles on Central Asia and the former USSR.

Michael MccGwire served as a senior fellow at the Brookings Institution from 1979 to 1990 and subsequently as the MacArthur Professor in the Global Security Programme at Cambridge University, where he remains a fellow in its Faculty of Social and Political Sciences. His publications include *Military Objectives in Soviet Foreign Policy* (1987) and *Perestroika and Soviet National Security* (1991).

George H. Quester is professor of government and politics at the University of Maryland, where he teaches courses on international relations, defense policy, and American foreign policy. Dr. Quester is the author of a number of books and articles on international relations and international security issues. He is the editor of *The Nuclear Challenge in Russia and the New States of Eurasia* (volume 6 of *The International Politics of Eurasia,* 1995) and coauthor of an article in *Economic Transition in Russia and the New States of Eurasia.*

Gilbert Rozman is Musgrave Professor of Sociology and director of the Council on Regional Studies at Princeton University. In 1996–97, he is a fellow at the Woodrow Wilson International Center for Scholars. His recent research has focused on regionalism in Northeast Asia.

Alvin Z. Rubinstein is professor of political science at the University of Pennsylvania and a senior fellow at the Foreign Policy Research Institute. His publications include: *Moscow's Third World Strategy* (1988) and *Regional Rivalries in the New Eurasia* (coeditor, 1995). His most recent publication is a coauthored book, *Russian Foreign Policy: From Empire to Nation-State* (1997).

Gertrude Schroeder is professor of economics emeritus at the University of Virginia. She is the author of numerous publications on the economy of the former Soviet Union and the economies of the post-Soviet states, including an article in *Economic Transition in Russia and the New States of Eurasia.* Dr. Schroeder focuses primarily on economic performance and reform.

Robert Sharlet is Chauncey Winters Professor of political science at Union College, and a member of the Professional Advisory Board of the Harriman Institute at Columbia University. From 1994 to 1996, he served as senior coordinator of the Rule of Law Consortium under the auspices of the U.S. Agency for International Development. His most recent book is *Soviet Constitutional Crisis* (1992).

Angela Stent is associate professor of government at Georgetown University. She has published widely on Soviet relations with Europe, East–West trade, and post-Soviet developments. Her latest book deals with German unification and the evolution of Russian–German relations in Europe.

Michael Turner is a Ph.D. candidate in the Department of Government and Politics at the University of Maryland at College Park and is currently teaching at Washington College (Chestertown, MD) and at George Mason University (Fairfax, VA). He is the coauthor of an article in *Political Culture and Civil Society in Russia and the New States of Eurasia* (volume 7 of *The International Politics of Eurasia,* 1995). He has a fellowship from the Institute for the Study of World Politics to complete his dissertation, entitled "Harsh Boundaries: The Politics of Illiberalism in Post-Communist Societies."

Celeste A. Wallander is associate professor of government and faculty associate at the Davis Center for Russian Studies and the Center for International Affairs at Harvard University. She received her B.A. in political science from Northwestern University and her Ph.D. from Yale University. She has written on Soviet use of military force and the rise and fall of Soviet interventionism. She is editor of *The Sources of Russian Foreign Policy after the Cold War* (1996) and is finishing a book on the role of international institutions in Russian–German security relations after the Cold War.

Zhen Kun Wang is a consultant working on the World Bank's *World Development Report* and was formerly a consultant to the Transition Economics Division in the Policy Research Department of the World Bank. She is the coauthor of *Foreign Trade in the Transition: The International Environment and Domestic Policy* (1996).

Preface

This book is the last in a series of ten volumes produced by the Russian Littoral Project, sponsored jointly by the University of Maryland at College Park and the Paul H. Nitze School of Advanced International Studies of the Johns Hopkins University. As directors of the project, we share the conviction that the transformation of the former Soviet republics into independent states demands systematic analysis of the determinants of the domestic and foreign policies of the new countries. This series of volumes is intended to provide a basis for comprehensive scholarly study of these issues.

This volume was shaped by our view that despite the dramatic growth of high-quality Western scholarship on post-Soviet developments, the interaction between external influences and trends in Russia and the other post-Soviet countries has not received systematic scholarly analysis. The influence of outside actors on post-Soviet affairs is poorly understood, although vigorous assertions about the connection are regularly voiced in response to Western policy makers' unavoidable need to deal with new developments in Eurasia. The lack of systematic study is due partly to the short interval that has elapsed since the breakup of the USSR, but it has other causes as well.

Most Western observers have yet to recognize the general need for systematic study of the interaction between the post-Soviet states and the outside world. To a large extent, Western specialists on the successor states have devoted their efforts to charting the torrents of exciting events inside these countries, leaving little time for broader-gauged studies. In addition, scholarly observers have always found it difficult to analyze international affairs as a process of interaction among decisions made in many states, rather than as the decisions taken by one state in response to other states whose policies are assumed to be more or less permanently fixed. In other words, the analysis of international relations has often been confused with the analysis of a given nation's foreign policy. Partly as a consequence, U.S. observers eager to influence American foreign policy have usually treated the issue of outside interaction with the post-Soviet states on a fragmentary, case-by-case basis. In addition, some of these observers have been preoccupied with the persisting controversy over whether to credit past U.S. administrations for the breakup of the Soviet empire—a topic that, though important, has tended to obscure the more urgent subject of post-1991 interactions between the Soviet successor states and the outside world. By adopting an interactive approach to the analysis of developments in Russia and the other new states of Eurasia, this volume will help remedy this critical deficiency in Western knowledge.

The purpose of the volume, and of the conference upon which it was based, was to provide a careful analysis of the following general issues: the content and evolution of the policies adopted by major international actors toward post-Soviet states; the linkages among the policies of these outside actors; and the nature and determinants of the responses to these policies from the Soviet successor states. Policy makers and citizens need a better grasp of the impact of external efforts to influence the domestic development and policies of the post-Soviet states. The main questions to be analyzed in this volume include the following: (1) How have international influences affected the approaches of the Soviet successor states to global and regional security issues, internal democratization, and the transition to capitalism? (2) In what particular instances have external policies actually advanced post-Soviet reforms, had no discernible impact, or provoked a counterproductive domestic backlash in the new states? and (3) Has a given state attached the greatest importance to promoting Eurasian diplomatic stability, democratization, or economic reform—aims that are sometimes contradictory rather than mutually reinforcing? The formulation of effective future external policies, whether toward the building of durable and democratic institutions, the granting of International Monetary Fund (IMF) loans, or NATO expansion, presupposes a sophisticated grasp of the ways in which Russia and the other new states are likely to respond to the initiatives of international actors.

We would like to thank the contributors to this volume for their help in making this phase of the Russian Littoral Project a success and for revising their papers in a timely fashion. We would also like to express our gratitude to the discussants, who prepared detailed written comments on the papers and greatly assisted in giving the conference coherence and momentum: George Breslauer, University of California at Berkeley; Daniel Kaufmann, Harvard University; Andrei Kortunov, Russian Science Foundation; Ambassador Jack Matlock, Columbia University; Michael MccGwire, Cambridge University; George Quester, University of Maryland; and Nikolai Rudensky, Institute for the Economy in Transition, Moscow.

We would also like to thank the MacArthur Foundation and the Smith Richardson Foundation for cosponsoring the conference. We would also like to thank the University of Maryland's Center for the Study of Post-Communist Societies and the Harrison Program on the Future Global Agenda for their assistance in sponsoring the conference. In addition, we are grateful to Janine Draschner and Trevor Wysong, the two executive directors of the Russian Littoral Project, for their skillful handling of the complex logistics of the conference on which this book is based and for their unstinting labor in preparing the final manuscript. For their invaluable assistance with the preparation of this book, we also thank Stephen Deets, Darya Pushkina, Melissa Rosser, and Michael Turner, all at the University of Maryland.

Russian Littoral Project

The objective of the Russian Littoral Project has been to foster an exchange of research and information in fields of study pertaining to the international politics of Eurasia. The interaction between the internal affairs and foreign policies of the new states has been studied in a series of workshops that took place in Washington, DC, San Diego, London, Central Asia, Ukraine, and other locations between 1993 and 1996. Over five hundred scholars, practitioners, and students were invited from the new states, North America, and Europe to present papers at the workshops.

Focusing on the interaction between the internal affairs and the foreign relations of the new states, the project workshops examined the impact of the following factors: history, national identity and ethnicity, religion, political culture and civil society, economics, foreign policy priorities and decision making, military issues, the nuclear question, and the comparative study of imperial collapse and the reconstitution of multinational states.

The Russian Littoral Project could not have been launched without the generous and timely contributions of the project's Coordinating Committee. We wish to thank the committee members for providing invaluable advice and expertise concerning the organization and intellectual substance of the project. The members of the Coordinating Committee are: Dr. Adeed Dawisha (George Mason University); Dr. Bartek Kaminski (University of Maryland and The World Bank); Dr. Catherine Kelleher (The Brookings Institution and the Department of Defense); Ms. Judith Kipper (The Brookings Institution and the Center for Strategic and International Studies); Dr. Nancy Lubin (Carnegie Mellon University and JNA Associates); Dr. Michael Mandelbaum (The School of Advanced International Studies); Dr. James Millar (The George Washington University); Dr. Peter Murrell (University of Maryland); Dr. Martha Brill Olcott (Colgate University); Dr. Ilya Prizel (The School of Advanced International Studies); Dr. George Quester (University of Maryland); Dr. Alvin Z. Rubinstein (University of Pennsylvania); Dr. Blair Ruble (The Kennan Institute); Dr. S. Frederick Starr (The Aspen Institute and the School of Advanced International Studies); Dr. Roman Szporluk (Harvard University); and Dr. Vladimir Tismaneanu (University of Maryland).

For funding the workshops on which several other volumes are based, we express our thanks to the MacArthur Foundation (particularly Kennette Benedict and Andrew Kuchins), the Pew Charitable Trusts (particularly Kevin Quigley and Peter Benda), the Smith Richardson Foundation (especially Mark Steinmeyer), the National Endowment for the Humanities, and the Ford Foundation (in particular Geoffrey Wiseman).

We also wish to thank President William Kirwan of the University of Maryland at College Park and President William C. Richardson of The Johns Hopkins University, who have given indispensable support to the project. Thanks are also due to Dean Irwin Goldstein, Associate Dean Stewart Edelstein, Director of the Office of International Affairs Marcus Franda, and Department of Government and Politics Chair Jonathan Wilkenfeld at the University of Maryland at College Park; to Provost Joseph Cooper and Vice-Provost for Academic Planning and Budget Stephen M. McClain at The Johns Hopkins University; to Professor George Packard, who helped launch the project during his final year as dean of the School of Advanced International Studies (SAIS), as well as to Dean Paul D. Wolfowitz and to Associate Dean Stephen Szabo, of the SAIS. Above all, Janine Draschner, who served as executive director of the project for four years, has our deepest thanks and respect for her endless patience, energy, and skill in sustaining the heavy burden of fund-raising, conference organization, and manuscript preparation throughout the heaviest phase of the project. In addition to Janine, a number of graduate and undergraduate students and staff members worked on the project throughout its four years, and we would like to single them out for praise and thanks: Ibrahim Arafat, Richard Cleland, Stephen Deets, Griffin Hathaway, Todd Perry, Darya Pushkina, Melissa Rosser, Michael Turner, Stacy VanDeveer, and Trevor Wysong at the University of Maryland and at SAIS, Florence Rotz and Stephen Guenther.

Finally, we are grateful to all the many staff at M.E. Sharpe who worked on the series throughout: above all to Patricia Kolb, whose knowledge of the area was matched only by her skill, good humor, and patience in shepherding the volumes through their various phases, to Ana Erlic and Elizabeth Granda for turning out really first-quality books, and to Evelyn Fazio, Carmen Chetti, Sue Lobel, Pat Zevola, Joan Zurell, Carol Johnson, Jim Gullikson, Margaret Dengler, Rosalie Kearns, Beth Levine, and Nancy Connick for all their assistance.

Karen Dawisha
University of Maryland
at College Park

Bruce Parrott
The Johns Hopkins University
School of Advanced International Studies

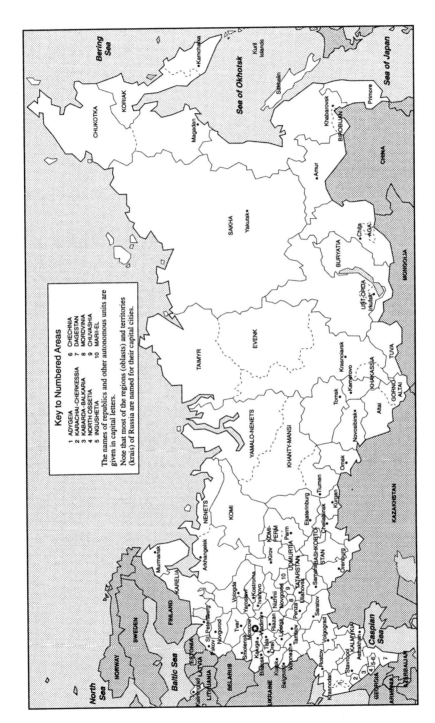

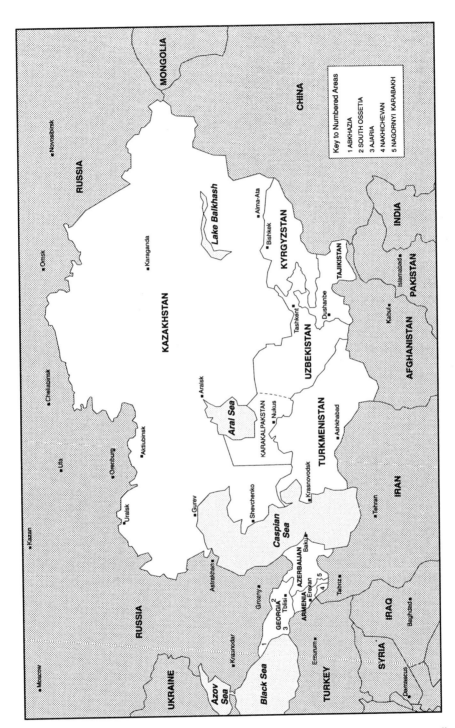

Key to Numbered Areas
1 ABKHAZIA
2 SOUTH OSSETIA
3 AJARIA
4 NAKHICHEVAN
5 NAGORNYI KARABAKH

THE
INTERNATIONAL DIMENSION
OF
POST-COMMUNIST
TRANSITIONS
IN
RUSSIA
AND THE
NEW STATES OF EURASIA

1

The Impact of the International Environment

Theoretical and Methodological Considerations

George W. Breslauer

The dramatic processes of change taking place in the newly independent states (NIS) of the former Soviet Union have generated a huge literature. Most such studies have been devoted to describing the changes. And most have focused principally on the *internal* determinants of the transformations taking place in that part of the world. This is understandable, given the powerful domestic forces—social, cultural, ethnic, and economic—unleashed by the collapse of communism, the dissolution of the Warsaw Pact and the Council on Mutual Economic Assistance (Comecon), and the disintegration of the Soviet Union. It also accords with an intuitive sense, shared by most specialists on comparative politics, that domestic factors are more likely to determine the trajectory of a country's development than are international influences. For these reasons, the first nine volumes in the important series coordinated by Karen Dawisha and Bruce Parrott have concentrated primarily—at points exclusively—on the internal determinants of change in both the domestic and foreign policies of these new states.

Sensibly, the present volume is devoted to somewhat righting the imbalance. The present volume takes an outside-in approach, exploring the international influences that have impinged on these states since 1991, and evaluating the extent to which those influences have shaped the trajectory of change within those states.

To be sure, a single volume could hardly do justice to such a huge topic. Where once there existed a single state—the USSR—there now stand fifteen juridically independent states. Those states, moreover, are very diverse in the extent and direction of changes undergone since the collapse of communism. Descriptive generalizations about the Baltic states scarcely apply to many of the states of what used to be called Soviet Central Asia. The scope of changes in

Armenia and Georgia is quite different from that in Belarus and Moldova. Hence, if the goal is to assess the impact of external influences, the "dependent variable" (that which is being influenced) is bound to vary greatly among the states in question. We do not have the luxury of easy generalizations about the causal impact of international factors on the newly independent states.

Moreover, the collapse of communism has ushered in a period during which many of these states are facing a plenitude of challenges, each of which may be affected differentially by international influences. While the casual observer may speak of the challenge of building "market democracies," closer inspection reveals that, additionally, these countries face the challenges of constructing new national identities and infusing these in their populations (nation building), of building state administrations that reliably coordinate public affairs (state building), of demilitarizing and restructuring (not just marketizing and privatizing) their economies, and of redefining their places in the international political and economic orders. All of these are long-term, transformative challenges that are being addressed differentially, and to varying degrees, in the new states of Eurasia.

In addition, almost all these states face short-term, circumstantial threats that urgently require amelioration. The need for environmental cleanup, though taking different forms, has reached emergency proportions throughout much of Russia, Ukraine, Belarus, and Central Asia. The threat of another nuclear accident on the order of the Chernobyl disaster of April 1986 is very real in Russia, Ukraine, Belarus, Lithuania, and Armenia. Toxic waste disposal is an ever-present challenge. The threat of the proliferation of nuclear weapons or nuclear materials is pervasive in the region. Health and health-care crises are pervasive as well.

A focus on systemic transformations and circumstantial crises can divert attention from still another way of conceiving the dependent variable: specific collectivities within the societies in question. When we discuss the success of marketization, democratization, nation building, state building, and demilitarization, we typically employ measures of progress that aggregate across sectors and collectivities. That is perhaps appropriate in specifying the extent to which a new system has come into being. But if we instead inquire into the subsets of the population that are the "winners" and the "losers" from the changes taking place, we have embraced a very different dependent variable. We might then explore the gender, ethnic, and/or class impact of the changes. Only a normative bias would lead one to define the systemic approach as intrinsically superior to the more socially differentiated focus. Hence, the first question to ask about the impact of the outside world is: "Impact on what?"[1]

In sum, when we reflect on the dependent variable for this volume, and for others that might follow, we must be very careful to specify the object of our study: Which countries are we considering? Which changes within those countries? Which of the several system-transformative challenges? Which of the circumstantial-ameliorative challenges? Which of the social collectivities that are affected by each of these?

Similar degrees of specificity are needed in identifying the independent variable for the study. Consider the several ways in which we might operationalize the concept, "the outside world." There are the constants: those features of the international political, military, cultural, and economic orders that are not likely to change, or to be willfully sacrificed, in the near term. Put differently, the international system has an impact on changes in the newly independent states regardless of the actions of governments. That system is today marked by a capitalist global economy in which much of the world's wealth and capital is concentrated, and in which multinational corporations make investment decisions, based on predictable criteria, that lead to a striking diffusion of capital, technologies, and products. The current international system is marked by a military order dominated by a nuclear superpower—the United States—and by many rising middle powers. It is marked by a cultural order dominated by Western mass-cultural products—from rock stars to athletic heroes to Hollywood movies to McDonald's hamburgers—and by international communication systems, such as CNN and the Internet, capable of instantly diffusing awareness of those products. Thus, when the Iron Curtain collapsed and fifteen new states mobilized to shape their futures, it was inevitable that their awareness of the brave new world they were entering would affect the hopes, fears, and perceptions of elites and masses alike. It was also inevitable that, to some extent, their options would be constrained willy-nilly by the broad contours of the international orders they were entering. From this standpoint, it was perhaps understandable that the euphoric anticipation of joining the West would be replaced within a few years by a certain measure of disillusion about the speed, extent, and costs of such an effort.

Another constant in the outside world was the geographic reality that Russia and the newly independent states bordered on *regional* orders or subsystems that could exercise significant influence on their domestic and foreign policy evolution. For Russia, attention would necessarily focus on both the European and East Asian regional orders, including, importantly, the Sino-Russian relationship and its interconnectedness with the East Asian wealth concentrated in Japan, South Korea, and Taiwan. Ukraine and Belarus, like Russia and the Baltic states, would necessarily be influenced greatly by the evolution of the all-European integration process. For the states of Central Asia, relations with the Muslim world would necessarily loom large from both a cultural and an economic standpoint. The fate of the Baltic states would necessarily be affected, perhaps determined, by their relationship with the states of northern Europe and Scandinavia. And all of the fourteen states other than Russia would have to face perhaps the dominant external influence on their trajectories of change: the looming presence of Great Russia itself. To be sure, none of these regional orders was either homogeneous or static; they were marked by internal conflicts and constant evolution and uncertainty. But their existence as points of concentration of diverse cultural, economic, political, and military forces was undeniable. In that respect they were constants that were bound to provide both opportunities and constraints. Policy changes and negotiated bargains were likely to take place within the parameters established by those preexisting constellations.

When we inquire into the impact of external factors on post-communist change, we may also concentrate on the variables: policies and choices made abroad that may have a direct positive or negative impact on post-communist changes. Those variables would include: (1) the official policies of other governments; (2) the policies of multilateral governmental groupings, such as the United Nations, the G-7 states, the Organization for Security and Cooperation in Europe (OSCE), The Organization of Petroleum Exporting Countries (OPEC), the Association of Southeast Asian Nations (ASEAN), etc.; (3) the policy choices of multilateral, nongovernmental organizations such as the World Bank, the International Monetary Fund (IMF), and the European Bank for Reconstruction and Development (EBRD); and (4) the decisions of single, nongovernmental actors, such as corporations, foundations, citizens' action organizations, and the like.

Suppose we have been careful to specify both the dependent and the independent variables that interest us. How then do we assess the causal relationship between the two? While diverse methodologies could be employed, the task is complicated by the short time frame within which we are working: 1991 to the present. This time frame makes it difficult to gather the evidence required to assess even the immediate impact of external influences. More importantly in the case of systemic transformation, short time frames make it difficult to know when to draw conclusions about progress. How much change over a five-year period is to be treated as indicative of progress rather than immobilism? What kinds of deviations from presumed progress are consistent with long-term success, and which kinds of deviations may be taken as signs that the project has been derailed?[2]

If we had the luxury of empirically grounded theories with which to work, we might be able to answer these questions with some confidence. We would then be in a position to specify indicators of progress based on a theory of long-term transition to a prospering market economy, a stable democracy, a cohesive nation-state, and the like. Much good work along these lines is being published, with fruitful debates over the relative impact on democratic consolidation of presidentialism and parliamentarism, plurality versus proportional representation electoral systems, rapid versus gradual strategies of economic reform, the relationship between political and economic reform, and so on. But the frequent need to qualify our generalizations, in light of distinctive features of the contexts in which these processes are taking place, signals the difficulty we face in assessing progress within the newly independent states in the future.

Indicators of progress are much easier to develop when dealing with circumstantial emergencies that require short-term amelioration; in these cases the short time-frame is less of a problem. We do not have to worry about how long it might take to "build" a "system." We can more readily evaluate progress in cleaning up toxic waste, in upgrading the safety systems on nuclear reactors, in closing down hopelessly dangerous reactors, in dismantling nuclear weapons, in distributing antibiotics in areas of epidemic, and so on. To be sure, transparency is not absolute, but it is relatively greater than when we try to assess the subjective orientations or prospective behavioral patterns of social groups. The interest groups to be addressed when dealing with ameliorative challenges are fewer and more obvious, while the relationship between assistance and impact is more immediate and apparent.

By contrast, when dealing with the system-building challenges, indicators of intermediate progress are more difficult to identify, the relationship between assistance and impact is confounded by the length of time it takes to judge progress, the interest groups are larger in number, more dispersed and less easy to bargain with, the causal chains are long and hard to anticipate, and the lack of a theory of transition makes it difficult to know what strategies are likely to work.

Admittedly, many economists are increasingly confident that they have identified a theory of economic transition that works in specifying near-term indicators of progress. The shock therapy approach is said to have worked in Poland and perhaps to be working in Russia. While some observers are inclined to bemoan the price paid by different social groupings for the progress made to date, it would appear that the experience of Poland does indeed vindicate the theory of rapid transition. In Russia, however, it remains very unclear whether progress to date is indicative of long-term success or of eventual backlash, both because of the type of market economy emerging in that country and because of the possibility of a breakdown of the political system under pressure from anti-democratic forces. Here too we face a deficit of deductive theory with which to work. Even if those economists are correct that the transition from a command economy to a market economy requires a series of specified measures implemented in a specified sequence, we lack a theory that would tell us the conditions under which the pursuit of such a program is compatible with democratic state building and liberal nation building in a post-Leninist context.

The chapters in this volume can be grouped according to the internal challenges on which they focus, the aspect of the outside world whose causal impact they are seeking to assess, the country or countries within the NIS and the outside world on which they concentrate, and the methodologies they employ. In some cases they also reach divergent conclusions, or propose clashing policies for the outside world to pursue.

The initial chapters of the volume concentrate on the foreign relations of Russia and the NIS. Most of them deal principally or exclusively with East–West relations; two of them focus, respectively, on East Asia and the Middle East. Some of them explore the roots of the policies of outside powers; others explore the impact of those policies on the foreign policies of Russia and other successor states. Some of them are explicitly policy prescriptive; others look to the future with greater detachment. All of them enrich our understanding of the complex forces at work in the international environment, and of the ways in which those forces might affect the integration or alienation of Russia and the newly independent states from the international system.

Chapter 3, by Alvin Z. Rubinstein, offers a panoramic overview of Russian foreign relations since the collapse of the USSR. He argues that Russian leaders' high expectations of Western policies have been dashed since they peaked in 1991–92, resulting in a widespread distrust of Western intentions in the military, political, and economic realms. He concludes that current Russian policy makers are trying to avoid overreaction to their disappointment and are pursuing policies that combine pursuit of integration into Western civilization with a hardheaded defense of Russian national security interests. Ultimately, according to Rubinstein, "whether [Russia's] mistrust turns into hostility may well depend on what the West does. The West's responsibility for cultivating a diplomacy of threat reduction must not be minimized." Thus, Rubinstein examines the interaction between Russian policy and U.S.–NATO responses, concluding that the latter has had a deleterious impact on the perspectives and calculations of Russian foreign policy makers.

The chapters by Michael MccGwire and Raymond L. Garthoff echo this viewpoint. In chapter 4, MccGwire analyzes in depth the issue of NATO's enlargement or expansion eastward, and concludes that such a step would be bound to elicit a sharply negative reaction in Moscow. His conclusion is that such a reaction would be counterproductive to the goals of peace and stability on the European continent. He instead proposes the construction of a new European security system into which Russia would be fully integrated, and within which the prevailing maxim would be "cooperative security." In sum, MccGwire focuses on the European regional subsystem, finds that it has had a profoundly negative impact on Russian foreign policy makers' perspectives, and argues that a restructuring of that regional security order could have a positive impact; indeed, it could integrate Russia into Europe in ways that would cement its status as a partner, not a foe.

In chapter 2, Garthoff also takes the interactionist approach, but covers a broader array of issues in East–West relations. He argues that U.S. efforts to influence the Russian transition have been most effective in areas concerned with short-term amelioration (nuclear disarmament of Ukraine and Kazakhstan, partial nuclear disarmament in Russia, nuclear reactor safety, etc.). However, Western policies have had only a marginal impact on the transformation of Russia's domestic political and economic orders. As for foreign policy, Garthoff is concerned that Western policies have been based on a double standard, leading Russian decision makers to conclude that they too must look out for themselves first and foremost. Garthoff shares Rubinstein's concern, and MccGwire's alarm, that, absent a shift in Western approaches to Russian foreign relations, Moscow's mistrust may turn into active hostility.

In contrast to the largely retrospective approach of Rubinstein and Garthoff, and sharing with MccGwire a concern for prescribing new approaches to international order, Celeste A. Wallander's chapter brings institutional theory to support and evaluate the prospects that multilateral organizations such as the United Nations and the Organization for Security and Cooperation in Europe (OSCE) might be employed to keep the peace within the "near abroad." She concludes that, to date, Russian policy makers have enjoyed a preponderance of deployable power in the area and have viewed multilateral peacekeeping institutions expediently rather than as ends in themselves. As long as this condition obtains, Western efforts to use all-European institutions to keep the peace *within* the former Soviet Union could prove counterproductive. However, to the extent that these conditions change, opportunities for crafting such a multilateral, external influence on interstate relations within the NIS could grow.

George H. Quester's chapter evaluates the likely direction of the foreign policy of the United States in response to events in the NIS. Testing three alternative models of the roots of U.S. foreign policy—power politics, liberalism, and Marxism—Quester concludes that liberal idealism is likely to predominate over balance of power and economic considerations in U.S. goals for Eurasia. This conclusion has important implications for our assessment of the political feasibility of security arrangements proposed by analysts and actors seeking to transform international and regional orders in order to deter, defend, or construct a partnership with Russia or other newly independent states. From the methodological perspective elaborated earlier in this introduction, Quester has developed a statement about the likely dynamics of one of the independent variables in the international environment. When coupled with the chapters by Rubinstein, MccGwire, and Garthoff, it has suggestive implications for assessing the conditions under which U.S. policy makers might provide Moscow with the reassurance and partnership those authors claim it needs and deserves.

The next two chapters analyze the dynamics of other regional subsystems within the international environment; they draw our attention away from the Western front toward the Far East and the Near East. Gilbert Rozman's chapter provides a trenchant specification of the dynamics of the Russia-China-Japan triangle and a number of scenarios for evolution or change within that triangular relationship. He argues that "a Sino-Russian-Japanese triangle is taking shape in which China occupies the pivotal corner." Kemal H. Karpat's chapter details the efforts of Turkey and Iran to influence post-Soviet Central Asia and the Caucasus and to broker the integration of these new states into competing regional and global orders. He argues that Turkey's secular Islamic model has enjoyed a competitive advantage in the NIS over the militant-Islamic model propagated by Iran, but that this situation could change as a result of changes in the policies of both the West and Russia toward the new states of this region.

In sum, by specifying the dynamics of two important regional subsystems, each of which is connected to a global system in which the West (the United

States and/or Europe) is hegemonic, Rozman and Karpat provide us with tools for speculation about the ways in which changes in these external variables could transform the foreign relations of Russia and the NIS.

Chapters 9 and 10 describe and analyze the origins and contents of U.S. and German efforts to influence change in Russia and the newly independent states. They are less concerned with documenting the impact of these policies on the actual trajectory of change within the newly independent states. Peter Dombrowski's chapter concentrates on bilateral governmental assistance: humanitarian, technical, and financial. The burden of his chapter is to explore the motives of German and U.S. politicians who negotiated, ratified, and implemented bilateral assistance agreements. Angela Stent, in turn, catalogs the variety of ways in which German leaders have tried to engage Russian, Ukrainian, and Kazakh leaders in order to foster political, economic, and nuclear stability within those countries, and in order to draw Russia in particular into European institutions.

The next three chapters deal, albeit in very different ways, with the role of the West in fostering the transition from the command to a market economy. Gertrude Schroeder's upbeat, capsule survey of changes in each of the newly independent states is geographically one of the most wide-ranging chapters in this volume. She is impressed by the extent to which system-transformative changes have been accomplished in five years, declaring these to be "a success story by and large." She views Western governmental, nongovernmental, and multilateral assistance to have been both substantial and salutary in inducing or assisting system transformation and in ameliorating certain conditions that have accompanied the shocks of transformation.

Chapter 12, by Bartlomiej Kaminski and Zhen Kun Wang, deals with a narrower issue: the relationship between IMF and World Bank support and progress in reforming a command economy. They use aggregated data about degrees of macroeconomic stabilization and institutional reform to rank the countries of both the NIS and of East Central Europe, and data about financial flows to look for correlations between reform and IMF/World Bank assistance. Their conclusion is that this external assistance is "very necessary although not sufficient" for achieving macroeconomic stabilization; they further suggest "a strong positive correlation between IMF/World Bank disbursements and progress in transition" [i.e., institutional transformation—GWB].

Yitzhak M. Brudny's chapter takes an entirely different approach to the issue. Focused solely on Russia, and employing neither economic nor statistical analysis, Brudny instead addresses the historical counterfactual: how different would Russian politics have been had Boris Yeltsin's government not embraced the policies of liberalization and stabilization urged upon it by external advisors and agencies? The question is both intriguing and fundamental to the further evaluation of the relationship between economic and political transformation. Disputing the claim that shock therapy destabilized Russian politics and led to the high polarization we witnessed during 1993–95, Brudny argues instead that the institutional legacy of Mikhail Gorbachev's perestroika, and the failure of Yeltsin's government to articulate a conception of liberal nationalism that could unify the nation and outflank the xenophobes, were the root causes of political instability. Hence, he concludes, avoidance of shock therapy would not have allowed the country to avoid high political polarization and dislocation.

Chapters 14 and 15, by Robert Sharlet and Nancy Lubin, evaluate the effectiveness of U.S. governmental and nongovernmental efforts to bring the rule of law to the newly independent states, with special, though not exclusive, attention to Russia. Both of them acknowledge that this task of system building is one that will take a very long time to consummate, and that success is anything but foreordained. They realize that five years is too short a period of time in which to change a mass culture and to build enduring institutions. However, they differ in their evaluations of the effectiveness of programs administered by different types of external organizations, with Lubin arguing forcefully that a large number of *small,* nongovernmental organizations (NGOs), pursuing highly specified and restricted tasks, are more likely to advance both ameliorative and transformative goals.[3]

Murray Feshbach's chapter is the only one that deals almost exclusively with the amelioration of circumstantial emergencies facing these states, rather than with system-building efforts. Focused entirely on Russia, Feshbach catalogs the magnitude of the environmental and health crises, and the specifics of Western assistance in these realms. His pessimistic conclusion is sobering indeed: that external assistance has been meager relative to the scope of the crises and that the situation will only further deteriorate, with perhaps apocalyptic consequences, if external assistance is not dramatically increased.

I began this chapter by arguing that the subject of external influences on the post-communist transitions is a vast one. A large number of processes are in train within the region, impinged upon by huge numbers and types of external influences. Assessing the interaction among and between the independent and dependent variables is itself a daunting enterprise, while the short time frame within which such an evaluation is taking place confounds the effort to draw firm conclusions. The skeptic, for example, can always respond to any conclusion about transformative processes with the warning: "Just wait." A comparison of the contents of this volume with an extensive list of important causal relationships worth exploring reveals how very much more work remains to be done. Nonetheless, this volume takes an important step forward in (1) detailing and evaluating the nature of forces within the international environments of Russia and the newly independent states; (2) exploring claims about the direct impact of some of these forces on aspects of transformation and amelioration; and (3) providing valuable analytical and methodological tools for building upon these results.

Notes

1. In the long run, of course, we will eventually want to know which social groups proved to be the winners and the losers in whatever systemic transformations take shape.

2. For example, is extreme concentration of wealth a typical feature of early capitalism, mitigated only later by a diffusion of wealth once economic growth has accelerated? Or is it a prelude to social turmoil, political instability, and economic stagnation?

3. Lubin's conclusions are consistent with my own sense that government is a blunt and wasteful instrument, and that a strategy of "comprehensive engagement" by community action groups may be warranted. See George W. Breslauer, "Aid to Russia: What Difference Can Western Policy Make?" in *The New Russia: Troubled Transformation,* ed. Gail W. Lapidus (Boulder, CO: Westview Press, 1994), pp. 223–244. In this article, I introduce the distinction between long-term transformative and short-term ameliorative challenges.

2

Western Efforts to Shape Post-Soviet Behavior

Contemporary Developments in Historical Perspective

Raymond L. Garthoff

International relations have assumed many forms throughout history, and the Cold War of 1946–90 has arguably not been the first or only "cold war." It was certainly not the first major political conflict to have combined ideological and geopolitical (realpolitik) elements. It does, however, have the distinction of being the first cold war so defined in its own time. More important, it was first to dominate global politics in a bipolar confrontation, with clearly defined major protagonists in the Soviet Union and the United States and the alliances they led for nearly half a century. It also was the first major conflict in the nuclear age, but while that factor may have helped to keep it a cold war rather than a hot one, it was neither the cause of the conflict nor of its conclusion. The unique feature of the great Cold War was that after dominating global politics for many years it came to a sudden and peaceful end. Soon after came the collapse of one of its protagonists—also peacefully, mirabile dictu.

The rapid disintegration of the Soviet Union so soon after the end of the Cold War has led many to blur the distinction, but the two were distinct phenomena. The Cold War had clearly ended by November 1990 with the Charter of Paris ratifying the reunification of Germany, celebrating the reunification of Europe, and marking the end of the bipolar global confrontation. The Soviet Union was deep in a revolutionary internal transformation that led to its disintegration, but that outcome was not a consequence of the revolutionary transformation of the external world. In other words, the end of the Cold War did not depend on (or, indeed, await) the fall of the Soviet system. What it did require was a fundamental change in the worldview of a Soviet leadership, under General Secretary Mikhail Gorbachev, willing to act on the basis of that changed perception. Moreover, abandonment not only of the Leninist Weltanschauung but also of many central elements of the Marxist–Leninist ideology as embodied internally in the Soviet system did underlie the failed attempt to reform the Communist Party and the Soviet political and economic system, and the failure of this attempted reform ultimately brought about the collapse of the Soviet state itself.

The end of the Cold War thus stemmed above all from the manifest failure of the Soviet communist worldview. It also, however, represented a successful conclusion to the Western policy of containment, which had, as its foremost exponent George Kennan had predicted, contained Soviet aggressive impulses until they were spent. In a deeper sense the failure of the Soviet system internally also soon led to the collapse of communist rule and disintegration of the Soviet Union. But, as Kennan had foreseen, it was the mellowing and transformation of the Soviet system even before its collapse that ended the Cold War.

In the first year or so of the post–Cold War world, from November 1990 to August (or even December) 1991, it remained the general expectation that the Soviet Union would continue as part of the new world order. Indeed, during the decisive final year of the dismantling of the confrontational structure of the Cold War, from the demolition of the Wall in Berlin and communist rule in Eastern Europe in November–December 1989 to the Paris Summit meeting of the Conference on Security and Cooperation in Europe (CSCE) issuance of a European Charter, and signature of a treaty reducing conventional forces in Europe (CFE) in November 1990, it was assumed by all that the new post–Cold War world order would include the Soviet Union as a partner. This new partnership was demonstrated in 1990–91 by the Soviet cooperation in the successful United Nations (UN) mandated rollback of Iraqi aggression against Kuwait, as well as the continuing liquidation of Cold War-sustained civil wars in Nicaragua, El Salvador, Cambodia, Angola, and Ethiopia (and the earlier Soviet withdrawal from Afghanistan). As late as October 1991, the United States and the Soviet Union jointly convened the long dormant Arab–Israeli peace conference in Madrid.

Thus, the subsequent early demise of the Soviet Union, although it surely underscored the outcome of the Cold War, was not a necessary element in it. Moreover, with the earlier end of the Soviet bloc in Eastern Europe and Soviet withdrawal from Third World arenas, the successful conclusion of forty-some years of containment was not accompanied or followed by a Western campaign to roll back Soviet rule within the USSR. To the contrary, the United States and other Western powers supported Gorbachev's efforts to constitute a voluntary union of the Soviet republics. President George Bush, it will be recalled, as late as 1 August 1991, deliberately sought to dampen sentiment for independence in Ukraine and other republics by stating in Kiev that "freedom is not the same as independence" and by praising Gorbachev's achievements, including explicitly the pending conclusion of a new Union Treaty, thus making clear the U.S. preference for a democratic, voluntary union of Soviet republics. Even when the three Baltic states—the incorporation of which into the Soviet Union in 1940 had never been formally accepted by the United States—had declared independence by 21 August 1991, President Bush held back from recognition until 2 September 1991, the same day that Gorbachev announced that the Soviet Union would do so, so that rather than being in the lead the United States was the thirty-seventh state to extend recognition.

In short, while the United States and its Western allies had long sought to contain and to end the "communist threat" and the Cold War, they did not seek to bring about the demise of the Soviet state. Moreover, while pursuing their own agenda toward reducing arms and encouraging democratization, the United States and the North Atlantic Treaty Organization (NATO) had essentially followed the lead of Gorbachev's Soviet Union, even cautiously and slowly, in moving from 1985 to 1990 to end the Cold War. Even those crucial steps that went beyond Gorbachev's design, notably the end of communist rule and of the Soviet-led bloc in Eastern Europe, came about as a consequence of Gorbachev's early encouragement and later acquiescence in internally generated change in those countries, rather than from Western initiative or pressure. To be sure, the West (and the NATO alliance) were victorious in the Cold War if only because they survived it, unlike the Warsaw Pact. More fundamentally, the Western system and its values survived and prospered while Soviet Communism soon collapsed. In that sense, clearly, the West won the Cold War, and certainly the traditional Soviet worldview of an inevitable struggle between two systems that had spawned the Cold War went down to total defeat. But in a broader sense, we all won the Cold War (as well as the avoidance of a hot war) by its peaceful termination.

This may seem an unduly long introduction to our subject, but I believe that in addressing Western efforts to change post-Soviet behavior attention must be given to the closely associated but separate phenomena of the end of the Cold War and the end of the Soviet Union. Western aims and actions (and some Russian reactions) have been heavily influenced by failure in many cases to remain cognizant of this distinction. Finally, not only was the Cold War in many respects unique, so too was the end of the Soviet Union. The Soviet Union was defeated by history, not by the Western powers. Moreover, Russia is not a defeated power but a reborn state liberated by the demise of the Soviet Union.

The bloodless dissolution of the Union of Soviet Socialist Republics on 26 December 1991, some seventy-four years after the Bolshevik Revolution (and sixty-nine years after the establishment of the USSR), was an extraordinary historical development. The peaceful passing of an empire from the world's stage without defeat in foreign or civil war, without a forceful struggle either among its leaders or among its constituent political entities, is, I believe, without historical precedent. This unique circumstance is also important in establishing the legacy of relationships among the successor states and of other countries with them.

The twelve constituent union republics of the USSR in December 1991 (the three Baltic states having seceded in August–September) became the successor states to the Soviet Union. Ironically, the very designation of the successors, as well as their territorial borders, was inherited from artificial Soviet political-administrative decisions. For example, until 1936 Kazakhstan and Kyrgyzstan had been autonomous republics in the Russian Socialist Federated Soviet Republic. The Central Asian and Transcaucasian republics are today recognized independent states, and Chechnya and Tatarstan are not, because the former were accorded the status of union republics. Crimea became part of Ukraine, and not of Russia, only because it had been a gift arranged by Nikita Khrushchev in 1954 on the three hundredth anniversary of the union of Ukraine with Russia. The breakaway Dniestr Republic (Trans-Dniester) is legally part of Moldova because it was separated from Ukraine and placed in Moldavia in 1944 by Joseph Stalin. Armenian-populated Nagorno-Karabagh similarly is part of Azerbaijan owing to Moscow decisions in 1921–23.

The decision to dissolve the USSR and leave twelve independent states was not a demand, or even the preference, of most of those republics. There had been a growing nationalism in several of the republics, and in parallel a growing desire in several republics for greater devolution of authority from the center. The most important development was the rivalry between Gorbachev, as leader of the Soviet Union, and Boris Yeltsin, as president of Russia, pitting the latter against the Union as a way of undercutting Gorbachev. The second crucial development was the growth of independence sentiment in Ukraine, inspired both by nationalist views in the Western Ukraine, and by a mistaken belief in Eastern Ukraine that economic difficulties would be alleviated if Moscow's dominating hand were removed. When Yeltsin (and the Belarusian leader Stanislau Shushkevich) agreed with Ukrainian leader Leonid Kravchuk on 8 December 1991 to dissolve the USSR and dismiss Gorbachev, Yeltsin would still have preferred to keep a voluntary union (particularly without Gorbachev). The leaders of the five Central Asian republics would have preferred the new union treaty, fearing the loss of Russian economic assistance more than they desired independence.

The clear preference of the United States and most Western powers for a renewed voluntary union stemmed primarily from concern over the potentially destabilizing consequences of a breakup of the Soviet Union, now no longer an adversary. This concern was especially strong with respect to control over its dispersed nuclear arsenal. The foremost Western effort was directed not at destroying the Soviet Union, but at preventing or at least cushioning its breakup. Concern over possible "loose nukes" would have been present under any circumstances of a disintegration of the Soviet Union, but it contributed to the Western preference to maintain a union in view of the fact that the Soviet Union was no longer regarded as a threat or rival.

The United States and other Western powers recognized that, whatever their own preferences, the fundamental political decisions within the Soviet Union and later among its successors would be made by the peoples or leaders of those states. Accordingly, efforts were made to deal with whatever leaders and whatever successor state or states should emerge. In the first U.S. statement of policy, on 12 December 1991, as a commonwealth of independent states was still form-ing, Secretary of State James Baker pledged that the United States "will work with those republics and any common entity which commit [themselves] to responsible security policies, democratic political practices, and free market economies." He noted that some republics seemed more prepared to take such a course than others, naming five: Russia, Ukraine, Kazakhstan, Armenia, and Kyrgyzstan. Although not then mentioned by Baker, particular attention was also given to a second set of countries defined by the presence of nuclear weapons on their territories: Russia, Ukraine, Kazakhstan, and Belarus. Application of these two criteria, which largely overlapped, led Baker to include on the itinerary of a trip he made to the region at that time five republics (all of the above named except Armenia). When eleven of the twelve republics (all except Georgia, which joined later) agreed on 21 December 1991 to create a Commonwealth of Independent States (CIS), the United States decided to recognize the indepen-dence of all twelve republics, but applying its mixed criteria to differentiate by establishing diplomatic relations with only six: Russia, Ukraine, Belarus, Kazakhstan, Kyrgyzstan, and Armenia. Although there was a logic to such dif-ferentiation, there also were difficulties and disadvantages: it was not easy to measure democratic standards; giving particular weight to countries having nu-clear weapons on their territories could operate against the U.S. objective of getting all nuclear weapons back to Russia; and most of the omitted republics were Muslim, even though they had not been excluded for that reason. Within weeks, this policy was quietly abandoned and diplomatic relations were estab-lished with all twelve republics.

Russia was, of course, the largest and most important of the successor states. Moreover, it was regarded for legal as well as political reasons as the sole "continuer" successor, inheriting the seat of the Soviet Union in the United Nations Security Council, and being recognized as the sole successor as a nu-clear-weapons state under the Nuclear Nonproliferation Treaty (NPT). It was also recognized as the sole successor signatory of the Intermediate-Range Nu-clear Forces Treaty (INF), and initially of the Antiballistic Missile Treaty (ABM), and the Strategic Arms Reduction Treaty (START I).

After considerable diplomatic effort, the United States, supported by the other Western powers, successfully persuaded Ukraine, Kazakhstan, and Belarus to agree to the withdrawal of all nuclear weapons present on their territory to Russia, and to sign the NPT as nonnuclear states. All tactical nuclear weapons were withdrawn within the first six months of 1992, and the last strategic nuclear warheads were withdrawn to Russia before the end of 1996. In Ukraine, in particular, giving up all claim to nuclear weapons was a controversial political issue in 1992–93. The United States, Germany, and the other Western powers, however, made clear that economic assistance and general development of rela-tions depended on resolution of this problem, and this bolstered Ukrainian recog-nition that it could not afford to be a nuclear power.

Western efforts to recentralize all nuclear weapons held by the former Soviet Union under control of Moscow were thus ultimately successful. Russia, too, had sought this outcome, but it was a combination of Western pressures and inducements that led Ukraine and Kazakhstan to agree. (Belarus had never objected, but also sought and shared in the direct economic assistance tied to withdrawal of the nuclear weapons and to enhancing security of remaining nonweapons nuclear facilities.)

The United States, with some direct support from other Western countries, has pursued a Cooperative Threat Reduction (CTR) program, widely known as the Nunn-Lugar program after its principal bipartisan senatorial sponsors. Initially geared mainly to facilitating the transfer of former Soviet nuclear weapons into Russia, it developed into a broader program to assist in safeguarding the reduction of Russian nuclear weapons and to enhance the security of nuclear materials. On the whole, it has made a very useful contribution to security.

The overriding Western objective had been to prevent the emergence of additional states possessing nuclear weapons, both to assure integrity and greater security of the former Soviet nuclear arsenal and to preclude an example for other potential new nuclear weapons states. The general (though not universal) international concern against nuclear proliferation, shared also by most Ukrainians, Belarusians, and Kazakhs, made it possible to present the matter as a step in meeting international standards of behavior rather than a sign of distrust toward these republics or partiality toward Russia. Secondary considerations involved arrangements for sharing former Soviet assets and reimbursement for the value of the fissionable materials salvaged from the warheads withdrawn, mainly through Russian supply of non-weapon grade nuclear fuel, facilitated by Western financial assistance.

The Western powers also sought to ensure that all successor states accepted relevant treaties of the Soviet Union, in particular the CFE treaty. Inasmuch as all the successor states were acquiring conventional armed forces, it was necessary that they agree among themselves on a division of the ceilings on holdings of major armaments assigned to the Soviet Union under that treaty. With some difficulty, but with a common desire to succeed, they did so by mid-1992. There were, of course, other frictions over division of the Soviet armed forces themselves, notably in Russian–Ukrainian disputes over possession (and basing) of the Black Sea Fleet and over control of strategic missiles and bombers. Local freebooting by various elements in Azerbaijan, Georgia, and even in the Russian Federation in Chechnya, led in 1992 to the loss of control of conventional weapons in a number of former Soviet garrisons. But overall, the transition from the Soviet armed forces to the armed forces of the successor states was surprisingly smooth. Although the Western powers did not become involved in the division of the Soviet armed forces among the successor states, they did play a role in encouraging Russian withdrawal from the Baltic states and continued withdrawal of former Soviet forces from eastern Germany and Poland, all completed on schedule before the end of 1994. Germany provided substantial assistance to resettling Soviet forces from Germany in Russia (continuing earlier assistance to the Soviet Union that had also included building military housing in the Soviet republics of Ukraine and Belorussia). The United States assisted in brokering an agreement between Latvia and Russia for continued Russian use until dismantling by 1999 of an important early-warning radar at Skrunda. The Western powers thereby played a limited but helpful role in the return of former Soviet military forces to Russia.

The Western powers thus encouraged and in some cases directly assisted in dealing with important tasks of managing the transition from the centralized Soviet state to twelve independent successors, in particular with respect to the very important issues of allocation of the armed forces and above all the nuclear weapons of the former Soviet Union. There have remained the less immediate but even more daunting problems of internal stabilization of these new independent states, the elaboration of the relationships among them, and the longer-term political and economic transformation of their societies.

The Western powers have broadly sought to influence the emerging policies of Russia, Ukraine, and other former Soviet republics.[1] The Western countries have, of course, been pursuing their own interests, including competitive efforts among themselves to develop economic relations with Russia and the other former Soviet republics. They have also sought to curb the potential influence of other countries, in particular Iran and other Islamic countries seeking to extend their own influence in the historically Muslim new states of Central Asia and Azerbaijan.

Overall, the Western powers have tended to see pursuit of their own interests in terms of pursuing common interests in stability and security, democratic development, and market economic reform. These objectives are assumed to represent common international interests including the best interests of Russia and the other new republics. In general and in principle they do represent values, objectives, and interests shared by these countries. Nonetheless, there were bound to be differences of view on concrete issues and applications of such general criteria. And it has been in this context that questions of the nature of the end of the Cold War, of Soviet Communism, and of the Soviet state arose.

The leaders of Russia (and the other new successor states to the Soviet Union) have naturally regarded themselves as the best and proper judges of their own interests. Initially, in 1992–93, the new leadership of Russia sought to be even more consistent new thinkers than the Gorbachev leadership of the Soviet Union that had contributed decisively to the end of the Cold War. Gradually, however, it became more and more the prevailing judgment in Russia that the West and the world were not so altruistic and indifferent to their own interests, nor so zealous in aiding Russia, as to make it feasible for Russia not to frame its policies in terms of serving Russian rather than common global interests. For example, while sharing a general common interest and having a concrete Russian interest in nonproliferation of nuclear and missile weapons, why should Russia not decide for itself whether the sale of nuclear power reactors to Iran or space-launch technology to India was compatible with those objectives? Moreover, those sales contravened no international or bilateral agreements, and indeed, in the case of the Iranian reactors, International Atomic Energy Agency (IAEA) safeguards were applied. The reactors were also the same type that the United States and South Korea were providing to North Korea. Why should the United States penalize Russia in terms of other economic relations if Russia made such sales in the few areas where it had competitive advantage? To be sure, only Western governments or entities they controlled, such as the International Monetary Fund (IMF), could decide on terms for credits to Russia (and the other successor republics). But why should the Western powers be arbiters of Russian economic (including foreign trade) decisions not related to those arrangements? To the extent that the Western powers have had the clout and could coerce Russia in such matters, the lesson was that power and pursuit of one's own interests were the way of the world and that Russia must act accordingly.

These illustrative examples are not meant to imply that the United States and Western powers should not pursue their own interests, nor that the interests of Russia and the United States will always coincide. The United States and France, for example, have also differed over trade with Iran and sales of nuclear reactors and space technology. The United States has, however, rarely sought to levy economic sanctions on its allies for trading with Iran, Iraq, Cuba, and North Korea—and when it has, as with recent legislation in effect prescribing a secondary boycott for such trade, it has provoked strong opposition. But no major power other than Russia is a recipient of direct economic assistance that can be curtailed as a sanction.

Moreover, the alliance partnerships with Japan, France, Germany, and other powers are better able to withstand disputes over sales of reactors and the like. Russian economic weakness and the frailty of a new and vague political partnership impose greater strains on relations, and on the internal political development of Russia itself. Moreover, the United States and other Western powers not only have very great political and economic clout; they also see themselves as the most powerful and experienced democracies and the leading market-economy countries. Sometimes more than example and experience, or husbanding of their own resources, seems to underlie Western policies toward the Soviet successor states. The Western powers tend to see themselves as the standard bearers of a victorious political/economic/ideological system and thereby empowered to judge what is best for Russia. To be sure, that idea is not expressed so baldly by Western governments (although it is by some individual Western politicians and commentators), but at least in Russian eyes it is seen as underlying the patronizing and sometimes hardball political posture of the West. In the extreme, it plays to a myth held by some in Russia that the West deliberately brought down the Soviet Union and is trying to keep Russia weak.

Did the West win the Cold War? The Soviet system certainly lost, but if that simply liberated the former republics of the USSR (including Russia as much as the others), why should they not enjoy the fruits of their freedom, above all the freedom to make their own decisions within the actual—not the idealized—standards of the world community?

The symbolic peace conference ending the Cold War was the 1990 Paris Summit meeting of the CSCE (now the Organization for Security and Cooperation in Europe, or OSCE). The Soviet Union had been accepted as an equal of the other great powers in formalizing the end to the division and residual occupation of Germany. The Paris Summit was much more akin to the Congress of Vienna in 1815 than to the Versailles Conference of 1919. The new world order included the Soviet Union, and later Russia (as the continuing successor state on the UN Security Council), as one of several equal great powers, rather than being a punitively imposed peace. Only a year later the Soviet Union was extinguished, but by internal and peaceful political action, not by defeat by the West or by any external adversary.

The Western powers have no mandate to dictate to Russia or the other successor states to the Soviet Union. They do have the right to serve their own interests, and those of the international community as they see them, and to encourage and assist the former Soviet states to develop and behave in ways that will serve the interests of those states and the international community. And they have the economic and political wherewithal in some cases either to induce or to press Russia and the other successor states. They should, however, wield their power in ways that will not generate avoidable grievances and suspicions that could far outweigh any constructive result.

It would be both unrealistic and unwise to urge that Western policy toward Russia and the other successor states should focus only on "carrots" and never on "sticks." In moving to accept the successor states into such institutions as the Council of Europe, for example, certain standards of observance of human rights have been required. (One of these, the abolition of the death penalty, on which Russia, Ukraine, and Latvia were all criticized in 1996 for slowness in moving to implement the standard, is incidentally one on which the United States would not qualify.) Often a combination of inducements as well as potential penalties is the best solution (as in the U.S. agreement to purchase Russian space booster technology as a quid pro quo for limiting the sale of Russian space technology to India). But the Western powers should avoid temptations to exploit Russian weakness by applying a double standard that implies that Russia is a defeated power or pariah.

The general overarching articulated objectives of the Western powers have been clear and not controversial, either in the West or for the most part in the dominant political strata of Russia, Ukraine, and the other successor states. In terms of the international political order, the principal objectives are to strengthen international cooperation, nonuse of force, stability, security, and mutually advantageous economic relations. The principal means is by drawing Russia and the other successor states into the world order. In terms of internal development, both on their own merits and as reinforcement for the desired international order, the main objectives have been stated to be political democratization, observance of human rights, and development of a free market economy. All of these objectives, especially those concerning the international order, have been subscribed to by all the successor states. The implementation of such principles in practice is, however, much more complex than it might seem (and by no means only in the behavior of the Soviet successor states). Moreover, the successor states are acknowledged to be in a transitional stage in working toward the achievement of the internal-development objectives.

It must also be noted that the successor states, including Russia as well as some never before independent states, are all striving to define their own identity and legitimacy. As noted earlier, even the territorial basis of the successor states in many cases is arbitrary. As in some earlier historical situations, for example the grant of independence to the former European colonies in Africa, the only real justification for the territorial integrity and borders of the new states is the legacy from earlier imperial fiat and demarcations. Yet that has proven (in Africa, to continue that illustration) to be the only shared basis that provides an alternative to clashing claims and chaos. Virtually all the violent conflicts in the former Soviet territory represent localized attempts to change the inherited territorial map: border area secessionist attempts by Chechnya in Russia, Nagorno-Karabagh in Azerbaijan, Abkhazia and South Ossetia in Georgia, and Trans-Dniester in Moldova. (Had the issue not been peacefully resolved, the Crimea, in Ukraine, would have followed the same pattern.) Moreover, in none of these cases (with the partial exception of Armenia in the case of Nagorno-Karabagh) have other successor republics been tempted to accept would-be defectors. The Russian government, in particular, has consistently reaffirmed the territorial integrity of Georgia, Moldova, and Ukraine. And no successor state, or any other government, has recognized the attempted secession of Chechnya from Russia. (The one exception has been the civil war in Tajikistan, pitting internal, regional, and political rivals against one another.)

The Western powers, too, have reaffirmed the territorial integrity as well as independence of each of the successor states, and sought to dissuade any country (in Eastern Europe as well as the space of the former Soviet Union) from raising territorial claims. One of the criteria for consideration of possible NATO membership is the absence of unresolved territorial claims.

The establishment in 1996 of close political ties between Russia and Belarus, though short of political unification, raised attention to the possibility of voluntary union by two or more of the independent successor states. Similarly, gradual steps toward closer coordination among some members of the CIS has raised a potential policy issue in the United States over how to regard any moves toward reestablishment of a confederal or other union among Russia and some of the other CIS members. To date, statements by U.S. officials have expressed the distinction that any voluntary association, including union, would be a matter for the decision of the states involved; what would be a source of concern to the international community would be any use of force to establish a union (or reestablish the Soviet Union). That is undoubtedly the correct position, although it skirts the tougher issues of possible coercion or pressure short of the threat or use of force.

Political democratization is a fine objective, but a difficult guideline for defining policy actions with respect to the transitional Soviet successor states. What if an avowed champion of democracy resorts to undemocratic political practices (as Yeltsin and most of the leaders of all of the successor states have done)? What if democratic processes such as popular elections bring to power Communists or others whose dedication to democracy is suspect? Former communists, although more or less reformed and expressing allegiance to democratic processes, have been elected in several Eastern European countries. In July 1996, the Communist, not former communist, candidate for the presidency of the Russian Federation, although losing the election, showed considerable strength. And President Yeltsin has on a number of occasions displayed an authoritarian approach. Only the future can tell us how soon and by what path democracy could become firmly rooted in Russia—and in each of the other former Soviet republics. The Western powers must of course deal with whatever government comes to power by democratic processes, and should seek to reinforce continued democratization so long as that is feasible.

Western statesmen, as well as Russian leaders, must bear in mind that pursuit of objectives of democratization and economic marketization must be sustained by the people and thus require a degree of social stability and measures to assure at least a minimum cushion or safety net for pensioners and others less able to learn and to compete in a new open and competitive economic system. The strongest support for communist and nationalist challenges to political and economic liberalization has come not from those privileged by the old order but from those most hurt and endangered by reform under the new order.

Among the most important, and elusive, aspects of democratization is the development of institutions constituting a political system (free press, political parties, clear distribution of authority), and a legal system (laws, a free and effective judiciary, police, absence of official corruption, and respect for the law). The Western powers have sought, both through government-sponsored and private-sector programs to educate and assist in developing such institutions, as discussed by Robert Sharlet in chapter 14.

Development of an economy operating on the basis of free market forces is a declared objective. One of the most powerful instruments of influence is Western economic assistance, principally through credits from such bodies as the International Monetary Fund and nongovernmental direct investment by Western companies. Here, too, the development of a stable environment for trade and investment, with known, clearly defined and predictable tax structures, property rights, and accountability is essential, and very difficult to establish.

For assisting both political and economic development in the successor states, the role of the Western powers is without clear precedent. They are welcomed by the authorities, and usually by counterparts, but the necessary supporting environment is often lacking. The lack of accepted ground rules that characterize the "wild capitalism" rampant in Russia today (as it is sometimes aptly termed there) makes it difficult to provide effective assistance or conduct business. In most of the other successor states this problem is not as great, owing to tighter governmental political and economic controls, but if and as economic reform gains, so does wild capitalism.

Especially in the early years (1992–93), a number of nongovernmental, academic Western economic experts had considerable influence on the Russian government and in some other successor states. Apart from dealing with an unfamiliar situation, their penchant for pressing economic reform even at great political and social cost sometimes created a considerable backlash.

The Western powers are seeking to develop both an economic system and a productive economy in the successor states, but they are also supportive of their own competing business interests. By far the largest part of U.S., and most Western, economic aid has been provided in the form of credits for Western purchases (as for U.S. grain) or technical assistance through U.S. and other Western companies. This does not mean that such assistance is not helpful, but it is not entirely altruistic. Even Western-financed construction (for example, German aid in building housing for resettled former Soviet military personnel in Russia) often use Turkish or Finnish workmen rather than Russians. Moreover, short-term credits require repayment or, more often, add to debt that must be rolled over and, presumably, eventually repaid.

The largest amounts of Western economic assistance have been given through multilateral organizations such as the International Monetary Fund, with fairly stringent conditions tying disbursement to continued onerous but necessary economic and financial reform measures. On the whole, this has been sound and has helped Russia (and some other former Soviet successor states) to keep up internal economic reform—which, in the final analysis, is the only way to effect the necessary overall transition to viable market economies. Western assistance to economic reform, depending on the outcome, will ultimately be judged the greatest element in determining whether the Western powers met their test of assisting the internal transformation of the former Soviet Union. (Western economic assistance is discussed much more fully in several later chapters of this volume, in particular those by Gertrude Schroeder, Bartlomiej Kaminski and Zhen Kun Wang, Peter Dombrowski, and Nancy Lubin.)

Measures apart from direct assistance are also important, and on the whole the West has not done so well in gearing its own practices to facilitate the transition of the former communist economies, and perhaps polities, to a market and democratic system. Western Europe has, understandably but unfortunately, been generally unwilling to give access to Eastern agricultural products. The United States, France, and others have been reluctant to grant Russia a share of the market for exportable conventional arms and aircraft and space technology. As a consequence, Russia and other successor states feel justified in ignoring Western calls for restraint, such as U.S. objections to the sale of Russian diesel submarines to Iran. The United States and South Korea denied Russia a chance to supply North Korea with nuclear reactors under the multilateral arrangements to replace those capable of producing highly enriched fissionable materials. That strengthened Russian resolve to press ahead in supplying the same type of reactors, under IAEA safeguards, to Iran.[2]

These few examples are cited merely to illustrate that when economic and political decisions on matters other than assistance to Russia are made by the Western powers, their impact on Russian interests, if considered at all, is but one of many competing political, military, economic, and commercial interests. Even more direct competitive commercial considerations are obvious in many other cases. Moreover, some vestiges of Cold War discrimination remain; the United States still applies the Jackson-Vanik Amendment to Russia, waiving its denial of most favored nation trade status only on the basis of annual renewal.

With all of their falterings and shortcomings, Western programs for direct support of economic and political development of the Soviet successor states have been making a substantial positive contribution, as discussed at greater length in several later chapters. Whether they have been sufficient, and equally whether the internal processes within the successor states will permit their contribution on the margin to be sufficient, remains to be seen. But on the whole, while falling far short of the scale of assistance of a new Marshall Plan, they have at least been a positive force.

As George Breslauer has noted, Western assistance has been more effective in dealing with more short-term ameliorative tasks, and less successful in meeting long-term transformative challenges. In part, this is due to the more clear relationship between assistance and results, with objectives, costs, and effects more easily measured and evaluated.[3] Politically it may also be easier to gain support in donor and recipient societies. The relationships between commitments and outcomes in meeting long-term transformative objectives are less clear, support in the donor society may be less strong, and it is more difficult to know which policies will succeed.

The Western powers have sought to promote democratic development in part through direct educational and exchange programs, and in part through support for the Yeltsin government (as the most democratic alternative, even if not consistently democratic in practice). In principle, and insofar as possible in practice, an attempt has been made to support the objectives of reform rather than any Russian (or other) leader or political program. Yet while criticizing some manifest shortcomings in performance, such as the Russian conduct of the war in

Chechnya, it has been very difficult to avoid alignment in support of Yeltsin (and Gorbachev before him) in such situations as the struggle between Yeltsin and a Communist Party challenger.

This discussion has focused on the efforts of the governments of the Western countries to shape post-Soviet behavior in the successor states. There is also, of course, a broader impact of the "Westernization" of the modern world and the cultural influence of the West (often, but not always, for the better) in the Soviet Union and its successors. That factor, over which we have little control, is also a consideration in internal debates in Russia and other successor states between avowed Westernizers and Slavophiles, or Eurasianists.

In the final analysis, the internal political and economic development of Russia, Ukraine, and the other Soviet successor states will depend on the internal dynamics of those societies. The West can influence these dynamics, but it cannot determine the outcome. In particular, it cannot prescribe the values, priorities, and decisions of the governments of these states, and efforts to do so risk not only failure but a backlash. Similarly, while political and economic programs of assistance designed to influence the direction of development are important, other actions of the West intended for other purposes may be as or more important. Specific Western actions undertaken for domestic political, economic, or commercial reasons, or intended to influence others in the international field, may loom larger in their impact on Russian decisions than those policies and actions designed for that purpose.

In terms of direct security issues, as noted earlier, the United States took a prompt lead in working with Russia (and to a lesser extent Ukraine, Kazakhstan, and Belarus) to enhance the security of nuclear facilities and materials. The major step in bilateral arms reduction has been the long-delayed efforts to ratify the START II Treaty. The United States has now done so, but the matter has become controversial in Russia owing mainly to two extraneous but not entirely unrelated issues: the U.S. pursuit of ballistic missile defense and the expansion of NATO. Bilateral U.S.–Russian talks have been held seeking to clarify the border between permitted development and deployment of nonstrategic theater missile defenses, and areas of development and deployment of strategic ballistic missile defenses banned by the ABM treaty. To date, however, these talks have not been able to resolve the issue because the United States seeks maximum latitude for its advanced theater missile defense programs. Beyond that, the strong calls in the United States for deployment of strategic missile defenses beyond the sharp constraints of the ABM Treaty raise real concerns in Moscow, inasmuch as those constraints constitute a fundamental assumption for the START reductions in strategic offensive arms.

The West, and in particular the United States, has not adequately recognized—and especially did not in 1992–93—that the honeymoon in relations with Russia, and the ardently pro-Western and internationalist "new thinking" of the Russian government was not foreordained or to be taken for granted. To have preserved this new course would have required not only a showing of Western readiness to offer significant assistance; no less important, it required Western policies that would validate, rather than undermine, the presumptions of the new thinking. This remains true, although now there is more of a realist national interest consensus in Russia, and it will be harder to demonstrate. Above all, the most important policy issue is the role to be accorded Russian national security and political interests. Regrettably, this is the area of greatest Western failure through its adoption of a priority for NATO enlargement over integration of Russia and the other successor states into European and global security arrangements, to which we shall turn presently.

This is not, however, the only indication of Western failure to take account of legitimate Russian interests. It may be useful to note a different example, one given almost no attention in the West. That Japan, an economic superpower, should seek in the wake of the victory in the Cold War to regain the so-called Northern Territories (the southern Kuril Islands) that it lost to Russia in 1945 is not surprising. The Western European countries have endorsed calls for a negotiated resolution of the issue between Russia and Japan, but have refrained from taking a position. The United States, however, without weighing the relative equities of the positions of the two sides, has endorsed the Japanese position since 1991. Yet the reasons that led the United States to support its ally Japan during the Cold War no longer apply. No longer does the United States have reason to wish to keep this issue alive and to prevent a Japanese–Russian détente; it should wish to see the issue resolved, on any terms acceptable to the two parties. (In 1956, the declassified archives now confirm, the United States placed direct pressure on Japan not to compromise and resolve the issue because it wished to keep Japan dependent and prevent a Japanese–Soviet rapprochement.) Both Japan and Russia have bases for their conflicting claims, but it would be prudent at least to consider the most relevant parallel and precedent: the final resolution of the Cold War territorial settlement in Europe on the basis of the status quo of the past half century. Germany accepted Russian and Polish sovereignty over the vast territorial gains of 1945 in heavily populated areas in Prussia and Pomerania; Japan could do the same over the barren southern Kurils. For the present discussion, however, my purpose is not to propose terms for resolving the issue, but to argue that the West (in this case above all the United States) should leave the issue for negotiation between the parties and not align itself in support of one against the other. Japan remains a U.S. ally, but Russia is now supposed to be a U.S. partner, too. The U.S. position was decided entirely by officials who wanted to reassure Japan, and who unthinkingly assumed the old Soviet position was anachronistic; in fact, the Russian position today is stronger. No one at the White House was even mindful of the gratuitous tilt toward Japan, first by Bush and then under Clinton, at a time the United States was seeking to encourage Russia to regard it as a new partner.[4]

Regrettably, despite good intentions, efforts to bring the successor states, and above all Russia, into the one world left after the end of the Cold War have faltered. Indeed, the spillover effects of ill-considered attempts to solve other international security problems without weighing realistically their impact on Russia and the other Soviet successor states threaten not only to outweigh the positive effects of the direct-support policies for internal reform but to create ominous new problems for both internal and external relationships of the former Soviet states.

The Western powers, with the United States in the lead, have moved to develop a new security architecture for Europe (still the heart of any new world order) based on NATO, rather than on the United Nations, OSCE, or some new organization. This was not a decision based on consideration, or weighing the available alternatives and predictable consequences. It was not even a decision deliberately to place NATO at the center of international security. In part it was a reaction to the failure of the new world order, foreseen by President Bush at the brief time of the triumph of the Gulf War, to emerge. In particular, the existing institutions (the United Nations, OSCE, the European Union, a "Contact Group" of great powers, and NATO) all failed to prevent a tragic civil war in the former Yugoslavia. The United States was uneasy that with the absence of a threat from the East, and apparent rapid movement toward unity in the West, there would be less room for a U.S. role and influence in Europe. NATO was seen as the one body that preserved a strong U.S. voice in Europe. NATO also appeared to be faltering in its search for a new raison d'être. And the states of Central and Eastern Europe released from the expired Warsaw Pact soon saw that the CSCE (even as the OSCE) was not being accorded a central role in security in place of the Warsaw Pact and NATO.

The initial attempt, even before the collapse of the Soviet Union, to create a North Atlantic Cooperation Council (NACC), largely overlapping membership and potentially functioning along with the CSCE, was not pursued beyond establishing a loose society of European states. The later NATO Partnership for Peace (PfP) offered a much more serious possibility by providing a flexible framework for developing military cooperation among members of NATO, Eastern Europe and former Soviet states, and interested neutrals in Europe. The PfP had embraced both the possibilities of becoming either an alternative to expansion of NATO membership or a path to it, by design of at least some of its authors, and it should have been implemented without prejudice to either future possibility. Moreover, after some hesitation, Russia (and all of the successor states) joined the PfP. But soon after the PfP had been launched and before its potential could be gauged and tested, it was overtaken in 1994 by a new initiative for expansion of NATO. The expansion (later termed "enlargement") of NATO was conceived by its principal authors (initially a minority in the political leadership and security establishments of the United States and Germany) as a way to do several things: first of all, to assure a continuity of and indeed an enlarged role for NATO; hence, too, (for Washington, DC) a key role for the United States in Europe, and (in Bonn) a politically acceptable framework for a growing German role in Central and Eastern Europe; to satisfy growing demands from the Poles and Czechs to be brought into NATO (supported by the large Polish- and Czech-American domestic political constituencies); and finally, to boost pro-Western, democratic and market societies in Central and Eastern Europe.

Another consideration, given increased attention after December 1993, was that a NATO enlargement would also be a hedge against the revival of a communist or nationalist regime in Moscow that might constitute a threat to countries in Eastern Europe. Some geopoliticians, notably Henry Kissinger and Zbigniew Brzezinski, gave this consideration greater weight, and even argued that NATO expansion was desirable now apart from a possible new threat simply because Russia remained a great power notwithstanding current weaknesses and that the West should act while Russia was still weak and could do little about it. This was not, however, the basis on which the decision was made in Washington, and duly in Brussels. To the contrary, it was argued that it would be in Russia's interests also to have a stable and democratic Eastern Europe. Moreover, the advocates of NATO expansion argued that it would placate the Eastern Europeans, involve no real expanded security requirements because there was no real Russian threat, and that adverse reaction in Russia could be contained by offering Russia a special role through a dialogue with NATO. It was a grievous error, for a number of reasons, including serious misjudgment as to the impact in Russia.

NATO enlargement, as the path to security for Eastern Europe and therefore for Europe as a whole, was not directed against Russia. Nonetheless, it did come to be depicted as at least in part a hedge against a resurgent threat from Russia. To many Russians, the renewal of the Western Cold War political-military alliance by absorbing the former members of the Warsaw Pact could only be seen as creating a new threat to Russia. Many believed, and others fanned opposition by claiming, that it would represent a direct military threat to Russia. Why else would NATO, with enormous conventional as well as nuclear superiority, feel it necessary to advance to the very borders of Russia itself?

The essence of the problem is not, however, that NATO expansion stirs unrealistic fears, but that it would not in fact serve legitimate Russian security interests. Expansion of NATO, excluding Russia, to provide security for Western and Eastern Europe means to exclude Russia from a meaningful participation in European security arrangements. If Russia is not offered membership in what is intended to be the central security body of Europe, it is not being given full and equal status as a power in the new world order. There is a problem feeding Russian misperceptions of a Western military threat, but there is an even more intractable problem in feeding valid Russian perceptions that their legitimate interests are not being given appropriate weight. To the substantial extent that this is not the Western purpose, there is all the more reason to seek some other means to meet Western (and Eastern European) purposes without persisting with a course that can only create a long-term problem with Russia—and, in one or another way, with the other successor states to the Soviet Union.

The argument that the expansion of NATO is necessary, or even helpful, to reinforce internal democratization in Central and Eastern Europe is at best misplaced. If NATO membership has that effect, it is secondary to the external security function of the alliance, and in any case surely the reinforcement of democratization in Russia and Ukraine is far more important and may be affected negatively by the enlargement of NATO. The argument for reassurance and inclusion in a security relationship is also even more important for Russia. Finally, the argument that NATO enlargement is a hedge against negative internal and external policy changes in Russia risks contributing precisely to such negative changes. Hedging should at the least not risk making political dangers more real; it can and should therefore be a contingent response if such changes occur, rather than a preemptive initiative when they have not arisen that may even help to bring about the undesired changes.

It remains to be seen, of course, whether and in what ways NATO will be enlarged. It is possible that despite continuing efforts no new candidate members will receive the unanimous acceptance of existing members. More likely will be an enlargement by the inclusion of at least three or four Central European (Visegrad) states. Further limited or gradual enlargement is less certain but may occur, in particular in the Balkans. Membership for the Baltic states would be most provocative to Russia. Any substantial enlargement would cause strains and tensions in Russia—possibly between Russia and some other states of the Near Abroad, and certainly between Russia and the West—to grow considerably. One conceivable course, although unlikely, would be a grand enlargement of NATO to include Russia and the Ukraine and other former Soviet successor states as well, if only because it might become easier than abandoning enlargement. That would, of course, defuse Russian–Western tensions, but it would also relegate NATO to another clone of the OSCE, NACC, and PfP. In such a case, a solution of the problems engendered by the enlargement of NATO could completely negate the original purpose. Most likely, however, is an incomplete enlargement of NATO leaving out Russia and several other former Soviet republics and other states in Eastern Europe, and leaving a residue of hostility and division in the region.

Relations of the United States and the other Western powers with Russia will of course continue, even if and as NATO expands, as will Western efforts to influence favorable developments within Russia and other successor states. These efforts will, however, be less effective and will have to overcome greater obstacles. Efforts underway to negotiate a charter between NATO and Russia will alone not be sufficient, but such an agreement can help and should be vigorously pursued. Even the path toward NATO enlargement has already made a mockery of the policy of the Bush and early Clinton administrations to create a post–Cold War partnership with Russia reaching from Vladivostok to Vancouver, and it is even undermining the conception of a Europe stretching from the Atlantic to the Urals celebrated at the Paris Summit of 1990 marking the end of the Cold War.

In the final analysis, the outcome of the transformation of the former Soviet successor states will thus be influenced not only by the overall impact of Western efforts to shape that transformation, but also by other Western efforts to serve other purposes that nonetheless have a serious impact on relations with Russia and the other successors and on their internal transformation. Inadvertent negative influences may swamp benign, deliberate, intentional policy directed toward shaping Russian policies and development, and perhaps that of other successor states. In another sense, the outcome of the internal transformation of these states, whether a success or a failure from the standpoints of internal and international stability, will in turn importantly affect the historical evaluation of Western policies. Even if other, internal factors are predominantly responsible for the outcome, as will probably be the case, success or failure—especially failure—will cast a long shadow back. Responsibility for who "lost" Russia could become an important political as well as historical question, even if the answer really rests mainly on the internal dynamics of the Russian (and other) societies.

As we examine the Western efforts to shape the behavior of the Soviet successor states over the first five years, it is evident that despite good intentions and many good deeds, long-term strategic vision and direction has been lacking. Short-term problems and ameliorative challenges have been met fairly well. But Western policies designed to meet long-term transformative challenges, especially with respect to the relationship of Russia to the international system, have not been handled well. The expansion of NATO at the expense of drawing Russia fully into the European security architecture is the most blatant and grievous error. The transformative challenges of internal development in Russia and the other successor states has also been less successfully addressed, but in this respect the role and responsibility of the external powers is less salient. In the long run, of course, the interaction of this internal development with the external environment will be decisive. The strategic task of the Western powers should be to facilitate, or at least not to take steps that make more difficult, such internal transformation in the desired direction. That will also contribute to more cooperative and less adversarial external relationships.

In historical perspective, it may be no easier than it is now to judge the effects of Western efforts to shape the policies and development of the Soviet successor states. Nonetheless, it is clear that some Western policies and actions are helpful, and others are not. Although the Western countries may not be able to determine the outcome, they do influence it. Western influence can be significant even if it is not determining. Negative influence, alas, is likely to be more evident than positive contributions. The least that can be asked of Western policies is that they not overburden and prejudice possibilities for a favorable outcome. Moreover, the question is evidently not merely one of contributing positively to a historical development in Eurasia. The West itself, and the world, have a tremendous stake in the outcome.

Notes

1. I do not in this chapter identify and apply models of policy or policy formation, or of international interaction, although I draw upon a number of them implicitly. In this connection, a few studies of Western policy influence on the Soviet Union are especially useful, taking account of the end of the Cold War and transformation of the international system, and the collapse of the Soviet Union and the succession of Russia and other republics. See Jack Snyder, "International Leverage on Soviet Domestic Change," *World Politics* 42, no. 1 (October 1989): pp. 1–30; George Breslauer and Philip Tetlock, ed., *Learning in U.S. and Soviet Foreign Policy* (Boulder, CO: Westview Press, 1991); and Roy Lubit, "Learning and Foreign Policy Change, the Undervalued Variable: Development of Soviet and American Security Policies" (unpublished manuscript, 1996). These and other discussions usually begin with the realist model and its variants, a neoliberal institutionalist model, a domestic (or bureaucratic) politics model, and a learning model. I see elements of each as useful, with particular attention to the perceptual as well as actual interaction of protagonists.

2. See also the discussion in chapter 3 of this volume by Alvin Z. Rubinstein.

3. See George W. Breslauer, "Aid to Russia: What Difference Can Western Policy Make?" in *The New Russia: Troubled Transformation,* ed. Gail Lapidus (Boulder, CO: Westview Press, 1995), pp. 223–44.

4. See my chapter, "A Diplomatic History of the Dispute," in *Northern Territories and Beyond: Russian, Japanese, and American Perspectives,* ed. James E. Goodby, Vladimir I. Ivanov, and Nubuo Shimotamai (Westport, CT: Praeger Publishers/Greenwood Press, 1995), pp. 11–26.

3

The Transformation of Russian Foreign Policy

Alvin Z. Rubinstein

Few would dispute the contention that Russia lost the twentieth century and that relative to other major powers it is in far worse condition now than when the century began. With the collapse of the Soviet Union in late December 1991 came the end of an extensive empire that had dominated much of the Eurasian heartland; the end of a repressive authoritarian system that had killed more of its own people than did the Nazi invaders in World War II; and the end of a tension-generating ecumenical ideology that had established a worldwide network of Moscow-oriented communist and procommunist parties and organizations. The Russia that emerged as "the continuer state" of the former Soviet Union (FSU) inherited a society in disarray, a demoralized, dispirited people, and a deteriorating, quasi-anarchical economy and political system. Still, it remained the largest of the fifteen newly independent republics and the most powerful by virtue of its possession of the preponderance of the old regime's nuclear and conventional forces and its own wealth of raw materials and energy.

That this new Russia lacked a coherent foreign policy was not surprising given its geostrategic and security challenges. It found itself shorn of a protective perimeter from the Baltic down to the Black Sea across Transcaucasia and Central Asia to Chinese Turkistan; bordered by eight of the fourteen weak and vulnerable Soviet republics that had acquired instant independence; faced with nationalisms whose conflicts had consequences for domestic as well as foreign policy; uneasy over Islam, heretofore regarded as the West's problem; and marginalized as a Middle East actor for the first time in several centuries, because it has been deprived of contiguity with Turkey and Iran in the Caucasus region and the border it had shared with Afghanistan for over 120 years. As a result, Russia had not only to rethink its relationship with regional powers such as Turkey, Iran, Pakistan, Saudi Arabia, and China, and how these impacted on the reconciliation with the United States and Western Europe, but also to reevaluate its military needs and economic situation in a new time of troubles.

The future came like an unwelcome guest for both Russia and the United States. Neither was prepared for rapid and dramatic changes in its strategic perspective or in the foreign policy that each had fashioned at enormous cost during the Cold War, and honed and tempered over a period of four decades. Bold strategic innovation—at once pragmatic and visionary—requires forethought and calculation, but neither Moscow nor Washington was up to the moment: neither acted in ways that might have set their ships of state on parallel courses. Instead, the tentative moves toward structural reconciliation were pursued without the determination and psychological affinity of a commitment to a shared goal.

Russian Expectations

The initial foreign policy orientation of Boris Yeltsin, the first president and the "father" of the Russian Federation, was unmistakably pro-Western. Yeltsin looked forward to a partnership with the United States that would go well beyond the path of reconciliation that had been pioneered by Mikhail Gorbachev. Yet, as Yeltsin's memoirs suggest, domestic politics—the conflict between the president and the parliament and the uncertainties and intense struggle over the character and pace of economic reforms—left him little time in 1992 and 1993 for foreign policy.[1] Unlike his predecessor, he left most of the specifics to his foreign minister. In Andrei Kozyrev, Yeltsin had a knowledgeable and politically congenial deputy who shared his desire for friendship with the West, integration in the world economy, and democratization of Russia. A forty-year-old middle-level official in the Department of International Organizations of the USSR Ministry of Foreign Affairs (MFA), Kozyrev hitched his star to Yeltsin's in 1990, at a time when this seemed a highly dubious career move.[2]

Kozyrev's foreign policy outlook and agenda emerged in his first published article as foreign minister. He hailed the advent of a new era for Russia. The harsh Bolshevik experiment, he said, had crushed the individual and divided mankind for a long time and must be considered a "total failure." But fortunately for Russia, in 1992, unlike 1917, "around us are not states exhausted by war and bristling against each other," but a civilized international community which values "human interests above all else and which is open to intercourse and cooperation." Our aim, declared Kozyrev, is "to become a full member of the international community," and to be viewed as a democratic, peace-loving state that poses "a threat neither to its own citizens nor to other countries." Proceeding to specifics, Kozyrev indicated that "the chief priority for Russian diplomacy is to shape the Commonwealth of Independent States" (CIS), whose viability will be far stronger if linked by "natural ties" than by "the shackles of the totalitarian system, which virtually turned us all into prisoners of one huge Gulag." Difficulties must be expected, but "we must simply learn to live as independent states and to look on one another as equal partners." With this explicit acceptance of the independence of the former union-republics of the Soviet Union, he called, in remarks directed as much toward the West as toward CIS members, for patience and goodwill in coping with "the whole complex package of problems that attend the processes of gaining of independence by all of us."[3]

His second major aim and expectation centered on nuclear issues. Here Kozyrev asserted that Russia bore a "special responsibility" to establish "reliable control over nuclear weapons" held by Belarus, Kazakhstan, and Ukraine, and thereby to ensure security both for Russia and for the other CIS states. He also spoke of the need to initiate "fruitful cooperation between Russia and the United States" in order "to achieve radical reductions in nuclear weapons," curtail the arms race, and "seek the way to minimal nuclear sufficiency with the prospect of the complete elimination of nuclear arsenals." At a UN disarmament conference in Geneva a month later, Kozyrev repeated some proposals which had been included in President Yeltsin's message to the participants—for example, the removal "from stand-by alert" of Russian and American strategic forces "trained at each other's territories and facilities," and the expansion of nuclear nonprolif-eration to include Ukraine, Kazakhstan, and Belarus, plus their joining the Nu-clear Nonproliferation Treaty (NPT) as non-nuclear powers.[4]

Third, he stressed Russia's aspirations to become part of the global econ-omy. It wanted and needed assistance to adapt to modern financial and eco-nomic norms of interaction, and to gain entry into leading organizations of the international community such as the International Monetary Fund (IMF). But the aid, cautioned Kozyrev, has to improve the population's standard of living, and credits must deliver tangible fruit. In a dismissive swipe at Gorbachev, he noted that "huge loans have been wasted" and scarce resources frittered away: "despite all the assurances and slogans" no real economic reform was carried out; "all perestroika's plans for economic transformation have resulted merely in cosmetic and haphazard repair of the administrative edict economy."[5] The presumption was that Yeltsin would not repeat Gorbachev's mistakes. He hoped that weeding out ideological and bureaucratic deadwood from rickety economic structures and advancing Russia's "brightest and best" from among the liberal intelligentsia (many of whom had experience in the West) would result in more effective reforms, particularly if the West provided the essential know-how and support. In this, like many another Russian liberals, he underes-timated the enormity of the challenges that faced Russia on the path to a market-oriented and prospering economy and overestimated the extent to which Western assistance could make a significant difference, and, indeed, how much the West would extend itself in order to make the significant difference. Kozyrev was working under the cloud of Russian history, in which no ruler had ever succeeded in pushing systemic reform without seriously endangering the stability of the state.

Yeltsin put the matter of needing Western assistance bluntly. During his first trip abroad as president (29 January–3 February 1992), he called on the United

States and other Western powers to support "Russia's economic reforms or face unknown consequences should the reforms fail."[6] (The linking of these warnings to his arms control proposals reminded the world of the possible consequences of unrest in the world's largest nuclear power.) Germany was already Russia's main source of assistance (the payoff from the July 1990 agreement at Zheleznovodsk between Chancellor Helmut Kohl and then president Mikhail Gorbachev which crafted the reunification of Germany in return for, inter alia, an economic aid package in excess of $10 billion). Like Gorbachev before him, Yeltsin viewed the bridge to Germany as one bringing not only goods and services, but political normalization with the European Union (EU), and possibly Japan as well.

Finally, Kozyrev's policy was predicated on Russia's being treated as a great power. Though fallen on hard times, the leadership, oriented as it was toward close collaboration with the West, believed that for a combination of strategic, military, and political reasons it would be accorded most-welcomed-nation treatment by the West, especially the G-7 group of industrialized powers (the United States, Germany, Japan, France, Great Britain, Italy, and Canada). What Moscow expected in the short term was not always immediately self-evident; but, certainly, it assumed massive flows of economic assistance and symbols suggestive of an evolving political partnership.

However, despite Kozyrev's agenda, coherence in Russia's foreign policy was difficult to discern. In the unfolding domestic political situation in Russia, individual ministries and, indeed, individuals close to Yeltsin often pursued their own bent, leading to even greater uncertainty as to what Russia's policy was and fueling intense disagreement. According to Nodari Simonia, a leading Russian scholar, the unresolved issue of power, the lack of consensus at the top, and pervasive "unprofessionalism, bureaucratization, and rampant corruption," all spelled confusion in dealing with the outside world. Russia's foreign policy, he noted, was "so inconsistent and variable as to give the impression that the nation" was pursuing "several foreign policies at the same time":

> For example, during 1992–93, foreign policy virtually became hostage to the politicking and confrontation of various social forces and power structures and even factions within the same structures (as on the issue of the Kurils, the Russian-speaking populations in the former republics, the attitude toward regional conflicts, and Western aid).[7]

Six months into 1992 the assault on Kozyrev began in earnest, but despite rampant rumors of his imminent resignation he remained Yeltsin's key foreign policy adviser until January 1996, when he was replaced by Evgenii Primakov. To allegations that he was excessively pro-Western, on one occasion Kozyrev made the following retort:

> You can drive a tank in the wrong lane defying traffic rules. But our choice is different: to progress according to generally accepted rules. They were invented by the West, and I'm a Westerner in this respect.

The West is rich, we need to be friends with it. But we will also maintain contact with the rest of the world, with no preferences. Thus the allegations about my pro-American orientation to the exclusion of everything else are rubbish.[8]

Another time, he denounced the "self-styled 'great-power boosters' " who speak of a "special path" for Russia:

But in essence this is a "center-swamp" that offers what is supposedly a less painful path of reforms in the shape of a semibureaucratic, semicapitalist and semimafia economy. In foreign policy, this takes the form of a position that is semiconfrontational with respect to the West and semiingratiating toward it, a position that gives the country an inferiority complex. . . .

The entire practice of our international activity refutes the trendy thesis of a pro-American tilt. At the same time, a pragmatic stocktaking of Russia's national interests in both West and East warns against the infantile disorder of anti-Americanism, which conceals either a nostalgia for the image of an enemy or an elementary inability to professionally defend our interests in any way other than confrontation.[9]

Difficulties with the United States did eventually develop, strengthening the ultranationalists and prompting Yeltsin to choose a replacement who would be more politically suitable in an election year.

Washington's Response

On Christmas day, 1991, Mikhail Gorbachev resigned as president, the Union of Soviet Socialist Republics was dissolved, and a new era began.

In his memoir, U.S. secretary of state James A. Baker III relates the mood in Moscow ten days earlier, when he witnessed Gorbachev's numbed and uncomprehending despair at the state of events, and Yeltsin's firm sense of growing power. In his discussion with Yeltsin, Baker sought to establish a standard to which the United States could hold the new leaders in the future. In the all-important realm of security, Yeltsin, he wrote, agreed "to work with the other republics on command and control, and storage of nuclear weapons; to take part in efforts for disabling nuclear weapons; to curb nuclear proliferation; and to cooperate with us to assure the speedy ratification of the START and CFE (Conventional Forces in Europe) treaties."[10] Baker found Yeltsin reassuring and remarkably candid, providing "an unprecedented outline of how the current launch system operated and how he envisioned the CIS system would operate."[11]

Although Washington had a politically congenial ruler in post-communist Moscow, it was virtually indifferent to the strategic opportunity at hand. In January 1992, instead of exploring suggestions that a "Marshall Plan" for Russia be devised, George Bush and James Baker set a more urgent priority—the reelection of the president. According to Harvey Sicherman, a Baker aide, the hopes of a New World Order perished "on the political playing fields of Pennsylvania":

When, by trumpeting the issue of health care and jobs, Democrat Harris Wofford clobbered the heavily favored former Republican attorney general, Richard Thornburgh, in an election for a Senate seat, the Bush administration's "neglect" of domestic issues became the theme of the year—and threw the White House into panic. On the defensive, Bush quickly rediscovered Japan's trading sins and rushed to Tokyo, where he lost his dinner on the lap of the Japanese prime minister. [And, it should be noted, he squandered an occasion—the fiftieth anniversary of Pearl Harbor—to reaffirm the enduring significance of the United States–Japan security relationship.] His "I Care" reelection campaign never recovered, and his foreign policy was the first casualty. Accused of not leading at home the way he led abroad, the president's answer was to stop leading abroad. It took Richard Nixon and the Senate Democrats to embarrass Bush into offering aid for Yeltsin.[12]

On 22 and 23 January 1992, after rejecting cosponsorship with the EU countries, Baker convened a meeting in Washington of forty-seven countries and seven international organizations to raise humanitarian aid for Russia and the countries of the former Soviet Union. He persuaded Bush to commit $645 million—a pittance given Russia's real economic needs. Anders Åslund, a Swedish economist who has been deeply involved in efforts to shape Russia's transformation to a market economy, argues that the humanitarian emergency was exaggerated, and that "the real issue of providing substantial financial support to help Russia move to a market economy was avoided."[13]

The full story of how and why Bush—and later Clinton—missed the boat on possibly fostering a profound transformation of Russia's socioeconomic system is still to be written. There is little doubt, however, that George Bush's ability to secure the peace fell victim to Ronald Reagan's success in waging the Cold War. The unparalleled deficits run up by Reagan's crusade against the "evil empire" deprived Bush of the means to place democracy and free markets on a sound footing in Russia: "Among other things, he inherited a national debt that had almost tripled in eight years, from $785 billion to $2.2 trillion"; interest on the debt exceeded $200 billion in 1992.[14] For whatever reasons, Bush was slow to mobilize the resources of the West and Japan to help Yeltsin return Russia to Europe, a process started under Gorbachev. No vision nurtured the high hopes that came with the end of the Cold War and the prospect of a sizable peace dividend—no Marshall Plan, no political partnership in the international arena, and no creation of "an American-Russian Defense Community" that would eliminate "the confrontation between nuclear forces," "phase out the secrecy between the two establishments," cooperate against nuclear proliferation, and "strengthen the understanding of the principle of civilian control of the military."[15]

A concerned Richard Nixon went public. In his speech on 11 March 1992, the former president declared that "freedom is on trial, and if freedom does not work, the Russian people are not going to return to communism, because it failed, but they will return . . . to a new despotism . . . which would have the overtones of imperialist Russian activities which have been traditional in Russian history" and that "could be a far more dangerous threat" to peace in the world than was the old Soviet totalitarianism. He stressed the importance of helping Russia move toward a "free market economy" and making the most of Yeltsin's leadership. Rating both Yeltsin and Gorbachev "as political heavyweights," he observed that Yeltsin, unlike Gorbachev, "has repudiated not just communism but socialism, as well," and has moved far beyond his predecessors in the field of arms control:

> Yeltsin is the most pro-Western leader in Russian history. Under those circumstances then, he deserves our help. Charity, it is said, begins at home and I agree. But aid to Russia, just speaking of Russia specifically, is not charity. We have to realize that if Yeltsin fails the alternative is not going to be somebody better, it's going to be somebody infinitely worse. We have to realize that if Yeltsin fails, the new despotism which will take its place will mean that the peace dividend is finished, we will have to rearm, and that's going to cost infinitely more than would the aid that we provide at the present time.[16]

Though he does not mention Nixon's speech in his book, Baker pressed Bush to commit the G-7 nations, the IMF, and the World Bank to a $24 billion package of financial assistance to Russia in 1992. This was announced 1 April 1992. But the package was poorly made. Russia was granted and encouraged to spend $11 billion in commodity credits, which weakened the ruble. All the while, the key item in the package was the $6 billion for a ruble stabilization fund that was to come from the IMF, which Russia joined on 27 April. "The IMF then disqualified Russia as a recipient of stabilization financing," notes Anders Åslund, "because it had received such large amounts of detrimental credits."[17] He blames this politically absurd sequence of conflicting credits on the IMF, whose handling of Russia's currency reform "could hardly be worse," and on the West, who gave all its attention to the details of the loans and not to the fulfillment of its promises. By the end of 1992, Russia's reforms had largely failed, and the reformers in Yeltsin's cabinet found themselves increasingly stymied by the resurgent bureaucratic, conservative nomenklatura-types who dominated the Duma and who tried on two occasions in 1993 to rid themselves of Yeltsin.

Regarding the difficulties of mobilizing the massive help that partisans of reform argued was needed to make a difference, Bush is alleged to have said, "We have the will but not the wallet." More likely he found the challenge too daunting to attempt.

In 1992, the thread connecting Bush and Clinton was their sense of the saliency of domestic issues and desire to downplay foreign affairs; in a few speeches, Clinton gave voice to aid for Russia in order to get the issue out of the way and permit himself to focus on the economy. The net effect was to relegate Russia to the sidelines for most of the campaign.

Thus, on 1 April 1992, Bill Clinton sounded Nixonian themes, calling for strong support of Yeltsin, accelerated efforts to speed Russia's transition to democracy and a market economy, privatization of key industries, and conversion of military production to civilian uses. After his election, Clinton did somewhat better than Bush had. He spoke out forcefully for Yeltsin against his opponents in the Duma, when they threatened him with impeachment in March 1993; and a month later, prior to their first summit meeting in Vancouver, Canada, he offered financial assistance as a demonstration of confidence. But the course he set was too prone to diversion.

The $28 billion financial package Clinton cobbled together in April 1993 sounded more impressive than it was in reality. Moreover, contends Jeffrey Sachs, "only a tiny fraction of the announced aid" ever arrived, and once again the IMF was found wanting:

> The last chance for the West in 1993 came in October, just after Yeltsin's coup [against the Duma]. The moment was critical for three reasons. First, Fedorov [the reformist finance minister] had an enormous opportunity for action and was moving rapidly to clean up the abuses of the budget and Central Bank. Second, the public was highly disoriented and needed a concrete sign of continuing reforms. Third, elections were on the horizon in just eight weeks.
>
> The IMF came back to Moscow in October with a degree of obtuseness unmatched in its sorry history in Russia. It rejected any immediate support on the grounds that the Russians had violated the monetary targets in August, under completely different political conditions. It took pride in saying, explicitly, that the forthcoming election should be of no relevance to the institution's lending timetable. It announced that it would not give any support in the fall, and would disburse funds in the first quarter of 1994.
>
> So the reformers went into the elections in December with rapidly growing public misunderstanding. They had avoided hyperinflation; yet they were blamed for the inflation nonetheless. They had fought corruption by ending many bureaucratic interventions in the economy, but they were blamed for corruption nonetheless. They had tried, over hard-line opposition, to shift government spending from wasteful subsidies to targeted social relief, but they were blamed for the absence of an adequate social safety net. They had succeeded in privatizing 80,000 enterprises, but were blamed for continued insecurity of property rights.[18]

The rise and fall of Russia's reformers is a complex and still incomplete story. Should Russia be "lost" to democracy, there will be endless postmortems: who was closer to the truth, the partisans of "shock therapy," such as Anders Åslund and Jeffrey Sachs, or the "gradualists," such as Padma Desai and Peter Murrell? What should U.S. policy—as opposed to political posturing—have been? Given the preoccupation of Bush in 1992 and Clinton in 1993 with domestic problems, and the absence of a Republican or Democratic party strategy for dealing with Russia, did not budgetary restraints, residual Cold War conceptions, and diffused presidential focus foreshadow the neglect of Yeltsin's real needs during Russia's fateful period of decision?

Yeltsin's hopes that the United States would use part of its peace dividend to finance Russia's democratic transformation and political integration into the West were disappointed in 1992 and dashed in 1993. Ironically, his biggest setback came from his staunchest supporter—President Bill Clinton.[19] It was Clinton who in 1993 twice helped Yeltsin surmount challenges from ultranationalists and antireformers in the parliament; but it was also Clinton who did little to accelerate the flow of promised aid to Yeltsin when he really needed it and who, by proposing NATO's expansion to the east in the fall, when Yeltsin was under attack at home, inadvertently strengthened Yeltsin's opponents, enabling them to dominate the December parliamentary elections.

This was the environmental context in which Russian officials and analysts began to debate the wisdom of Kozyrev's foreign and defense policy and the essentials of what should constitute Russia's national interest.

A Foreign Policy for Russia

At first, Russia's foreign policy debate centered on two competing conceptions—Atlanticism and Eurasianism. Each was persuasive, and a part of Russia's history. The Atlanticists, epitomized by Kozyrev and his adherents in the MFA, argued that the West's goodwill and support were crucial to the success of Russia's economic reforms, promotion of democracy, and integration into Western civilization and international institutions. Kozyrev emphasized that Russia had "painlessly" replaced the Soviet Union in the United Nations and its affiliated organizations, developed close ties to the G-7 nations, thus ensuring Russia's entry into the IMF, and had moved relations with the United States "from the sphere of rapprochement to the sphere of friendly and, in the future, allied relations."[20] In interviews with Russian and foreign journalists, he acknowledged the many difficult problems that Russia faced, but kept them located within this overall framework of friendship with the West.[21]

Initially, Kozyrev's main critics were adherents of the Eurasianist school. Not a new phenomenon in Russia's political and philosophical landscape, Eurasianism first appeared in the late nineteenth century and reemerged in Russian émigré circles during the 1920s and 1930s. The current debate was started by a member of Yeltsin's foreign policy team, State Counsellor Sergei Stankevich. He called the Atlanticist approach "rational, pragmatic, and natural: That's where the credits are, that's where the aid is, and that's where the advanced technology is."[22] But he cautioned that a policy of pragmatism "that is not balanced by a healthy idealism will most likely degenerate into cynicism." He envisaged a mission for Russia that would "initiate and maintain a multilateral dialogue of cultures, civilizations, and states." Given its geographic and geopolitical boundaries, Russia, he said, must strike a new balance of Western and Eastern orientations which means strengthening "our positions in the East, rectifying the obvious distortion caused by the creators [Gorbachev and Shevardnadze] of the conception of the 'common European home.' "[23]

Stankevich recommended a differentiated approach to CIS partners, distinguishing between those who intended to go their own way and those "for whom the Commonwealth is a fundamental historical choice"; a strong policy of defending the rights of Russians living in the near abroad; and cultivation of close ties with "traditional partners," such as Mexico and Brazil, South Africa, Greece and Turkey, and India and China. Stankevich's moderate brand of Eurasianism was neither antidemocratic nor really anti-Western; what divided him and Kozyrev was mainly a matter of emphasis.

There were many critics, with a wide range of discontents. Georgii Arbatov, director of the USA and Canada Institute (ISKRAN), ridiculed assumptions of U.S. readiness to share advanced technology and to create a joint Russian-American ballistic missile defense program.[24] Andranik Migranian of the CIS Center of the Russian Academy of Sciences (RAN) attacked Kozyrev's reluctance to declare "the entire geopolitical space of the former USSR" a sphere of "vital interest" in which Russia must be more decisively engaged in curbing conflicts and ensuring stability; he advocated the promulgation of a "Monroe Doctrine" for the area, similar to that which the United States had enunciated in the early nineteenth century for the entire Western hemisphere.[25] Leading newspaper commentators sustained the assault on the MFA: Yurii Glukhov of *Pravda* derided the "egghead" scholars planning to commit Russian troops to UN multinational peacekeeping forces, "a lousy situation [in which] we can at best hope to play the role of the West's hired hands and mercenaries."[26] Aleksandr Vasilyev of *Komsomol'skaya Pravda* called Kozyrev "an idealist" who had invented a so-called "civilized world" in the West to suit his imagined fancies; he noted with approval that U.S. pressure on Russia to cancel the sale of rocket technology to India on the grounds that it could contribute to proliferation had been rejected, though only after bitter "infighting in the Moscow corridors of power."[27] The list was long, and the criticisms continued throughout 1992 and 1993. Kozyrev's general approach had Yeltsin's support, but on a few issues— for example, Iran, Iraq, and relations with Japan and the possible return of the Kuril Islands—Kozyrev had to yield to nationalistic pressures.[28]

Early in his tenure, Kozyrev set the MFA the task of identifying the country's national interests. In February 1992 it circulated the first draft of a document entitled "On the Concept of Russian Foreign Policy." During the year, there was extensive debate of its principles and focus, but against the backdrop of the two severe domestic challenges to Yeltsin's rule nothing fundamental changed in the realm of foreign policy. Still, Kozyrev's uneasiness over the growing influence of the nationalists led him to deliver a wake-up call at a meeting of the Conference on Security and Cooperation in Europe (CSCE) in Stockholm in mid-December 1992. Reminiscent of Orson Welles's *War of the Worlds* radio broadcast in 1938 was Kozyrev's shocking speech to his foreign colleagues, in which he solemnly declared that Russia's tradition in Asia set limits on its rapprochement with Europe, deplored the West's military buildup in the Baltic states, assured Serbia of Russia's full support, and advocated the immediate reintegration into a new federation of all former Soviet republics. He then hastened to reassure all present that none of this was true, that he had merely hoped to emphasize the urgent need for a prompt upgrading of Western help in order to strengthen the beleaguered reformers and democrats in Moscow.[29]

One month later, Kozyrev submitted a revision of the document to the Duma.[30] The key tenets included:

— "The settling of conflicts around Russia" and safeguarding the human and minority rights of ethnic Russians and the Russian-speaking population in nearby countries;
— "the preservation of the unity and territorial integrity of the Russian Federation";
— the declaration that the entire territory of the former Soviet Union was a vital sphere within which Russia's interests cannot be denied or ignored;
— CIS's transformation "into an effective interstate formation of sovereign subjects of international association, based on commonality of interests and voluntary participation in various forms of cooperation";
— support for arms control and disarmament measures, including implementation of the START II Treaty, concentration of all nuclear forces on the territory of the FSU in the hands of Russia, control over the export of missile technology, and adoption of the Chemical and Biological Weapons Conventions;
— strengthened relations with the United States and Western Europe;
— fostering of closer ties with the nations of Asia.

The "Concept" document presented an optimistic view of global trends and implicitly of Russia's relationship with the United States and the rest of the West. It posited that the new Russian state was of a "democratic nature" and shared "a common understanding of the basic values of world civilization and commonality of interests in maintaining peace and security''; that "Russia does not take an a priori view of any state as hostile, nor as being friendly, but rather proceeds from the desire to build maximally friendly and mutually beneficial relations with all"; and that the "primary source of global and regional threats in the coming decades" is to be found in the Third World. Kozyrev's optimistic outlook, which was by no means universally shared in Moscow, may have been at its peak on 22 June 1994, when he signed the Partnership for Peace (PfP) Framework Document, signifying Russia's intention to cooperate fully with NATO and, at some time in the future, to become a full-fledged member.[31]

However, the course of Russian–American relations has been less than roseate. Already by 1994 tensions not mentioned in the Concept document were assuming greater prominence: tensions over nuclear issues, relations with Iran and India, rivalry in the Caucasus, Bosnia, foreign assistance, membership in international organizations (governmental and nongovernmental), and NATO's PfP proposal itself. All of this was a reflection of the slowing down of, and disenchantment in Russia with, the reformist impulses toward democracy and a market economy.

Kozyrev himself called attention to these emerging tendencies and said that if there was to be real partnership between the West and Russia there must, "in practical terms," be policy adjustments along the following lines:[32]

— "Institutional gaps" needed to be closed, with Russia being made a member of the G-7 industrial nations;
— NATO's future must be rethought, because it no longer had to defend against the military threat for which it was created; its Partnership for Peace proposal served to bring Russia "closer to the alliance for now," but it "should not stimulate NATO-centrism among the alliance's policymakers or NATO-mania among impatient candidates for membership," both of whom have a stake in portraying Russia as a threat to European security;
— CSCE (renamed in December 1994 the Organization for Security and Cooperation in Europe, or OSCE) should be transformed into a post-Cold War system for European–American cooperation and security;
— the rules of partnership dictated "the need not only to inform one another of decisions made, but also to agree on approaches beforehand. It would be hard to accept an interpretation of partnership in which one side demands that the other coordinate its every step with it while the former retains complete freedom for itself. Partners must have mutual respect for each other's interests and concerns." He cited Bosnia as an example of a regional conflict on which there had not been adequate consultation between Russia and the United States;
— more respect should be shown for Russia's efforts to master "complex, ambiguous situations" similar to those that the United States "more than once had to deal with . . . in Europe and Latin America"; Russia did not talk gleefully of U.S. difficulties and mistakes in Somalia, but "some people in the West" had done precisely that regarding the Russian role in Abkhazia. [Note: After December 1994, Kozyrev could have mentioned Chechnya as well.]

In Kozyrev's admonitions lay imbedded the outlines of Russia's emerging conception of its national interest. The conflicting outlooks of Russia and the United States, their erupting frictions, could not indefinitely hide behind professions of good intentions.

The evolution of Russia's approach to its security will be examined here with respect to the following issue areas:

- Commonwealth of Independent States (CIS)
- Partnership for Peace (PfP)
- the nuclear complex
- East Asia

Commonwealth of Independent States (CIS)

On 3 December 1991, on the eve of the dissolution of the USSR, an agreement was signed by Russia, Belarus, and Ukraine, creating the Commonwealth of Independent States (CIS). Concerned at being left out, non-Slavic republics pressed for membership, and on 23 December Azerbaijan, Armenia, Kazakhstan, Kyrgyzstan, Moldova, Tajikistan, Turkmenistan, and Uzbekistan become members as well (Georgia joined in 1993). Only the Baltic states—Estonia, Latvia, and Lithuania—elected to go their own way.

In his first official statement as foreign minister, Kozyrev described the situation in the area around Russia as "something that could probably be called the 'near' abroad."[33] The term came to mean, variously, the non-Russian republics of the FSU; ethnic Russians (*russkie*), Russian-speakers (*russko-iazychenie*), or Russian citizens (*rossiskie*) living in those republics; and the geopolitical space that Russia came increasingly to regard as its "natural" sphere of influence and region of special security significance. Thus, the "near abroad" has demographic, linguistic, political, and strategic connotations that resonate strongly in Russian domestic and foreign policy. In light of these factors, plus the role of historical memory and economic linkages in foreign policy formation, it is not surprising that most Russians agreed with Kozyrev when he said, "The chief priority for Russian diplomacy is to shape the Commonwealth of Independent States." Over the years, Yeltsin and his foreign ministers (Andrei Kozyrev, January 1992–January 1996; Evgenii Primakov, January 1996–) have probably devoted more attention to CIS affairs than to all other foreign policy issues combined.

With the end of the USSR, Russia lost about 24 percent of its territory and almost 40 percent of its population. More than 75 percent of the estimated 25 million Russians in the near abroad reside in Ukraine, Belarus, and Kazakhstan, hence the critical impact of developments in these countries on the condition of the Russian/Russian-speaking minority. Thus far, the emigration of Russians from the near abroad, predominantly from Central Asia, has occurred in a relatively orderly way. The present ethnic and interrepublic tensions in Central Asia may foreshadow danger for the independence of the newly independent republics. For Russia, Kazakhstan is, in many respects, the key to the future of the region. A landlocked territory about four times the size of Texas, rich in energy and natural resources, with a population of some 18 million, it suffers from a north–south ethnic divide. Under President Nursultan Nazarbaev, the government has so far deflected the rumblings of discontent among the non-Kazakh population (49 percent), which lives primarily in the northern part of the country, contiguous to Russia. This uneasy coexistence of Slavs and Kazakhs occasionally shows signs of breaking down. However, as long as power is retained by Nazarbaev, a masterful politician who is pursuing a not-too-subtle but deft process of "Kazakhification" of key ministries and institutions, Moscow and Almaty have more in common than not, and a mutual though asymmetrical interest in the territorial and political status quo. To its credit, Moscow has worked hard to make the accommodation work, particularly in the nuclear-military fields.

According to Aleksei Arbatov, director of the Center for Geopolitical and Military Forecasts and a member of the Duma's Defense Committee, Russia's primary objectives are to promote political stability and to prevent and limit conflicts on the territory of the FSU, lest they threaten Russia's security:

> The maximum task (desired) is economic and political integration on the basis of equal rights, voluntary actions, and mutual advantage for the CIS countries, above all Russia, Ukraine, Kazakhstan, and Belarus. If the desired turns out to be unattainable, the minimum task (vitally important for the Russian Federation) is to prevent the appearance of a hostile coalition of other republics, which will inevitably try to gain support from outside.[34]

Given its extraordinarily large number of active and latent border problems— both external and internal—Russia faces a nightmarish prospect of mapmaking and border negotiations for years to come. One estimate placed the number of violent conflicts on the geographic space of the FSU at about 180.[35] At present, Russia has settled borders only with Belarus and Finland, and territorial claims with China appear close to settlement.

Moscow's haste, therefore, to confirm CIS military-security arrangements is understandable. Initially, it was especially important to convince Ukraine, Kazakhstan, and Belarus to relinquish the nuclear weapons in their possession and to accede to the NPT as nonnuclear states.[36] Discreet but firm assistance from the United States helped accomplish this expeditiously.

Far more difficult has been the reconfiguration of Russian conventional forces with those of CIS members. The attempt in 1992 to create a highly integrated CIS alliance structure modeled on NATO was a failure.[37] In establishing relations with CIS members, Russian planners faced a number of problems: how to restructure their forces and force deployments within the constraints of substantially reduced resources; how to balance CIS members' requests for assistance with Russia's own internal military needs; how to fashion military agreements that would not be viewed as threatening by Russia's dependent clients; and how to legitimate the retention of military installations in member states, especially in Kazakhstan.

The Russian military doctrine adopted in November 1993 focused on preventing strife in the near abroad; it attributed the threats to "social, political, territorial, religious, national, ethnic and other conflicts and the desire of a number of states to want to resolve them by means of armed conflict"; to "territorial claims on Russia or its allies"; and to "suppression of the rights, freedoms, and legitimate interests of citizens of the Russian Federation" living in CIS states.[38] Thus far, Russian involvement and peacekeeping operations have been prompted by requests from beleaguered governments—for example, in Tajikistan, Georgia, and

Armenia—and not from victimized Russians. This leads Raymond Garthoff to conclude that "the new Russian military interest in strengthening CIS military ties and in a limited Russian forward deployment and involvement in the CIS clearly seems to stem more from defensive concerns than from expansive ambitions."[39]

Russia currently has approximately 100,000 troops and border guards in other CIS countries. Most of them are engaged in Georgia, Moldova, and Tajikistan in peacekeeping operations (in Russian, *mirotvorchestvo*—"creation of peace"— which encompasses the ideas of peacekeeping, peacemaking, and conflict management, and is therefore broader than Western terminology implies). The first Russian deployments took place in the summer of 1992 in Georgia "to separate the warring Ossetians, who aspired to unification with their brethren in Russia, from the Georgian militia, which was fighting to hold Georgia together."[40] Separatist movements in South Ossetia and Abkhazia exacerbated Georgia's internal civil strife and led to the ouster of the country's first independent president, Zviad Gamsakhurdia. The current leadership, headed by former Soviet foreign minister Eduard Shevardnadze, has come to regard the 20,000 Russian peacekeepers in these areas as the price its country must pay to preserve Georgia's territorial integrity. Bilateral treaties were signed in February 1994 permitting Russia to maintain permanent military bases in Georgia and to station troops along the border with Turkey. For Moscow, emerging from the fog of uncertainty that characterized Yeltsin's policy in 1992 and 1993, the experience confirms the time-tested practice of exploiting ethnic rivalries to inject its influence into Transcaucasia's polyglot political arena.

Like Shevardnadze, leaders in Moldova and Tajikistan have requested Russian peacekeepers as the price of political survival against rebellious factions. The two operations have succeeded in containing the fighting (less so in Tajikistan), but fallen "short of addressing the causes of the conflicts and of providing solutions."[41] They have also enhanced Moscow's status as an honest broker and deepened the dependency of the requesting governments.

Attempts to provide the CIS peacekeeping operations with a UN imprimatur have eluded agreement, basically for two reasons: on the one hand, the OSCE countries do not wish to concede to Russia freedom of action throughout the FSU; and, on the other hand, Moscow refuses to allow OSCE the automatic involvement in the political process which it presumes for its own peacekeepers or to grant the OSCE any control over Russia's freedom of action in CIS space. However, in July 1994, in a limited accommodation, the UN Security Council endorsed the deployment of Russian peacekeepers to Abkhazia, together with a small number of UN military observers. For the moment, this makeshift accord is holding.

Moscow also signed collective security agreements with all CIS countries except Turkmenistan, which uses a bilateral treaty to regularize the presence of Russian troops along its borders with Iran and Afghanistan. These agreements have provided Russia with important basing facilities in Kazakhstan, Armenia, Georgia, and Tajikistan.

In the economic realm, Moscow's efforts at promoting integration have met with less success. A large number of interstate and interministerial treaties and agreements have been negotiated, and a Treaty on Economic Union, signed in Moscow on 24 September 1994 by nine of the republics, envisages the gradual reduction and eventual abolition of all customs tariffs, a payments union, and interlocking cooperative economic arrangements; but the progress is more apparent than actual, as the following may illustrate.

First, in early 1996, the Customs Union still consisted only of Russia and Belarus. Then, on 29 March, Kazakhstan and Kyrgyzstan joined with Russia and Belarus to form an economic union. Integration is a distant goal. In the short term, Yeltsin seeks to breathe life into the Commonwealth, calm Russians in the near abroad, and show himself capable of reforging close relationships with newly independent FSU republics. Second, Deputy Prime Minister Aleksei Bolshakov, chairman of a governmental commission on Russian–CIS cooperation, acknowledged that CIS integration was proceeding with difficulty, only 22 percent of Russia's total exports going to the CIS. Indeed, according to data provided by CIS Executive Secretary Ivan Korotchena, "the CIS' share in Russia's foreign commodity turnover amounted to only 24 percent, while the rest belonged to third countries"; whereas, at the end of the Soviet period, "inter-republic ties accounted for 58 percent of Russia's commodity turnover." This trend is likely to continue; that is, "the CIS countries' foreign commodity turnover with the near abroad will decline, while that with the far abroad will conversely increase."[42] Third, there has been little movement in passing compatible tax legislation and commercial codes in all CIS states. Finally, there is the parlous condition of the "transit monopoly" of the Trans-Siberian Railroad and the major ports of the Russian Federation "connected to it on the Baltic, Black, Azov, and White Seas and in the Far East"; as the rail system and rolling stock deteriorate faster than their replacement and modernization, there is much less expansion, and CIS states are looking for alternative routes for Euroasian traffic and trade through Turkey, Iran, and China.[43]

Russia's quest for a "special role" in Transcaucasia and Central Asia is further motivated by the vast oil reserves of the Caspian Sea Basin, the disposition of which Moscow seeks to dominate. The far from settled key issue revolves around the legal status of the Caspian. With Turkmenistan's support, Russia and Iran, relying on their 1921 and 1940 treaties, contend that the Caspian Sea is a closed body of water—that is, a lake—"and therefore its resources are common property of all the states bordering the Caspian and an object of their joint use." However,

> other states bordering the Caspian—Azerbaijan and Kazakhstan—feel that the Caspian is a closed sea. The status of a lake presupposes the common possession of the Caspian, its shelf, mineral wealth, etc., while the status of a sea, in conformity with the UN Convention on Maritime Law, establishes the sovereign rights of each of the states bordering the Caspian to its own "economic zone"—its part of the mineral wealth, shelf, territorial waters, etc.[44]

The stakes are enormous, economically and strategically. Possession of the oil is not as important as control of the oil pipelines. For the moment, Russia holds the strongest cards. In recognition of this, in October 1995, the Clinton administration influenced Azerbaijan's president Gaidar Aliev to agree to have two new pipelines built to transport Azeri oil: one, a Russian pipeline from Baku to Novorossiisk, across the northern Caucasus, the other, across Georgia to Turkey. Given the unrest in the Caucasus, the Russian pipeline is the more likely candidate for early construction. To counterbalance this tilt toward Russia, the United States disputes Russia's contention about the nature of the Caspian Sea. But uncertainties will cloud the investment environment and affect political maneuvering for years to come.

Beyond doubt, however, is the CIS's centrality in Moscow's foreign and security policies. President Yeltsin issued a sweeping decree, dated 14 September 1995, on "The Affirmation of the Strategic Course of the Russian Federation with Member States of the CIS," which sets forth the major objectives of Russian policy.[45] According to this decree, the goal of Russia's relations with the states of the CIS should be "to create an economically and politically integrated alliance of states capable of achieving a worthy place in world society." As the dominant power in this alliance, Russia should take the lead in forging "a new system of inter-state political and economic relations over the territory of the post-Soviet expanse." Soon after taking office, Foreign Minister Evgenii Primakov underscored the importance of Russia's relations with the CIS states and emphasized that "their sovereignty is irreversible, but this does not rule out the development of reintegration tendencies in the economic sphere." At a summit meeting of the heads of CIS states in Moscow in January 1996, Yeltsin declared that "a trend toward voluntary integration has finally taken shape among the countries of the Commonwealth."[46] In an obvious reaction to the calls for reintegration of the republics of the FSU by ultranationalist members of the new Duma elected the previous month, Kazakhstan's President Nazarbaev stressed that "it is now impossible to restore the Soviet state in its old borders without violence. Such attempts will undermine stability and sovereignty, call into question economic and social progress, and run counter to the long-term interests of the Commonwealth."[47]

Given the weaknesses of most CIS states, a cooperative strategy serves their interests as well as Russia's. As long as Moscow is seeking security and not a new empire, does not threaten their independence, and promotes the CIS as one of the world's larger organizations, governments with otherwise limited resources have a greater opportunity to voice their common concerns than any one of them singly. On the other hand, if Moscow's policy is seen as excessively intrusive, or if economic improvements do not come about quickly enough as a result of greater integration, the Russian strategy of pressured cooptation will encounter strong resistance.

Russia's policy toward the CIS satisfies the United States' stated opposition to coercion and intimidation of neighboring states, and for the time being it is not a major source of tension. According to Deputy Secretary of State Strobe Talbott, who is primarily responsible for Clinton's policy toward Russia, "We will endorse regional cooperation only so long as it is truly and totally voluntary and only if it opens doors to the outside world."[48]

Partnership for Peace

For centuries, Russia's foreign policy, particularly in Europe, was driven primarily by a sense of strategic vulnerability and a quest for secure borders. The profound changes in Europe and Eurasia since 1991 require that Moscow rethink its security policy. Aleksei Arbatov offered a thoughtful perspective:

> The withdrawal of Russian armed forces from the center of Europe over a distance of 1,500 kilometers, from Magdeburg to Smolensk, led to an unfamiliar state of strategic vulnerability: For the first time in hundreds of years, Moscow Oblast ceased to be deep in the heartland and became the advance frontier. On the other hand, this was also an unprecedented advantage, because it separated the forces of the Western military powers and Russia over a vast distance . . .
>
> The maintenance and legal consolidation of this separation is one of the main objectives of the Russian national strategy of security. . . . This means that one of the pillars of the new European security system should be the guaranteed neutral and non-nuclear status, independence, and sovereignty of the "double belt" of East European states and western republics of the former USSR. For many centuries these countries served as the bridgehead for Western aggression against Russia or for Russian aggression against the West. In the future Western Europe, the United States, and Russia should become the guarantors of the neutrality and security of these countries and turn them into a bridge for economic and political cooperation between Russia and the West.[49]

Arbatov's strategic logic was commendable; but the best of foreign policy logic can be upset by unpredictable events.

Yeltsin and Kozyrev had assumed, perhaps naively, as they embarked on an unequivocally pro-Western course, that the end of the Cold War and dissolution of the FSU implied the end of NATO as well. However, in the fall of 1993, stymied by an inability to pass a health care bill and criticized abroad for waffling on Somalia, Haiti, and Bosnia, President Clinton looked for a new foreign policy doctrine to enhance his sagging prestige. In a series of rapid-fire speeches, the Clinton Doctrine of Enlargement emerged: on 21 September, National Security Adviser Anthony Lake proclaimed the shift from containment to enlargement; on 23 September, UN Ambassador Madeline K. Albright stressed the moral and multilateral bases of a U.S. policy wedded to a strong United Nations; and on 27 September, President Clinton added a universal dimension to the aims of enlargement. But to satisfy NATO allies uneasy over U.S. intentions in Europe and to allay the anxieties of East Europeans who feared a Russian revival, a specifically European focus was needed. The resulting solution may perhaps best be described in words George F. Kennan used to deplore Washington's attempt to deal with Moscow at a different time, in different circumstances, but with consequences that were momentous then—and could well be again:

> A new era had begun in the Russian capital. Once again, as so often in the course of these rapidly moving events, Washington—troubled, hesitant, and ill-informed—had spoken, reluctantly, into the past.[50]

At a NATO summit meeting in Brussels on 10 and 11 January 1994, President Clinton formally proclaimed the Partnership for Peace (PfP) proposal, which held out the prospect of NATO membership for Central Europe, the Baltic states, and the republics of the FSU, including Russia. At once an invitation to join in the evolutionary process of the "enlargement" of NATO, it was also a dampener of expectations, leaving purposely vague the timing and procedure for admission.

Foreign Minister Kozyrev generally supported the initiative, notwithstanding the findings published in late November 1993 by the Foreign Intelligence Service (then headed by Evgenii Primakov), saying that NATO's expansion to the proximity of Russian borders would occasion "a drastic revision of all defense concepts" because of the threats to Russia's vital interests.[51] (The Foreign Intelligence Service assumed the external functions of the KGB and, like its American counterpart, prepares analytical assessments of international threats.) On signing the PfP Framework Document in Brussels on 22 June 1994, Kozyrev repeated his assumptions, which were soon to create problems between NATO and Russia; namely, that the initiative would involve treating the two former Cold War adversaries on an equal footing and that it would provide NATO "an opportunity *to continue its adaptation to the real needs of European security,* to dovetail its activities with those of the CSCE [renamed the OSCE after 1 January 1995] which plays the key role in matters concerning European security and cooperation."[52] At the CSCE summit in Budapest six months later, an irate Yeltsin, reacting to domestic pressure and criticism of his passive policy in Bosnia, reversed the previous decision to reaffirm Russian participation in PfP and warned of the dangers of a "cold peace." In May 1995, after meeting with Clinton in Moscow on the occasion of the fiftieth anniversary of the victory over Nazi Germany, Yeltsin displayed a more conciliatory tone and said that Russia would resume the PfP process toward eventual membership but was opposed to any rapid expansion. In late September, NATO presented Russia with a draft proposal for a "Political Framework for NATO-Russia Relations." But between that and actual membership for any of the suppliants, many years lie ahead.

For the time being Russia has bowed to delay as the better part of wisdom. Among Russian officials and analysts the broad consensus opposing NATO's expansion was reinforced by the U.S.-led NATO air strikes against Bosnian Serb positions in August–September 1995. The demonstration of power brought the fighting to an end, leading to the Dayton Accords and de facto partition of Bosnia; but it also infuriated the Duma, which called for reconsideration of PfP, a unilateral withdrawal from UN sanctions against Yugoslavia (Serbia), and reassessment of Russia's foreign policy options.

Russian leaders have no ready answers to NATO's unforeseen post–Cold War challenge. PfP comes at a time of systemic turmoil and persisting marginalization in Europe. (Even Russia's grudging admission to the Council of Europe in January 1996 may come a cropper, if its government fails to abolish capital punishment within three years.) It serves as a catalyst for the resurgent ultranationalism that underlies the outlook of its opponents and militates against meaningful security cooperation with the West.

The PfP proposal, which was made without consideration of its effect on Russia, has had chilling consequences for Russian–American relations. It reopened a psychological, if not ideological, division, which can only complicate the task of securing peace in Europe. Designed to buttress President Clinton's domestic position and give him a freer hand to push needed economic reforms, it has ironically proved to be a boon for the military-industrial complex—both in the United States and Russia. Russian reactions have been varied and often bitter. Prime Minister Viktor Chernomyrdin warned that it will split Europe. Among Russian democrats who had seen NATO as an institution that was important for the promotion of stability in Europe, there is now a sense of betrayal. As for the ultranationalists, the anti-American Vladimir Zhirinovsky and his ilk view PfP as a threat to Russia and evidence of "American expansionism in the Slav world."[53] Far fewer in number are those who suggest that Russia look at it positively: the European specialist, Dmitrii Trenin, for example, says "it is obvious that Russia will not acquire any veto in Europe. Instead of this we should chart a course toward convergence and close interaction between NATO and the Russian Federation."[54]

Although few Russians support NATO expansion, even among the critics there is a general understanding that PfP can contribute toward some Russian goals:

- avoidance of isolation in Europe;
- closing of the institutional gaps between Russia and the West and improving the domestic environment for reform and economic changes;
- Russian engagement in the process of forging some kind of useful strategic relationship with NATO;
- a Russian voice in the establishment of a European collective security organization, which has OSCE as its core.

Nevertheless, there is no warrant for expecting Russia's elite to ameliorate its deep and abiding mistrust of PfP. Any extension to the east of a powerful military alliance could hardly be viewed as other than a threat by Russian military planners and political leaders. At a minimum, the spillover from the PfP issue has had an effect on official thinking about security. First, Moscow will look more closely at its nuclear deterrent, as has been recommended by retired Lieutenant General Aleksandr Lebed.[55] With START II facing a problematic future, the shift away from a "no first use" nuclear policy, which was approved as Russian military doctrine in November 1993, could become even more pronounced. To compensate for the weakness of its conventional forces, Moscow has embraced the Western-style concept of deterrence and "NATO's old 'flexible response.' "[56] According to this new doctrine, certain kinds of countries are placed on notice as being liable to attack with nuclear weapons, specifically those who "join, NATO or the WEU or 'support' any Western intervention in Russia or the 'near abroad', for example, by giving rights of passage or bases."[57]

Second, opposition to PfP has accelerated efforts to transform CIS into a security system tightly controlled by Russia. At a press conference on 9 September 1995, Yeltsin said that Russia was ready to create a new military-political bloc with the CIS states, patterned after the Warsaw Pact. Of the president's decree of 14 September on Russia's Strategic Course toward the CIS, one observer noted that it "stands out among the flow of edicts" that he signs almost every day "in that it has come about amid practical actions and events which, as it were, have de facto outlined the contours" of Russia's strategy in the CIS.[58] It has intensified bilateral contacts with close CIS partners. Thus, during a visit to Belarus in early December 1995, Defense Minister Pavel Grachev signed eighteen bilateral military agreements and asserted that "Moscow retains the right to initiate creation of another military-political bloc, not to implement provisions of the CFE treaty, nor START I and START II, and to revise its position concerning flank restrictions."[59] A month later, Grachev signed sixteen such agreements with Kazakhstan.

Third, PfP has heightened fears of a new and enlarged anti-Russian coalition forming, not only in Europe but also among disaffected members of CIS's southern flank. Many Russians believe the American initiative is a pretext for increasing the U.S. military position in Europe. The Cold War may be over, but, according to Georgii Arbatov, its legacy "remains a nest of dangerous mines on the path of Russian–American reconciliation."[60] For First Deputy Defense Minister Andrei Kokoshin, PfP's enlargement is a "containment" policy, though "this time its target is not communism . . . but Russia as a great state and even as a certain type of civilization that made a huge contribution to the evolution of world culture."[61] Andranik Migranian, a Yeltsin adviser, warned his countrymen against allowing Russia to be "strategically isolated. We must not ignore even the theoretical possibility of creation of a 'cordon sanitaire' between Europe and Russia and the threat of excluding Russia from Europe."[62] The more the Americans try to convince the Russians "of the inevitability and desirability of NATO's eastward expansion," the greater the tendency in Moscow, notes a

Russian report on the Russia-U.S.–NATO Seminar, to see in PfP a conscious design "to isolate Russia and eliminate her from decision making of key European issues."[63]

Fourth, PfP may spawn a new arms race. Shock and outrage greeted Andrei Kokoshin when he told a gathering of dedicated Western Atlanticists that "many spheres of arms limitation and reduction would be severely—and maybe mortally—affected by NATO expansion to the East."[64] As far back as December 1994, Aleksandr Konovalev, director of the Center for Military Policy and Systems Analysis of the USA and Canada Institute, had observed that such a NATO development would result in CFE losing all meaning and in greater reliance on tactical nuclear weapons, as Russia sought to find the cheapest way to compensate for the imbalance of conventional capability.[65]

Lastly, Moscow has become increasingly mistrustful of the West. Its experience in Bosnia, belated admission to the Council of Europe, and exclusion from the G-7 all contribute to an uneasy suspicion that it is being manipulated into the demeaning position of a supplicant, an attitude that inevitably redounds to the benefit of the most regressive political elements in Russian society.

The Nuclear Complex

One of the vivid metaphors for the relationship between Moscow and Washington during the Cold War was of two scorpions in a bottle, each the center of the other's attention and preoccupation, knowing one wrong move would be fatal to both. In the post–Cold War era, Russia and America are no longer obsessed with one another. They are out of the bottle, but still in possession of the deadly stings that could bring sudden catastrophe. And for the indefinite future, their capabilities, which cannot be overlooked or wished away, link them in a common cause of nuclear security management. For several reasons, Russia's nuclear condition is of even greater concern to the United States than it was during the Cold War: erosion of centralized control has increased the risks of weapons grade fissionable material being diverted to foreign and rogue sources; economic disruption and turmoil have loosened bureaucratic and managerial regulation, heightening the threat of nuclear accidents and pollution; the downsizing of nuclear arsenals demands more resources than did their development and upkeep; and, in an era of fiscal constraints, storage and disposal are at risk from neglect and misplaced attention.

Every aspect of the multifaceted nuclear challenge impacts on all the others:

— The reduction and dismantling of strategic missiles and delivery systems, as mandated by the START I and START II treaties;

— the dismantling of nuclear warheads taken from strategic missiles, and the disposal of the fissionable material extracted therefrom;

— restraining nuclear proliferation by obtaining more nearly universal ad-

herence to the NPT, which was indefinitely extended at the review conference held in May 1995;
— an end to all nuclear testing, the aim of the Comprehensive Test Ban
  Treaty (CTBT);
— the denuclearization of Belarus, Kazakhstan, and Ukraine by the end of
  the century, and their adherence to the NPT;
— disposal of nuclear waste in ways that preclude the material's being used
  to make weapons or pollute the environment;
— prevention of nuclear smuggling of fissionable material that may be
  stolen or sold from inadequately policed stockpiles in the FSU;
— avoidance of other Chernobyls by enhancing the safety of Soviet-built
  power reactors in Eastern Europe and the FSU;
— establishment of suitable verification of all of the above.

Concerted action by the United States and Russia is the key to the success of
these objectives, the specifics of which have been widely discussed in the scholarly literature.[66] Denuclearization entails enormous costs and is mind-boggling
in its complexity, which is as much political as military and technical.

An example of the difficulties can be seen in the efforts of Russia and America to reduce their nuclear stockpiles. Trouble is looming over the ratification of
START II, which was only ratified by the U.S. Senate in January 1996, a full
three years after it had been signed by presidents George Bush and Boris
Yeltsin.[67] Although Yeltsin submitted the treaty to the Duma in June 1995,
ratification is far from assured. The increasingly nationalistic legislative body
has criticized the treaty for placing an excessive financial burden on the budget:
Russia will have to commit scarce resources to destroy the land-based, multiple
warhead ICBMs, replace or downsize some of them to carry single warheads,
and make them silo-based rather than mobile. Some officials have suggested
extending the SALT II time frame beyond the year 2003 so that weapons need
not be withdrawn before the end of their usefulness; others tie approval of the
treaty to strict implementation of the Anti-Ballistic Missile (ABM) treaty.
Mikhail Gorbachev warns that Russians believe NATO is "a war machine that is
trying to take advantage of our troubled political and economic situation" and
that its projected expansion "is seen as a fundamental violation of Western
guarantees after Russia dissolved the Warsaw Pact and agreed to German unification."[68] Vladimir Lukin, chairman of the Duma's Foreign Affairs Committee,
is one of a small minority who believe, like Mikhail S. Vinogradov, director of
Research of the Committee of Scientists for Global Security (an analogue to the
Arms Control Association in the United States), that Russia should sign the
treaty because, with all its shortcomings, it enables Russia to maintain an adequate deterrent:

> Russia is not the USSR: its economic potential is less than the Soviet potential
> by a factor of almost two, the gross national product is seven times less than

the American GNP, and the financial and demographic difficulties are well known also. Objective factors could prevent Russia having by the year 2003 even 3,000 warheads as part of the SOA (strategic offensive arms). What kind of correlation of SOA is safer for Russia ... 9,000 warheads against fewer than 3,000 or 3,500 against 3,000?[69]

START II, however, is not a model agreement. For one thing, it calls for the destruction only of delivery systems (missiles and bombers), not the warheads they carry. For another, the permissible limits at the end of the downsizing leave each side with 3,000 to 3,500 long-range nuclear weapons—far more than the number of feasible targets. Also, although both sides are, in fact, dismantling large numbers of warheads, "not just from strategic weapons but from short-range and medium-range ones too," the process is not subject to verification, leaving unresolved questions of accountability and credibility.[70]

Still, the treaty's advantages may, in time, come to be accepted even by ultranationalists, because its terms are such as to leave Russia with nuclear equivalence with the United States, a deterrent potent enough to safeguard Russia against likely enemies in the decades to come, a central role in the global management of nuclear issues, and a military expenditure on nuclear forces that is affordable, given Russia's economic circumstances.

The START agreements are important for what they reveal about Russia's foreign policy and its relations with the United States. First, Russia has, as far as can be determined, lived up to its treaty obligations. In addition to mandated reductions in strategic systems, it has demonstrated a readiness to cooperate with the United States in securing a CTBT and maintaining the ABM treaty. Russian–American cooperation was successful in obtaining the accession of Belarus, Kazakhstan, and Ukraine to denuclearization; if sustained, their relinquishment of the nuclear capabilities they inherited when the USSR collapsed will enhance strategic stability in the region.

Second, Russia needs considerable assistance if it is to be an effective partner in managing nuclear problems. Notwithstanding an uncertain domestic situation and irrespective of political outlook, its leadership may come to accept the advantages of reducing nuclear warheads, relying on an assured deterrent at a much lower quantitative level than before, safeguarding the stockpiles of fissionable material, and neutralizing weapons grade nuclear waste. This will, however, be expensive. For example, the U.S. government has concluded that it may cost about $36 billion just to maintain the safety of the radioactive waste stored in the underground tanks at the Department of Energy's Hanford site in Washington State. In the foreseeable future, no Russian government will have such sums to allocate for its own nuclear dumps. The Clinton administration's proposal to allocate $330 million over six years to help Russia institute new security measures at nuclear storage sites will not go very far toward solving the problem. Also at risk, without substantial U.S. assistance, is the program for dismantling nuclear warheads and neutralizing their plutonium or highly enriched uranium cores.

At the end of 1991, Congress passed farsighted and unprecedented legislation for underwriting the dismantlement of Soviet nuclear weapons—the Soviet Nuclear Threat Reduction Act, also known as the Cooperative Threat Reduction (CTR) program, but generally referred to as the Nunn-Lugar bill, in recognition of its two cosponsors, Senator Sam Nunn (D-GA) and Senator Richard Lugar (R-IN). It allotted funds from the Department of Defense budget to help Russia, Ukraine, Kazakhstan, and Belarus establish "chain-of-custody cooperation to improve fissile materials control and accountability systems, customs controls, storage facilities for dismantled nuclear warhead components, and safe and secure rail transport of fissile materials"; in addition, it stipulated that "special reciprocal monitoring and safeguard procedures also will be required if Russia and the United States can agree on how to assure each other that warheads are being dismantled and that excess fissile materials will not be re-used for weapons."[71]

To achieve these ambitious objectives, Congress provided about $1.2 billion between 1992 and 1995, of which less than $400 million had been spent as of December 1995. This rate of expenditure is far too low, and future funding is not likely to increase greatly, given the reluctance of Congress to fund assistance to the FSU. While there is some progress, according to the General Accounting Office, "CTR assistance provided as of June 1995 had been limited and the program still had to overcome numerous challenges and problems to achieve its long-term objectives" (such as the construction of nuclear storage facilities and the establishment of efficient procedures in working with the Russians).[72] A similar equivocal evaluation appertains to the 215 nonnuclear-oriented bilateral programs undertaken in the FSU by twenty-three departments and agencies of the U.S. government during the period from 1990 through 31 December 1994.[73]

Third, Russia knows that nuclear arms control is no panacea, that it offers no "magic bullet" for security. Cheating is always possible, as the Krasnoyarsk affair demonstrated. In 1979, the Politburo decided to locate the completed radars at the Krasnoyarsk facility in central Siberia east of the Ural Mountains in a way that violated the 1972 ABM Treaty; that is, the radars were oriented not toward outer space, as Moscow contended, but toward the horizon, for use as an early warning against missile attack.[74] But one hopes that the Russian leadership realizes that if used intelligently and imaginatively arms control might, in combination with force modernization, research and development, effective verification procedures, and skillful diplomacy, help it and the United States safely navigate the shoals of nuclear insecurity, and avoid another ruinous runaway arms race.

Finally, having been, in Robert Blackwill's words, "both overpromised and underdelivered," Russia distrusts the West. Its national security elite

> was showered with promises . . . of strategic partnership that would make Russia a crucial player in the creation of the "new world order." . . . Expectations went through the roof in Moscow's foreign affairs and defense establish-

ments as these elites waited for specific ideas from Washington and major West European capitals on how this lofty task might be accomplished. What they got instead was repeated and vague rhetoric and a series of exclusionary steps that mirrored Western ambivalence about including Russia systematically in its decisionmaking processes.[75]

Russia has reason to feel isolated, alienated, and ignored. Fred Ikle' has warned that "those who see the ABM and START treaties as the cornerstone of nuclear security cannot have thought far ahead"; old strategic suppositions must be jettisoned and new approaches considered, with Russia an integral party to the new opportunity offered by the collapse of the Soviet empire.[76] But far from being drawn into closer consultations with the United States and its allies on nuclear and security issues, Russia remains on the fringe, and nowhere is this more evident than in East Asia.

East Asia

Russia is "the sick man" of Asia. A status quo power, no longer a threat to neighboring states, and lacking the capabilities or regional opportunities that facilitated imperial advances in the eighteenth and nineteenth centuries, it finds itself locked into a low-cost strategy and a policy of accommodation.

In the late Gorbachev period, Moscow embarked on a policy of normalizing relations with Japan, China, and South Korea. However, the Soviet regime did not survive long enough to institute the reforms at home that might have attracted substantial Asian investment, complete the negotiations for a return of the "northern territories" of Etorofu, Kunashiri, Shikotan, and the Habomais to Japan, or engage South Korea in a major way in Siberia's economic development.

In the post-Soviet period, Moscow places much of the blame for its troubled relationship with Japan on the United States. After some tentative overtures to Tokyo to settle the territorial issue of the disputed islands, Yeltsin backed away. Like Gorbachev, he was not willing or strong enough domestically to strike a bargain with Japan in the face of nationalist opposition. Moscow believes that Japan has toughened its stand, with U.S. encouragement, because of Russia's weakened position. Far from trying to broker a Japanese–Russian reconciliation and ease tensions in Northeast Asia, the United States, according to Russian nationalists, is eager to keep the animosity alive—witness its then ambassador to Russia, Thomas Pickering, upholding Japanese claims on the eve of the December 1995 Russian parliamentary elections. Pickering's comment, made in response to a question, may have stoked ultra-nationalist passions, but it merely reaffirmed long-established U.S. policy. Henry Trofimenko, the veteran Russian America-watcher, chides some of his colleagues for their "harebrained" view that the United States should somehow help Russia out of its predicament:

The American leadership is quite satisfied with the in-built tensions in Russian–Japanese relations. Those tensions deny Japan the possibility to play balance of power politics in the Russia-Japan-America equation, in other words, to use the Russian connection to ease itself out of U.S. political domination of Japan . . .

The freeze in Russian relations with Japan is tremendously beneficial to U.S. strategic planners: they can continue to use Japan as America's military base in the North Pacific—a base that pays for itself—and at the same time not worry very much that commercial frictions will move Japan to initiate any drastic change in relations with the United States.[77]

Moreover, he argues, Washington's promotion of NATO's expansion to the east is coupled with efforts to bring NATO and Japan into closer cooperation, thereby "squeezing Russia from two sides."

A similarly doleful perspective dominates Russian assessments of developments on the Korean peninsula, where Russia finds its influence at the lowest ebb in this century. The division of Korea at the end of World War II, intended as a temporary line of demarcation between Soviet and American forces, ushered in a period of almost forty-five years of preeminent Soviet control over North Korea. By the late 1980s, Soviet influence had lessened significantly, as Gorbachev extended his "new thinking" to improve relations with South Korea, in the process alienating North Korea. Yeltsin continued to court Seoul and neglect Pyongyang. As matters turned out, Moscow had viewed South Korea too hopefully, for Seoul lost economic interest in Russia once the USSR collapsed. This has left Moscow odd capital out regarding developments on the peninsula, even though its aims are less intrusive or ambitious than any of the other powers in the region. Certainly, Russia has nothing to gain from a new conflict, and favors a peaceful unification of the two Koreas, a denuclearized peninsula, effective inspection by the International Atomic Energy Agency (IAEA) of North Korea's nuclear reactors, a decrease in tensions between North and South Korea, and the eventual withdrawal of all foreign military forces from the Korean peninsula.

But Russia no longer has the leverage or the wherewithal to play a major role; its alignment with the United States against its former ally, North Korea, has brought virtually nothing in return from Washington. When presidents Yeltsin and Clinton met in Moscow in January 1994, their joint statement agreed that the presence of nuclear weapons on the Korean peninsula would pose a threat to regional security, and called on North Korea to accept IAEA inspections in accordance with its commitment to the NPT. However, by the latter part of 1995, Russia had become resentful over what it regarded as U.S. (and South Korean) indifference to its interests and status as a regional great power. Believing that it would be included in the diplomatic efforts to manage the North Korean nuclear crisis, Moscow had given North Korea the required one year's notice in September 1995 of its intention to terminate the 1961 Soviet–North Korean defense treaty. In the months prior to that, Moscow had supported the U.S. initiative to convince North Korea to accept two

light-water reactors as replacements for North Korea's current graphite, pluto-
nium-capable reactors. From mid-1994 until the official announcement on June 13,
1995 that South Korea would provide the two light-water reactors under the aegis of
an international consortium operating through the Korean Energy Development Organization (KEDO), created specifically for this purpose, Moscow lobbied hard in
Washington, Seoul, and Pyongyang for some of the commercial contracts.[78]
Washington's lack of interest came as a severe disappointment. Indeed, according to
the *Wall Street Journal*, Kozyrev had even offered to cancel the $800 million
contract for the construction of a light-water nuclear reactor and power plant that
Moscow had signed with Iran in early 1995, in return "for $200 million in alternative
nuclear work," that is, for "a piece of a new deal to give nuclear-power equipment to
North Korea."[79] This would, it might be noted, have again made Moscow an active
player in the high-stakes Korean power game. Secretary of State Warren Christopher
never considered the offer seriously. Nor, in all likelihood, did North Korea, which
had excellent reasons to craft a settlement of the nuclear crisis with the United States
directly, and little reason to trust or respect Russia.

For its part, Moscow feels bitter about Washington's squeezing it out of the
nuclear market, and angered at Seoul's shabby treatment. Not only did South
Korea refuse to reschedule the debt Russia had incurred from the 1991 extension
of a $3 billion credit, but it has not satisfactorily resolved the disposition of the
former Soviet embassy compound, which was nationalized in 1970 without compensation. Moscow rejects as totally inadequate the amount Seoul now offers,
though officials hint at a compromise under which Russia would accept land to
build a new embassy and South Korea would finance its construction.

Russia's economic marginalization is nowhere more symbolically evident
than in its continued exclusion from the eighteen-nation organization for Asian-
Pacific Economic Cooperation (APEC), which was established in 1989 by the
United States and Asian states committed to free trade and economic cooperation. Nor is Russia (or China, for that matter) likely in the foreseeable future to
be admitted to the World Trade Organization (WTO), the successor to the General Agreement on Tariffs and Trade (GATT). Despite all of this, some Russian
liberals profess confidence in Russia's long-term economic prospects in Asia.[80]

The cornerstone of Russian policy in East Asia is China. Gorbachev's tentative political normalization in the late 1980s has given way to an emerging
entente. Nothing exemplifies the determination of Moscow and Beijing to consolidate their relationship more than the complete demarcation of the former
Soviet–Chinese border, that is, not just the Russo-Chinese part, but China's
border with Kyrgyzstan, Tajikistan, and Kazakhstan as well. The agreements
signed during Yeltsin's visit to China in April 1996 also included provisions for
mutual reductions of military forces along the border. They greatly reinforce an
expanding arms relationship. Eager to sell in hard currency markets and largely
outmaneuvered and outfinanced by Western competitors in lucrative Middle East
and Asian markets, Russia has opened its arsenal of high-tech conventional

weapons and air defense systems to China. In early 1996, by way of example, Russian sources confirmed that Moscow is supplying China with Su-27 fighter-interceptors, a combat plane that is considered on a par with the latest Western models.[81] Advanced weaponry is the coin of the Russian realm. Moreover, Russia and China are reaching agreements on nuclear cooperation, which is to include construction of a nuclear power plant, a uranium enrichment plant, and uranium mining and processing, among other projects. This deepening relationship with China is Russia's strategic response to Washington's indifference. For the moment, cautionary voices against too hasty an arming, training, and modernization of China's armed forces are largely ignored and overruled. The consequences for Russian–American relations will not be insignificant.

Conclusion

For the first time in generations, Russian interests are defined in regional rather than global terms. If there is a theoretical formulation that shapes the way Russian analysts look at the world, it is realpolitik, the assessment of which nations can threaten the domestic security of Russia proper. The result is a view of Russian national security interests that places the highest priority on the CIS states, next on relations with the United States and the West European powers, then China and India, followed by the Eastern European countries and the Middle East. This view of national priorities seems to be widely accepted across the Russian political spectrum, and it offers important insights into the long-term patterns that may emerge in Russian diplomacy.

It is already clear that Russia seeks to reestablish its status as a great power balancing competing interests in a multipolar world. At his first press conference after being appointed foreign minister, Evgenii Primakov reasserted this intention. In practice this will likely mean that Russia will utilize its position in the Eurasian heartland to act as power broker and prevent the emergence of hostile coalitions in Europe, Central Asia, or East Asia. And though Russia has neither the capability nor the present inclination to reabsorb any of the CIS regions by force, it will use all the other instruments at its disposal to ensure that the domestic and foreign policy priorities of these states are congenial to Russian national interests.

We cannot, of course, be certain that Russia's relatively unthreatening course in world affairs will continue. A change in domestic orientation could restructure foreign policy priorities. Thus, a more chauvinistic government in Moscow, anti-Western and anticapitalist, would find favor among the entrenched elements of the old nomenklatura who are still influential in the security forces, local government, and the military. Yet, given Russia's economic and military weakness, there are limits to what such a regime could undertake. Jack Matlock, former U.S. ambassador to the Soviet Union, insists that neither Gennadi Zyuganov (the leader of the Russian Communist Party) nor

Vladimir Zhirinovsky (the head of the Liberal-Democratic Party), "nor for that matter any other Russian politician, can rebuild the Communist system or the Russian empire. Russia no longer has the capacity for either, and if their rhetoric fails to recognize that reality, then the problem is with the rhetoric, not the reality."[82]

In the past, Russia's quest for security was used to justify a policy of expansion; and the expansionist policy was justified in terms of security. On the eve of a new millennium, the parallels between the military-political situation of late Imperial Russia and the former Soviet Union, on the one hand, and post-Soviet Russia, on the other, are worth noting: the erratic attempts to restructure the economy and society in order, among other reasons, to strengthen the military's capability at a less crippling cost; a sense of technological inferiority; and pervasive feelings of being an outsider in the concert of major powers.

Russian officials of different persuasions but well-disposed toward reconciliation with the West have objected to Russia's being slighted diplomatically and economically by those who profess friendship and partnership. Vladimir Lukin criticizes the United States for trying to exclude Russia from markets where it might have an advantage: ". . . nonproliferation is one thing, trying to monopolize the world market for nuclear technology and squeezing us out of it is quite another."[83] To this might be added the market for conventional weapons as well. Aleksandr Bovin, Russia's ambassador to Israel and a figure who has been close to the centers of power since Khrushchev's time, cited Washington's neglect of Moscow on matters relating to the Arab–Israeli peace process and initiatives in the Middle East in general: "Our American friends often forget about cosponsorship and prefer to go it alone."[84] Sergei Rogov, director of ISKRAN, contends that NATO expansion would "revive military brinkmanship and the arms race between Russia and the West," as well as helping the neo-imperial groups in Russian politics.[85] And Viktor Kremenyuk, one of the most consistently moderate and thoughtful of Moscow's elite specialists on the United States, expressed uneasiness at the way Russia had been treated during the Bosnian conflict, concluding that:

> As far as Russia is concerned, it has learned a good lesson: It can preserve its international importance and authority not if it submissively demonstrates its pliability and "readiness for solidarity" but, on the contrary, if it upholds firmly and resolutely, although with the preservation of diplomatic tact, legitimate historical and geopolitical interests and is prepared to begin a multilateral settlement of the conflict, not dragging along in the rear of the Contact Group but boldly taking advantage of specific opportunities . . .
> Russian policy 1992–1995 could confuse anyone. It was prepared so often to go so far to accommodate the United States (although there has been no particular need for this) that American policymakers were of the perfectly natural opinion that it was not prepared generally for any independent role or for any independent actions. At each meeting the Americans were for several years assured that Russia had practically no questions which would complicate its relations with the United States (this applied even to so delicate a sphere as

the CIS or the "near abroad"), and now it is suddenly ascertained that Russia is speaking about some special interests that it has in Europe, in the Balkans, in the Persian Gulf, in North Korea, and so forth. The puzzlement of the American president . . . is perfectly understandable.[86]

The long and short of the matter is the overriding question: Is Russia a foe or a friend? Is it to be viewed as a partner in creating a viable security system, or as the principal problem? Of course, Russia's domestic politics will affect its foreign policy, but whether its mistrust turns into hostility may well depend on what the West does. The West's responsibility for cultivating a diplomacy of threat reduction must not be minimized.

The present state of flux in Russia can easily yield unduly optimistic or pessimistic assessments of the future of Russian–American relations. But it would not be amiss to emphasize that the developments that gave rise to the Cold War at the end of World War II are gone, never to return. And this alone recommends a measure of optimism.

Notes

1. Boris Yeltsin, *Boris Yeltsin: The Struggle for Russia* (New York: Times Books, 1994), passim.

2. But events soon showed the wisdom of Kozyrev's choice. In May 1990, Yeltsin was elected chairman (Speaker) of the Supreme Soviet of the Russian Soviet Federated Republic (RSFSR). In June, two months after Gorbachev had agreed to negotiations to replace the USSR with a loose confederation of union republics, Yeltsin pushed a Declaration on the Sovereignty of Russia. In June 1991, he was elected president of the RSFSR by an overwhelming majority.

After the abortive coup by his key associates in August 1991, a weakened Gorbachev could do little to forestall the rush to independence of the non-Russian union republics. On 25 December 1991, the RSFSR was renamed the Russian Federation, and Gorbachev resigned as president of the USSR, which was officially dissolved on 31 December 1991.

3. Andrei Kozyrev, "Transformed Russia in a New World," *Izvestiia*, 2 January 1992, p. 3, as translated in Foreign Broadcast Information Service (hereafter referred to as FBIS, FBIS/SOV/Russia), 2 January 1992, p. 77.

4. FBIS/SOV/Arms Control and Disarmament, 13 February 1992, p. 1.

5. Kozyrev, "Transformed Russia in a New World," p. 3.

6. Suzanne Crow, "Russian Federation Faces Foreign Policy Dilemmas," *RFE/RL Research Report* (6 March 1992): p. 17.

7. Nodari A. Simonia, "Priorities of Russia's Foreign Policy and the Way It Works," in *The Making of Foreign Policy in Russia and the New States of Eurasia*, ed. Adeed Dawisha and Karen Dawisha (Armonk, NY: M.E. Sharpe, 1995), p. 23.

8. FBIS/SOV/Russia, 5 June 1992, p. 27.

9. Andrei Kozyrev, *Rossiiskie vesti*, 3 December 1992, p. 2, as translated in *The Current Digest of the Post-Soviet Press* (hereafter referred to as *CDPSP*), 44, no. 48 (1992): p. 14.

10. James A. Baker III, *The Politics of Diplomacy: Revolution, War and Peace 1989–1992* (New York: G.P. Putnam's Sons, 1995), p. 571.

11. Ibid. p. 572.

12. Harvey Sicherman, "Winning the Peace," *Orbis* 38, no. 4 (Fall 1994): pp. 525–26.

13. Anders Åslund, *How Russia Became a Market Economy* (Washington, DC: Brookings Institution, 1995), p. 217. On Baker's timidity in aiding Russia, see also William Safire, "Baker's Big Bash," *New York Times,* 23 January 1992.

14. TRB, "Reagan's Heir," *New Republic* (23 March 1992): p. 6.

15. The idea of a defense community came from an undersecretary of defense in the Reagan administration. Fred Ikle', "Comrade in Arms," *New York Times* (31 December 1991).

16. Richard M. Nixon, speech delivered at a conference held at the Nixon Library in Washington, DC on 11 March 1992.

17. Åslund, *How Russia Became a Market Economy,* p. 218.

18. Jeffrey Sachs, "Betrayal," *New Republic* (31 January 1994): pp. 14, 16. For a different and less apocalytic interpretation, see, for example, Gertrude Schroeder's chapter in this volume; see also Yegor Gaidar, Yeltsin's reform-minded prime minister in 1992, in Yegor Gaidar and Karl Otto Pohl, *Russian Reform/International Money* (Cambridge, MA: MIT Press, 1995).

19. For example, see Michael Cox, "The Necessary Partnership? The Clinton Presidency and Post-Soviet Russia," *International Affairs,* 50, no. 4 (1994): pp. 635–58.

20. Andrei Kozyrev, "Challenge of Transformation," *Izvestiia,* 1 April 1992, p. 6, in FBIS/Sov/Russia, 1 April 1992, p. 19.

21. See *Komsomol'skaia Pravda,* 9 June 1992, and *Le Monde,* 8 June 1992.

22. Sergei Stankevich, "A Power in Search of Itself," *Nezavisimaia gazeta,* 28 March 1992, in *CDPSP* 44, no. 13 (29 April 1992): p. 1.

23. Ibid., p. 2.

24. Georgii Arbatov, *Izvestiia,* 10 February 1992, in FBIS/SOV/Arms Control and Disarmament, 20 February 1992, pp. 1–3.

25. Andranik Migranian, "Real and Illusory Guidelines in Foreign Policy," *Rossiiskaia gazeta,* 4 August 1992, in *CDPSP* 44, no. 32 (9 September 1992): pp. 1–3.

26. Yurii Glukhov, *Pravda,* 8 September 1992, p. 3.

27. Aleksandr Vasilyev, "Russia's Foreign Policy: No Trump Cards with Kozyrev?" *Komsomol'skaia Pravda,* 3 September 1992, p. 3, in FBIS/Sov/Russia International Affairs, 4 September 1992, p. 15.

28. For example, Alexei G. Arbatov, "Russia's Foreign Policy Alternatives," *International Security* 18, no. 2 (Fall 1993): p. 24.

29. William Safire, "Kozyrev's Wake-up Slap," *New York Times,* 17 December 1992.

30. For the English version, see "Foreign Policy Concept of the Russian Federation," FBIS/USR/Central Eurasia, 25 March 1993, pp. 1–20.

31. Andrei Kozyrev, "Russia and NATO: A Partnership for a United and Peaceful Europe," *NATO Review,* no. 4 (August 1994): pp. 3–6.

32. Andrei Kozyrev, "The Lagging Partnership," *Foreign Affairs* 73, no. 3 (May–June 1994): pp. 65–68.

33. Kozyrev, "Transformed Russia in a New World," p. 78.

34. Aleksei A. Arbatov, "An Empire or a Great Power?" *New Times,* no. 50 (December 1992): p. 20.

35. Olga Glezer et al., "The Updated Political Map of the CIS," *Moscow News,* no. 14 (5–12 April 1992): p. 8.

36. Karen Dawisha and Bruce Parrott, *Russia and the New States of Eurasia* (New York: Cambridge University Press, 1994), chap. 8.

37. For an account of the early months, see Sergei Rogov et al., "Commonwealth Defense Arrangements and International Security," a joint paper prepared by the Institute

of the USA and Canada of the Russian Academy of Sciences (ISKRAN) and the Center for Naval Analyses (Washington, DC), June 1992.

38. As quoted in Raymond L. Garthoff, "Russian Military Doctrine and Deployments," in *State Building and Military Power in Russia and the New States of Eurasia,* ed. Bruce Parrott (Armonk: M.E. Sharpe, 1995), p. 57.

39. Garthoff, "Russian Military Doctrine and Deployments," p. 60.

40. Maxim Shahenkov, "Russian Peacekeeping in the 'Near Abroad,' " *Survival* 36, no. 3 (Autumn 1994): p. 52.

41. Ibid., p. 53.

42. *Delovoi Mir,* 8 December 1995, pp. 1–2, in FBIS/SOV/Interregional Affairs, 26 December 1995, p. 3.

43. Aleksei Chichkin, "Will the Great Siberia Give Way to Its Competitors? Euroasian Transit Could Be Shifted to Central Asia," *Rossiiskaia gazeta,* 14 October 1995, p. 15, in FBIS/SOV/Russian National Affairs, 6 November 1995, pp. 35–37.

44. Mekhman Gafarly, *Nezavisimaia gazeta,* 6 December 1995, p. 3, in FBIS/SOV/ International Affairs, 21 December 1995, p. 12.

45. English language summaries are provided in the *Washington Times* (22 September 1995) and by Kathleen Mihalisko, "Yeltsin Outlines Strategy for a Renewed Superpower," *Prism: A Bi-Weekly on the Post-Soviet States,* 1, no. 21, pt. 1 (6 October 1995). A Russian copy appeared in *DipKur'er,* no. 16/18 (August 1995): pp. 76–83, a Russian language journal, which may be published in Austria.

46. Moscow ITAR-TASS, 19 January 1996 in FBIS/SOV/Interregional Affairs, 19 January 1996, p. 19.

47. FBIS/SOV/Interregional Affairs, 19 January 1996, p. 18.

48. Strobe Talbott, "Terms of Engagement," *New York Times,* 4 February 1996, p. E13.

49. Aleksei Arbatov, "Russia: National Security in the 1990s," *Mirovaia ekonomika i mezhdunarodnye otnosheniia,* nos. 8–9 (August–September 1994), in FBIS/USR/Russia, 29 November 1994, pp. 54–55.

50. George Kennan, *Russia Leaves the War* (Princeton, NJ: Princeton University Press, 1956), p. 517.

51. "Yevgeniy Primakov Stirs the Waters: World Reaction to the Russian Intelligence Service's Report," *Nezavisimaia gazeta,* 30 November 1993, p. 1, in FBIS/SOV/ Russia International Affairs, 1 December 1993, p. 13. "Prospects for NATO Expansion and Russian Interests: Foreign Intelligence Service Report," *Izvestiia,* 26 November 1993, p. 4, in FBIS/SOV/Russia International Affairs, 26 November 1993, pp. 6–8. See also, "Opravdano li rasshireniye NATO?" *Nezavisimaia gazeta,* 26 November 1993, pp. 1, 3.

52. Kozyrev, "Russia and NATO," p. 4. Italics added. As initially envisaged under NATO's invitation to the countries of Europe "to deepen their political and military ties and to contribute further to the strengthening of security within the Euro-Atlantic area," Partnership for Peace stressed the following objectives: 1) "facilitation of transparency in national defence planning and budgeting processes"; 2) "ensuring democratic control of defence forces"; 3) maintaining the capability to contribute to UN and CSCE operations; 4) developing "cooperative military relations with NATO, for the purpose of joint planning, training, and exercises in order to strengthen their ability to undertake missions in the fields of peacekeeping, search and rescue, humanitarian operations, and others as may subsequently be agreed"; and 5) developing armed forces that are better able to operate with those of NATO's. "Partnership for Peace: Framework Document," NATO Press Release M-1 (94)2. Before the end of 1994, enlargement completely overshadowed the menu of activities and aims offered PfP's participants.

53. For example, see elaborations of Zhirinovsky's views in Andrei Baturin, "Tanets s Metloi v Ispolnenii Zhirinovskogo," *Izvestiia,* 1 February 1994; Jacob W. Kipp, "The Zhirinovskii Threat," *Foreign Affairs* 73, no. 3 May–June 1994: p. 74; and FBIS/Sov/Russia International Affairs, 24 October 1995, p. 17.

54. Dmitrii Trenin, "Will NATO Expand Eastward?—And What Should Russia's Policy Be in this Regard?" *Novoe vremya,* no. 43 (October 1994): pp. 18–20, in FBIS/SOV/Russia International Affairs, 8 November 1994, p. 12.

55."Lebed Offers Cure for NATO Enlargement Plans," Moscow Interfax in English, 14 December 1995, in FBIS/SOV/Russia International Affairs, 15 December 1995, p. 21.

56. George Quester, ed., *The Nuclear Challenge in Russia and the New States of Eurasia* (Armonk: M.E. Sharpe, 1995), p. 256; see also the essays by Steven E. Miller, pp. 97–98, and John W.R. Lepingwell, pp. 105–7.

57. Charles Dick, "The Military Doctrine of the Russian Federation," *Jane's Intelligence Review,* no. 1 (January 1994): p. 2. Special Report.

58. Leonid Velekhov, "A New 'Warsaw Pact': To Be or not To Be?" *Segodnia,* 21 September 1995, p. 9, in FBIS/SOV/Russia International Affairs, 25 September 1995, p. 24. See also A.A. Yazkova, *Mirovaia ekonomika i mezhdunarodnye otnosheniia,* no. 4 (April 1995): pp. 102–10.

59. FBIS/SOV/Russia International Affairs, 11 December 1995, p. 29.

60. Georgii Arbatov, "Rossiisko-Amerikanskie Otnosheniia," *Nezavisimaia gazeta,* 14 April 1994.

61. Cited in FBIS/SOV/Russia International Affairs, 23 October 1995, p. 20.

62. Cited in FBIS/SOV/Russia, 30 March 1994, p. 66.

63. Cited in *S.Sh.A.: ekonomika, politika, ideologiia* (October 1995): pp. 74–76, as reported in FBIS/SOV/International Affairs, 30 November 1995, p. 1.

64. Rick Atkinson, "Russian Official Assails NATO Expansion Plans, Warning of Sharper Conflict," *Washington Post,* 4 February 1996, p. A30.

65. Aleksandr Konovalev, "Toward a New Partition of Europe? Russia and the North Atlantic Alliance," *Nezavisimaia gazeta,* 7 December 1994, p. 5, in FBIS/SOV/Russia International Affairs, 6 January 1995, p. 22.

66. A few recent works are: Graham T. Allison et al., *Avoiding Nuclear Anarchy* (Cambridge, MA: MIT Press, 1996); Vladimir Babak and Guy Degany, "The Nuclear Legacy of the Former Soviet Union," Research Paper 76 (Jerusalem: Center for Russian, Eurasian, and East European Research, Spring 1994); Robert D. Blackwill, Rodric Braithwaite, and Akihito Tanaka, *Engaging Russia* (Washington, DC: The Brookings Institution, 1995); Quester, *The Nuclear Challenge in Russia and the New States of Eurasia;* Konstantin E. Sorokin, "Russia after the Crisis: The Nuclear Strategy Debate," *Orbis* 38, no. 1 (Winter 1994): pp. 19–40; and Eric Arnett, ed., *Nuclear Weapons After the Comprehensive Test Ban: Implications for Modernization and Proliferation* (New York: Oxford University Press/SIPRI, 1996).

67. Start I was signed by former presidents George Bush and Mikhail Gorbachev on 31 July 1991 in Moscow, but did not go into effect until late 1994, when the former Soviet republics of Ukraine, Kazakhstan, and Belarus signed the NPT and agreed to become nonnuclear members, divesting themselves of nuclear weapons by the end of the century.

68. Mikhail S. Gorbachev, "NATO's Plans Threaten START-II," *New York Times,* 10 February 1996, p. 23.

69. Mikhail S. Vinogradov, "The START-II Treaty Is Essential: Dragging Out Its Ratification Is Not in Russia's Interests," *Nezavisimaia gazeta,* 17 November 1995, pp. 1–2, in FBIS/SOV/International Affairs, 30 November 1995, p. 2.

70. "Finish What You Have STARTed," *Economist,* 27 January 1996, p. 18.

71. James E. Goodby, "Dismantling the Nuclear Weapons Legacy of the Cold War," *Strategic Forum,* no. 19 (February 1995): p. 4; see also James E. Nolan, ed., *Global Engagement: Cooperation and Security in the 21st Century* (Washington, DC: Brookings Institution, 1994), chaps. 2, 15, and 16. In another realm—that of negotiating a global treaty banning chemical weapons—Moscow has repeatedly told Washington that it cannot carry out the treaty's elaborate provisions without U.S. assistance.

72. Harold J. Johnson of the General Accounting Office (GAO), testimony before the Committee on International Relations, House of Representatives, 15 December 1995, in GAO/T-NSIAD-96–78, pp. 1–6.

73. See *Former Soviet Union: U.S. Bilateral Program Lacks Effective Coordination,* GAO/NSIAD-95–10, (7 February 1995); *Former Soviet Union: An Update on Coordination of U.S. Assistance and Economic Cooperation Programs,* GAO/NSIAD-96–16 (1996); and *Former Soviet Union: Information on U.S. Bilateral Program Funding,* GAO/NSIAD-96–37 (1996).

74. After years of denial, Moscow acknowledged its violation of the treaty. On 24 October 1989, Foreign Minister Eduard Shevardnadze told the Supreme Soviet that it took the government a long time "to learn all the truth of the project. Finally, we saw it clearly: The station had been built on the wrong site, not where it should have been . . . representing, to put it bluntly, a violation of the ABM Treaty." See *New York Times,* 25 October 1989.

75. Blackwill et al., *Engaging Russia* (typescript version), p. 9.

76. Fred Charles Ikle', "The Second Coming of the Nuclear Age," *Foreign Affairs,* 75, no. 1 (January–February 1996): pp. 126–27.

77. Henry Trofimenko, "U.S.–Russian Relations in East Asia: A View from Moscow," in *Imperial Decline,* ed. Stephen Blank and Alvin Z. Rubinstein (Durham, NC: Duke University Press, forthcoming), typescript version, pp. 34–36.

78. For example, FBIS/SOV/Russia International Affairs, 10 August 1994, pp. 10–11, and FBIS/SOV/Russia International Affairs, 26 August 1994, p. 3.

79. Carla Anne Robbins, *Wall Street Journal,* 5 May 1995, p. 14.

80. Andrei Kozyrev, *Preobrazhenie* (Transformation) (Moscow: Mezhdunarodnye Otnosheniya, 1995) pp. 230–40.

81. *Kommersant-Daily,* 7 February 1996, pp. 1, 4, in FBIS/SOV/Russia International Affairs, 8 February 1996, pp. 19–20.

82. Jack F. Matlock Jr., "The Russian Prospect," *New York Review of Books,* 29 February 1996, p. 46.

83. Quoted in *Economist,* 8 April 1995, p. 45. See also Aleksandr Golts, "Russia Is Tired of Being Lectured," *Krasnaia zvezda,* 27 June 1996, p. 2, in FBIS/SOV/Russia International Affairs, 30 January 1996, pp. 14–6.

84. *Moskovskie Novosti,* no. 2 (14–21 January 1996): p. 13, in FBIS/SOV/Russia International Affairs, 19 January 1996, p. 27.

85. As quoted in Bruce Clark, "NATO and Russia Enter 'Cold Peace' Amid Expansion Plans," *Financial Times,* 12 September 1995, p. 2.

86. Viktor A. Kremenyuk, "United States–Russia: Conflict or Cooperation in the Former Yugoslavia?" *S.Sh.A.: ekonomika, politika, ideologiia,* no. 11 (November 1995), pp. 56–64, in FBIS/SOV/Russia International Affairs, 13 December 1995, pp. 22–23.

4

Russia and Security in Europe

Michael MccGwire

Security in Europe is an unwieldy subject, ranging from matters of institutional architecture to what we mean by the word "security" itself, from the geographical scope of Europe to how such security is best achieved. The aspect that concerns this chapter is the perceived threat of Russia to that security, a question I address in the context of extending North Atlantic Treaty Organization (NATO) to include former members of the Warsaw Pact.

This policy (announced in January 1994) was not the result of an objective review process designed to strengthen NATO and enhance security in Europe. Rather, it was a by-product of U.S. domestic politics with an admixture of intra-alliance trade-offs. Since implementation of the policy lay some distance off in the future, agreement on this issue was conceded at a time when the West was seriously at odds over Bosnia.

The policy was not without its critics, particularly among those who were knowledgeable of Russia or had experience of dealing with the former Soviet Union.[1] For example, in May 1995 a group of retired senior State Department officials took the unusual step of writing to the U.S. secretary of state, expressing their collective opinion that the policy risked "endangering the long term viability of NATO, significantly exacerbating the instability that now exists in the zone that lies between Germany and Russia."[2] They considered that promising to extend NATO membership to the Czech Republic, Hungary, and Poland would "convince most Russians that the United States and the West [were] attempting to isolate, encircle, and subordinate them, rather than integrating them into a new European systems of collective security."[3]

The eighteen signatories included Jack F. Matlock, recently retired as ambassador to Moscow, six others who had served as ambassador to one or more East European countries, plus a former under secretary of state, and two directors of Policy Plans. But the most notable member of this prestigious and tough-minded group of foreign policy professionals was Paul H. Nitze, who had been closely involved in national security affairs at the highest levels throughout the Cold War. He is the last man to be unduly solicitous about Moscow's sensibilities.[4]

The Clinton administration responded to these and other more public criticisms in an article by Deputy Secretary of State Strobe Talbott, which was published in August 1995.[5] I therefore start this essay by considering the arguments advanced in favor of extending NATO, before moving on to a formal assessment of current and future threats to security in Europe. I end by suggesting certain principles that should underlie any policy that is intended to enhance security in Europe in the years ahead.

Limitations on length have forced me to omit discussion of other NATO initiatives, such as the Partnership for Peace (PfP), and policy initiatives by other Europe-based organizations such as the European Union (EU), the Western European Union (WEU),[6] and the Organization (originally Conference) for Security and Cooperation in Europe (OSCE; originally called the Conference on Security and Cooperation in Europe). Readers seeking information on these matters should refer to the chapters in this volume by Raymond L. Garthoff, Alvin Z. Rubinstein, and Angela Stent,[7] which also shed light on the political processes that prompted the Clinton administration to adopt this controversial policy.[8]

The Official Rationale for Extending NATO

Strobe Talbott gave three main reasons for NATO's decision; another four have been advanced by the many advocates of that policy.[9] The first official reason is an "ought" statement. While acknowledging that the threat NATO was created to counter has been eliminated, Talbott states that collective defense remains (1) an imperative, and (2) should be extended to new democracies that have regained their independence. There is no explanation of *why* NATO should be extended in this way.[10] Nor is there any mention of which state might need to be deterred or defended against at some future date, but the meaning is inescapable. NATO ought to incorporate former members of the Warsaw Pact so as to increase NATO's collective defense capability against the potential threat of a resurgent Russia.[11]

In an attempt to dilute this interpretation, Strobe Talbott noted that the enlargement of NATO is not a new issue and makes the surprising claim that the reasons for and consequences of the progressive growth of the alliance between 1949 and 1982 strengthen the case for doing so now.[12] The evidence does not support that claim.

The accession of Greece and Turkey in 1952 formalized an evolving situation that reached back to the start of the Cold War in 1947–48, at which time the United States took over from the United Kingdom in Greece, deployed a newly formed fleet to the eastern Mediterranean, and began building up Turkey's military capability. Their joining NATO formally committed the two countries to active collective defense, clarified the command structure in the eastern Mediterranean, and tightened the ring of containment, but did not substantially change the bilateral relationships.

When West Germany joined NATO in 1955 (via membership of the WEU in 1954 and agreement that it should rearm), American, British, and French forces had been stationed on its territory for ten years, initially as armies of occupation and subsequently deployed against the threat of Soviet aggression. Spain did not join NATO until 1982, following Franco's death, before which its membership had been vetoed by European members. However, the United States had long before established a significant military presence in the country, including operational air bases, numerous support facilities, and the equipping of Spanish forces.

Not one of these cases provides an argument for eastward expansion today. What is more, NATO's history actively undermines the most prominent of the unofficial arguments, which claims that NATO extension would "project stability" to the east, and that a failure to do so will actually import instability. One could imagine that NATO is some kind of all-purpose floor covering that will effortlessly upgrade the uncarpeted rooms of the European home, and without which the termites will take over. But the lesson of the last fifty years is somewhat different.

The most important factor in bringing stability in the wake of World War II to what became NATO Europe was the vast disparity in wealth and resources enjoyed by the United States in relation to the countries that had been devastated or impoverished by war, a disparity that provided powerful political and economic leverage in the postwar decade. The Marshall Plan and other assistance programs were major examples, but it also took the form of direct financial pressure, as when France and Italy were forced to evict communist parties from their parliaments in 1947, or of clandestine payments, as in the 1948 Italian elections.[13] Although some countries were already members of NATO when they received U.S. military assistance, the programs were all bilateral and the leverage lay with the United States.

The political situation (civil war) in Greece was stabilized using U.S. resources, and since the fight was with communism, people weren't too fussy about the means. Only when stability had been restored did Greece join NATO. Similarly, Turkey joined NATO after the bilateral aid programs had taken effect. But its membership in NATO, along with Britain and Greece, did not prevent Turkey from mounting a military invasion of Cyprus in 1974 and taking over the northern part of the island. Nor did NATO membership deter a military junta from seizing power in Athens (1967–74). Similarly, NATO showed more concern than pleasure when, in 1974, a putsch brought an end to half a century of dictatorship in Portugal.

Given this kind of evidence (and the confrontation between Greece and Turkey over islands in the Aegean in February 1996),[14] the claim that membership in NATO would dampen aggressive nationalism and promote democracy is unpersuasive. So, too, is the claim that membership in NATO would prevent the renationalization of defense policies among former members of the Warsaw Pact. One has only to consider the persistence of strongly individualistic national defense policies among the existing members of NATO, from the days of the Suez crisis to the continuing Yugoslav imbroglio, to see the weakness of this argument. In any case, the PfP program was specifically designed to achieve many of the military and defense-related benefits that are claimed for NATO expansion.

Turning to the other main reasons advanced by the Clinton administration, both are aspirational. It is claimed that "the prospect of membership" provides an incentive for the Central and East European (CEE) and other FSU states to (1) strengthen democratization and legal institutions, ensure civilian control of their armed forces, liberalize their economies, and respect human rights, including those of their national minorities; and (2) resolve disputes peacefully and contribute to peacekeeping operations.

These criteria apply equally to membership of the EU and WEU; therefore, the pertinence of these two reasons depends on the argument that the EU is not yet ready to expand further and that economic harmonization is anyway more difficult, while the WEU, lacking U.S. participation, is not militarily meaningful. For that argument to stand up, the incentive of NATO membership would have to be offered to all FSU republics west of the Urals, especially those who would otherwise be unlikely to adopt the criteria. That is clearly not the case and, in practical terms, the incentive is only available to the four Visegrad states (Poland, Hungary, Slovakia, and the Czech Republic), three of whom are already on track. Are we to suppose that without that incentive, those countries would reverse their present policies? A variant of the official incentive argument is the claim that membership in NATO is needed to reassure states that still have some way to go to meet EU requirements. Again, are we to suppose that without such reassurance they would abandon their efforts? And where would they turn?

Lastly, NATO expansion has been justified for reasons that have to do with Germany. Some see expansion as a way of binding Germany firmly into Europe, the only alternative being German hegemony over CEE. It is argued that there will only be a real Europe when there has been a deep and wide-ranging reconciliation between Germany and Poland.[15] Others see NATO expansion as less dangerous than a race between Russia and Germany to fill the security vacuum, which they consider as otherwise inevitable. But accepting that German reconciliation with Poland is important, it is even more important with Russia, and that could be threatened by NATO expansion. And why does reconciliation require Poland to be a member of NATO? German reconciliation with France was achieved primarily through economic means, binding the two together in the European Coal and Steel Community and then the EEC. And is a Russo-German race to fill a so-called security vacuum the necessary alternative to extending NATO? Or is that just another assertion to support a favored policy?

The extent to which the arguments advanced for extending NATO rely on assertion, slogan, or sentiment is notable. Writing in *Foreign Affairs,* a key member of the Clinton administration asserts that "expansion of NATO is an essential consequence of the rising of the Iron Curtain" and, without any further justification, moves to discuss the new security architecture to be built around that central pillar.[16] The metaphor of "a security vacuum" assumes a physical reality; the catch phrase "project stability" is taken to resolve the complex questions concerning the very nature of political and social stability and how to ensure it. And there is a sentimental, if somewhat selective assumption of common European values, allowing "the wrongs of Yalta" to be translated into a right to join NATO.[17]

The difficulty in developing a persuasive case for the expansion of NATO is only to be expected, as the policy is not the product of a dispassionate political–military analysis of the threat to security in Europe. Rather, the policy is a tactical response to the challenge by the isolationist tendency in the U.S. domestic debate over the cost-effectiveness of continued participation in NATO. The promise to expand NATO was needed to craft a coalition of sentiment and interests in Congress that would be strong enough to ensure the continued funding of an American military presence in Europe.[18] But to justify such a policy in terms of security in Europe rather than U.S. global policy, it was necessary to gloss over the costs and magnify the supposed benefits.[19]

For old and new members alike, the economic costs would be substantial,[20] but these will be insignificant compared to the political costs of expansion. The most obvious is the inevitable Russian reaction to the idea of incorporating former members of the Warsaw Pact into NATO. But there are also the divisive effects of drawing new lines across Europe, whereby existing economic and cultural differences are reinforced and exaggerated by Western-determined political–military and geostrategic considerations.[21] The political costs of such stratification are inherent, but they will be greatly magnified by the Russian reaction to NATO enlargement.

In that respect, the denial practiced by these advocates of extension is almost total, as evidenced by the internal contradiction in their argument. The stated objective is to enhance security in Europe. It is accepted that there is no Russian threat to the EEC states "for the next decade or more."[22] There is general agreement that the security of Europe requires the integration of the republics of the FSU, especially Russia, into a stable security system.[23] Yet it is widely recognized that Moscow will be worried by the hostile implications of NATO expansion and that Russia has "legitimate concerns" about this development.[24]

Suggestions on how to square this circle by alleviating those concerns have been of three kinds. One addresses the problem directly with ideas as to how Moscow might be propitiated or reassured: for example, by renegotiating the

1990 treaty on conventional forces in Europe and by according Russia special status vis-à-vis NATO and within PfP; by combining the expansion of NATO with a new transcontinental and transoceanic security architecture in which Russia would have a major place;[25] and by refraining from deploying troops and nuclear weapons from existing member states to the territory of new members.[26] It is also argued that the United States should make greater use of OSCE and ensure that it plays a more important role in European security,[27] a suggestion that is vitiated by the concurrent insistence that OSCE can neither replace NATO nor can NATO be in any way beholden to OSCE.[28]

A second response is that, in the event, Russia's concerns will be allayed by the transparency of the expansion process. Moscow will be fully informed of bilateral negotiations with future new members and of subsequent agreements concerning force structures, deployments, and command arrangements.[29] It is not explained *why* this transparency should allay Russia's concern over the adverse effects of enlargement.

The third kind of response consists of "ought" statements. Russia *ought* to recognize that NATO is an explicitly defensive alliance; that expansion is an inevitable evolutionary development; that it is in no way anti-Russian; that it is in Russia's interests to accept the inevitable and to actively seek reconciliation with the CEE states.

Two of these approaches are almost willful in their inability to see Moscow's side of this European dilemma and to admit the consequences of ignoring its legitimate concerns. In particular, they slight the problems that will inevitably be created if NATO extends its eastern perimeter to the Ukrainian border.[30] The Russo–Ukrainian relationship is already fraught with difficulties and potential dangers, and the enlargement of NATO will inject a destabilizing factor into an evolving and delicately balanced situation.

The Threat to Security in Europe

The conflicting agendas underlying the debate on NATO expansion remind us that the concepts of threat and security are highly subjective and that one country's security can be another's insecurity. For that reason it is counterproductive to focus on the security concerns of one or a few states. Security must be seen in relation to the whole of Europe, which, for the purpose of this analysis, is taken to extend from the Atlantic to the Urals—the general area covered by the CFE treaty.

It is unlikely that each nation or ethnocommunity will enjoy the same level of micro-security, if only for reasons of political geography. But they all have a common interest in the macro-security environment, whether in Europe or at the global level, since this will inevitably affect security at the micro level. Security in Europe depends largely on the state of relations between the major powers.

Potential threats to security in Europe fall into three main categories. One is related to Russia's political and territorial aspirations. Another has to do with nuclear weapons and the control of fissile material. The third is the possible breakdown of political and civil order in the process of transforming socialist societies into market economies and democracies. It is this last threat which is said to require the expansion of NATO membership.

The Breakdown of Order

From everyone's point of view, security in Europe requires peace in Europe. The Yugoslav conflict illustrates vividly how the breakdown of political and civil order can threaten peace by spreading to neighboring states, by drawing other countries into the conflict, and by generating refugee flows and an illegal arms trade.

For quite some time, a general war in the Balkans seemed a live possibility, and the danger has not yet passed. The ineffectiveness of the European Community's efforts at conflict resolution following the declaration of independence by the republics of Slovenia and Croatia in June 1991, the inability of the major European powers to agree even on the question of recognition, and the steady slide to war in the Republic of Bosnia-Herzegovina, raised serious doubts as to whether the conflict could be contained.

Similarly, the disintegration of the Soviet Union in the second half of 1991 allowed long-standing claims between and within the constituent republics of the USSR to blaze into open conflict, as in the war between Armenia and Azerbaijan over Nagorno-Karabagh, or secessionist wars in Georgia. The potential for disorder was high in other parts of central and eastern Europe, where pressures "to right historical wrongs" had been held in check by the Warsaw Pact. However, while historical animosities may contribute to the savagery of a conflict, to blame them solely for the breakdown in order is to ignore structural factors. The socialist societies in central and eastern Europe are having to cope with the domestic problems involved in transforming themselves into market economies and democracies, while being denied the security of Comecon and having to operate as best they can in a continuously changing economic environment.

There are actual or potential crises of political authority and fragmentation throughout the central and eastern parts of Europe, and the appropriate way for outsiders to respond to these competing claims and incipient conflicts is not at all clear. As the West has discovered in Yugoslavia, the difficulty lies as much in conceptualizing the problem correctly as in devising ways of dealing with it. We are "seeking solutions to a set of problems that are not (and perhaps cannot be) fully understood in any simple causal sense."[31]

We can, however, be certain that in the event of breakdowns of this kind in central and eastern Europe, the nature of Russian involvement in Western attempts to resolve or contain the situation will be crucial to the outcome. The experience of the last ten years and the history of the last two hundred indicate that peace in Europe depends very largely on the extent to which the major powers are able to collaborate effectively on resolving the various problems that arise in the area. We have seen it in Yugoslavia with the Five Nation Contact Group, and we saw it in the first half of the nineteenth century with the Concert of Europe.

In short, "Europe cannot be made stable without Russian agreement and direct involvement."[32] Any Western policy designed to prevent the breakdown of political and civil order in central and eastern Europe must therefore provide for the cooperative involvement of Russia. Given our poor understanding of the problem and the absence of any proven solution, a Western policy that does not respect that principle can only increase the threat of political disorder, leading to wider conflict in the rest of Europe.

Nuclear Weapons and Materials

There are two very different issues here. The one that has attracted the most attention is the danger of unintended nuclear proliferation (the "loose nukes" problem), which extends from concern about the control of fissile material, through the mechanics of transferring to Russia the nuclear assets deployed in Kazakhstan, Ukraine, and Belarus,[33] to procedures for dismantling nuclear weapon systems and warheads, and the verification of disarmament agreements. Coming within this general category is concern for the continuing safety and effectiveness of command-and-control systems and procedures for the operational strategic missile forces.

In 1991–92, the United States approached this problem with imaginative generosity, recognizing that it was in its own interest to enable what would be a difficult, costly, and lengthy process. While it is proceeding more slowly than hoped, significant progress has been made and the process was reaffirmed at the Moscow Summit in May 1995. It is, however, an inescapable fact that the continued success of the process depends absolutely on full and willing Russian cooperation.

The other and, in the longer term, more important nuclear issue is the Russian attitude regarding the utility of such weapons. Towards the end of the 1960s, the evolving military situation prompted a shift in Soviet nuclear requirements from "strategic superiority" to "parity at as low a level as could be negotiated." In January 1986, this was carried to its logical conclusion with a formal arms-control proposal that all nuclear weapons should be eliminated within fifteen years.[34] (As the Soviets did not subscribe to Western deterrence theory, they did not believe that nuclear weapons prevented nuclear war; rather, they recognized that it was nuclear weapons that made nuclear war possible. Since their overriding concern was to avoid nuclear war, the aim of eliminating nuclear weapons was only logical.) This policy objective was carried over from Soviet to Russian strategic policy and was reaffirmed by Boris Yeltsin in October 1994.[35]

Quite separately, in the wake of the Gulf War, the U.S. national security establishment came to recognize that nuclear weapons in the hands of an unfriendly Third World state could negate the global reach of America's conventional forces. There was general agreement that U.S. nuclear forces should thenceforth be deemphasized, with an influential body of opinion arguing for their progressive marginalization, leading to the progressive atrophying of the nuclear instrument.[36] A small (but prestigious) group were actually recommending elimination.[37]

In other words, in 1993–94, a conjunction of unrelated circumstances (the post–Cold War hiatus, the Gulf War, Soviet nuclear doctrine) opened a window of opportunity for the nuclear powers to adopt the firm and serious policy goal of eliminating nuclear weapons, and to embark on the process of achieving that goal within twenty to thirty years.

However, for the objective of a nuclear weapons-free world to be adopted, it is necessary that both the United States and Russia should consider the elimination of nuclear weapons to be in their interests. Unfortunately, in the last two to three years, Moscow has become increasingly frustrated by its exclusion from the key European decision-making processes and by the failure of the United States to deliver promises of a new strategic partnership that would make Russia a critical player in the creation of a new world order.[38] Not only has Washington excluded Moscow from a meaningful role, but it has gone on to insist on the extension of NATO, a military alliance with an explicitly anti-Soviet (and hence anti-Russian) orientation.

Faced by a stronger NATO to the west and China's mass armies to the east, can Russia really afford to relinquish the great equalizer, its nuclear capability? Reflecting the reality of this concern, the Russian military has adopted a policy of nuclear-first-use—reversing the doctrine that ruled in the 1970s and 1980s. But it is not only relative military capabilities that is shaping Moscow's attitude towards nuclear weapons. The experience of Yugoslavia, where history gives Russia's regional interests a special edge, demonstrated that the only way to get Washington's attention was by obduracy, and this reopened the long-standing debate on how best to handle the United States.

In the Soviet era, it was generally believed that Washington's willingness to negotiate (to cooperate, even) on various issues in the first half of the 1970s was a direct result of the Soviets having achieved a measure of strategic (i.e., nuclear) parity. In the internal Soviet debate that followed the collapse of détente and the U.S. return to Cold War at the beginning of the 1980s, a strong case was made for an intransigent stance, on the grounds that Washington mistook conciliation and concessions for weakness and, rather than reciprocate, would seek to exploit it.[39] To many Russians, this assessment is seen to have been borne out by the outcome of the conciliatory policies adopted by Mikhail Gorbachev and Eduard Shevardnadze from 1987 onward.

Even more widespread is the belief that the United States only responds to strength, be it economic or military. This implies that it is essential for Russia to retain the nuclear trappings of the former Soviet nuclear power. This does not necessarily mean that it would refuse to join with the United States in a joint statement embracing the goal of eliminating nuclear weapons, but it does mean that Russia has moved from being the leading advocate of that policy to a country that will need to be persuaded.

Meanwhile, there are disturbing indications that all is not well with other aspects of the nuclear relationship. Ratification of SALT II is still held up by the Russian Duma, because of the treaty's relatively unfavorable terms and because the U.S. Congress is once again pushing for antiballistic missile defenses that would breach the ABM treaty.[40] And although Russia would have nothing to gain and much to lose by the failure of the Comprehensive Test Ban (CTB) treaty, in the most recent negotiations, it was adopting a newly negative attitude.[41]

Russia's Political and Territorial Aspirations

Dispassionate analysis of its aspirations is handicapped by the fact that Russia, whether tsarist or communist, has long served as a bogeyman for the West. One reason has been the ideological divide: conservative absolutism versus liberal constitutionalism in the nineteenth century; and authoritarian socialism versus democratic capitalism in the twentieth. That divide, added to a racist image (Mongol hordes) and the often brutal nature of Russia's domestic regime, certainly reinforced the idea of a bogeyman. But the more important reason was the tenacious belief that Russia was inherently expansionist, in a way that other great powers were not. That belief persisted despite the fact that it was France in the nineteenth century and Germany in the twentieth which set out to conquer and control the whole of Europe. And that it was Russia's armies which not only repelled the aggressors at immense cost, but were largely responsible for the enemy's defeat on his native soil.

The charge of expansionism was initially promoted by Great Britain in the nineteenth century, concerned about a possible threat to its interests in the eastern Mediterranean and its lines of communication with India and the Far East. The charge was resurrected in 1946, when it was combined with the Marxist vision of a socialist world to justify Washington's claim that Soviet communism was set on military world domination.[42] And one of the features of Western rhetoric during the Cold War was the extent to which Russia and Soviet communism were held equally to blame for the evil in the world.[43] As a consequence, Russia remains a bogeyman today.[44]

If, therefore, we are to assess the threat posed by Russia to security in Europe in the twenty-first century, we must first clarify the historical record, setting Russian behavior in the context of its times, and clear away the distortions of Cold War propaganda.

Is Russia Inherently Expansionist?

The European global expansion that would come to dominate the world in the first half of the twentieth century began to gather momentum in the sixteenth. States bordering the Atlantic Ocean expanded overseas; Russia, hemmed in to the west and south, expanded over land to the east. Russian policy was no more expansionist than that of other Western (or Westernized) powers, and in the latter part of the four-hundred-year period it was less so.

Russian colonial expansion had largely run its course by 1885, when the "grab for Africa" by the Western Europeans was just getting under way. Russian involvement in China had trailed by more than forty years that of the western maritime powers, who had engaged in two punitive wars in 1839–42 and 1858–60 in the attempt to force the failing Manchu empire to open its hinterland to trade and investment. Russian penetration of northern China was halted and reversed in 1905 after war with Japan, while the Western (or Westernized) assault on China continued in various forms until 1945. Tsarist imperial expansion was just part of the general pattern of European behavior, and the objection that the western Europeans ultimately withdrew from their overseas empires is only partly true. To the indigenous peoples of the Americas,[45] Australia, New Zealand, and South Africa, the European colonists are still very much in place.

In Europe, Russia's frontiers had been largely established by the end of the eighteenth century, by which time it had finally pushed back the Swedish and Polish–Lithuanian empires to the west and the Ottoman Empire to the south. The period of the Napoleonic wars added Bessarabia and the Transcaucasian territories of the Persian Empire, and detached Finland from Sweden to become an autonomous grand duchy beholden to the tsar. The war also brought Russia into Europe, with its armies campaigning in northern Italy and finally in France. At the time of Napoleon's defeat in 1814, Russia was the most powerful continental power.

Once Russia had pushed back the borders of encroaching empires, the possession of European territory ceased to be an end in itself, as long as influence and security could be achieved by other means. As a grand duchy (1809), Finland was allowed to keep its own laws and institutions; these were respected by Russia for nearly a century. Reestablishing Poland as a separate kingdom under the tsar (1815) was another, if less successful, example of an alternative to full incorporation into the Russian Empire.[46]

It is of course true that Russia (like Austria, the other directly adjacent power) hoped to gain influence and its share of territory from the long-delayed breakup of the Ottoman Empire,[47] besides which it had a genuine and politically popular concern for the fate of its fellow Slavs and/or Orthodox coreligionists living under the "Ottoman yoke."[48] But Russia had no great incentive to territorial aggrandizement. Its objective in the Balkans was not to acquire more possessions, but to facilitate and hasten the emergence from Turkish rule of Christian nation-states that would turn to Russia for protection and would heed its interests.[49]

In other words, Russia was conforming to contemporary Great Power norms as it jostled for power, influence, and security in Europe, using its armed forces to promote and protect its interests. So did other powers, including the United States when, through war in 1845–48, it acquired the half of newly independent Mexico that extended six hundred to nine hundred miles north of the Rio Grande and Gilla Rivers.[50] The American dream of an even larger Union was frustrated by Canadian federation in 1867, but that same year it agreed to buy Alaska from the Russians, who had decided to withdraw from North America.[51] In the Caribbean, the spoils of the war with Spain (1898) were Puerto Rico and a protectorate over Cuba.[52] Thereafter, the United States made it clear that it saw the Caribbean basin as its own fiefdom, and proceeded to act accordingly. In 1903, the Panamanian isthmus was detached from Columbia, and the United States acquired the territory through which the canal would run.

In sum, the evidence does not support the claim that Russian policies in the nineteenth and early twentieth centuries were driven by an urge to expansion. Nor does the pattern change under communism. It was World War II—a war they did their best to avoid—that brought the Russians into Europe. At the end of the war they withdrew forces that, in the process of driving back the Germans, had advanced about 250 miles into Norway; they withdrew from Finland, Yugoslavia, Czechoslovakia, and the strategically located island of Bornholm in the Baltic Sea; they agreed to four-power control of Berlin, a city captured by the Soviets at immense cost and well behind their lines; at British request, they made Bulgaria withdraw its army from Thrace and the Aegean coast; and they refused help to the grassroots communist insurgency in Greece. In the 1950s the Soviet Union relinquished military bases in Porkala, Finland, and in Port Arthur, China; and it withdrew from Austria.

That is not the behavior of a country set on military domination of the world, and those who make that claim must also explain why the Russians did not exploit other opportunities for expansion that came their way.[53] For example, why didn't they move into Afghanistan in 1958, in response to the formation of the Central Treaty Organization (CENTO), which linked Iran and Pakistan in an anti-Soviet alliance?[54] It was at this time that the United States and Britain intervened militarily in Lebanon and Jordan. Why didn't they take over Xinjiang in the mid-1960s, while China was embroiled in its cultural revolution? In the late 1960s, with more than half a million Americans tied down in Vietnam, the British committed to withdrawing from east of Suez; with the U.S. tilt to China and the arming of Iran yet to come, why didn't the Soviets use their local military preponderance to achieve gains in Iran? And if the invasion of Afghanistan in 1979 was an example of planned expansion, why did the Soviet Union choose to mount the operation at short notice in midwinter and only use limited force?

But the most persuasive refutation of the existence of any Russian urge to military world domination lies in the structure, posture, and deployment of Soviet forces during this period. This is not the place for a detailed exposition, but it can be said with certainty that Soviet military requirements between 1948 and 1986 were shaped by the reasonable assumption that war with the West—world war—was at least possible. Throughout the period, the Soviets' overriding concern was the danger of world war—a war they absolutely wanted to avoid, but could not afford to lose. They could not afford to lose because U.S. statements and Western capabilities made it clear that in such a war the capitalist objective would be to overthrow the Soviet system.[55]

While the charge of unbridled Russian expansion stemmed from a partisan reading of nineteenth-century history, the image of a Soviet urge to military aggression was reinforced by the tendency to equate Communist Russia after World War II with Nazi Germany in the 1930s. In fact, the post–World War I analogue for the Soviet Union in 1945–53 was not the defeated and disgruntled German nation of the 1920s, whose damaged pride allowed the rise of Hitler and his policy of courting war in order to harvest the fruits of victory. For the Soviets, who lost more than twenty million dead in defeating Hitler's armies, the appropriate analogue was the British and French, whose victory over the Germans in World War I cost them so dearly that they went to extreme lengths in the 1920s and 1930s to avoid precipitating another such war.

Eastern Europe

Soviet forces entered Eastern Europe in the course of achieving final victory over the Axis armies, who fought as tenaciously in retreat as they had when advancing one thousand miles into Soviet territory. Germany did not capitulate until its armies went down to defeat on their native soil, and the Soviet advance through Eastern Europe was a prerequisite for that defeat.

Joseph Stalin had always made it clear that Russia's immediate aims in World War II were to defeat the Axis powers and to secure the country's western frontiers. The validity of the latter objective was accepted by Franklin D. Roosevelt and Winston Churchill, who acquiesced in the reincorporation of the Baltic states and agreed to Poland's physical displacement westward, aligning its eastern boundary with the 1919 Curzon Line.[56] The longer-range Soviet objective was to keep Russia strong and Germany weak, with German reparations and a Soviet sphere of influence in Eastern Europe as essential means to that end. This, too, was accepted by Roosevelt and Churchill, who acknowledged, explicitly or implicitly, the primacy of the Soviet Union's political interest in the countries of the region.

Except in the most general terms, Stalin did not have clear-cut plans for the countries that came to comprise the Warsaw Pact.[57] The basic requirement was to establish a buffer between the USSR and the resurgent Germany that could be expected to emerge in fifteen to twenty years, and this implied governments that were amicably disposed toward the Soviet Union, or at least not hostile. This would not be easy to achieve, since Romania and (to a much lesser extent) Hungary had fought against Russia in both world wars, and there was a centuries-old enmity with Poland, whose government had been actively hostile in the interwar years.[58]

However, having been welcomed as liberators in Eastern Europe, the Soviets probably genuinely believed that governments that represented the mass of the people would be positively disposed toward the Soviet Union, a Marxist prediction that seemed to have been validated in Albania and Yugoslavia, and again by the free elections held in Czechoslovakia in 1946. The pattern that finally emerged in Eastern Europe was not preordained, despite the ideological prejudice that the interests of the working class could only be properly represented by the world communist movement led from Moscow. Given the case of Finland and the differentiated Soviet approach to the other countries in 1945–47, it is likely that Stalin was prepared to live with a variety of left-leaning or resolutely neutral regimes. Communist control of the state apparatus was not seen as uniformly mandatory, although it may well have been the inevitable outcome for most countries.

This relatively relaxed approach changed abruptly in 1947–48, following the Truman Declaration in March 1947, matched by Andrei F. Zhdanov's "two camps" doctrine in September. This led to a switch in Soviet threat assessments from Germany in fifteen to twenty years' time to the more immediate danger of a capitalist coalition led by the Anglo-Saxon powers that would be ready for war in 1953. Eastern Europe must now serve as a defensive glacis in both military and ideological terms, and the latter requirement evoked the worst kind of centrally enforced Stalinist orthodoxy.

During the next twenty-five years Eastern Europe evolved from an ideological glacis to a cross between an ideological empire and an alliance, and it became an important part of the metropolitan core of the growing socialist system and growing world communist movement. At the same time, its importance as a military glacis increased steadily as contingency plans were reshaped to reflect changes in Soviet military doctrine about the probability and likely nature of a world war.

However, by 1985, Soviet interests in Eastern Europe were badly out of balance. Economically, the area was a net burden; and in all six countries, large sections of the populace were more or less openly hostile to the government apparatus. There were strong arguments on political, ideological, and economic grounds for the Soviet Union to get out of Eastern Europe, the loss of face notwithstanding.

The obstacle to such a move was the area's vital importance in Soviet plans for the contingency of world war. That obstacle was, however, removed in January 1987 by a reformulation of Soviet military doctrine that effectively ruled out the possibility of world war and required the military to plan on the assumption that war would be avoided or prevented by political means. This lifted the requirement for Soviet forces to be deployed in Eastern Europe; by May 1987, discussions were afoot within the Warsaw Pact about unilateral force reductions and the ultimate withdrawal of Soviet forces. East European party chiefs had already been told by Gorbachev that they could not expect Soviet military intervention to keep them in power.[59]

The pattern of events in 1987–88 argue strongly that the Gorbachev leadership deliberately set in motion the process that would lead to the collapse of communist rule throughout Eastern Europe by the end of 1989, and Moscow appears to have actively abetted the process whereby popular forces removed existing Communist Party regimes from power, the East German case being the most blatant.[60] This is not to say that the Soviets foresaw the rapidity with which events would move, but it is certain that Moscow addressed the possibility of some kind of unified Germany as far back as mid-1987, and the final outcome is likely to have been less of a surprise in the Soviet Union than in the West.

The Near Abroad

While it is possible to be reasonably definite about Russian attitudes toward the former members of the Warsaw Pact, its aspirations in relation to the "near abroad"—a euphemism for the other fourteen republics of the former Soviet Union (FSU)—are less easily defined, if only because they differ so greatly with respect to the different entities.[61]

In the ebb and flow of rival empires, virtually all the European territories of tsarist Russia had been acquired by the end of the eighteenth century. (To put that date in perspective, it was some fifty years before the United States incorporated the western third of its continental territory, three-quarters of that area having been yielded by Mexico under various forms of duress, including war.) To the east of the Black Sea and south of the Caucasus, the Russian border with Persia was agreed upon in 1828 (the border with Turkey was finalized in 1878), while the Caucasus (including Chechnya) had been occupied by 1859. To the east of the Caspian, the Turkic Khanates had been mainly conquered by 1885. (In timing, this compares with the U.S. annexation of Midway, Samoa, the Hawaiian Islands, and Wake in 1867–99, plus the fruits of the war with Spain in 1898–99.)

In the wake of World War I, the collapse of Russia's armies, the Bolshevik Revolution, and the eastward advance of the Central Powers deep into Russia, parts of the tsarist empire took the opportunity to secede, but only the three Baltic states were successful in breaking away for any length of time. Georgia, Armenia, and Azerbaijan had been reincorporated by 1922, as had the eastern parts of Byelorussia and Ukraine, the western parts being absorbed by Poland. But the latter were recovered in 1939–40 when, for largely strategic reasons, the

Soviets colluded with Germany so as to reincorporate the eastern parts of Poland (the population being largely Byelorussian and Ukrainian), plus Bessarabia (Moldavia) and the three Baltic states. The extra depth provided by the latter made the fragile difference between failure and success in the subsequent defense of Leningrad. By the end of World War II, most of the tsarist territory had been regained, the legitimacy of the postwar frontiers having been endorsed by Roosevelt and Churchill.

This means that at the time of its disintegration at the end of 1991, the Soviet Union was the contemporary manifestation of a state entity that had, for the most part, existed in its current form for some two hundred years, an entity that within the living memory of a quarter of its population had been successfully defended against foreign invasion at a very great cost. Given that historical background, the most striking aspect of the dissolution of the Soviet Union is the peaceable nature of the process, particularly when compared to the examples of the Russian and American civil wars, and the British, French, and Portuguese withdrawals from empire.

This may be explained in part by the emphasis on national identity that stemmed from Marxist theory, the Soviet Union comprising fifteen union republics, each dominated by a single ethnic group, with its own government and representation in the Council of Nationalities in Moscow. It was often claimed that the USSR was a union of more than one hundred nationalities, and many of the union republics contained within their borders "autonomous" republics, regions, and districts with concentrations of other ethnic groups. But most of the nationalities were very small, and in practical terms just over half the Soviet population was Russian, another 20 percent was also Slav (Ukrainian and Byelorussian), 20 percent were traditional Islamic peoples, 3 percent were Christian Caucasian (Armenians and Georgians), and 3 percent were Balts.

The union republics ranged in size from tiny Estonia (with a population of 1.6 million at the end of the 1980s) to the Russian Federation (population 147.0 million, roughly half the total of the USSR), stretching from the Baltic to the Pacific. In the main, the Russian Federation (RSFSR) comprised the territories that made up tsarist Russia at the end of the seventeenth century, while the other fourteen union republics comprised additions to the empire during the eighteenth and nineteenth centuries.

In 1989, the newly elected Supreme Soviet in Moscow was already reworking the law on the federal relationship that linked the fifteen republics in a single union and delimited the division of powers; it was also preparing a new law, which had hitherto not existed (and does not exist in many federal states), on the mechanics of secession. This required that two-thirds of the voters in the republic in question opt for secession and that there be a five-year transition period during which the political, military, and economic terms would be negotiated. This measured approach was, however, overtaken by the disintegrating forces of perestroika, glasnost, democratization, and the relaxation of Soviet control in Europe. The process was hastened when Boris Yeltsin exploited the issue in his struggle with Gorbachev, and became irreversible when Yeltsin withdrew the Russian Federation from the Union, which had the effect of denying Gorbachev a power base while enhancing his own.

Somewhat in the same way that the Soviet Union chose to walk away from the political, economic, and military burden of Eastern Europe, the Russian Federation chose to walk away from the massive economic and political problems of the USSR. The general acceptability of that policy decision was demonstrated by the lack of support for the August 1991 coup that had been intended to prevent it from happening, and Yeltsin's subsequent (if short-lived) popularity.

Certain conclusions can be drawn from this brief historical review and from subsequent events in the former Soviet Union. First, while there may be calls to restore Russia's "greatness," the political drive to reconstitute the Soviet Union or the tsarist empire is absent, as is the military capability to do so.[62] Second, Russia has long-standing and legitimate interests in the former republics; these include geostrategic concerns and the continuing presence of some 25 million Russians who were living outside the borders of the RSFSR. Moscow will, therefore, take a close and direct interest in their affairs, just as the United States does with events in Central America and the Caribbean, although Russia lacks the overwhelming military and economic predominance enjoyed by the United States in that region. And third, there are persuasive indicators that Russia will conform to existing norms of great power behavior, such as they are.

By the end of 1988, it was already becoming clear that Moscow saw the Baltic states as a special case and would be wiling to negotiate an orderly secession if it did not jeopardize the larger Union. By virtue of their location, ethnic makeup, and existing infrastructure, the Baltic states were ideally suited to serve as the major economic interface between western Europe and the Soviet Union. Meanwhile, the strategic imperatives that had justified their annexation in 1940 and retention after the war had ceased to apply once it was decided that world war would be averted by political means. It was therefore appropriate for Moscow to view the Baltic republics in terms of the Soviet–Finnish relationship, which had proved to be a satisfactory way of achieving physical security, while opening the Soviet Union to Western technology and trade.[63]

In 1991, 41 percent of the population of Kazhakhstan was Russian, compared to only 37 percent native Kazakhs, and the Russian population was largely concentrated in the northern part of the republic, adjoining the Russian Federation. In the throes of dissolution, it would have been very simple for Moscow to have annexed that region to the RSFSR, but it chose not to.

There were sizable Russian minorities in the Baltic states (Estonia—36 percent; Latvia—28 percent). Moscow has nevertheless met its obligations to withdraw all Russian forces (albeit under Western pressure) and has relied on negotiations to achieve compromises in the Baltic states' restrictive citizenship policies that were designed to disadvantage and often exclude ethnic Russians.

Despite Russia's relative preponderance, the complicated process of apportioning the Union's assets among the fifteen Republics has been achieved with surprisingly little rancor. This is most notable in respect to military resources, where Russia had to consider its external security requirements, as well as the zero-sum implications of the internal apportionment.

The case of the Black Sea Fleet and its base at Sevastopol is particularly relevant. Russia conquered the Khanate of Crimea in the 1780s, and in the 1920s the Crimea was designated an autonomous republic within the Russian Federation. For domestic political reasons, Khrushchev (himself a Ukrainian) transferred the Crimea to Ukraine in 1954. Despite the suspect legality of this transfer, the fact that 75 percent of the Crimea's population is Russian, and the absence of a comparable naval base on the Russian Black Sea coast (Ukraine has Odessa), Moscow has relied on intensive negotiations rather than populist pressure or military force to resolve this contentious issue.

While these examples (and others noted by Raymond L. Garthoff in chapter 2 of this volume) are reassuring, the vexed question of Russia's long-term relationship with Ukraine and Belarus remains uncertain. To some extent, Yeltsin was playing politics when, four weeks before the formal dissolution of the USSR, he agreed to join with the other two Slavic republics in creating the Commonwealth of Independent States.[64] But the agreement also reflected an assumption that by virtue of their shared ethnicity and common history, there was some affinity of interests between the three.[65]

Not that their relations have always been amicable. Both countries declared independence at the time of the Russian Revolution. Most of Ukraine was White territory; it supported the Polish invasion of Russia, and in the wake of the Red victory, some 650,000 fled the country as refugees. Ukraine suffered disproportionately from collectivization and significant numbers supported the Germans in 1941, who were able to raise a Ukrainian division. There was no shortage of collaborators to head the puppet regimes established by the Nazis[66] and, after the war, U.S.-supported Ukrainian partisans were active in the Carpathians through 1952.[67]

Nevertheless, there is a significant measure of interdependence between them which, in the case of Belarus, is close to dependency. The relationship with Ukraine is more complex, not least because of the difference between the eastern and western parts of the country, particularly in terms of their respective links with Russia and with Poland, forged by the circumstances of history, which is also reflected in religious orientation. But both states are of crucial geostrategic concern to Russia. Whereas in the past, Byelorussia and Ukraine provided defense in depth, Moscow is now within 250 miles of its western border, while its southern flank has been exposed to hostile reinforcement by sea.[68]

Overall Assessment

The historical record does not support the belief that Russia is inherently expansionist; there is no reason to suppose that it has an urge to add to its existing territories.[69] It does, however, see the former republics of the Soviet Union as coming within its national security zone, and Moscow would react strongly to any attempt to turn them against Russia or to move them any further away than a position of strict neutrality.[70]

Russia's attitude toward these new states will be conditioned by its assessment of the overall security environment and where it stands in relation to the West in general, and the United States in particular, on the continuum that runs between valued partner and potential enemy. As regards to Russia's attitude toward Ukraine, there are appropriate analogies in both ethnocultural and geopolitical terms. One is Britain's attitude toward the Irish Free State when it was flirting with Germany in 1939–40. Another is how the United States views Canada. One can envision the reaction in Washington if it were believed that Ottawa was being weaned away from its traditional stance of a compliant ally.

There is no reason to suppose that Russia has any aspirations in respect to the countries of Eastern Europe, other than the natural interests of a great power in a nearby area with which it has long-standing historical and cultural links. By the same token, Moscow will react against attempts to draw those countries into a potentially opposing bloc.

Where Russia does have large—and largely unfulfilled—aspirations is in the level of respect it should be accorded by virtue of its history, its physical and intellectual resources, and its geopolitical situation. Despite having fallen on hard times, Russia continues to insist on great power status, a claim that has overwhelming domestic support.

The widespread disillusion over the massive disparity between Western promises and deliveries since the dissolution of the Soviet Union, and the move toward political democratization and economic liberation, is exacerbated by a Western triumphalism that allows Russia no credit for the "new political thinking" that led to the end of the Cold War and opened the possibility of a new security regime in Europe. Nor was Moscow given any credit for the unilateral force cuts and subsequent concessions that enabled the treaty on conventional forces in Europe (CFE) to be negotiated; Western practice was to pocket concessions and ask for more. And when the dissolution of the Soviet Union and the Warsaw Pact invalidated the treaty's carefully wrought balances, the West insisted that its terms must stand, to Russia's serious disadvantage.[71] Add to this the fact that SALT II focused on U.S. concerns and committed the Russians to new expenditures, and it is unsurprising that the Gorbachev and Yeltsin leaderships are both vulnerable to the politically dangerous charge of having pandered to the Americans and of selling their own people short.

An Overview of the Threat

Having bewailed the absence of democracy in Russia for the past two hundred years, it would be ironic if the West were to jeopardize security in Europe by ignoring the strongly held objections of Russians at all levels of society to the extension of NATO, some of which are quoted or cited by Alvin Z. Rubinstein and Angela Stent (in chapters 3 and 9 of this volume, respectively).[72]

Russia's aspirations are not extravagant. It wants to be treated as a fully paid-up member of the international community and accorded the respect due to its past achievements, current capabilities, and future potential. It wants to have due account taken of its opinions and sensibilities in international affairs, especially in central and eastern Europe; to enjoy a cooperative relationship with the Western powers, particularly the United States; to promote the OSCE as the primary vehicle for ensuring cooperative security and preventing conflict in Europe; to establish a mutually supportive political and economic relationship with the former republics of the Soviet Union; to receive the sustained economic and political assistance needed to transform Russia into a market economy and a democracy. And (of steadily increasing importance), Russia does *not* want to find itself disadvantaged by the political–military realignment of former members of the Warsaw Pact.

Russia's aspirations are not unreasonable and, in themselves, present no threat to security in Europe. A constructive relationship with Russia does, however, depend on the West's capacity to meet those concerns. Our ability to avert the real and present dangers to security in Europe depends on the continuing existence of that relationship.

The possible breakdown of political and social order in the new or newly liberated communist states is one such danger. The proximate reasons for such breakdown are poorly understood, but there is a clear link with economic factors, domestic and foreign. Besides the timely involvement of mediation and conflict prevention services by international organizations and others, the most effective means of averting this threat is likely to be the politically sensitive provision of appropriate (i.e., nondoctrinaire) forms of economic and financial support and assistance. It has still to be demonstrated that the PfP program has any relevance to this threat.

One thing is certain, however. Unless the major powers cooperate in responding to potential and actual breakdowns of order, security in Europe will be undermined. If the major powers (including Russia) do not present a united front in seeking practical solutions that respect the realities of the situation, and in implementing and enforcing their agreed-upon decision, the virus is likely to spread.

Similarly, to avert both aspects of the nuclear threat requires wholehearted Russian cooperation. As regards "loose nukes," it is already difficult to achieve the levels of efficiency and veracity needed to control and verify the ongoing dismantling and destruction process. The problems would be nearly insurmountable if the Russians followed the letter rather than the spirit of the various agreements, or withdrew their active cooperation. The Russians have the further option of deferring action on the grounds that the U.S. Congress is actively considering programs that will breach the terms of the 1972 Antiballistic Missile (ABM) treaty.[73]

If Russian cooperation is withdrawn, there is a significant danger that all that has been achieved since 1990 in terms of halting and reversing the buildup of nuclear arsenals will be lost, and with it the possibility of eliminating nuclear weapons. Whether or not a nuclear-weapons-free world is politically feasible, the possibility of a new and more deadly nuclear arms race (this time including space-based systems), is a danger to be avoided at all costs.

Retrospective analysis of the last forty years has shown how close the world came to accidental and inadvertent nuclear war during that period.[74] We are unlikely to be so lucky the second time around, as we will be involved in a multipolar game, where there is even less understanding between players and a greatly increased possibility of systems failures. Meanwhile, the dynamics of a new nuclear arms race and its associated doctrines will kill off the still-tender shoots of cooperation and conciliation, and ensure that the international system reverts to the confrontational policies of the Cold War years.

In short, the primary threat to security in Europe is the withdrawal of Russian cooperation. This would be brought about by steadily mounting frustration at what Russia sees as Western bad faith and the increasingly uneven nature of its relationship with the West in general and the United States in particular.

Principles for Action

It is perhaps understandable that many in the West are reluctant to pander to what they see as unwarranted Russian sensitivities, particularly if it means neglecting the preferences of other states with whom they feel a greater affinity. But that is to ignore the prior and more important question, which is how security in Europe will be affected by enlarging NATO.

This chapter started with the collective judgment of former senior State Department officials that the enlargement of NATO threatened Washington's cooperative relationship with Moscow, an opinion shared by the Russian elite, who, for that and other cogent reasons, are strongly opposed to the policy.[75] The chapter went on to argue that Russian cooperation is essential if the major powers are to respond effectively to the threat of breakdown of political and civil order in former communist states, and if the various aspects of the nuclear problem are to be dealt with successfully.

The corollary is that if Russian cooperation is withdrawn, macro-security in Europe (and in the wider world) will be undermined. So, too, will the micro-security of individual countries in the region, because the very nature of Russia's political and strategic interests in the former republics will change adversely. At the same time, the international and domestic constraints on pursuing those interests through political, economic, and military means will be weakened or removed completely, as the security of the Russian homeland assumes its traditional place at the head of Moscow's concerns.

In seeking the psychological comfort of NATO membership, the Visegrad four and their Western sponsors are ignoring the harsh realities of international politics, where one country's security is another's insecurity. Will Poland really feel more secure in the front line of a redivided and rearmed Europe? And can the claims of cultural affinity justify jeopardizing the security of the newly independent states of the FSU? What will happen to tiny Estonia, strategically located across the southwestern approaches to St. Petersburg? And what kind of political and economic pressures will Moscow bring to bear on Ukraine?

In short, the enlargement of NATO will have serious repercussions for the security of nonmember states, both directly and through adverse political developments in Russia. The latter are of vital concern to Russia's neighbors and to its own citizens, and the situation is still in flux. There continues to be the danger that a sense of unfairness, when added to the existing feeling of national humiliation, the high unemployment, and low and falling living standards, will generate a fully fledged Weimar syndrome. At the very least it will weaken the movement for democratic reform and strengthen those who wish to reincorporate the other Slav republics.[76]

Clearly, it is nonsense to claim that the future composition of NATO is solely a matter for its present members. The prevalence of this attitude underlines the need for rethinking our approach to security in Europe.

Thinking about Security in Europe

It was Gorbachev's "new political thinking about international relations" that underlay the fundamental changes in the second half of the 1980s and brought about the Soviet withdrawal from Eastern Europe and the Cold War.[77] The West was happy to garner the fruits of those changes, but dismissed the new thinking, with its emphasis on cooperation rather than competition, as utopian propaganda. And while the NATO summit in July 1990 recognized the Soviet Union as a partner in building security in Europe and the concept of "cooperative security" assumed a new prominence in Western discourse, cooperation as between equals was only on offer when vital interests were at stake, as in the redeployment and disposal of the FSU's nuclear assets. This implies that before we can develop a new way of thinking about security in Europe, we must rid ourselves of Cold War habits of thought.

The concept of war lay at the heart of Cold War thinking. World War II practice ensured that threat assessments focused on worst-case rather than most likely Soviet behavior, assessments that were then made concrete by the assumptions justifying nuclear deterrence. As a result of Munich, compromise was seen as appeasement and the emphasis was on military rather than diplomatic solutions. As in war, strategy and tactics were zero sum, while the negative objective of containment (exclusion and blockade) ruled out positive inducements to cooperative Soviet behavior.

Many of these attitudes persist today and we have yet to admit the reality of self-fulfilling prophecies.[78] We emphasize military responses to worst-case contingencies, brushing aside the adverse long-term consequences, and neglect opportunities to structure the future through political means. We have still to accept that by unilaterally seeking to improve our own security we automatically reduce the security of others, meanwhile diminishing overall security by increasing the danger of conflict.

These age-old principles remind us that in rethinking security in Europe, we should not overlook the political arrangements that worked well in earlier times, such as neutral states and buffer zones. The Concert of Europe has already been mentioned, but we need to eschew its corollary—balance-of-power politics. These are inherently adversarial and divisive. Rather than a balance of power, we should think of balancing interests.

Balancing Interests

There are four entities whose security interests need to be weighed and reconciled: Russia, the United States, Western Europe, and newly independent central and eastern Europe (including the FSU republics). All four have a vital interest in peace in Europe, but that peace depends absolutely on constructive cooperation between the major powers.

All three European entities favor strongly a continued U.S. military presence. The American interest is less clear and "the NATO enlargement debate is really a debate . . . over whether, when, and how to anchor the United States in Europe . . ."[79] It was because the isolationists and budget cutters in Congress put the answer to those questions in doubt that the internationalist wing of the U.S. defense debate sought additional support. They found it in a coalition of interests that viewed Russia—whether tsarist, communist, or quasi-democratic—as an inherent threat to the region. The price of that support was the enlargement of NATO.

Such enlargement will, however, violate Russia's legitimate interests and already threatens cooperation between the major powers. Having voluntarily withdrawn from Eastern Europe and joined in the dismantling of its former empire, Russia had to accept NATO as a historical fact, but was not alone in believing there was agreement that former members of the Warsaw Pact would remain militarily nonaligned.[80] With justification, Russia sees the proposed enlargement not only as a threat to its interests but as a serious breach of trust.

It thus falls to Western Europe to be the "balancer" between the interests of Washington and Moscow. While they face no territorial threat in the foreseeable future, the countries of Western Europe consider a continued U.S. presence to be essential to the long-term security of the greater European region. It is also clear that constructive cooperation by Moscow is essential to that security. This means taking active steps to avert the danger of Russia being driven to adopt an assertively defensive stance that would lead to renewed confrontation and new divisions in Europe.

These differing interests could be reconciled if the Western Europeans were to provide a justification, other than enlarging NATO, for congressional funding of U.S. forces in Europe. U.S. internationalists agree with the isolationists that the continuing defense of Europe is the primary responsibility of the European members of the alliance, but they also see the U.S. presence there as an essential element of America's global military posture.[81] As demonstrated in the Gulf War, NATO has a new importance for the United States as a forward base and staging post, but that war also showed the European powers joining with the United States in defending common interests outside the NATO area.[82]

If the major European members were willing to spin off from the WEU a semiformal alliance structure that would commit those powers to joint operations with the United States outside the NATO area, that direct military contribution combined with the indirect contribution of basing rights could be considered to balance out the financial cost of the U.S. military presence in Europe.[83] This would likely enlist the support of conservative isolationists in Congress, removing the need for support by the coalition pressing for NATO enlargement.[84] From the European viewpoint, a contribution of this kind would compensate for U.S. limitations in the field of peacekeeping, while providing more direct access to the U.S. policy process.

This leaves the interests of the central and eastern European states to be considered. Since the micro-security of individual countries depends ultimately on the macro-security of the region, the security interests of each and all the CEE states will be best served by a binding declaration of neutrality, guaranteed by the major powers in a multilateral treaty.[85] Europe is still in transition, feeling its way from Cold War confrontation to some kind of cooperative security structure. Competitive alliance building would be fatal and, for the time being at least, the role of the CEE must be that of a neutral buffer zone, preferably girdered by a lattice of nonaggression and arms-limitation treaties. Military neutrality need not, however, exclude membership of other groupings.[86]

Cooperative Security

It would be foolish to pretend that NATO would respond in kind should Russia take military action against neighboring states, such as Estonia or Ukraine. The independence of those states depends on the effectiveness of the encompassing cooperative security regime, and the latter's viability requires that Russia feels secure. Cooperative security is based on the principles of partnership and reassurance.[87] It is clearly the opposite to reassurance if one of the nominal partners (NATO) sets out to increase what is already a preponderance of effective military power in Europe.[88]

At this time, Russia's need is more for psychological than physical security, and that can only be provided through constructive partnership, primarily with NATO and the United States. This is widely acknowledged and there are a range of relatively simple institutional adjustments that would "recognize Russia as a great European power with which NATO should engage extensively" by providing the necessary consultative mechanisms.[89] Preferably codified in treaty form, this would be a two-way street, giving NATO the routine opportunity to discuss with Moscow security developments in the region stretching from the Atlantic to the Urals (including the CIS).

However, despite the rhetoric of partnership, the trend since 1991 has been away from recognizing Russia's need for symbolic equality as a great power. This was exemplified by the PfP program, which provided an obvious opportunity for according Russia the special treatment warranted by its existing military capability, its latent power, and the record of consultation between Washington and Moscow, established over some twenty-five years. Instead, as if deliberately to humiliate, NATO insisted that Russia should observe exactly the same arrangements as tiny Estonia and Tajikistan.[90] Another example was U.S. reluctance to recognize Russia as a major player in dealing with the Bosnian conflict. Similarly, Washington continues to resist Moscow's proposals for providing OSCE with a management structure that would allow the organization an effective role in crisis prevention while recognizing Russia as a great European power.[91]

The responsibility for remedying this deteriorating situation lies squarely with Britain and France. Russia is in no position to take remedial action: moreover, democratization has made it harder for Moscow to acquiesce meekly in what is widely seen as unfair treatment and a breach of trust. America *is* in a position to take action, but lacks the capacity to do so; as so often, this foreign policy issue is enmeshed in U.S. domestic politics.

By virtue of their agreement to the policy of enlargement, Britain, France, and Germany are as much to blame for the present situation as America.[92] They also have the greater stake in security in Europe, and they possess the capacity to reverse this dangerous trend. If the Europeans work together, they can ensure Russian participation in security decision making in Europe and, by making firm commitments, they can reshape the Washington debate about Europe's place in U.S. global strategy.

The most immediate requirement is to challenge the complacent acceptance of past policy decisions, a complacency that is manifest in the assertions by the proponents of NATO expansion that Russia will just have to like it or lump it. It is equally evident in the cynics' claim that once the financial implications are understood, Congress will never authorize it; by then, of course, the damage will be done.

History may not repeat itself exactly, but parallels have already been drawn between current developments in Russia and those in Germany during the Weimar period. There are also parallels between the situation in Washington in 1993–94 and that in 1945–46. Both were times of public debate about America's global role in the wake of a war from which the United States emerged supreme; times when a decision was taken that shaped future relations with Moscow.[93]

Both decisions identified Russia as a potential enemy—implicitly in 1994 and explicitly in 1946.[94] By 1948, each side was amply fulfilling the other's prophecies, and Korea merely confirmed the Western prognosis.[95] As we move toward the year 2000, Russian relations with Iran could provide the same kind of confirmation (albeit in a lower key), while space-based ballistic-missile defenses would echo the U.S. atomic monopoly. We might even find Russia and China lined up together against the West, only this time bound by an identity of interests, rather than the brittle ties of ideology.[96]

That is speculation, but the actual and opportunity costs of the Cold War in terms of human suffering were too real to risk repeating the experience. That is, however, the direction in which we are heading. Whether or not the Weimar syndrome takes hold, the adverse effect on Russia's legitimate interests of extending NATO and our implicit designation of Russia as a potential enemy are a certain recipe for acrimony and dissension, rather than the cooperative engagement on which security in Europe must perforce depend.

Notes

1. In a review of opinion among members of NATO, Philip Gordon observed that students of Russian politics, many of them former Sovietologists, generally opposed the enlargement, while those who originate from or interact with Central Europe had more sympathy for the proposal. "NATO's Grey Zone," *Prospect,* no. 8 (April 1996): p. 68.

2. A copy of the letter, dated 3 May 1955, was published in *New York Review of Books* (21 September 1995): p. 75. The original letter enclosed a draft of the article by Ambassador Jonathon Dean, "Losing Russia or Keeping NATO: Must We Choose?" that was due to appear in *Arms Control Today* (June 1995).

3. At this same period, Senator Richard G. Lugar gave as his informed opinion that "Russians . . . see United States policy on NATO enlargement as part of a larger shift in U.S. policy designed to squeeze Russia out of Europe. In their minds, enlargement is linked to the U.S. support for Bosnian Muslims, as well as Ukraine. These moves have been seen as part of a larger strategic design to consolidate the geostrategic gains of the Cold War at Russia's expense." *NATO's Future: Problems, Threats, and U.S. Interests,* Senate Committee on Foreign Relations: Hearings before the Subcommittee on European Affairs, 27 April, 3 May, (Washington, DC: U.S. Government Printing Office, 1995), p. 47.

4. A significant aspect of the debate is the number of former Cold War warriors and anti-Soviet Hawks who now oppose NATO extension, in addition to those who signed the letter to the secretary of state. See, for example, the testimony of Arnold Horelick and Fred C. Ikle´ at the Lugar hearings, reprinted in *NATO's Future,* pp. 11–25.

5. Strobe Talbott, "Why NATO Should Grow," *New York Review of Books* (10 Au-

gust 1995): p. 27. This article reminded me of those in the Communist Party house organ *Kommunist,* where the losers in an internal Soviet debate were required to recant publicly by expounding the official party line.

6. Although they both originated in the late 1940s and had overlapping member-ships, the WEU and EU were quite separate in purpose and function. The distinction is captured by their original designations as a "Treaty Organization" (a defensive alliance) and a "Community" (of economic interests), respectively.

7. For an excellent history of the various organizations, unions, conferences, and programs through September 1994, see Catherine M. Kelleher, *The Future of European Security: An Interim Assessment* (Washington, DC: Brookings Institution, 1995). See also Centre for Defence Studies, *A Common Foreign and Security Policy for Europe: The Inter-Governmental Conference of 1996 (CDS-IGC)* (London: Kings College, July 1995); House of Commons Defence Committee, *The Future of NATO: The 1994 Summit and Its Consequences* (London: July 1995); Lawrence Martin and John Roper, eds., *Towards a Common Defence Policy* (Paris: Institute for Security Studies, WEU, 1995).

8. I give my interpretation of those processes in the final section of this chapter.

9. See Michael E. Brown, "The Flawed Logic of NATO Expansion," *Survival,* 37, no. 1 (Spring 1995): pp. 36–40. Brown discusses six main strategic and political argu-ments for expansion, the last (not considered here) being the need for WEU and NATO membership to be coextensive.

10. At the Lugar Senate Hearings, Fred C. Ikle´ observed that NATO was "not a free trade area or a club for democracies." *NATO's Future,* p. 21.

11. Jonathon Dean notes that "NATO leaders do not speak much in public about . . . insuring against a resurgent Russia, but it is much in their thoughts." He goes on to give chapter and verse. Dean, "Losing Russia," pp. 3–4.

12. Talbott, "Why NATO Should Grow," p. 28.

13. November 1956 provided a telling example of U.S. financial clout, when Britain was forced to break off the Suez operation.

14. It is relevant to the claims being made for NATO membership that Assistant Secretary of State Richard Holbrooke, having berated the Europeans for their inactivity, gave Washington (*not* NATO) credit for defusing this potential conflict.

15. Zbigniew Brzezinski, "A Plan for Europe," *Foreign Affairs* (January/February 1995): p. 30.

16. Richard Holbrooke, "America: A European Power," *Foreign Affairs* (March/April 1995): p. 42. At the time of writing, Holbrooke was assistant secretary of state for European affairs, before which he was U.S. ambassador in Bonn.

17. Jane M.O. Sharp, "Reassuring Central Europe," in *About Turn, Forward March in Europe,* ed. Jane M.O. Sharpe (London: Institute for Public Policy Research, 1996), draft chapter, p. 2. Her writing assumes that the West has an unquestioned obligation "to right the wrongs of Yalta." Understandably, the advocacy of the ethnic lobbies is motivated more by sentiment than by dispassionate political analysis.

18. For the background see Paul R.S. Gerhard, *The United States and European Security* (London: IISS, February 1994): Adelphi Paper no. 237, particularly pp. 37, 67–68.

19. This is not surprising, as the debate on extending NATO had "not focused on what it was going to cost." Testimony by Ambassador Matlock, Lugar Hearings, reprinted in *NATO's Future,* p. 87.

20. See *Study on NATO Enlargement* (London: BASIC, 1995): Research Report 95.2, October 1995. It cites Richard L. Kugler, "The Defence Program Question: The Military and Budgetary Dimensions of NATO Expansion," a paper presented at a symposium on NATO, Fort McNair, Washington, DC, 24–25 April 1995.

21. Zbigniew Brzezinski refers to the need for "strategic differentiation," quoting Senator Richard Lugar in "A Plan for Europe," p. 29.

22. This is the administration's line. See also General William Odom's testimony at the Lugar Hearings, reprinted in *NATO's Future,* p. 27; Brzezinski, "A Plan for Europe," pp. 34–36; Holbrooke, "America: A European Power," p. 45.

23. Holbrooke, "America: A European Power," p. 50.

24. Brzezinski, "A Plan for Europe," p. 34.

25. Ibid., pp. 35–36; Jane M.O. Sharp, "Tasks for NATO: Move East and Revise the CFE," *The World Today* (London: Royal Institute of International Affairs, 1995): pp. 67–70.

26. Henry Kissinger, cited by R.T. Davis, letter to *New York Review of Books,* 21 September 1995, p. 74.

27. Brzezinski, "A Plan for Europe," p. 35; Holbrooke, "America: A European Power," p. 48.

28. Holbrooke, "America: A European Power," p. 48.

29. Ibid., p. 45.

30. See, for example, Brzezinski, "A Plan for Europe," pp. 38–39, and Holbrooke, "America: A European Power," pp. 50–51.

31. Abram and Antonia Chayes discuss this problem in the introduction to *Preventing Conflict in the Post-Communist World: Mobilizing International and Regional Organizations,* ed. Abram Chayes and Antonia Chayes (Washington, DC: Brookings Institution, 1996): pp. 1–6. See also the chapters by Keitha S. Fine, Jean E. Manas, and Wolfgang Reinicke.

32. Robert D. Blackwill, "Russia and the West," in *Engaging Russia,* ed. Robert D. Blackwill, Roderic Braithwaite, and Akhito Tanaka (New York: The Trilateral Commission, 1995): p. 42.

33. On 1 June 1996, it was announced that the last nuclear warheads had been transferred from Ukrainian territory. *Disarmament Diplomacy,* no. 6 (Bradford, U.K.: DFAX, June 1996): pp. 40–41. The transfer of warheads from Kazakhstan was completed in the spring of 1995, and from Belarus before that.

34. Michael MccGwire, *Perestroika and Soviet National Security* (Washington, DC: Brookings Institution, 1991): pp. 60, 194–204.

35. Through 1992, Russia continued to advocate complete nuclear disarmament. At the United Nations in September 1994, Yeltsin advocated further cuts in strategic weapons beyond SALT II, in order to provide for the eventual possibility of a nuclear weapons free world.

36. See Stephen A. Cambone and Patrick G. Garrity, "The Future of U.S. Nuclear Policy," *Survival,* 36, no. 4 (Winter 1994–95): pp. 74–77.

37. General Andrew J. Goodpaster, *An Evolving U.S. Nuclear Posture* (Washington, DC: Henry L. Stimson Center, Second Report of the Steering Committee Project on Eliminating Weapons of Mass Destruction, December 1995).

38. For an excellent summary of the West's failure to deliver on exaggerated promises and Russia's disenchantment with how it has been excluded from the policy formulation process, see Blackwill, "Russia and the West," pp. 15–17. See also Raymond L. Garthoff (chapter 2) and Alvin Z. Rubinstein (chapter 3) in this volume.

39. MccGwire, *Perestroika,* p. 122.

40. The United States only ratified START II in January 1996. For a review of the congressional politics underlying these issues, see John Steinbruner, "Unrealized Promise, Avoidable Trouble: The Unwitting Drift of International Security," *Brookings Review,* vol. 13, no. 4 (Fall 1995): pp. 10–13. See also Raymond L. Garthoff (chapter 2) in this volume.

41. Rebecca Johnson, *Comprehensive Test Ban Treaty: The End Game* (London: Disarmament Intelligence Review, April 1996), Acronym no. 9, p. 31.

42. Marxism-Leninism was always explicit that the capitalist system was destined to fail and would be replaced by world socialism. But it spoke in terms of historical inevitability, of inexorable social forces, not of military conquest. Indeed, once the civil war was behind them, the Soviets consistently refuted the idea that war by itself caused revolution, or that revolution could be exported. Military forces were needed to defend socialist gains against attempts to reverse them. This requirement was vividly demonstrated by the intervention of counterrevolutionary capitalist forces during 1918–21 and was revalidated many times thereafter. But the idea of communist world domination was a capitalist bogey and not a Marxist-Leninist concept.

43. A particular feature of Western rhetoric during the Cold War was the underlying and often explicit assumption that the Communist Soviet Union and tsarist Russia were all of a piece. For an example, see Vice President Bush's speech in Vienna on 21 September 1983, summarized in MccGwire, *Perestroika,* p. 113. See also Winston Churchill's statement in 1942, when proposing a Council of Europe, that "it would be a measureless disaster if Russian barbarism overlaid the culture of the ancient states of Europe," quoted by Jean E. Manas in "The Council of Europe's Democracy Ideal and the Challenge of Ethno-National Strife," in *Preventing Conflict in the Post-Communist World,* ed. Chayes and Chayes, p. 103. Most recently, the debate on the National Reconstruction Act passed in February 1995 by the Republican-dominated House of Representatives made it clear that the expansion of NATO was motivated by traditional fears of Russia. Dean, "Losing Russia," p. 6.

44. For a current example, see chapter 8, Kemal H. Karpat, in this volume.

45. It is estimated that before the year 1600, something like one million Native Americans lived north of the Rio Grande. In 1783, the newly independent United States had a settler population of a little more than three million. Geoffrey Barraclough, ed., *The Times Atlas of World History* (London: Times Books, 1979), pp. 220, 236.

46. The persistent problem of Poland, a traditional enemy for hundreds of years, has been likened to England's "Irish problem." But, unlike the Irish, the Poles were a military threat in their own right, as was demonstrated anew in 1918–20. They were also the spearhead and the avenue of the more general political, military, and social threat that lay beyond.

47. It was, of course, the British and French who profited from the collapse of the Ottoman Empire.

48. In the war of 1827–28, Russia made the greatest military contribution to the liberation of Orthodox Greece. The terms of the subsequent peace also confirmed the autonomy (under Ottoman suzerainty) of Serbia and the two Romanian principalities.

49. The Turkish straits were a partial exception. A large part of Russia's exports passed that way, but by the nineteenth century the primary concern was to prevent the passage of unfriendly warships into the Black Sea. The existing legal regime allowed Turkey, when at war, to grant passage to whom it chose, as it did to Russia's opponents in 1853–56, 1877–78, and 1914. In 1918–21 the straits were a primary route for British and French intervention forces and for supplies to the White Army. In the absence of an effective regime excluding warships of nonriparian powers, physical control of the straits was the only certain way of preventing passage.

50. What is now California, Nevada, Utah, Colorado, Arizona, New Mexico, and Texas.

51. The Russians had crossed over into Alaska in the eighteenth century, moving south along the coast, where they met the Spaniards coming north from California. Claim to the area that is now Oregon, Washington State, and British Columbia was for a time in dispute.

52. In the Pacific, the war yielded the Philippines and Guam as spoils. It also justified the formal annexation of Hawaii and Wake, thus completing the "life line" to China.

53. That claim was still being made by senior government officials in 1983–84, despite its obvious absurdity. This view was widely held in the first Reagan administration and it seems to have been believed that the Soviets had embarked on the necessary military buildup in the wake of the Cuban missile crisis. See, for example, statements by Secretary of Defense Caspar Weinberger on *Face the Nation*, CBS television, 13 March 1983; Caspar Weinberger interview, *USA Today*, 11 August 1983; Fred Hiatt, "Pentagon Sees Space Buildup by Soviets," *Washington Post*, 11 April 1984.

54. This could be seen as breaching the Soviet-Iranian treaty of 1921.

55. Michael MccGwire, *Military Objectives in Soviet Foreign Policy* (Washington, DC: Brookings Institution, 1987): pp. 15–20.

56. The British had already given de facto recognition of Russia's claims to the Baltic states in 1942. Roy Douglas, *From War to Cold War: 1942–48* (New York: St. Martin's Press, 1981): pp. 7–9, 188.

57. Isaac Deutscher, *Stalin: A Political Biography* (New York: Pelican Books, 1970): pp. 522–24; John Lewis Gaddis, *The United States and the Origins of the Cold War* (New York: Columbia University Press, 1972): pp. 90, 139, 143, 157, 168, 202, 354–55; Lynn Davis, *The Cold War Begins: Soviet-American Conflict over Eastern Europe* (Princeton, NJ: Princeton University Press, 1974): pp. 143, 165, 171, 390; Voytech Mastny, *Russia's Road to the Cold War* (New York: Columbia University Press, 1979): pp. 121, 147, 158; William Taubman, *Stalin's American Policy: From Entente to Détente to Cold War* (New York: W.W. Norton, 1982): pp. 68, 121, 147, 158.

58. Romania served as the southern springboard for Hitler's invasion and provided some thirty divisions and incurred nearly half a million casualties, as it sought to extend its frontier to the River Bugg. Hungary had joined the Axis in November 1940, and its troops fought against Yugoslavia as well as the Soviets, while its transportation system was essential to the supply of both the Balkan and the Russian fronts.

59. In late 1986. MccGwire, *Perestroika*, pp. 355–63.

60. Karen Dawisha, *Eastern Europe, Gorbachev and Reform: The Great Challenge*, 2d ed. (New York: Cambridge University Press, 1988): chap. 7.

61. In chapter 3 of this volume, Alvin Z. Rubinstein discusses this issue in the section "Commonwealth of Independent States."

62. Roderic Braithwaite (formerly British ambassador in Moscow) points out that the collapse of the Soviet Union was a failure not only of the Communist system, but of something much older: the Russian political and economic tradition evolved over many centuries. Roderic Braithwaite, "Russia's Future and Western Policy," *Engaging Russia*, p. 69. Jack Matlock (former U.S. ambassador) is adamant that the Soviet system cannot be rebuilt and that the Russian empire cannot be reconstituted. Jack Matlock, "The Russian Prospect," *New York Review of Books*, 43, no. 4 (29 February 1996): p. 46.

63. See MccGwire, *Perestroika*, pp. 352–53.

64. The agreement was signed on 3 December 1992. As the result of pressure from the non-Slavic republics, membership in the CIS was extended to eight of them on 23 December 1992, the three Baltic states and Georgia declining to join. Georgia joined (under pressure from Russia) in 1993.

65. Russia had its origins in the ninth-century state centered on Kiev (now capital of Ukraine) and subsequently reemerged centered on Moscow, which shook off the Mongol yoke in 1480. The eastern parts of the original state (including Kiev) were recovered from the Polish-Lithuanian empire in the sixteenth and seventeenth centuries, the western parts (including Byelorussia and the rest of Ukraine) toward the end of the eighteenth century.

66. Most of the collaborators, both Ukrainian and Byelorussian, had withdrawn with

the Germans and ended up in refugee camps, where they were recruited by British and U.S. intelligence. By 1946, the Western allies were working closely with General Gehlen, former chief of German intelligence on the Eastern Front, as they sought to build up their knowledge of the Soviet Union. John Loftus, *The Belarus Secret: Richard Helms and the CIA* (New York: Alfred Knopf, 1982): pp. 11–12, 54–57, 61–66.

67. Western intelligence had started infiltrating refugees back into their home countries in 1946. The Carpathian operation was part of an attempt to establish partisan capabilities in nine East European countries and Soviet republics, none of which were successful. The Soviets eliminated the last of the Ukrainian partisans in late 1952. Thomas Powers, *The Man who Kept the Secrets* (New York: Alfred Knopf, 1979): pp. 39–43; Loftus, *The Belarus Secret,* p. 79.

68. The Black Sea provided the main route for Western intervention forces and supplies in 1918–21.

69. In this context, it is relevant that the demarcation of the former Soviet-Chinese border (i.e., including China's border with Kazakhstan, Tajikistan, and Kyrgyzstan), which was initiated by Gorbachev in 1985, was formally agreed to in April 1996. See chapter 7, by Gilbert Rozman, in this volume.

70. For a succinct survey of Russia's dealings with the other republics, see Blackwill, "Russia and the West," *Engaging Russia,* pp. 9–15. See also chapter 8, by Kemal H. Karpat, in this volume.

71. The West persisted in this stand for four years, but finally agreed to some adjustment of Soviet force levels on "the flanks" at the First Review Conference on the CFE treaty, which was held in May 1996.

72. See also the reports by the Office of Research and Media Reaction, U.S. Information Agency, *The New European Security Architecture* (Washington, DC: U.S. Information Agency, September 1955): p. 24, and *Four Russian Regions View the United States* (Washington, DC: U.S. Information Agency, May 1996, R-2–96): pp. 21–27.

73. See Steinbruner, "Unrealized Promise, Avoidable Trouble," pp. 10–13, and Raymond L. Garthoff (chapter 2) in this volume. The U.S. Strategic Defense Initiative (Star Wars) announced by President Reagan in March 1983 would have breached both the letter and the spirit of the ABM Treaty, as understood by the Americans who negotiated it.

74. See, for example, Bruce G. Blair, *The Logic of Accidental War* (Washington, DC: Brookings Institution, 1993) pp. 22–26, 186–94; Scott D. Sagan, *The Limits of Safety: Organizations, Accidents, and Nuclear Weapons* (Princeton, NJ: Princeton University Press, 1993).

75. For a summary, see Blackwill, "Russia and the West, p. 18.

76. The possibility of a Weimar syndrome was raised by Sergei Karaganov in "Where is Russia Going?" in *Foreign and Defence Policies in a New Era,* PRIF Report 34 (Frankfurt: Peace Research Institute Frankfurt, April 1994) p. 7, quoted by Kelleher in *The Future of European Security.* See also Blackwill, "Russia and the West," p. 19.

77. The "new thinking" was prompted by the new possibility of human extinction, the most immediate threat being the increasing danger of nuclear war. This led to the conclusion that a radically different approach to international relations was essential, particularly as regards the question of security. For a synopsis of the new thinking, see MccGwire, *Perestroika,* pp. 179–86. For the effects of that thinking on Soviet military and foreign policy behavior, see also MccGwire, *Perestroika,* chaps. 6–9.

78. Pro-Western Soviet elites insist that enlarging NATO to include former members of the Warsaw Pact would produce a self-fulfilling prophecy—a hostile and revisionist Russia intent on overturning an emerging European security system that it regarded as profoundly inimical to its vital national interests. Blackwill, "Russia and the West," p. 19.

79. *NATO's Future,* p. 47.

80. This belief is shared by various American officials, including Jack Matlock, former U.S. ambassador to Moscow, who has spoken of a "geopolitical deal" that NATO would not move eastward. Quoted by Philip Zelokow (who thinks otherwise) in "NATO Expansion Wasn't Ruled Out," *International Herald Tribune,* 28 July 1995.

81. This draws on the argument made by Paul Gerhard, in *The United States and European Security,* p. 37.

82. NATO was also important as a political-military forum and the organizational template for joint operations with European allies outside the NATO area.

83. At $98 billion, the combined defense expenditure of France, Germany, and Britain constitutes two-thirds of the estimated total expenditure by EU members in 1996. It compares to the U.S. expenditure of $279 billion (both in 1994 dollars). See "Table of Defence Expenditure Estimates for 1996," in Martin and Roper, *Towards a Common Defence Policy,* pp. 48–49. The commitment need not be limited to those three countries and could be extended to other members "ready and willing" to contribute to such operations, particularly peacekeeping. Recent organizational innovations in NATO and the WEU, including the Combined Joint Task Force concept, will make it easier to move in this direction.

84. Janne E. Nolan identifies three disparate sets of principles in the American security debate, which she labels Pax Americana, isolationism, and multilateralism. She notes that only the liberal theory of isolationism advocates true disengagement, while the conservative isolationists accept intervention as necessary to impose American values. In practical military terms, there is convergence between Pax Americana and conservative isolationism. Janne E. Nolan, "Cooperative Security in the United States," in *Global Engagement: Cooperation and Security in the 21st Century,* ed. Janne E. Nolan (Washington, DC: Brookings Institution, 1994): pp. 508–11.

85. This would be comparable in some ways to the 1955 treaty between Austria and the four occupying powers, although that only forbade union with Germany. However, a condition of Soviet withdrawal was the Austrian Constitutional Law on Neutrality, which committed Austria to permanent neutrality. House of Commons Defence Committee, *The Future of NATO,* p. 72.

86. The argument that Moscow would find Visegrad membership in the EU even more objectionable than membership in NATO is based on the silent assumption that Russia has an urge to invade those countries.

87. See Nolan, "The Concept of Cooperative Security" in *Global Engagement,* pp. 1–8.

88. For example, in the fall of 1993, the U.S. Congress approved the so-called Brown amendment, which stipulated that the four Visegrad states would thenceforth benefit from the special cooperative privileges in logistics and weapons acquisition otherwise reserved to NATO members. Noted by Brzezinski, "A Plan for Europe," p. 40.

89. Blackwill, "Russia and the West," pp. 40–43. He suggests weekly meetings with the North Atlantic Council, represented by a troika comprising the United States, Britain/France/Germany (on a rotating basis), and one other member. There would also be regular gatherings with NATO's Defence Planning Committee, the Nuclear Planning Group, and corresponding frequent meetings among defense and foreign ministers. Catherine Kelleher suggests Russian membership of the informal but legitimated core NATO groupings, the Quad (United States, United Kingdom, France, Germany) and Quint (the Quad plus Italy), which allow for special consultation in crisis and action as appropriate. See Kelleher, "Cooperative Security in Europe" in *Global Engagement,* ed. Janne E. Nolan, pp. 332–44. She also stresses the value of architectural redundancy and the importance of a multiplicity of relationships (pp. 299–300).

90. Russia's proposal for additional bilateral provisions to reflect its special role and

unique need was publicly rejected by NATO's leaders. Kelleher, *The Future of European Security,* p. 97. For the terms of Partnership for Peace, see Appendix B of that work.

91. Blackwill suggests a managing body of seven permanent members (Britain, France, Germany, United States, Poland, Russia, and Ukraine) with four or five rotating members. Blackwill, *Engaging Russia,* p. 50.

92. For a pungent comment on how the three European powers were preoccupied with domestic concerns, rather than the problems of security in Europe, see Blackwill, "Russia and the West," pp. 32–34, 41. See also Kelleher, *The Future of European Security,* chaps. 4 and 5 for an extended discussion of the institutional and national politics that shaped the outcome.

93. Both in 1945–46 and in 1993–94, a relatively weak Democratic president was coming up to a mid-term election, in which control of both the House and the Senate would pass to the Republicans. In both cases, there was strong Republican pressure to reduce government spending, combined with criticism of the administration's policy and stance vis-à-vis Moscow.

94. Early in 1946, the Truman administration embarked on a new policy that had the effect of moving the Soviet Union from the category of an estranged ally to a potential enemy. Gaddis, *The United States and the Origins of the Cold War,* pp. 313–23, 356; Daniel Yergin, *Shattered Peace: The Origins of the Cold War and the National Security State* (Boston: Houghton Mifflin, 1977), pp. 11, 241–45; Taubman, *Stalin's American Policy,* p. 8.

95. How this came about is explained in Melvyn P. Lefler, "U.S. Foreign Policy," and Michael MccGwire, "Soviet Foreign Policy," in *Origins of the Cold War: An International History,* ed. Melvyn P. Lefler and David S. Painter (New York: Routledge, 1994): pp. 18–76.

96. See chapter 7, by Gilbert Rozman, in this volume.

5

Conflict Resolution and Peace Operations in the Former Soviet Union

Is There a Role for Security Institutions?

Celeste A. Wallander

The demise of the Soviet Union created a rather stark and inescapable geopolitical reality on the territory of the historical Russian empire. Instead of one centralized state, fifteen independent states occupy territory which is divided even further by ethnic and religious differences and subdivided into subnational administrative units. Combined with the fact that these fifteen countries also had to create new domestic state structures under conditions amenable neither to democratization nor compromise, these factors produced political conflicts with the potential for militarization. Consequently, there is a genuine problem of instability which threatens regional and international security.

In addition, the form of the demise of the Soviet Union left another inescapable geopolitical reality: these fifteen states are far from equal in size and power. Russia emerged from the Soviet interlude as not only one of the largest countries in the world, but far larger and more powerful than its new neighbors. The potential for a mode of security relations based on hegemony and run according to Russian power and interests is significant.

Nevertheless, two factors work against such a style of security relations. The first is the reality of instability, which creates potentially common interests and stakes in cooperative conflict prevention and resolution and which constrains the effectiveness of unilateral use of military force to achieve security. It may be possible to deter a neighboring country from launching a military attack across the border, but it is more difficult to coerce a neighbor into having a stable government. It may be possible to occupy a neighbor and impose a solution, but in the modern world the governance costs of empire and even hegemony can be quite high, and the economic and political benefits less compelling.[1] Insofar as many modern security problems have their roots in conditions requiring joint action over a long period of time for resolution, multilateral security strategies can prove more efficient than unilateral military threats or action.

The second factor working against Russian hegemony and unilateralism is Russia's interest in a continually changing and evolving system of multilateral economic, political, and security institutions. This interest ranges from the purely instrumental, as in obtaining financial assistance from the International Monetary Fund (IMF) or access to the General Agreement on Trade and Tariffs (GATT) trade regime, to the less tangible, as in Russia's efforts to become a major player in leading multilateral organizations such as the Group of Seven (G-7).

Taken together, these two factors create the potential that Russia would choose multilateral strategies to deal with security issues, problems, and threats in its relations with the other newly independent countries of the former Soviet Union (FSU). In the discussion that follows I first briefly explain some of the now-familiar security issues which arose with the breakup of the Soviet Union. I then outline a theory of the role of institutions in sustaining multilateral security strategies. In the third section, I explain why security strategies and institutions need to be differentiated according to different underlying strategic situations, and assess in greater detail the variety and variation in peace operations. Finally, I turn to Russian thinking and practice on peace operations and assess the role of international institutions in current cases and in Russia's security relations with its neighbors in more general terms. In conclusion, I argue that because the conflicts in the former Soviet Union entail a substantial degree of security inter-dependence, Russian decision makers have sought to use international organizations for conflict prevention, peacekeeping, and peace enforcement. However, I show that Russian political and military leaders have not been reluctant to obscure the conceptual and practical distinctions between peacekeeping and peace enforcement which form the basis for an effective and legitimate role for international organizations and multilateral approaches in local and regional conflicts. This has enabled Russia to use ostensibly legitimate multilateral instruments to a limited degree for assertive and narrow Russian interests. Nonetheless, I also conclude that on balance, international organizations have played an important role by contributing to transparency about Russian behavior and by establishing multilateral rules of the game which, if not always observed, give the international community some basis for assessing Russia's intentions and ambitions.

Security Relations Among the Post-Soviet States

Although the leaders of the Soviet republics divorced in haste in December 1991 in order to escape the dual grip of the centralized Soviet and entrenched communist system, the founding and early documents of the Commonwealth of Independent States (CIS) show at least some concern and thought for the difficult realities of security independence among the post-Soviet states. Following the 8

December 1991 and 21 December 1991 agreements establishing the Commonwealth of Independent States, the CIS members recognized the right of each state to establish its own military forces in Minsk on 30 December 1991. At the same time, however, they agreed to maintain overall strategic forces under CIS command, and to establish common procedures for border troops. Thus, while beginning to go their own ways with respect to national defense forces, the former Soviet states acknowledged and made vague provision for military forces and procedures to deal with areas where security relations were interdependent in important ways. This was further acknowledged and addressed at a meeting in Kiev, Ukraine, in March 1992, where the members further specified their individual and common borders and border troops, and where they agreed to the creation of CIS peacekeeping forces for dealing with conflicts in the former Soviet states. Finally, on 15 May 1992, in Tashkent, Uzbekistan, a subset of the CIS member states[2] signed the Treaty on Collective Security, which declared that if one of the participating states is the object of aggression by any state or group of states, this would be aggression against all participating states, which are committed to giving necessary assistance, including military.

The importance of these agreements is twofold. First, they demonstrate that early on, some of the former Soviet states perceived security issues and problems for which they felt it was important to have the capacity to address multilaterally. Second, at least in principle, the basis exists in terms of international law and norms for multilateral peace operations in the countries of the former Soviet Union.

At the same time, the states of the former Soviet Union joined international and regional institutions, many of which have rules and resources for dealing with political–military conflict. The states of the former Soviet Union joined these institutions by one of three routes. First, Russia joined all the organizations in which the Soviet Union had been a member automatically as a result of the decision by the international community to recognize Russia as the legal "continuing successor" state to the Soviet Union. Second, the other former Soviet republics joined open institutions such as the United Nations, the Organization for Security and Cooperation in Europe (OSCE), and the North Atlantic Coordination Council (NACC) virtually automatically.[3] For these types of institutions, there is a presumption that barring egregious violations of international norms, all states of all types have a right to membership and are included. Third, institutions which have stricter performance criteria and conditions for membership accepted post-Soviet states on a case-by-case basis. Thus, for example, membership in the Council of Europe requires certain strong commitments from aspiring members on provisions for democratic institutions and rules about human rights, such as abolishing the death penalty. Consequently, not all the former Soviet states are members: Russia, for example, was accepted into the Council of Europe only in 1995. And in contrast to NACC, which accepted all the former Warsaw Pact states and former Soviet republics, membership in Partnership for

Peace (PfP) requires the negotiation of an explicit treaty which commits each member to meet certain obligations in terms of military cooperation, transparency, and progress toward democratic control of military forces. In this regard, one could see the North Atlantic Treaty Organization (NATO) as merely one of the more selective limited membership institutions, along with the European Union. Its performance criteria include not only qualities such as democratic control of military forces, but also that new members contribute to the security of the membership as a whole.

The first, and in many regards typical, post-Soviet conflict in the newly independent states was the civil war in Nagorno-Karabagh. The population of this autonomous region, located entirely within the republic of Azerbaijan, was Armenian. Armed conflict between the local population—aided by Armenia—and the Azeri government began in 1988. Soviet forces remained in the region, although they did not play an active role in preventing conflict. In February 1992, the remaining Soviet forces were withdrawn, and various Russian government proposals were advanced for UN and CIS peace operations. By that time, Nagorno-Karabagh's objective of joining Armenia changed to one of a new independent state.

Meanwhile, Azerbaijani President Abulfez Elchibey was working to reduce rather than permit Russian military presence in his country and involve the OSCE in resolving the conflict in Nagorno-Karabagh. Consequently, from May 1992 to June 1993, when he was overthrown in a coup, Russia contributed to the conditions which weakened his hold on power. Military forces from both Nagorno-Karabagh and Armenia occupied the narrow band of Azerbaijan's territory which had divided the two. With a pro-Russian government in power in Baku, Azerbaijan joined the CIS and Russian forces were permitted to operate a radar station in Azerbaijan. However, the Azerbaijani government has proven somewhat less malleable than at first glance and has since resisted a purely Russian or CIS peace operation. In December 1994, Russia agreed to a OSCE peacekeeping force, but this has never been implemented. Instead, actual OSCE involvement has been limited to observer missions and mediation under the active nine-member Minsk group convened in 1992.

The conflict in Tajikistan began as a civil war among distinct regional groups. An uneasy power sharing developed in the late-Gorbachev and immediate post-Soviet periods as an arrangement between the groups which had traditionally held power as republic leaders in the Soviet Union and opposition groups broke down in March 1992 and quickly escalated to full-scale internal war by that summer. While a multilateral decision to use foreign (Russian and Uzbek) troops came first in September 1992, that is somewhat misleading, since Soviet troops controlled by the Russian government never left. Both the 201st Motorized Rifle Division and the (formerly KGB) border troops were transferred to Russian control when the Russian military forces were formed in May 1992. These forces were increasingly focused on defending the border with Afghanistan, from which Tajik opposition forces sometimes launched attacks. Although the presence of some 25,000 troops under Russian command on the border has not enabled the government to eliminate the opposition, the amount of internal fighting in Tajikistan decreased and has leveled out. Since 1994, Russia has pressed the Tajik government to negotiate in good faith and compromise with opposition forces, but with little success.

The conflict in Moldova centers on the secessionist attempts of ethnic Russians living in a section of the country east of the Dniestr river (thus the self-proclaimed name of Pridniestrovye, or Trans-Dniester). Claiming to be acting to defend themselves against Moldova's intentions to merge either politically or culturally with Romania, local Russians created their own militia armed with equipment from the Soviet Fourteenth Army, which was deployed in the region. Ethnic Russians were in fact a minority in Trans-Dniester, as were Ukrainians, but the separatists were concentrated in key urban areas. In late 1991 and early 1992, the Trans-Dniester militia carried out military operations to extend its control over the entire territory, which entailed military operations against Moldovan towns and villages. In March 1992 the Moldovan government committed its military forces to suppressing the conflict, but its forces were inferior to those of the militia which was clearly supplied and supported by the Fourteenth Army. In April 1992, Russian president Boris Yeltsin subordinated the Fourteenth Army to Russian command, and thus its conduct became Russian responsibility. Despite Russian government statements calling for a peaceful settlement and noninterference, the Fourteenth Army continued to aid the separatists until June 1992, when they officially took on the role of separating the Trans-Dniester military and Moldovan forces. By this time, however, the Trans-Dniester political and military authorities had gained control over their entire region. In July 1992, Yeltsin and Moldovan president Mircea Snegur signed a bilateral agreement establishing a peacekeeping force comprised of Russian (1,500 troops), Moldovan, and Trans-Dniester forces and establishing a negotiation process. Although a long-term political settlement has not been reached, Russia has on several occasions repeated its commitment to withdraw the Russian remnants of the Fourteenth Army from Moldova. A Russian promise to live up to this commitment was one of the conditions it accepted in order to achieve Council of Europe membership in 1995.

Georgia has been the location of two post-Soviet ethnic/territorial conflicts. A separatist movement in South Ossetia (seeking to join North Ossetia in the Russian Federation) was stabilized in July 1992 with a trilateral agreement and deployment of Russian (1,000), Georgian (350), and South Ossetian (500) peacekeeping troops, although at the cost to Georgia of greater Ossetian autonomy. More serious has been the separatist war in Abkhazia, which had briefly held a form of republic status in the 1920s but at the time of Georgian independence in 1991 was an autonomous republic within that country.[4] In the summer of 1992, the Abkhazian soviet declared its independence. The military conflict began in August when Georgian military forces under command of General Tengiz Kitovani entered the regional capital Sukhumi claiming to have orders from Georgian president Eduard Shevardnadze to find government officials who had been kidnapped by overthrown Georgian president Zviad Gamsakhurdia. Instead of dealing only with that mandate, Georgian forces engaged in fighting with Abkhazian forces. In the ensuing conflict from 1992 to 1993, the small Abkhazian forces defeated and drove out the numerically superior Georgian forces. This led to early speculation and now substantial evidence that the Abkhazian forces benefited from not only Russian supplies and training, but active and direct Russian military planning and support, especially from combat aircraft and helicopters.[5] Russia clearly used Georgia's vulnerability to destabilize the country in order to force Georgian concessions, including joining the CIS and permitting Russian military bases. In May 1994 the parties signed a cease-fire agreement which provided for a CIS peacekeeping force (which in practice has been entirely Russian) monitored by UN observers.

It is important to note as well, however, that many political security conflicts in the former Soviet Union which could have become militarized have not escalated. First and foremost is the example of the security interdependence created by the deployment of strategic nuclear weapons in three of the newly independent states (Ukraine, Kazakhstan, and Belarus), which were not nuclear "continuing successor" states according to international law (Russia alone held that designation). Following intense Western diplomatic activity and given genuine doubts about the wisdom of unilaterally disarming, all three states have lived up to their commitments to become nonnuclear states. Similarly, a political and military conflict between Russia and Ukraine over the division of the Black Sea Fleet and the status of Crimea within Ukraine, while not as of this writing entirely settled, has been handled by intensive negotiations, rather than a resort to force. And despite lingering resentment and Russian presence, all Russian military forces have been withdrawn from Lithuania, Latvia, and Estonia and all three Baltic states have made compromises in their citizenship and social policies to accommodate Russians living in their states.

In addition to these specific cases, it is important to note the larger question of Russian interests, intentions, and policies toward the countries of the former Soviet Union. Ultimately, the question for the rest of the world is whether Russia has accepted the independent existence of the Soviet successor states, or whether behind its efforts to create and develop the CIS and to manage conflicts on its borders lie an expansionist policy meant to reconstitute the Russian and Soviet empire. In particular, this question has centered on whether the stated Russian policies for integration are merely a cover for imperial reconstitution.[6] If Russian intentions are unalterably imperial, then there is little common ground for security cooperation; at most, Russia would use international institutions as cover and for legitimacy. In this regard, however, the involvement of international institutions in conflicts in the former Soviet Union can play a role in answering the substantive question of what Russia's intentions are. Since the international rules of the game are inconsistent with imperial ambitions, and institutional procedures should constrain aggressive policies and methods, institutional involvement should provide information about Russian intentions and behavior which—while never guaranteed—should assist in other states' assessments.

Clearly the demise of the Soviet Union did not eliminate the interrelated nature of security among the post-Soviet states. The common borders, mixed populations, instabilities of transition from communism, and division and deployment of Soviet forces among multiple countries created common as well as competing security interests. At the same time, Russia's power and increasingly assertive definition of its national interests and sphere of influence in Eurasia just as clearly favored Russian unilateralism and coercion. Under these conditions, what role could there be for international institutions in post-Soviet conflicts?

Security Relations and Institutional Theory

Strategic and security interdependence create the conditions under which states may find it in their interests to cooperate, and thus make use of security institutions, rather than act unilaterally to achieve their objectives. Strategic interdependence is a situation in which outcomes are determined by the choices of two or more states, while security interdependence obtains when states can be jointly better or worse off—that is, when security interests are not zero-sum.[7] These interdependencies mean that national decision makers make choices based not only on their preferences, but also based on their assessments of the intentions and likely choices of other states.

Therefore, a fundamental problem in security relations is that there is uncertainty about the likely intentions and policy choices of other states. If a decision maker knew the preferences and intentions of others, he or she could confidently choose multilateral cooperative security strategies when dealing with states which shared common security interests and intentions, and could avoid being exploited by expansionist or hostile states. In particular, if decision makers could confidently identify jointly acceptable solutions short of war and knew ahead of time who would prevail in a military conflict, we would expect them to always reach a political bargain short of war.[8]

In reality, of course, decision makers know neither the true intentions of other states, nor the precise costs and outcomes of military conflict. This uncertainty makes strategic choice difficult, and the problem is to get information in order to choose a strategy most effectively. Choosing security strategies, therefore, entails assessing not merely the balance of power. Since outcomes will be affected by the choices of others, states need to take the interests, preferences, and likely strategies of other states into account.

Strategic and security interdependence create the possibility for cooperative security strategies, but they do not guarantee that states will have identical or substantially compatible security interests. If security interests vary, then the underlying obstacles to cooperation and the ways in which those obstacles may be overcome will vary as well. Even when states can see substantial common security interests they may not be able to realize them. The most commonly recognized obstacle to cooperation in security relations is the fear of being exploited, or the temptation to exploit others' cooperation. For example, the risk in entering into a cease-fire arrangement is that other warring parties might violate the cease-fire in order to use an advantageous military situation and achieve territorial gains which cannot be easily reversed.[9]

However, it is a serious mistake to assume that these kinds of obstacles are the only or even the most important reasons why states may find it difficult to pursue cooperative and multilateral security strategies. In many instances, states do not have exploitative intentions and would not diverge from a multilateral arrangement even given the opportunity once they were confident that the other parties had similar intentions. The obstacles to cooperation can be severe nonetheless, and political and military conflicts may not be resolved. First, there always remains an underlying uncertainty about the degree to which other states see it in their short- and long-term interests to refrain from unilateral or military solutions to security problems. This uncertainty can be reduced, but it can never be eliminated.[10] Second, while agreements may be self-enforcing and reliable once achieved, they are often extremely difficult to achieve in the first place. Even conflicting sides that genuinely seek a peaceful and negotiated settlement should be expected to bargain for the best terms they can get, and it is likely that different provisions have different advantages and disadvantages for all the different parties. Bargaining always entails a mix of common and competing interests: a common interest in reaching an agreement does not preclude competing interests over the precise terms of the agreement.[11] This is likely to be especially true in security relations that involve a mix of political and military issues, such as election procedures and disarmament schedules. This creates the possibility that the parties to such a conflict resolution process will begin to suspect that the other parties are not committed to a multilateral solution. It is extremely difficult to distinguish between states which are bargaining in good faith but are actively seeking their best deal, and those which are bargaining with no intention of abiding by an agreement at all.

Thus, returning to the example of observing a cease-fire, we can see that there can be genuine obstacles to security cooperation and conflict resolution even if the parties do not intend to exploit one another. Parties to a conflict may genuinely wish to extricate themselves, but may find it difficult to do so because they cannot be certain about the intentions of the other states, and because the establishment of a cease-fire itself is part of a bargaining process in which decision makers are seeking to achieve advantageous terms in the agreement.

Finally, an assessment of conflict resolution and security cooperation is complicated by the fact that states are often not merely concerned with reducing uncertainty, guarding against exploitation, and overcoming negotiation dynamics to achieve an agreement. Quite often, and perhaps nearly always, parties to such a process are concerned with altering the costs and benefits associated with different options and outcomes. Getting parties in a civil war to agree to a schedule of free and fair elections, for example, may entail not merely monitoring for transparency and sanctions for violating the rules, but it may require the promise of financial assistance to a government freely and fairly elected. It certainly entails the long-term task of establishing and maintaining institutions that encourage previously warring parties to continue to play by the political rules of the game because they are confident that others will also remain committed to cooperative and political means.[12]

If it is the case that all of these situations are possible, states are in an even worse position with respect to security cooperation than any of these problems individually would pose. If you have to worry not only that it may be difficult to negotiate the terms of a cease-fire because the different parties want different things, and you have to at least allow the possibility that one or more of the parties may seek to enter the agreement only in order to exploit it, security cooperation becomes very complicated indeed. If you are trying to structure a peace settlement to encourage free and fair elections and minority rights, while at the same time entertaining the option of military sanctions against parties who may resort to force or commit war crimes, it is difficult to play the role of an honest and neutral broker.

So it is not merely complexity which makes it difficult to approach conflict resolution and peace operations in political–military conflicts, but the fact that different underlying problems call for different policy solutions and instruments. Solving the problem created by the attempts by one or more parties to exploit cooperation or restraint—as the Bosnian Serbs did repeatedly from 1992 to 1995—requires monitoring and a credible commitment to retaliate and sanction those who violate agreements. Solving the problem created by competition over the precise terms of a political and military settlement requires sustained and neutral good faith negotiations. Solving the long-term problem of creating a political and economic framework in which the parties can see and are confident of the benefits and safety of future cooperation requires substantial political and military resources and a long-term commitment by third parties.

The simple response to this problem might be simply to layer all of the alternative strategies. However, there are two problems with this idea. First, it is very expensive to deal with all the contingencies, as it would require substantial military forces, economic sanctions, sustained diplomacy, the involvement of development and international financial agencies, and so on. While there may be instances when the stakes of a conflict are deemed sufficiently great to warrant a comprehensive commitment of international resources, those instances are few. Even today there remains substantial doubt about whether such a commitment in Bosnia is worth it. It would be truly tragic, however, to avoid all conflict resolution efforts because all conflicts do not inspire a full-scale, layered strategy. Sometimes, conflict resolution can be quite successful by addressing a more limited set of problems.[13]

Second, a layered or comprehensive approach will fail when the multiple instruments and policies are contradictory or even mutually destructive. As I will discuss in the next section, peacekeeping missions are qualitatively different from those of peace enforcement in such a way that peacekeeping can contribute to conflict resolution only if all the parties are confident that its real role or mission is not peace enforcement. This will be very difficult, if not impossible, to accomplish if a comprehensive approach includes a mix of instruments. The troubled story of the United Nations' Protection Force (UNPROFOR) in Bosnia—which mixed humanitarian assistance, peacekeeping, and peace enforcement missions—provides a stark lesson.

Given this rather daunting discussion of obstacles to security cooperation, it is perhaps not surprising that security analysts tend to discount the potential for cooperation in security relations. That, however, overlooks two factors which make security cooperation more likely: the often quite substantial benefits arising from security interdependence, and the availability and role of international institutions in security affairs.

Institutions are "persistent and connected sets of rules (formal and informal) that prescribe behavioral roles, constrain activity, and shape expectations."[14] International institutions by and large have no enforcement powers, although the European Union and United Nations Security Council are partial exceptions. They generally affect social behavior by altering states' strategic environments, rather than through strict enforcement in the sense of domestic political institutions.[15] Institutions serve as monitoring mechanisms, provide negotiating structures and focal points in cases of distributive bargaining, enhance the information available to states assessing their choices of strategies, and allow states to credibly signal threats, promises, intentions, and capabilities. Although there has been little study of the role of institutions in security relations, there is no reason why international security institutions cannot exist and have substantial effects.[16]

The realities of strategic and security interdependence mean that states might be able to pursue more ambitious security objectives through multilateral security strategies if international institutions help them reduce uncertainty about others' capabilities, intentions, actions, and strategies. When states abide by informal institutions such as respect for sovereignty and diplomatic immunity, they signal that their intentions are not in conflict with fundamental operating assumptions under which other states operate. Modern formalized institutions such as the United Nations, OSCE, or NATO provide for regular contact among states. As ongoing arenas for multilateral discussion, these organizations allow states to exchange information and provide a framework for assessing the reliability of that information. An established framework of negotiation makes it easier for states to evaluate patterns of policies, and thus intentions.

Institutions also enhance the credibility of threats and promises, both of which are important in security relations. For members, an institution can support promises to cooperate by permitting monitoring of behavior and by enmeshing the members in an ongoing process that reduces the chances of a single devastating act of noncooperation. Institutions also reinforce the credibility of threats to retaliate for violating agreements among members because potential exploiters know that their actions are less likely to go undetected. In general, by establishing monitoring and information, institutions guard against the problem of opportunistic behavior.[17]

The obstacles to conflict resolution are substantial under any circumstances. In internal wars and ethnic conflicts, fear, distrust, and uncertainty generate especially intractable obstacles.[18] Further complicating matters is the issue of Russian interests and strategies. The question of conflict resolution and the role of institutions in post-Soviet international and internal conflicts is not only whether those institutions provide resources, but whether Russia will use them.

There are therefore three crucial variables in the effectiveness and extensiveness of security institutions in managing security conflict and cooperation among the post-Soviet states. The first dimension is whether there are sufficient common interests among both the states involved, including of course Russia, and the outside parties through their involvement in international security institutions to create a cooperative bargaining space. The second dimension is whether the nature of the stakes and opportunities offer Russia a reasonable policy instrument through international institutions. Institutions are effective only insofar as they are seen as legitimate and valuable by nation-states. Since institutions have little enforcement power and depend ultimately on the willingness of states to work within their rules, they are effective only at the discretion of their members. Therefore, the legitimacy and efficacy of security institutions is a valuable asset which cannot be squandered. Third, the form of institutions varies, and it matters. This means that in thinking about the potential role of institutions in conflict resolution in the former Soviet Union, we have to distinguish between different problems and instruments.

Peace Operations and Conflict Resolution

The scholarly and practical analysis of different peace operations, their characteristics, and requirements has become quite well-developed in the aftermath of the Cold War. In the years since 1991, distinctions between different types of political and military peace operations have become the focus of study and proposals for policy change, while the practical and real-case distinctions remain often very difficult to make.

The crucial distinction which is at the heart of recent discussions is that between Chapter VI and Chapter VII operations (these terms refer to the UN Charter). Chapter VI authorizes the general secretary and member states to employ peaceful means for preventative diplomacy and what has been called "peacemaking" though active diplomacy in existing conflicts. Chapter VII provides for classic collective security operations whereby the UN Security Council is empowered to pass resolutions calling upon members to use any means, including military coercion, to impose peace settlements and enforce them. The best-known UN peace operation is peacekeeping, but the term does not directly appear in the UN Charter. Instead, as practice and policy, it has evolved over time from the UN's Chapter VI powers and responsibilities for contributing to the peaceful settlement of disputes. In particular, the instrument of peacekeeping arose because the Security Council was largely paralyzed by U.S.–Soviet hostility and could not conduct more proactive and forceful peace operations as provided for under Chapter VII. It was therefore always a limited tool meant for use under circumscribed conditions to achieve limited objectives.

Thus, in his major post–Cold War policy statement "An Agenda for Peace," UN secretary general Boutros Boutros-Ghali clearly distinguished among these different peace operations.[19] During the Cold War, the clarity of these distinctions was not terribly important, because traditional peacekeeping was basically all the United Nations could hope to accomplish, given the effect of U.S.–Soviet rivalry on the effectiveness of the Security Council. Traditional peacekeeping (first employed to monitor the end to hostilities in Israel in 1948) is based on three principles: consent of the parties to the conflict, impartiality of the peacekeeping forces, and nonuse of military force—except in case of self-defense. Because it involves more than diplomacy and political negotiations, peacekeeping missions are sometimes referred to as "Chapter VI-and-a-half" operations.[20] However, although certainly a military operation, peacekeeping functions precisely because it is sought and valued by all the parties to the conflict, and because the actual military forces deployed are seen as neutral and impartial. The fundamental purpose of peacekeeping operations is to give the warring parties confidence that their desire for a political solution is genuinely held by the other parties as well, and that their military restraint will not be disastrously exploited. Peacekeeping operations, therefore, fall under the category of security problems in which the disputants are not determined to achieve their objectives through force but face obstacles of uncertainty and competitive bargaining incentives which make reaching an agreement difficult, as discussed in the previous section. Peacekeeping forces have neither the mandate nor the capacity to punish cease-fire violations, because at the point of punishing one party they might no longer be seen as impartial. Peacekeeping operations, therefore, depend for their effectiveness on two assets: (1) the fundamental desire of warring parties to seek a negotiated solution; and (2) the system of consent, strict impartiality, and self-defense which makes the peacekeeping forces not at all a threat and only an asset to those parties.

Peacekeeping is distinct from conflict prevention (or preventive diplomacy) and peacemaking in that the former is a military operation, while as Chapter VI operations the latter two are diplomatic and political. Obviously, any reasonable hope for a peace settlement and lasting peace will have to join a peacekeeping operation with political mediation and diplomacy as well as "peacebuilding," which is a long-term commitment to create the political, economic, and social conditions for lasting peace.[21] Furthermore, peacekeeping operations may coexist with and even make possible humanitarian assistance missions.

But just as clearly, peacekeeping operations must be kept distinct from peace enforcement, or even humanitarian intervention, which fall under Chapter VII.[22] If consent, impartiality, and self-defense are what make peacekeeping work, use of force against any one of the parties undermines and may destroy this foundation. Even if one of the parties to a conflict is much deserving of sanctions and the Security Council agrees to authorize such missions—as it did against Iraq in 1990—the sanctioned party is hardly likely to see such operations as justified. This would all be academic were these distinctions unrelated to practice, but there is a qualitative difference between Chapter VI and Chapter VII operations that changes both the military and political terms of conflict resolution. As we have learned so tragically in Somalia and Bosnia, the military requirements and political processes of the two types of missions differ fundamentally.

Finally, we should note that peacemaking and peace enforcement are different concepts and different policies, although they are often used interchangeably. Peacemaking refers to diplomatic activity in the course of a conflict which is meant to get the parties to agree to a settlement. It does not imply the use or even threat of military force, in contrast to peace enforcement. Peace enforcement as envisioned by the United Nations in Chapter VII derives directly from the UN's role as an institution of collective security. In collective security systems, members commit themselves to the peaceful and political solutions of disputes and pledge to take multilateral action against any member which violates that pledge.[23] Thus, collective security systems are based on some authority and provision for peace enforcement operations. This is an important distinction for analyzing Russian thinking and policy on peace operations, as I will explain in the following section.

Although I have pointed out the definitional and operational distinctions among different peace operations, it is important to recognize that the trend since the end of the Cold War has been to mix missions and operations in practice. Greater visibility of international and internal conflicts has created stronger motives for humanitarian missions which sometimes require enforcement elements, while the explosion of post-communist internal conflicts has strongly extended both the number and ambitions of peace operations. UNPROFOR and the Implementation Force (IFOR) operations in Bosnia exemplify this mixing of missions, as they have combined peacebuilding, peacekeeping, humanitarian assistance, and enforcement.[24]

Thus, it would be misleading to claim that there was a single international system or norm for peacekeeping as distinct from other peace operations, and judge Russian behavior against that. To a certain extent, the mixing of Russian doctrine and practice which I will discuss in the next section reflects that of the international community at large.

Nevertheless, the analytical distinctions are important for thinking about conflict resolution in the former Soviet Union because they are related to the effectiveness and legitimacy of international security institutions. The political terms of Chapter VI and Chapter VII conflict resolution are fundamentally and qualitatively different. In Chapter VI operations, the objective is to create and support a process in which the parties can achieve a self-enforcing agreement. This may entail offering incentives for honest bargaining and constructive proposals as well as support for long-term peacebuilding, but the focus remains mediation and facilitation.

In peace enforcement situations, there are, roughly speaking, two options. Either a settlement will be chosen multilaterally within the bounds of international laws and institutions such as the United Nations, or it will be chosen and enforced according to the interests of the predominant state. One of the achievements of the international community in the twentieth century has been the creation of a system for the former, and its greatest failing has been how rarely multilateral enforcement according to international laws, norms, and procedures has been used.

So the question for peace operations and conflict resolution in the former Soviet Union is first whether Russia can and does serve as an honest and neutral mediator in those situations which are amenable to Chapter VI-type peace operations. If so, the use and effectiveness of international institutions that are based upon and reinforce preventive diplomacy, peacemaking, peacekeeping, and peacebuilding should be both possible and desirable. The second question is whether in those situations which appear to require Chapter VII-type solutions— that is, where conflict arises not from competition, uncertainty, instability, and the like but from aggression by one party—can and do international institutions encourage multilateral and rule-based enforcement and intervention, or are Russian power and interests the basis for solutions?

Peacekeeping and Conflict Resolution in the Former Soviet Union

The obstacles to assessing Russian policy and practice in peace operations becomes immediately apparent when one tries to distinguish concepts, instruments, and policies as I have done in the preceding section. The first problem is simply one of language. Russian officials and political analysts have often used two different terms in referring to peace operations: *podderzhanie mira* (peacekeeping) and *mirotvorchestvo* (usually translated as peacemaking, but literally "peace creation"). Russian policy and doctrine also recognizes and uses the concept *kollektivnaia bezopasnost'* (collective security). As the preceding section discussed, at least in terms of theory and international law, the first two terms refer to two different policies, such that podderzhanie mira should refer to the interposition of invited, neutral forces (*voiska po podderzhaniiu mira*) for monitoring an established cease-fire to facilitate associated peace negotiations. In the same framework, *mirotvorchestvo* should then refer to diplomatic and political efforts to achieve peace settlements.

In Russian usage and policy, however, there is considerable confusion. First, the tendency of Russian officials and political analysts is to use the two terms interchangeably.[25] This would not be terribly problematic, since, as I have explained, both peacekeeping and peacemaking derive from the UN's Chapter VI and are reasonable complementary policies: maintaining a cease-fire without proactive policies to reach a settlement is not very helpful, though better than continued fighting.

Indeed, the conclusion that some observers have drawn that Russian policy in the near abroad is duplicitous and insidious because "peacekeeping" and "peacemaking" are used interchangeably betrays a certain lack of understanding. A Russian presidential declaration signed in September 1995 on security relations among the CIS states lists three national security tasks of the CIS: (1) collective security, (2) security of state borders, and (3) resolution of conflicts on CIS territory.[26] In discussing the third policy, the document uses the term *mirotvorchestvo* to refer to "the settlement and prevention of conflicts in the CIS states preferably by peaceful political-diplomatic means."[27] It goes on to state that this should be accomplished with the cooperation and participation of the UN and OSCE, although with the understanding that this region is of primary interest to Russia.

Thus, the problem is not in the interchangeability of terms in which Russia seeks to blend peacekeeping and peacemaking against international laws and norms. The two are quite related in international usage and practice as well. The real problems with Russian policy and practice in peace operations lies elsewhere: with the mixing of peacekeeping and collective security operations, the strong military element in Russian peacemaking practice, the refusal to accept international standards of peacekeeping (neutrality and impartiality in particular), and the claim to a special Russian role by right of its national security interests.

This blending is apparent in all the militarized conflicts in the former Soviet Union, but is most apparent in peace operations in Tajikistan. Although many Russians and Western analysts refer loosely to operations in Tajikistan as "peacekeeping," the missions actually operate as collective security and border defense forces. The latter were authorized in January 1993 when the civil war in Tajikistan had become extended to conflicts across the Afghan border. The former were authorized in September 1993 through an agreement among Russia, Tajikistan, Kazakhstan, Kyrgyzstan, and Uzbekistan. The form and legal basis for this agreement was the May 1992 Tashkent agreement on collective security. As forces for collective defense, therefore, the operations would not have to meet criteria for peacekeeping forces such as impartiality and deployment after the achievement of a cease-fire, conditions which they clearly do not meet. The problem is that at the last moment, the wording of the agreement was changed to provide for "peacekeeping forces,"[28] although neither the purpose nor form of the operations were changed. The agreement on the deployment of "collective peacekeeping forces" is of further significance because it serves as a precedent for subsequent peace operations.

This became clear in the negotiations on a CIS peacekeeping force for Abkhazia. The UN was involved in seeking an end to the conflict as early as 1993 and was active both in seeking a cease-fire and in sending observers. But UN secretary general Boutros-Ghali refrained from sending a peacekeeping force even after a Russian-brokered cease-fire agreement in December 1993 because the agreement on the terms of such a force and the likelihood of movement to a political settlement were so weak. Meanwhile, after exerting substantial pressure on Shevardnadze and leaving him few options, Russia had obtained a CIS agreement to deploy peacekeeping forces under the March 1992 CIS agreement and the September 1993 agreement's provisions. The parties agreed that if the UN did not supply a force, then the CIS force would be sent. In practice, a contingent of 3,000 Russian peacekeepers were sent in June 1994 after a quadripartite agreement (among Abkhazia, Georgia, Russia, and the UN) was signed in April 1994.

Reluctant to bow out of a crisis in which the UN had been so involved, the UN thus took the apparent middle ground (which was in fact a qualitatively new step) of tacitly approving of the CIS peacekeeping force on the condition that UN observers would monitor the operation.[29] In doing so, the UN is now associated with a peacekeeping force that clearly violates the norm of neutrality and impartiality. That said, however, one should note that Russia appears to be taking seriously some of the constraints which an internationally mandated peacekeeping force implies. Most recently, Russia has refused to take on an active peace enforcement role in returning Georgian refugees to Abkhazia by pointing out that such operations would exceed the peacekeeping mandate and would require a UN decision.[30]

Despite the fact that both Russian peacemaking and peacekeeping clearly violate fundamental rules and norms of international security institutions such as the UN and OSCE, Russia has consistently sought to obtain legitimacy and even funding for its peace operations efforts in conflicts in the former Soviet Union while trying to ensure that international involvement will not substantially constrain Russian options. For example, although Russia has allowed and participated in ongoing OSCE conflict resolution efforts in Nagorno-Karabagh, including an agreement in principle in December 1994 for the deployment of an OSCE peacekeeping force, Russia has prevented the actual deployment of such a force. At the same time, however, OSCE observers have remained active in Nagorno-Karabagh, Moldova, South Ossetia, Abkhazia, and Tajikistan. In addition to UN observers in Abkhazia, the UN has been involved in both observer missions and negotiation efforts in Tajikistan. Similarly, although the Russian military attack in Chechnya has clearly violated important OSCE rules (including those on notification of military movements and on nonuse of military forces for internal security), Russia subsequently permitted substantial OSCE observer and assistance missions, even when the result was a highly critical report on Russian human rights violations.[31]

This conjunction of substantial violations yet consistent involvement of international institutions by Russia in peace operations indicates that Russian leaders do see institutions as instrumental for security objectives. This is exemplified by Russia's efforts to have the CIS recognized as a "regional organization" under Chapter VIII of the UN Charter. Russian officials emphasize that these conflicts on their borders are a genuine security threat and must be dealt with one way or another. We seek international involvement, said a foreign ministry official, but other than Nagorno-Karabagh—clearly because of Azerbaijan and its oil wealth—the West has been unwilling to send forces. We support proposals to increase linkages between the UN, OSCE, and CIS to make peacekeeping effective, but it is effective peacekeeping that we need.[32] It is the opportunity created by the UN's Agenda for Peace and the potential to develop the CIS as a Chapter VIII regional organization, said another government official, which will both settle the question of the status of these forces under the UN and permit an effective resolution of these conflicts.[33]

Although the UN decision to become involved in the CIS operation in Abkhazia might appear to be a way to impose multilateral constraints on the CIS while meeting Russian demands for effective peacekeeping, allowing the CIS to operate as a UN Chapter VIII regional institution entails substantial legitimacy and control problems for the UN and the international community. Recognition as a regional organization would permit the CIS a greater and more active scope of peacekeeping activities, as well as the right to recommend enforcement measures. This is problematic, for if there is a dominant power at a regional level, it is too easy for a regional recommendation to be a thinly disguised legitimization of that dominant power's use of force to get its security interests. As one authority on international law writes:

> Unlike the UN, regional organizations could be dominated by a single state or an ideological bloc; they could, in other words, be coterminous with a great power and its closest allies. In such cases, the distinction between the action by the organization and the action taken by certain member states with the blessing of the organization makes no difference ... the regional organization, although no more than a thinly disguised power bloc, could legitimate military action against a geographically proximate member.[34]

This is, then, an important distinction. The UN and other international security institutions have been used by their members and international staffs to remain quite involved in conflict prevention, observation, and mediation in CIS conflicts. In this regard, it is deemed more valuable to be involved than to completely disavow conflict resolution in the area. In order to preserve the value of its legitimacy, however, the UN in particular has limited the degree to which Russia can claim a UN mandate in its operations. The cost of this balance between engagement and distance has been a more proactive Russian role in peace operations and a substantial reduction in the legitimacy and value of peacekeeping in the region. Although Russia's style of peace operations may have been more "effective" in stabilizing conflicts and getting peace settlements, there is very little question that these have not been effective multilateral solutions to security threats and that international institutions have played a very limited role.

How did this situation arise? There is, of course, the well-documented shift to a more nationalist definition of Russian interests and assertion of Russian preferences in relations with the near abroad.[35] In this regard, the mixing of peacekeeping, peacemaking, and peace enforcement serves Russian interests by lending a cast of international legitimacy to policies that permit Russia either to impose its own preferred solutions or to achieve concessions from CIS countries. At the same time, however, two other factors contributed to the mixing of peace operations and Russia's ability to make unilateral use of the leverage they afford. First, these political-military conflicts increased in number and scope over time. On a political level, these threatened upheaval and refugees.[36] On a military level, they raised the real and numerous possibilities of escalation from local wars. During the Cold War, escalation from local wars was one of the major threat scenarios in Soviet military planning, and this potential plays a very significant part in current Russian military doctrine.[37] Since 1992, therefore, conflicts in the CIS have risen to the top of Russian national security concerns.

Second, while the Russian interests at stake grew, the willingness of the international community to become involved in militarized conflicts remained tightly constrained.[38] While the UN and OSCE have been active in conducting conflict prevention and observer missions in the former Soviet Union, and have offered to provide peacekeeping forces when requisite preconditions are met (especially given the establishment of a cease-fire), the ability of these institutions to operate in the murky areas between peacemaking, peacekeeping, and peace enforcement remained limited and problematic.[39] Thus, it should be recognized that it is not at all clear that the international community could have handled all these conflicts any more cleanly or effectively with reference to its own repertoire of peace operations.

The significant role of international institutions has not been at the peace enforcement or peacekeeping end of the peace operations spectrum, however. That is, we have to recognize that their role has been minimized by Russian preferences and power when it comes to robust functions such as sanctioning and military oversight. Since 1994, however, the UN and OSCE in particular have played an increasingly significant role in facilitating transparency, conflict prevention, and negotiations in not-yet-militarized political disputes in the former

Soviet Union. The importance of political compromises in Russia's relations with the Baltic states and Ukraine should not be ignored.

Given that Russia has since 1994 appeared to increase the value it places on pressing parties toward a settlement in Moldova, Tajikistan, Georgia, and Nagorno-Karabagh, UN and OSCE strengths in these more political and facilitative institutional functions might become significant in the next period of post-Soviet conflict resolution.

Conclusion

As my outline of an institutional approach to security issues expects, the existence of substantial security interdependence among the post-Soviet states does create the potential that multilateral strategies to cope with political and military conflicts may be valuable to states. Even Russia, with its strikingly predominant power in the post-Soviet space, has pursued multilateral solutions to security problems.

Two limitations to the role of institutions become immediately apparent, however. First, in cases where the stakes are high or Russian preferences are strong, Russia is not going to be substantially or directly constrained by prevailing international rules or norms. Peace operations that are primarily military in character or which entail elements of enforcement will not be directly affected by institutional rules or procedures—certainly not to the same degree as they are affected by unilateral Russian policies. The Russian government's view of institutions remains primarily instrumental and practical, rather than normative and comprehensive. Russian leaders seek to use the legitimacy of international institutions, but they are not particularly bound by a long-term commitment to the maintenance of the norms and rules of post–Cold War security institutions. The greater impact of institutions on countries such as Germany arises from precisely this normative, comprehensive, and long-term stake in the legitimacy and functioning of Western-based security institutions.[40]

The second limitation on the role of international security institutions in conflicts in the former Soviet Union arises because, ironically, the form and functions of institutional rules and procedures do matter and are taken seriously by their members. In particular, the rules and understanding of the role and effectiveness of peacekeeping missions has constrained their usefulness in the former Soviet Union. Effective multilateral instruments are valuable and are not to be squandered in situations where their legitimacy will be undermined. It is precisely because member states and the institutions themselves take seriously both the value of different kinds of peace operations and the role of their legitimacy in contributing to their effectiveness that international institutions have played so little a role in Russian peacekeeping and peace enforcement. Given the mixing of instruments and missions that Russia has preferred and for the most part successfully implemented, international reticence was the right policy. It has preserved the legitimacy and effectiveness of the political and facilitative roles of the UN and OSCE, which may prove a more long-lasting and valuable asset.

Notes

I am grateful to Jonathan Aves, Karen Dawisha, Larry Forster, Raymond Garthoff, Gunnar Klinga, Bruce Parrott, George Quester, and participants at the Russian Littoral Project Conference, 6–8 June 1996, for their extremely helpful comments. All arguments and remaining errors are my responsibility. This research was supported by the National Council for Soviet and East European Research, which, however, is not responsible for the content or findings of this paper.

1. David Lake, "The Rise, Fall, and Future of the Russian Empire: A Theoretical Interpretation," in *The End of Empire? The Transformation of the USSR in Comparative Perspective,* ed. Karen Dawisha and Bruce Parrott (Armonk, NY: M.E. Sharpe, 1996).
2. The signatories to the Tashkent Treaty on Collective Security were Armenia, Kazakhstan, Kyrgyzstan, Russia, Tajikistan, and Uzbekistan. They were subsequently joined by Azerbaijan, Belarus, and Georgia. The notable holdouts remain Moldova, Ukraine, and Turkmenistan. Turkmenistan has signed a bilateral mutual defense treaty with Russia.
3. In January 1995, the Conference on Security and Cooperation in Europe (CSCE) changed its name to the Organization for Security and Cooperation in Europe (OSCE). For the sake of consistency, I will use OSCE throughout this chapter to refer to this security institution.
4. On Abkhazia's complicated history, see Georgui Otyrba, "The Regional Signifi-cance of the Georgian-Abkhazian Conflict," in *National Identity and Ethnicity in Russia and the New States of Eurasia,* ed. Roman Szporluk (Armonk, NY: M.E. Sharpe, 1994), pp. 281–309.
5. Catherine Dale, "The Case of Abkhazia (Georgia)," in *Peacekeeping and the Role of Russia in Eurasia,* ed. Lena Jonson and Clive Archer (Boulder, CO: Westview, 1996), pp. 121–37; Dmitri Trofimov, "The Conflict in Abkhazia: Roots and Main Driving Forces," in *Crisis Management in the CIS: Whither Russia?,* ed. Hans-Georg Ehrhart, Anna Kreikemeyer, and Andrei Zagorski (Baden-Baden: Nomos Verlagsgesellschaft, 1995), pp. 75–90.
6. For detailed assessments of this question, see Alvin Z. Rubinstein, "The Transfor-mation of Russian Foreign Policy," and Michael MccGwire, "Russia and Security in Europe," both in this volume.
7. Celeste A. Wallander, "International Institutions and Modern Security Strategies," *Problems of Communism* 41, nos. 1–2 (January–April 1992): pp. 44–63.
8. James Fearon, "Rationalist Explanations for War," *International Organization* 49, no. 3 (Summer 1996): pp. 379–414.
9. The underlying strategic situation and obstacle to cooperation thus described are called "collaboration games." See Lisa L. Martin, "Interests, Power, and Multilateralism," *International Organization* 46, no. 4 (Autumn 1992): p. 776.
10. These are known as problems of transparency.
11. I follow the standard practice in the theoretical literature in calling these types of obstacles to security cooperation "coordination problems."
12. Stephen John Stedman and Donald Rothchild, "Peace Operations: From Short-Term to Long-Term Commitment," paper presented at the meeting of the International Studies Association in San Diego, CA, 16–20 April 1996.

13. See studies of UN peacekeeping such as Virginia Page Fortna, "Success and Failure in Southern Africa: Peacekeeping in Namibia and Angola," in Daniel and Hayes, *Beyond Traditional Peacekeeping,* ed. Donald Daniel and Bradd Hayes (New York: Macmillan, 1995); see also John Stedman, "UN Intervention in Civil Wars: Imperatives of Choice and Strategy," in Daniel and Hayes, *Beyond Traditional Peacekeeping.*

14. Robert O. Keohane, *International Institutions and State Power* (Boulder, CO: Westview Press, 1989).

15. Even institutions that operate on the domestic level, and therefore have enforcement power, affect social behavior largely as strategic constraints. See Ronald Rogowski, "Institutions as Constraints on Strategic Choice," paper prepared for the annual meeting of the American Political Science Association, Chicago, IL, 30 August–3 September 1995.

16. For a dissenting view, see John Mearsheimer, "The False Promise of International Institutions," *International Security* 19, no. 3 (Winter 1994): pp. 1–43. There is a growing body of theoretical and empirical work on international security institutions. See John Duffield, "International Regimes and Alliance Behavior: Explaining NATO Conventional Force Levels," *International Organization* 46, no. 4 (Autumn 1992): pp. 819–55; Celeste A. Wallander and Robert O. Keohane, "An Institutional Approach to Alliance Theory," Center for International Affairs, Working Paper 95–2, April 1995; Celeste A. Wallander, "Balance and Institutions: German-Russian Security Relations after the Cold War" (manuscript).

17. Beth V. Yarborough and Robert M. Yarborough, "International Institutions and the New Economics of Organization," *International Organization* 44, no. 2 (Spring 1990): p. 240.

18. James Fearon, "Commitment Problems and the Spread of Ethnic Conflict," in *Ethnic Fears and Global Engagement: The International Spread and Management of Ethnic Conflict,* ed. David A. Lake and Donald Rothchild (Princeton: Princeton University Press, forthcoming); Barbara Walter, "The Resolution of Civil Wars: Why Negotiations Fail" (Ph.D. diss., University of Chicago, December 1994.)

19. Boutros Boutros-Ghali, *An Agenda for Peace* (New York: United Nations, 1992).

20. Larry Forster, "U.S. Peace Operations: A Primer," *Harvard International Review* (Summer 1996, 18, no. 4): p. 3.

21. Stedman and Rothchild, "Peace Operations," p. 27–28.

22. On the similarity of peace enforcement and humanitarian intervention (as distinct from humanitarian assistance), see Forster, "U.S. Peace Operations," p. 4.

23. Arnold Wolfers, "Collective Defense Versus Collective Security," in *Discord and Collaboration: Essays on International Politics* (Baltimore, MD: Johns Hopkins University Press, 1962), p. 182.

24. This is not merely my critique, but is recognized within the UN. See, for example, Boutros Boutros-Ghali, "UN Peacekeeping: An Introduction," *Brown Journal of World Affairs,* 3, no. 1 (Winter–Spring 1996): pp. 17–21, for a self-critical assessment.

25. Maxim Shashenkov, "Russian Peacekeeping in the 'Near Abroad'," *Survival* 36, no. 3 (Autumn 1994): pp. 46–69; see especially p. 65, n. 1.

26. "Strategicheskii kurs Rossii s gosudarstvami-uchastnikami Sodruzhestva Nezavisimykh Gosudarstv," 14 September 1995, ukaz no. 940, pp. 3–4.

27. Ibid. p. 4.

28. Anna Kreikemeyer and Andrei Zagorski, "The Commonwealth of Independent States (CIS)," in Johnson and Archer, *Peacekeeping and the Role of Russia in Eurasia,* p. 158.

29. Paul Taylor and Karen Smith, "The United Nations (UN)," in Johnson and Archer, *Peacekeeping and the Role of Russia in Eurasia,* p. 205.

30. "Russia Again Rejects Police Powers for Troops in Abkhazia," *Jamestown Monitor* (electronic version), 2, no. 67 (4 April 1996).

31. "Chechnya: The OSCE Excoriates Moscow," *Prism* (electronic version), 2, no. 7 (5 April 1996).

32. Official of the Russian Foreign Ministry, interview by author, Moscow, Russia, 26 May 1994.

33. Member of Presidential Advisory Council, interview by author, Moscow, Russia, 27 May 1994.

34. Tom J. Farer, "The Role of Regional Collective Security Arrangements," in *Collective Security in a Changing World,* ed. Thomas G. Weiss (Boulder, CO: Lynne Rienner, 1993), p. 164. I should note that the specific case which led him to the quoted discussion was the U.S. use of the Organization of American States (OAS) to sanction the U.S. blockade of Cuba in 1962.

35. Fiona Hill and Pamela Jewett, "Back in the USSR: Russia's Intervention in the Internal Affairs of the Former Soviet Republics and the Implications for United States Policy Toward Russia," working paper of the Strengthening Democratic Institutions Project, Kennedy School of Government, Harvard University, January 1994; Bruce D. Porter and Carol R. Saivetz, "The Once and Future Empire: Russia and the 'Near Abroad'," *Washington Quarterly* 17, no. 3: pp. 75–90.

36. Shashenkov, "Russian Peacekeeping," p. 49.

37. On the role of local wars and conflict in Soviet military doctrine, see Michael MccGwire, *Military Objectives in Soviet Foreign Policy* (Washington, DC: Brookings Institution, 1987), esp. chaps. 2, 3, and 10. The Russian military doctrine's discussion of escalation and local wars is in "Osnovnye polozheniia voyennoi doktrini rossiiskoi federatsii," pp. 17–8. It is the original text of the government decree, November 1993. It was not published.

38. Natalia Tsvetkova, "Peacekeeping in the Former Soviet Union: Russia and the International Community in the CIS," paper presented to the Seventh Annual Meeting of the Academic Council on the United Nations System in The Hague, Netherlands, June 1994.

39. This remains a crucial problem in Bosnia, with gray areas on whether IFOR should become actively involved in enforcing the terms of the Dayton agreement. See Mike O'Connor, "New Refugee Conflict Points Up Flaw in Bosnia Pact," *New York Times,* 29 April 1996, p. A3.

40. This comparison is documented in Wallander, "Balance and Institutions."

6

The Roots of American Goals for Eurasia

George H. Quester

This will be an attempt to sort out some of basic nature of how Americans relate to the world as a predictor of U.S. policies toward the countries that comprise the former Soviet Union.

When the United States still confronted a hostile and powerful unified USSR during the Cold War, there was indeed much debate inside the United States, and outside, about what had really determined U.S. foreign policy—the successes like the Marshall Plan, and the failures like the intervention in Vietnam. Now that the Cold War is over, some of the same debate has to be projected forward to account for U.S. foreign policy without such a unified Soviet adversary.

Three different theories of U.S. foreign policy—realist, liberal, and radical— will be evaluated to determine whether they can account for choices made since 1989, and for what they can predict for the future. Each of them will be shown to encounter complications, but the argument will be made that the liberal drives of American democracy are still more persuasive as an explanation than alternative theories.

The Importance of Surprise

One very important aspect of any such analysis may seem quite obvious, that Americans were very much taken by surprise by the tearing down of the Berlin Wall, the collapse of the Warsaw Pact, and then the subsequent collapse of communist rule in Moscow and the breakup of the Soviet Union. It is difficult to find any social scientists, regardless of ideological disposition, who would have ventured to predict such a dramatic Western victory in the Cold War.

George Kennan has been widely congratulated for having been the definer of the theory of containment, and for thus having his vision somehow verified.[1] Yet anyone rereading Kennan's 1947 "X" article will note some ways in which it does not fit so well with what actually happened.[2]

To begin, the implication of Kennan's argument was that it would take only a decade or so of holding back communist expansion for the Leninists to lose their confidence in the historical inevitability of revolution spreading throughout the world. In the event, it was to take more than four decades for Soviet Communism to fall.

What made communism collapse in 1989, moreover, was hardly that it was being "contained" and not spreading, since one could still easily enough mark communist advances on any map of Central America, Africa, and the Philippines. The military resistance of the United States and the Western alliance undoubtedly increased the economic and other burdens of Moscow's desire for spreading the revolution. Yet communism collapsed not because of some disproof of its inevitable expansion, but because of its broader failings back in the areas it had so long governed, its political and economic and social defects all across Eastern Europe, and in Moscow itself.

Until the dramatic events of 1989, the normal U.S. and Western perception was indeed that containment was working much less than perfectly. All through the Cold War, when the public opinion poll question was posed as to whether "we were winning the Cold War," the normal American answer was "no."[3] The victory was a surprise, its totality was a total surprise. American students who had to study the text of the Soviet constitution would giggle over the fact that it specifically allowed for secession by the separate republics; as with the other "guarantees" of Soviet constitutional law since Stalin, nothing seemed further from reality in terms of what would actually ever be allowed.

One theory was indeed dramatically confirmed in 1989, but again in reverse of the normal apprehensions: the domino theory. This had often been ridiculed by the American left as a fixation of John Foster Dulles or Richard Nixon, as a specious argument that a lack of resolve of Americans in Vietnam or anywhere else might somehow undermine resistance to communism everywhere. Yet the weakness of the East German regime's resistance to anticommunist demonstrators surely then undermined the Communists in Czechoslovakia and Romania, and then finally in Moscow itself. This dramatic falling of dominoes, in a direction eliminating rather than spreading communist rule, thus indeed caught everyone by surprise. The years since then have also been beset by some more surprises to complicate U.S. attitudes and policies, and here the unexpected has been more disappointing. The collapse of the Soviet Union, the realization of the right to secede by the Baltic and other republics, had come as a pleasant surprise. But the unexpected follow-ons have often been less pleasant.

If any American had been asked, merely as a *contingent* hypothetical question, whether the disappearance of the Soviet Union would thus increase or decrease peace in the world, the response would most surely have been optimistic. The same would have been true for what the likely economic impact of such a change would have been. If we had been asked whether free elections in the countries liberated from dictatorial communist rule would see former communists winning such elections fairly, the expectation would again have been that surely this was not going to happen.

The years from 1989 to 1996 have thus beset the U.S. government and people with a series of disappointments—that is, negative surprises. The economies of the components of the former Soviet Union, and of the former members of the Warsaw Pact, have not improved as much, when freed of Marxist command-economy controls, as many Westerners might have assumed. The general expectation might have been for something comparable to the West German economic miracle after the deutsche mark was introduced in 1948, to replace a currency for which the Soviets had control of the printing presses, or for something like the improvements in China under Deng Xiaoping; but (for a wide variety of reasons) the actual economic changes are now widely portrayed as disappointing.

The question is often posed today, as it was during the Cold War, on whether Americans attach higher priority to the attainment of political freedom around the world or to economic prosperity. *If* there had been any need to choose, Americans would most probably have rated political freedom as the most important. But they had every reason to believe that political freedom would bring along economic improvements as well.

The economic results of this ending of communist rule may indeed be somewhat debatable; and in another decade there may finally be such a general improvement that everyone discards talk of economic disappointment.

But much more definitely a disappointment has been the resurgence of ethnic conflicts in such countries, with the most horrible illustrations of course coming in the former Yugoslavia, but with parallel conflict across the Caucasian region of the former Soviet Union, and with serious worries about ethnic nationalism and conflict along other lines of contact.[4]

Whatever else Americans felt about communism, most would have given Stalin and his successors credit for deemphasizing ethnic conflict. One of the few axioms that Western liberals and Soviet-led Communists shared was that ethnic disputes were folly, that the kind of ethnic nationalism that had produced Fascist Italy and Nazi Germany had to be avoided. On the Western side of the Cold War lines of confrontation, the memories of Nazism, fear of communism, and the prosperity of the West European economic miracle, all combined to make Germans and Frenchmen and others bury their ancient hatreds. To the east of the Iron Curtain, it seemed that everyone was similarly being taught to believe that "all men are brothers," and that "workers of the world" should unite, as the class struggle was all that mattered, and disputes about language or religion were silly.

During the Cold War, the remaining ethnic conflicts, such as those between Israelis and Arabs, or Pakistanis and Indians, or Protestants and Catholics in Northern Ireland, thus seemed the anomalous exceptions. If communism had to be given credit for anything, it could be praised for having taught Azeris and Armenians to live together in peace, so most Americans would have thought. To discover, after seventy years of Marxist rule, that these groups still knew how to organize massacres of each other, and still wanted to do so, surely has had to be a disappointment for Americans. To discover that the kinds of ethnic hatred that produced World War II were to be given a fresh hearing all across the former Soviet Union, often with the same symbolisms that had been harnessed by the Nazis, has come as a shock to all.

One can translate this general theme of surprise and disappointment fairly easily into domestic politics by putting one's self into the position of George Bush. If President Bush had known in 1988 how the Cold War would end in his first term, he might have had every reason to expect to be reelected four years later. But Bill Clinton was to beat George Bush precisely on the theme that Bush had been paying too much attention to foreign policy, that foreign policy was now "bad news."

Unpredictabilities

The task here is thus to try to predict what Americans will want to achieve with regard to the former Soviet Union and its immediate neighbors, how much they will want to intervene, and on what side, and for what reasons. As with all of U.S. foreign policy around the globe, prediction here is not easy.

The initial point has to be repeated and stressed, that such predictions are made all the more difficult because so little of what happened in 1989, or since, was predicted. What Americans think they intend to do, what they plan about and speculate about, is always a partial, albeit somewhat imperfect, clue to what will actually be done. But even this kind of clue is missing here, when no one has foreseen that the Berlin Wall would come down, or that Estonians would be drafting difficult citizenship requirements for Russian speakers, or that Azeris and Armenians would be killing each other, or that Russian soldiers would be fighting their way into a place no one had ever heard of, called Chechnya.

When the Cold War was still unhappily in place, when it looked like the Berlin Wall would remain standing for at least another century, one could at least deal with the projections forward of various schools of American thought, with their recommendations and predictions of how the United States would deal with the military, political, economic, and social implications of the superpower confrontation.

Now that the Cold War is over, one way to try to assess what *is* happening in U.S. policy, and what *will* happen in the future, is to project forward these same very broad and general schools of thought.[5]

At the risk of enormous oversimplification, three such kinds of interpretation of American foreign policy will thus be elaborated here, just as they were elaborated during the Cold War: first, a realist view, by which all countries are basically the same, acting in pursuit of power; second, what could be labeled a liberal view, by which the United States has been an unusually good and benevolent country, importantly because it is a political democracy at home; and finally, still getting a hearing in the universities of Latin America, Western Europe, and Japan, what could be called a radical or Marxist view, by which the United States has been driven by the problems and demands of capitalism and thus has been a source of trouble and conflict in the world.

A "Realist" Interpretation

The first point of view to be outlined here would be that espoused over the years since World War II by scholars like Hans Morgenthau,[6] Kenneth Waltz,[7] and Henry Kissinger.[8] By this interpretation, all nations are basically alike, in that they all seek power, and fear power in the hands of others; and the domestic political arrangements of each of the countries, whether they be democratic or Stalinist or fascist, makes relatively little difference. If the generalization were not to hold that all such countries *seek* power, it would still be the case, by the view presented by the later neorealists, that each state must at least be wary of any accumulations of power in the hands of others.[9] The anarchic nature of international relations makes it dangerous for any state not to be on guard against what another state would do.

Quite consistent with such a realist interpretation of the major foreign policies would be an introduction then of the concepts and notions of geopolitics. This term is sometimes used to suggest nothing more than that a knowledge of geography is very important in the study of international relations. But more concretely, as in the writings of Halford Mackinder,[10] this is a theory that the geographical distributions of land and water on the surface of this earth offer a key to the amassing of power.

While Alfred Thayer Mahan might also have been seen as a geopolitical theorist, with his publication of *The Influence of Sea Power on History* in 1890,[11] he in effect had offered the diametrically opposite key to global power from what Mackinder and the later geopoliticians (for example, Karl Haushofer)[12] were to project. Mahan had argued that whoever controlled the seas would control the world. Mackinder offered an assessment much less reassuring for Britons or for Americans, that whoever controlled the center of Eurasia could exploit this to control the rest of this greatest of continents (the "world island"), and from this would be able to dominate the world.

Mackinder's lecture in 1904 was merely bringing to the surface what British government officials had viewed all through the nineteenth century as "the great game,"[13] the task of keeping tsarist Russia from exploiting its central position in Eurasia, from which it might strike in the direction of India, or Korea and Japan, or Scandinavia, or Turkey or Central Europe. Whoever controlled the interior lines of communication had the military advantage by such theories, able to strike in any direction. The British navy, rather than having some kind of advantage, would then be hard-pressed to bring forces to the right place at the right time, to rebuff any advances into the peninsulas sticking out from Eurasia.[14]

A realist theory of power politics had always dictated that Britain (and/or the United States) be concerned to keep adversarial hegemonic accumulations of power from being combined. Britain would have to intervene to prevent France from conquering Spain, just as it had earlier worked to keep Spain from conquering France. A balance-of-power strategy entailed intervening again and again on the weaker side, propping up the weaker so that it would not be conquered and absorbed by the stronger.[15]

Yet the peculiar geopolitical shapes of continental geography thus threatened that power could not be balanced here. If the tsar, or the successors of the tsar, could dominate the interior of Eurasia, they could accumulate enough force, working from this central position, to make it very difficult for a state like Britain to keep power divided and balanced.

Mackinder had warned that the geopolitical threat posed by Russia would become particularly acute once the interior lines of communication were completed. With the Trans-Siberian Railroad about to be opened, he delivered his pessimistic lectures about what this meant for Britain, the lectures that made his reputation. Mackinder included a prediction that was indeed to be monumentally wrong, that the Trans-Siberian Railroad would only be the first, and that "the century will not be old before all Asia is covered with railways."[16]

In the event, these railroads were never built, an important factor being some of the wars that Mackinder's theories had predicted. But military technology had moved along, during and after World War I, to offer a new reinforcement for interior mobility independent of railroad tracks: the tank. As Soviet Russia was to accumulate some 80,000 tanks in the Warsaw Pact, as Soviet-built tanks stormed into Seoul in 1950 and into Saigon in 1975, and rolled into Budapest and Prague in 1956 and 1968, one could easily enough see a realization of the geopolitical problem presented in 1904.

By the theories of power politics, the U.S. postwar commitment to containment and alliances was thus little more than the Americans inheriting the great game. Unable to get power into balance in the outside world, because Moscow controlled the center of that world and so much of its manpower and resources, the United States could not sit back during the Cold War, but had to commit and deploy its forces forward, to hold the line. Or at least it would have had to make this kind of force commitment if military technology had not put forward another tool, the atomic bomb, perhaps even more revolutionary than the tank.

If nuclear weapons had *not* been invented, the United States would thus have had but two choices after 1945, to trust in the intentions of Joseph Stalin (such a trust would have violated the basic assumptions of realist power-politics theory, as well as flying in the face of what anyone of more liberal assumptions saw happening), or to invest enormous manpower and economic capacity to defend South Korea, Western Europe, and all the other peninsulas that were geographically so vulnerable to attack.

Since nuclear weapons had indeed been invented, however, the United States made extensive use of a third choice, thus relying on threats of nuclear escalation and nuclear retaliation to deter the conventional attacks that Moscow might otherwise have launched. Such nuclear weapons allowed for containment, for the preservation of Western Europe and other places against an imposition of Moscow's rule, at a much lower cost. Such an exploitation of atomic weapons for "extended nuclear deterrence" may then have exempted the United States and its allies from a tremendous diversion of resources.[17]

In truth, it could be argued that nuclear weapons made possible the West German economic miracle and West European economic miracle that followed 1948, producing levels of economic growth and prosperity exceeding anything that the world had seen before. Without the threat of nuclear escalation, the steel that went into Volkswagens and into steel mills would instead have had to go into Western tanks, somehow to counter all the tanks assembled for the Warsaw Pact. What went into capital goods, or into consumer goods, would have had to go into military goods.

As we now try to project what U.S. attitudes are likely to be toward the former Soviet Union, and what they ideally *should* be, one must then immediately introduce the complications produced by the existence of nuclear weapons. Such weapons may have made the management of Cold War power conflict easier for the United States, as the successor to Britain in the great game; but they also make policy choices more complicated and difficult now that the Warsaw pact has been dissolved, and the Soviet Union has been broken up.

To repeat, if nuclear weapons had never been invented, the United States or Britain would have had every reason to foster a division of what had been the Russian Empire, and then Stalin and company's "evil empire." "Divide and conquer" is an old maxim of power politics, and it (even if it only for the moment meant "divide and escape the risk of being conquered") would have suggested supporting the independence of Ukraine or Kazakhstan.

To impose two huge and important conditions, *if* power was the determinant of behavior here, and *if* nuclear weapons did not exist, Washington would thus have to welcome every secession that occurred, in Georgia, in Chechnya, in Siberia, and so on. The more that the old Russian Empire was divided against itself, the safer it would be for Poland,[18] Finland, and any other nation along the edges of the old empire, and the easier it would be for the United States to relax its military guard.

The goal would be to reduce Russia, and to keep reducing it, at least until some other power, perhaps China, Germany, or Japan, replaced it as a threat, whereupon Russia would again be reinforced and reenlisted as an ally, in the endless game of the balance of power. Once the Russian geopolitical threat was gone, once another state had become the major threat to U.S. power and interests, the desire to weaken or fragment Russia would be gone.

A portion of the analysis offered by realpolitik thinkers since 1989, for example by Henry Kissinger,[19] indeed pursues such a line, assigning a very great importance to guarding the independence of Ukraine and Belarus, as well as the Baltic and Asian republics; if nothing else, this reduces the central Eurasian threat to all the rest of the world.[20]

For such an analysis, it would matter very little if Russia were governed by liberal democrats, and Ukraine by unrepentant Marxists. The United States would be enhanced in relative power for as long as Ukraine was independent of Moscow's rule, for as long as Russian and Ukrainian forces were more in opposition than in coalition.

Yet, even from the purest military-power perspective, the addition of nuclear weapons to the scene has had to alter calculations here. One can never forget that Moscow, in addition to threatening all the world in terms of geopolitics and traditional conventional military power, possesses a nuclear arsenal that could, in less than an hour, destroy the entire globe. And, since any major nuclear war anywhere threatens to impose damage all across this globe, one must then have very mixed feelings about seeing this aggregate of nuclear power divided against itself.

A confrontation between Ukrainian tanks and Russian tanks, or between a Ukrainian Black Sea Fleet and a Russian Black Sea Fleet is one thing, perhaps very much to be welcomed. A confrontation between Russian and Ukrainian *nuclear* forces is something altogether different, and very much to be feared, even from the most narrow and selfish interests of a country like the United States.

A few realist analysts might indeed welcome an independent nuclear force in Ukraine, Belarus, or Kazakhstan, and perhaps elsewhere in countries confronting Russian military power,[21] but this is surely a sentiment counter to the intuitions of most Americans.[22]

Nuclear weapons are very different from other weapons in that their destructiveness is hardly likely to be contained to the immediate battlefield confrontation in which they are employed. If nuclear weapons were ever to come into use between Ukraine and Russia, or between Chechnya and Russia, there are no guarantees that harm would not befall North America. The nuclear missiles that Ukraine inherited from the former Soviet Union, and then dragged its heels about surrendering, happened to have been aimed at targets in North America; if nothing else, this bizarre situation underscored how much the nuclear factor had altered the "divide and benefit thereby" reasoning of traditional power politics.

Even if *all* the Soviet nuclear arsenal had been retained from the outset on *Russian* territory, the nuclear factor would still have had to somewhat alter U.S. power calculations here. Without the nuclear factor, it would have served the selfish national interests of Americans to see even Russia fractionated and divided. Riots and demonstrations and civil war in the streets of Moscow itself would have been welcome, since a country convulsed in such internal division is inevitably less able to dispatch armored divisions to invade other territories.

Such a turmoil within Russia itself would perhaps even have allowed the

United States to introduce its own military and economic power to dominate the situation. We could then impose U.S. influence on Russia itself, finally "conquering" what Hitler and Napoleon had failed to conquer.

But the addition of nuclear weapons had almost from the start established a new logic by which *no one* could thereafter dare to occupy Moscow and conquer Russia, anymore than anyone might again dare to occupy Washington and try to conquer the United States. The nuclear arsenals of the superpowers, by the elementary logic of basic deterrence and mutual assured destruction, dictated that one always had to offer their regimes some reason to withhold the horrendous last-gasp retaliation they could inflict. One presumptively had to exercise constant care to avoid putting the other side into a position of "use them or lose them" with regard to its thermonuclear intercontinental missiles. One had to have a care for the *other* side's command-and-control apparatus, putting one's own self in the shoes of the Soviet leadership.

As what was indeed one of the biggest surprises of the end of the Cold War, one then has to note how the collapse of the Soviet Union, as the civilian supporters of Boris Yeltsin stood up to Soviet tanks, thus violated many of the premises of basic nuclear deterrence just noted here above. In a nonnuclear world, the United States should have welcomed, and fomented, such demonstrations in the streets of Moscow. In the nuclear world as it actually existed, the United States should not have dared to welcome any such developments, out of the simple fear of whether this would lead to nuclear war.

The Central Intelligence Agency (CIA) did not bring Yeltsin to power, and did not in any direct way cause the turmoil within the USSR. As most Americans however, welcomed this turmoil (much more probably from the liberal motives to be discussed next, rather than from power-politics motives), they in effect forgot the nuclear threat, or simply could not do anything about it.

Yet the nuclear threat is illustrated all too well by some of the rumors and uncertainties about who was in control of the Soviet nuclear weapons release codes during the Communist Party coup attempt, as Gorbachev was held under house arrest in Yalta.[23] And it was then illustrated even more by the suicide of Marshal Akhrameev immediately after the coup. Akhrameev, often viewed as a relatively moderate and reasonable member of the Soviet military leadership, nonetheless saw the events of 1989 to 1991 as disowning all that he had lived and worked for. The classic fear of basic nuclear deterrence was that some such military leader, seeing his political cause suffering so total a defeat, would not just commit suicide, but would drag down the world by imposing the appropriate retaliation.

Nuclear deterrence has always predicted that the loser in a conventional power struggle would impose a horrendous *nuclear* second-strike retaliation on the winner, with this therefore deterring the prospective winner from exploiting its advantages in the first place. But the grand winners in the Cold War, by power considerations (and by ideological considerations to be introduced), were the United States and its NATO allies, and Soviet nuclear retaliation was not inflicted.

Aside from the complications introduced by nuclear weapons, one must add one other asymmetry by which the United States might wish to befriend Russia in the breakup of the Soviet Union, rather than befriending its new neighbors—that is, by which the United States might need to support the *larger* state here, rather than the smaller states. The UN Charter gives a veto in Security Council deliberations to the five permanent members, defined in the Charter as the United States, the United Kingdom, France, the Republic of China, and the Union of Soviet Socialist Republics.

The wording of the Charter was already twisted in 1970 when the People's Republic of China was allowed to assume the seat that was literally designated for the Republic of China; and the same happened then in 1991 when the Russian Federation replaced the USSR.

The most doctrinaire of the power-politics analysts would assign little or no importance, of course, to the UN Charter or to the votes of the Security Council. But a slightly more sophisticated realist would indeed attach weight to international law as yet another power tool. If there is indeed some political advantage to having international law and UN Security Council resolutions as a backing, then it is valuable for the United States, when confronting Iraq or Cuba or any other state, to win a positive Russian and Chinese vote (or at the minimum an abstention, so that the desired resolution is not vetoed).

The nuclear factor and the UN factor (many have noted the coincidence that the five permanent members of the Security Council just happen to be the states openly in possession of nuclear weapons, the five states that the Nuclear Nonproliferation Treaty allows to retain such weapons) thus complicate what might otherwise have been the right pattern for the United States to pursue power.

But for these two considerations, one might want the CIA and Western radio broadcasts to encourage even further division within Russia itself, with Chechnya being the model. Except for these two considerations, it might be much easier to favor the expansion of NATO to all the East European countries (and all the former components of the Soviet Union) that would like to be members. And/or it might be much easier for Americans to relax into a noninvolved isolation, as power in Eurasia was more and more balanced against itself.

Because nuclear weapons do exist, however, the United States may have to be more cautious about expanding NATO, perhaps preferring expansion of the non-military European Union instead, the model adopted thus far by Finland and Sweden (again there may also be other more liberal and less power-oriented reasons to favor EU over NATO expansion).[24] Because nuclear weapons do exist, the United States cannot push for a maximum of division within the former Soviet Union or within what is now Russia. Because such weapons exist, the United States cannot relax about international security issues, cannot let a balance of power facilitate a return to isolation.

A Liberal Interpretation

We have come to the point where entirely different perspectives on U.S. foreign policy scream out to be heard. Do Americans really want their country to be as powerful as possible? The mere mention of the phrase "world policeman" typically causes voters and congressmen to race in an opposite direction. And one remembers that President Bush, having presided over the Western victory which unified Germany and dismantled the communist coalition, and then having defeated Saddam Hussein's aggression in Iraq, went on to lose the 1992 election, to an opponent who accused Bush of spending too much time on foreign policy.[25]

There are some Indian and Chinese analysts of international relations who, having read their Morgenthau carefully, warn the world that the United States is out to establish a power hegemony;[26] and one can find similar projections in Moscow.[27] Yet much of East Asia, and much of the world, is just as concerned that the United States will retreat rather than advance, will avoid accumulating power, will pull back its troops and aircraft carriers.[28]

We must turn then to the second broad interpretation of all of U.S. foreign policy, by which Americans care little for power, but care rather for the advancement of democracy and prosperity around the world.

This second line of analysis would be that by which the outside world would label most Americans as "liberal" (a phrase which Americans themselves apply in a very different sense, to what the world might call "social democrats"). Liberal in the global sense would thus very much include Thomas Jefferson and Barry Goldwater and Ronald Reagan; that is, all Americans who harbor a distrust of governmental power and a faith in the individual, people who regard the American political and economic and cultural experience as one of the great successes of world history, and who (being generous in light of their own good fortune) would like to share this with other peoples and nations in the world.

What Americans most centrally have wanted to share is political democracy, the principal of government by the consent of the governed. If such democratic governments opted for more state intervention, for democratic socialism, as were the voter's choices for decades in Scandinavia or India, there would be little problem, as long as these voters were free to change their mind and as long as elected governments did not abolish elections. The economic by-products of free elections might or might not soon enough be a substantial turn to free markets and prosperity, if the voters would be persuaded by the economic example of the United States, as well as the all-important political example.

Power-politics analysts often speak of "vital interests," the preservation of the United State's own self-government and prosperity, as if these were the *only* goals for which U.S. power would ever be deployed. But a broader sense of U.S. national interest here would include the welfare and happiness of peoples abroad as an end in itself, something which Americans have cared about in the past, and may well care about in the future.[29]

By such an interpretation of the events since 1989, and of the entire Cold War, those Americans who could spare the time to master the details would support every component of the former Soviet Union that was achieving political democracy, and would oppose any that were sliding toward fascism, a new form of Marxist dictatorship, or toward an intolerance based on religious fundamentalism. By this kind of an interpretation, Americans were never anti-Russian during the Cold War, but only anti-Soviet and anti-communist, seeing Lenin and Stalin and their successors as dictators who had forced themselves on the Russians, and on everyone else, against the people's will.

By this kind of an interpretation of American character, the taking down of the Berlin Wall, and the breakups of the Warsaw Pact and Soviet Union, were indeed tremendous victories; they were not so much power victories for the United States, however, but victories for the Germans, Hungarians, and Estonians and even for the Russians themselves.[30]

This victory was indeed total, total beyond anyone's dreams, but here again we must then turn to some serious problems. To begin, Americans have been swamped by the number of new democracies that deserve attention. Who is having an election this month, and under what new rules? Where is democracy being truly implemented, and where do we instead see former Communists or others bending the rules to try to win such elections unfairly? Where is the public enthused about democracy, and about the economic changes that come with it? And where are the same publics, to Americans' dismay, instead voicing complaints and disenchantment, a general sense of disappointment? And how much economic assistance will be required to relieve such disappointment, to make up for the ecological and other damage inflicted in the decades of the Marxist dictatorships' command economies?

As a counterfactual, one could thus speculate about what the U.S. attitudes and behavior might have been if *only one* communist-governed country (perhaps Hungary?) had been freed to leave the Warsaw Pact, or if just the Baltic republics had been released from the Soviet Union, with Gorbachev continuing to govern the rest of the USSR as a nominally communist country.

Under such circumstances, one might predict that Hungary, and/or Lithuania, Latvia, and Estonia, would have been showered with attention and with help. The West would have paid great attention to how free elections were working and to how the electoral issues were being phrased. Americans, and Germans and Swedes and Finns and so on, would have been ready to offer more substantial economic assistance, to be sure that these first examples of a post-communist society proved a success.

With a patient sense that all the rest of the communist world might be liberated over a longer period of time, perhaps one or two such countries per decade, it would have seemed important to take proper care of each of these positive "dominoes."

But the way that *all* the dominoes fell so quickly after 1989 has rather saturated and overloaded the attention span of the typical generous and liberal American, leaving him or her unaware of the latest from Romania or Uzbekistan, if he or she ever was aware of how Uzbeks differed from Russians.

Americans are generous and warm-spirited, by this second interpretation, and actually averse to exercising power over or dominating others; but there obviously have to be some limits to human generosity. The immigration restrictions the United States imposes are only the most obvious example of the bounds of generosity here. The inadequacy of the economic assistance offered, and of the trade barriers lowered, supply another example, if only because there are now *so many* plausible needs for economic assistance.

Americans are very fully prepared to share their political success with the world, wishing that all countries have the benefits of free elections and freedom of the press and speech. They hope that the economic concomitants of this will also spread. But Americans are not so willing to share *all* of their economic prosperity—for example, the portion due to a rich soil not overburdened by population. Hence, the immigration barriers for anyone who is an economic refugee rather than a political refugee.

Things get even more complicated when the principle of self-government gets interlinked with ethnic subdivisions that most Americans have never heard of. The American commitment to political democracy normally amounts to an endorsement of self-determination, the idea that ethnic groups should be the deciders of what state they are part of. As demonstrated already at the end of World War I, however, such Wilsonian principles are often difficult to implement where ethnic groups are intermixed in very complicated ways, where the economic interests of a group work in exactly the opposite direction from their desires for ethnic union, or where the ethnic minorities are so minimal in size as to escape attention (much less achieve an economic or political viability as a separate state unit).[31]

Because of their historical independence, and the principled stand that had been taken by all U.S. presidents, including Franklin Roosevelt, the Baltic republics of Lithuania, Latvia, and Estonia thus had a more ready claim on the attention of Americans and thus, a greater likelihood of winning support for self-determination and independence. The official policy of the United States, before the Soviet Union collapsed when *all* the member republics elected to secede, was basically to recognize Soviet unity rather than oppose it, *except* for the Baltic republics.

Perhaps there was additionally little of a special status in the way Americans saw Ukraine and Belarus, ironically in part because Stalin had insisted on getting separate UN memberships for these republics. But the attention span of Americans, and of other political liberals around the world, has surely then been strained for the separate Asian republics of the USSR, and even more for the multitude of separate ethnic nationalities and autonomous republics comprising what was previously the Russian Federated Soviet Socialist Republic, today's Russian Federation.

Thus, Americans will obviously not have an inexhaustible sympathy for the right to self-determination of ethnic groups. Just as their sympathy for Scottish independence from Britain cannot be high on any list of priority concerns (and infinitely less will be the sympathy for demands from Shetland Islanders for independence then from Scotland), so the official policy of the U.S. government, and the sympathies of Americans in general, were not such as to press for independence for Kazakhstan and Tajikistan from the old Soviet Union. If the USSR had not broken up so spontaneously and surprisingly, U.S. concerns might have indeed been directed to the obvious case of the Baltic republics.

Yet, just as the Monroe Doctrine made Americans feel very different about a Latin American state once it had achieved independence, there would be a difference between U.S. attitudes before and after the so totally unexpected fragmentation of the Soviet Union. Once all the former Soviet Socialist Republics had in fact achieved this independence, with membership in the United Nations and full de jure U.S. diplomatic recognition, Americans would indeed become more hooked to defending these independences, at least until it was shown clearly that Kazakhstan or Belarus or some other republic truly again wanted to merge with Russia.

Yet, as the next drawing of the line here, the U.S. government and people then would have wanted what remained of Russia to stay together. Anyone attempting to educate Americans on additional differences and gradations here has had an uphill battle, for at least two reasons.

First, Americans are notoriously uninformed about, and uninterested in, the details of ethnicities around the world, because U.S. educational systems place a very low stress on knowledge of history or geography, and of facts in general.[32]

Second, all the recent discoveries of ethnic disputes, as in Armenia, Azerbaijan, and the former Yugoslavia, have come with the bad news that wars and their human misery are not gone with the end of the Cold War, but have, if anything, becomes somewhat more prevalent. Americans have more generally regarded the ethnic disputes of the outside world as a great waste of human effort, producing wars and massacres. To repeat, one of the few important propositions that the liberal and Marxist perspectives shared was that such ethnic disputes were never genuine, were never really worth fighting about.

Some more complications might be projected with American feelings about religion. Americans are more religious than most of Europe, at least by the data on church attendance or self-description. But they are also happily divided in their religious beliefs, checking and balancing each other in the manner that Madison described in his "Tenth Federalist," producing strong rules on religious freedom and separation of church and state.

One of the earliest intrusions of Americans into the former Soviet Union has indeed come with young missionaries of various Protestant denominations, intent on converting Russians to a Western version of Christianity (thereby upsetting older hard-line Communists, representatives of the Russian Orthodox and other Orthodox churches, and local Muslim clerics).[33]

Also possibly intruding into the former Soviet Union are of course the various strands of militant Islamic belief, some of which are quite intolerant of other religions.

It is not easy to sort out how all this will affect the overall attitudes of the American people and their government. Americans were always critical of the heavy-handed atheism of the communist world, and stood up for freedom of religion. At the same time, given their own history, Americans disapprove of religious people waging wars because of their faith, just as they scoff at and disapprove of wars about the language people speak.

When Americans thus speak of "freedom of religion," they in the end probably put slightly more emphasis on the "freedom" than the "religion." Rather than taking sides between Baptist or Mormon missionaries and Russian Orthodox bishops, Americans are more likely to rally simply to principles of tolerance and individual free choice, to oppose every faction—Islamic, Orthodox, Marxist, or whatever—that would use government force to impose a religion or ban it.

Americans, to repeat, will have trouble digesting all the details here, with most of them being quite unaware of what kinds of young Americans are headed for the former Soviet Union as missionaries. When such ethnic or religious conflicts do indeed result in war, however, it then becomes much more difficult to remain ignorant about whether Chechens are the same as Russians, or are not. And here one must then introduce an important additional factor (what is sometimes today called "the CNN factor") into the determination of how Americans will feel about the former Soviet Union.[34]

Where the media, and now most importantly the television medium, bring direct evidence of human misery from any part of the world, the generous and liberal instincts of Americans are additionally mobilized. And when the same media evidence suggests that the democratic local wishes of a people are being frustrated and punished by brute military force, then this American sympathy may also fasten on the issues of democracy and self-determination.

Just as there were other portions of Africa suffering from starvation, when Ethiopia and then Somalia captured so much American sympathy, there may be other ethnic minorities within Russia, or elsewhere within the former Soviet Union, who seem to care about self-determination, and are willing to plunge their region into guerrilla war to contest for this. Yet CNN and other American television cameras were in Somalia and not in the Sudan, and they have been in Chechnya more than in Abkhazia.

It may be a sad commentary on the Wilsonian instincts of American liberal feelings that these will be mobilized only when the news media capture their attention for a fleeting moment. Because so much of the world was able to contest for self-government so suddenly, because Americans do not spend that much time digesting the details of the world, and because television has become the principal means by which they know anything, the commitment of the American public to the components of the former Soviet Union will be shockingly uneven.

Another inevitable complication in the American feelings about the outside world needs to be introduced here. The liberal American world outlook may include a generous identification with peoples everywhere, expecting that they all should benefit from democracy and self-government. Yet it is altogether natural that Americans will identify the most with people they resemble, with distant cousins, with the regions from which their ancestors came.

At the extreme this could become what Samuel Huntington has outlined as a future "clash of civilizations," as considerations of ethnicity and culture become intertwined with political sympathy and identification.[35] The typical American assumes that democracy can work anywhere in the world; Huntington would instead be among those seeing close links between culture and whether a people can handle democracy, and will be likely to stick to it.

Yet there are more basic ethnic ties of simple human identification, unrelated to whether any particular foreign culture supports or conflicts with democracy. The American entry into World War I was thus complicated by the presence of large numbers of German-Americans and Irish-Americans, leaning in the opposite direction from Americans of British ancestry. And an important initial stimulus for the Cold War thus stemmed from the fact that Buffalo and Detroit and Chicago had large concentrations of Polish-Americans, people who regarded it as an outrage, even more than the rest of Americans, that Poland had been liberated from Hitler only to be governed by Stalin. Greek-Americans have special feelings about Cyprus, and Jewish Americans tend to be strong supporters of Israel (but also have had strong feelings in the past about the anti-Semitism that showed up in the tsar's Russia, and in the Soviet Union of Stalin and his successors).

Compared to the issues of Northern Ireland or Cyprus or Israel, these special ethnic feelings of such "hyphenated Americans" will now play a less central role in U.S. policies toward the former Soviet Union. There are no large concentrations of Russians or Ukrainians in the United States to lobby their congressmen in one direction or the other. The sympathy Americans feel for the Baltic republics may reflect the ethnic biases of Scandinavian and German-origin Americans somewhat, as the Baltics are seen as western Europeans rather than as an appropriate part of the Slavic world; but there are no significant voting blocs of Estonian-Americans, and so on.

Where anti-Semitism reemerges in any of the components of the former Soviet Union, one might anticipate a slightly stronger impact on U.S. politics, but the sad historical pattern is that such resurgences are almost as likely in Ukraine (or in Poland?) as in Russia.

Yet one more complication needs to be introduced here. To repeat, except for the nuclear factor, the power-politics approach might have suggested supporting any and every state, or fragment of state, confronting Russia, on the old principle of opposing the potential hegemon. The liberal approach, constrained by the limits of information and potential endlessness of the local popular demands for separation, would instead be to let the chips fall where they may, large or small.

If Belarusians[36] or Ukrainians freely wanted, as Slavs, to merge with Russia, then Americans would not want to oppose this, but would want indeed to expedite it, just as they supported the reunion of Germany, and support the potential unification of Europe. The same would hold true if any of the *other* newly independent states of the former Soviet Union wanted, of their own free will, to become part of a single political state together with the Russians.

So far, so good. But what if, pending the sorting out of all the real feelings of the peoples here, it were obvious that some of the former Soviet republics were more democratic in their internal processes, while others were instead maintaining the more dictatorial processes of the old USSR? In particular, what if the largest and most geopolitically threatening of the components, Russia, were also to be one of the most genuinely democratic, while some of the smaller and less threatening components were largely being governed irrespective of their populations' wishes, by thinly disguised former Communists, or by what amount to neofascists or simple warlords?

In any confrontation around the world between a democracy and a dictatorship, it would be the normal instinct of Americans to back the democracy, with greater economic assistance, with a greater likelihood of military and political backing, with a deeper and more genuine human sympathy.

Because of the difficulties of obtaining and processing information, as noted above, it will not be easy for most Americans to keep track of how democratic processes and freedom of speech and press are faring in Russia, and even less easy to track this in Ukraine or Kazakhstan. Good news in one year is followed by bad news in another, and vice versa.

What if a more stable pattern sets in, however, by which Russia seems to have adopted the political and economic "American model" more than the newly independent states on its littoral?[37] One might then expect American sympathies to align in almost exactly the opposite direction from the realistic considerations advocated, for example, by Henry Kissinger. Rather than identifying with "little Ukraine" against the "Russian hegemon," we might see the United States identifying with "democratic Russia" against "nondemocratic Ukraine."

The sorting out of policies would be easier, of course, if the prospective contest was between a "democratic Estonia" and a "nondemocratic Russia." Here the considerations of liberalism and balance-of-power thinking would both lean in favor of Estonia (but with worries about nuclear command and control still complicating the realist power position).

The processes of political evolution after the fall of communism are more ongoing and dynamic, of course, rather than once-and-for-all.[38] Just as with outside-world assessments of the Weimar Republic in Germany, Americans looking at today's Russia will have to contemplate an incomplete case of democracy, with much greater free speech and deference to will of the voters, but with the military forces sometimes seemingly adopting policies all on their own;[39] and even among the civilians some of the attitudes come across as more in the

Russian imperialistic tradition, and less as a democratic concern for the self-determination wishes of others.

Could it indeed be that preserving democracy in Russia will thus require tolerating a Russian intolerance of self-determination for some other ethnic group, a group most Americans probably have never heard of? If the great majority of voters choose to be intolerant of the separatist wishes of a minority, theories of democracy do not have a ready answer as to which side is correct; and the liberal instincts of Americans in the 1990s may thus confront puzzles and choices as difficult as Woodrow Wilson had faced at Versailles.

And what if today's Russia, like Weimar Germany, waxes indignant about the status of ethnic kinsman abroad? Weimar's concern for Germans in Poland or in Czechoslovakia may have paved the way for the Nazis, but it was not inevitable that democracy would fail in Germany, and such ethnic concerns were hardly so unnatural even in a democracy. The Russians' concerns for the rights of ethnic Russians in Estonia or Kazakhstan are similarly not any sure sign that democracy is doomed in Moscow.[40]

The issues in Moldova, Chechnya, and Estonia thus pose difficult choices and problems of assessment for any liberal outsider. Just as a power-politics interpretation of American relations with the former Soviet Union can no longer be so simple and straightforward, neither can a liberal approach. If Americans care for democracy and self-government in this entire area for the longer run, some shorter-term compromises may be inevitable.

Marxist Interpretations

The dramatic collapse of Marxist regimes in all the countries we are considering here might suggest that little or no attention should be given to what had been taught in the universities of these countries under communist rule, an interpretation of U.S. foreign policy as the product of the defects of capitalism. Yet, even if such an interpretation now produces yawns among Russian or Ukrainian students, it still has a great appeal for many West European and U.S. faculty and students, and it must be addressed for what it would predict.[41]

Americans who regard themselves as radicals or Marxists might indeed draw some solace from the grumbling and disappointment that one witnesses in the eastern European and former Soviet countries, and from the periodic electoral resurgences of former Communists, in parties renamed or not renamed. Perhaps the Marxist sense of priority was not so wrong after all, by which socialism's economic guarantees and equality were more important than free elections or free market choice. Time will tell whether the voters in any free election in these countries would really vote to return to the situation before 1989; but the more important question here is what such an interpretation would have predicted about U.S. policy.

A radical interpreter of U.S. policies might also sense some vindication in the reluctance of the United States, and also of Western Europe, to lower tariffs sufficiently on the agricultural and other goods that the former communist countries could be the most cost-effective for the moment in exporting. Rather than bolstering democracy in the former Warsaw Pact area, we are bolstering our own farm incomes behind remaining protectionist barriers.[42]

Yet the special role assigned to agricultural interests in the United States and in the European Union is much more a demonstration of the peculiar voting rules of the parliaments involved, and of a tradition where a special cultural role is assigned to agriculture, and less a demonstration of the pernicious workings of capitalism. To be sure, what is involved is a basic form of material greed, but a radical theory of U.S. foreign policy is based on more than simple human greed.

Rather than a simple retention of *some* tariff barriers (which most Republicans and most Democrats are indeed inclined to continue lowering), a Marxist theory of the totality of U.S. policy toward the former Soviet Union should have *predicted* here what the power-politics theory *recommends,* that the United States would play the game of divide and conquer to the maximum. The ultimate goal would have been different, to open up markets for American products and thus to relieve pressures on American capitalism (rather than to guard against any hegemonic Russian military power), but the result should have been the same: a policy of seeking to weaken any and all local regimes that could stand up against the demands of the United States.

By this theory, rather than caring about free elections, U.S. pressure would have been directed to free markets, to opening up opportunities for American sales and American investments. (By the same theory, of course, the United States should also be shrugging off Chinese human rights violations, as long as Beijing opens itself to American investments and sales.) By this theory, power is pursued as the accessory to economic needs, and any endorsement of free election and self-government is basically window dressing.

The U.S. interest in opening the former Soviet Union to free international trade is undeniable, but the difficult point is, as always, whether this is entirely for the benefit of U.S. capitalism, or mostly rather because this is seen as serving the material well-being of Russians and Estonians, and so on, and as reinforcing political democracy. As throughout the Cold War, in interpretations of the Marshall Plan and GATT, and other proposals for free trade, the issue between liberals and Marxists has been about which is the tail and which is the dog here—the political concern for people's freedom, or the concern for exports and profits?[43]

We must return once more here to how Americans more generally balance economic and political considerations. The typical American (by the liberal view) wishes other people well, hoping that they can share in the benefits of political freedom, as well as in the prosperity produced by consumer-oriented free markets. If an American *had* to choose, he or she would assign political freedom the higher priority, but most Americans would expect the two, sooner or later, to advance together, as each furthers the other.

It has thus been somewhat perplexing to see great economic success in the liberalization of markets in Communist China, and relatively less growth in political freedom. Yet the hope remains that the freeing up of markets will *inevitably* erode the political constraints, as well.

It has conversely been perplexing, in the former Soviet Union, to have economic improvements seemingly lagging as political liberalization is introduced. Again, the long-term hope is that political freedom will bring economic results.

How would most Americans react if Russia had resembled China, or if it came to resemble China in the future, with great economic growth and a frustration of anything like full democracy? Those who are power-oriented have painted such a scenario as very threatening, because of the military use that a dictatorial Russian government (or perhaps *any* Russian government) might make of such economic inputs. The American who is oriented to a liberal worldview would more probably again find it simply perplexing.

The Marxists used to claim that the United States, under President Truman, had provoked the Cold War by aggressively engaging Stalin's Soviet Union. If Americans at the end of the twentieth century are not in the mood to engage Russia in any such confrontation, this would hardly seem to support such radical theories. The United States is *not* pressing its influence in the former Soviet Union as hard as Marxist-Leninist theories would have predicted. Some Russians are now claiming that American pressure is severe and unreasonable, but they are more likely to phrase this as a power-politics argument than as the workings of capitalism.

On a more trivial point of nomenclature, one senses a last gasp of the left-of-center interpretation of events whenever one hears the remaining communist forces during the coup of 1991, and since, referred to as the "conservative" forces in Russian politics, and hears those who wish to reform the political and economic system referred to as "radical reformers." Most of us have lived through decades of seeing anyone who questioned the government's role in economics and in the rest of individuals' lives labeled "conservative," and seeing the "radical" or "reform" phrase applied instead to those who saw a bigger role for government; this would then indeed be an amazing turnaround.[44]

In some part, of course, it is a desire somehow to get back over to the "winning side" of historical momentum, but it comes from many of the same analysts who predicted that the East Germans would never want to sacrifice the benefits of socialism by merging into West Germany and that communism might be governing the Soviet Union for all of the foreseeable future, in large part because most of its residents had become accustomed to it.

Some Tentative Conclusions

The ethnic and nuclear dimensions of what was the Soviet Union complicate what all three theories of U.S. foreign policy drives would have recommended.

It has been argued here that U.S. policies fall more into a liberal framework than into any realistic pursuit of power, and that this in the same moment serves to negate the Marxist or radical analysis. Today, one hardly sees the United States so eager to be the world's policeman, to develop an imperial hegemony. Rather than running after power, Americans are more often seen as running away from it.

Power-politics theories of international behavior would recommend a leaning toward isolation only when one faces no external threats *and* when one has no opportunity to build up one's own empire. Having been relieved of the threat of Soviet hegemony, however, Americans are not interested in establishing a hegemony of their own, and are not intent on dominating the world militarily.

As noted, the liberal commitment to democracy must also wrestle with impulses toward isolation or nonengagement, because active foreign policy has always been seen as a threat to democracy and liberty at home, and because of mere fatigue with the burdens of the world. There have thus been, and will continue to be, limits to how much support and sacrifice Americans are ready to assign to the protection of political freedoms across the former Soviet Union; but these will stem largely from a basic American inability to absorb the details of all the successes here since 1989, the successes which of course are still always partial, and perhaps therefore needing support.

Notes

1. For an example of such an analysis extolling Kennan as a predictor here, see Wilson D. Miscamble, *George F. Kennan and the Making of American Foreign Policy* (Princeton, NJ: Princeton University Press, 1992).

2. "X" (George F. Kennan), "The Sources of Soviet Conduct," *Foreign Affairs* 25, no. 4 (July 1947): pp. 169–82.

3. Polls on "Cold War" cited in George Gallup, *The Gallup Polls: Public Opinion 1935–1971* (New York: Random House, 1973).

4. A widely cited example is John Mearsheimer, "Back to the Future: Instability In Europe After the Cold War," *International Security* 15, no. 1 (Summer 1990): pp. 5–56.

5. For an extended analysis of these basic tendencies, see Richard N. Haass, "Paradigm Lost," *Foreign Affairs* 74, no. 1 (January–February 1995): pp. 43–58.

6. Hans J. Morgenthau, *Politics Among Nations* (New York: Alfred A. Knopf, 1978).

7. Kenneth N. Waltz, *Man, the State, and War* (New York: Columbia University Press, 1959).

8. Henry A. Kissinger, *Diplomacy* (New York: Simon and Schuster, 1994).

9. See Kenneth N. Waltz, *Theory of International Politics* (Reading, MA: Addison-Wesley, 1979).

10. Halford J. Mackinder, lecture, January 25, 1904, published as "The Geographical Pivot of History," *Geographic Journal* 27 (1904): pp. 421–44, reprinted in Halford J. Mackinder, *The Scope and Methods of Geography and the Geographical Pivot of History* (London: Royal Geographical Society, 1969).

11. Alfred Thayer Mahan, *The Influence of Sea Power Upon History* (Boston: Little Brown, 1890).

12. On Karl Haushofer, see Andreas Dorpalen, *The World of General Haushofer: Geopolitics in Action* (Port Washington, NY: Kennikat Press, 1966).

13. This strategic interaction is outlined in Peter Hopkirk, *The Great Game* (New York: Kodansha International, 1992).

14. A provocative analysis of the earlier period is to be found in Edward Ingram, *Commitment to Empire* (New York: Oxford University Press, 1981).

15. A useful explication of the concept of balance of power can be found in Ernst B. Haas, "The Balance of Power: Prescription, Concept or Propaganda," *World Politics* 5, no. 4 (July 1953): pp. 442–77, and Arnold Wolfers, *Discord and Collaboration* (Baltimore: Johns Hopkins University Press, 1962), chap. 8.

16. Mackinder, *The Scope and Methods of Geography*, p. 41.

17. On the implications of such extended deterrence, see Ivo Daalder, *The Nature and Practice of Flexible Response* (New York: Columbia University Press, 1991).

18. See Sherman W. Garnett, "Poland: Bulwark or Bridge?" *Foreign Policy*, no. 102 (Spring 1996): pp. 66–82.

19. Kissinger, *Diplomacy*, pp. 813–20.

20. Another example of this kind of reasoning can be found in Zbigniew Brzezinski, "The Premature Partnership," *Foreign Affairs* 73, no. 2 (March–April 1994): pp. 67–82.

21. See, for example, John Mearsheimer, "The Case for a Ukrainian Nuclear Deterrent," *Foreign Affairs* 72, no. 3 (Summer 1993): pp. 50–66.

22. The more mainstream arguments are presented well in Steven E. Miller, "The Case Against a Ukrainian Nuclear Deterrent," *Foreign Affairs* 72, no. 3 (Summer 1993): pp. 67–80.

23. The issues of Soviet command and control here are dissected in John J.R. Lepingwell, "Soviet Civil-Military Relations and the August Coup," *World Politics* 44, no. 4 (July 1992): pp. 529–72.

24. On the trade-offs among various ways of integrating the Central European countries, see Zbigniew Brzezinski, "A Plan for Europe," *Foreign Affairs* 74, no. 1 (January–February 1995): pp. 20–42.

25. The lessons of Bush's defeat for the general prediction of U.S. foreign policy are explored in Thomas Omestad, "Why Bush Lost," *Foreign Policy*, no. 89 (Winter 1992–93): pp. 70–81.

26. A Chinese example is mentioned in Nicholas Kristof, "The Rise of China," *Foreign Affairs* 72, no. 5 (November–December 1993): p. 73.

27. See William C. Wohlforth, *The Elusive Balance* (Ithaca, NY: Cornell University Press, 1993).

28. For some Southeast Asian views, see Michael Vatikiotis, "Yankee Please Stay," *Far Eastern Economic Review* (13 December 1990): p. 32.

29. Useful examples of such a liberal analysis of the drives of American foreign policy are to be found in Tony Smith, *America's Mission* (Princeton, NJ: Princeton University Press, 1994): and David Fromkin, *In the Time of the Americans* (New York: Alfred A. Knopf, 1995).

30. A very detailed and readable account of these events can be found in Philip Zelikow and Condoleezza Rice, *Germany Unified and Europe Transformed* (Cambridge, MA: Harvard University Press, 1995).

31. Some of the inherent difficulties with ethnic self-determination are discussed in Gidon Gottlieb, "Nations Without States," *Foreign Affairs* 73, no. 3 (May–June 1994): pp. 100–12.

32. A perceptive and nuanced discussion of the political implications of public information here can be found in Jeremy D. Rosner, "The Know-Nothings Know Something," *Foreign Policy*, no. 101 (Winter 1995–96): pp. 116–29.

33. See Michael Bourdeaux, ed., *The Politics of Religion in Russia and the New States of Eurasia* (Armonk, NY: M.E. Sharpe, 1995), on the potential new issues emerging on religion within the former Soviet Union.

34. On the overall significance of the media for shaping American foreign policy

attitudes, see Patrick O'Heffernan, *Mass Media and American Foreign Policy* (Norwood, NJ: Ablex, 1991), and Michael Arlen, *The Living Room War* (New York: Viking Press, 1969).

35. See Samuel P. Huntington, "The Clash of Civilizations?" *Foreign Affairs* 72, no. 3 (Summer 1993): pp. 22–49. The more particular significance of the ethnic feelings of "hyphenated Americans" is discussed in Yossi Shain, "Multicultural Foreign Policy," *Foreign Policy,* no. 100 (Fall 1995): pp. 69–87.

36. Current developments in Belarus are outlined in George Sanford, "Belarus on the Road to Nationhood," *Survival* 38, no. 1 (Spring 1996): pp. 131–53.

37. An optimistic projection can be found in Stephen Sestanovich, "Russia Turns the Corner," *Foreign Affairs* 73, no. 1 (January–February 1994): pp. 83–98.

38. See Philip Zelikow, "Beyond Boris Yeltsin," *Foreign Affairs* 73, no. 1 (January–February 1994): pp. 44–55.

39. An interesting analysis is presented in Benjamin S. Lambeth, "Russia's Wounded Military," *Foreign Affairs* 74, no. 2 (March–April 1995): pp. 86–98.

40. Some analogies between Weimar Germany and post-1991 Russia are pursued by Kissinger, *Diplomacy,* pp. 271–72.

41. An interesting collection of such viewpoints is presented in Ralph Summy and Michael E. Stalla, ed., *Why the Cold War Ended* (Westport, CT: Greenwood Press, 1995).

42. Agricultural policy issues are discussed in Robert Paarlberg, "Agricultural Policy," in *U.S. Foreign Policy: The Search for a New Role,* ed. Robert J. Art and Seyom Brown (New York: MacMillan, 1993), pp. 192–212.

43. See Benjamin J. Cohen, *The Question of Imperialism* (New York: Basic Books, 1973).

44. For an illustration of this use of terminology, see William Pfaff, "Redefining World Power," *Foreign Affairs* 70, no. 1 (February 1991): pp. 39–40.

7

China, Japan, and the Post-Soviet Upheaval

Global Opportunities and Regional Risks

Gilbert Rozman

The strategic-triangle of China, Japan, and Russia is emerging as an important part of the strategic quadrangle of China, Japan, Russia, and the United States. Although of the four triangles found in the quadrangle it is the one most often overlooked, it has many distinctive and important characteristics. As the sole triangle without the United States, it reveals the dynamics of a three-way relationship among neighbors, non-Western great powers, and traditional rivals. It presents a different perspective on Russia as well as on its two principal Asian rivals of the past century.

Observers can choose among three distinct ways of viewing this triangle: (1) as an environment fostering cross-border economic integration; (2) as a framework for regional and, at times, global geopolitical readjustment; and (3) as a context for confronting civilizational barriers. Reflecting the instability of the period 1992–96, these three separate perspectives provide sharply different images of how this millennium is drawing to an end.

While this chapter considers all three viewpoints, it argues that, for the time being, the global and regional geopolitical readjustment looms foremost for policy makers in Moscow and Beijing, whose interactions are playing the lead role in triangular relations. Geopolitics are driving bilateral improvements, geoeconomics play a supporting role, and geocultural concerns bring deeply felt but mostly minor complications. When economic forces gather steam once Russian growth resumes, we can anticipate that Japan's influence on Russia and, thus, the triangle will increase. Eventually, cultural differences will acquire new meaning, too, shifting from the apprehensions of public opinion manipulated by local or opposition leaders to the challenges of institution building. Nevertheless, even if in the next decade Japan and Russia reach a state of full normalization and cultural forces resulting from frequent contact work more directly against Russo-

Chinese ties, the Sino-Russian geopolitical partnership is likely to remain the most prominent binding force in the Northeast Asia triangle.

The upheaval in the former Soviet Union has, together with the rise of China as a self-confident world power and the reactive politics of Japan in a transitional period of coalition governments, transformed great power relations in Northeast Asia in just a few years. Advocates of economic integration have suggested that this is leading to "borderlessness" and a healthy boost for regionalism.[1] Others who follow strategic thinking have warned of a "vacuum," inviting scarcely concealed expansionist aspirations.[2] Finally, those who pay attention to a wider range of forces point to a complex process, some stressing jockeying for short-term advantage as a new balance of power takes shape and others focusing on positioning one's country in a long-term "clash of civilizations."[3] The situation is fluid, eliciting conflicting interpretations. What is clear is that over a five-year period following Mikhail Gorbachev's long-anticipated, but disappointing, visit to Tokyo in April 1991 and the failure of the conservative putsch in Moscow in August 1991 on which Chinese leaders appear to have pinned their hopes, bilateral and regional relations have turned in new directions. Moreover, as the fog of inconsistent Russian foreign policy and dashed expectations has begun to lift, there seems little doubt that a Sino-Russian-Japanese triangle is taking shape in which China occupies the pivotal corner.

In the waning years of the Soviet Union after Gorbachev had declared his government's intent of entering the Asia-Pacific region, Beijing and Tokyo proposed conditions for sponsoring this new regional relationship. Tokyo both joined with Washington in linking its support to demilitarization, democratization, and a shift to a market economy, and added its own condition of progress on the bilateral dispute over four islands. Beijing reasserted its three conditions for normalization (related to the Soviet military role in Afghanistan, Cambodia, and the northern border area from Mongolia east) and made modest claims for territorial demarcation where river currents may have changed over the decades. Beijing's offer proved to be more attractive. In addition, the mind-set of a majority of those who assumed power in Moscow gave China the edge. Its long border with the Soviet Union/Russia, its costly rivalry with the Soviet Union, its far greater prominence in postwar thinking, its military potential, and its long-term prospects based on population and growth rates made China the obvious favorite. As a result, Japan did not gain much leverage in the emerging triangle and did not manage to use the post-Soviet transformation to its advantage in gaining international stature, strengthening its regional base, or solidifying its national identity. In contrast, China's leaders focused precisely on these three goals and became, perhaps, the primary beneficiaries of the post-Soviet upheaval. Through a new partnership with Russia, new patterns of cross-border commerce, large-scale migration of Chinese, military purchases and cooperation, and the ups and downs of debates in both countries on their mutual relevance, China looms as an ever larger presence for Russia. Time is on China's side, but there may be setbacks if it acts precipitously and frightens Russia or a combination of its neighbors.

This chapter looks chronologically at the Sino-Russian-Japanese great power triangle as seen through three periods: (1) Russia's (and before that the Soviet Union's last gasp) leaning to the West, culminating in 1992; (2) Russia's assertion of its Eurasian identity in the search for balance while continuing to give preference to the West through 1995; and (3) the first signs of a shift toward a more demonstrative and proactive foreign policy supporting clearly defined national interests in anticipation of the presidential elections of June–July 1996. For each period, the chapter treats economic, geopolitical, and civilizational factors. It reviews the separate bilateral relations and compares them, while assessing the impact of the triangle, in its formative stage, on global politics and on regional transformation. The analysis draws heavily on the views in each of the three countries on changing relations within this triangular context.[4]

The Period of Russia's Pro-Western Leanings

We can observe an inverse relationship between Beijing's cooling response toward the Gorbachev leadership and Tokyo's warming interest. In both cases a turning point was reached in 1987, followed by an open shift of direction in 1989 and intensifying concern through 1991. At the outset of the Gorbachev era, it was Beijing that harbored greater hopes. Eager for an economic reformer to take charge in Moscow, those in China's Communist elite who regarded a shake-up as essential for serious reform to begin looked with favor on many of Gorbachev's early initiatives.[5] Two goals were foremost in their mind: to raise China's international stature, above all achieving a more balanced strategic triangle with the United States and the Soviet Union; and to strengthen legitimation for socialism at home and abroad through a global process of socialist economic reform producing high rates of growth. Meanwhile, Japan's political establishment led the doubters about Gorbachev in the Western camp, distrusting glasnost and showy human rights breakthroughs as symbolic gestures to excite "Gorbymania" among gullible Westerners. They feared that perestroika would result only in some fine-tuning of an economy still concentrated on the military-industrial complex.[6] The Japanese were preoccupied with the question of whether the Soviet threat would end, the symbolic test for which was a willingness to negotiate in good faith a return of the four islands known as the northern territories. This test became the equivalent of one of Japan's famous entrance exams: it became the benchmark for realizing a bright future, with the potential to release Japan from its postwar dependency on the United States so that it could become a "normal" country. Ironically, Moscow's concessions on all three of Beijing's demands for normalization came amidst growing alarm in China about the direction of Soviet policies, while more cautious agreements only to discuss the territorial question led to a flurry of speculation in Japan about how a breakthrough could soon be reached. Part of the explanation no doubt lies in the contrast between the fears of China's Communist Party conservatives that Gorbachev's domestic policies were undermining the very foundation of communist rule,[7] and the delayed, but palpable, optimism among all but the far right and far left in Japan that the Gorbachev reform course was genuine.[8] Yet, also significant for two rising powers closely attuned to the balance between the world's two superpowers was the powerful imagery of Moscow's "new thinking": the contest between the superpowers would end, the Soviet Union would enter the "European common house," and universal principles of humanism without need for vigilance against the West would guide future diplomacy.[9] Geopolitics lay at the core of Beijing's and Tokyo's shifting reactions.

Before the Tiananmen crackdown Beijing's discomfort with new thinking was muted. It was uncertain at first over the implications. It was intent on preparations for the summit in Beijing that would crown the success of normalization. And it was split; reformers in China's leadership were still emboldened, Zhao Ziyang taking care not to alienate the international capitalist community. Feeling encircled after 4 June 1989 and resenting Gorbachev's barely veiled rebuke of China's leaders for repressing the very students who had greeted him as a hero of reform, the more united post-Tiananmen leadership demanded a sharper critique of Russian policies, especially in internal circulation publications.[10] The rise of Boris Yeltsin as a critic of communist rule after the loss of Eastern Europe to communism added to the sense of alarm, especially that the balance of global power would turn unfavorably away from China. At the same time Japan was becoming reconciled to the role of reluctant supporter, within the G-7 context, of first Gorbachev and then Yeltsin. By lowering the priority of a solution to the territorial squabble in 1989 under a policy of "expanded equilibrium," Tokyo signaled its willingness to improve relations as long as a dialogue over its concerns was advancing.

When the Soviet breakup was in progress, fears were expressed in China that Russia would look to Japan first in the region while Sino-Russian relations would see little development beyond businesslike economic ties. Under these circumstances Beijing would face the threat of a joint plan by the United States, Russia, and Japan to control China.[11] The strategy of "peaceful evolution" would gain momentum, leaving China further isolated. But by the spring of 1992 Chinese analysts concluded a momentous debate over the meaning of the collapse of the Soviet Union and Communist Party rule there with the surprising assertion that the international environment was more favorable than at any previous time for China. In opposition to those who attributed the collapse to humanistic thought and other influences of the West and glasnost, reformers blamed it on the failure to become part of the world economy and to satisfy consumer aspirations. As a counterargument to the call for greater Chinese vigilance against a growing threat of containment in which Russia would join, they insisted that China would gain maneuverability.[12] Reasserting what Deng Xiaoping had indicated in 1990, they said that the bilateral course begun with normalization would continue no matter what change occurred in their neighbor to the north.[13] To the new Russian government China's leaders signaled their readiness to develop all-around ties, with greatly expanded cross-border commerce playing a leading role. In turn, Russia signaled to China its commitment to build on the hard-won foundation of normalization and, even more, that China—not Japan would be its first priority in the region. Thus, at a time when Foreign Minister Andrei Kozyrev was championing a foreign policy leaning heavily on the West as part of a government led by Prime Minister Egor Gaidar that counted on massive financial assistance for "shock therapy," Sino-Russian relations emerged virtually unscathed. Given Yeltsin's real power base and Russia's fundamental national interests, Chinese analysts voiced confidence that one-sided dependency on the West would not last. Yet they predicted that the condition of a strong United States on the offensive and a weak Russia on the defensive could be maintained for a very long time.[14]

Paradoxically, China's relations with Russia improved even as Chinese sources ridiculed shock therapy and warned that Russia should shift its course of leaning to the West, and Japan's relations with Russia soured at the very time the fit between the two countries seemed most ideal and, along with the other members of the G-7, Japan committed itself to what appeared to be a large package of multilateral and bilateral assistance. Especially in 1992, before the bubble economy burst, Japan was flush with capital, envied for its superior technology and management, and confident of its capacity to emerge as an economic superpower coupled with a strong political voice in reshaping the world order. It was ready to give priority to nearby areas. This provided a good match with Russia's thirst for foreign capital and know-how for the transition to a market economy; the priority status given to technological and managerial restructuring of Russia's industrial plant, including conversion of much of the military-industrial complex; and Russia's desire to make the Far East and Siberia a dynamic part of the Asia-Pacific region. Yet, as 1992 unfolded, Russo-Japanese relations deteriorated. In early summer the Supreme Soviet held hearings lambasting Japan for its territorial pretensions, which may be seen as the first salvo in a more nationalistic foreign policy directed also against the United States and Western Europe.[15] The nadir in bilateral relations occurred in September when, on only a few days notice, Yeltsin canceled his planned trip to Japan without even a fig leaf of diplomatic cover to conceal the strident nationalistic message that this was what Tokyo deserved for pressuring Moscow.

How do we explain the contrasting paths of Sino-Russian and Russo-Japanese relations in a period when Russia was, in most respects, following a pro-Western foreign policy and when its internal reform required good ties to both neighbors and G-7 countries? Was this little more than throwing a bone to keep the nationalistic forces at bay in order to preserve the forward thrust of an internationalist foreign policy? After all, observers argued, Japan had overplayed its hand, producing an emotional backlash in Russia. Did the Yeltsin administration actually welcome the outcome because its sense of the national interest, even if vaguely defined, gave precedence to China over Japan? From the beginning this was a coalition government combining Russian nationalism (with an important say by the military and the security forces) and Western-style reformism, and the former forces largely opted for ties with China. Indeed, even before the fall of the Soviet Union, was not a new understanding gradually emerging of relations with China on both a regional and global level that left Japan on the periphery? In retrospect, we may conclude that a global geopolitical realignment was under way that even the upheaval of 1991 could not derail.

Despite the varied interpretations by Western analysts of the significance of Sino-Soviet and Sino-Russian relations in this transitional period, closer Sino-Russian relations were consistent with new reasoning about national interests in both countries. This reasoning has often been overlooked. Analysts have pointed to the strong and mostly unwelcome Soviet impact on China during the Gorbachev era, leading to impatience, demonstrations, and the Tiananmen repression; the strong and unexpected Chinese impact on the Soviet Union during the same period, leading to accelerated reform and the breakup of the country;[16] the close call in 1991 of a reversal of reform in the Soviet Union, with China's encouragement, that almost produced a renewal of the Sino-Soviet alliance in all but name;[17] and the persistence of constraints from 1992 on Sino-Russian cooperation consistent with the notion that Russia had become a problem for China rather than a player, as if the strategic triangles involving the United States, the Soviet Union or Russia, and China, and the United States, the Soviet Union or Russia, and Japan had simply ceased to exist.[18] Yes, a strategic quadrangle was taking shape, but, no, the triangles themselves were not losing significance. All of these unexpected impacts and close calls obscure the reality that, through ups and downs, China and Russia were coming together in pursuit of their fundamental national interests as understood by those best positioned to define them.

According to Chinese sources, the United States in 1992 sought to use the breakup of the Soviet Union and its resounding victory in the Persian Gulf War to achieve one-country hegemony in the world, or at least to join together with Germany and Japan to establish a monopoly triangle giving the West global dominance. The prime target was China, to be subjected to concentrated pressure. This strategy was bound to fail, Beijing insisted. Instead, China found itself in a favorable international environment able to wait for Russia to come calling and then to play the "Russia card" at the same time as a record windfall of foreign investments and export expansion made its economic boom the envy of the world.[19] With Deng Xiaoping taking the offensive on economic reform in his southern journey of January 1992 and Jiang Zemin guiding the ideological review, China is credited with drawing the correct historical lessons. China did what it could to keep Russia out of the Western camp, and it was gratified with the outcome.

The dynamics of bilateral relations already in place for several years proved to have lasting value in removing the threat of isolation to China. We need only look back to the Soviet commentaries at the time of the fortieth anniversary of the Chinese Revolution in October 1989 or during Li Peng's visit of May 1990. While much of the world continued to chastise China's leadership for its repression in June 1989, Russian moderates publicly asserted that, after struggling so long and hard to achieve normalization, leaders of the two countries must not repeat past mistakes so costly to their two nations. They had paid such a huge price for mistakes on both sides that they must refrain from condemning or even teaching each other. Seen in this light, the "powerful impulse" to Sino-Soviet relations from Li Peng's visit contributed not only concretely through specific agreements on economics, science and technology, and arms and military confidence but also through the psychology of sticking by each other as the basis for Sino-Russian relations.[20] A geopolitical adjustment was occurring that went well beyond normalization, and it was capable of overcoming ideological and political twists.

In the final months of 1991 and the first months of 1992 China's leaders were not happy with the direction of Russian foreign policy. But they responded patiently with a pledge of continuity, recognizing that since Russia's most pressing need was to stabilize its economy, China, by pledging its cooperation, would win appreciation. The trade agreement of March 1992 met urgent Russian needs: supplying consumer goods and helping to stabilize the Russian Far East. As spring approached the Chinese could see the situation changing before their eyes: shock therapy was failing and Russia was beginning to seek balance in its foreign relations. On 6 October 1992 a conference of more than forty experts convened at the Chinese Academy of Social Sciences in Beijing. It concluded that Russia's foreign policy already had made the transition from leaning to one side to a new model—"xikao, dongjin, nanxia" (rely on the West, enter the East, and head to the South). Proceeding carefully, Russia was bent on restoring its great power influence. This boded well for China. Looking ahead, conference participants predicted the rise of nationalism and a tougher assertion of Russia's national interests.[21] Japan's loss as a result of Yeltsin's decision to cancel his visit signaled to the Chinese observers a new Russian approach, one with positive implications for China.

Increasingly, Japan followed the U.S. lead in supporting Russia's economic transition, although it was less optimistic that the reforms would work and more concerned that Russia should take additional steps to break resolutely with the past. Finally, encouraged by a series of overtures in the fall of 1991 and the winter of 1992, the Japanese allowed their hopes for a compromise on the territorial dispute to rise. After all, economic recovery in Russia appeared unimaginable without the involvement of the world's second economic superpower, and the first superpower—caught in a recession and turning inward in an election year to face its own economic problems—shared this view. However, after Foreign Minister Kozyrev's visit in March 1992 fell well short of what Deputy

Foreign Minister Georgii Kunadze, a reform-oriented Japan specialist, had publicly advocated and of what Kozyrev himself in December had encouraged the Japanese ambassador to Russia to expect,[22] the mood turned more cautious. When Yeltsin suddenly postponed his visit in September, Japan's Foreign Ministry recognized that the tide had turned, that the conservative faction in Russia had made a comeback. The ministry, however, refused to accept this as a proper explanation for rude conduct. A high-ranking official reiterated the importance of progress on the islands, pointing to the absence of a peace treaty between the two countries as a reason for Japan's restraint in offering assistance.[23] Meanwhile, many Japanese were asking if aid to Russia was really justified. They wondered what could account for tension in this bilateral relationship when the Cold War had already ended.[24]

What was missing from these puzzled reactions was any sense of a great power struggle involving China. While Japanese analysts often commented on the pressure from the United States or the G-7 meetings to increase assistance to Russia, and even of the danger of Japan becoming isolated if it did not contribute its share,[25] they scarcely envisioned what the Chinese placed right in the forefront: the reconfiguration of great power relations in which Russia was tempted by other options besides depending on Japan. The Japanese had become accustomed to seeing China as a developing country within a world on the path to economic integration.

Among the methods adopted in Japan to break the logjam were trilateral cooperation (including the United States) to find an acceptable compromise on the disputed territories or on a broad agenda ranging from security and arms reduction to the environment and resources, and energetic public relations work centered in Moscow and the Russian Far East. The trilateral project codirected by Graham Allison, Hiroshi Kimura, and Konstantin Sarkisov in the summer of 1992 listed scenarios for achieving fully normalized relations and concrete actions governments serious about normalization and constructing a trilateral relationship should be taking now.[26] Only weeks after its findings were delivered to the heads of the three governments, however, Yeltsin decided not to travel to Japan, giving the various scenarios for negotiations no chance at all. A May 1993 trilateral conference at the U.S. Institute of Peace brought together decision makers, academics, and analysts in search of a more comprehensive agenda,[27] but with no more success. Efforts by Japan's Foreign Ministry to analyze Russian public opinion and to prepare public relations information to shed new light on the territorial dispute and on the realities of postwar Japan also made little impression against the nationalist assault mounted against Japan throughout Russia.

In 1991, accompanying the Persian Gulf War, and in 1992, following the breakup of the Soviet Union, images of the "new world order" became the craze.[28] Among the great powers, Japan was seen as firmly enrolled, although its export-oriented economic policies and reluctant dispatch of peacekeeping forces left room for improvement. Russia was usually depicted as quickly taking its place, which would have to be secured by economic stabilization and elections to replace a parliament representative of the old era. And China was regarded as, for the time being, left outside. But it would presumably succumb before long by virtue of its full-steam integration into the global economy, the untenability of its isolation from the great power consensus, and the inevitable replacement of an aging leadership. These expectations fared poorly in the face of new realities. Instead, Sino-Russian relations began to grow closer without improvements in Sino-American ties; Russo-Japanese relations failed to advance and, for a time at least, worsened; and international politics witnessed a new jockeying for place in a global power struggle, including the growing reality of several great power triangles.

While many expected that global economic integration with a regional emphasis on Sino-Japanese ties and Russo-Japanese ties would overwhelm other forces, the first period reveals a different outcome in which economics was only one of several determinants. Geopolitical concerns made a quick return, galvanized by Russia's economic chaos and the Chinese Communists' insistence on an ideology of great-power nationalism. Civilizational factors such as Sino-Russian fears remained largely in the background, but not for long.

The Period of Russia's Eurasian Balance

Boris Yeltsin left no doubt about his desire for a new equilibrium in Russian foreign policy when he visited, in succession, South Korea, China, and India from October 1992 to January 1993. In Seoul, one message relayed to the world was that Russia had other options besides Japan. In Beijing, Yeltsin proclaimed that Russia would not be used by the United States in its relations with China— relations between great countries and countries in the same neighborhood. Suddenly China became prominent in two of Russia's priorities: as a great power whose ties helped to achieve a global equilibrium necessary for Russia to pursue its national interests; and as a neighbor, while not actually in the targeted priority of the near abroad, close enough to deserve a special place in the effort to secure Russia's borders. In India, Yeltsin formally declared the beginning of equilibrium policies balancing East and West.

One of the central themes of this dawn of a new epoch in bilateral relations was military cooperation. Among the institutional interests drawing China and Russia together, the defense sector in both countries was prominent. Large military-industrial enterprises in Siberia and the Far East sold accumulated reserves to China in exchange for consumer goods. After some hesitation, Moscow anticipated that through substantial sales of Russian military hardware and technology to China it could make some headway in sustaining a defense sector having little success in conversion. Any detailed chronology of Russo-Chinese relations in Yeltsin's first term would inevitably highlight the frequent agreements on military matters and their spillover effect on improved relations.[29] Later the energy sector became another interest group with a strong stake in Chinese trade. Russia gained a share in supplying China's Three Gorges megaproject and agreed to sell natural gas from the Sakha Republic (Yakutia) through a pipeline to China. In contrast, Russian interest groups, such as the fishing industry, with a stake in Japan were much weaker, but prospects for multinational (including the United States) development of Sakhalin shelf oil and natural gas could heighten their influence.

The upgrading of relations with China was preceded by an understanding between the two countries in the handling of relations with Central Asia. It did not take Moscow long to recognize that with tens of millions of Russians living outside the borders of Russia and non-Slavic leaders ruling over many of them that the near abroad, one part of which encompasses the five newly independent countries of Central Asia, matters most of all. Beijing reassured Moscow, expressing its respect for Russia's influence in the region and its continued claim to great power status. While Western analysts such as Robert Scalapino and Robert Legvold foresaw a new competition in inner Asia, heating up the Sino-Russian rivalry,[30] China, with Xinjiang its biggest worry about separatism on the mainland, and Russia, concentrating on Kazakhstan first, quickly achieved a consensus in 1992 and stuck to it closely. In contrast, Russia's American partnership seemed to offer only criticisms of Russian assertiveness in Central Asia. It appeared threatening because of the mounting talk about incorporation of Eastern European countries into NATO, and it lost nationalistic appeal because of the sympathy inside Russia with Serbia as opposed to America's favoritism for Bosnia as the recognized government in the main battle zone of the former Yugoslavia. Bill Clinton's campaign talk and initial policies emphasizing human rights, especially as they applied to interethnic relations, frightened the Russians as well as the Chinese.[31]

Both China and Japan became significant actors in the Central Asian economies. On the one hand, Japan was too far away and the five countries of the region were too cautious about capitalist reforms to give it great leverage. On the other, even when Chinese shuttle traders created a backlash through aggressive and often unscrupulous methods, there was little doubt that Chinese commercial ties would continue to shape the region. The Russian-Chinese-Central Asian triangle would prevail, as in agreements on security matters during the group summit in Shanghai in April 1996 and in compromises on energy pipelines that had the potential to loosen Moscow's grip on the region.

Boris Yeltsin's December 1992 visit to Beijing accelerated the improvement in bilateral relations at the macrolevel and the microlevel. At the level of state-to-state relations concerned with geopolitical themes, there was a meeting of the minds. Moscow conveyed to Beijing that a "stable and flourishing China answers Russia's interests,"[32] and Beijing communicated its desire for stability and economic growth to return to Russia. The foundation of this improved relationship is the mutual respect of two great powers. According to Li Jingjie, deputy director of the Institute of Central Asia, Russia, and Eastern Europe in the Chinese Academy of Social Sciences, neither side experiences humiliation from the other: "In the view from China, Russia today is the first country, which for more than 300 years accepts China as a partner with equal rights . . . China does not extract benefit from the crisis in Russia in order to intensify external pressure."[33] This mood continued as China strove to create a "peaceful and stable environment" and Russia a "zone of good neighborliness."

At the level of cross-border relations, the two countries, which had based earlier ties on planned and carefully regulated contacts, allowed spontaneity to reign. They ushered in an age of visaless crossings, direct ties between enterprises and organizations, and decentralization of authority to local governments. Already in 1992, when trade between Russia and other countries was falling sharply, Sino-Russian trade, especially barter exchange across a porous border, grew rapidly. In 1993 this growth accelerated for a time, leading, especially in China, to optimistic extrapolations of these trends and predictions of a close fit between two complementary economies.[34]

As opposed to the worldview espoused initially by Andrei Kozyrev, conservatives and moderates alike gravitated to the rallying cry of national interests. Somehow in the short-term thirst for Western assistance, Russia, it was agreed, had failed to define and pursue its own national interests. From afar, in Moscow, this not only meant reducing dependence on the United States, it also pointed to China as a source of balance. As Alexei Voskressenski reported, "many Russian analysts consider the PRC to be perhaps the only mighty country on which Russia can rely in trying to strengthen its position in the Asia-Pacific region. Neither the United States nor Japan would support such Russian activity, because doing so would narrow their own spheres of influence."[35] The logic was clear. The PRC wanted to offset Japan's regional role. Russia needed balance versus Japan and the West.[36] Russia and the PRC had to form closer relations. Two triangles were at play. In one case, the United States shifted its preference from China to the Soviet Union and later Russia; then the PRC turned toward the Soviet Union and, especially after the dust of the transition settled, to Russia; and, in turn, Russia began to shift to the PRC. In the other case, China calculated that Japan was its chief rival and it turned to Russia, which reciprocated.

Classic signs of strategic triangles were reported in one Chinese article after another. By the spring of 1993 Chinese analysts recognized that Russia already had switched to an equilibrium diplomacy facing East and West. This was only natural because the United States, as the only superpower, sought world hegemony, although it could not afford this status. Even in the Persian Gulf War the United States, as a debtor nation, had to play a "beggar" role, an authoritative Chinese source explains.[37] Meanwhile, allies deserted the United States after the Soviet military threat ended. Above all, Japan had its own designs on building an Asian economic sphere with itself on top. Given the complexity of contradictions and latent conflicts in Asia, there was ample room to maneuver for a country such as China. Russia became prized as a force that made it easier for China to maneuver—a corner along with China in Asia's great power triangles.

In the final months of 1993 and the first part of 1994 the emerging Sino-Russian relationship was put to a severe test. The economic model that had produced a boom in small-scale barter trade, open borders, and spontaneity from below proved wanting. Public opinion, above all in the Far East, blamed the Chinese, and often powerful forces in China, whether they were governmental or criminal, for selling shoddy goods. Local governors catered to the rising discontent with demagogic accusations. Illegal aliens streaming across the border were featured as the centerpiece in warnings about the "yellow peril."[38] Without reliable numbers, estimates grew well beyond the realm of possibility, into the millions of Chinese illegally residing in Russia. When sweeps in search of them occurred, only small numbers were actually found. Continued progress in border demarcations by a joint committee aroused the same governors to rail against giving away Russian territory,[39] despite the small extent of the anticipated transfers and the existence of a formal agreement between Moscow and Beijing of 1991 and ratified in 1992. When Russia rescinded visaless entries, followed by sharp drops in border crossings and trade, there could be no doubt that the early model of economic relations had failed.[40]

Leaders in Moscow and Beijing responded to the cross-border chaos by reaffirming bilateral relations. Although mass alarm in Russia was slow to recede, Chinese authorities responded quite patiently. They accepted many of the criticisms and agreed to work closely with their Russian counterparts to make improved relations a more long-term, serious business.[41] Among the many visits by officials, no doubt the most significant was Jiang Zemin's trip to Russia in September 1994. It came after the generally positive atmosphere at the April hearings in the State Duma on Sino-Russian relations. On the Russian side, the December 1993 elections had ushered in a more nationalistic legislature, including both critics of China as a threat and advocates of closer ties to China. At the very least, China represented the lesser of two evils to many nationalists. On the Chinese side, we should not overlook personal ties to Russia among the generation in their sixties and seventies. Many of the top leaders had studied in Russia as part of the student generation of the 1950s. Although neither Deng Xiaoping nor Boris Yeltsin could be identified with the personal networks linking the two countries, the Chinese party secretary, premier, and foreign minister were but a few of the leaders who had once lived in Russia and were now well positioned for personal diplomacy. At a time when foreign policy was poorly institutionalized in Moscow (there were competing ministries and even rival factions in the Foreign Ministry with insufficient coordination), opportunities were great for informal relations linked to emotional attachments (*ganqing*). This particularly sets Sino-Russian relations apart from Russo-Japanese relations, which are handicapped by weak personal connections.

Throughout much of 1993, 1994, and 1995 Japanese officials and analysts kept finding glimmers of hope in relations with Russia. Every sign of increased stability or legitimacy for the presidency or the parliament, economic stabilization, or renewed interest expressed in official visits seemed to offer some prospect of a breakthrough. It was easy to find excuses for why a little more time would be needed for Russia's internal complexities to be settled and then things could start to improve. Other analysts distinguished long-term prospects from short-term ones, arguing that the elite would eventually seek legitimacy more from economic growth than from nationalism, and that would push ties to Japan to the forefront. In the meantime, they added, Tokyo must refrain from playing into the hands of the nationalists by pushing hard. Some even suggested that Japan's Foreign Ministry was willing to let the problem of the northern territories die, as it shifted direction.[42]

Worrying that passivity would do Japan little good, those most deeply engaged in the decade-long effort to improve relations urged a proactive stance. If the outcome in Russia remained uncertain between "dangerous nationalism" and "realistic nationalism," Japan must energetically work to tip the balance by helping to establish an international cooperative system reassuring to Russians demanding a strong country.[43] Moscow played on this concern. First Deputy Premier Oleg Soskovets explained that Japan's insistence on a territorial agreement only aroused "spiritual friction" (*seishinteki masatsu*) on the Russian side. The two countries should develop a partnership with closer ties, he proposed, as a step toward a breakthrough in diplomacy to Russia.[44] Gradually this message grew more tiresome as the Japanese found little appreciation for the assistance, including humanitarian aid, that they were providing. At the end of 1995, without any media outpouring of gratitude, an additional $500 million in humanitarian credits was awaited in Russia.[45] Compared to the United States, China and Japan viewed Russia less in ideological terms and more as a great power impinging on their own national interest. Since the Chinese had stopped thinking of their own brand of socialism as an ideology—using it instead to assess the historical merits and demerits of the ideas of various leaders, to deduce policies from established principles, or to make foreign policy choices—they had no reason to apply an ideological test to Russia. To the extent that they felt threatened by the collapse of socialism and of the Soviet Union, it was because of the dual impact of these events on the legitimacy of the leadership by the Chinese Communist Party and on the balance of world power. When China's leaders were persuaded within a year or two that their party's legitimacy no longer had much to do with perceptions of the Soviet Union and that they were gaining rather than losing in the changing balance of power, they could relax. For the Japanese, the antipathy toward Russian and Soviet imperialism was more deeply rooted. Since they were not stirred, as Americans were, by the concepts of "communism" and "democracy," they did not make a 180-degree shift from rejecting the "evil empire" to welcoming the most important convert to the road to democracy. Instead, they remained vigilant, only to see their fears confirmed by the "barbarous" conduct of Yeltsin in canceling his visit. Even as the Ministry of Foreign Affairs shifted to a stance close to those of European countries and the United States, the public and the media found repeated fault with the new Russia, transferring anti-Soviet feelings with little regard for ideology. As Hakamada Shigeki, a Japanese expert on Russia and Russo-Japanese relations argued, the Japanese people were more forgiving of Chinese authorities for the Tiananmen incident of June 1989 and less tolerant of Boris Yeltsin for the parliamentary shooting incident of October 1993 because they were driven by deep-seated emotions toward the two countries.[46] While the Russian threat may have changed its outward appearance, it had not disappeared for the Japanese. In late 1994 and most of 1995 the Sino-Russian-Japanese triangle stabilized. China entered a constructive partnership with Russia, upgrading relations in comparison to the first years of the Yeltsin presidency. This gave China some leverage; for example, in 1995 it finally secured a commitment to go forward with the Tumenjiang project to establish at the juncture of the China's Jilin Province, Russia's Primorskii krai, and northern North Korea an international city, which at last would give Northeast China an outlet to the Sea of Japan. In contrast, Japan had little to show for its pursuit of normalization. But, in fact, the agreement in principle on Tumenjiang did not guarantee that there would be much near-term follow-up, while Japan's vital role in bankrolling huge international loans kept tensions under control.

Chinese sources seemed to find some satisfaction in the dismal state of Russo-Japanese relations, as they smugly highlighted contradictions in the Russo-American partner relations. While for many years China had supported Japan's territorial claims against the Soviet Union, Beijing grew silent on this issue, to Moscow's satisfaction. Neither country really wanted to see Japan become a permanent member of the Security Council with veto power; so they took satisfaction that among the current select group of five, each of them was not alone in obfuscating the issue by speaking of the need for gradual and complex changes in the process of UN reform. They even shared the same basic critique of Japan: that it will not reconcile itself to the realities of World War II—the condemnation of its aggressive conduct and the territorial arrangement that followed the war. Moreover, neither China nor Russia currently recognizes Japan's right to become a normal power, whose military expenditures reflect the strength of its national economy and whose strong voice can be respected as that of a political great power. Yet, China takes care not to suggest that it is teaming with Russia against Japan.

When the geometry of great power relations is extended to a triangle or quadrangle including the United States, we can observe a contrast in Chinese and Japanese perceptions. Even as Japan habitually coordinates its principal foreign policies with the United States and gives the impression of offering assistance to

Russia in part at the urging of Washington, the Japanese rarely express support for working closely with their American ally to establish a new world order. The Chinese, on the other hand, are constantly pointing to the contradictions in the Russo-American partnership and in Japanese-American relations, analyzing their consequences for China, and searching for the best strategy to undermine American leadership. The logic is that of jockeying for expanded power and influence: Russia losing its great power status and harming its national interests, Russia then readjusting its policies, restoring its great power position, reestablishing its sphere of influence, and resisting the United States although not to the point of open opposition.[47] Russians and Chinese are speaking a shared language, both determined to limit America's vast power and to prevent Japan's from growing.

During the period 1993–95, economic integration within this triangle became increasingly divorced from geopolitical calculations. The economics were taken largely for granted, as in China's treatment of Japan, or dismissed as a matter for the distant future, as in Japan's treatment of Russia. Meanwhile, civilizational factors began to play a larger role, as in Russian fears of a "yellow peril" and Japanese concern about China emerging either as an economic superpower capable of overwhelming their country or as a post-Deng site of chaos, inducing millions of refugees to flee and overwhelm Japan in a different manner.[48]

On the Eve of a New Era

After the December 1995 elections to the State Duma and the quick replacement of Andrei Kozyrev with Evgenii Primakov as foreign minister observers searched for signs of a new foreign policy. Were they to be found in the campaign rhetoric of the late autumn? in the votes of the elected parliament? in policy adjustments by Yeltsin? or in the global overlap of critical leadership changes and elections, beginning with the March elections for president in Taiwan which Beijing tried to influence by a show of military intimidation? When prior to the June election Russia's economic course held steady and international credit began flowing at a faster rate, the possibility rose that economic forces more than nationalistic ones would shape the future. Civilizational forces, however, could affect the balance. National governments and the public were not always in sync in their reaction to these forces.

If, as stated above, we concluded that Japan's government was in front of the Japanese public in working to improve relations with Russia, then there is no less reason to conclude that Russia's government was ahead of the Russian public in bolstering relations with China. China did not figure importantly in the fall 1995 election campaigns, and when it did appear the image was more often that of a problem for Russia than of a partner. According to Moscow State University's Vilya Gel'bras's review of the rhetoric of the various parties, only a minority of the communists appealed to a positive image of China.[49] The central government is more positive than the politicians, who vary from those hesitant to voice the negative sentiments felt by much of the population to those ready to incite public opinion against the Chinese. Among local officials, Evgenii Nazdratenko, governor of Primorskii krai, has jarred Moscow with his denunciation of the demarcation agreement and inflammatory language about China. Newly elected with a strong popular mandate in December 1995, he stands as an obstacle to the next stage of Sino-Russian relations. Despite the devolution of power in the Russian Federation from the center, Moscow's geostrategic priorities make a showdown with Nazdratenko likely. The Far East is too divided and Moscow's levers of control too powerful to allow populist misgivings to put a brake on high priorities of foreign relations.

Reassuring to both the center and the most exposed localities, however, is the prospect of diversification of ties with Asia. In the first half of the 1990s South Korea gained prominence for its expanded ties to the Russian Far East and Siberia, while hopes rose for closer ties with Singapore, Taiwan, Hong Kong, and the members of the Association of Southeast Asian Nations (ASEAN). Meanwhile, economic ties with North Korea declined. Until the standoff on the Korean peninsula is resolved, the long-term role of Korean interests in Russia may be hard to gauge. Other countries will find it tempting to work through Chinese trading networks. Indeed, Heilongjiang Province has turned for assistance to firms from southern Chinese provinces and beyond the jurisdiction of the PRC to revive its tarnished reputation after the chaos in cross-border barter trade of 1993. Given their labor shortages, their proximity to the PRC, and the foothold already secured by energetic Chinese traders, Siberia and the Far East will find it difficult to develop strong links with other parts of Asia without a large role for PRC firms. Diversification in search of markets and investments will somewhat attenuate the influence of the PRC but not reduce it sharply.

Beijing and Moscow also have an incentive to find success in a common model of post-socialist development distinct from that identified with the West. Russians who for a decade have sought inspiration from China's successes in economic reform keep coming back to aspects of that model that are supposedly promising for their own country: a state corporatist system, special economic zones separated from other more vulnerable areas, heavy foreign investment without much political spillover, resistance to Western individualism, and so on. Yet China's reforms are not so popular that they obscure worries about the attendant corruption, Communist Party authoritarianism, and denial of human rights. Meanwhile, Beijing desires Russian reform success not only because of its effect on the geopolitical balance, but because it may reinforce the idea that a separate model of development—whether called "market socialism" or not—is viable.

The reelection of Boris Yeltsin as president promises to strengthen the voice of Moscow domestically and internationally. Although its capabilities are reduced by the state of the economy and the military, Moscow will be looking for ways to project its power in accord with still-inflated perceptions of Russia's national interests. Without becoming dependent on China, it is likely to intensify this bilateral partnership as a means to greater regional and global influence.

Washington can exert a profound effect on the Sino-Russo-Japanese triangle, forcing each of the players to make strategic adjustments. The future of U.S.–Chinese relations is particularly important. If Washington moves toward containment, it will drive China closer to Russia and perhaps alarm Japan into becoming a more active player in the region. If it opts for what some may call appeasement of China, Moscow may eventually become concerned about the consequences. Alternatively, Washington may become aroused by Moscow's behavior and, finding no common ground with Beijing, begin to press Tokyo more closely to coordinate a response aimed at both continental powers. As long as Tokyo's ties with Moscow remain weak and Beijing makes little effort to reassure Tokyo about its long-range intentions, Tokyo will seek reassurance in the United States—that is, the strategic quadrangle.

What may matter most for the next few years is how Russia decides to approach the other powers. Multiple images compete for the attention of the Russian people. At least four images of Russia's place as one of the great powers early in the next century have appeared at one time or another over the past several years across the Russian political spectrum: (1) Russia should revive on its own, suspicious of or even hostile to all of the other great powers; (2) Russia should rely primarily on China, while regarding the United States and Japan with suspicion; (3) Russia should seek balance—between the United States and China, between China and Japan, and between the United States, the European Community, and Japan; and (4) Russia should rely primarily on the United States, working together with the European Community and Japan, without relaxing its guard toward China. These views reflect different degrees of nationalism or internationalism. They also vary in their perception of the principal threat to Russian national interests.

The first perception, which might be deduced from Vladimir Zhirinovsky's invectives against all of the great powers, treats China and Japan alike as potential foes. This captures much of the rhetoric in the media of the Russian Far East over the past few years. The attitude that Moscow's priority should be to reestablish the Soviet Union regardless of what other great powers think is consistent with this outlook. Nonetheless, while this reaction may be an understandable reflection of the anger felt about the state to which Russia had sunk, it offers no solution apart from military blackmail. The North Korean model lacks appeal.

The second approach is rooted in nostalgia for the postwar state after the relaxation of Stalinism's worst excesses and before the stagnation of Leonid Brezhnev's decrepit years. For a time Russia and China stood together when Russia reveled in its claims as a rising superpower. This approach demonstrates a way of thinking common today among Communists and other types of Russian nationalists, which recognizes the West as the principal threat and China as the lesser of two evils. A similar view about the potential for the Sino-Russian partnership is gaining prominence in China, too.

> China's "foreign coordination system" could be of greater use to Russia as an "important parameter" . . . good relations between China and Russia will have a synthesis effect for China, whether in using the Russian market or affecting the Western power balance. . . . In essence, the United States and Japan do not want China to gain in power. At the end of this century, the United States wishes to gain the upper hand in the Chinese market by using the three-way money capital of America, Japan and South Korea . . . by the years 2020–2030, whether China lies low or not, America and the West will want to contain China's development momentum . . . if China recognises this in theory, then in practice it can accumulate force and not be misled by temporary phenomena so that when the flood arrives, China can build an invincible Great Wall of steel.[50]

The Chinese model lacks sufficient appeal in Russia for this approach to be of lasting interest.

The third approach in search of an all-around balance is likely to be the means to optimal flexibility. Evgenii Primakov, Kozyrev's successor from January 1996, has long prepared to champion this way of thinking. As Director of the Institute of Oriental Studies from 1978 and, under Gorbachev, as director of the premier world affairs institute, the Institute of World Economy and International Relations, he gave priority to reshaping Russian thinking and, ultimately, policy to the East, including Japan. So far, however, Russia has not gained maneuverability with Japan.

Enthusiasm for the United States and the West, required for the fourth approach, is also doubtful. The time has passed when many Russians trusted the West to meet their country's major economic needs. Even if economic growth begins and markets in the West and Japan become increasingly important, it is unlikely that a high degree of internationalism or trust will soon reemerge. We can anticipate continued interest in balancing the superpower status of the United States, marked by distrust.

Only one concern, the "China threat," could conceivably tilt the balance toward the West or Japan. Indeed, beginning in 1993 articles on the China threat became quite prominent in the Russian press.[51] Of all the great powers only Russia truly is worried about the imminent danger of Chinese migrants overrunning their homeland, of Chinese territorial ambitions severing huge areas now under its sovereignty, of Chinese organized crime gaining a widespread foothold in the land, and of ecological damage or ethnic wars spreading across a long border. If for many Russians the China threat is real, then why does China seem to be so important for Russian diplomacy? The answer is, according to much of the rhetoric, that Moscow's primary goal is to regain its status as the capital of a great power. Both Moscow and Beijing seek the maneuverability and influence of strategic triangles when facing Washington and even Tokyo. A new world order represents a threat, but a strategic triangle or quadrangle with the assurance of each other's presence offers the right geometry for our time. The geopolitical dimension stands out because the economic integration of Russia and China or Japan is advancing slowly and in an irregular fashion. Plans to invest heavily in Russia's natural resources failed to develop as expected, mostly because of Russian internal bickering and fear of exploitation. Joint ventures between large enterprises for purposes of production rarely materialized, as neither Russia nor China accomplished the reform of its state-owned enterprises predicted in 1992–93. Third parties rich in capital and technology were needed to assist Russia and China in working together. But the two were prone to compete for attention when it came to dealing with Japan, and China was the big winner. In economic relations, Japan and China were drawing much closer together than Russia was with either of the others. Japan would have been comfortable capitalizing on this in the form of closer all-around ties. It was China that felt itself more inclined to Russia, in part in order to limit this economic impact from spreading. Yet, with the Russian Far East wary of becoming a periphery in the emerging "Greater China," China is not likely to gain soon the economic balance and leverage that some were predicting.

On all sides there was a perception that ties between Russia and China or Japan cross civilizational boundaries. Russians in the Far East consider themselves Europeans, who are deserving of extra support from Moscow because of their strategic situation on the border not with Slavic nations or Central Asians but with the peoples of the Asia-Pacific region who pose a civilizational challenge. Chinese, too—especially those in the south who were rapidly becoming part of the global economy—were not attracted to Russia. Few were interested in studying Russian. They were playing for much more predictable commercial stakes in other regions. Meanwhile, the Japanese had transferred their antipathy from Soviets to Russians, finding little encouragement in their contacts with sailors, who once allowed off ship had the reputation of stealing whatever they could get their hands on, and with officials, who could offer few if any reassurances. Since the Chinese and the Japanese acknowledged a shared civilization, these circumstances would seem to have been favorable for a close bond between them within the context of the strategic triangle. Nonetheless, their expanding economic cooperation did not come without tensions. Japan's inability to bring closure to the war memories of its neighbors left in place something akin to a civilizational barrier—a deep-seated mistrust between peoples in which they attribute to the other a historical propensity toward militarism and deviousness. Fifty years after the end of the war China's leaders seek an advantage from manipulating these feelings for their geopolitical aspirations.

Taken together, the slowness of economic integration involving Russia, the lack of progress toward a reconciliation among civilizations, and the suspicious geopolitical reasoning of China and Russia have left a strategic triangle still at an early stage of formation. It has not become a very active force globally. At the same time, the Sino-Russian partnership is invoked by the Chinese and Russians to limit other global arrangements from becoming more active. With Japan ever present as a challenge, the triangle has become a central factor in official Chinese consciousness. Russia, too, is incorporating it into new geopolitical reasoning. The Sino-Russian-Japanese triangle looms as a force for the future.

Notes

1. This optimism appears particularly in nonofficial, nonbusiness Japanese sources. One recent example is Ogawa Yuhei and Kowata Shinji, *KanNihonkai keizai: Saizensen* (Tokyo: Nihon hyoronsha, 1995).

2. This is a frequent warning in Russia, as in a recent article by Aleksandr Chudodeev, "Vilia Gel'bras: Rossiiskoe mogushchestvo prirastat' dolzhno Sibir'iu i Dal'nim Vostokom," *Segodnia* 31 January 1996, p. 5.

3. Chinese sources concentrate on competition among great powers, while not ignoring the rise of Eastern civilization (*dongfang wenming*) in a world dominated by Western civilization. A running commentary on the balance of power can be found in the monthly *Shijie jingji yu zhengzhi* (formerly *Shijie jingji yu zhengzhi neican*). Of course, the United States became the site of the popular debate on clashing civilizations, as launched in Samuel P. Huntington, "The Clash of Civilizations?" *Foreign Affairs* vol. 72, no. 3 (Summer 1993): pp. 22–49.

4. An example of the informative materials available is a 148–page annotated chronology in Chinese prepared in Japan by Chen Hui, a Beijing specialist on Russia. *Russo-Chinese Relations: 1991–1995,* Occasional Papers on Changes in the Slavic-Eurasian World (Slavic Research Center, Hokkaido University, 1996).

5. "Yao jiachang Sulian Dongou guojia lishi he xianzhuang de yanjiu," *Sulian lishi wenti,* no. 2 (1986): p. 1; Liu Keming, "Heluxiaofu zhizheng shiqi Sulian shehuizhuyi de jige wenti," *Sulian dongou wenti,* no. 1 (1986): p. 141.

6. Gilbert Rozman, *Japan's Response to the Gorbachev Era: A Rising Superpower Views a Declining One* (Princeton, NJ: Princeton University Press, 1992), pp. 98–108.

7. Yan Sun, *The Chinese Reassessment of Socialism, 1976–1992* (Princeton, NJ: Princeton University Press, 1995), pp. 237–57.

8. Togo Kazuhiko, *NichiRo shinjidai e no joso: dakai no kagi o motomete* (Tokyo: Simul Press, 1992).

9. Chen Rishan, "Gaige bulu panshan: Zhengzhi jingji weiji shenzhong Sulian zhengzhi jingji gaige gaiyao," *Shiboliya yanjiu,* no. 3 (1991): pp. 1–12.

10. Journals on the Soviet Union continued to be *neibu* or internal circulation with few exceptions, as were some of the leading journals on international relations. See Gilbert Rozman, "China's Soviet Watchers in the 1980s: A New Era in Scholarship," *World Politics,* 37 (July 1985): pp. 435–74.

11. Zheng Biao, "Sulian jieti dui dongbeiya de yingxiang," *Dongbeiya luntan,* no. 2 (1992): pp. 85–86.

12. Xu Zhixin, "Yuan Sulian diqu de weiqi yu xifang de yuanzhu," *Dongou Zhongya yanjiu,* no. 3 (1992): pp. 37–41.

13. The importance of "Deng Xiaoping's counsel" is stressed in Steven M. Goldstein, "Nationalism and Internationalism: Sino-Soviet Relations," in *Chinese Foreign Policy: Theory and Practice,* ed. Thomas W. Robinson and David Shambaugh (Oxford: Clarendon Press, 1994): pp. 259–62.

14. Liu Yichang and Xu Xiaojun, "Muqian guoji guanxi de zhuyao tezheng he fazhan qushi," *Shijie jingji yu zhengzhi,* no. 4 (1992): p. 34.

15. Hakamada Shigeki and Hyodo Nagao, "NichiRo kankei dakai wa sogo ninshiki no zesei kara," *Gaiko forum* no. 50 (November 1992): p. 9.

16. Nancy Bernkopf Tucker, "China as a Factor in the Collapse of the Soviet Empire," *Political Science Quarterly* vol. 110, no. 4 (Winter 1995–96): pp. 501–18.

17. John W. Garver, "The Chinese Communist Party and the Collapse of Soviet Communism," *China Quarterly,* no. 133 (March 1993): pp. 1–26.

18. Robert Legvold, "Russia and the Strategic Triangle," in *The Strategic Quadrangle: Russia, China, Japan, and the United States in East Asia,* ed. Michael Mandelbaum (New York: Council on Foreign Relations Press, 1995), p. 37; Michael Mandelbaum, "Introduction," ibid., p. 9.

19. Wang Huaining, "Shijie zhengzhi jingji xingshi," *Shijie jingji yu zhengzhi,* no. 2 (1993): pp. 1–3.

20. Sergei Goncharov, "Ot soiuza cherez vrazhdebnost'—k dobrososedstvu: 40 let sovetski-kitaiskikh otnoshenii," *Literaturnaia gazeta* (4 October 1989): p. 14; Evgenii Bazhanov, "Konets 'kitaiskogo sindroma,' " *Novoe. vremia,* no. 19 (4 May 1990): pp. 5–6.

21. "Dangqian Eluosi xingshi zuotanhui," *Dongou Zhongya yanjiu,* no. 6 (1992): pp. 88–94.

22. "Islands," *Japan Times Weekly International Edition,* 17–23 February 1992, p. 6.

23. Saito Kunihiko, "Eritsin Roshia daitoryo no hoNichi enki to kongo no NichiRo kankei," *Sekai keizai hyoron,* no. 11 (1992): pp. 8–18.

24. Hiroshi Kimura, "Hold It There: Is Aid to Russia Justified?" *Japan Times Weekly International Edition,* 5–11 April 1993, p. 9; Sugimori Koji, "NichiRo ga tekitai shinai jidai," *Voice* (July 1993): pp. 182–91.

25. Gilbert Rozman, "Japanese Views of the Great Powers in the New World Order," in *Old Nations, New World: Conceptions of World Order,* ed. David Jacobson (Boulder, CO: Westview Press, 1994): pp. 23–27.

26. Graham Allison, Hiroshi Kimura, and Konstantin Sarkisov, "Beyond Cold War to Trilateral Cooperation in the Asia-Pacific Region: Scenarios for New Relationships between Japan, Russia, and the United States" (Strengthening Democratic Institutions Project; Harvard University: Cambridge, MA: 1992).

27. Vladimir I. Ivanov, "Japan, Russia, and the United States: Prospects for Cooperative Relations in the New Era" (Washington, DC: United States Institute of Peace, 1993).

28. Among the most careful formulations was Joseph S. Nye Jr., "What New World Order?" *Foreign Affairs* 71, no. 2 (Spring 1992): pp. 83–96.

29. Hui, *Russo-Chinese Relations: 1991–1995.*

30. Legvold, "Russia and the Strategic Triangle," pp. 50–51.

31. A.D. Bogaturov, "Vvedenie," in *"Novoe Zarubezh'e" i shansy rossiisko-amerikanskogo partnerstva,* vol. 14, (Moscow: Rossiiskii nauchnyi fond, 1993): p. 3.

32. Mikhail Karpov, "Interesam Rossii otvechaet stabil'nyi i protsvetaiushchii Kitai," *Nezavisimaia gazeta,* 10 December 1992.

33. Li Jingjie, "Model' budushchego," *Rossiia i ATR,* no. 1 (1996): p. 25.

34. Li Jingjie, "Xin shiqi de Zhong-E guanxi," *Dongou Zhongya yanjiu,* no. 1 (1994): pp. 8–17.

35. Alexei D. Voskressenski, "New Dimensions in the Post–Cold War Russian-PRC-American Relationship," *Issues & Studies* 31, no. 2 (February 1995). p. 44.

36. Aleksei Voskresenski, "Vyzov KNR i rossiiskie interesy," *Nezavisimaia gazeta,* 16 September 1994.

37. Yan Zhu, "Sulian jietihou shijie xingshi fazhan quxiang," *Shijie jingji yu zhengzhi,* no. 5 (1993): pp. 1–4.

38. Sergei Filonenko, "Migratsionnye protsessy v Vostochnoi Azii," *Vladivostok,* 29 September 1994, p. 2.

39. "Khabarovsk Governor Denounces Border Agreement with China," *RA Report,* no. 17 (1994): p. 48.

40. Peter Kirkow, "Regional Warlordism in Russia: The Case of Primorskii Krai," *Europe-Asia Studies* 47, no. 6 (1995): p. 925.

41. Liu Baorong, "Zhong-E jingmao hezuo jinru tiaozheng shiqi," *Guoji maoyi* (October 1994): pp. 26–28.

42. "Hoppo ryodo mondai no 'shizenshi' o nerau Gaimusho," *Foresight* (August 1994): p. 35.

43. Hakamada Shigeki, " 'Kiken na nashonarizumu' ka 'genjitsuteki nashonarizumu' ka," *Foresight* (December 1994): pp. 74–75.

44. " 'Sosukobetsu shi hoNichi' ooki na igi," *Sankei shimbun,* 13 December 1994, p. 2.

45. B. Afonin, "Nuzhen proryv v storonu progressa: Rossiisko-Iaponskie torgovo-ekonomicheskie sviazi," *Rossiia i ATR,* no. 1 (1996): p. 9.

46. Hakamada Shigeki, "Nihon no kimyo na 'nejire gensho,' " *Foresight* (March 1995): pp. 56–57.

47. Xiao Guang and Xin Bo, "Luelun E-Mei 'huoban guanxi,' " *Dongou Zhongya yanjiu,* no. 6 (1994): pp. 62–63.

48. Tsuyuki Takao, "21 seiki wa Chugoku no jidai da," *Gekkan Asahi* (June 1993): pp. 45–49.

49. Vilya Gel'bras, unpublished manuscript, in "Great Power Identities in Northeast Asia: China, Russia, and Japan Face Each Other," ed. Gilbert Rozman (unpublished).

50. Liu Jinghua, "The Rise of China and Choice of Foreign Strategy by the Years 2020–2030," *Strategy and Management,* no. 2 (1995): pp. 125–26.

51. Aleksei Tarasov, "Sibir'—tol'ko dlia russkikh?" *Izvestiia,* 2 November 1993, pp. 4–5.

8

The Role of Turkey and Iran in Incorporating the Former Soviet Republics into the World System

Kemal H. Karpat

Introduction

The disintegration of the Soviet Union unleashed overnight two mutually complementary processes of reintegration of the new independent states of Central Asia and the Caucasus into region blocs which emerged as a consequence of the disintegration and the world international and economic system. Turkey and Iran, located at the southern flank of the former Soviet Union and linked to Central Asia and the Caucasus by historical, cultural, and ethnic ties, were drawn almost immediately into this process of reintegration and assumed a variety of roles, based not upon any predetermined plan but according to the dialectic of international forces and the new states' search for support to consolidate their independence and statehood.

The policies of Turkey and Iran towards the new states were conditioned partly by their own national interests and historical and ethnocultural perceptions of the area, but mostly by their position, ties, and ideological relations to at least three geographic-cultural and economic blocs. The first and dominant international bloc is the Western one, led by the United States and Western Europe, which may be joined at times, paradoxical as it may sound, by Russia, if the latter deems that certain foreign relations of Central Asia and the Caucasus serve its own interests. The second bloc is regional, is led by Turkey and Iran, and is supported by other regional states such as Pakistan, Afghanistan, and India, although India more often than not follows its own independent policy. The third bloc may be called Islamic, for it includes in addition to the countries in the second bloc Saudi Arabia, the Persian Gulf states, and, to a lesser extent, Malaysia and Indonesia. This third bloc, although relatively large in size, does not have a formal structure or extensive influence; nevertheless, it provides a useful outlet for both Turkey and Iran to court the support of the Muslim countries in order to advance their own agendas in the area while permitting other Islamic states to seek Central Asian and Caucasian support for their own security and interests—for example, Saudi Arabia versus Iran. Despite the growing appeal of Malaysia and Indonesia as relatively successful economic models and pluralist, pragmatic modern Islamic societies for Central Asia, they will not be studied here. Instead, this study will focus mainly on the relationship of Turkey and Iran with some of the former Soviet republics, and their role in opening up the former Soviet southern republics to the world. These are the Central Asian (except for Tajikistan), Caucasian, and Black Sea republics. Russia's policies in Central Asia and the Caucasus are seminal but will be studied in relation to those of Iran and Turkey rather than separately. It must be emphasized, however, that the relations between Russia on one hand and Turkey and Iran, respectively, on the other gained both momentum and diversity after 1991, as conditioned by their changed positions toward each other and Central Asia and the Caucasus. Prior to 1991 Turkey and Iran conducted limited bilateral relations with the USSR, as both countries feared communism as well as its territorial expansionism and sought Western help. Turkey joined the North Atlantic Treaty Organization (NATO) in 1952 and faithfully followed its policies, while Iran, along with Turkey and Pakistan, became part of the Central Treaty Organization (CENTO), until Ayatollah Khomeini's revolution of 1979 rendered that organization meaningless. The inevitable political and ideological estrangement of Iran from the United States after 1980 and the hostage trauma led the Iranians to seek some sort of accommodation with the USSR, while Turkey enjoyed renewed interest and backing as a Muslim antidote to Iran's perceived Islamic militancy. The end of the war in Afghanistan removed a major obstacle to Iranian-Soviet/Russian rapprochement, which the disintegration of 1991 accelerated and reconditioned. Meanwhile Turkey, after undergoing a rather rude awakening to the fact that the diminished role of NATO made precarious her presence in the Western alliance, regained a new stature as a stable Western ally in a region divided into new blocs and subject to the uncertain future of the Russian Federation and the Muslim fundamentalist movements.

It must be noted from the very start that the terms "Islam," "Muslim," or "Islamic" used in this study describe only the culture and faith of the individuals and not their countries' foreign policy, although common faith, language, culture, and history seem to have facilitated relations between Turkey and Iran and the new neighbor states. Indeed, Turkey and Iran historically have had unique and close ties with Central Asia and the Caucasus—and Ukraine, in the case of Turkey—and have relied strongly on them to renew their relations with and even influence the area's economic and political life. The specific nature of these historical relations and their compatibility with future aspirations have, in fact, facilitated to some extent the success of Turco-Iranian relations with the contemporary new states, but did not determine them. The ultimate outcome of these relations was determined by the new perception of the world and one's own group position in it as part of a territorial national state and the subsequent sense of "national interest." These are old truths for the West but are new for the Islamic world, forced to divide itself into a series of ethnoterritorial states.[1] Persia dominated for centuries parts of Central Asia and the eastern Caucasus, but after the sixteenth century its promotion of Shiism as a political ideology of expansion alienated it from the bulk of the Muslims, even in areas such as Azerbaijan, where it was able to convert a substantial part of the population to Shiism. Shiism turned Iran into a political enemy of the Central Asian khanates, as the Safavids defeated the newly emerging Uzbek state only to be crushed by the Ottoman sultan Selim I (1512–20) at the battle of Chaldyran; the victory permitted the revival of the Uzbek state and the establishment of a long alliance.

Politics and religion not only distanced Central Asia further from Persia but also pushed it closer to the Ottomans by adding a new political weight to their common linguistic and cultural ties. These are key background issues which cannot be ignored by any student of the contemporary affairs of the area. Persia eventually transformed itself into Iran in order to camouflage the rule of the Persian minority over a variety of Turkic, Arabic, and Kurdish groups, and its use of Shiism along with the Persian language to assimilate its minorities. In sum, the concept of Iran was basically a modernist scheme designed to transform the multiethnic Persian empire into a Farsi nation-state; in a similar way the Young Turks used Ottomanism-Islamism to Turkify the multiethnic Ottoman state. Moreover, historically speaking, Persia was not a land of destination, but of transit, for the Muslims of Central Asia and the Caucasus to reach the shores of the Mediterranean, Marmara, and Black Seas, which were the terminals of the Silk Road.

The conversion of the bulk of Central Asian Turks to Islam in the tenth century further increased the attraction and influence of the western Islamic lands because of the obligation of *hajji* (pilgrimage to Mecca at least once in a lifetime) and the influence of the travel infrastructure necessary to support the pilgrimage. The communications of Central Asia, the Volga region, and Siberia with western Asia increased, as did the number of lodges along the pilgrimage road, which served not only as sanctuaries and work colonies for the pilgrims' support but also as outposts to disseminate the faith. Eventually, pilgrims avoided crossing Persia and preferred to use the Ottoman-held land. In the process Istanbul became such a semisacred place that Central Asians considered a pilgrimage to Mecca incomplete without a stop in Istanbul. Istanbul became the seat of the caliphate in 1517, and the fact that the sultan-caliph, the spokesman for the Orthodox Sunni Islam, appeared to be the only Muslim ruler who could do something for the Muslims of Russia after the period 1552–1783 increased the influence of Istanbul without giving rise to fears that the sultan-caliph may seek to substitute his rule for the tsar's as Persia's rulers had attempted to do many times. The Ottoman sultans never ruled Central Asia and the eastern Caucasus but instead appeared as disinterested defenders of the Central Asians' religious freedoms. Moreover, Istanbul was also a center of Islamic culture and learning, and after the 1850s it appeared increasingly as the source of reform, revival, and religious-national rejuvenation. It attracted hundreds of modernist (*jadidist*) intellectuals from Russia proper, the Caucasus, and Central Asia, including the famous Bukharan poet-modernist, Abdurrauf Fitrat, who wrote (ca. 1911) his seminal *munazara* (a dialogue about modernity) in Istanbul.

The disintegration of the USSR found Turkey and Iran in a markedly different situation from that prevailing in 1917, when the Bolshevik regime completely cut off all the Muslims under its rule from communicating with the rest of the world. Turkey had abolished (in 1922 and 1924, respectively) the sultanate and caliphate, whose incumbents personified the faith that was the main bond between eastern and western Turks. Turkey had become a territorial national state guided by national interest and a political identity derived chiefly from ethnolinguistic roots; without a written rule, Islam in Turkey gradually would become one of the sources of national culture, personal ethics, and morality. Meanwhile Iran, after an intensive campaign of Persianization under the Pahlavi dynasty, abolished the monarchy in the revolution of 1979, whose leaders defined themselves as the revolutionary promoters of the return of all the faithful to the fundamental grassroots of Islam. Shiism was ignored outwardly but was in essence the driving force behind Iran's new Muslim internationalism. Thus, following different ideological and philosophical paths, Turkey and Iran had become republics, as would all the new states of the former USSR.

On balance, the Muslims of Central Asia and the Caucasus appeared closer to the Turks of Turkey. They shared not only common linguistic and cultural-historical ties but also the secular pragmatic outlook of their elites and citizenship in territorial ethnolinguistic states, however arbitrary their boundaries and limited their experience in independent national statehood. Even the Sunni Tajiks, despite their Persian language, are closer to the rest of Central Asia than to Iran, as their leaders have repeatedly indicated. In sum, the relations between the Central Asians/Caucasians and Turkey and Iran were facilitated by their historic cultural ties, but conditioned and determined largely by their respective political and ethnolinguistic transformations in the period 1917–91. In more than one way, all sides had changed, although many preserved the memory of the Soviet days.

The collapse of the Soviet Union put an end to seventy years of complete segregation of Central Asia and the Caucasus from Iran and Turkey and seemed to have revived overnight the old ties, but the reality was different from the image. In a visit to the grave (mosque) of Aslan Bab(a) (the mentor of Ahmed Yesevi) near the town of Otrar in Kazakstan in 1989, I was astonished to hear the old worshipers at the mosque greet visitors from abroad with the cry "*jetpis jylyn bitti*" ("a seventy year wait has ended"), while both younger Kazaks and the visitors looked puzzled by this outburst of sentimentality. Indeed, the dominant theme at these reunions, which I witnessed repeatedly, was not the joy of finding long-lost brothers but the anxious search for friends and allies, regardless of nationality or faith, who could help the Central Asians overcome as soon as possible the ravages of political oppression and economic backwardness. The oft-expressed view of scholars accustomed to echoing the Soviet line, that the Central Asians regretted the end of communist rule, did not appear to be correct except maybe at the beginning and in isolated cases, at least as witnessed by this writer.[2] Moreover, the Central Asians did not soon turn against each other (an excuse used by Russia to justify interventionism) and proved to be able to govern themselves and to learn to run their industries without Russian leadership. True, the collapse of the USSR and sudden independence initially had caused a high degree of perplexity, for the Soviets and Russians had taught the natives that their presence in the area was permanent and that the natives (often called in private "black donkeys") had no capacity to govern themselves without Russian directives. These artificial perceptions began to disintegrate rapidly after 1993, however, as the new states realized that Russia was too weak economically, and too concerned politically about the possible reaction of the European community of civilized nations, which it wanted to join, to attempt to revive the defunct USSR.

The international and interregional relations of the new states intensified and subtle changes were made. For instance, the Central Asian states abandoned the old formula, "Kazakstan and Central Asia," for the shorter "Central Asia," making Kazakstan an organic part of this cultural-political bloc. The move further enhanced Kazakstan's chance to become the leader of the area and pushed aside the old concept of "Turkestan" (southern Central Asia) put forth by Uzbekistan in order to promote its own regional leadership. The relative eclipse of Uzbekistan as a regional leader was also due to Uzbekistan's view of China as a model of development and its late acceptance of economic reforms as well as to President Islam Karimov's autocratic rule. By contrast, Kazakstan's signing of the Nuclear Nonproliferation Treaty (NPT) in 1993 and its prompt sale and delivery to the United States of about 600 kilograms of uranium from Ust'-Kamenogorsk in 1994—the material was flown immediately to the Dover airbase in Delaware, then trucked to Oak Ridge, Tennessee—encouraged the United States to support Nursultan Nazarbaev as the preferred leader of Central Asia. There is no question that Nazarbaev proved to be an exceptionally capable and foresighted leader as much as an adept manipulator of Russia's fears and ambitions. However, there is no clear indication that the Western, and especially the United States', interest in the Caucasus and Central Asia is deep and lasting. Kazakstan enjoyed a high degree of popularity in the United States as long as it harbored nuclear weapons and displayed an economic attraction. But the historical, cultural, and even strategic center of gravity in Central Asia is Uzbekistan, and sooner or later it will gain its due recognition, as indicated by the warming relations between Washington and Tashkent and the recent visit of Karimov to the United States. The situation may change, and the Western interest in Central Asia may increase drastically, if China's dormant ambitions in Central Asia are revived and Russia remains militarily and economically too weak to stem Chinese expansion, however improbable it may appear now. The desirability of a Central Asian self-defensive and self-supporting bloc against Chinese expansion westward—or against a revived Russia's move southward—may in the long run determine the Western policy in this area. For the time being the Western interest, even if formal, is vital in consolidating the area's independence and statehood. However, up to now the Western interest in the area, if measured in financial terms, has been minimal—except in Armenia, which has received enough help to rank it as one of the top five countries receiving U.S. aid. The U.S. Congress has prevented Azerbaijan from receiving aid on one of the clumsiest and most unjust of pretexts, while Uzbekistan and Turkmenistan received no help. In the latter case the lack of projects, the initial Uzbek orientation toward China as an economic model, and Turkmenistan's economic closeness to Iran, as well as apparent unfamiliarity with aid procedures, played some role in obstructing Western economic aid.

The Phases of Integration into the World

The integration of the newly independent states of the former Soviet Union into the global diplomatic and economic web can be divided into two distinct phases. The first phase lasted from independence until the end of 1993 and the start of 1994, and the second began thereafter. During the first period the West—notably, the United States—was caught unprepared by the sudden collapse of the USSR; lacking even elementary information about the area, Western nations showed considerable reluctance to become involved in its affairs for fear of being pulled into ethnic warfare and civil disorders, epitomized by the war in Tajikistan. It is now well known that the Russians were at least partly responsible for the Tajik war and that the attacks on Mesketians (Turks of Ahiska in Georgia deported to Central Asia in 1944) in Uzbekistan were staged by the KGB in order to impress upon the world the need for a Russian presence in the area. In a similar way Russian and Soviet foreign policy makers portrayed the bogey of Islamic fundamentalism as directed against Western civilization and Christianity, thereby justifying their violent suppression.[3] As late as 1989, for example, on a visit to Tashkent, Mikhail Gorbachev lambasted Islam as a reactionary and oppressive faith, and this charge was followed up with attacks in the Soviet press and from its local pundits.

During the first period Turkey was designated, as clearly indicated by U.S. president George Bush's statement during a visit to that country in 1992, a model of development and a cultural antidote to Iran's fundamentalist Islam. Turkey accepted its role enthusiastically because of its long-standing ties with the Muslims of Russia and its desire to reinforce its NATO membership, which the collapse of the USSR had made even more tenuous. Meanwhile Iran, relatively isolated by U.S. policy and still recuperating from the war with Iraq, remained relatively passive and undecided as to what policy to pursue. Iran's posture was essentially defensive, for the rise of independent ethnic nation-states on its borders, notably in the Caucasus, posed grave dangers to its territorial integrity, as shall be indicated.

The second phase in the process of incorporating the former Soviet states into the world political economic system took place after 1994, when the United States and Europe became actively involved in the lives of those nations. At least two key issues prompted the Western involvement—namely, the realization that the Muslim states of the former USSR possessed rich deposits of oil, gas, coal, gold, and other minerals,[4] and the Russian policy of keeping only a military and economic foothold in the area without contributing much to the new states' development and welfare. During this second phase Turkey turned from an independent actor enjoying freedom of political and economic initiative to a partner of Western interests. At the same time, Iran, deprived of allies, achieved a rather close rapprochement to Russia in order to, among other things, prevent the ethnic nationalist policy of Azerbaijan from creating separatist movements among the Azeri population in Iran and use economic incentives to counter Turkey's cultural penetration of Central Asia. Russian backing and Iran's own economic muscle enhanced its unique advantage of providing direct land access to the Indian Ocean for the Central Asian and Caucasian states once their need to export gas and oil abroad became evident. Even so, Iran appeared to be a land of transit, as in the past, while Turkey emerged as the terminal gate for loading and shipping the oil and gas to the Western world, a position Turkey probably will retain until Russia can provide a safe alternative passage to Western markets, which is unlikely to happen soon.

The second phase of incorporation was also characterized by several internal developments: the intensification of regional interstate relations, the absence of ethnic strife, and especially the adaptation of both the natives and the Russians to the new circumstances. The emigration of many Russians, including qualified personnel who could not accept their minority status or were unwilling to learn the native language, had a rather important political and demographic impact. By raising the numerical proportions of the natives, it enhanced their claim that they were the permanent masters of their lands. After *Nezavisimaia gazeta* reported that some 400,000 people migrated to Russia from Kazakstan in 1994 alone, the newspaper stressed once again the demographic fact now facing the Russian Federation, that the "situation is not as bad for Muslims in Russia. . . . [Their] birth rate is significantly higher than [their] death rate, and [their] population density is increasing, as is the percentage of Muslims in their traditional areas. . . . Muslim families are bigger, stronger, and healthier than Russian families."[5] Today the percentage of ethnic Kazaks might have reached 51 to 52 percent, while that of ethnic Russians likely has fallen to 30 to 33 percent. The Russians in Kazakstan appear to have accepted their new situation.

A study conducted by the Russian Institute of Strategic Studies indicated that only one out of ten Russians living in Kazakstan's cities felt that Russia was his or her homeland but that one of two indicated that the former Soviet Union was his or her homeland (a rather interesting political nostalgia); meanwhile, 83.4 percent of Kazaks said Kazakstan was their homeland.[6] According to the same survey, 28.2 percent of Kazaks placed priority on independent statehood; 21.8 percent wanted to be part of the Eurasian nation proposed by President Nazarbaev, and only 14.7 percent preferred the Commonwealth of Independent States (CIS). Meanwhile, 24.4 percent of the ethnic Russians wanted to see Kazakstan as part of a revived USSR, 21.5 percent as part of the CIS, 20.6 percent as a former union republic, and 15.1 percent as part of Eurasia; 32 percent of Kazaks and 11 percent of Russians agreed to transferring the nation's capital from Almaty to Akmola.[7] In both cases there were undecided respondents. In a rather interesting and meaningful act of ethnic reconciliation in Kazakstan, only a small percentage of Russians and Kazaks recognized the right to territorial autonomy for Russians, and only 7.4 percent of the Kazaks wanted to see the Russians leave the country. In other words, the results of that survey imply that many ethnic Russians would live as a minority with assured rights and freedoms in a potentially prosperous Kazakstan rather than immigrate to a Russia with an uncertain future and a bleak economy.

The Role of Turkey and Iran in World Economic Integration

During the period 1991–93 Turkey played a key role in bringing the Central Asian and Caucasian states into the international diplomatic circuit, while Iran sought to revive these states' traditional cultural and religious identities by appeals to Islam and past association to Persian culture. On balance, Iran's initial messianic efforts to portray itself as the "center and aspiration and the Mecca" of all Muslims, to quote a recent article, seemed to have been less successful than the Turkish and Saudi efforts to promote Islam as the faith and culture of the citizens of the new states.[8] However, during the past three years Iran has successfully used its relations with Turkmenistan not only to expand its economic ties with this country, with which it shares a long border, but also to prove to the rest of Central Asia that it is interested primarily in mutually beneficial economic relations rather than ideological conquest. The recently completed railway connection has brought Iran economically closer to Central Asia and has given a new impetus to its bilateral relations with the countries in the region. The growing de facto entente between Russia and Iran has helped consolidate Tehran's position in the area but without undermining—at least for the time being—Turkey's position. The combined effect of the appeals by all these Muslim states, plus Pakistan, each one playing the Islamic card to promote its own national interest in the area, was to rehabilitate the Muslim identity and cultural self-respect of the ex-Soviet Muslims and to bring them into the mainstream of world relations. It was clear from the very beginning that the Central Asians displayed secular attitudes and were interested in the material welfare and progress that their coreligionists from abroad could bring them. Even the Sunni Tajiks, despite their Farsi language, appeared to prefer the Turkish model of statehood and economic development to Iranian proselytizing.

The politics of oil and gas in Central Asia and the Caspian provided an excellent avenue for the incorporation of the ex-Soviet republics into the world economic-political system. It proved the primacy of economics in defining international relations, and the value of independent territorial statehood in enabling a nation to monopolize the use of its natural resources. It also highlighted the crucial role Turkey and Iran could play in assuring the political and economic future—and possibly the survival—of the Muslim-Turkic states of the former Soviet Union, and demonstrated as well that neither Iran nor Turkey possessed the political, military, and economic capability to determine by itself the economic and political course of the former republics. The crucial fact, to repeat, is that practically all the Muslim republics of the former USSR (and of the Russian federation) are landlocked; their exit is commanded first by Iran and second by Turkey, though Turkey is not contiguous with any of these areas, except for Nakhichevan (cut off from its mother country, Azerbaijan, by the Armenian corridor), but has a crucial position on the Mediterranean and Black Seas.

Contrary to some opinions, Turkey was reluctant to establish relations with the Turkic lands of the USSR during the periods of glasnost and perestroika. In fact, then premier Turgut Özal declared undiplomatically during a visit to New York that Turkey had little affinity for predominantly Shiite Azerbaijan. (He barely survived the outcry caused by his remarks, which demonstrated his lack of historical knowledge.) With the independence of the new states a fait accompli by 1991, however, Turkey drastically changed its position and was instrumental in promoting the new states' admission to the United Nations, the Conference on Security and Cooperation in Europe (CSCE), the International Monetary Fund (IMF), and other international bodies. Among the first countries to establish diplomatic relations with the new states, Turkey facilitated their doing the same with the rest of the world.[9] It donated a building in Ankara to house the diplomatic missions of the cash-strapped new states and engaged in a massive program to train their diplomatic and civil service personnel.

The Turkish penetration of Central Asia and Azerbaijan during the period 1991–93 was rapid, multisided, and profound, for both the West and Russia—which came to believe its own anti-Islamic propaganda—regarded Turkey as the only suitable Islamic model of development and secular statehood for them.[10] The position of the West and Russia towards the involvement of Turkey and Iran in the life of the new Muslim states determined the scope and impact of each country's involvement. Turkey was by far the chief beneficiary of the great powers' support and attempted to draw the utmost benefit from it.

Turkey lent strong support to President Abulfez Elchibey, the pan-Turkic leader of the Popular Front in Azerbaijan, who was elected to the presidency in 1992. However, Elchibey was ousted for giving anti-Russian and anti-Iranian policies—including a prediction that Iran would disintegrate and the Azeris of Iran would be freed—and was replaced in 1993 by Gaidar Aliev, the former Communist master of Azerbaijan. Elchibey's removal was engineered by Russia with the tacit support of Iran; and it dealt a devastating blow to Turkish influence in Azerbaijan, which already was rapidly declining because of Turkey's inability to stop the Armenian advance into Azerbaijan. Nevertheless, Azeri-Turkish relations resumed shortly thereafter because of public pressure in both countries and because Azerbaijan realized Turkey was indispensable to its survival as an ethnic national state and member of the international community. For instance, Turkish support has allowed Azerbaijan to resist Russian demands for military bases on its soil.

The oil question proved to be the axis around which revolved the complex relationship between national interest, the new state's incorporation into the world economic system, and the roles of Turkey and Iran. It also produced a Byzantine labyrinth of maneuvers and showed Russian contempt for established contracts, and displays of arrogance, all in the name of national interests and power politics. Soon after the disintegration of the USSR, the Ministry of Petroleum in Moscow divided into five lots the Caspian Sea shelf, which hitherto had been explored entirely by Azeri oil men, now giving one lot each to Turkmenistan, Kazakstan, and Russia. Azerbaijan's share included the Guneshli, Chiraq, Azeri, and Neftyanie Kammi fields, and the newly discovered one of Kaypaz, all about twenty to thirty-five miles from the Apsheron Peninsula coast, on which Baku is located. The issue remained dormant until 20 September 1994, when an international consortium headed by British Petroleum and Amoco, in which Russia's Lukoil (80 percent of whose capital belongs to the state) and Turkey had shares, signed an exploration contract with the government of Azerbaijan.[11] Meanwhile, President Aliev had traveled to London, where he was promised generous economic assistance and support, encouraging him to resist more resolutely Russian calls for closer cooperation. The news about the consortium produced a very negative reaction from the Russian Foreign Ministry, which invoked the Iran–USSR treaties of 1921 and 1940 on fishing and navigation to claim that the Caspian Sea was a closed sea and any decision to explore and exploit its riches should rest on the unanimous agreement of all five littoral states.[12] The idea of a Caspian Sea organization had been put forth first by Iran's president Hashemi Rafsanjani during his visit to Moscow in 1992 but was ignored at the time, as Russia was overly confident that its long-entrenched position on the Caspian was more or less permanent. Now the Organization for Regional Cooperation of Caspian Countries was formed through the efforts of the Russian Foreign and Defense Ministries, the KGB, and Iran, to keep the West, especially Turkey, from establishing a strong economic foothold in the Caspian.

Prime Minister Viktor Chernomyrdin, speaking on behalf of the Russian industrialists and satisfied with the 10 percent given to Lukoil (they were afraid of being left out altogether), assured Aliev that Russia had no intention of opposing the implementation of the consortium oil agreement. However, Russian Foreign Minister Andrei Kozyrev, supported by foreign intelligence chief Evgenii Primakov, condemned the agreement as illegal, accused the Russian industrialists of greed and lack of patriotism, and persuaded President Boris Yeltsin to issue a secret directive—which Chernomyrdin refused to sign—to protect the Russian interests in the Caspian and the "provisions of international law."[13]

After Russia sent a strong memo to the British government criticizing the consortium and threatening to undertake a variety of unspecified measures, the West finally allowed Turkey to play its Black Sea card. Turkey announced to the world that it was taking the necessary measures to defend the environment and the safety of its citizens by subjecting the passage of oil tankers and other ships through the Bosporus and the Dardanelles to new regulations. The Montreux Convention of 1926 had left the defense of the two straits to Turkey, but gave users unlimited freedom of passage. The only requirement for passage was notification. In 1994, however, Turkey declared that it had the right to authorize passage, imposed a twenty-four hour notification, demanded the stationing of a pilot on the passing ships, and implied that it might even levy a fee to clean and protect the environment. If one considers that the number of vessels using the straits had increased to 16,000 by 1993, from about half that number just ten years earlier, that all the beaches of Istanbul are polluted by tar, and that incidents of collision are frequent, a rationale for the measures is self-evident. Nevertheless, by backing Turkey, the West acquired a rather effective but potentially dangerous means to force Russia, half of whose maritime trade passes through the straits, to respect the rights of the new states.

In 1994, Azerbaijan successfully took the initiative to secure the acquiescence of Iran and Turkey to the consortium. On a four-day visit to Iran in July 1994, President Aliev signed a declaration to deepen bilateral relations with Iran in the political, economic, and cultural fields and then eight other agreements to build a railroad from Orduabad to Menjan and to lay a gas pipeline from Khvoy to Orduabad. Iran promised to support Azerbaijan in its Nagorno-Karabagh dispute with Armenia but refused to discuss any question related to southern Azerbaijan, even rejecting Aliev's demand to visit Tabriz, its capital, and refused to give any assurances that Iran will not build a gas pipeline to Armenia.[14] Soon afterwards, Saudi Arabia entered the picture by promising to finance twenty-four programs in Azerbaijan worth $15 billion, hoping to entangle Iran more deeply in the politics and economics of Central Asia and the Caucasus and lessen its grip on the Gulf area, or at least to secure a bargaining chip.[15] The Iranians and Azeris agreed to set up a commission to supervise the implementation of their agreements, including those signed by President Rafsanjani in 1993 but never enforced.

Earlier in 1994 Aliev had made his first official visit to Turkey. As a gesture of reconciliation, he assured the Turks that they would receive a share in the consortium—the share went up, according to unconfirmed reports, from 3 to 5 percent—provided that Turkey accept as "natural and inevitable" Azeri membership in the CIS, claiming it would be difficult to sever two-hundred-year-old ties to Russia. In exchange, Aliev received from Turkey $250 million of credit for long-term exports and a promise for an additional $600 million, plus a gift of 100,000 tons of grain and more on loan, to be turned into grants if necessary. Moreover, Azerbaijan and Turkey signed sixteen agreements, including one on Development of Friendship and Multifaced Cooperation, Article 5 of which stated that if one of the parties became subject to aggression, the other would take necessary "effective" measures and provide assistance to the other in conformity with the UN Charter. Turkey had every interest in preserving its self-styled image as a caring brother to the Azeris.

The "contract of the century," as the Azeri oil consortium was dubbed, continued to involve the West in the Caucasus and bring the new states further into the limelight of world politics. On 10 November 1995, Azerbaijan signed a second oil consortium agreement, which included Pennzoil (USA), Agip (Italy), and Lukoil (Russia), to operate the Karabagh field (estimated to have from 80 to 120 million metric tons of oil), fanning further the discord between the Russian Foreign Ministry, which insisted that the riches of the former USSR belong to Russia, and the fuel and energy chiefs, supported by Chernomyrdin, who were more than happy with Lukoil's huge (35 percent) share in the second consortium and the right to operate the field.[16]

The geographical layout of the oil pipelines was potentially the most important phase of the oil deal, for the control of the pipelines has infinite economic, military, and political implications. The oil reserves in the fields assigned to the first consortium are estimated modestly to be 500 million metric tons, and because the extraction is truly cost effective, for each $1 billion invested, the return is roughly $10 to $15 billion.[17] Consequently, the owners of the pipeline can impose rather high fees on the oil flowing through their territory. Russia, which controls the existing pipeline to the Black Sea port of Novorossiisk through Dagestan and Chechnya that will also transport the oil from Chevron's fields in Tengiz in Kazakstan, naturally insisted that all new pipelines follow the same route. Azerbaijan and Turkey, on the other hand, advocated that the Baku-Supsa (Georgia) route be lengthened to Ceyhan (on Turkey's Mediterranean coast), and even though the United States opposed the Baku-Iran-Turkey pipeline, presidents Suleyman Demirel and Gaidar Aliev both declared in 1994 that Turkey had an indisputable right to lay a pipeline through its territory.

The long dispute was finally resolved in October 1995. The Azerbaijan International Operating Company (AIOC) determined that the first oil—95,000 barrels a day—will start flowing late in 1996 and will be exported through Russia and Georgia, the line eventually to be extended to Ceyhan. The repercussions of the oil and pipeline deals created price wars between Russia and Georgia, affected the war in Chechnya, had something to do with the attempt on Eduard

Shevardnadze's life, and prompted a phone call from President Clinton to Aliev, advising him to accept both the Russian and Georgian pipelines. The pipeline and oil deals are far from being settled definitively. The Russian press has blamed the United States for being behind this "intrigue, which they are cleverly calling . . . a compromise . . . although in reality Russia is the loser."[18] Indeed, Russia was made to pay for its manipulation of the Sadaval, the organization that Russia backed in 1992–93 to unite the Azeri Lezgians with their "brothers" in Dagestan in the Russian Federation and thus destabilize Azerbaijan and weaken Elchibey. In 1994 Aliev claimed that the pipeline to Novorossiisk was unsafe because it passed through two hundred miles of hostile Lezgian-Dagestani territory, and consequently Azerbaijan preferred the southern route through Georgia and Turkey.

The battle over the oil consortiums and the pipelines in Azerbaijan awakened Chevron to the importance of the pipelines (the company had plunged into the operation of the Tengiz fields without paying much attention to transportation issues), and it also introduced Mobil into the oil business of Kazakstan. Chevron is exporting barely 20,000 barrels of oil from its Tengiz fields, but reportedly it is planning to lay a pipeline across the Caspian and through Azerbaijan to Georgia and Turkey. Meanwhile, because Georgia expects to earn several times more money from the oil flow than from its tax revenues of just $250 million annually, it has sought to improve relations with Turkey, which is already supplying Georgia with a substantial amount of hard currency thanks to business tourism.

Oil politics brought Azerbaijan into world politics—it recently joined the Partnership for Peace—and highlighted the crucial position and role of Turkey in the area, forcing Iran to side with Russia. In the short run the oil deals allowed Azerbaijan to somewhat isolate Armenia, as Russia and Iran, the main supporters of Yerevan, had to distance themselves somehow from their protégé (actually an unloved pawn) in order to safeguard their economic interests in Azerbaijan. Nevertheless, their long-range interests call for maintaining a strong foothold in Armenia so that Russia can use Armenia to put military pressure on Azerbaijan, despite the Minsk group and European peace efforts, and Iran can use Armenia to quell any Azeri separatist initiative among its own Turks. Armenia, in turn, looks upon the Russian military bases on its territory (and in Georgia) as a possible springboard for a Russian advance into the Middle East, which would allow Armenia to occupy eastern Anatolia.[19] This political fantasy, nourished by the Armenian diaspora in United States and France, along with pressure from Azerbaijan, has compelled Turkey to cut off Armenia's land communication (limited air communication has been restored) with the rest of the world.

Exclusion from the oil deals and from trade with Turkey has ravaged Armenia's economy and prompted an exodus of its people to Russia, Europe, and the United States, slowly turning the Armenian military "victory" in Karabagh into a political and economic defeat. Although Armenia massacred thousands of innocent civilians and occupied one-fifth of Azeri territory, from which it ousted one million Muslims, it could escape isolation and improve its world standing by coming to terms with Azerbaijan. Following the 1994 meeting of the Council of Foreign Affairs of the Organization for Security and Cooperation in Europe (OSCE) in Budapest, the representatives of Azerbaijan and Armenia met in Amsterdam. Armenian President Ter Petrosian declared that the Armenians of Karabagh were prepared to make concessions (but not on the status of the province or the Azeri corridor of Lachin, which links Armenia to Karabagh) by taking the Dayton agreements as a model.

Meanwhile, Iran's claim to be a disinterested advocate of all Muslim causes has been buffeted by its policy of friendship with Armenia, which is dictated by its own national interest but in the end negatively affects Azerbaijan. Iran was able to hide its pro-Armenian policies until the 1994 downing of an Iranian C-130 transport plane by Armenians (who mistook it for an Azeri plane) not only caused public revulsion against Armenia in Iran but also reinforced claims that Iran was providing secret military help to Yerevan despite assuring the Muslim world of the contrary. Although Iran continues to be troubled by the growing ethnic consciousness among its Turkic groups (Azeris, Turkmens, etc.), awakened by the rise of national territorial states north of the Iranian border, President Aliev assured Iran that Azerbaijan considers "sacred" any territory under Iranian jurisdiction. In addition, relations between Georgia and Turkey have continued to expand. In January 1994 Georgian president Eduard Shevardnadze and President Aslan Abashidze of the autonomous Republic of Adzaria, a Muslim enclave on the border with Turkey, visited Ankara to sign a declaration of solidarity and cooperation. Shevardnadze lauded Turkey's efforts to stabilize the situation in Georgia and received a $50 million loan, promises of electricity, and other assistance. (President Abashidze offered to go to Abkhazia to mediate that enclave's conflict with Georgia but was turned down by Tbilisi, probably out of fear that the "mediation" might turn into collaboration between the two Muslim enclaves of Georgia.)

An abundance of resources has played a crucial role in integrating other states into the world political system, sometimes through Iran and Turkey. Kazakstan, the recipient of by far the largest amount of foreign aid from the United States and investment from abroad, has played an astute diplomatic game. President Nazarbaev has sought to accommodate Russia militarily, economically, and politically—even taking a position against Turkey when he supported passage of the pipeline through Russia—at the same time he has worked for the rapid economic development and nationalization of Kazakstan. Nazarbaev has rejected all efforts to impose the economic sanctions on Iran advocated by the United States, while striving to build regional interstate organizations, as will be discussed later. Nazarbaev signed an agreement with an international consortium comprised of Mobil, Shell, Total Agip, British Gas, and British Petroleum/Statoil to conduct exploratory surveys in the northern Caspian Sea, and in 1994 Nazarbaev signed another contract with British Gas and Agip for the exploration-exploitation of the Karachaganak field, which has at least 650 million tons of gas condensate and 200 million tons of oil, in the northwest part of the country. Still, Kazakstan has insisted that these two Western companies come to terms with Russia's Gazprom to secure the transportation of gas and oil. To supplement the Central Asian Economic Council that regulates trade between the five member states, Nazarbaev has proposed a Eurasian Union, partly to overcome the numerous shortcomings of the CIS and possibly to downgrade Russia's domination of the latter. In a conference on "Eurasian Space: Using Integration Potential" held on 20 September 1994, Nazarbaev insisted integration not be limited to trade and economics. (It should be noted that in the Eurasian Union Kazakstan favors, all states would maintain their territorial integrity, but Islam Karimov's proposed Turkestan would consist of a territorial union similar to the one created by Russia in the 1860s.)

It was, however, Turkmenistan that signed first the truly major Central Asian contract with Iran. President Saparmurad Niyazov (known now as Turkmenbashi—the head of the Turkmen) visited Tehran in the fall of 1994 and signed a contract to build a four-thousand-kilometer pipeline to carry gas to Turkey and Europe via Iran.[20] The pipeline will take years to build and will cost $7 billion. Although the United States opposes it, Turkey will accept it—not only for financial reasons but also in order to decrease its own dependency on Russia, whose gas pipelines to Turkey have been periodically pirated by Ukraine, causing costly shortages in Ankara and Istanbul, which prefer to use gas instead of pollution-causing cheap Arab oil. Turkmenistan shares a six-hundred-mile border with Iran, with which it has had long trade relations, and more recently has improved its land communication. The Ashkhabad-Mashhad-Tehran highway was opened in 1991, and the three-hundred-mile Tajan-Sarkhs-Mashhad railway is expected to be completed in 1996, giving Turkmenistan access to the Indian Ocean. Uzbekistan and Kazakstan hope to use this transportation system to ship their goods overseas, as indicated by a series of agreements.[21] Meanwhile, the Caspian Sea Shipping Company, established in 1992, is linking the ports of the five littoral countries to each other and to the Indian Ocean.[22]

Although Iranian trade with Central Asia has been rather limited, it is expected to increase rapidly as Turkmenistan begins to earn hard currency. Indeed, partly to counteract the growing economic presence of Iran, President Turkmenbashi has invited businessmen from Germany and Great Britain to Turkmenistan. A British delegation from twenty firms, headed by Minister of Energy Timothy Egger, visited Ashkhabad in mid-1995 and promised Turkmenistan liberal credits to build gas pipelines and railways and conveyed, on behalf of British Prime Minister John Major, "feelings of eternal friendship and brotherhood," mentioning Iran's failure to build even a single structure in the country.[23] Obviously, British participation in the economic "great game" now unfolding is intended to prevent Iran from taking the lead in building the pipeline, but the British also have concluded a series of agreements on education, science, and culture and signed memoranda of cooperation in exploring sources of gas and oil energy. The truth is that Iran, besides being immersed in dire economic problems of its own, does not have the capital, organization, and know-how to play a major economic or political role in the new states of the former Soviet Union.

As this survey of economic activities in the southern republics and their underlying political, social, and cultural implications clearly has demonstrated, the new Muslim states of Central Asia and the Caucasus have linked themselves to the outside world through lucrative relations and powerful partners, such as the United States, Britain, Germany, and France. (France has actually established a sort of economic-diplomatic monopoly over Uzbekistan.) There are also lesser partners such as Israel, which has been visited by several Central Asian heads of state, including Kazakstan's Nazarbaev, who balanced his trip there with a visit to Yasir Arafat. In addition, Japan, China, and India are preparing their own separate plans to carry Central Asian oil to the Pacific and build refineries in Kazakstan, but all these Asian countries are bound to play secondary roles because of their limited influence in the area, in contrast to Russia, apparently still the main political actor. The incorporation of the Central Asian and Azeri states into the world cultural, economic, and political system was backed and generalized by scores of exchange programs with Europe and the United States; the Fulbright and International Research & Exchanges Board programs alone brought over one thousand scholars and officials to the West between 1991 and 1995, and the Turkish exchange program will be mentioned later.

The opening of the Central Asian and Caucasian republics, especially the southern ones, to the world was evaluated by a group of experts at the Social Science Institute, the think tank established by Mikhail Gorbachev at Moscow State University. Citing the Baku oil deal and the de facto change in the status of the Turkish straits, those experts claimed that the Western countries had used the oil companies to influence the new states to "fling their doors open to the West and open windows to the Mediterranean," ominously adding that political unrest was the only means to stop or slow down Western investment there.[24] The experts named Turkey the "new regional leader," and because Turkey controls the Russian exit to the Mediterranean, they called upon Russia to balance it by establishing a strong foothold in Armenia by building military bases there.[25] Finally, they likened the impact on Russia of the new routes out of Central Asia to the way the discovery of routes to India around Africa ultimately pushed the Italian city-states to the periphery of European politics. Russian political elites seem to have a permanent great power psychosis that leads them to rely on power to solve any problem involving the Muslims (while taking advantage of their wealth), probably including a military showdown when they are ready for it.

It would be wrong to portray Turkey and Iran as permanent rivals and competitors who can be played against each other at will. The two countries know full well that a strong Russia is a threat to their existence, as made clear by Vladimir Zhirinovsky's speeches, and that, as proven by history, Armenia has always been a pawn in Russia's southern politics to the detriment of both Iran and Turkey. Consequently, in response to the rising Russian nationalist tide, their presidents held a series of meetings in 1993 and 1994 in order to settle Iranian–Turkish differences and coordinate policies in Central Asia and the Caucasus.[26] It was under these conditions that in 1994 Gaidar Aliev was able to renew, improve, and place Azerbaijan's relations with Iran and Turkey on equal terms rather than openly favor Turkey, as his predecessor, President Elchibey, had done.

International and Regional Organizations

The relatively small, ethnically divided populations of the new states of Central Asia and the Caucasus, as well as their landlocked position, economic weakness, and domineering national bureaucracies, expose them to internal and external pressures. As a result, these states have regarded membership in international bodies and the establishment of regional organizations as the prime means for offsetting potential foreign threats, or courting support, as the case may be, from their big neighbors—Russia and China (and Iran)—for which they are no military match, individually or collectively. The total populations of Kazakstan, Uzbekistan, Turkmenistan, Kyrgyzstan, Azerbaijan, and Tajikistan consist of roughly 65 million people, more or less equal to the populations of Turkey and Iran and far below those of Russia and China.

Because the independent existence of the Central Asian and Caucasian republics offers Turkey and Iran a safety zone against Russia and China, however, both Turkey and Iran, whatever their differences, have done their best to consolidate the independent statehood of their northern brethren. The dormant Economic Cooperation Organization (ECO), which originally included Iran, Turkey, Pakistan, and Afghanistan, was expanded to include the Central Asian states and Azerbaijan.[27] ECO membership opened the way for the new states to reincorporate themselves into the Islamic Middle Eastern world to which they had belonged for millennia.[28] This symbolic reincorporation facilitated for the Central Asians the pilgrimage to Mecca, instruction in religion, student exchanges, and the like,[29] but the ECO's grandiose plans to expand communication and transportation, lower tariffs among member nations, and establish banking facilities have materialized only in part and primarily as the consequence of lateral agreements rather than regional pacts. Iran, which stands to benefit most from it, has been the most dedicated advocate of the ECO.

Personal relations, not well-planned projects, accounted for much of the interaction between Turkey and Iran and the new states. The president of Turkey visited the area in 1991, followed by Iran's Rafsanjani in 1992, and a summit meeting held in Ashkabad led to other meetings that spelled out the policies of the new states toward Turkey and Iran. By 1992 it became clear that the Turkic states chose to follow Turkey's secular, ethnonational, pro-European path of development while maintaining close relations with Iran. The choice of Turkey as a model stimulated cooperation among the Turkic states, creating a de facto economic and cultural Turkic bloc, but there was no open or covert commitment to Pan-Turkism, which conflicts with the idea of ethnonational statehood. The rise of the ethnic and linguistic factors as the principal link between the new states of Central Asia in 1991–92 and the subordination of Islam to them as a cultural ingredient left Iran no other alternative but to play its own Islamic card, minimizing the Shiite differences while upholding the virtues of the Persian language and culture, especially in dealing with the Tajiks. Perhaps inadvertently, Iran helped raise the importance of ethnicity and language as the prime sources of identity. The revolutionary fundamentalism of Iran, the conservative revivalist Wahhabism of Saudi Arabia, and the orthodoxy of Pakistan, all alien to the Central Asian understanding of Islam, neutralized each other (or at best limited each to isolated footholds) and prevented the formation of an Islamic international political organization, however remote the possibility.

In January 1992 Turkey established the Turkish International Cooperation Agency (TICA). Its purpose is to develop a "legal framework for liberalization . . . democratization . . . [and] management cadres . . . necessary to help the new republics adjust to the outside world not only politically and economically but also socially and culturally," and, of course, to consolidate Turkey's position in the Turkic states.[30] Meanwhile the Exim (export-import) Bank, with a revolving credit of $1.2 billion, encouraged investment in gas and oil exploration, transportation, telecommunications, and a variety of smaller consumer-goods industries such as clothing, shoes, and supermarkets. In mid-1992 alone, 220 firms received financing, while by 1995 the figure had increased to 350, according to a conference report. In 1993, bilateral trade between Kazakstan and Turkey increased by 300 percent over 1992, amounting to $112 million, and the total cost of projects assumed by Turkey was over $1 billion. Turkey also concluded economic and cultural agreements with all the other republics; consequently, beginning in 1992, some 10,000 exchange students were enrolled in Turkey's fifty-three universities. (Students who failed the courses were trained and given capital to open small businesses in their country of origin, preferably in association with a financing firm in Turkey.) Meanwhile, trade between Turkey and Russia reached $2 billion, according to official figures; unregistered private trading probably was three times that amount.

The Central Asians became more interested in establishing regional organizations after 1992–93 as they became more confident that "a return to the empire," as Nazarbaev put it, would not occur. As mentioned, they established the Economic Union, which did not seem to yield much result. Then, however, the Central Asian states were forced out of the ruble zone in 1993, and each country had to issue its own separate currency. Russia provoked this monetary crisis to benefit itself in economic relations with the former Soviet republics without realizing that the move would consolidate their economic and political independence and stimulate the drive to establish regional associations.

When President Nazarbaev paid an official visit to Turkey in October 1994, he signed the Treaty of Friendship and Cooperation. He further stated publicly that the time had arrived to create an organization that would include Turkey and the Turkic-speaking states of Central Asia and work for peace without being directed against anyone. As if to stress his Turkic affiliation, Nazarbaev prolonged his visit in Turkey through the Turkic summit held on 18–19 October 1994. There, the heads of the six states (Azerbaijan included) proclaimed in their declaration that their relations had developed significantly since the first summit held in Ankara in 1992 and needed to progress further.[31] They reaffirmed their common historical, cultural, and linguistic ties and stated that their views on solving regional problems were in harmony and that they would act in accord with the charter of the United Nations and other international bodies. They also condemned Armenia for its acts in Azerbaijan and called for an early solution of the United Nations Cyprian and Bosnian conflicts.[32] The heads of state symbolically described their interstate cooperation as reestablishing the Silk Road—that is, a sure way to produce prosperity and stability for the region. Moscow expressed its fears that such meetings incited Pan–Turkic sentiments, only to be told by President Demirel of Turkey that such accusations were unfounded, but that Turkey would come to the aid of Azerbaijan if, as threatened, Moscow imposed sanctions on Baku.

The Turkic summit meeting, held at the request of Turkey just on the eve of the CIS summit, was designed to demonstrate to Russia that Turkey exerted a special influence over the region. At the CIS meeting following the Turkic summit, Nazarbaev proposed the establishment of the aforementioned Eurasian Union, and Russia complained about the growing segregation of the Turkic countries along national and ethnic lines. In order to remind Turkey of the danger of ethnic politics, Russia subsequently convened a conference on the situation of the Kurds in Russia (a bare one hundred thousand people, many of whom had been deported to Central Asia in 1944) and abroad. Formally, the conference was organized by the Association of Kurds in the CIS, the Kurdish Workers' Party (PKK), and the Institute of Eastern Studies of the Russian Academy of Sciences, but in reality it was supported by Russia.[33] Turkey lodged a strong protest against Russia's use of the Kurds to pressure Turkey and then embarked even more assiduously on preparations for the next summit meeting of Turkic states, to be held in Bishkek, Kyrgyzstan, in August 1995.

Probably as a reaction to these inter-Turkic developments and as a warning to Turkey not to go too far, Russia and Armenia held their own military exercises, allegedly in response to Turkish military exercises conducted on the frontier of Armenia in the winter of 1995. Although Russian defense minister Pavel Grachev paid an official visit to Armenia, he was not able to intimidate Turkey, as Marshal Shaposhnikov had in 1993. Then, Shaposhnikov's warnings that Armenia was part of the CIS defense system had quelled Turkey's posturing about taking action against Armenian attacks on Azerbaijan.[34] In fact, Russia was concerned about a whole chain of military relations Turkey had established with the new states, including Uzbekistan and Kazakstan.

In August 1994 the Kazak and Turkish ministers of defense concluded a preliminary military cooperation agreement, which Nazarbaev described as not conflicting or interfering with Russia and other countries.[35] Later in 1995, following his well-established method of involving Kazakstan in as many international agreements as possible without alienating Russia, Nazarbaev agreed to join the Russian-Belarusian customs union, described Russia as his country's strategic partner, and supported the passage of the oil pipeline from Kazakstan to the Black Sea through Russia's territory. At the same time, he announced that his administration will move to Akmola, the new capital favored by Kazak nationalists, in 1997.[36] Remaining close to Russia both in appearance and essence, Nazarbaev still has managed to expand his country's relations not only with its neighbors but also with the West, which has far surpassed Turkey as a source of investment and trade. Indeed, Kazakstan has appointed an ambassador to the European Union in Brussels. The EU accounts for 28.5 percent of Kazakstan's foreign trade, and the Netherlands ranks second only to Russia as the recipient of Kazak exports.

After the CIS summit meeting of 10 February 1995 adjourned and Russia's President Yeltsin departed, the presidents of Kazakstan, Kyrgyzstan, and Uzbekistan met and laid the groundwork for what could be the first truly meaningful regional bloc. They created an Interstate Council composed of the three presidents, a Council of Foreign Ministers, and a Central Asian Bank of Cooperation with a capital of $10 million. The three countries, searching for ways to economic integration, held another meeting at Tashauz, Turkmenistan, which Turkmenistan attended despite declaring its "permanent neutrality," and the three agreed to follow different ways of development, respect each other's territorial integrity and sovereignty, and consolidate their participation in the Interstate Council on the Aral Sea.[37] In short, the regional policy of the Central Asian States was following, more or less, the pattern proposed by Nazarbaev after the 8 December 1991 meeting of Russia, Ukraine, and Belarus in Minsk. When the Central Asian heads of states met at Ashkhabad and asked to join the CIS, because they could not face the insurmountable difficulties of being suddenly severed from the long-dominant Slavic bloc, Nazarbaev proposed the creation of a transnational union to coordinate regional cooperation and balance the Slavic group. The policies, meetings, and organizations subsequently established by the Central Asians all seem to have conformed to Nazarbaev's strategy of appearing to draw close to Russia while in fact balancing it.

It is too early to assess the impact of Turkmenistan's decree of permanent neutrality in its constitution, which the United Nations, in an unprecedented act, ratified. Lately, Turkmenistan has taken an active part in bringing together the warring parties in Tajikistan. It also has changed the name of the country's chief

Russian-language newspaper from *Turkmenskaia Iskra* (Spark) to *Nitralny Turkmenistan* (Neutral Turkmenistan) and adopted the motto "Follow me, my united people," coined by its leader. Is Turkmenistan becoming a political and economic dissident from the rest of Central Asia in order to reserve for itself the economic benefits of following Iranian and Russian suggestions? It is too early to volunteer a guess. Information about the latest Uzbek-Kazak-Kyrgyz summit, held at Djambul on 15 December 1995, is too scanty for an in-depth analysis. Nazarbaev's warning to Yeltsin that the re-creation of the defunct USSR will be a tragedy for everybody, however, indicates that the Central Asian states view themselves no longer as docile satellites of Russia but as independent members of the international comity of nations.

The Black Sea Basin Organization

The politics of the Black Sea countries has not received the international attention it deserves despite the area's crucial importance to the defense of West Europe and the future of the former Soviet republics. Until 1989–91 the Black Sea littoral was divided almost in half between Turkey (ca. 1200 kilometers) and the Soviet bloc. After 1991 the old Soviet portion was subdivided between Russia, Ukraine, Bulgaria, and Romania. Turkey became the main riparian state, consolidating further the position it enjoyed through control of the straits; the de facto amendment of the Montreux Convention in 1994 has been mentioned. Until the peace of *Küçük Kaynarca* in 1774 which sealed the Russian conquest of the northern Black Sea littoral from the Ottoman Empire, of course, the Black Sea had been a Turkish mare nostrum and the Ottoman government had been able to establish ethnic, religious, and political outposts—and centers of influence—along the littoral in the Caucasus, Crimea, and Moldova. After 1774, although many potential sources of Turkish influence in the Caucasus and Crimea were gradually liquidated or neutralized, population movements brought in others, such as the Gagauz of Moldova.

The Gagauz are the descendants of the Seljukian Turks from Anatolia, who, fleeing the Mongols, settled (ca. 1263–65) on the western shores of the Black Sea. During the Byzantine reconquest of the Balkans from the remnants of the Fourth Crusade (ca. 1261–70), many of these Seljukian Turks converted to Orthodox Christianity. Now known as the Gagauz, they became part of the Ottoman Empire (ca. 1390–92) and remained so until the nineteenth century. When the Turks lost Bessarabia (the historical name of southeastern Moldova) to Russia through the peace of Bucharest in 1812, according to the treaty terms, the predominantly Muslim population of the south (mostly Nogai remnants of the Cumans and Golden Horde) were resettled in the north Caucasus and mainly in Dobruja, south of the Danube, which was still part of the Ottoman state.[38] Russia, in turn, settled Gagauz and Bulgarian immigrants in the place of departing Muslims in what amounted to an informal exchange of Muslim and Christian populations, most of whom were ethnically Turks. The Turkish dialect still spoken by the Gagauz is the closest to the language spoken in Turkey, as are their customs and attitudes. In fact, Turkey opened schools in the Gagauz areas of Bessarabia while the province was part of Romania from 1918 to 1944. Afterward, however, Turkey was cut off entirely from the area until 1989, for during Soviet rule the southern part of Bessarabia was made part of Ukraine's Odessa oblast. That move deprived Moldova of access to the Black Sea and split the historic *Gagauz yeri* (homeland of the Gagauz, as they call it) in two: about 160,000 live in Moldova in about twenty-five villages and towns, while 60,000 are left in Ukraine.

The disintegration of the USSR in 1991 added new dimensions to the Turkish initiative to establish the Organization for Black Sea Economic Cooperation (BSEC).[39] Turkey had taken the initiative in 1990 in order to increase its regional influence and thus counteract its expected marginalization in NATO with the end of the Cold War. Following an official invitation by Turkey, representatives of the USSR, Bulgaria, and Romania joined their Turkish counterparts in Ankara on 19 December 1990 and agreed on a basic constitutive act. After the disintegration of the USSR one year later, Azerbaijan, Georgia, Ukraine, and Moldova joined, as did Greece and Yugoslavia. Thus BSEC became a kind of vehicle for incorporating the new states of the Black Sea into the world economic and political system,[40] and its final constitutive act was signed on 25 June 1992 by all the heads of state. The organization's primary aims were to achieve multilateral cooperation in the region based on market economy principles, and to strengthen the signatories' connection with Europe in accord with the Helsinki Act, Charter of Paris for a New Europe, the CSCE, and so on, but without competing with the European Community (now Union).[41] Turkey is not yet a member of the EU but was admitted to the Customs Union in March 1996. The signatories stressed again and again the fact that the organization was European and a part of the emerging European structures, and that it would uphold democracy, the rule of law, and human rights, and that it would resort only to peaceful means to solve the many conflicts in the area.[42]

Although the success of the Black Sea organization was limited by the delaying tactics of Greece and Russia, both of which feared Turkish ascendancy to the rank of regional power, it nonetheless played a crucial role in helping Turkey develop bilateral relations with Ukraine and Moldova and thus helped solve the simmering Gagauz conflict. Ukraine was reluctant to establish close relations with Turkey for historical reasons (Ottoman rule and the situation of southern Moldova in addition to the status of the Gagauz). Moldova, on the other hand, needed regional support because ethnic Russians in its Tiraspol region, backed by the Fourteenth Russian Army of General Aleksandr Lebed, had declared independence. Consequently, Moldova used the friendship of Turkey to counterbalance pressure from the Russian military and the hawks who desired the establishment of permanent military bases in this westernmost outpost of the former Soviet

Union. Although Moldova has been Slavicized to some extent, it definitely is not a Slavic country, as anyone who has visited the area would know. In fact, 65 percent of Moldova's population speaks Romanian and has a Latin culture. Turkey is aware that Ukraine and Moldova are of crucial importance to its own security and trade and that their independence is the best guarantee against the revival of the Russian Empire, so Turkey has done its best to strengthen their independent statehood. Besides establishing diplomatic relations at all levels, Turkey has opened its frontiers to visitors from the area, provided economic assistance to their governments, established flights to Kiev and Kishinev (Chishinau), and encouraged cultural exchanges.

The Gagauz separatist endeavors created a difficult problem for Moldova. The Gagauz nomenklatura, backed by Russia and, to some extent, Ukraine (a large Russian force was stationed in Bolgrad just south of the Moldovan-Gagauz-Ukrainian border), had declared their territory a republic as early as 1989–90.[43] The subsequent effort by the Moldovan army to liquidate the Gagauz "republic" was stopped short by Russian troops, turning the Gagauz rebels into Russia's and Ukraine's military stooges. The Moldovan government found itself squeezed from the east and southwest by two separatist forces, the ethnic Russians of Tiraspol and the Gagauz, both backed by Russia. Turkey played a decisive role by using persuasion and economic incentives to convince the Gagauz leaders and the Moldovan authorities to solve their conflicts peacefully. The continual visits by Turkish businessmen and intellectuals to the Gagauz and vice versa, the exchange of students, and common linguistic ties, despite differences of religion, helped the Gagauz overcome their feeling of isolation and give up their reliance on Russia. When the Gagauz–Moldovan conflict finally was resolved in 1995, the Gagauz (who constitute about 42 percent of the population in the district assigned to them) agreed to recognize Moldovan authority in exchange for extensive cultural and administrative autonomy and the right to secede if Moldova unites with Romania. (The reconciliation was greatly facilitated by the decision of Moldovan president Mircea Snegur's party to renounce eunification with Romania and his subsequent electoral victory, which put to rest Gagauz fears of Romanian chauvinism.)[44] Western diplomatic fora responded to Moldova's application to join the Council of Europe—it was the first of the former Soviet republics to apply, in July 1995—by making good treatment of the minorities a preliminary condition and supporting an "independent and united Moldova." The United States made clear that it had an interest in the early withdrawal of the Fourteenth Russian Army from Moldovan territory, but the rebel Trans-Dniester Republic of Tiraspol held elections and referenda to legalize its independent status and opposed a Yeltsin–Snegur agreement to withdraw the army. As late as January 1996 some members of the Russian Duma visited the area and voiced support for the separatists.[45] Moldova, meanwhile, tried to soothe Russian fears by declaring that it would not join NATO. For its part, Ukraine, which holds territory in northern Bukovina and southern Moldova that was recognized as part of Romania from 1918 to 1944 (except for a short interlude from 1940 to 1941), has since kept aloof from the strife. Should Romania eventually claim this territory Ukraine will need Russia's support, and it also faces in Crimea the separatist claims of ethnic Russians.

The Turkish role in the Ukrainian opening and integration into the rest of the world has been dependent on the policies of Europe, for Turkey does not have the economic, cultural, and historical resources to affect such matters on its own. The West took a rather late interest in consolidating Ukrainian independence and helping its economic development, and Ukraine proved hesitant in defining its relations with Russia, its own identity, and its economic policies. Unlike Moldova and the Central Asian and Caucasian nations, the Ukrainians do not differ much from the Russians in language, history, and/or religion except in the predominantly Catholic western part of the land. Nevertheless, President Leonid Kuchma, contrary to all expectations, began to move away from Moscow, changing his country from a fraternal nation to a good neighbor to just a neighbor.[46]

Ukrainian trade with Russia has been halved; gas imports will be reduced from 56 billion cubic meters in 1994 to 50 billion in 1996; and Ukraine has been admitted to the Council of Europe. In December 1995 Kuchma traveled to Latin America and then to Britain. British Prime Minister John Major welcomed Ukraine's expanding relations with the United Kingdom, Europe, and the European Union, and promised to visit Ukraine, as did U.S. vice president Al Gore. President Kuchma also held important talks with President Chirac of France, Prime Minister Helmut Kohl of Germany, and many other dignitaries during the funeral of French president François Mitterrand.[47] Moreover, the chairman of People's Rukh party, Viacheslav Chornovil, declared at the sixth party convention that Ukrainization must be forged to create a true Ukrainian nation even though dire economic conditions seem to have made many Ukrainians lose interest in independence. Still, Ukraine decided to stay out of the CIS customs union.

The Tatars of Crimea are both a link as well as a source of possible discord between Turkey and Ukraine. Crimea was part of the Ottoman state from 1475 to 1774, and the descendants of Crimean immigrants in Turkey are estimated accurately to number around three to five million. (Some estimates are exaggerated to the point of leaving no Turks in Turkey.) Meanwhile, about three hundred thousand Crimean Muslims out of a total of about one million living in Central Asia, where they were expelled by Stalin in 1944, have returned to their homeland and created tensions among the Russian-dominated Crimean legislature, the Ukrainian government, and the Muslim Crimeans. The returnee's grievances include their legal status, their dire economic situation, and the fact that their properties have not been returned, as well as their lack of full equality with the rest of the Crimeans. The well-organized Crimean lobby in Turkey has exerted considerable pressure on the Turkish government to secure from the Ukrainian authorities favorable terms for their kin in Crimea. Nevertheless, the Muslim *mejlis* (council) in Crimea decided to side with the Ukrainians, thus bolstering the strength of the non-Russian population from 25 to 35 percent but without any obvious benefit for the Crimeans, at least for the time being. As this example once again indicates, Turkey's position of leadership in the BSEC has not received wide enough acceptance to make the organization a truly effective interregional body, mainly because Russia fears marginalization in an area it regards as vital to its status as a super- or global power.

(The record of freedom for the press and opposition parties, fair elections, and human rights leaves much to be desired throughout the new republics, but did not prevent their admission into European bodies. The subject, interesting as it may be, was left out of this paper because, despite formal conditions to abide by the rules of democracy, none of the governments [except to some extent for Moldova] paid attention to it. The violation of democratic pledges seems to have neither speeded up nor delayed the integration of the new states into the European system, for as usual, realpolitik has prevailed over democratic idealism.)

Conclusions

Turkey, and to a much lesser extent Iran, played key roles in paving the way for incorporating the new states of the former Soviet Union into the world political and economic system. In the process both countries had a chance to enhance, in proportion to their influence, their own regional stature and interests. Religious, ethnic, and historical ties between the new republics and Turkey and Iran facilitated their contacts but had little impact in determining the ultimate success of Turkish or Iranian efforts. The key factor that determined the level of their success was their affiliation—or alienation—from the West. That affiliation was measured, as in the case of Turkey, by the degree of commitment to secularism, democracy, and economic and political-cultural modernization, as well as to upholding sincerely the national ethnic identity and sovereignty of the new states. Turkey represented a Westernized model of modernization which proved to have a definitive appeal over the Iranian-traditionalist-imperial-Islamic model. The symbol of this preference was the acceptance of the Latin alphabet by all the Turkic-speaking republics, including the Gagauz Republic and Uzbekistan, the latter hesitantly agreeing to adopt it by the end of the century. In effect, the major Turkic groups in the world are committed to using the Latin script. Contrary to a variety of dire predictions, Islam proved to be a potent force only if associated with and supplementing national identity and culture. In other words, Islam in the former Soviet Union, to the dismay of Iran and Saudi Arabia, has ceased to be an independent constant factor of politics—at least for the time being.

The Islamophobia, which had such a distorting effect on Western policies towards the Muslim countries, was shared fully and to an even worse degree by the Russians.[48] Recently and belatedly, however, the Russians have come to view Islam in the former Soviet Union as a moderate, pluralist, and regionalist form of faith rather than a monolithic extension of Middle Eastern Islam or, most improbably, of Iranian fundamentalism.[49] This simple discovery, echoed in several conferences on Islam in Russia, may have revolutionary implications for Russia's future policies. With at least 20 million Muslim citizens of its own living in the Caucasus, Tatarstan, Bashkirdistan, Siberia, and so on, and surrounded by several Muslim states to the south, Russia has come to the realization that it has more to win than lose by acting as the Muslims' friend, and many communist candidates—including the presidential aspirant Gennadi Zyuganov—advocated that approach during the 1995 election campaign.

Turkey was able to act as intermediary in the incorporation of the Muslim-Turkic republics of the former USSR into the world system because the Western powers strongly encouraged Turkey to do so and Russia acquiesced to their will. The Russians saw Turkey's role as an alternative to Iran's fundamentalism and realized it was too late to do anything about it anyhow. Without question the decision of Gorbachev, and to some extent of Yeltsin and Andrei Kozyrev, to become part of the Western world also had much to do with Russia's willingness to let Turkey pull Central Asia and the Caucasus into the political and economic fold of Europe. Andranik Migranian, an influential member of Russia's Presidential Council, attributed the "unilateral" concessions made by Russia to the West during Gorbachev and Yeltsin's first years to the hope of receiving aid, achieving a basic unity of goals with United States and Europe, and becoming part of the civilized world. In the process, Migranian claimed, administrative borders became political ones, and Russia turned inward, hoping to stay away from the problems and conflicts of the former republics.

Migranian blamed the Foreign Ministry and especially Foreign Minister Kozyrev for pursuing a defeatist policy that prevented the USSR and then Russia from making its military might into tangible economic and political assets in Europe and elsewhere.[50] He seemed to think that the foreign policy of Russia in the former republics and members of the Warsaw Pact should aim at reversing the incorporation of the former republics into the world economy and society. As indicated throughout this study, relations between Russia and Turkey, except for their excellent trade relationship, are being made increasingly tense by the complex affairs of the former Soviet republics. Although it may be too late to do so, Russia actually is attempting to recoup many of the "losses" incurred during its own efforts to become part of the Western world and is trying to pull the new states along as it inches out of the system it once idealized. Just as Turkey helped the West to bring the new states into the world system, Iran may now help Russia to pull them out. If Russia decides to abandon the democratization program and revive the defunct empire, Iran may be compelled to review its ties to Russia and realign its policies with Turkey in accordance with their historical experience. The vicious circle of Iranian, Russian, and Turkish politics may be thus closed once more.

Notes

1. This key issue, aside from some sources mentioned below, has received scant attention. See James P. Piscatori, *Islam in a World of Nation-States* (Cambridge: Cambridge University Press, 1986); Adeed Dawisha, ed. *Islam in Foreign Policy* (Cambridge: Cambridge University Press, 1983).

2. The nostalgia for Soviet rule was described in Martha B. Olcott, "Central Asia's Post-Empire Politics," *Orbis* 36, no. 2 (Spring 1992): p. 253 ff.

3. There is a striking similarity in the attitudes of the tsarist administrators and Soviet satraps towards Islam. Both claimed that it was a reactionary and destructive force, ignoring the most elementary fact that the first truly enlightened modernists of the nineteenth century, such as Shiabeddin Marjani and Ismail Gaspirali, just to name two, came from among Russia's Muslims and influenced profoundly and positively Ottoman and Russian Islamic modernism. The fundamentalist movements in Russia, such as the Caucasian Muridism of Sheyh Shamil, were essentially political movements of liberation which are still continuing, as indicated by the Chechen revolt. It is interesting to note also that even sophisticated Russian scholars claiming detachment and objectivity have described the natives' deep attachment to their ways of life as a regressive consequence of their Islamic faith rather than a cultural self-defense against Russian-Soviet assimilationist campaigns. See, for instance, Sergei P. Poliakov, *Everyday Islam: Religion and Tradition in Rural Central Asia* (Armonk, NY: M.E. Sharpe, 1991).

4. It is a strange coincidence that the oil reserves in the republics of the former USSR are concentrated in the Muslim republics, such as Azerbaijan and Kazakhstan. Even in the Russian Federation the two Muslim autonomous republics, Tatarstan and Bashkirstan, have rich oil deposits. "Europe makes good cars and we give them good oil to run them, so this is a good partnership, if we get our share of the deal," an Azeri told this writer.

5. *The Current Digest of the Post-Soviet Press* (hereafter *CD*) 47, no. 4 (1995): pp. 20–21; *CD* 47, no. 10 (1995): p. 15. The Voronezh province was so alarmed by the number of newcomers that it sought to limit the immigrants' number. It should be noted that some publications continue to reproduce the Soviet demographic data which places the Kazakhs at 42 percent and Russians at 37 percent of the population while indicating that the Russian population had decreased by 500,000 or about 9 percent in 1989–1995. *Monitor* (Open Society Institute) 10 March, 1996.

6. *CD* 47–48 (1995): pp. 16 ff. For a behavioral study of Central Asian attitudes towards democracy, identity, ethnicity, and so on, see Nancy Lubin, *Central Asians Take Stock* (Washington, DC: U.S. Institute for Peace, 1995).

7. Ibid.

8. Hanna Yousif Freij, "State Interests versus the Umma: Iranian Policy in Central Asia," *Middle East Journal* 5, no. 1 (Winter 1996): p. 81.

9. Kemal H. Karpat, "The Foreign Policy of the Central Asian States, Turkey, and Iran," in *Turkish Foreign Policy: Recent Developments,* ed. Kemal H. Karpat (Madison, WI: 1996), pp. 101 ff; Kemal H. Karpat, "The Socio-Political Environment Conditioning the Foreign Policy of the Central Asian States," in *The Making of Foreign Policy in Russia and the New States of Eurasia,* ed. Adeed Dawisha and Karen Dawisha, (Armonk, NY: M.E. Sharpe, 1995).

10. Ian O. Lesser, *Turkey's New Geopolitics: From the Balkans to Western China* (Boulder, CO: Westview Press, 1993); Graham E. Fuller, *Central Asia: The New Geopolitics* (Santa Monica, CA: Rand, 1992); Hafeez Malik, ed., *Central Asia: Its Strategic Importance and Future Prospects* (New York: St. Martin's Press, 1994). For a short but informed report on Turkish activities in Central Asia, see Lowell Bezanis, "Turkey Runs Up the Flag," *Transition* 1, no. 24 (29 December 1995).

11. *CD* 46, no. 39 (1994) and *CD* 46, no. 41 (1994).

12. *CD* 46, no. 39 (1994) and *CD* 47, no. 45 (1995).

13. *CD* 46, no. 27 (1994) and *CD* 46, no. 41 (1994). An appraisal of the contract appeared in *Nezavisimaia gazeta,* 27 October 1994, and is reproduced in part in *CD* 46, no. 43 (1994).

14. *CD* 47, no. 45 (1995).

15. *CD* 46, no. 33 (1994). Under Saudi pressure, the Islamic Charity Fund of the League of Islamic States provided care to thirteen thousand refugees and promised to finance a large clinic and to build fifteen hundred apartment buildings in Baku.

16. The Azeris told this writer in Baku that the amount of oil reserves is several billion metric tons. When asked, the late rector of Azerbaijan Petroleum University, Tawfik Aliev, did not support the above figure but insisted that Azerbaijan had the know-how and manufactured the equipment for the entire oil industry of the former USSR. In any case, the oil deal deserves far greater attention and study than we were able to devote to it. For further information see *CD* 46, nos. 38, 40, 46, and 47, and *CD* 47, nos. 21, 34, passim.

17. *Pravda,* 10 October 1995.

18. *RFE/RL Daily Report,* 2 January 1996; *Pravda,* 10 October 1995.

19. The Armenian diaspora is doing its best to provoke Turkey. In a meeting in Istanbul in 1994, the then foreign minister of Armenia, Raffi Hovannisian, representing the most extremist irredentist U.S. group, launched an incredibly insulting attack on Turkey. This episode was one of the reasons Ter Petrosian, the president of Armenia, ousted his foreign minister and tried to forge a new foreign policy for Armenia in accord with the prevailing political and economic realities of the area rather than the bellicose dreams of the diaspora. Petrosian has refused to grant dual citizenship to diaspora Armenians and in 1995 outlawed the Dashnak party, the standard bearer of Armenian irredentism. Meanwhile, budget revenues in Armenia fell to $21.6 million (it was $44 million in 1993) and nominal wages per month dropped to $15.60; in addition, the country forfeited any share of oil pipeline revenues. But Armenia receives generous aid from the United States.

20. *CD* 46, no. 34 (1994); see also *CD* 47, nos. 34, 40.

21. Freij, "State Interests," pp. 78–79.

22. *CD* 46, no. 2 (1994); see also *CD.* vol. 46, nos. 38, 39, and 40 (1994).

23. *CD* 47, no. 7 (1995): p. 25. See also *US-Kazakstan Monitor,* vol. 1, no. 5 (October–November 1994).

24. *CD* 46, no. 43 (1994): pp. 10–11. The *Economist* reported (2 December 1995) that Iran is planning to establish several free trade zones along its northern border, including one at Sarakhs.

25. These views were expressed at a conference organized by the Foreign Policy Institute of the Russian Foreign Ministry and its Turkish counterpart titled, significantly, "Russia and Turkey: Rivals or Partners." The conference, closed to the public, was held in Ankara in May 1995, and there Russian participants accused Turkey of "Pan-Turkist" aims and of being the tool of the "corrupting, decadent" West which had destroyed Russia. The Turks responded in kind. The second part of the conference, held in Istanbul, dealt with economic issues and was open to the public.

26. Late in 1993, as Russian near abroad policy threatened to become aggressive and politicians talked about expanding Russian borders to the Indian Ocean and Mediterranean, Ankara and Tehran came together to patch up their differences. Both countries appeared to agree that the PKK (the Kurdish Workers Party ruled by the Kurdish marxist guerrillas) was a threat to their stability and that Russia successfully had manipulated to keep both Turkey and Iran from mediating in the Karabagh conflict. Both countries have established visa requirements for Azeri citizens and vice versa.

27. *CD* 45, nos. 43, 51 (1993).

28. Iran formally recognized the seven states on 25 December 1991, well after they

declared their independence, lest demands for border changes and a disorderly breakup of the USSR create turmoil and demands for ethnic reunification in the north of Iranian Azerbaijan, which shares the same language and ethnicity as the former Soviet Azerbaijan, and actual border changes. A. Ehteshami, "New Frontiers: Iran, the GCC, and the CCARs," in *From the Gulf to Central Asia,* ed. Anoushiravan Ehteshami (Exeter: Exeter University Press, 1994): p. 94.

29. For the ideological battle between various varieties of Islamic fundamentalism and the Central Asian response, see Ahmed Rashid, *The Resurgence of Central Asia—Islam or Nationalism?* (London: 1994).

30. Umut Arik, "The New Independent States and Turkish Foreign Policy," in Karpat, *Turkish Foreign Policy,* p. 38. Arik, a former ambassador to Tokyo, was the head of TICA until his appointment as ambassador to Italy late in 1996. See also *CD* 45, no. 23 (1993).

31. *Sabah,* 20 October 1994; *CD* 46, no. 42.

32. *CD* 46, no. 9.

33. *CD* 47, no. 3 (1994).

34. Karpat, "The Foreign Policy of the Central Asian States, Turkey, and Iran" pp. 101 ff.

35. *CD* 46, no. 32 (1994).

36. *Daily Report,* 16 January 1996. Practically all the Russian names of streets and villages in Kazakstan have been changed to Kazak, including that of Yermak. (Yermak Timofeyevich was the conqueror of Siberia.)

37. *CD* 47, no. 10 (1995).

38. On the history of the Gagauz, see Kemal H. Karpat, "The Seljukid Origin of the Gagauzes," *Etnograficheskoe obozrenie* 4 (July–August 1994): pp. 36–43.

39. Oral Sander, "Turkey and the Organization for Black Sea Cooperation," in Karpat, *Turkish Foreign Policy,* pp. 61 ff.

40. Oktay Ozuye, "Black Sea Economic Cooperation," *Mediterranean Quarterly* 3, no. 3 (1992): p. 50 ff.

41. Ibid.

42. Sander, "Turkey and the Organization for Black Sea Cooperation," p. 71.

43. For these recent developments, see Kemal H. Karpat, "Gagauzlar," *Islam Ansiklopedisi* (Istanbul, The Diyanet Foundation: 1996).

44. Information collected by this writer during visits to Moldova in 1992 and 1994.

45. The Moldovan parliament renounced unity with Romania late in December 1994 under the pressure of President Mircea Snegur, who had won the national elections with an independence platform opposing the nationalist party's demands for reunification with Romania. The Gagauz, in turn, held a local referendum and an election, which ended in the ousting of Stefan Topal and his group, the leaders of the separatist drive. The Gagauz will have three languages—Gagauz, Romanian, and Russian—and their own flag and anthem. See *CD* 47, nos. 8, 10, and 13 (1995).

46. *CD* 47, no. 46 (1995).

47. *FBIS,* 28 December 1995 and 16 January 1996.

48. For the enduring strength of some of the old cliches about the power of Islam, see Raphael Israeli, "Return to Source: The Republics of Central Asia and the Middle East," *Central Asian Survey* 13, no. 1 (1994): pp. 19 ff. See also, for a different perspective, Lowell Bezanis, "Exploiting the Fear of Militant Islam," *Transition* 1, no. 24 (29 December 1994): pp. 6–8.

49. Russia has realized belatedly that Turkish Islam, promoted extensively as a supplement of ethnic national identity, is far more politically potent than pure religion. The old Pan-Slavists of Russia effectively proved a similar point with their use of Orthodox Christianity in the nineteenth-century Balkans.

50. *Nezavisimaia gazeta,* 24 January 1994; *CD* 46, no. 6 (1994).

9

Germany and the Post-Soviet States

Angela Stent

The Legacies of History and Unification

Germany's stake in the outcome of the post-Soviet transformation is greater than that of its other Western partners because of the legacies of history and geography. The Soviet role in German unification, Russia's proximity to Germany, and the reality that these two countries between them are bound to dominate the European continent ensure that Berlin will remain an important player in Russia's post-communist future. However, despite the significance of Russia for Germany, Germany's willingness and ability to focus on relations with Russia and the other post-Soviet states has been limited by the unexpectedly onerous economic and political burdens of integrating the former East Germany into the new Federal Republic and by its concern about developments in neighboring Central European states. Moreover, both countries are preoccupied with their own domestic problems in this transitional period after the end of the Cold War, and neither has yet developed a clear concept of what role it will play in the Europe of the twenty-first century.

Germany occupies a unique place among Russia's Western partners because of the legacies of the past and the dramatic events linking German reunification with the collapse of communism and of the Soviet Union. Russia and Germany have, during this century, developed a complex network of ties and multilayered interactions. The interwar history of Soviet–German cooperation—Rapallo, the secret military collaboration between the Red Army and the "Black" Reichswehr before Hitler's accession and the Nazi–Soviet Pact from 1939 to 1941—provide one historical model. The Cold War years present another. For forty years, the Federal Republic faced hostile Soviet troops on its borders. It depended on the USSR for its contacts with the German Democratic Republic. The GDR depended on the Soviet Union for its very survival. As Leonid Brezhnev unceremoniously reminded East German leader Erich Honecker: "We have troops in your country, Erich. I'm telling you openly, never forget this: the GDR can't exist with its power and strength without us, without the Soviet Union. Without us there is no GDR."[1]

German unification reversed these patterns of dependence. Once Moscow had allowed the Berlin Wall to fall, had agreed to unification and to permitting a united Germany to remain in NATO, the new Germany became a fully sovereign state for the first time since 1945. But the price for unification was significant German financial and logistical commitments to the USSR which have outlasted the collapse of the Soviet Union. Moreover, although Germany no longer has Russian troops on its border and is, in fact, a comfortable one thousand miles away from Russia, Bonn remains acutely conscious of its political obligations toward Moscow. This is partly because the USSR allowed Germany to unify and partly because the Germans appreciate that the demise of the GDR contributed to the collapse of the USSR itself. By the same token, however, and given Moscow's conviction of its right to be fully compensated for these concessions, expectations of what the Federal Republic owed Russia and how much it would assist its transition were considerably exaggerated.

Like its allies, Germany was greatly disconcerted by the breakup of the Soviet Union. Chancellor Helmut Kohl and Foreign Minister Hans-Dietrich Genscher had developed close personal ties with Soviet President Mikhail Gorbachev and Foreign Minister Eduard Shevardnadze during the intense period of negotiations over German unification.[2]

To the Germans, Gorbachev became *berechenbar* (calculable), a man whose behavior was predictable and in whom the Germans had great confidence. The twenty-year Soviet–German Treaty on Good Neighborliness, Partnership, and Co-operation, signed in November 1990 epitomized the rapid change from Cold War to cooperation. The treaty envisaged a close political and economic partnership between the two states and the emergence of a peaceful Europe in which both countries would play a major role.[3] Thus, the August 1991 putsch and the events that followed it greatly disturbed the Germans not only because they began to realize that their preferred interlocutor's position was in jeopardy, but because they feared the impact of the breakup of the Soviet Union on the withdrawal of 580,000 Soviet troops and their dependents from East German soil. As the prospect of disorder in the former Soviet space grew, their main preoccupation was the uninterrupted and orderly departure of Soviet soldiers from united Germany.

The collapse of the Soviet Union forced Germany to face a number of unpleasant realities. Although Germany and its European partners had confronted potential conflict with Soviet Communism for forty years, they had also grown to understand the Soviet mentality and had developed a comfortable modus vivendi with Gorbachev's USSR. The end of the Soviet Union meant setting foot on an unknown and uncertain terrain with no accepted rules of the game. Moreover, the USSR had disintegrated because of Gorbachev's inability to rein in nationalist forces in the non-Russian republics.

The end of communism meant the resurgence of powerful and unpredictable nationalist forces in parts of the Soviet Union barely known to or understood by the West. This was particularly uncomfortable for Germany, which had spent four decades fighting its own nationalist demons and the legacy of the Third Reich, downplaying the significance of nationalism and seeking to inculcate in its population a European, as opposed to a German, identity. After all, was not the twentieth century the ultimate testimony to the evils of nationalism? No Western European country felt comfortable with the fact that nationalism and ethnicity appeared to be a defining characteristic of the immediate post-communist search for identity in Eastern Europe and the former Soviet Union.

Reunified Germany and reborn Russia became new states within one year of each other. Neither Germany nor Russia have natural borders, and both countries' historical struggles to establish viable national identities within uncertain boundaries had in the past led to instability and war in Europe. Thus, the two countries were politically and geographically new but searching for their benign, as opposed to aggressive, historical roots. United Germany in 1990 was a country with new borders for whom history (prior to 1945) offered little guidance in redefining national identity or national interest (the same was true for Russia). For forty years, West Germany had concentrated on becoming a stable democracy and deliberately eschewed a major international role. It pursued a limited foreign policy, circumscribed by Four-Power occupation rights focusing on NATO, the European Community and, after 1969, Ostpolitik. Germany had become a successful example of a *Zivilmacht,* a civilian power, one in which the use of military force was not a defining element of its statehood; rather, Germany focused on its political–economic role internationally.[4]

After unification, however, Germany's neighbors and allies expected it to assume new responsibilities commensurate with its increased size, economic weight, and attainment of full sovereignty. In particular, the United States believed that, given its economic might and strategic location in the center of Europe, united Germany should assume the primary responsibility for assisting the former communist countries in their political and economic transitions. Thus Germany, which was initially reluctant to take on a more active international role, was compelled to redefine its Ostpolitik and to reconceptualize its priorities.

The greatest challenge that continues to confront Bonn is how to balance its interest in stability and the development of viable market societies in Central Europe, on the one hand, and in Russia and other successor states, on the other, given its limited resources. Germany has sought to transform the legacy of Soviet–West German and Soviet–East German ties into a workable post-communist partnership without alarming the newly emerging democracies of Central and Eastern Europe.

Given Germany's wariness about assuming the burdens of a great power in Europe and fully aware of the historical ghosts of Rapallo and the residual fears of Central European states sandwiched between a powerful Germany and an ailing but nuclear Russia, Germany has sought to multilateralize its role in the former Soviet Union as much as possible.[5] It has, above all, emphasized its role as a member of the European Union (EU) in its relations with the former communist states and has sought to shift the burdens of assisting the newly independent states to the EU. The desire not to "go it alone" in Russia is a constant theme in German foreign policy. Indeed, from the German perspective, Russia is by far the most important post-Soviet state both strategically and economically. It is also the most significant in terms of its potential negative impact: concern about Russia's ability to destabilize the lands to the east of Germany—and ultimately Germany itself—through the export of nuclear proliferation, environmental dangers, organized crime, and refugees. Through its weakness, therefore, Russia has paradoxically gained greater power to disturb European security.

From a Russian perspective, the United States may well be the most important Western interlocutor politically and militarily, and also the only country that can bestow on Russia the international legitimacy it seeks; but Germany is Russia's most important economic partner and one which continues to have an abiding interest in engagement, because of the legacies on history, geography, and reunification.

German Objectives in the Post-Soviet States

Given its traumatic experiences with the impact of economic crisis and societal dislocation on Germany's body politic during the Weimar Republic, Germany has sought to assist the post-Soviet states in bringing stability to a chaotic situation. Without a successful Russian transition, Bonn feels that it will ultimately be difficult for its neighbors in Central and Eastern Europe to prosper. Thus, Germany's primary objective has been to find partners within the Russian government with whom it could build a predictable relationship. Despite Chancellor Kohl's discomfort at Gorbachev's departure, he steadily built up strong personal ties with President Boris Yeltsin, viewing his continuation in power as the major guarantor of stability and *berechenbarkeit* (predictability).

Germany, like its West European partners and like the United States, is also committed to promoting Russia's political transition to a democratic, pluralist *Rechtsstaat* (society based on the rule of law.) The process of democratization is, however, inherently destabilizing, particularly after seventy-four years of communism and centuries of tsarist autocracy, which suppressed the growth of civil society. In the five years since the collapse of communism, there have been instances when Germany—like its other western partners—has countenanced breaches of the democratic process and violations of the principle of the rule of law for the sake of stability, defined as ensuring that antireformist forces—be they communist or nationalist—do not come to power. The most obvious examples were the support given to Yeltsin in his violent confrontation with the Congress of Peoples' Deputies in October 1993 and the overt endorsement of his candidacy in the 1996 presidential elections. Official German government public reticence on the December 1994 invasion of Chechnya and the war that continued until October 1996 is another facet of this policy. While German public opinion was at times vocal in its criticisms of Yeltsin's retreat on democratic reforms, the government itself was supportive, viewing him as the best hope for Russia's further moves toward democracy and guarantor of stability.

Germany, like its EU partners, has also supported Russia's economic transition to a market economy. Beyond financial assistance, it has provided training for Russian business managers and has sponsored a variety of programs to educate the public about how a market works and how the private sector should be run. Germany also hopes to profit economically from its role in Russia's private sector. Germany's other major goal has been to integrate Russia into international economic institutions, convinced that the more anchored it is in the world economy, the more incentive it will have to continue on the path toward reform.

Germany has also been involved in Russia's third transition—from an imperial to a postimperial state. It has sought to influence Moscow's foreign policy by promoting Russia's inclusion in European security structures such as NATO's Partnership for Peace (PfP) program. It has tried to engage Russia in European structures in ways that minimize Central Europe's perception of threats emanating from possible Russian desires to reassert its hegemony in the area. However, Bonn has at times found that the simultaneous pursuit of security and stability for Central Europe, on the one hand, and for Russia, on the other, can be mutually contradictory. What makes Russia more secure often makes Central Europe less secure, and vice versa.

Germany has also encouraged Russia to pursue a policy toward the Commonwealth of Independent States (CIS) that respects their sovereignty, although the Bonn government remains skeptical about the ultimate viability of some of the post-Soviet states, particularly those like Belarus which have sought reintegration with Russia. Nevertheless, Germany, like its NATO partners, has accepted Russia's role as military "peacekeeper" in conflict regions such as Tajikistan, Moldova, or Nagorno-Karabagh because no outside country or multilateral organization is willing to become militarily involved in ethnic conflicts in the former Soviet space.

Germany's objectives in the other CIS states also focus on stabilizing the newly independent countries and minimizing the risks of ethnic or civil strife. From Bonn's perspective, Ukraine is the second most important state after Russia. Bonn was initially wary about whether Ukraine would indeed survive as an independent state, but has more recently become more actively involved in supporting democracy and a market economy in that country. It has also become more involved in Kazakhstan. It has actively participated in the economic and political transformation of the Baltic states and has sought to act as a mediator in some of the disputes between Russia and the Baltics. Germany's degree of interest in the CIS is determined by how important the individual states are to Russia; by their economic resources and their environmental problems; by the presence of a significant ethnic German population, as is the case in Ukraine and

Kazakhstan; and by their potential for adversely affecting European stability, including the question of nuclear weapons.

Thus, Germany's objectives in the post-Soviet states largely derive from its impact as Europe's most powerful economy and from its growing political influence on the continent. Germany can, on some level, take a more distanced, dispassionate view of Russia now than it could during the Cold War, because Russia no longer directly threatens its security. But Russia's indirect ability to destabilize the countries around Germany remains a primary driving force behind Bonn's commitment to promote stability in the region.

German Policies and Outcomes

Politics and Foreign Policy

When Gorbachev, Shevardnadze, and their few domestic allies agreed to German unification and to a united Germany's remaining in NATO, they expected not only an economic payoff for abandoning the sine qua non of their postwar foreign policy but also envisaged a political quid pro quo. They believed that Germany would champion their inclusion in a new European security system, one in which the Soviet Union could still play a major role, despite the demise of the Warsaw Pact. Kohl and his colleagues were aware of this Soviet expectation; they did little to disabuse Gorbachev and his supporters of these hopes, and reiterated their commitment to including the USSR in new European structures.

This promise, however, became increasingly difficult to keep, as Germany focused on the financial and political pressures of integrating Eastern Germany and the USSR disintegrated. By 1992, Russian commentators realized that, in order to even contemplate a new role in Europe, the country had first to confront major domestic and foreign policy challenges. They began to fear that, with unification achieved, Germany would distance itself from Russia, particularly once the troops were withdrawn from Eastern Germany.[6] Indeed, Russia's main concern after 1991 was not of Germany's assertiveness, but of German disinterest. Despite occasional laments about the rise of neo-Nazi movements in Germany, the Russian government was more concerned about engaging Germany than criticizing it.[7] As one analyst soberly noted, "It is very clear that the FRG is far less prepared to cooperate with today's Russia than it was with the former Soviet Union—the most negative influence on the development of our bilateral relations is the situation of political instability and severe, protracted economic crisis in Russia."[8]

Germany, like its Western partners, sought simultaneously to reassure Russia about its continuing interest in bilateral relations and to insulate itself, as far as possible, from the political turmoil throughout the country. It struggled to understand the new Russian dynamics, to find an adequate conceptual basis for comprehending what was happening as Russia embarked on its zigzag, post-Soviet path. In the absence of clear rules of the game or new institutions—let alone understanding of the rapidly evolving chain of command—Germany, like the United States, clung to a familiar aspect of bilateral relations—summitry and the cultivation of close personal ties with the new leadership.

The Kohl administration had begun to deal with Yeltsin even before the breakup of the USSR. Yeltsin made his first state visit as president of Russia to Germany for a summit in November 1991 at which the main items on the bilateral agenda were the withdrawal of Soviet troops and the fate of ethnic Germans in Russia and other republics. Although Kohl's discomfort at welcoming him was evident at the arrival ceremonies, the meeting produced a joint declaration dealing with economic, political, and military questions. Despite skepticism about what Yeltsin's true intentions were and whether he was indeed committed to a consistent reform program, the general German reaction was encouraging.[9]

Initial caution about the Russian president gave way, within a year, to a conviction on the part of the German government that Boris Yeltsin, whatever his flaws as Russia's first democratically elected leader, represented the West's best hope of continuing reform and movement away from communism. In Germany's case, it was particularly important to identify a partner whom Bonn could support as long as Soviet troops remained on its territory. By the December 1992 summit, therefore, the new, personalized bilateral relationship was consolidated. During Kohl's first post-Soviet summit in Moscow, the German chancellor promised additional economic rewards—a new DM 550 million loan, more German involvement in the oil and gas sector, deferral of transfer ruble payments from outstanding GDR-Soviet debts, rescheduling of Russia's debt, most of which was owed to Germany, and more payments of compensation for Nazi victims—in return for an acceleration of the withdrawal of troops by four months, to September 1994.[10] The troop withdrawals proceeded on time, unaffected by the domestic upheavals within Russia. This was a major success story in post-Communist Russian-German relations.

At this summit, Yeltsin also pledged to permit the restoration of the Volga Autonomous Republic so that the two million ethnic Germans who had been exiled during World War II and were living in Siberia and Central Asia would be encouraged to return to what had once been their home. Germany sought to limit immigration because of the economic and social strains of unification and a growing domestic antiforeigner sentiment. But, Yeltsin was not able to fulfill his promise, largely because of opposition among Russians in the Saratov area to the return of large numbers of Germans. However, the desire to find a solution to the plight of ethnic Germans—other than emigration—remained an incentive for continued German involvement in Russia and elicited further millions of marks to encourage the improvement of the material conditions both for ethnic Germans and others in the regions where they lived.[11]

Another longer-term potential source of conflict between Germany and Russia is the future of the Kaliningrad exclave, an issue that has significant implications for European security. Annexed from Germany by the USSR in 1945, the once-productive agricultural region, home to some of Prussia's great Junker families, became a highly militarized Soviet garrison zone and environmental disaster area. But after the collapse of the USSR, the Kaliningrad oblast, which now houses Russia's only warm-water port, is physically separated from Russia, sandwiched between Lithuania and Poland. Given its precarious strategic location and the desire of some Germans originally from the area to assist in its economic development, the Russian government has been particularly sensitive about German attempts to play a more visible role in Kaliningrad.

The German government has reiterated that it has no territorial claims on Kaliningrad. It has given financial assistance to the fifteen thousand ethnic Germans and their families who have relocated to Kaliningrad instead of emigrating to Germany. It has also responded to the call made by the Kaliningrad oblast's former governor, Yuri Matochkin, for the creation of a free economic zone by encouraging German industry to invest in the area. Nevertheless, Russia remains suspicious, and has refused to permit Germany to open a consulate in the area, a request that former Foreign Minister Andrei Kozyrev described as a "relapse into the German urge to the East."[12] Meanwhile, both the Poles and Lithuanians are concerned about heavy Russian troop concentrations in the area, invoking these issues to reinforce their requests for more security guarantees from the West. The Kaliningrad issue, therefore, symbolizes both powerful historical memories on both sides and the difficulties of dealing with post-Soviet geographical realities.[13]

When Yeltsin visited Bonn in May 1994, the Russian president was concerned about whether German interest would wane once Russian troops had withdrawn. Chancellor Kohl went out of his way to reassure his Russian guests that this would not be so.[14] Indeed, new issues of bilateral concern ensured continuing German involvement in Russia because they directly affected Germany—nuclear smuggling and illegal exports of drugs and conventional weapons.[15] These problems, plus an ongoing dispute about cultural artifacts taken by the Soviets from Germany at the end of the war and never returned, were of a different order of magnitude than troop withdrawals, but nevertheless had both material and symbolic importance.[16]

Multilateral Ties

German policy toward Russia involved two tracks—the bilateral and the multilateral. Bonn increasingly sought to Europeanize its relations with Russia, to include it both in European and international structures. This would relieve Germany of what it viewed as a substantial and unlimited economic burden and would possibly curb a reassertion of imperial interests by anchoring Russia firmly in what the Moscow leadership called the "community of civilized nations." Germany had persuaded its G-7 allies to invite Gorbachev to their London summit in 1991, the first time that a Soviet leader had attended such a conference. The concrete economic results were meager, but the political symbolism was important and the Soviet leader gained a Western commitment to granting associate status to the USSR in the IMF and in the World Bank.[17]

After the demise of the Soviet Union, Bonn continued to press its allies to admit Russia to the exclusive club of the world's wealthiest industrial countries—even though, on the face of it, Russia's economic qualifications were dubious. But Germany realized, perhaps more than its partners, that Russia expected to be rewarded for renouncing communism and the Soviet Union and helping to end the Cold War. As Foreign Minister Andrei Kozyrev said early on, "Our choice is . . . to progress according to generally accepted rules. They were invented by the West, and I'm a Westernizer in this respect. The West is rich, we need to be friends with it . . . It's the club of first-rate states Russia must rightfully belong to."[18] Attending the "political" sessions of the G-7 group was equivalent to giving Russia associate membership of the club. The association with the G-7 paid off. It led to new loans, assistance for improving safety conditions at nuclear reactor sites, debt rescheduling, high technology cooperation, and other benefits.[19]

Germany also worked hard to promote ties between Russia and the European Union, emphasizing that its role in Russia as an EU member was as important— if not more so—as its bilateral role. Apart from the EU TACIS and PHARE programs—providing technical and economic assistance to all post-communist states—Germany shepherded the negotiations for an EU-Russia agreement. While Germany championed the association agreements with the Central European countries—a prerequisite for full membership—it recognized that Russia could not hope to join the EU, but could benefit from closer economic ties. The 1994 Partnership and Cooperation Agreement between Russia and the EU was signed in 1994, envisaging a move toward freer trade by 1998.[20] Beyond this agreement, however, the EU has not developed a common Ostpolitik toward Russia. Each country pursues its own economic and political ties with Russia, and there has been little discussion within the EU of formulating a longer-term Ostpolitik, although all member countries share common goals of promoting stability, markets, and democracy. Bilateral ties between member countries and the CIS states continue to determine the parameters of the relationship.

Including Russia in the G-7 and promoting closer ties with the EU went some way toward embedding Russia economically in a wider global and European network; but it did not address the issue of Russia's political role in Europe and its place in an evolving post-communist European security structure. The collapse of the Warsaw Pact and of the Soviet Union created a major dilemma for the emerging Russian state. It had to find a new identity as a nonimperial, major regional power whose interests were determined by nonideological factors, at a time when the rebirth of nationalism and ethnic identity was the central and often destabilizing factor in all of the former communist countries.[21] The most pressing issue was how to conduct relations with the newly independent states that had for centuries been part of the Russian empire and the USSR. The psychological shock of losing the internal Soviet empire and the difficulty of accepting the CIS states as foreign countries is a challenge that will preoccupy generations of post-Soviet Russians. It is an issue over which Germany and other Western states have limited influence, and it became increasingly clear that the West was willing to accept Russia's de facto right to a sphere of influence in the former Soviet states.

European Security and NATO

Germany had more influence, however, over the question of Russia's role in Europe. By the end of 1992, Russia had begun to assert its right to great power status—whatever that meant for an unstable, economically weak country with a vast nuclear arsenal and a military that was in the midst of a major identity crisis.[22] It sought inclusion in the major decision-making structures in Europe. Having lost its old alliances, it sought new partners. The Yeltsin government also grew wary of being isolated while its former Warsaw Pact partners were integrated into the West. Despite Russia's hope that the new Germany would become the harbinger of an inclusive new security system in Europe, it became increasingly clear that it was premature to speak of replacing the old institutions with new ones. Since Germany's postwar rehabilitation and success were so intimately connected with its role in the European community and in NATO, the German government was committed to maintaining and strengthening existing Western institutions, including NATO. But what, if any, was Russia's position in these institutions?

There was no satisfactory German answer to this question because Russia itself was uncertain about where it belonged in Europe. In the absence of a clear vision on both sides of the Atlantic on these questions, the West turned to existing institutions, seeking to devise ways of including the post-communist states in them. Its first act, the creation of the North Atlantic Cooperation Council (NACC) at the December 1991 NATO summit, was to invite all the post-Soviet states (including those not in Europe) to join an ongoing security dialogue at NATO headquarters. However, the NACC was a discussion forum more than an institution promoting security. As the war in the former Yugoslavia spread, as ethnic conflicts on the territory of the former Soviet Union increased, and as aggressively nationalistic rhetoric emanated from certain parts of the Russian political spectrum, the Central European states became increasingly alarmed about their security. Without any collective military organization they felt vulnerable to sudden changes in Russia and sought rapid integration in Western institutions as a means both of protecting themselves against revived Russia imperial ambitions and cementing their own fragile democratic transitions.

Thus, NATO became the focus of discussions on how to integrate the post-communist states into European security structures. The first, American-inspired solution, the Partnership for Peace (PfP) was an attempt to begin the process of enlarging NATO without addressing the question of full NATO membership. Announced at the January 1994 NATO summit, PfP is a military cooperation program involving joint exercises and the possibility of eventual full NATO membership for some. States whose goal was full NATO membership could begin to shape their own military organizations, doctrines, and civil–military relations to conform to NATO standards. Members could not only engage in joint maneuvers, but could consult with NATO in time of crisis.[23] PfP thus provides many of the benefits of NATO membership but without the security guarantees of Article 5 of the NATO treaty ensuring collective defense if a member is attacked. It was an interim solution designed to delay the far more contentious issues of full NATO membership for some—but not all—of the post-communist states.

The Bonn government was divided on the issue of how to include Russia. The central question was and remains: Is it possible to create structures that can simultaneously reassure and satisfy the security needs of both East-Central Europe and Russia? For the Central Europeans, the solution was clear: given centuries of Russian suppression of their independence, full NATO membership was the only guarantee that, in the twenty-first century, they would remain sovereign states able to enjoy full self-determination. Since EU membership would take longer than they had initially hoped, and since the EU could not provide for their military security, NATO was the answer. There were many in the German government, particularly in the Defense Ministry, who concurred with this view. One of the most articulate advocates of NATO enlargement was Defense Minister Volker Ruehe:

> Now that they (Central Europe) have liberated themselves from Soviet hegemony, the time has come to extend the benefits, help them live by Western standards, consolidate democracy and the rule of law. . . . This is the very essence of the concept of extending NATO and the European Union to the East. Without democracy, stability and free market economy, this geographic part of Europe will remain vulnerable to the old problems of conflicting historical resentments, ambitions, and territorial and ethnic disputes. . . . We cannot save reform in Russia by placing reform in Central and Eastern Europe at risk.[24]

This point was not, however, universally accepted. Critics argued that Russia posed less of a threat to Central Europe than at any time in the past three centuries. Expanding NATO to the Polish–Ukrainian border would inevitably provoke a Russian counterreaction and would redivide Europe. This in turn would intensify Russian desires to exert more influence over the CIS states, particularly Ukraine, because of its sense of isolation. There cannot be a truly viable European security system that excludes Russia.[25] Proponents of NATO expansion in the West countered that NATO expansion should be accompanied by a separate treaty between NATO and Russia so as to minimize Russian concerns.[26]

The Russian government and most foreign policy specialists were skeptical about PfP and opposed to NATO expansion. Kozyrev repeatedly warned against NATO enlargement, stressing that an all-European security system should replace NATO.[27] In 1995, he spelled out a more detailed plan for a NATO–Russian partnership involving "a mechanism for consultations at all levels."[28] Kozyrev's successor, Evgenii Primakov, was more outspoken in his criticism of NATO enlargement, as was First Deputy Defense Minister Andrei Kokoshin. Calling NATO expansion "unacceptable," Kokoshin added that "Russia's firm position on nonexpansion of NATO has already yielded certain fruit. It is stimulating differences on this question in political circles in Germany, France, and other countries."[29] Indeed, some Russian political observers believe that NATO enlargement is a consequence of Germany's failure to take the initiative in creating a post-Soviet European security system.

There were significant differences of opinion within the German government about how far to push NATO enlargement and about its very advisability. The Foreign Ministry was more cautious in its advocacy and Chancellor Kohl himself, addressing the Wehrkundetagung in February 1996, advocated moving slowly on expansion, precisely because of its effects on Russia, stressing that Yeltsin had legitimate concerns about what NATO enlargement would mean.[30] These remarks caused considerable debate both within Germany and within the NATO alliance. They also highlighted the fact that Kohl continued to stress Germany's special ties to Russia and its responsibility for promoting stability there. He was also more willing to show official support for Yeltsin's candidacy in the June 1996 presidential election than were President Clinton and other Western leaders.

Thus, four and a half years after the breakup of the USSR, Germany had succeeded in promoting Russia's acceptance into international economic organizations and NATO's Partnership for Peace, and had secured treaties between Russia and the EU and Russian acceptance into the Council of Europe. The question of Russia's future place in European security structures remained, however, unanswered. Russia's participation in the Bosnia Implementation Force (IFOR), which involved Russian troops being subordinate to NATO command and considerable intelligence sharing, indicated that, shorn of rhetoric, and out of the limelight, Russia and NATO could in fact cooperate quite well on the ground. Defense Minister Ruehe recognized this when he offered Russia a "privileged" partnership with NATO but admonished that "it is up to the leaders and people of Russia themselves to make proper choices."[31]

Economic Ties

Germany's most important and direct contribution to post-Soviet Russia has been its role as the largest donor to the NIS. When the USSR collapsed, Germany had committed $52 billion in aid, most of which went to Russia and was

tied to the unification treaties. It involved $23 billion in credit and export guaran-
tees, $11.4 billion in grants, including humanitarian and technical assistance, a
$4.5 billion to a larger G-7 package, $2.4 billion in energy investment projects,
and $10.7 billion to cover the GDR's transfer ruble balance.[32] More contribu-
tions followed, but Germany was reluctant to promise any new aid packages
because of the financial burdens of unification. Since Russia owed more of its
debt to Germany than to any other country, Bonn was wary of making further
loans and was active in seeking to reschedule repayments.[33] The German government also assisted Russia's transition in other ways, particularly in the dismantling of nuclear weapons, building a center to employ Russian nuclear
scientists to deter them from selling their services to Third World countries, and
in working out a new legal system.

The major lesson that Germany, like its Western partners, learned from its
experience with aid was that its impact was marginal, given the enormous economic problems of transition. Certain types of aid—particularly humanitarian
—were quite effective, especially when German officials were able to monitor the
entire process from Germany to the end user. Technical assistance, especially
when carried out on a small scale, was also effective. However, too much of the
initial aid fell into the wrong hands and disappeared down a "black hole," making
its way to offshore bank accounts held both by the old nomenklatura and by the
new rich. The Russians' attitude toward German assistance was ambivalent. On
the one hand, they disliked the humiliation of having to ask for aid. On the other,
they complained that Germany had not given them enough, in view of the concessions they had made during the unification process. Ultimately, German aid
helped Russia to avoid further economic distress; but it could not solve Russia's
economic problems or guarantee a viable transition to a market society.[34]

Private sector involvement in the Russian economy was much more important
in promoting and ensuring a transition to a market economy, and Russian expectations about German firms were initially very high. After all, during the Cold
War, Germany had become Russia's most important trading partner and had
often disagreed with the United States over trade restrictions aimed at the Soviet
Union. But the German private sector proved to be considerably more cautious
than that in the United States after the collapse of the Soviet Union, because of
the unpredictability of developments and the absence of a legal structure and a
commercial code. Bilateral trade fell, although Germany remained Russia's most
important trading partner, accounting for 17 percent of total trade turnover.[35]
There was much business activity and signing of joint venture agreements, but
German firms remained cautious. By 1994 Mercedes-Benz had its largest foreign
dealership in Russia, and East Germans who knew the Soviet market much better
than West Germans were employed in a variety of ways in promoting German–
Russian trade. But the fact remained that delays, uncertainty about the chain of
command, and concern about rising crime, as well as Russia's liquidity problems, were major deterrents. Russian commentators were well aware of the

German hesitation to invest and realized that Russia would first have to put its own economic house in order if it wanted to increase private sector foreign activity.[36]

Germany and the NIS

Ukraine

Although Germany's primary focus has been Russia, it has also become more involved in other post-Soviet states. Ukraine and Kazakhstan are its most important partners, both because of their size and strategic locations and also because they have significant ethnic German minorities. Germany's major concerns have been the destabilizing potential of Ukraine, a country bordering Central Europe, in which the combination of a large nuclear stockpile and potential domestic ethnic conflicts and tensions between Ukraine and Russia could have a major impact on the security of Germany's eastern neighbors and thus on Germany itself. Bonn has also been very concerned about the security implications of huge environmental problems, particularly the safety of the nuclear reactors at Chernobyl and other nuclear power plants which could threaten the health of a billion Europeans.

Germany, like its allies, greeted the breakup of the Soviet Union with a great deal of apprehension. The challenge of unification made it especially sensitive to the impact of potential disruptions from the east on their own stabilizing efforts at home. German leaders were wary of the specter of former party apparatchiks with unknown agendas becoming leaders of post-communist, ethnically diverse, countries, one of whose central motivating forces was anti-Russian nationalism. They were extremely cautious in their initial approaches to Ukraine. But history and geography also propelled them toward involvement in Ukraine.[37] Moreover, Bavaria—in which most of the postwar Ukrainian émigré community in Germany had settled—had embarked on its own program of economic and political ties with Ukraine even before the breakup of the Soviet Union.[38]

Germany's major bilateral concerns focused on persuading the Ukrainians to commit themselves to giving up their weapons and sign the Nuclear Nonproliferation Treaty (NPT), both of which they did in 1994, and on Ukraine's debts. Since Ukraine owed a proportion of the Soviet debt, and Germany was Ukraine's largest creditor, this was a key issue for Bonn. Moreover, the fate of ethnic Germans who had been deported from Ukraine during the war and sought to return was also a major bilateral question.[39] Germany's initial experiences in Ukraine were less than satisfactory because of Ukraine's reluctance both to embark on economic reform and to give up its nuclear weapons. Once Ukraine signed the NPT at the end of 1994, relations between Bonn and Kiev improved. But the difficulties of debt rescheduling and Ukraine's failure to introduce a program of economic reform under President Leonid Kravchuk complicated ties.

Moreover, Kravchuk reneged on an initial promise he had made to resettle ethnic Germans from Central Asia in Ukraine, thus placing pressure on Bonn to admit more immigrants, provoking German threats to cut back on its assistance to Ukraine.[40]

The German government provided aid to Ukraine both as part of the initial unification package in which most of the housing for Soviet soldiers returning from East Germany was to be built in Ukraine and in subsequent negotiations over ethnic Germans, export credits, and training programs for returning soldiers. It also encouraged the EU to offer Ukraine a Partnership and Cooperation agreement in 1994, but insisted that this and other EU and G-7 agreements be linked to Ukrainian promises about improving nuclear power plant safety and closing down reactors at Chernobyl. As Foreign Minister Kinkel said, saving the environment on the territory of the former Soviet Union was "a key concern in German foreign policy."[41] After President Leonid Kuchma's election in 1994, and his commitment to pursue economic reform, the German government was more forthcoming both in bilateral aid and in its support for multilateral efforts in the World Bank and IMF. But it remains cautious because of Ukraine's slow progress in both political and economic reform. The German private sector has also been reticent, although some entrepreneurs have benefited from the close economic links between the GDR and the Ukrainian SSR that existed prior to 1989.

The other major area of German involvement has been in security matters, where the German government has supervised the retraining of officers returning to Ukraine from East Germany and, since 1993, has been involved in a program of bilateral military cooperation. It has also provided financial assistance for dismantling nuclear weapons and transferring them to Russia. Thus, after a tentative start, Germany has made a commitment to support Ukraine's transition. Its degree of activism and influence has been limited by Ukraine's own difficulties in developing a viable national identity and pursuing domestic and foreign policies that move beyond the obsession with Russia. The Ukrainian government and population initially held exaggerated expectations about Germany's enthusiasm and commitment to their independence and prosperity, and were disappointed that Germany was not more forthcoming. But the pace of German activity picked up in 1995 and 1996, as Ukraine appeared more willing to pursue economic reforms and political democratization. Germany is likely to become more involved as Ukraine moves further along in its transition.

Kazakhstan

Bonn's interest in Kazakhstan is a result of issues that are similar to those motivating its activities in Ukraine. The first is Kazakhstan's size and its geostrategic role as a Muslim state on the border of Europe and Asia. The second is the nuclear arsenal remaining on its territory. The third is the population of six hundred thousand ethnic Germans who were deported during the war from the

Volga to Kazakhstan. Even though Kazakhstan does not have the direct potential to threaten European security and stability as do Russia and Ukraine, it could, nevertheless, export half a million unwanted ethnic Germans. Its nuclear arsenal was also a subject of concern. Finally, in contrast to Ukraine, Kazakhstan is a resource-rich country, with oil, gas, and a major potential role in the Caspian Sea basin, one from which German companies could benefit.

President Nursultan Nazarbaev has been quite successful in engaging the West in a dialogue, and in realizing which issues will attract Western attention. Germany's first government assistance to Kazakhstan came in 1993, and most of the financial assistance has been earmarked for modernization programs and for improving the situation of ethnic Germans. Germans—who form the third largest ethnic group after Kazakhs and Russians—have been adversely affected by some of the language legislation and Kazakhization of the country. According to one Russian report, half of the German population has left or is trying to leave.[42] Instead of going to Russia—where the government has been slow to reestablish the Volga Republic—they are migrating to Germany. In 1995, further economic assistance was provided for German cultural revival.[43]

Germany's relations with Kazakhstan remain cautious partly because it has seen few results from its aid program and partly because the process of democratization in Kazakhstan has largely stopped. Nevertheless, geopolitical considerations and concern about emigration of ethnic Germans and about the role of Islam in this part of the world will ensure a continued German role.

New Issues: The Transition from Past to Future

The issues that continue to preoccupy Germany and Russia are largely legacies of the Cold War. However, while these problems persist, they coexist with a growing number of new, post–Cold War issues whose impact has yet to make itself fully felt. Economic and social issues largely beyond the purview of governments—a result of the growing "privatization" of Russian foreign policy—will increasingly affect German–Russian ties.

The first issue in this transitional era is the growing role of Russian companies—especially energy companies—in Germany and the rest of Europe. Gazprom, the Russian gas giant, formerly headed by Prime Minister Viktor Chernomyrdin, has in the past few years entered into a number of joint ventures with European gas companies, particularly Wintershall, a German rival to Ruhrgas which, until recently, dominated energy ties with the former Soviet Union, and the Wintershall–Gazprom partnership is growing. In the future, Gazprom and other Russian energy companies will increase their role in European gas markets and also will become more involved in the European energy infrastructure.

A more diffuse, albeit major issue, is the growing role of Russian organized crime in Germany. Even if one discounts the more lurid tales, it is undeniable that, in major cities like Berlin and Frankfurt, Russian mafias are active and impinge on many aspects of daily German life. Substantial numbers of "new" Russian businessmen, blue-collar migrants, students, and criminals have come to Germany in the past five years. Many are engaged in legitimate activities, but some have exported their organized crime networks and practices. Moreover, a significant portion of Russian flight capital—some of which is the product of money laundering, drug trafficking, and other criminal activities—has found its way into German banks. These large sums of money and the people who control them have the potential to affect German society and financial stability in a number of ways. Thus, complex societal interactions—which governments can only partially control—will influence German–Russian relations in ways that are not amenable to traditional diplomatic solutions.

Probably the biggest question mark that hangs over Russian–German relations as they enter the twenty-first century is the issue of generational change. The men who fought the Cold War and united Germany were products of World War II and their political consciousness was profoundly affected by it. But Gorbachev, Yeltsin, and Kohl are the last of that generation. The Germans who initiated the first steps toward a rapprochement with the USSR in the 1960s and 1970s approached Moscow with a mixture of guilt for the devastation of World War II and a sense of responsibility for making amends. Moreover, Kohl and his generation feel a profound sense of gratitude toward Gorbachev and the Russian people for making unification possible. The older generation in Russia has similarly feared Germans and has also experienced a continuing sense of pride for defeating Germany in 1945, despite the upheavals of Stalinism.

Once this generation is gone, this special relationship will no longer exist. Younger Germans will not feel the same sense of responsibility or engagement in Russia. It could become "just another country," reasonably far away and potentially troublesome. Younger Russians will also have more distanced feelings about Germany. Without the commitment and mutual love–hate relationship that created a powerful symbiosis for their predecessors, the next generation of Russian and German leaders may simultaneously be more detached and more willing to reexamine the entire basis of their relationship.

Prospects

The Germans have realized since 1991 that it is extremely difficult to formulate and implement a coherent foreign and foreign economic policy toward a country in the throes of a major upheaval which itself is still deciding what its role in the former Soviet space and in Europe should be. Yet Russia's size, potential negative impact on European stability—as well as its considerable economic wealth and ultimate potential to play a major, positive international role—will ensure that Germany remains involved. There are few discussions among the German political class similar to those in the United States, where a growing number of politicians and commentators have questioned why America should bother with a weak, unpredictable Russia. The German government and population accept that they do not have the luxury of debating this issue, at least for the present.

In the next few years, Germany will concentrate on issues closer to home—the future of the Maastricht Treaty and the outcome of the European Union's Intergovernmental Conference, which began in 1996. This process will ultimately decide whether the EU will move successfully into the next century, or whether Germany may rethink its role in Europe. Meanwhile, Germany will await developments in Russia before any qualitatively new relationship can emerge from the disorganization of the post-Soviet situation. Russia itself has become more stable since 1992 and has achieved a new foreign policy consensus in which Germany has a significant role.[44] But Russia is also widening its horizons to seek more partnerships in Asia and other areas. Meanwhile, the question of future European security structures will evolve, but tensions with Russia over NATO enlargement and a future NATO–Russian partnership will continue. Determining Russia's place in a post-communist Europe is a matter of decades, not years.

Germany and Russia will undoubtedly play a more assertive role in the Europe of the twenty-first century. Despite all the problems connected with integrating eastern Germany and dealing with an unpredictable Russia, Germany is committed to building a partnership with Russia and to promoting stability in the post-Soviet states. But as new economic and social issues interact with more traditional security concerns and begin to determine the future of the relationship, it is inevitable that the old ties that bind Germany and Russia will become weaker. The end of the twentieth century leaves us with more questions than answers as we contemplate the future relationship between Berlin and Moscow.

Notes

1. Conversation between Leonid Brezhnev and Erich Honecker, 28 July 1970, in Jochen Staadt, *Auf hoechster Stufe: Gespraeche mit Erich Honecker* (Berlin: Transit, 1995), pp. 13–14.

2. For descriptions of these developments and of the importance of personal relationships, see Horst Teltschik, *329 Tage: Innenansichten der Einigung* (Berlin: Siedler Verlag, 1991); Mikhail Gorbachev, *Zhizn' i Reformy* (Moscow: Novosti, 1995), vol. 2, chap. 22.

3. For the text of the treaty see Karl Kaiser, ed., *Deutschlands Vereinigung* (Bergisch Gladbach: Gustav-Lubbe Verlag, 1991), pp. 260–68.

4. See Hanns Maull, "Grossmacht Deutschland: Annmerkung und Thesen," in *Die Zukunft der deutschen Aussenpolitik,* ed. Karl Kaiser and Hanns Maull (Bonn: Europa-Union Verlag, 1993), pp. 53–72.

5. See Angela Stent, "Between Moscow and Bonn: East-Central Europe in Transition," in Congress of the United States, Joint Economic Committee, *East-Central European Economies in Transition* (Armonk, NY: M.E. Sharpe, 1995).

6. Sergei Karaganov, "Vizit Kanzlera: Konets Pauzy?" *Moskovskie novosti,* 14 December 1992.

7. "Kozyrev warnt vor nationalistischen Stimmungen in bieden Laendern," *Frankfurter Allgemeine Zeitung (FAZ),* October 1992.

8. K. Viatkin, "Rossiia i Germaniia: Potentsial sotrudnichestva," *Mirovaia ekonomika i mezhdunarodnie otnosheniia,* no. 4 (1994): p. 104.

9. Iurii Shpakov, "Trudnyi gost'," *Moskovskie novosti,* 1 December 1991; for the text of the agreements, see "Besuch des Praesidentem von Russland," *Bulletin* (Bonn), no. 133 (25 November 1991): pp. 1081–88.

10. Statement of Chancellor Kohl to the Moscow press, in *Bulletin* (Bonn), no. 139 (22 December 1992): p. 1268.

11. See Pavel Shinkarenko, "Nemsti na Volge," *Rossiiskie vesti,* 4 August 1992; *Die Welt,* 1 March 1993.

12. *Der Spiegel,* 21 March 1993, p. 145.

13. For a broader discussion of these issues, see *Die Zukunft des Gebiets Kaliningrad (Koenigsberg)* (Cologne: Bundesinstitut fuer ostwissenschaftliche und internationale Studien, 1993).

14. German Information Center (New York), "The Week in Germany," 13 May 1994; *Nezavisimaia gazeta,* 11, 13, and 18 May 1994.

15. *Economist,* 20 August 1994.

16. For a Russian view of the dispute of cultural artifacts, see interview with Deputy Minister of Culture Mikhail Schvidkoi in *Suedeutsche Zeitung,* 11–12 May 1994.

17. See Heinrich Vogel, "The London Summit and the Soviet Union," *Aussenpolitik* (English ed.) 42, no 4 (1991): pp. 315–25.

18. Interview with Andrei Kozyrev, *Moscow News,* no. 23 (7–14 June 1992): p. 14.

19. See "Wirtschaftsgipfel Tokio: Politische Erklaerung," in *Bulletin* (Bonn), 16 July 1993; *Welt Am Sonntag,* 10 July 1994.

20. Interview with Boris Yeltsin, Moscow Radio, 24 June 1994, in *FBIS-SOV-94–123,* 27 June 1994, p. 5.

21. For a more extensive discussion of these themes, see Angela Stent, Thane Gustafson, and Daniel Yergin, "The Return of Great Power," in *Russia 2010,* ed. Daniel Yergin and Thane Gustafson (New York: Vintage, 1994), chap. 15.

22. For a discussion of the various Russian interpretations of "great power" status, see Hannes Adomeit, "Russia as a Great Power," *International Affairs* (London) 71, no. 1 (January 1995): pp. 35–68.

23. For more details of the program, see Catherine McArdle Kelleher, *The Future of European Security* (Washington, DC: Brookings, 1995), chap. 4.

24. Volker Ruehe, "America and Europe: Common Challenges and Common Answers," lecture at Georgetown University, 2 March 1995, pp. 9–10.

25. For a summary of the main arguments for and against NATO expansion, see Council on Foreign Relations Task Force, *Should NATO Expand?* (New York: Council on Foreign Relations, 1995).

26. See Ronald Asmus, Richard Kugler, and F. Stephen Larrabee, "NATO Expansion: The Next Steps," *Survival* 37, no. 1 (Spring 1995): pp. 7–33.

27. Andrei Kozyrev, "Obshcheevropeiskoe partnerstvo," *Nezavisimaia gazeta,* 2 March 1994.

28. Andrei Kozyrev, "Partnership or Cold Peace?" *Foreign Policy,* no. 99 (Summer 1995): p. 14.

29. *Krasnaia zvezda,* 7 February 1996.

30. Helmut Kohl, speech to the thirty-third Munich Conference on Security Policy, reprinted in *Bulletin,* no. 15 (14 February 1996): pp. 165–268.

31. Volker Ruehe, "The New NATO," speech at the Johns Hopkins School of Advanced International Studies, 30 April 1996, reprinted in *Statements and Speeches* (German Information Center: New York) 19, no. 7, p. 4.

32. German Information Center (New York), "German Support for the Transition to Democracy and Market Economy in the Former Soviet Union," June 1992.

33. The Deutsche Bank has been leading rescheduling negotiations in the London Club. In November 1995, it was agreed that Russia could extend the repayment of its main $25.5 billion debt for twenty-five years. *FAZ,* 18 November 1995.

34. For a fuller discussion of these issues, see Angela Stent, "Russia's Economic Revolution and the West," *Survival* 37, no. 1 (Spring 1995): pp. 121–43.

35. Vyacheslav Kevorkov, "Rossiia-Germaniia: Padenie ob´emov tovarooborota," *Izvestiia,* 14 October 1993; *FAZ,* 11 May 1994.

36. For a fuller discussion of these issues, see Sergei Karaganov, *Whither Western Aid to Russia* (Guetersloh, Germany: Bertelsmann Foundation Publishers, 1994), p. 28.

37. Ukraine and Germany have had a complicated historical relationship, particularly in the twentieth century, when some Ukrainian groups collaborated with the Nazis in seeking to defeat Soviet Communism. See Frank Golczewski, "Die Ukraine im Zweiten Weltkrieg," in *Geschichte der Ukraine,* ed. Frank Golczewski (Göttingen: Vandenhoeck und Ruprecht, 1993).

38. Interview with German Interior Minister (and Bavarian patriot) Edmund Stoiber, *Die Welt,* 2 May 1992.

39. Vladimir Sergeichuk, "Nemtsy v Ukraine," *Pravda Ukrainy,* 14 March 1992.

40. *Der Spiegel,* no. 11 (1993): p. 148; *Sueddeutsche Zeitung,* 16 March 1993.

41. *FAZ,* 22 June 1994.

42. *Izvestiia,* 12 April 1994.

43. "Almaty Kazakh television first Program Network in Russian," 26 June 1995, in *FBIS-SOV-95-123.*

44. For an elaboration of these themes, see Angela Stent and Lilia Shevstova, "Russia's Election: No Turning Back," *Foreign Policy* (Summer 1996): pp. 92–109.

10

German and American Assistance to the Post-Soviet Transition

Peter Dombrowski

Since the collapse of the Soviet Union in 1992, the United States and Germany have provided Russia and the other newly independent states (NIS) of the former Soviet Union (FSU) with billions of dollars in assistance.[1] Both countries have pursued a three-track strategy for channeling economic assistance to the region.[2] First, both reorganized their foreign assistance programs to route bilateral funds to the transitional economies. Second, both helped mobilize international assistance through multilateral organizations (the International Monetary Fund, World Bank Group, and the European Union) and the bilateral programs of other members of the Organization for Economic Cooperation and Development (OECD).[3] Third, both used official trade and investment promotion programs to encourage private firms to conduct business in the region. Given space limitations, this chapter analyzes bilateral assistance programs rather than the entire range of German and American support for the transition.[4]

By many measures American and German bilateral assistance programs have been successful. Germany and the United States rank as the first and second largest official bilateral donors in terms of monies committed and disbursed.[5] Several individual programs have met or exceeded initial objectives. Germany's housing construction for ex-Soviet troops formerly stationed in eastern Germany, for example, built more housing units than were originally planned. American programs for dismantling and safeguarding nuclear weapons have helped reduce the dangers of proliferation.[6] Multilateral assistance programs have played important roles in stabilizing economic crises and financing the transformation process.[7] Although private firms have been reluctant to commit resources to the region as a whole, individual newly independent states and specific economic sectors have benefited from international trade and investment.

Important differences can be discerned in the two countries' bilateral pro-

Table 10.1

German Official Net Bilateral Disbursements to the Newly Independent States (in millions of U.S.$)

	1991	1992	1993	1994	Disbursements per capita (dollars), 1994
Armenia	—	—	0.5	3.1	0.84
Azerbaijan	—	—	0.8	2.9	0.39
Belarus	184.0	244.0	465.5	285.5	27.45
Georgia	—	—	15.3	188.0	34.81
Kazakhstan	111.5	4.9	275.2	275.8	16.42
Kyrgyzstan	—	—	—	2.3	0.51
Moldova	—	—	2.9	−0.5	—
Russia	520.0	1501.6	9,087.5	6,024.7	40.60
Tajikistan	—	—	0.7	0.6	0.10
Turkmenistan	—	—	—	22.7	5.16
Ukraine	364.9	538.8	894.9	448.4	8.64
Uzbekistan	—	—	—	11.7	0.52
Unallocated	521.9	188.7	815.3	17.7	—
Total	1,702.3	2,478.0	11,558.6	7,282.9	25.5

Sources: Adapted from Organization for Economic Cooperation and Development, *Aid and Other Resource Flows to the Central and Eastern European Countries and the New Independent States of the Former Soviet Union (1990–94)* (Paris: OECD, 1996), annex Tables 11 and 13, pp. 41, 43; and Organization for Economic Cooperation and Development, *Aid and Other Resource Flows to the Central and Eastern European Countries and the New Independent States of the Former Soviet Union in 1991 and 1992* (Paris: OECD, 1994), Tables 7 and 8, pp. 14–15.

Note: Disbursements per capita for 1994 (column 5) were arrived at by dividing the official net bilateral disbursement for each country by the 1994 population of that country.

grams. Both Germany and the United States have claimed to promote the emergence of popularly elected, market-oriented regimes with their official assistance programs. In practice, they have each pursued specific foreign policy objectives in addition to the underlying goal of regime transformation.[8] Policy objectives in both countries have changed over time, initially in response to the dissolution of the Soviet Union, then in response to crises such as the coup against the Yeltsin government, the halting pace of reform, and the emergence of a less Western-oriented Russian foreign policy.

Aggregate assistance figures are especially revealing (see Tables 10.1 and 10.2). Germany has disbursed more money but it has concentrated on programs related to the unification process. The United States has disbursed less in the aggregate, but it has devoted more resources to the transition itself. More U.S. assistance has been in the form of grants, while Germany has offered relatively more credits. Although each country has channeled large amounts of assistance

Table 10.2

American Official Net Bilateral Disbursements to the Newly Independent States (in millions of U.S.$)

	1991	1992	1993	1994	Disbursements per capita (dollars), 1994
Armenia	—	16.0	62.0	86.0	23.24
Azerbaijan	—	—	—	13.0	1.73
Belarus	—	22.0	74.0	27.0	2.60
Georgia	—	—	72.0	53.0	9.81
Kazakhstan	—	2.0	9.0	12.0	0.71
Kyrgyzstan	—	1.0	59.0	22.0	4.89
Moldova	—	9.0	25.0	21.0	4.77
Russia	—	26.0	1,158.0	174.0	1.17
Tajikistan	—	10.0	17.0	18.0	3.10
Turkmenistan	—	5.0	24.0	13.0	2.95
Ukraine	—	8.0	67.0	99.0	1.91
Uzbekistan	—	—	1.0	4.0	0.18
Unallocated	3.0	94.0	359.0	728.0	—
Total	3.0	193.0	1,927.0	1,270.0	4.45

Sources: Adapted from Organization for Economic Cooperation and Development, *Aid and Other Resource Flows to the Central and Eastern European Countries and the New Independent States of the Former Soviet Union (1990–94)* (Paris: OECD, 1996), annex Tables 11 and 13, pp. 41, 43; and Organization for Economic Cooperation and Development, *Aid and Other Resource Flows to the Central and Eastern European Countries and the New Independent States of the Former Soviet Union in 1991 and 1992* (Paris: OECD, 1994), Tables 7 and 8, pp. 14–15.

Note: Disbursements per capita (dollars) for 1994 were arrived at by dividing the official net American disbursement for each country by the 1994 population of that country.

to the Russian Federation, the Clinton administration has increasingly shifted its commitments to Ukraine.[9]

Despite their successes, German and American programs have not met the expectations of some advocates of Western assistance.[10] Less money has been disbursed than was promised. Assistance has often been tied to securing commercial and political benefits. Coordination within and between programs has been limited. Some critics in Germany, the United States, and the recipient countries claim that too much (or too little!) assistance has been conditioned on policy performance goals.

Meanwhile, political developments in both the donor and recipient countries have weakened the domestic consensus for funding assistance programs; as a result, the size and scope of both German and American assistance programs have been reduced in the last several years. Even more to the point, despite bilateral and multilateral assistance programs, the political and economic transformations remain fragile and, at times, appear threatened by domestic instabilities, leading some politicians and commentators to question the appropriateness of assistance programs.

Why have German and American bilateral assistance strategies not met the initial expectations of either the donors or the recipients? This chapter argues that differences in timing, types, and quantity of each country's assistance can be understood only with reference to both the international and domestic levels of analysis.[11] Neither the evolving international environment during the collapse of the Soviet Union nor subsequent internal political developments in both donor and recipient countries alone can explain the performance of bilateral assistance programs. Viewed together, however, they can help explain the successes and failures of American and German programs.

To illustrate this argument, this chapter examines the negotiation, ratification, and implementation of the key decisions underpinning U.S. and German assistance programs:[12] the Freedom Support Act of 1992 in the United States and the economic components of the German-Soviet Treaty on Good Neighborly Relations, Partnership, and Cooperation in 1991.[13] It does not, however, provide a comprehensive account of all German and American programs implemented during the post-1989 period. The analysis begins with German assistance programs because they preceded and influenced those of the United States and other donors.

Treaty on Good Neighborly Relations, Partnership, and Cooperation

Germany's initial response to glasnost and perestroika in the late 1980s was cautious optimism. German officials recognized opportunities in the gradual changes taking place in the Soviet Union earlier than their counterparts in the United States. Especially in Central and Eastern European Countries (CEEC), Germany sought to extend the complex web of political, economic, and social interactions that had characterized German foreign policy since the emergence of Ostpolitik under Chancellor Willy Brandt.

Initially, the Kohl government's willingness to exploit opportunities in the CEEC did not extend to the German Democratic Republic (GDR) or to the Soviet Union.[14] Few believed Gorbachev's reforms would lead to regime change in GDR, much less unification. Some critics have even charged that the Kohl government was too willing to support the status quo in its sister state.[15] This bias extended to the Soviet Union; for decades the German foreign policy establishment had recognized that the keys to stability in the CEEC lay in Moscow. As Gorbachev's "new thinking" gained the upper hand, German foreign policy specialists remained conscious of the Soviet military forces stationed in the GDR.

In 1989 the German government was shaken by events in Poland and Hungary; massive emigration and large demonstrations in major cities highlighted the

GDR's political and economic bankruptcy. Chancellor Kohl, prodded by Foreign Minister Hans Dieter Genscher and advisors such as Horst Telchick, was among the first to recognize that a historic moment was at hand. Once Kohl became convinced that the Soviet Union would not interfere with the ongoing revolutions, he began contemplating unification. His political situation encouraged an active strategy; with elections upcoming and strong challenges to the Christian Democratic Union (CDU) from the Social Democratic Party and the Republikaners, Kohl hoped for foreign policy successes to boost his campaign.[16]

The most visible sign of Kohl's shift came when the Ten Point Plan for unification was announced on 28 November 1989. By envisioning a gradual unification process proceeding over seven to ten years, the Kohl government became the driving force behind unification and the terms under which it took place. As the following discussion will make clear, the German–Soviet economic arrangements that emerged from the unification process laid the groundwork for German financial assistance to the Soviet Union and then the former Soviet republics including, most importantly, Russia.[17]

Negotiation Stage

In June 1989 Helmut Kohl and Mikhail Gorbachev had negotiated the Bonn Declaration—eleven substantive agreements on trade, investment, hot-line arrangements, and other issues. The specific agreements are less significant for our purposes than a private conversation reported to have taken place between the two leaders. Here Chancellor Kohl first raised the issue of unification. Gorbachev responded not with alarm, but with concern for his country's economic difficulties and with a question: Would the Chancellor respond favorably to a request for urgent economic help if he, Mikhail Gorbachev, asked?[18]

Although the accuracy of Kohl's remembrances are open to debate, something momentous clearly had occurred. Each had apparently acknowledged his primary objective—unification for Kohl, reviving the Soviet Union for Gorbachev—and each did not shrink from the implications of the other's position. In effect, the two leaders opened the door to sustained negotiations over the conditions for reunifying Germany.

Over the next year discussions devoted to economic assistance were sporadic. Periodically, Eduard Schevardnadze, Gorbachev's foreign minister, or one of Gorbachev's other deputies would ask for new assistance or remind the Germans that past promises should be kept. In the midst of the GDR crisis of January 1990, for example, Shevardnadze pressed Bonn to honor what Gorbachev believed was Chancellor Kohl's June 1989 offer of assistance. Chancellor Kohl then arranged for the Agriculture Ministry to ship 152,000 tons of foodstuffs to the Soviet Union at highly subsidized prices.[19] In May 1990, Prime Minister Ryzhokov pressed Chancellor Kohl for hard currency credits and as much as DM

20 billion in long-term assistance.[20] One Soviet expert on German affairs, Nikolia Portugalov, aptly if unofficially, summarized the period:

> I won't mince my words: We hope that the partnership—indeed friendship—with united Germany, that the German economy, and Germany private investments will save us from the catastrophe that threatens us.[21]

Soviet motivations for asking for German assistance were more complex than indicated by Portugalov, however. Obviously, on the most straightforward level, the Gorbachev regime needed to muddle through the mounting economic crisis—hard currency could help postpone the possibility of collapse. Gorbachev and his inner circle also needed something to show for agreeing to German unification. After all, the Soviet Union would be giving up its most visible spoil of World War II. On a deeper level, Gorbachev may still have hoped to reform socialism and save the Communist Party by transforming the Soviet Union from within. German funds could help buy more time for glasnost and perestroika to overcome the forces of resistance within the Soviet state and the Communist Party.

In mid-July Chancellor Kohl and Secretary Gorbachev held a series of bilateral meetings in Moscow and then Zheleznovodsk in the Caucasus. Kohl and Gorbachev first met in Moscow to discuss the details of a Treaty of Cooperation and Friendship between the USSR and Germany. Discussions involved the future of NATO, the military status of a newly unified Germany, and the removal of Soviet troops from the GDR. Gorbachev's deputy prime minister, Stepan Sitaryan, and Theo Waigel, the German finance minister, discussed economic matters.[22] Little was accomplished, however, as Waigel reiterated Germany's unwillingness to offer further economic assistance aside from the multilateral pledges of early July and the amounts already offered by Germany over the last twelve months. For his part, Sitaryan stressed the severe financial crisis facing the Soviet Union.

In Zheleznovodsk, Kohl and Gorbachev focused on economic issues in addition to continuing negotiations on NATO and other bilateral questions. They agreed to discuss the GDR's financial obligations and future German support for Gorbachev's internal reforms at a later date.[23] Some reports suggest that Kohl also promised DM 1.25 billion to offset the cost of Soviet troops in the GDR and another DM 220 million in food subsidies.[24] Although they agreed that the forthcoming cooperation treaty should settle financial considerations, neither mentioned this in his final press statement.

Final discussions over German financial obligations to the Soviet Union began in August 1990.[25] Participants met under the pressure of completing bilateral German–Soviet arrangements prior to signing the Two-Plus-Four Agreement on 12 September. Negotiations involved the "interim stationing and status" of Soviet troops in the former GDR and the "transition treaty on financial arrangements for withdrawing Soviet forces."[26]

A decisive exchange occurred on 27 August.[27] Shevardnadze wrote to Genscher claiming that it was technically impossible for the Soviet military to withdraw from the GDR within the three to four year period envisioned earlier; he argued that it might take more than five years. By Shevardnadze's account, Gorbachev's earlier promise had been contingent on large-scale Western assistance that had not materialized. Moreover, security guarantees written into the prospective treaties were inadequate. In short, Gorbachev played his trump card—Soviet troops stationed in Germany—at the most propitious moment, barely a month before the final Two-Plus-Four agreement.

Over the next week, the Soviet Union increased the pressure on Kohl's foreign policy team by gradually escalating their demands. On 5 September the Soviet ambassador delivered an itemized list of expectations that totaled DM 36 billion (about $20 billion). Only months before, German economic officials had projected Soviet costs at only DM 4.25 million over four years.

With this, the two leaders resumed personal diplomacy. On 7 September Chancellor Kohl and Secretary Gorbachev haggled over the exact amount of assistance necessary to ensure the orderly withdrawal of Soviet troops from the GDR. Circumstances favored Gorbachev's position because of (1) the Soviet troops in the GDR and (2) the German chancellor's political stake in the Two-Plus-Four agreement. Yet even as Gorbachev threatened to abandon the process, Kohl remained reluctant to meet Soviet demands.[28]

Ultimately, however, Chancellor Kohl sweetened the DM 12 billion figure arrived at by Waigel with an interest free DM 3 billion credit. He also hinted that Germany would provide economic assistance to the Soviet Union in the future. As Philip Zelikow and Condoleezza Rice conclude: "Overwhelmed by events and eager to achieve a quick settlement with Moscow, the West Germans did not mount an effective resistance when, finally, Moscow named a price."[29] The figure agreed upon by Kohl formed the basis for German bilateral assistance to the Soviet Union and its legal successor, Russia.

Ratification Stage

Ratification of Germany's bilateral settlement with the Soviet Union was swift. On 30 October 1990 the Bundestag approved the treaty governing the fate of Soviet troops on the territory of the former GDR. In particular, they agreed to the Kohl–Gorbachev plan to withdraw all Soviet troops from inside unified Germany by the end of 1994.[30] In return, the Bundestag appropriated DM 13.5 billion, ostensibly to cover the costs associated with maintaining and withdrawing the Soviet troops in the former GDR.

On 2 December 1990, the first post–World War II all-German elections confirmed public support for the policies of the Kohl government, including arrangements with the Soviet Union. The CDU/CSU/FDP alliance won a major victory in both the western Länder and the former GDR. The only major party that had opposed quick unification, the Green Party, failed to meet the 5 percent threshold necessary to remain in the Bundestag.[31] Interestingly, the SPD, the mass party alternative to Kohl's CDU/CSU/FDP coalition and policies, offered, and continues to offer, only muted criticisms of Kohl's unification policies and, more important for this chapter, the general thrust of the Federal Republic's policies toward Russia and bilateral assistance programs.

Implementation Stage

In 1990 nearly 550,000 Soviet citizens (approximately 340,000 soldiers and their civilian dependents) were living in the former GDR.[32] Implementation of the German–Soviet Good Neighbor Treaty depended upon their return to the Soviet Union by December 1994. The return of so many troops to the Soviet Union presented an enormous practical problem: given existing housing shortages and financial difficulties, where would the returnees live? In the Treaty on Good Neighborly Relations, the Federal Republic had agreed to construct housing for demobilized soldiers once stationed in the GDR.

Germany had promised to build 36,000 housing units (4 million square meters) at a cost of DM 7.8 billion and pledged an additional DM 200 million to be spent on training programs for demobilized Russian officers. Early on, officials associated housing construction with officer training programs because they believed that demobilized Soviet soldiers might work in the housing sector.[33] In December 1992, Chancellor Kohl offered an additional DM 550 million to accelerate the final withdrawal date from 31 December 1994 to 31 August 1994.[34]

In less than five years Germany built over 45,000 housing units in Russia, Ukraine, and Belarus.[35] More units were built than were originally promised for slightly more money than originally planned. Individual housing projects were completed on time and according to Soviet-era specifications.[36] When it became clear that preparing demobilized Soviet officers to serve in the housing sector was impractical, they were trained in computer literacy, business management and other potentially marketable skills. By 19 December 1994, Germany had trained over 3,000 ex-Soviet officers and built nine training centers in cities including Moscow and St. Petersburg.[37]

Although the Housing Construction Program was not the largest German program in terms of deutsche marks spent or the one most directly related to German support for the post-communist transition, it was of practical and symbolic importance to the Soviet (then post-Soviet) leaders and the international community as a whole. From an international perspective, the program was "Germany's contribution to the restructuring of Russia's military posture . . . which is in its own but also European interest."[38] Moreover, Germany's Housing Construction Program was unique among bilateral assistance programs.[39]

Table 10.3

German Bilateral Disbursements and Commitments to the Former Soviet Union (in billions of U.S.$)

Subsidies and unilateral transfers:

Support for troop withdrawal and aid for reintegration	10.3
Humanitarian aid	2.5
Consultations, training, and other technical aid	0.6

Credits, credit guarantees, and Hermes credit guarantees:

Guarantees for untied credits	5.6
Hermes export guarantees	23.7
Development aid	0.1
Multilateral debt restructuring	8.8

Transfer ruble balance:

Settlement of claims by the former GDR or the five eastern Länder resulting from foreign trade agreements with the former Soviet Union	14.7

Cost of financing investment projects:

Yamburg (natural gas) and Krivoi Rog (ore) projects	2.5

Total: 68.8

Source: German Information Center, "German Support for the Reform Process in the Former Soviet Union and the Countries of Central, Southeastern and Eastern Europe" (New York: German Information Center, March 1995), pp. 1–2.

Note: All DM figures have been calculated in U.S. dollars at rate of DM 1.40.

Aftermath

According to official German sources, between 1989 and early 1995 Germany provided over DM 100 billion (about $71 billion) in grants, credits, export guarantees, and transfer ruble balances to the former Soviet Union (see Table 10.3). Over $68 billion was direct bilateral assistance to the newly independent states.[40] Much of this sum was associated with the German–Soviet settlement during the unification process—the Housing Construction Project, the Transfer Ruble Program, and the Yamburg/Krivoi Rog industrial projects. For example, "of the $2.5 billion in official assistance disbursed in 1993, $1.5 billion" related to "obligations undertaken in the context of German unification."[41]

With the fluidity of the Soviet–Russian political situation and the relative paucity of international support for the post-communist transition, Germany quickly tired of bearing a disproportionate share of the bilateral assistance burden. The costs of unification were already straining the Federal Republic's fiscal situation—most accounts suggest that since unification the Federal Republic has spent a minimum of DM 100 million each year on the five eastern Länder. Thus, as early as 1991,[42] it began strongly encouraging other bilateral donors, the European Union (EU), and the international financial institutions to assume larger burdens. At the Tokyo Summit in mid-1993 Chancellor Kohl pressed more publicly for greater contributions from the United States and Japan.[43]

By December 1993, however, Germany began demonstrating signs that it was impatient with developments in the successor states and Boris Yeltsin's Russia in particular. New bilateral assistance programs and disbursements were not forthcoming. Eventually, other countries even began asking Germany to contribute more. For example, after traveling to Russia, Kyrgyzstan, and Kazakhstan following the strong showing of Vladimir Zhirinovsky's Liberal-Democratic Party in the Russia's parliamentary elections, Vice President Al Gore stopped in Bonn for consultations with Helmut Kohl. American accounts suggest that Gore attempted without success to convince Kohl to increase German assistance to the Yeltsin government.[44] Chancellor Kohl's developing personal relationship with Boris Yeltsin and his financial incentives to speed up the Soviet troop withdrawal[45] were important symbolically, but they could not substitute for increased German bilateral assistance to the transition.

With the major assistance projects associated with unification coming to a close, Germany has declined to initiate major new bilateral programs. Aside from technical assistance,[46] decreasing amounts of export and investment credits,[47] and its share of multilateral debt relief,[48] Germany now contributes relatively little direct bilateral assistance. It apparently prefers to contribute indirect assistance through the international financial institutions (IFI), the European Bank for Reconstruction and Development (EBRD), and the European Union's TACIS program. Indeed, Germany has been a vigorous internal advocate of stronger EU–Russian relations (including EU assistance programs).[49]

Some German officials suggest that the Federal Republic's relatively modest postunification bilateral commitment to the newly independent states can be attributed to a conscious effort to subordinate German policies to those of the European Union.[50] Although this observation may understate the roles of domestic budget problems and lingering uncertainties about the Yeltsin government in determining German bilateral assistance policies, it does suggest the interconnectedness of German and European preferences with regard to the FSU.[51] It also calls into question common distinctions between the "private" goods associated with bilateral assistance programs and the "public" goods associated with multilateral assistance policies. At least with regard to German-EU-NIS relations, the public goods accruing from EU programs may substitute for the private goods achieved by bilateral policies.

Finally, if the Kohl government's push for unification dominated its initial allocation of bilateral assistance to the Soviet Union, more traditional political and economic factors have motivated Germany's policies toward Russia and the other newly independent states. On the economic side, Germany has been interested in the region's emerging markets, postunification relations between the former Council for Mutual Economic Assistance (CMEA) countries and the eastern Länder, possible access to raw materials, and new investment opportunities based on inexpensive labor.[52] Yet because German economic relations with Russia remain underdeveloped, some analysts have concluded that "without a stabilization of the economic situation, without sufficient progress toward the transformation of the economic and political systems and without permanent structural change no enduring upturn in foreign economic relations is possible."[53] Moreover, they believe the transformation task "is one that Russia must accomplish itself."[54] If this attitude is common among German policy elites, it may help explain the Federal Republic's emphasis on the political aspects of assistance—efforts to integrate Russia into European-wide institutions, completing programs associated with unification, and providing for ethnic Germans living in NIS territories[55]—over large-scale bilateral programs designed to support the transition.

In contrast to Germany's sometimes lukewarm support for the Soviet successor states and the Yeltsin government in particular, the United States accelerated its own bilateral assistance programs following Gorbachev's demise. With the Freedom Support Act and the Nunn-Lugar programs, the United States initiated a series of major programs which, barring unforeseen political crises, will continue at least to the turn of the century.[56]

The Freedom Support Act

As Mikhail Gorbachev's reforms helped unleash the "velvet" revolutions in central and eastern Europe and undermined internal support for his own regime, the Bush administration wrestled with how to encourage change without being prematurely optimistic.[57] Even as Germany negotiated its assistance in the context of unification in 1989 and 1990, President Bush rebuffed Gorbachev's initial pleas for economic assistance.[58] Beginning in 1989 Mikhail Gorbachev began asking for U.S. economic assistance with increasing desperation.[59] Yet until relatively late in the Bush presidency—following the failed coup and the beginning of the American presidential campaign—Soviet and then NIS requests fell on unsympathetic ears. One official advising a more aggressive strategy may have been Ambassador Jack Matlock in Moscow; he had concluded by early 1989 that it "was the time to bring our economic might to bear," especially with regard to Soviet energy production, agriculture, and space technology.[60] He stopped well short, however, of advocating large amounts of U.S. bilateral assistance.

Negotiation Stage

According to James Baker, a turning point in the Bush administration's approach to the Soviet Union, a switch "from confrontation to dialogue, to cooperation," followed his one-on-one meeting at Jackson Hole with Soviet Foreign Minister Eduard Schevardnadze in September 1989.[61] Soon thereafter Baker began arguing that the administration wanted the "true revolution" of perestroika to succeed, but that this was possible only through the efforts of the Soviet themselves. For Baker, a new Soviet–American relationship could then emerge from a search for "mutual advantages" in a free Europe, reduced regional conflict, the transformation of Soviet society, and U.S. technical assistance for economic reforms.

The first concrete opportunity to implement this new thinking came at the Malta Summit in December 1989. President Bush presented a list of propositions including promises to move "beyond containment" by granting most-favored nation (MFN) status to the Soviet Union, asking Congress to remove legislative prohibitions against offering the Soviet Union credits, and sponsoring the Soviet Union for observer status at the General Agreement on Tariffs and Trade (GATT).[62] When Gorbachev then asked for economic support for perestroika, Bush responded with a qualified yes: indirect support was possible, but direct aid was not yet feasible. Some argue that Bush feared that Gorbachev would ask for direct assistance, so he forestalled the possibility by praising the Soviet leadership's opposition to "handouts."[63] The Bush administration offered only modest amounts of humanitarian and technical assistance while promising to normalize U.S.–Soviet economic relations by removing Cold War restrictions on trade and investment. Gorbachev apparently returned home believing "he had won Bush's support for his program" and used this to his advantage within the Politburo.[64]

The next development in the negotiations stage was the decision to move beyond economic normalization, humanitarian aid, and technical assistance to a full-fledged program of economic assistance. The process was exceedingly slow and by no means preordained. Between the Malta Summit in 1989 and the early 1992 legislative proposal that became the Freedom Support Act, the United States vacillated on assistance depending, in part, on the evolving Soviet political situation. Jack Matlock, the American ambassador to the Soviet Union, summarized the administration's mood in deploring "the swing to the right in Gorbachev's political behavior that began in 1990 . . . [and the] . . . frequent vacillation between reform and reaction—between liberals and hard-liners—and the obvious efforts to appease the hard-liners."[65]

After the August coup hastened the demise of the Soviet Union and signaled Russian president Boris Yeltsin's ascendancy, the official American attitude toward direct assistance shifted. When Baker met with Yeltsin in February 1992, he found that the Russian president had "staked his personal prestige" on reforms that were "serious and credible in terms of its financial and economic components."[66] Baker consequently promised to press the international community to ante up more assistance and push his own government to support a ruble stabilization fund, technical assistance, and other considerations. In return, he advised Yeltsin to practice fiscal austerity, meet external obligations, and work with the

World Bank and the International Monetary Fund. This, then, was the final "negotiation" leading to direct, nonhumanitarian assistance to the post-communist transition.

The shift in U.S. policy did not occur quickly enough or offer sufficient support for the Yeltsin regime, according to some American critics; debates during this period prefigured arguments over American policies toward the FSU that would appear again and again in the Clinton administration. In early 1992, former president Richard Nixon, for example, repeatedly castigated the Bush administration in public for failing to provide meaningful assistance to the newly independent states.[67] Much of Nixon's analysis hinged on the assumption that if the Yeltsin regime failed, it would be replaced by one less amicable to broad U.S. national interests. Other observers wondered, however, if U.S. policy toward Russia and the other Soviet successor states should be dependent upon the fate of a single regime or even the worst case assumption that Yeltsin's successors would be more threatening to the United States. Although Nixon helped initiate this debate, it has continued into the Clinton administration and received new life each time Russia has experienced a major political or economic crisis.[68] It is also important to note that perspectives focusing on the relative amounts of U.S. assistance have been challenged by those who argue that virtually any support is too much given the nation's domestic problems.

Amid these discussions, President Bush proposed a comprehensive assistance package, the Freedom Support Act, to increase the U.S. IMF quota by $12 billion, authorize a $3 billion ruble stabilization fund from IMF resources, and provide for $470 million in bilateral humanitarian and technical assistance on 1 April 1992.[69] The Bush and Clinton administrations subsequently developed major programs for the newly independent states in trade and investment, business and economic development, training and exchanges, democratization, energy and the environment, social and humanitarian areas, and security, as well as smaller projects such as funding the Eurasia Foundation.[70]

Ratification Stage

The Bush administration's legislative campaign to "ratify" the Freedom Support Act began with a rousing success. In June 1992 Russian president Boris Yeltsin spoke movingly of his commitment to investigate the fate of U.S. Vietnam-era prisoners of war within the Soviet era archives before a joint session of Congress. American legislators responded with ovations.[71] Boris Yeltsin's performance had been scripted by President Bush and Secretary of State Baker to achieve maximum support from Congress.[72] The president himself had suggested (and the secretary of state had informed Yeltsin) that the Russian president should address the POW issue if he hoped to win congressional support for increased economic assistance. Baker later claimed that the speech was "a political masterstroke that instantly won over a reluctant Congress and paved the way of the Freedom Support Act."[73]

The legislation itself had been crafted to be "a vehicle around which we could coalesce public support—and votes on the Hill."[74] But Baker, before introducing the draft legislation, had also sought "government-wide consensus," no easy task given the number of agencies contributing assistance. One key aspect of the legislation—the ruble stabilization fund—required the support of the Treasury Department. The Yeltsin government and the Bush administration cooperated to win Treasury's support by having Egor Gaidar make the case for a stabilization fund directly to U.S. Treasury officials. Shortly thereafter, opposition to the fund quieted.

Baker also introduced the Freedom Support Act legislation when it would have maximum effect on both the U.S. and the Russian domestic political processes.[75] Baker took into consideration the congressional budget cycle (especially the unique problems associated with funding foreign assistance), the schedule of the Russian parliament, and, as befitting someone experienced in campaign politics, the weekly media cycle. In each case, Baker turned necessity—domestic political cycles—into virtue by timing the legislative announcement to achieve maximum visibility for the administration's program.

The legislative battle over the Freedom Support Act was heated. Although congressional reaction had been generally favorable initially, a minority of legislators had serious reservations. Senator Dennis Deconcini, for example, opposed the legislation on domestic grounds: "Before we pour more money into solving the problems abroad, we must turn our attention to the long-neglected problems here at home."[76] Others sought to impose conditions in return for assistance; Senator Larry Pressler offered (and had accepted) an amendment to the Senate bill on the withdrawal of Soviet troops from the Baltic states. Ultimately, however, with strong personal support from senior foreign policy officials,[77] the bill passed on 24 October 1992 with relatively minor modifications.[78]

Implementation Stage

When President Bush lost the 1992 presidential election, implementation of the Freedom Support Act fell to the incoming Clinton administration. Although President Clinton raised the visibility of FSU assistance—for example, by appointing Strobe Talbott as aid coordinator and pledging increased assistance in meetings with Boris Yeltsin—Freedom Support Act implementation suffered. Over the next several years, the U.S. government had trouble fulfilling even the original Freedom Support Act commitments of the Bush administration, much less the grander promises of President Clinton.

The implementation problem was straightforward: U.S. aid programs and agencies designed to help reconstruct Europe after World War II and then to promote development in the less-developed countries were not especially well-suited to providing assistance to former communist countries. The administrative, congressional, and regulatory rules and procedures that constrained the implementation were varied and complex. In particular, two issues were important: (1) the difficulty of coordinating the diverse programs through which U.S. assistance was channeled, and (2) the decision to provide a large portion of assistance in the form of credits rather than grants.

Coordination

U.S. foreign assistance programs are fragmented; assistance programs to the newly independent states are no exception. The number of agencies involved in foreign assistance complicated the shifting mission of assistance programs; by the U.S. Agency for International Development's count, over thirty-five public agencies and numerous private groups provide funds or in-kind assistance to the former Soviet republics. The U.S. channels most bilateral assistance through the U.S. Agency for International Development (USAID).[79] USAID works with the Department of State, the Treasury Department, the Defense Department, the Export-Import (EXIM)Bank, the Overseas Private Investment Corporation (OPIC), and other agencies to disburse assistance. Interagency working groups attempt to coordinate American assistance programs and cooperate with international donors. Despite these procedures, newspaper accounts, congressional testimony, and USAID internal audits all suggest that the U.S. assistance programs have encountered bureaucratic, organizational, and political obstacles in assisting the transition.[80]

Although the Bush administration recognized its coordination difficulties, its solution—the creation of an aid coordinator by the Freedom Support Act—was inadequate to the task. In May 1993 President Clinton appointed an aid coordinator (Strobe Talbott) within the Department of State. The president granted Talbott wide authority to design, coordinate, manage, and mediate U.S. assistance programs. In practice, however, the coordinator's role has been limited. First, relatively little money is under his direct control. Second, several major assistance programs do not fall under the Freedom Support Act (for example, the Cooperative Threat Reduction or Nunn-Lugar program). Third, for many programs, implementing agencies maintain relative autonomy from the coordinator's office. Finally, traditional foreign policy management structures—the National Security Council staff, for example—remain extremely influential.[81] Even the administrative reforms accompanying the Clinton administration's appointment of Richard Morningstar as the special advisor to the president and the secretary of state on assistance in 1995 has not fully addressed the difficulties of managing U.S. assistance programs.[82] The aid coordinator has not had sufficient authority over personnel, policy decisions, or budgets to bring coherence to U.S. assistance programs.

USAID and the State Department also established new centralized procedures to coordinate assistance to the former Soviet Union.[83] With the variety of U.S. assistance initiatives, the size of the recipient countries, and the geography of the newly independent states, centralization has been problematic. Relatively inexperienced field personnel and a dearth of high-quality, timely information have occasionally undermined management reforms. Compounding these difficulties, the American presence in the former Soviet republics grew rapidly following the decision to provide assistance;[84] new personnel and programs had to be integrated into a coherent approach to assistance nearly simultaneously.

Credits

When the focus first shifted to direct bilateral assistance for the former Soviet Union, officials scrambled to find ways to channel funding to the region. The Freedom Support Act itself had not provided sufficient resources for a major increase in official flows to the former Soviet Union. As the Congressional Research Service noted, "the main source of 'new money' . . . was the humanitarian and technical assistance programs" included in the legislation.[85] If the Clinton administration was to make good on its promises to Boris Yeltsin and the international community, it would have to rely on other sources of funding.

One convenient possibility was existing agricultural credit guarantee programs. Indeed, between fiscal year 1991 and fiscal year 1993, agricultural credit guarantees accounted for over $5.5 billion in U.S. "assistance." The Freedom Support Act encouraged agricultural credit guarantees (through the GSM-102 program) by modifying several statutory and administrative impediments to providing funds to the FSU.[86] If credit programs, including those of OPIC and the Export-Import Bank as well as agricultural programs administered by the Department of Agriculture, represented a convenient conduit for U.S. funds and a boon for American business interests, they were also in demand from the Gorbachev and Yeltsin governments, at least initially. Throughout the early transition period, both had asked the U.S. government to continue and increase credits.

Agricultural credit guarantees represented a mixed blessing, however. At best, agricultural imports alleviated short-term food shortages in the immediate crisis period. Yet, in the longer-term, Russia did not necessarily need to accumulate more external debt beyond the $80 billion already owed to international creditors.[87] Extending new dollar credits to a borrower experiencing hard currency shortages was, in many ways, counterproductive. Moreover, agricultural imports undermine efforts to develop internal agricultural markets. Credits exacerbated external debt repayment and may have retarded agricultural development.

If the newly independent states failed to repay guaranteed credits, costs accrued to the U.S. government. It would be liable for the overdue NIS debts. As a result, the program might then be discontinued or, given political realities, endanger other unrelated assistance programs. In late 1992 and early 1994 Russia began to default on GSM-102 guaranteed credits; the United States thus paid out over $1 billion in claims and rescheduled Russia's outstanding GSM-102 debts.[88]

Repayment difficulties reduced congressional support for other nonagricultural assistance programs and consumed vast amounts of energy trying to reach new repayments agreements. During the winter of 1992–93, for example, renegotiations sidetracked the United States and Russia from more pressing issues such as European security arrangements and the Bosnian crisis.

In short, while extending the FSU credits was politically and administratively expedient for the U.S. government, it was not necessarily an effective strategy for supporting reforms. It may have undermined implementation efforts, by making U.S. assistance programs appear self-serving and unresponsive to NIS needs. On the other hand, however, both the Soviet Union under Mikhail Gorbachev and the Russian Federation under Boris Yeltsin repeatedly requested assistance from the United States and other international donors. To refuse assistance, even in the form of credits, would have had political and symbolic significance far beyond the contribution of such programs to the actual transformation process.

Aftermath

By October 1995 the U.S. government had budgeted $8.05 billion for assistance to the newly independent stataes. Of this total it had obligated $7.31 billion and expended $5.12 billion.[89] Russia was by far the largest recipient among the newly independent states; Boris Yeltsin's government received nearly 50 percent of the total expenditures (and proportional amounts of other assistance types) provided by the United States.[90] As with Germany, the United States also gave assistance to the successor states indirectly through its contributions to the World Bank, the International Monetary Fund, the EBRD, and through multilateral debt renegotiations. With the exception of contributions to the EBRD ($350 million committed, less than $270 million appropriated),[91] the State Department accounting of U.S. assistance does not provide figures for the total multilateral contribution of the U.S. government. (See Table 10.4.)

Not all U.S. bilateral assistance derives directly from the Freedom Support Act, of course. But the Freedom Support Act broke the taboo of providing large-scale assistance to the Soviet Union (and then the FSU). In particular, it authorized commercial financing and credit programs administered by the U.S. Department of Agriculture (USDA), EXIM Bank, and OPIC to begin developing projects for the region. The USDA, EXIM Bank, and OPIC financing and insurance programs equaled $2.528, $3.276, and $0.547 billion, respectively for a grand total of $6.351 billion as of October 1995.[92]

As Jeffrey Sachs has repeatedly and eloquently argued, however, "it is one thing to announce aid, and another to deliver it."[93] Under President Clinton the United States has helped lead Western summits that resulted in huge promises but meager results. In 1992 and 1993 American-led donor coalitions offered $24 billion and $28 billion, respectively. Sachs claims that by 1994 only $4 billion of the 1993 figure had reached the newly independent states. More recent data on

Table 10.4

American Bilateral Expenditures and Commitments to the Former Soviet Union, by Agency (in billions of U.S.$, as of 30 September 1995)

U.S. Agency for International Development	1.468
U.S. Department of Commerce	0.013
Overseas Private Investment Corporation (OPIC)	N/A
U.S. Export-Import Bank	N/A
U.S. Information Agency	0.181
U.S. Trade and Development Agency	0.026
U.S. Department of Defense	0.324
U.S. Department of Energy	0.061
U.S. Department of Agriculture	2.815
Humanitarian shipments (government and private)	1.355
Other agencies	0.106
Total	6.349

Source: Adapted from U.S. Department of State, *U.S. Government Assistance to and Cooperative Activities with the New Independent States of the Former Soviet Union* (Washington, DC: Department of State, April 1996), pp. 204–5. Table does not include commercial financing and insurance provided by the Overseas Private Investment Corporation (OPIC) or the U.S. Export-Import Bank.

expenditures, as discussed above, suggest that the United States, at least, has improved it's expenditure rate for funds promised to the FSU. By October 1995, the United States had expended nearly 63 percent of the funds that Congress had budgeted under the Freedom Support Act.

The effect of U.S. implementation problems upon the officials and populace of the newly independent states, and especially Russia, was dramatic. For domestic reasons, the new Russian government had originally pursued a policy of "demonstrative cooperation" or "ingratiating accommodation" toward the United States in 1992.[94] Within eighteen months, however, the accommodationist policy had worn thin. As Raymond Garthoff has argued:

> There was much debate, some promise, but little delivery of Western economic assistance to Russia. The ultracooperative, ingratiating Russian policy toward the West did not yield the economic assistance expected (whether realistically is another question). In the West, the promise of economic assistance was tied to implementation of far-reaching Russian economic reform, which the Russians did not believe they could undertake without massive assistance, leading to a circular process in which little was done.[95]

By April 1993, political opportunists such as Russian Vice President Aleksandr V. Rutskoi had begun criticizing the United States and his own government by claiming that 60 percent of western assistance had been siphoned off by the "commercial structure."[96] Yeltsin himself soon pursued less accommodationist policies, although not quickly enough to satisfy critics. Subsequently, Russia's periodic foreign policy and defense challenges to the West—in Bosnia, the "near abroad," and, most significantly, Chechnya—and its emerging policies on military planning and restructuring[97] have undermined remaining support for further bilateral assistance.

Domestic budget difficulties in the United States and the ongoing political uncertainties in Russia have led Congress to gradually lower Freedom Support Act appropriations. Freedom Support Act funding peaked in fiscal year (FY) 1994 at $2.5 billion. In 1995 funding fell to $850 million—nearly a two-thirds reduction, while the FY 1996 appropriation dropped to $641 million—a one-quarter reduction.[98] The Clinton administration requested $1 million less for FY 1997 ($640 million) but in June 1996 the U.S. House of Representatives voted to slash programs to $590 million.[99] Following Boris Yeltsin's victory, the U.S. Senate voted in favor of the entire $640 million requested by the Clinton administration.

Since the Freedom Support Act's origins in the Bush administration, American assistance to the FSU has been marked by controversies both within government and among the wider policy community. Generally, the debate has remained in line with the more or less traditional divisions in post-World War II U.S. foreign policy—those fearful of the Soviet Union or a resurgent Russia claim that anyone who supports more assistance and greater engagement is "soft" on the Soviet/Russian leadership. The Clinton administration has been especially vulnerable to charges that it is "soft" on Russia because its point man on post-Soviet affairs has been Strobe Talbott, a close personal friend of the president. First as aid coordinator and then as deputy assistant secretary of state, Talbott has advocated an engaged policy laced with incentives for good behavior.[100] He has maintained this position throughout even the worst crises of the post-Soviet period, including the coup attempt against Boris Yeltsin and the Russian invasion of Chechnya. If the Clinton administration has maintained a strong relationship with the Yeltsin government, its efforts to provide assistance under the auspices of the Freedom Support Act have been limited by Congress. Appropriations have been reduced, despite the unfinished nature of the transition and America's real national security interests in the region.

Conclusion

Five years after the revolutions of 1989, the transition toward democracy and markets proceeds slowly while the ability of the United States and Germany to influence outcomes has waned. Communists or former Communists have returned to power in the Russian Duma; several leading candidates in the 1996 Russian elections disavowed, in many respects, many of the reformist policies of Boris Yeltsin. Meanwhile, security arrangements remain unsettled. The possibility of NATO expansion in Central and Eastern Europe threatens Russia but fails to offer adequate security guarantees to those countries that would be most threatened by a resurgent Russia. Pan-European security initiatives such as the Organization for Security and Cooperation in Europe (OSCE) and the West European Union remain underdeveloped. Although progress has been made, continuing political and economic instabilities remain a real possibility.

German and American bilateral assistance programs to the Soviet Union were negotiated under fundamentally different sets of circumstances. German negotiations took place in the context of reunification; if the original assistance package was not a bribe or payment (as most Germans accounts stress), it was linked explicitly to the withdrawal of Soviet troops from the former GDR. For Germany, Soviet assistance contributed to the historical process of reconstituting the German nation, breaking down the remaining artificial barriers separating the German people, and restoring formal sovereignty to German territory.

For the United States, the stakes were also high, but not as immediately pressing as for Germany. By the time the Bush administration proposed the Freedom Support Act in 1991, many bilateral issues had already been resolved to the advantage of the United States. Although Gorbachev had attempted to obtain quid pro quos for cooperating on arms control, regional conflicts, and other issues, he was operating from increasingly untenable domestic and international positions. At home, the internal logics of perestroika and glasnost had already unleashed the forces that would lead to the Soviet Union's dissolution. Abroad, events within the former Warsaw Pact had already spun out of Moscow's control.

The final collapse of the Soviet Union, leading to Boris Yeltsin's accession to power in Russia, ultimately made the Germans more cautious about providing assistance to the region. Mikhail Gorbachev had made unification possible; Boris Yeltsin could only complete the implementation of the previous agreement. This reality, combined with the increasingly perilous political and economic situation in the FSU, helped dissuade Germany from providing large amounts of bilateral assistance to the Yeltsin government. The Soviet Union's demise had the opposite effect on the United States. For the first time, the United States agreed to provide significant amounts of bilateral assistance, in part because ideological obstacles to assistance were no longer as strong.

Both Germany and the United States sought, in the long run, to influence developments within the Soviet Union and then the former Soviet Union. If rhetorically they pledged to assist the transition toward a market-oriented economy and a more democratic political system, in practice they each focused on more pragmatic objectives. Germany's first priority was to complete the Soviet troop withdrawal by mid-1994. Only secondarily did it seek to secure economic opportunities for German firms and the rights of ethnic Germans living in Russian territory. The United States focused on securing issues related to strategic weapons, nuclear materials, and the implementation of arms control agreements. It also allowed domestic political concerns (for example, the appeasement of congressional agricultural interests) to influence the types and timing of U.S.

assistance programs. There is evidence to suggest that these circumstances will not continue in the years ahead.

Notes

I would like to thank the Alexander von Humboldt Foundation for financial support and India Gray for research assistance on this project.

1. This paper concentrates on the Soviet Union and, following its breakup, Russia, the largest of the fifteen newly independent states. Substantial amounts of aid have been supplied by both Germany and the United States to these other countries (especially Ukraine, Kazakhstan, and the Baltics), but these are left aside in the interest of space.

2. Defining what constitutes "assistance" is complex issue. This chapter generally follows conventions developed in the context of international assistance for central and eastern Europe in Krzysztof J. Ners and Ingrid T. Buxell, *Assistance to the Transition Survey 1995* (New York: Institute for East–West Studies, 1995), pp. 22–3. Most importantly, the term "assistance" is used to denote all resource transfers to the region while aid refers specifically to grant and concessional forms of assistance.

3. Germany and the United States have also helped sponsor the incorporation of the new states into international economic regimes and organizations.

4. See Peter Dombrowski, "Dismantling Communism: American, German and International Assistance to the Post-Soviet Transition," manuscript.

5. With regard to assistance to central and eastern Europe, the Institute for East–West Studies has warned that "there are manifest difficulties with regard to the collection and compilation of accurate data on assistance flows. Thus all quoted assistance figures should be treated with caution." This admonition holds true for assistance to the FSU as well. Ners and Buxell, *Assistance to the Transition Survey* 1995, p. 26. One critical problem in comparing figures is the distinction between monies "committed" or promised and monies "disbursed" or provided. No single international agency collects and disseminates data on both commitments and disbursements on a regular basis. Although the Organization for Economic Cooperation and Development (OECD) publishes information on disbursements, its most recent analysis includes data only to 1993. OECD, *Aid and Other Resource Flows to the Central and Eastern European Countries and the New Independent States of the Former Soviet Union in 1992 and 1993* (Paris: OECD, 1995). Figures reported directly by aid donors including the United States often do not follow the conventions recognized by the OECD or other international agencies.

6. For a recent assessment of the Nunn-Lugar programs, see Jason D. Ellis, "Dollar Diplomacy and Nuclear Non-Proliferation: The Case of Nunn-Lugar," paper presented at the 1996 annual meeting of the International Studies Association, San Diego, CA, 16–20 April 1996.

7. For excellent overviews see Bartlomiej Kaminski and Zhen Kun Wang, "External Finance, Policy Conditionalities, and Transition from Central Planning," and Gertrude Schroeder, "The Economic Transformation Process in the Post-Soviet States: The Role of Outside Actors," both in this volume.

8. Germany, for example, initially focused on ensuring the smooth exit of Soviet troops from the former German Democratic Republic (GDR) while the United States concentrated on projects related to ex-Soviet nuclear programs.

9. Ukraine now ranks as the third largest recipient of U.S. assistance, behind Israel and Egypt but ahead of the Russian Federation. Jane Perlez, "Despite U.S. Hope and Help, Ukraine's Star Fades," *New York Times,* 27 June 1996, p. A2.

10. According to Alvin Z. Rubinstein, for example, the Bush administration "missed the boat on the possibility of fostering a profound transformation of Russia's socioeconomic transformation," at least in part, because it failed to provide sufficient bilateral assistance and "mobilize the resources of the West." See Alvin Z. Rubinstein, "The Transformation of Russian Foreign Policy"] in this volume. Extensive critiques of the Bush and the Clinton administrations initiatives as well as international efforts can be found in Jeffrey Sachs, "Betrayal: How Clinton Failed Russia," *New Republic* (31 January 1994): pp. 14, 16; Marshall I. Goldman, *Lost Opportunity: Why Economic Reforms Have Not Worked* (New York: W.W. Norton and Company, 1994), esp. pp. 213–28; and Anders Åslund, *How Russia Became a Market Economy* (Washington, DC: Brookings Institution, 1995), pp. 215–20.

11. On the theoretical logic underlying this analysis see Robert D. Putnam, "Diplomacy and Domestic Politics: The Logic of Two-Level Games," *International Organization,* 42 (Summer 1988): pp. 427–60; and Peter B. Evans, Harold K. Jacobson, and Robert D. Putnam, *Double-Edged Diplomacy: Bargaining and Domestic Politics* (Berkeley: University of California Press, 1993). For a more explicit application of these concept to the post-Soviet transition see Peter Dombrowski, "The Game Boards of Two-Level Diplomacy: International Assistance to the Post-Soviet Transition," presented at the 1996 annual meeting of the International Studies Association, San Diego, CA, 16–20 April 1996.

12. Even when interactions between states assume the formal characteristics of negotiations, analytic power is gained by disaggregating the process into stages. See, for example, Janice Gross Stein, "Getting to the Table: The Triggers, Stages, Functions, and Consequences of Prenegotiation," *International Journal* 44 (Spring 1989): pp. 475–504. ,

13. Given the limits of space, this analysis does not provide a narrative covering the ebb and flow of the "negotiations." Nor does it explore the relationship between the decision to provide aid and other broader developments such as the creation of a new European security "architecture" or the interrelationship between German and American strategies.

14. In part because the conventional wisdom in West Germany discounted the susceptibility of the GDR to internal upheavals already evident in Poland in early 1989. By this analysis, the GDR lacked a strong dissident movement, its leadership had balked at Gorbachev's reforms, the Stasi remained powerful, and the political culture was characterized by passivity. Stephen F. Szabo, *The Diplomacy of German Unification* (New York: St. Martin's Press, 1992), p. 35.

15. Garton Ash argues, for example, that West Germany's Deutschlandpolitik was ambiguous on the question of promoting political change in the GDR; its relativistic policy of looking at the GDR's "bright side" (p. 210) in order to achieve "normalisation" between the two states, at best, encouraged stability in government-to-government relations (pp. 183–84) and, at worst, prolonged the ability of the SED to hold onto power. Further, West Germany preferred "stability to liberty" throughout central and eastern Europe (pp. 279–98). Timothy Garton Ash, *In Europe's Name: Germany and the Divided Continent* (New York: Vintage Books, 1994).

16. Szabo, *The Diplomacy of German Unification,* pp. 25–26.

17. Economic assistance was only one part of the international settlement regarding German unification. Other issues (troop withdrawals, NATO membership, etc.) consumed more of the time and effort of the diplomatic participants in the Two-Plus-Four negotiations and, even, the bilateral discussions between Chancellor Kohl and Secretary Gorbachev.

18. Garton Ash, *In Europe's Name,* pp. 117–18.

19. Ibid., p. 350.

20. Philip Zelikow and Condoleezza Rice, *Germany Unified and Europe Trans-*

formed: A Study in Statecraft (Cambridge, MA: Harvard University Press, 1995), pp. 258–59.

21. Quoted by Alexandr Kokeev, "Moscow and Bonn: From Confrontation to Partnership," in *In from the Cold: Germany, Russia and the Future of Europe,* ed. Vladimir Baranovsky and Hans-Joachim Spanger (Boulder, CO: Westview Press, 1992), p. 229.

22. Zelikow and Rice, *Germany Unified and Europe Transformed,* pp. 337–38.

23. Ibid., p. 340.

24. Elizabeth Pond, *Beyond the Wall: Germany's Road to Unification* (Washington, DC: Brookings Institution, 1993), p. 223.

25. See "Money for the Soviet Union," in Zelikow and Rice, *Germany Unified and Europe Transformed,* pp. 347–52.

26. Zelikow and Rice, *Germany Unified and Europe Transformed,* p. 349.

27. Ibid., pp. 349–50.

28. Finance Minister Waigel and Sitaryan reached an impasse at DM 11–12 billion on the German side, DM 16–18 billion on the Soviet side. Kohl and Gorbachev agreed to speak again in three days. Zelikow and Rice, *Germany Unified and Europe Transformed,* p. 352.

29. Ibid., p. 352.

30. Ultimately, the final Soviet troops withdrew in August 1994, several months ahead of the original schedule.

31. The Green party from the five eastern Länder won eight seats, however. Henry Ashby Turner, *Germany from Partition to Unification* (New Haven, CT: Yale University Press, 1992), p. 254.

32. Fred Oldenburg, *Germany's Interest in Russian Stability,* Bericht des Bundesinstituts für ostwissenschaftliche und internationale Studien (BOIST), no. 33–1993, (Cologne: BIOST, 1993) p. 25.

33. German official, interview by author, Foreign Ministry, Bonn, Germany, 26 April 1995.

34. "Germany's Housing and Retraining Programmes for the Russian Armed Forces Leaving Germany," draft copy of speech to be given by German Foreign Ministry official, fall 1994.

35. Kreditanstalt für Weideraufbau (KfW), Consulting Konsortium Wohnungsbau (CWU), and Arbeitsgemeinschaft zur Projekt vorbereitung des Wohnungsbau programms (ARGE WOBAU), *Das Wohnungbau-Programm in der Russichen Foderation der Republik Weissrussland und der Ulraine* (Frankfurt am Main: KfW, 1994), p. ii.

36. German official, interview by author, German Foreign Ministry, Bonn, Germany, 26 April 1994.

37. "Germany's Housing and Retraining Programmes," p. 3.

38. Oldenburg, *Germany's Interest in Russian Stability,* p. 25.

39. In late 1993 aid officials from a number of donor countries met to discuss ideas and programs for housing returning or demobilized Soviet troops, but little cooperation resulted from these discussions. The United States floated a proposal for a voucher system that was not appealing to German officials. Denmark informed the other donors of its own "holistic" approach combining housing, employment, and other social programs in a village outside St. Petersburg. German official, interview.

40. Figure derived from a summary provided in the German Information Center, "German Support for the Reform Process in the Former Soviet Union and the Countries of Central, Southeastern and Eastern Europe," March 1995, pp. 1–2.

41. Letter to the Organization for Economic Cooperation and Development (OECD) from the German Economics Min'stry dated 26 May 1995, p. 3. The letter is in the author's possession.

42. Ian Murray, "Bonn Treaties Help Moscow," *Times* (London), 26 April 1991, p. 16.

43. See, for example, "Bonn: Germany, Supportive of Yeltsin, Pushes for a 'Micro' Aid Approach that Would Help Ordinary Russians," *Christian Science Monitor,* 24 March 1993, p. 13; and "Clinton and Kohl Agree Russia is Top Priority," *Los Angeles Times,* 27 March 1993, p. A16.

44. Richard L. Berke, "U.S. Asks Germany to Push Russia Aid," *New York Times,* 19 December 1993.

45. See Angela Stent, "Russia and Post-Communist Europe," in this volume.

46. Germany provides approximately DM 75 million in technical assistance per year to Russia and smaller amounts to other the NIS. For details, see Bundesministerium für Wirtschaft, *Die Beratung Mittel- und Osteuropas beim Aufbau von Demokratie und sozialer Marktwirtschaft: Konzept und Beratungsprogramme der Bundesregierung* (Bonn: Bundesministerium für Wirtschaft in Zussamenarbeit mit der Kreditanstalt für Wiederaufbau, April 1995), esp. pp. 21–54 on technical assistance for Russia, Ukraine, and Belarus.

47. For example, Hermes budgets for the CIS fell from DM 4.0 billion in 1993 to DM 2.3 billion in 1996. Jeffrey Anderson and Celeste A. Wallander, "In the Shadow of the Wall: Germany's Eastern Trade Policy After Unification," Harvard University Center for International Affairs Working Paper 96–3 (April 1996), p. 34.

48. "Russian Debt: Join the Club," *Economist,* 4 May 1996, p. 75.

49. For details, see Heinz Timmerman, *Die Beziehungen EU-Russland: Voraussetzungen und Perspektiven von Partnerschaft und Kooperation,* Berichte des Bundesinstituts für ostwissenschaftliche und internationale Studien (BIOST) no. 60–1994 (Cologne: BIOST, 1994), esp. pp. 7–10.

50. German officials, interviews by author, Foreign Ministry, Bonn, Germany, May 1996.

51. On the complex German–EU relationship, see Simon Bulmer and William E. Patterson, "Germany in the European Union: Gentle Giant or Emerging Leader?" *International Affairs* 72 (January 1996): pp. 9–32.

52. On these arguments and the German-Russian economic relations more generally, see Hans-Hermann Höhmann and Christian Meier, *Deutsch-russiche Wirtschaftsbeziehungen: Stand, Probleme, Perspektiven,* Pt. I, no. 55–1994 (Cologne: BIOST, 1994).

53. Ibid., p. 29.

54. Ibid.

55. Oldenburg, *Germany's Interest in Russian Stability,* esp. pp. 13–16.

56. For an excellent account of the Nunn-Lugar programs, see Ellis, "Dollar Diplomacy and Nuclear Non-Proliferation."

57. On the Bush administration's approach to the Soviet Union, see Michael R. Beschloss and Strobe Talbott, *At the Highest Levels: The Inside Story of the End of the Cold War* (Boston: Little, Brown and Company, 1993).

58. Anatoly Dobrynin claims that "[a]lthough it is not well known, [Gorbachev] spared no effort to secure financial and moral support for his reforms from the United States and from the new President Bush personally as a way of supporting his regime and his popularity at home." Anatoly Dobrynin, *In Confidence: Moscow's Ambassador to America's Six Cold War Presidents (1962–1986)* (New York: Times Books, 1995), p. 634.

59. Following the August 1991 coup attempt, Russian president Boris Yeltsin and the heads of other former Soviet republics also pressed the United States and other western countries.

60. Jack F. Matlock Jr., *Autopsy on an Empire: The American Ambassador's Account*

of the Collapse of the Soviet Union (New York: Random House, 1995), pp. 176–82.

61. James A. Baker, *The Politics of Diplomacy: Revolution, War and Peace, 1982–1992,* (New York: G.P. Putnam and Sons, 1995), p. 153.

62. Raymond L. Garthoff, *The Great Transition: American-Soviet Relations and the End of the Cold War* (Washington, DC: Brookings Institution, 1994), pp. 405–7.

63. Beschloss and Talbott, *At the Highest Level,* p. 160.

64. Ibid., p. 60.

65. George F. Kennan, "Witness to the Fall," *New York Review of Books,* vol. 42 (16 November 1995): p. 8.

66. Baker, *The Politics of Diplomacy,* p. 655.

67. See Rubinstein, "The Transformation of Russian Foreign Policy," for more on former president Nixon's intervention into the debate of the Bush administration's assistance policies.

68. For example, Strobe Talbott, President Clinton's chief advisor on the former Soviet Union, has often been accused of being excessively pro-Yeltsin and pro-Russia, sometimes to the detriment of American long-term interests. Michael Dobbs, "Mission to Moscow: Is Strobe Talbott the Right Architect for the U.S.'s Russia Policy," *Washington Post National Weekly Edition,* 10–16 June 1996, pp. 6–9.

69. In addition to bilateral aid, the Bush administration also supported the $24 billion aid package offered by the G-7 nations in 1992.

70. For a complete description of Freedom Support Act programs, see U.S. Department of State, *U.S. Government Assistance to and Cooperative Activities with the New Independent States of the Former Soviet Union* (Washington, DC: Department of State, April 1996).

71. Pamela Pressler, "Yeltsin Charges onto Capitol Hill, Charms the Life out of Cold War," *Congressional Quarterly Weekly Report* 50, no. 25 (20 June 1992): pp. 1813–18.

72. Baker, *The Politics of Diplomacy,* pp. 652–54.

73. Ibid., p. 653.

74. Ibid., p. 656.

75. Ibid., p. 657.

76. "Aid to the Former Soviet Union," *Congressional Digest,* 79, no. 8–9 (August–September, 1992): p. 207.

77. Baker, for example, quickly called Senate Foreign Relations committee members and persuaded them to support the administration's position when Senator Jesse Helms offered an amendment to require collateral for all multinational loans to the newly independent states. Pamela Fessler, "Senate Panel, With Baker's Help, Approves Aid to Former Soviet," *Congressional Quarterly Weekly Report* 50, no. 20 (16 May 1992): p. 1358.

78. For details on the House, Senate, and Conference reports see Curt Tarnoff, "Freedom Support Act of 1992: A Foreign Aid Program for the Soviet Union," *CRS Issue Brief* (updated 3 November 1993).

79. On USAID's role, see Agency for International Development, *Development and the National Interest: U.S. Economic Assistance into the 21st Century: A Report by the Administrator* (Washington, DC: USAID, 1989).

80. U.S. General Accounting Office, *Foreign Assistance: AID Strategic Direction and Continued Management Improvements Needed,* GAO/NSIAD-93–106 (Washington, DC: GAO, June 1993).

81. For details, see U.S. General Accounting Office, *Former Soviet Union: U.S. Bilateral Program Lacks Effective Coordination* GAO/NSIAD-95–10 (Washington, DC: GAO, February 1995).

82. Memorandum on the Charter of the Special Advisor to the President and to the

Secretary of State on Assistance to the New Independent States (NIS) of the Former Soviet Union and Coordinator of NIS Assistance, 5 April 1995, reprinted in U.S. Department of State, *U.S. Government Assistance to and Cooperative Activities with the New Independent States of the Former Soviet Union,* pp. 7–8.

83. The principal innovation was top-down management; "program planning, implementation, and management authority would be retained in Washington, DC, rather than delegated to U.S. personnel in-country" as with other U.S. aid programs. U.S. General Accounting Office, *Former Soviet Union: Assistance by the United States and Other Donors,* GAO/NSIAD-93–101 (Washington, DC: GAO, December 1992), p. 7.

84. By April 1992, the State Department had opened fourteen new embassies in the newly independent states and increased its personnel from the Cold War high of 233 diplomats to 340 personnel. The Commerce Department had added fifty trade promotion officials and the Department of Agriculture had sent a large number of advisors. Dana Priest, "Coming to Grips with the New World Order," *Washington Post,* 20 April 1992, p. A17.

85. Curt Tarnoff, "Freedom Support Act of 1992: A Foreign Aid Program for the Former Soviet Union," *CRS Issue Brief* IB92081 (3 November 1992): p. CRS-5.

86. Ibid., pp. 13–15.

87. On the promise and pitfalls associated with U.S. credit guarantee programs for the NIS, see U.S. General Accounting Office, *Former Soviet Union: Agricultural Reform and Food Situation in its Successor States,* GAO/GGD-94–17 (Washington, DC: GAO, 1994), esp. pp. 42–50.

88. U.S. General Accounting Office, *Former Soviet Union: Creditworthiness of Successor Sates and U.S. Export Credit Guarantees,* GAO/GGD-95–60 (February 1995), p. 8.

89. U.S. Department of State, *U.S. Government Assistance to and Cooperative Activities with the New Independent States of the Former Soviet Union,* pp. 200–5.

90. Ibid., p. 205.

91. Ibid., p. 126.

92. Ibid., p. 206.

93. Sachs, "Betrayal: How Clinton Failed Russia," p. 14.

94. Garthoff, *The Great Transition,* p. 779.

95. Ibid.

96. Celestine Bohlen, "One Year Later, Russians Doubt West's Aid Total," *New York Times,* 4 April 1993, p. A1.

97. Michael R. Gordon, "As Its World Narrows, Russia Seeks a New Mission," *New York Times,* (30 November 1993), p. A1.

98. U.S. Department of State, *U.S. Government Assistance to and Cooperative Activities with the New Independent States of the Former Soviet Union,* p. 3.

99. Carrol J. Doherty, "House Passes Foreign Aid Bill Curbing Loan Agencies," *Congressional Quarterly Weekly Report* (15 June 1996): pp. 1697–98.

100. On Talbott's role in the Clinton administration, see Steven Erlanger, "Russia Vote Is a Testing Time for Key Friend of Clinton's," *New York Times,* 8 June 1996, p. 1; and Dobbs, "Mission to Moscow," pp. 6–10.

11

The Economic Transformation Process in the Post-Soviet States

The Role of Outside Actors

Gertrude Schroeder

The sudden appearance of fifteen independent states from the wreckage of the collapsed Soviet state at the end of 1991 presented the rest of the world with an adjustment crisis of an unprecedented character. Simultaneously, the disintegration of the Soviet state entailed a massive societal shock for the political leaderships and peoples of the new states so abruptly catapulted into the international arena. In the subsequent five years, foreign actors have become involved in the economic affairs of the new states to a rapidly increasing extent and in numerous ways, as the new states have sought to further their declared objective of becoming "normal" societies with "normal" (market) economies integrated into the international community. In this brief period, they have made significant progress toward that goal, but in different ways and degrees among them. Although the pattern and extent of progress necessarily has been driven and conditioned largely by domestic politics, the role of outside actors—broadly defined—has been strongly influential, indeed, in a sense even decisive, in shaping and sustaining the ongoing transformation process. But their impact potential could have been even greater.

The West has consistently encouraged the new states in their efforts to create market economies and join the rest of the world in a web of normal economic relationships. It has pursued a policy of inclusion, admitting them with remarkable speed to membership in international economic organizations, and has extended normal trading privileges to them for the most part. It also has provided substantial financial assistance and through numerous channels has been the source of a massive transfer of human capital (economic expertise and market economy know-how) that has been indispensable to the conduct of economic reform. Unfortunately, however, these Western contributions have been obscured by a mass of publicity about flaws in implementing particular technical assistance programs and about whether massive financial aid should have been given in particular situations. This chapter aims to provide some perspective on the considerations and issues involved.

The Initial Situation

The circumstances under which the new states began their journey toward their goal of creating well-functioning market economies integrated into the international community could hardly have been less auspicious. The immediate legacy of the disintegration of the Soviet state was a near-catastrophic macroeconomic crisis in each country, requiring the inexperienced new governments and bureaucracies immediately to have to formulate policies to deal with its manifestations—consumer markets in massive disarray, rapidly accelerating inflation; falling production, foreign trade, and living standards; and looming financial collapse. Moreover, the new states shared a common currency—the Soviet (Russian) ruble—and a huge collective foreign debt. The issues involved in economic policy making to deal with the crisis and also to further the declared long-run goal were those appropriate for an embryonic but malperforming market economy. But economic illiteracy was enormous and pervasive. The supply of people in the new governments who understood the complex issues and policy options involved was exceedingly small, even in Russia—the proclaimed successor state to the USSR—and nearly nonexistent elsewhere. The "economics" that had been taught in Soviet schools was not really economics at all, but rather the study of the techniques of state central planning and management of an economy.[1] Macroeconomics was absent in such studies, as was analysis of the behavior of households and firms under conditions of economic freedom. Even in Russia, where expertise was greatest, it was to be found only at senior levels in a few key organizations and academic institutions.

Lack of in-depth understanding of monetary and financial phenomena and market behavior was a great handicap for would-be builders of a market economy. By and large, the general public seemed to be supportive of a market economy with privately owned property, but after many decades of living under communism its understanding of what those terms implied was superficial at best. Having never had to sell their products, purchase their inputs, seek out investors, or worry about the bottom line, business firms almost totally lacked any sense of how to behave in a market environment. Fortunately, some progress toward acquiring these understandings had been made and a little experience gained during the preceding few years of Mikhail Gorbachev's perestroika. Finally, along with unsuitably trained human capital, the new states inherited large stocks of greatly outmoded physical capital and abused land, both deployed in patterns almost totally unsuited to a modern market economy functioning in a competitive international environment.

In a similar vein, the abrupt and unanticipated disintegration of the seemingly monolithic Soviet state and economy into fifteen new states, each with its own polity and economy, also caught the outside world almost totally unprepared, presenting it with its own species of decision making and adjustment crisis. International organizations, governments, and actors from the private sector confronted the need to respond quickly in some way to the manifest economic crises in the greatly diverse post-Soviet states. While having gained relevant experience in dealing with developing countries, and more directly in 1990–91 through involvement with the post-communist economies of Eastern Europe, key international organizations (the International Monetary Fund and the World Bank) lacked both direct experience and in-depth knowledge and understanding of the former Soviet republics, where the economic legacies from their past tight integration into a unified economy and polity were far more onerous than those inherited in east-central Europe. In particular, the insulation of individuals and firms from the outside world had been much greater in the post-Soviet states. Similar paucity of experience and expertise also was present in the decision-making strata of Western governments, where the dimensions of the societal transformation being attempted were not fully comprehended. Fortunately, however, the new states began the transformation in a climate of international goodwill. They were speedily given diplomatic recognition, and nearly all of them were admitted to membership in the United Nations (UN) and in key international economic organizations in their first year of independence. Numerous actors from the private sector soon stepped forward also.

Although the objectives of assistance were clear and noncontroversial in the West—to promote democratic institutions and market economies in the new states—the details of how to proceed were not, nor could they reasonably have been expected to be so, given the surprise and the precipitous nature of the Soviet Union's demise. Specifically, what kinds of assistance were really needed where, when, and in what amounts? By whom and how could assistance be effectively implemented? What conditions, if any, should be attached to the delivery of such aid? Despite all the murkiness, major Western governments quickly pledged tens of billions in assistance to the new states, mainly in the form of debt rescheduling and export credits and guarantees.[2] There had been no time to devise and implement a detailed program of coordinated Western support. Meanwhile, with such direct financial assistance as actually materialized (a total of at least $17.5 billion in loans and grants during 1992), along with a plethora of often conflicting advice from Western academics and other advisors, the inexperienced and greatly overburdened governments in the new states began to take actions to further their own political–economic agendas and to deal with immediate economic crises. The need for a coordinated and differentiated approach to international assistance soon became evident.

With regard to assistance in the form of detailed advice on economic policy, no Western consensus existed, other than on a few broad fundamentals. Western academics were debating the relative merits of two general approaches to making the transformation from central planning to markets, labeled "shock therapy" and "gradualism."[3] Advocates of the former approach argue that the state should move quickly to liberalize prices, economic activity, and foreign trade and to stabilize the currency, whereas their opponents believe that those actions should be spread over a long period of time. There were also vociferous arguments over the merits of alternative approaches to privatization of the pervasively state-owned property and land in the former socialist economies. Obviously, the kind and pattern of assistance that would be needed would depend on the paths and programs actually chosen in the new states, where these same issues also were highly controversial and deeply enmeshed in their emerging politics.

Both in the new states and in the West, policy makers, their advisors, and the general public grossly underestimated both the burden of the past and the magnitude of the tasks ahead. People in the former Soviet republics seemed to believe that their newfound ability to pursue their own perceived national economic interests would soon bring the prosperity that never materialized under the old order dominated by Moscow. They also hoped for and probably expected substantial Western material assistance in making the transformation, especially in light of the early grandiose promises of support. In the West, the task of economic transformation generally was viewed as fairly simple—of getting a few things done right; although there would be costs, of course, they probably would not be too great, and benefits soon would be clearly visible. Foreign technical assistance obviously would be needed, and many people were ready to offer advice. But both domestic and foreign actors failed adequately to appreciate the political–economic forces that would be unleashed in each state by newfound independence in decision making and by the trade shock resulting from the abrupt disintegration of a closely integrated common market, as other former republics suddenly were turned into "foreign" countries.

Mutual Learning

In the past five years, we have been witnessing a complex, interactive process of mutual learning. Policy makers in the new states have learned much from their own experience in creating a market-based economy with whatever speed and configuration the political process permitted. Households and business firms in these countries have learned a lot simply by having to function in the messy, market-oriented environments that have emerged. But the outside world has contributed enormously to this learning process. After all, the experience with market economies, their many complex institutions, and the diverse roles of governments in their functioning exists on the outside, as does the economic expertise to understand the workings of the market and to prescribe public policy to improve its performance. But there, too, policy prescriptions are often controversial; there are usually difficult economic and social trade-offs, and politics ultimately decides.

Western expertise, broadly defined, has been actively sought by the new states in their quest to integrate with the outside world, but also has been volunteered by outside actors in their efforts to assist or participate in that process. The channels of learning from the West have been numerous and diverse. First, there are the many international organizations that the new states moved quickly to join—those associated with the UN, the Bretton Woods institutions (the IMF and the International Bank for Reconstruction and Development), the European Bank for Reconstruction and Development (EBRD), and some regional bodies such as the Economic Commission for Europe (ECE) in the case of the Baltic states and the Economic Cooperation Organization (ECO) and the Asian and Islamic Development Banks in the case of the states of Central Asia. The European Union (EU) and the Organization for Economic Cooperation and Development (OECD) also have become active players. The EU's TACIS and PHARE initiatives to provide technical assistance have meant extensive involvement with local actors in the former Soviet Union (FSU). Probably the most important channels of learning, however, have been the expanding relationships with the IMF and the World Bank and more recently the EBRD. In connection with their primary role as providers of financing, these institutions have become involved in a wide range of activities that entail extensive and continuing dialogue and interaction with policy makers, government and business institutions, business firms, and numerous private individuals.[4] The IMF now has formal assistance programs in place in all post-Soviet states except Turkmenistan, and resident missions have been set up in most states. The process of negotiating the initial programs and their follow-ons has had a crucially important technical assistance spinoff by helping to build local understanding and expertise in economics and the ways of market economies. Given its wider scope of involvement, the World Bank's activities have facilitated learning for an even larger and more diverse clientele. The Bank now has field offices in eight of the post-Soviet states. By the end of 1994, its training arm—the Economic Development Institute—had organized market-oriented training workshops that had involved nearly four thousand participants including government officials and enterprise managers. The Bank's activities as part of its lending for specific sectoral projects likewise have entailed extensive dialogue with thousands of local actors over extended periods.

Similarly, bilateral assistance endeavors undertaken by Western governments have provided a vehicle for transfer of market-economy know-how, with Germany, the United States, and Japan being the major players, but with the United States having the most extensive array of programs. During 1991–94, twenty-three U.S. government agencies implemented 215 programs in the FSU.[5] With regard to noncommodity, noncredit programs, the U.S. Agency for International Development played the major role, with some twenty ongoing programs in 1995. While some of them directly funded education and training for FSU nationals, most of the rest, as well as many others implemented by various agencies, also involved extensive, close, and continuing interaction with local people

(Peace Corps). Even credit programs, which took the lion's share of U.S. assistance, involved interactions conducive to learning. U.S. programs have been implemented in all of the new states, with Russia having received over half ($6.6 billion) of the funds expended through September 1995 under noncredit (grant) programs as well as those entailing credits, insurance, and loan guarantees. Germany has funded a massive program to provide housing for troops returned from East Germany, as well as considerable technical assistance. Japan has been developing active, hands-on programs focusing on business enterprises in the Russian Far East. The Swedish government, in effect, helped to finance a crash course in macroeconomic policy for dozens of young Russians as part of its support for the Sachs/Åslund group of Western advisors to the Russian government in 1992–93.

In turn, the international organizations and the participants in bilateral assistance programs have also learned much in the process. Thus, they now have much more in-depth knowledge about the physical and behavioral legacies from the old Soviet order, legacies that differ significantly among the post-Soviet states. No longer do any of the major tasks of transformation seem relatively simple. They have learned that changing the habits and mind-sets of employees in the numerous government bureaucracies with which they must deal is a slow, painful, and frustrating business. They have learned that the specifics of reform policies and programs are usually highly controversial among domestic participants, even though consensus may exist on the desired goals and long-run outcomes. They now perceive that general "textbook" solutions or those based directly on "another country's" experience may require modification to take into account the peculiarities of the communist legacy in each state. Finally, they have learned, hopefully, to avoid some of the inevitable mistakes of the initial years of involvement.[6] For instance, the perceived failure of donors, especially of technical aid, to involve the recipient country's experts in all phases of project development has been a frequent complaint, especially from local intellectuals.

In addition to official actors through formal programs of international organizations and governments, a variety of actors from the private and business sectors have been involved in this process of mutual learning. Private universities and foundations have helped to organize student and faculty exchanges and also have served as conduits for public funds. Under such programs, for example, several thousand students from the post-Soviet states were studying in the United States in 1995. Other countries have similar programs. Professional associations—of economists, lawyers, bankers, accountants, and others—have provided opportunities through internships, sponsorship to attend professional meetings, and the like to help educate their counterparts in the new states in the ways of a market economy. In addition, while in search of markets for their products, the new states have sought actively to obtain bilateral trade and cooperation agreements with a wide array of Western countries and their organizations such as the European Union, with much learning taking place in the process. Perhaps even more important are the numerous contacts between local and foreign government and business officials that have occurred in the day-to-day process of promoting and conducting foreign trade. Much market know-how has been communicated to local firms by the many hundreds of foreign businessmen in search of profitable foreign investment opportunities. Even though the amount of investment has been small, many people may be getting messages about what it takes to attract large amounts of capital in a competitive global economy; above all, there needs to be a reasonable degree of political stability and a business-friendly climate protective of private property. With the vastly expanded freedom of action accorded them as reforms have proceeded, business firms in the new states have accumulated market experience in the process of seeking foreign customers, suppliers, and partners and in operating the rapidly growing number of joint ventures with partners outside the former USSR. By 1995, registered joint ventures in the post-Soviet countries numbered in the tens of thousands, compared with only a few thousand in 1991.

Criticism and Response

With its large and crucial human capital transfer rarely recognized, official assistance provided by the OECD countries to the FSU has come in for widespread criticism, indeed even apocalyptic condemnation. Thus, Jeffrey Sachs writes, "Without doubt, the Western neglect of the Russian economic crisis is the greatest foreign policy failing in decades."[7] In a similar vein, Constantine Menges states, "However, judging by the results attained in comparison with the enormous opportunities and resources spent, these assistance efforts may one day be considered one of the greatest and most costly failures in contemporary history."[8] Above all, perhaps, the Western assistance effort has been faulted for being far too meager and for consisting largely of credits rather than grants, as did Marshall Plan aid to Western Europe after World War II. During 1992–94, total disbursements under credit offerings to the states of the FSU totaled $31.4 billion (see Table 11.1). An additional several billion dollars were received in 1995 and the first half of 1996. Nearly 28 percent represented multilateral financing principally from the IMF and World Bank; 15 percent was bilateral aid, and the rest was private lending with government guarantees. These outlays were debt-creating, with only about one-tenth of multilateral and bilateral credits consisting of concessionary loans. Three-fourths of the disbursements went to Russia, with Ukraine and Kazakhstan being the next largest recipients. In addition, Russia, which assumed the old Soviet debt of some $80 billion in exchange for Soviet assets abroad, has been given debt relief through periodic rescheduling of principal amounting to some $40 to $45 billion during 1992–95, with another major rescheduling taking place in 1996.

Grants have been provided on a much smaller scale. Total official grants to the new states during 1992–95 exceeded $12 billion, however, with the United

Table 11.1

Disbursement of Assistance to States of the FSU, 1992–94, and Cumulative Foreign Direct Investment, 1992–95 (in millions of U.S. $)

Country	Credits, 1992–1994				Grants 1992–94	Cumulative foreign direct investment, 1992–95
	Multilateral	Bilateral	Other[a]	Total		
Estonia	131	16	39	186	171	646
Latvia	265	67	30	362	138	323
Lithuania	304	81	42	426	102	73
Russia	5,642	2,448	15,787	23,877	8,026	3,900
Ukraine	621	330	985	1,936	1,004	950
Belarus	326	219	400	945	523	52
Moldova	318	110	0	428	52	86
Armenia	125	51	0	176	249	10
Georgia	143	76	39	258	214	N/A
Azerbaijan	8	59	0	68	75	110
Kazakhstan	492	346	371	1,209	60	719
Uzbekistan	5	570	75	650	29	250
Kyrgyzstan	168	98	0	266	139	25
Turkmenistan	53	155	158	365	14	N/A
Tajikistan	64	206	0	270	61	25
Total	8,664	4,832	17,926	31,422	10,445	7,169

Source: For credits and grants, see World Bank, *World Debt Tables 1996*, vol. 2 (Washington, DC: World Bank, 1996); for foreign direct investment, see World Bank, *World Development Report 1996: From Plan to Market* (Washington, DC: World Bank, 1996), p. 64.

Note: Columns and rows may not add up to totals due to rounding.

[a]Disbursements by private creditors on loans guaranteed by a public entity.

States and Germany being the major donors. As of the end of September 1995, the United States had disbursed $5.2 billion in grants to the post-Soviet states, nearly half of it to Russia (see Table 11.2). Somewhat over half consisted of food assistance, another quarter was humanitarian aid, and the rest could be regarded as mainly technical assistance supplied by diverse agencies under a variety of programs. Although Germany has given grants of more than double the U.S. total, most of the funds were spent before 1992 in connection with housing and resettlement programs to effect the withdrawal of Soviet troops from East Germany.[9]

In all, credits plus grants disbursed during 1992–95 to the fifteen new states amounted to some $50 billion; commitments were perhaps over twice that sum. While the total of all assistance to the new states (including debt rescheduling) represented a minuscule fraction of OECD countries' GDP, it is a large amount—over $100 billion during 1992–95. Moreover, it represented a signifi-

Table 11.2

U.S. Government Assistance to Post-Soviet States—Cumulative Disbursements through 30 September 1995 (in millions of U.S. $)

Country	Food assistance	All other	Total	Total per capita
Estonia	N/A	N/A	26	12
Latvia	N/A	N/A	33	13
Lithuania	N/A	N/A	44	11
Russia	1,257	1,145	2,402	16
Ukraine	130	330	460	9
Belarus	229	53	282	27
Moldova	104	46	150	34
Armenia	335	170	505	136
Georgia	299	89	388	72
Azerbaijan	42	30	72	10
Kazakhstan	35	135	170	10
Uzbekistan	5	32	37	2
Kyrgyzstan	166	95	221	49
Turkmenistan	105	19	124	28
Tajikistan	107	29	136	23
Total	2,815	2,405	5,220	18

Source: U.S. Department of State, *U.S. Government Assistance to and Cooperative Activities With the New Independent States of the Former Soviet Union*, Fiscal Year 1995 Annual Report (Washington, DC: U.S. Department of State, April 1996); U.S. Department of State, *SEED ACT Implementation Report for FY 1995* (Washington, DC: U.S. Department of State, February 1996). Data for Baltic states refer to obligations rather than expenditures. Per capita figures are based on mid-1994 population data.

cant share of each of the recipients' total GDP,[10] in this respect comparing favorably with the Marshall Plan effort for postwar Western Europe. Substantial disbursements are continuing in 1996, especially to Russia and Ukraine. Regarding funding in support of the economic reform process, in particular, an in-depth study by the IMF concludes that no IMF-supported program has failed due to lack of availability of external finance, nor has inadequate foreign financing set back the reform process in the FSU.[11] Another study finds that where a credible reform program was in place, the required external finance was made available.[12] In a recent example, Western governments put together substantial assistance packages for both Ukraine and Russia in 1994–95, when propitious political conditions for accelerating economic reform emerged.

Besides lack of both long-range strategic vision and generosity in providing money, critics of Western involvement in the FSU, particularly regarding the role played by international financial institutions, have faulted those involved for giving "wrongheaded" advice to these fragile governments in their efforts to move to market economies. Broadly speaking, that advice has been to move as quickly as possible to liberalize, stabilize, and privatize their economies. Although the issues are complex and controversial among economists, much of such criticism about the quality of economic advice reflects the critic's ideological stance or his position in the shock therapy versus gradualism debates. Such critics, moreover, have yet to come up with alternative approaches that would do the job within any reasonable time frame.[13] With the passage of time, however, a body of experience has accumulated to provide convincing evidence that the rewards in terms of revival of growth, investment, and foreign trade come soonest to states that move quickly and decisively to stabilize and liberalize their economies.[14] Some critics also cite instances of alleged bad advice in specific cases. Regarding the ruble zone, for example, Jeffrey Sachs writes that the IMF in 1992 "pressed hard" for its retention,[15] an account that the organization disputes.[16] Although the ruble zone was effectively ended by Russian actions in the following year, one should remember that at the time the question of when, how, and whether or not to end it was a highly emotional and controversial issue within Russia and in most of the other republics.[17]

Critics in both donor and recipient countries have argued that the multilateral institutions have established unduly onerous economic conditionality requirements for their lending, thus failing adequately to allow for the economic, social, and political realities in these countries following the USSR's abrupt disintegration. They have also maintained that excessive emphasis was being put on macroeconomic stabilization, to the relative neglect of the microeconomic institution building essential to sustaining it. The use of the IMF's standard conditionality requirements for lending in support of policy programs has come in for particular attack by some Western advisors as well as within recipient constituencies. In the process of mutual learning, however, conditionality has evolved to mitigate some of this criticism.[18] Thus, in early 1993, the IMF created a new lending facility—the Systemic Transformation Facility (STF)—designed to assist the reform process in FSU states. Its use speeds up the arrival of funds and also appreciably eases the targets and repayment schedules set forth in stabilization and reform programs that are agreed to by the recipient government. For example, targets for reducing inflation and budget deficits are set at levels easier to achieve than would be acceptable under the usual IMF lending arrangement—the Standby Agreement. Virtually all of the FSU states have availed themselves of this new opportunity. Moreover, IMF programs now include targeted progress on a broad range of reforms in addition to those designed to stabilize the value of currencies. But as experience has accumulated with the FSU in particular, critics are now arguing that such a "soft" conditionality program is doing more harm than good.[19] The World Bank—the other principal lender under a wide array of microeconomic programs—also has adjusted its approaches and practices to better allow for the particularities of the situation in the post-Soviet states and has developed closer relationships with the IMF in order to speak with a common voice.[20]

Finally, Western assistance endeavors have been widely faulted for numerous flaws in coordination and implementation, especially technical assistance programs. Early on it became clear that the periodic conclaves of the G-7 were much too broad a forum to effectively coordinate the diverse assistance being offered to the fifteen states of the FSU by the numerous multilateral and bilateral donors. Acting on a suggestion of the Japanese prime minister at a Conference on Assistance to States of the Former Soviet Union in October 1992, the World Bank inaugurated a process of convening consultative groups of donors for individual states or groups of states that are undertaking market-oriented reforms. These groups meet with representatives of the country concerned to work out the amount and kind of assistance needed, arrange for its financing by prospective donors, and coordinate its delivery. This process also has promoted closer cooperation among the international organizations, who now can speak with one voice in dealing with recipient governments.

In the United States, there has been much criticism of the lack of coordination among the many federal agencies involved in assistance programs, a failure that evidently has resulted in considerable duplication, waste, and reduced effectiveness of U.S. bilateral programs in meeting their goals. Even though the enabling legislation for U.S. assistance (the Freedom Support Act of 1992) provided for appointment of an overall coordinator, disputes among the dozens of agencies involved frustrated the process, leading to an audit by the General Accounting Office (GAO) in 1994 and congressional requests for investigation.[21] A follow-up GAO report in 1995 described significant improvements.[22] Finally, implementation of the numerous and diverse technical assistance efforts has been faulted on many counts: for example, too large a share of funds going to donor nationals and companies; overpaid, ignorant, and "arrogant" Western consultants; failure to take the recipient country's perceived national interests sufficiently into account; unprepared government and business officials in recipient states; and possibly most sensitive of all for recipients, failure by donors sufficiently to enlist and involve local participants in all phases of a project.[23] It would seem that many of these shortcomings were probably unavoidable in the early stages of the assistance effort. The implementation of technical aid programs should improve, however, as both donor personnel and recipient entities gain knowledge and experience in working together and as the reform process itself evolves in those countries, as evidently has been the case with assistance programs in Eastern Europe.[24]

Two Sore Points

As the reform process has unfolded with differing speeds and patterns in the new states, two areas of interaction with the international community have emerged both as crucially important in the long run and as sore points in the short run. They are (1) the flow of direct foreign investment into these states and (2) the access to Western markets for their products. The governments in all states have actively sought foreign investment and have adopted legislation designed to promote it. Yet inflow has amounted to a mere trickle—$1.2 billion in 1992, $1.3 billion in 1993, $2.0 billion in 1994, and some $2.7 billion in 1995.[25] All FSU countries remain near the top in lists of degree of risk for foreign investors,[26] who continue to be deterred by perceived very high degrees of political risk in the region, uncertainties about property rights, taxes and regulations, and the poor state of the infrastructure needed to support profitable operations. The leaderships in the new states have expressed considerable disappointment at the meager flow of investment; indeed, in some states (Russia, for instance), disappointment seems also to have a tinge of resentment. In contrast, however, one hears charges there that foreign investment amounts to plunder, especially in the case of natural resources. The largest flows expressed per capita and as percentages of GDP have gone to the Baltic states, notably Estonia, which have moved most rapidly to create a policy environment conducive to the growth of investment, both domestic and foreign.[27] Nevertheless, despite their small number, foreign investors have contributed importantly to the acquisition of market know-how in the region in the short run; in the longer term they can prove vital to the revival of economic growth there, as they have elsewhere. But leaderships in many of the new states have yet to grasp the fact that they will have to compete vigorously for such investment in a global arena, where investors can move funds rapidly in search of their best return.

An often-heard complaint by government officials in the new states is that while preaching free trade, the developed Western countries have "unfairly" restricted access to their markets by erecting a variety of barriers to exports from the new states. On becoming independent, these states inherited the discriminatory trade regime vis-à-vis OECD markets that had applied to the Soviet Union. Except for the Baltics, the early Western response to the issue of market access was rather slow and uneven.[28] Although the EU, the countries belonging to the European Free Trade Association (EFTA), Canada, and Japan accorded the new states most-favored nation (MFN) status almost immediately, the United States did so only over a period of more than two years, and Azerbaijan has yet to acquire that status. Similar delays characterized their coverage under the General System of Preferences (GSP), which accords special tariff concessions to relatively low-income, developing countries, and the process is still not completed. Probably even more important than the level of tariffs in influencing market access, however, are the numerous nontariff barriers that prevail in OECD countries' trade regimes (quantitative restrictions on imports, import "fees," antidumping provisions). The restrictions imposed by the EU's Common Agricultural Policy (CAP) have been a particular grievance for would-be exporters of farm products to the West. While it is uncertain how much harm restrictions on market access have done to the FSU economies up to now, it is clear that their persistence has not fostered goodwill toward the West. On the other hand, the fast-reforming Baltic states clearly benefited from the multiple arrangements that greatly improved their access to OECD markets. In the long run, as the transformation proceeds, market-opening measures will be critically important to economic recovery in the region and are, in any case, also in the long-run economic interests of Western countries themselves. Progress toward normalizing trade relationships between FSU states and OECD countries is being made through such devices as Partnership and Cooperation Agreements with the EU, which over half the new states have signed. A major additional step will be their admission to membership in the World Trade Organization (WTO), for which over half have already applied.

The Reform Process and Outside Actors

Since independence, economic reform has proceeded in all of the new states, but in widely differing ways and with greatly diverse outcomes. No state has sought to leave the institutions of the Soviet command economy intact. In general, reforms have proceeded in fits and starts through a complex interactive process of actions from above (the government) and from below (individuals and firms). As a result of the considerable learning that took place during the last years of the USSR,[29] governments and, by and large, their populations now accept the fact that joining the rest of the world as normal countries requires that they develop relatively open market economies, which clearly are the only ones that work tolerably well in the modern world and deliver the prosperity they all want. Despite the economic hardships for many people up to now in the transformation process and their evident nostalgia for the seeming security of the old order, the necessity for a market economy has been accepted, and reforms have aimed to bring it about. Thus, in steadfastly conditioning assistance (other than humanitarian aid) to progress on market-oriented reforms, the West has been reinforcing a domestic political choice and not imposing one. In the words of a Russian spokesman,

> The move to democracy, to formation of a civil society and socially-oriented market economy came as a result of a long and painful search which is now the historical choice of the peoples of Russia. This move is (1) not externally imposed on Russia and is not a result of outside pressure and (2) is not contingent upon the aims of any particular political leaders or groups. Therefore, despite possible fluctuations in political developments, Russia's movement along the path of democratic transformation and economic reform is not reversible.[30]

The West has not attempted to impose on the new states a particular model for a market economy or to prescribe the path to achieve it. Each state, dictated by its own initial conditions and political processes, has chosen its own model and rate of speed. Their choices have ranged from the relatively fast, Europe-oriented reforms of the Baltic states to the glacially paced, state-oriented choice of some

Central Asian states. Throughout, however, the West has delivered a clear and consistent message—that the sine qua non for creating successful market economies are liberalization, stabilization, and privatization, the three "pillars" of reform. Western assistance has been targeted toward putting those pillars in place, not merely by providing funds, but also by seeking to spread understanding of the economics that underpins those three concepts.

Aside from broad goals, the reform process in the new states has proceeded amidst much controversy—among intellectuals, within governments and legislatures, and between those bodies. Indeed, the issues debated in those states often mirror those argued among academics in the West over the speed and sequencing of reforms. On a more detailed level, the fiercest controversies have raged over the content of particular reform programs and legislation, especially that concerned with the role of the government and with privatization of state-owned property and land, where strongly entrenched economic and bureaucratic interests are at stake. A variety of approaches has emerged from these internal debates over the political economy of reforms. Again, the West has not sought to impose a particular approach, but rather to support the one chosen and to work with the new state as best it could. In some countries, the nature of the role that should be played by outside actors itself has been controversial at times, especially when issues of national pride or national "patrimony" are perceived to be involved. Conflicting domestic interests also come to the fore in debates over trade policies and provisions for foreign investment and production-sharing arrangements. Finally, although integration into the international community has been accepted everywhere as a goal, the relative role to be played by economic integration (understood variously) with other states of the FSU is controversial, both within Russia and in the non-Russian states.

Economic reforms in the states of the FSU have proceeded not by grand, overall designs and time schedules (as in the famous "500-day" plan of 1990), but rather piecemeal in each state in a process of accomplishing the politically and socially feasible, with increasing diversity characteristic of the process in 1992, 1993, and the first half of 1994. Since then, as a result of learning from their own and other reforming countries' experience, a greater commonality of approach became visible as reforms speeded up in several states. In particular, their leaders seem to have learned that taming inflation is essential to the much-desired revival of production. The pattern of interaction with outside actors may be described similarly, most prominently involvement with the international financial institutions. But the matter is more complex than that, because up to now these bodies, the IMF especially, have served in diverse ways both to catalyze economic reform and to support, discipline, and sustain the process. The potential availability of external funds for essential imports and as a source of noninflationary financing of budget deficits has made it easier for the political leaderships to embark on comprehensive reforms. At the same time, the conditionality attached to such funding has helped to strengthen the backbones of reformers as they struggle to keep often painful reform policies on track. Nonetheless, the strength of the domestic political will to implement and sustain economic reforms has been the most decisive factor in shaping the process in each state. We now sketch briefly how the course of economic reform has evolved in each state,[31] focusing on the role of outside actors.

The Baltic States

Just as they were pioneers in the breakup of the Soviet Union, Estonia, Latvia, and Lithuania have led the way in the post-Soviet years in economic reform and integration with the international community. They have adhered steadfastly to three goals—democratic politics, a market economy, and rejoining Europe. Pursuit of these goals has rested on a solid societal consensus for reforms, which has survived several changes of government leadership, even though the details of particular programs to implement the reforms have been subjected to vigorous internal debates in each state. From independence, the three states have had strong moral support from the West, along with active cooperation and considerable financial assistance. Historic cultural ties to their Nordic neighbors have been an important asset, also.

The three states wanted to become members of Western institutions, especially European ones, as quickly as possible. They joined the IMF and the World Bank in 1992 and the EBRD in 1993. In 1995, they signed association agreements with the European Union and have now had applications for full membership accepted, with negotiations over the terms underway. In pursuit of greater market access and integration, they signed free-trade agreements with most EFTA members in 1992–93 and with the EU in 1994. Finally, all three states now are actively negotiating the terms for admission to the WTO. Consistent with their rush toward Europe, the Baltic states from the beginning have refused to join the Russia-dominated Commonwealth of Independent States (CIS), for which stance they paid the high, short-term cost of having to pay world market prices for energy supplies from Russia.

Because of diverse internal political developments, the three states by no means have moved in lockstep. Economic reform has been pursued most persistently and vigorously in Estonia, the most economically advanced economy with the most steadfast commitment to reform. The Baltics had gotten a head start with liberalizing their economies during 1990–91 and were actively pursuing programs of reform at the time of independence.[32] Having their own national currencies was high on their agendas. The three states left the ruble zone in June 1992, with each state choosing different monetary arrangements. The Baltics have worked closely since independence with the international financial institutions, whose policy advice, extensive technical assistance, and financial support have been crucial to the success of stabilization programs. The word "dialogue," rather than "diktat," needs to be stressed here, however. Thus, the Estonian government early on opted to move more quickly than its IMF consultants had thought prudent.[33]

In September–October 1992, the IMF approved standby (SBA) funding agreements for the Baltic states with subsequent renewals. These are normal IMF facilities that provide for loans targeted to specific reform goals during the period, usually one year. The states also took advantage of the STF opportunity to obtain additional financing after it became available in 1993. Lithuania's SBA was replaced in late 1994 with an extended funds facility (EFF), which provides IMF funds to support a three-year program of specified reform targets. Besides direct IMF funds, the Baltics have received substantial financial support for their reform programs from other multilateral institutions and bilateral donors, especially the EU, Sweden, and Denmark. Through 30 September 1995, the United States had obligated $103 million in grant assistance to the Baltic states.[34] Overall, the total external assistance of about $1 billion, the largest on a per capita basis among FSU countries, seems to have been timely and adequate, and on the whole, the objectives of IMF-negotiated reform programs have been met.

Driven by domestic politics, but with consistent support from outside, economic reforms have made remarkable strides. Although much remains to be done, the three states now have reasonably well-functioning market economies open to the outside world. In 1995, the private sector accounted for 55 to 60 percent of GDP, compared with about 10 percent in 1990. Small-scale privatization is nearly completed, and state divestiture is well under way for large firms under diverse programs. With Estonia well ahead, the economies have been liberalized and nearly stabilized at levels achieved in the reformist countries of Eastern Europe, with annual inflation rates of 27 to 36 percent in 1995. The economies started to recover in 1994, and growth continued in 1995 with significant desirable structural change also visible, especially in Estonia. Remarkable reorientation of foreign trade has taken place—from 85 percent or more of it conducted with other Soviet republics in 1990 to only a third with the FSU in 1994 for Estonia, 53 percent for Latvia, and 60 percent in Lithuania.[35] This trend evidently continued in 1995. Finally, the Baltics—with Estonia far in the lead— have attracted a growing inflow of foreign direct investment, again the greatest per capita among the post-Soviet states.

Russia

From the outset, the government of the Russian Federation has been committed to and has led the way among CIS states toward a market economy integrated into the global economy. Although Russia has come a long way toward achieving that goal, it has done so amid ferocious domestic controversy, not over the goal per se (albeit perhaps variously understood), but over the design and implementation of the numerous measures taken to bring it about. Throughout the period, reformers in the government have had to do continuous battle with bureaucratic opponents within the government, with conservative legislatures, and with politically powerful vested interests in the economy.[36] Despite all this, Russia has managed to effect a truly radical economic reform, but one that has been implemented only gradually. Its path has been neither shock therapy nor gradualism as usually understood in the Western debates, but a uniquely Russian path, with the ebb and flow of politics dictating the timing, strategy, and outcomes. The West has steadfastly encouraged Russia's efforts to become a normal state, not only with words, but with measures for inclusion and substantial financial support. But the size, content, and timing of such support has become the subject of much, often-heated controversy, both within Russia and in the West.

The Russian government's choice to implement bold economic reform has had the unwavering endorsement of Western leaders, support that surely was welcomed by Russia's reformers. Moreover, Western governments have moved quickly to integrate Russia into the international community. Russia became a member of the IMF and World Bank in June 1992 and of the EBRD and International Finance Corporation (IFC) in the following year. President Yeltsin was invited to participate in some of the discussions at each of the G-7 summits during 1992–96, although his request to become the eighth member has yet to be granted. At these fora, the Western governments applauded Russia's progress on economic reform, promised varying kinds of financial assistance, and voiced support for Russia's admission to the GATT and its successor, the WTO,[37] which when accomplished will make Russia a normal participant in the global trading system. Finally, MFN and GSP status was given to Russia by most OECD countries in 1992 and 1993, thus ending most of the discrimination that had applied to the USSR. Russia has yet to sign a free-trade agreement with any major Western country, but it signed a Partnership and Cooperation Agreement with the EU in 1994. As successor to the USSR, Russia acquired associate membership in the GATT, and its application for membership in the WTO has been accepted. Nevertheless, alleged lack of adequate access to Western markets has been a sore point in Russia's dealings with the West.

The West responded to Russia's plea for financial assistance early on with announcements of a major aid package of $24 billion in April 1992 and another partially overlapping package totaling $43.4 billion in April 1993. The packages included multilateral loans and a ruble stabilization fund to be provided with conditionality by the international financial institutions, bilateral aid largely in the form of export credits, and debt relief. These high profile announcements doubtless raised expectations in Russia. Although bilateral commitments and debt relief were largely implemented, only about 15 percent of the multilateral commitments were disbursed in 1992–93, because the requisite conditionality targets were not being met by wide margins.[38]

A spirited controversy has arisen with regard to that outcome. One side argues, in effect, that the multilateral organizations should have provided the committed funds anyway, in order to ease the domestic pain of reducing the huge budget deficit—an essential step needed to bring down inflation, because the deficit was being financed by printing money. Adherents to this view believe that the IMF's conditions were too tough and should have been relaxed in recognition of Russia's particularly difficult financial situation. They also believe that foreign financing would serve to support the reformers by reducing the political opposition to economic and political reforms, thus helping to ensure their continuance.[39] Putting the issue most dramatically and making comparisons with the Marshall Plan, Jeffrey Sachs, a prominent Western advisor to the Russian government during this period, declares, "Not only the Russian economy, but also Russian democracy has been put recklessly at risk by Western neglect."[40]

An alternative view maintains that in 1992–93 the Russian reformers clearly did not have the requisite political consensus to implement a bold macro-stabilization effort, because it would have necessitated drastic reductions in subsidies to industrial enterprises and to farms, thus raising the specter of mass unemployment. Adherents also argue that reducing inflation was not the government's top priority in 1992–93; rather, once the economy had been substantially liberalized in early 1992, the reformers wanted to push their bold privatization program forward as rapidly as feasible.[41] Spokesmen for this alternative view point out that provision of international funds necessarily has to be made contingent upon carrying out economic policies that will ensure their repayment, stem capital flight, and foster economic recovery and development over the longer term. They believe, moreover, that by helping to maintain economic and financial discipline, conditionality strengthens rather than weakens the hand of the reformers.[42] In addition, they question the propriety of using international funds to "buy" (in effect) political support for reforms in member states. In doing so, the West could be seen to be interfering in the internal political affairs of Russia, something Russians themselves strongly oppose. The author supports this alternative view. Also, although the addition of several billion rubles to Russian budget revenues in 1992–93 likely would have knocked a few points off the monthly inflation rate, stabilization probably could not have been achieved, given the early stage of related reforms, an unwillingness to impose hard budget constraints on firms and farms, and insufficient learning. Finally, the impact of Western assistance for budget support on Russian political processes during these formative years would seem marginal at best. Rather than using international funds Western governments, of course, could have provided larger grants or concessionary loans directly to support the Russian budget or currency, but the political will to do so was not there; after all, how best to provide financial aid to Russia was not all that clear among the G-7 as well as within domestic constituencies. Ultimately, the international financial organizations were given the primary role; after all, they were set up to provide technical and financial assistance to member countries in urgent need of economic policy reform to foster long-run development.

The Russian government has been in a dialogue with the IMF since November 1991, a dialogue that has contributed importantly to the building of intellectual understanding of macroeconomics in the economic ministries and the central bank.[43] The first standby agreement became effective in August 1992, followed by two STF arrangements in 1993–94; a total of $4.2 billion was disbursed under these agreements in 1992–94.[44] A second standby agreement was signed in April 1995, under which about $5.1 billion was disbursed in 1995. At the end of March 1996, a three-year extended funds facility was approved, with monthly program monitoring by the IMF of the $4 billion scheduled for disbursement in 1996. In addition, official and private creditors have provided more than $20 billion in loans, and the Paris and London Clubs agreed to a rescheduling of payments on the principal of Russia's external debt in each year from 1992 to 1996. In all, such debt relief amounted to some $40 to $45 billion during 1992–95. The United States has given grants totaling over $2 billion, while other countries, mainly Germany, have provided some $6 billion. Western governments and organizations have funded a substantial amount of technical assistance, which has significantly facilitated implementation of reforms, as even Russian critics agree.[45] Specifically, with regard to voucher privatization, the program's designers state, "There is no doubt that American technical assistance vastly improved the quality and the speed of Russian privatization."[46]

In its seemingly chaotic way, Russia has transformed its economy fundamentally in a short five years.[47] The state's monopoly over ownership of property, allocation of resources, and foreign trade has been shattered. The private sector—with its numerous new businesses as well as some 120,000 privatized firms—now accounts for over 60 percent of gross domestic product (GDP). Inflation has been brought down from a monthly average of 20 percent in 1992–93 to 10 percent in 1994, and to 7 percent in 1995; it averaged 3 percent through mid-1996. Most Western forecasters expect economic growth to resume in 1997. Russia has maintained a positive balance of trade and now conducts well over half of its trade with non-FSU states, compared with only 40 percent in 1990. Foreign direct investment, though, totaled only $3.9 billion in 1992–95, but 12,400 joint ventures with Western partners were operating in 1995. Accumulating evidence points to a gradual shift in attitudes and behavior of both households and firms away from accepting state paternalism as normal and toward self-reliance for economic well-being. Through adoption of a new civil code, a legal basis for a private-enterprise, market-based economy has been put in place, although the process is far from completed. The mix of output has shifted appreciably from greatly excessive emphasis on industrial and military production toward the services sector. Rudimentary financial markets, while still fragile, have become strong enough to help to discipline macroeconomic policy. The process of overcoming the egregious economic distortions and physical legacies from seventy years of central planning, however, has barely begun. While the credit for the substantial progress made in the first stages of reform must go to the Russians, the role of the many and diverse outside actors has been strongly positive. Their involvement has greatly facilitated the vast learning that is essential to accomplishing Russia's self-set goal of becoming a normal state integrated into the global economy. Given the acute societal stress that has been a part of the transformation process thus far, it should be no surprise to observe among Russians both nostalgia for a perceived less stressful past order and a proclivity to blame outsiders for the pain.

Western Republics

The economic reform process has evolved quite differently in Ukraine, Belarus, and Moldova, largely for reasons of domestic politics, and so has the pattern of their interaction with the world beyond the FSU. In all three states, little progress was made in 1992 and most of 1993, but the process accelerated in 1994–95, most prominently in Ukraine. With their expressed intent to move toward market economies integrated into the global economy in normal ways, the three countries were admitted to membership in the international financial institutions in June–September 1992. MFN status was accorded them almost immediately after independence by the EU and EFTA countries, followed by the United States in mid-1992 for Ukraine and Moldova and in January 1993 for Belarus. GSP status was given to them by the EU in January 1993. All three have applied for membership in the WTO, with discussions currently under way.

Ukraine

In the first two and a half years of independence, Ukraine was explicitly committed to a policy of a gradual move toward a socially oriented market economy. In practice, however, gradualism amounted to gross mismanagement, as inadequate efforts to stabilize the national currency (introduced in November 1992) produced hyperinflation, as privatization proceeded feebly and sporadically, and as perhaps half of all economic activity was drawn into the unofficial economy as a consequence.[48] During this period the inflow of Western assistance was minimal, limited almost exclusively to export credits and bilateral aid, much of it related to nuclear weapons disposal and to matters connected with the Chernobyl nuclear power plant.

The situation changed radically after mid-1994 with the election of Leonid Kuchma as president and his launching of comprehensive economic reform. Ukraine figured prominently in G-7 discussions at the Naples Summit in July, when a package of $4 billion was offered to assist continued reform. To support Kuchma's program, the IMF approved an STF credit line of $365 million in October and the World Bank committed to a large rehabilitation loan in December. A standby agreement with the IMF was approved in April 1995 along with a second payment under the STF, while the World Bank committed to substantial lending for balance-of-payments support. Under these arrangements, Ukraine received about $2 billion in 1995. At the end of the year, because a credible program was not in place for 1996, the IMF suspended disbursements under the standby agreement until the Ukrainian parliament passed the 1996 budget; they were resumed in April 1996. Besides financial assistance, the IMF and World Bank have provided government officials with a crash course in market economics and macroeconomic policy making, deemed by one observer to have been "a decisive element" in the design and implementation of reform.[49] The U.S. substantially increased its technical assistance to Ukraine in 1995, as did the EU.

Under its new program, Ukraine has greatly liberalized its economy, speeded up privatization markedly, and made notable progress in stabilization. The results are to be seen in a significant slowing of the fall in output in 1995, the privatization of about one-third of medium and small firms, and sharply higher numbers of private farms and privatized apartments. Most importantly, the rate of inflation has dropped from 400 percent in 1994 to 182 percent in 1995, with monthly rates averaging about 5 percent through mid-1996. Foreign investment rose by some $265 million in 1995, bringing the total, however, to less than $1 billion since independence.[50] A liberal law on foreign investment was adopted in early 1996. Despite remarkable progress relative to past years, Ukraine's current efforts to implement radical economic reform remain deeply controversial, with the reformist Kuchma government in conflict with a conservative legislature and with only a dim understanding of economic issues in the state bureaucracy and among the general population. In this valiant effort to salvage Ukraine's economy, the support of the West has been timely and crucial, not least its efforts through many technical assistance channels to speed up the learning process among key groups of domestic actors.[51] Ukraine has signed a Partnership and Cooperation Agreement with the EU, and there is now open discussion in Ukraine of the possibility of eventual EU membership.

Belarus

Commitment to economic reform on the part of the Belarusian government has been erratic and weak. Instead, it has seemed far more interested in cementing some kind of an economic union with Russia. The latest of several attempts to do so culminated in a set of agreements signed in early 1996. Nonetheless, the government's reform efforts were sufficient to persuade the IMF to approve an STF arrangement, effective in July 1993, in support of reform and the introduction of a separate currency. A standby agreement was adopted in early 1995. In early 1996, however the IMF suspended payments under the standby agreement, citing lack of progress in developing credible economic policy for 1996. Under these arrangements, plus modest credits from the international banks, Belarus received $326 million during 1992–94. Through the end of fiscal year 1995, the United States provided $282 million in aid, most of it in the form of food and humanitarian grants.

Although moderate progress has been made in liberalizing the economy, privatization has proceeded glacially, and almost no reform has taken place in agriculture. The economy is far from being stabilized, with inflation amounting to 710 percent in 1995, although the monthly rate in the first half of 1996 has averaged only 4 percent. The private sector accounted for only about one-eighth of GDP in 1995. Over two-thirds of the labor force was employed in state enterprises and unreformed collective farms in 1995. The services share in GDP has actually fallen at the expense of industry. Although Belarus was accorded MFN and GSP status by Western countries in 1992–93, the share of its trade with non-FSU states has fallen, and only a trickle of foreign investment has flowed into the country.

Moldova

Despite a series of natural disasters and the conflict over the status of Trans-Dniester, the Moldovan government has maintained a strong commitment to economic reform and has made considerable progress, especially since introduction of its own currency in November 1993. This stance has won it substantial encouragement and support from the international community. After disbursing emergency drought-assistance credits in February 1993, the IMF effected an STF arrangement in September and converted it to a two-year standby funding agreement at the end of the year. The standby was extended in March 1995, with negotiations underway for a two-year Enhanced Structural Adjustment Facility (ESAF) arrangement. During 1992–95, the international financial institutions have disbursed more than $200 million in credits. The United States has had a variety of endeavors in Moldova, providing it with $150 million in grants through fiscal year 1995, mainly in the form of food assistance. U.S. technical assistance to the privatization effort has been deemed indispensable by Moldovan officials.

Moldova has liberalized its economy to about the same degree as has Russia, but it has been much slower to privatize. In 1995, state enterprises still employed nearly 40 percent of the labor force, and the private sector accounted for less than a third of GDP. Moldova's most notable achievement has been its success in bringing down inflation to only 24 percent in 1995, comparable to rates in the Baltic states. Although GDP declined only slightly in 1995, desirable structural changes have yet to take place. The share of the service sector has actually declined at the expense of agriculture. Despite a moderately liberal trade regime and the receipt of MFN and GSP status from the West, Moldova still conducts well over 90 percent of its trade with the FSU. Although there was some 412 registered joint ventures at the end of 1994, foreign investment through 1995 totaled only about $86 million.

Transcaucasia

Armenia, Azerbaijan, and Georgia may be treated together, because their postindependence experience has many similarities, as do their interactions with the international community. During 1992–93, and into early 1994, the governments of these states were preoccupied with military conflicts, which were accompanied by periods of hyperinflation and the largest declines in economic activity among FSU states. Nonetheless, Transcaucasia managed to make some progress in economic reform; Armenia and Georgia are judged to have achieved greater liberalization and privatization of their economies overall during 1992–95 than did all of Central Asia, Ukraine, and Belarus.[52] National currencies were introduced in 1992–93, but inflation accelerated in all states of Transcaucasia. With an easing of military conflicts, reform speeded up markedly in late 1994 and 1995, when adoption of comprehensive reform programs led the IMF to approve STF credits with conditions designed to bring rapid stabilization and to help lay the foundations for market economies. STF funding was approved for Armenia and Georgia in December 1994 and for Azerbaijan in April 1995, when standby funding was also approved for Armenia on concessional terms. In March 1996, three-year ESAF arrangements were approved for all three states. Georgia's president, Eduard Shevardnadze, hailed the agreement as a vote of confidence in the state's independence. Along with substantial funding, the IMF staff has provided extensive technical assistance, especially for Armenia, and World Bank lending has also been stepped up. In early 1996, the three states signed Partnership and Cooperation Agreements with the EU, which will implement additional technical assistance.

The Transcaucasian states have received substantial amounts of U.S. aid, especially food and humanitarian aid components. As of 30 September 1995, Armenia had been given $505 million and Georgia $388 million, but Azerbaijan (because of its use of force and its blockade against Armenia) received only $72 million. On a per capita basis, Armenia and Georgia were the top recipients of U.S. aid among FSU states. Technical assistance programs, which account for about one-fifth of the total, are helping to provide the training and know-how needed for building market-oriented economies and democratic societies.

Under their newly adopted comprehensive reform programs, the three states have made substantial progress in liberalizing their economies, especially in Azerbaijan, which had lagged earlier. Armenia and Georgia had already privatized most of their agricultural land and housing, but privatization elsewhere has moved forward slowly, as well. The most remarkable success has been in stabilization, with inflation rates in 1995 ranging between 25 and 85 percent, according to official data, compared with quadruple-digit or higher rates in 1994. Monthly rates in the low single-digits were being maintained through mid-1996. Economic growth was positive in Armenia in 1994 and 1995. As is to be expected, given the experiences since independence, restructuring of production and reorganization of enterprises has yet to occur, and the vast bulk of trade is still conducted with the FSU.

Central Asia

In terms of their proclivity to implement economic reform, the five Central Asian states may be grouped into moderate reformers (Kyrgyzstan and Kazakhstan), a latecomer to moderate reform (Uzbekistan), and very slow reformers (Tajikistan and Turkmenistan). The extent and pattern of involvement of Central Asian states with the international financial institutions and bilateral donors are closely related to their reformist stance. In their search for markets and foreign investment, all of them have been interacting extensively with non-FSU countries, their Islamic neighbors in particular, with whom they have negotiated a number of trade agreements. All three states have joined the Economic Cooperation Organization, a regional body that aims to promote cooperation in trade, transportation, and economic development for members. Kazakhstan, Uzbekistan, and Kyrgyzstan have also joined the Asian Development Bank, and the first two have applied for membership in the WTO.

Kyrgyzstan

Kyrgyzstan has led Central Asia in commitment to implement economic reform and has made by far the most progress. This stance, along with its democratic politics, has won it substantial Western assistance, but not as yet much direct foreign investment. The introduction of its own currency in May 1993 was supported by STF and standby arrangements with the IMF. In July 1994, an ESAF arrangement was negotiated to support a comprehensive program of systemic reforms over four years. Through the end of 1994, multilateral and bilateral donors had disbursed nearly $200 million in loans, and the United States had provided $221 million in grants through 30 September 1995, the third largest among FSU states on a per capita basis. The new state has been receiving extensive amounts of technical assistance from a variety of donors. After a rather rocky start, the country has been adhering to its IMF-supported program reasonably well. Its economy is liberalized about to the same degree as in Latvia and Lithuania. The inflation rate of 32 percent in 1995 was also at Baltic levels. A marked slowing of the decline in GDP and a structural shift toward the service sector also has been occurring. Privatization of small firms and housing is nearing completion, and agricultural reform is well under way. The private sector contributed about 40 percent of GDP in 1995.

Kazakhstan

Kazakhstan has followed a much slower and more erratic path of reform than has Kyrgyzstan. The pragmatic president of Kazakhstan, Nursultan Nazarbaev, had been able to make sufficient progress to persuade the IMF to support the reform program with an STF in July 1993, in anticipation of the introduction of a national currency in November. A standby arrangement took effect in January 1994 and was renewed in 1995. In July 1996, the IMF approved an ESAF credit to underpin a three-year program of systemic reform and restructuring. Bilateral creditors have provided financing about equal to that of the multilateral creditors, and Kazakhstan's progress in economic reform, plus its natural wealth, has brought in an even larger amount of private credits. Total credits disbursed from all sources amounted to nearly $1.2 billion during 1992–94. The United States has an extensive array of aid projects in Kazakhstan, with cumulative disbursements totaling $170 million at the end of September 1995. Technical assistance comprised over half of the total. The country has also attracted the greatest amount of direct foreign investment of any post-Soviet state except Russia and Ukraine, and on a per capita basis it is second after Estonia. Along with credits, the IMF and the World Bank have provided the government and its central bank with a large and steady flow of technical assistance; both have resident missions in Almaty.

With this assistance and a stable commitment by President Nazarbaev to pushing reforms forward, Kazakhstan has made considerable progress, and can boast the most liberalized economy in Central Asia after Kyrgyzstan. A focus on stabilization after mid-1994 brought the rate of inflation down to 60 percent in 1995 from over 1,900 percent in 1994. Privatization has been controversial, slow, and erratic, however, and the private sector accounted for only about one-quarter of GDP in 1995. The decline in GDP and industrial output also slowed appreciably, and the balance of trade was positive. A rather sizable shift in employment to the services sector has been taking place, as well as a moderate shift toward the West in the geographical direction of foreign trade, although trade with the FSU still dominates.

Uzbekistan

Since independence, Uzbekistan has been following its own distinctive road to a market economy, which might be termed "state-managed gradualism." In 1992 and 1993, the government focused on policies to make the country self-sufficient in energy and food and, with hard currency earnings from exports of cotton and nonferrous metals, to modernize its industry and improve cotton yields. Following a partial liberalization of prices in early 1992, the government maintained extensive controls on prices and economic activity, most prominently on external trade. These policies, along with an authoritarian political regime, greatly restrained the role of outside actors, including foreign investors. In early 1994, however, President Islam Karimov embarked on a far more reformist course, aimed initially to bring down the triple-digit rates of inflation and halt the rapid depreciation of the country's new currency, which was introduced in November 1993. Negotiations with the IMF to provide technical and financial support for the new program culminated in approval of an STF in January 1995, followed by a standby arrangement at the end of the year. The World Bank also made large loans available. President Karimov hailed this agreement as a vote of confidence in the irreversibility of the reform. In all, creditors, mainly bilateral, had disbursed $650 million through the end of 1994. Because of Uzbekistan's policies and politics, the United States had through the end of September 1995 provided a mere $37 million in grants, mostly for technical assistance.

Considerable liberalization has taken place and privatization has speeded up under the new program, although the private sector contributed only about 30 percent of GDP in 1995. Inflation has dropped from nearly 1,300 percent in 1994 to perhaps about 125 percent in 1995. GDP declined by only 1 percent, and industrial output continued to rise. Under its assorted policies, the country is now nearly self-sufficient in energy and food, the service sector as a share of GDP has increased significantly, and less than 75 percent of foreign trade was conducted with FSU states in 1994, compared with 90 percent in 1990. Foreign investment, which has been actively encouraged, has picked up since 1994, especially through the government-favored means of forming joint ventures.

Tajikistan and Turkmenistan

Tajikistan and Turkmenistan have been the slowest reformers among the post-Soviet states. Tajikistan, where civil war has raged much of the time since independence, is somewhat farther along in economic reform than is Turkmenistan, whose authoritarian president seems to see little need for comprehensive reform. Although the IMF has been in consultation with the governments in the two states, no programs had resulted through 1995. The two states had received $118 million in financing from international financial institutions and $361 million from a few bilateral donors. Through September 1995 the United States had provided $260 million in aid, mostly food. Foreign investment has been negligible. In May 1996, however, the IMF approved a standby credit in support of a newly adopted economic reform program for Tajikistan.

While the two countries have freed many prices and allow the formation of new private businesses, pervasive state controls remain in effect, especially over foreign trade. Privatization, although sanctioned by legislation, has been little implemented. The notably poor official statistics show steady declines in output and extremely high inflation through 1995. Introduction of national currencies—in November 1993 in Turkmenistan and in May 1995 in Tajikistan—did not serve as catalysts for stabilization and reform, as was the case in other Central Asian countries. The economies in the two states have been kept afloat largely because they have been able to export raw materials on the world market, as is reflected in some reduction in the shares of their trade that is conducted with FSU states.

Conclusions

The sudden and unexpected breakup of the USSR at the end of 1991 delivered a massive societal shock to the peoples of the fifteen independent states that emerged. During the past five years, they have been attempting to carry out diverse societal transformations—to build new worlds to replace defunct Soviet worlds. They have had to build simultaneously new nations, new states and politics, and new economies, starting from the deformed organizational structures and the human and physical capital in place on their territories. With varying degrees of zeal, they have been trying to become normal countries with normal (market) economies interacting in the international community of sovereign states in normal ways. These are daunting tasks, given the egregious legacies of many decades of abnormality. Despite the social trauma and many visible problems and shortcomings, the first five years are a success story by and large, rather than the failure that is perceived by many observers. This positive assessment applies to economic reform in particular and is formulated with the abysmal state of affairs at the outset of independence and with the enormity and complexity of the political–economic task being undertaken always kept in mind. Many outside actors have been involved in this success story, so the fact that the West is often blamed for the pain that has been part of the reform process should be no surprise; in fact, both scapegoating and finger-pointing is to be expected.

The new states have chosen diverse strategies for economic reform, ranging from the state-managed gradualism of much of Central Asia and Belarus to the fast-paced, comprehensive path taken by the Baltic states, most prominently by Estonia. After five years, the outcomes are also widely diverse. Thus, as is the case for the transition economies in east-central Europe, the experience of post-Soviet states sheds some empirical light on the much muddled Western debates over shock therapy versus gradualism as reform strategies for ex-Communist states. This experience shows clearly that countries that move most rapidly to stabilize and liberalize their economies, encourage the entry of new firms, and open their economies to world markets are the ones that will reap the rewards of reform most quickly.[53] They come in the form of a revival of economic growth, desirable structural changes in the composition of GDP, a speedy reorientation of foreign trade away from past patterns, greater foreign assistance, and increasing direct foreign investment. Thus, the economic revival and trade reorientation observed in the Baltic states, which opted for a fast pace of reform, stands in marked contrast to the continued economic stagnation in much of Central Asia, which has taken a far more gradualist approach. Similarly, the present economic situation in relatively reformist Russia, full of blemishes though it may be, can be compared with the much worse situation in Ukraine, a self-proclaimed gradualist reformer during its first two and a half years of independence.

The precipitous disintegration of the monolithic Soviet Union into fifteen sovereign countries caught Western governments almost totally by surprise. Speedy response to this radically new situation was clearly and urgently needed, but there had been no time to devise a grand strategic vision, let alone to formulate agreed-upon programs for implementing it. Two determinants quickly appeared: (1) the new states desired to become normal members of the international economic and political community and needed assistance in doing so; and (2) the West decided that it was in its own interest to welcome the new states and help them to create market economies, consensual governance, and civil societies. Although the objectives were clear and not controversial, how to assist the process was not, but the need to act speedily to address the manifest economic crises in the region was evident.

Fortunately, the West had created in the postwar years several international institutions which were in place to provide both financial assistance and policy and technical advice—the IMF and World Bank, the EBRD, the EC, and OECD. It was agreed that, aside from humanitarian aid, provision of financial assistance was to be conditioned on the progress of economic and political reform, that the IMF, World Bank, and EBRD were to have the leading role with respect to furthering economic reform, and that individual governments would supplement such help with additional loans and grants under whatever conditions they wished to set. Many private organizations also joined in the assistance endeavor. While major Western governments have been in agreement on this overall approach to assisting the new states, they have not always seen eye to eye on the details, such as the amounts of assistance commitments and the terms of conditionality that should be imposed. At the several summits of Western leaders, the United States has often pressed for greater bilateral commitments and less stringent conditionality from the international financial institutions. Bilateral donors have often geared their assistance to particular domestic agendas, such as support for their exporters or, for Germany, removal of Soviet/Russian troops from East Germany and, for the United States, their removal from the Baltic states.

In fundamental ways, the many outside actors from the West have contributed a great deal to the progress in economic reform that has been made in this brief period. The West has consistently pursued policies of inclusion of each of the new states in the established organizations of the international order. Western governments and their assorted organizations have moved quickly to interact in many arenas with the fledgling governments in the new states, thus helping to shore up their newfound independence. The West has provided living examples, and not just theoretical models, of how market economies function in all their diversities and with their many costs and benefits. The numerous actors from the public and private sectors in the West, along with their international organizations, have participated in a massive transfer of human capital—that is, of market economy know-how—to the new states; this input has been essential to their progress in economic reform. Much mutual learning has taken place in the process. More specifically, officials in the new states have stated that Western technical assistance has been indispensable to putting many of the nuts and bolts of market economies in place. The West has steadfastly encouraged market-oriented reforms in the new states and has geared its assistance to that end. Although emphasis on the pillars of reform—liberalization, stabilization, privatization—necessarily has been a consistent theme, the West has tolerated and even supported diversity in approaches among the new states.

The West has made substantial financial assistance available to the post-Soviet states since their independence at the end of 1991. In all, total aid during 1992–95 probably amounted to over $100 billion, provided through credits, debt relief, and grants, with the first two dominating overwhelmingly. Meager though the total may seem relative to the OECD countries' total GDP, the availability of these external funds has been a strong positive factor in supporting the reform process in the countries of the FSU. Multilateral organizations, notably the IMF and the World Bank, not only have been major sources for finance and technical assistance, but also have both catalyzed and sustained the reform process through the conditionalities attached to that finance. Bilateral donors have sometimes geared their assistance to progress in both economic and political reform. But economic reform necessarily must be driven primarily by domestic politics. When those politics produced a readiness to undertake comprehensive reforms, the needed external financing has been made available. Whether this holds for Russia in 1992–93, however, is a matter of some controversy. The essential issue is whether the course of Russian politics and the present state of economic reforms would have been materially altered had Russia been given the promised additional billions of dollars in those years. I think not.[54] In 1995–96, when the political conditions in support of stabilization were far more favorable, substantial financial support was made available by multilateral and bilateral donors on favorable terms.[55]

On the whole, the West has been generous with funding for an array of technical assistance programs, which have greatly facilitated the reform process. Unfortunately, their implementation has been flawed, probably unavoidable given the urgent need to respond and the lack of mutual experience in the early years. These mistakes and shortcomings produced a storm of criticism, which, however well deserved, has tended to obscure the benefits of these endeavors to both donors and recipients. Better coordination, more effective targeting, and greater attention to the sensitivities of recipients surely would have produced a more effective use of donor resources vis-à-vis their objectives. Despite remarkable progress to date, economic transformation in the post-Soviet states still has a long way to go, and the process is bound to be slow, to proceed in fits and starts, and perhaps even with some setbacks. It is crucial to the success of this mammoth endeavor that the West remain cooperative, supportive, and actively engaged. George Breslauer has suggested a sensible strategy of selective engagement by governments and comprehensive engagement by private actors.[56] It would seem appropriate for governments to focus on assistance programs that have mutual benefits, such as those relating to the environment, nuclear safety, and weapons destruction. Another focus might be on programs, such as defense conversion, that are multipurpose, in that they foster economic reform as well as other aspects of societal transformation. Western governments should generously support their international financial institutions, for they now have the requisite expertise and experience and should continue to be key actors in furthering the process of economic transformation. The new states will continue to require large amounts of technical assistance for some years in a variety of areas. Both governments and nongovernmental organizations should fund them generously to the extent that the states can absorb it. Assistance should be targeted toward helping them become members of the WTO as quickly as feasible. This will enhance market access, provide some protection against imposition of arbitrary trade barriers, and afford strong political support for maintaining a liberal trade regime. Urgent attention needs to be given to better coordination of the numerous channels through which technical assistance is rendered, so that the increasingly scarce funds likely to be made available can be used most effectively. Waste, duplication, and conflicting programs are in nobody's interest. Moreover, the kind of assistance that is needed will change as the reforms evolve in each state. Finally, the West must be patient and must formulate reasonable expectations in assessing progress, with the legacies of history always in mind. A societal transformation process of the enormity that is being attempted in the new states—the dimensions of which still are not fully comprehended in the West—is bound to take a long time and to be quite messy. But the creation of reasonably well-functioning economies and democratic societies integrated into the international order is a mutual, long-run interest.

Notes

1. For discussions of the education of economists in the Soviet Union, see Pekka Sutela, *Economic Thought and Economic Reform in the Soviet Union* (Cambridge: Cambridge University Press, 1991): and Michael Alexeev, Clifford Gaddy, and Jim Leitzel, "Economics in the Former Soviet Union," *Journal of Economic Perspectives,* 6, no. 2 (Spring 1992): pp. 137–48.

2. "Aiding the Commonwealth of Independent States: A Bridge Loan too Far," *Transition,* 3, no. 1 (January 1992): p. 4.

3. For a flavor of this debate, often heated and muddled, see Josef C. Brada, "The Transformation from Communism to Capitalism: How Far? How Fast?" *Post-Soviet Affairs* 9, no. 2 (April–June 1993): pp. 87–110; Peter Murrell, "What Is Shock Therapy? What Did It Do in Poland and Russia?" *Post-Soviet Affairs* 9, no. 2 (April–June 1993), pp. 111–40; and Herman W. Hoen, " 'Shock vs. Gradualism' in Central Europe Reconsidered," *Comparative Economic Studies* 38, no. 1 (Spring 1996): pp. 1–20.

4. For a survey of the range of involvements of the World Bank and its institutions, see Christine J. Wallich, "What's Right and Wrong with World Bank Involvement in Eastern Europe," *Journal of Comparative Economics* 20, no. 1 (February 1995): pp. 57–94.

5. Summary descriptions of these programs are given in U.S. General Accounting Office, *Former Soviet Union: Information on U.S. Bilateral Program Funding* (Washington, DC: GAO/NSIAD 96–37, December 1995). For a summary of OECD countries' programs, see OECD *Assistance Programmes for Central and Eastern Europe and the Former Soviet Union,* (Paris: OECD), 1996.

6. For a flavor of the problems surrounding technical assistance efforts at the outset, see Robert Sharlet, "Bringing the Rule of Law to Russia and the NIS: The Role of the West in the Transformation of the Post-Soviet Legal Systems," in this volume.

7. Jeffrey Sachs, "Consolidating Capitalism," *Foreign Policy* (Spring 1995): p. 60.

8. Constantine C. Menges, "U.S. Aid to Russia, 1992–1996: A First Assessment of Results" (Washington, DC: George Washington University, 26 February 1996), mimeo, p. 33.

9. For more detail on Germany's assistance to the post-Soviet states, see Peter Dombrowski, "German and American Assistance to the Post-Soviet Transition," in this volume.

10. For details on this and other related issues, see Bartlomiej Kaminski and Zhen Kun Wang, "External Finance, Policy Conditionalities, and Transition from Central Planning," in this volume.

11. Daniel A. Citrin and Ashok K. Lahiri, ed., *Policy Experience and Issues in the Baltics, Russia, and Other Countries of the Former Soviet Union,* IMF Occasional Paper 133, (Washington, DC: IMF December 1995), pp. 15–6.

12. Bartlomiej Kaminski and Zhen Kun Wang, "External Assistance and Progress in Transition," World Development Report background paper (Washington, DC: World Bank, December 1995).

13. For a more extended discussion of these issues, see Josef C. Brada, Roland Schoenfeld, and Ben Slay, "The Role of International Financial Institutions in Central and Eastern Europe," *Journal of Comparative Economics* 20, no. 1 (February 1995): pp. 49–56.

14. Martha de Melo, Cevdet Denizer, and Alan Gelb, *From Plan to Market: Patterns of Transition* (Washington, DC: World Bank, Policy Research Working Paper 1564, January 1996); Bartlomiej Kaminski, Zhen Kun Wang, and Alan Winters, "Trade Performance Depends on Bold Reforms," *Transition* 6, nos. 9–10 (September–October 1995): pp. 17–9; Stanley Fischer, Ratna Shay, and Carlos A. Vegh, "Transition and Growth in Transition Economies: The Early Experience," *Journal of Economic Perspectives* 10, no. 2 (Spring 1996): pp. 45–66; and World Bank, *World Development Report 1996: From Plan to Market* (Washington, DC: World Bank, 1996).

15. Jeffrey Sachs, "Russia's Struggle with Stabilization," *Transition* 5, no. 5 (May-June 1994): pp. 7–9.

16. Ernesto Hernandez-Cata, "Russia and the IMF: The Political Economy of Macrostabilization," in Citrin and Lahiri *Policy Experience and Issues in the Baltics, Russia, and Other Countries of the Former Soviet Union,* p. 119.

17. Linda S. Goldberg, Barry W. Ickes, and Randi Ryterman, "Departure from the Ruble Zone: The Implications of Adopting Independent Currencies," *World Economy* 17, no. 3 (May 1994): pp. 291–322; James H. Noren and Robin Watson, "Interrepublic Economic Relations after the Disintegration of the USSR," *Soviet Economy* 8, no. 2 (April–June 1992): pp. 89–139; and Brigitte Granville, "Farewell Ruble Zone," in *Russian Economic Reform at Risk,* ed. Anders Åslund (London: Pinter, 1995), pp. 65–88.

18. Salvatore Zecchini, "The Role of International Financial Institutions in the Transition Process," *Journal of Comparative Economics* 20, no. 1 (February 1995): pp. 125–33.

19. Marek Dabrowski, *Western Aid Conditionality and the Post-Communist Transition* (Warsaw: Center for Social and Economic Research (CASE), Studies and Analyses 37–1995).

20. Kermal Dervis, Marcelo Selowsky, and Christine Wallich, "The Transition in Central and Eastern Europe and the Former Soviet Union," in *The Evolving Role of the World Bank: Helping Meet the Challenge of Development,* ed. K. Sarwar Lateef (Washington, DC: World Bank, 1995), pp. 119–53; "Lending to Russia: A New Challenge to the World Bank. An Interview with Managing Director Ernest Stern," *Transition* 4, no. 6 (July August 1993): pp. 1–4.

21. U.S. General Accounting Office, *Former Soviet Union: U.S. Bilateral Program Lacks Effective Coordination* (Washington, DC: GAO/NSIAD-95–10, February 1995); *U.S. Foreign Assistance: Assessment of Selected U.S. AID Projects in Russia* (Washington, DC: GAO/NSIAD/95–156, August 1995).

22. U.S. General Accounting Office, *Former Soviet Union: An Update on Coordination of U.S. Assistance and Economic Cooperation Programs* (Washington, DC: GAO/NSIAD/96–16, December 1995).

23. "The Russian Report," an independent assessment presented by a team of Russians at a conference on U.S. Aid to Russia, 1992–1996: A First Assessment of Results, George Washington University, Washington, DC, 26 February 1996, mimeo; Ariel Cohen, "Aid Russia, but Reform the U.S. Program," *Problems of Post-Communism*, 42, no. 3 (May–June 1995): pp. 32–35.

24. Janine R. Wedel, "U.S. Aid to Central and Eastern Europe: Results and Recommendations," *Problems of Post-Communism* 42, no. 3 (May–June 1995): pp. 45–50.

25. World Bank, *World Debt Tables, 1996,* 2 (Washington, DC: World Bank, 1996); de Melo et al., *From Plan to Market,* p. 64.

26. *Transition* 5, no. 9 (November–December 1994): p. 14.

27. John Hansen and Piritta Sorsa, "Estonia: A Shining Star From the Baltics," in *Trade in the New Independent States,* (Studies of Economies in Transformation, no. 13) ed. Constantine Michalopoulos and David G. Tarr (Washington, DC: World Bank, No. 13, 1994), pp. 115–32.

28. Bartlomiej Kaminski, "Trade Performance and Access to OECD Markets," in Michalopoulos and Tarr, *Trade in the New Independent States,* pp. 237–80.

29. George W. Breslauer, "Soviet Economic Reforms: Ideology, Politics and Learning," *Soviet Economy* 6, no. 3 (July–September 1990): pp. 252–80.

30. "The Russian Report," p. 8.

31. For more detail on the reform process in individual states, see Gertrude Schroeder, "Economic Transition in the Post-Soviet Republics: An Overview," in *Economic Transition in Russia and the New States of Eurasia,* ed. Bartlomiej Kaminski (Armonk, NY: M.E. Sharpe, 1996), pp. 11–41.

32. For more details see Saisa Lainela and Pekka Sutela, *The Baltic Economies in Transition* (Helsinki: Bank of Finland, 1994); and Raphael Shen, *Restructuring the Baltic Economies: Disengaging Fifty Years of Integration With the USSR* (Westport, CT: Praeger, 1994).

33. Ardo H. Hanson, "Comment on Chapter 5: The Political Economy of Macroeconomic and Foreign Trade Policy in Estonia," in Michalopoulos and Tarr, *Trade in the New Independent States,* pp. 133–40.

34. For details of the modest U.S. assistance to the Baltic states, see U.S. Department of State, *FY1995 SEED Act Implementation Report* (Washington, DC: U.S. Department of State, February 1996).

35. Misha V. Belkindas and Olga V. Ivanova, *Foreign Trade in the USSR and Successor States* (Washington, DC: World Bank, 1995): pp. 61–65.

36. For details see Anders Åslund, *How Russia Became a Market Economy* (Washington, DC: Brookings Institution, 1995); and Egor Gaidar and Karl Otto Pohl, *Russian Reform/International Money* (Cambridge, MA: MIT Press, 1995): pp. 1–54.

37. For a summary of the discussions about Russian assistance at successive summits, see John P. Hardt and Gretchen R. Rodkey, "Global Integration and the Convergence of Interests Among Key Actors in the West, Russia, Ukraine, and the Commonwealth of Independent States," in Kaminski, *Economic Transition in Russia and the New States of Eurasia,* pp. 357–385.

38. Edward Brau, "External Financial Assistance: The Record and Issues," in Citrin

and Lahiri, ed., *Policy Experience and Issues in the Baltics, Russia, and Other Countries of the Former Soviet Union,* pp. 103–16.

39. Jeffrey Sachs, "Why Russia Has Failed to Stabilize," in Åslund, *Russian Economic Reform at Risk,* pp. 53–63; Åslund, *How Russia Became a Market Economy,* pp. 214–20; Jeffrey Sachs, "Western Financial Assistance and Russia's Reform," in *Making Markets: Economic Transformation in Eastern Europe and the Post-Soviet States,* ed. Shafiquil Islam and Michael Mandelbaum (New York: Council on Foreign Relations Press, 1993), pp. 143–81; Brigitte Granville, *The Success of Russian Economic Reforms* (London: Royal Institute of International Affairs, 1995): pp. 52–70.

40. Sachs, "Consolidating Capitalism," p. 60.

41. Support for this position can be found in Gaidar and Pohl, *Russian Reform/International Money,* pp. 21–54.

42. Ernesto Hernandez-Cata, "Russia and the IMF: The Political Economy of Macro-Stabilization," *Problems of Post-Communism* 42, no. 3 (May–June 1995): pp. 19–26; Stanislaw Gomulka, "The IMF-Supported Programs of Poland and Russia, 1990–1993: Principles, Errors, and Results," *Journal of Comparative Economics* 20, no. 3 (June 1995): pp. 316–46; Dabrowski, *Western Aid Conditionality and the Post-Communist Transition,* pp. 15–16.

43. Alexei V. Mozhin, "Russia's Negotiations with the IMF," in *Changing the Economic System in Russia,* ed. Anders Åslund and Richard Layard (New York: St. Martin's Press, 1993): pp. 65–71; Hernandez-Cata, "Russia and the IMF," pp. 19–21.

44. Under the two G-7 aid packages, the IMF was to have provided $6 billion for a ruble stabilization fund and an additional $4 billion under the standby agreement. These funds were not disbursed because the Russian government did not adhere to the agreed-upon conditionality. Edvard Brav, footnote 38 in Citrin and Lahiri, ed. *Policy Experience and Issues in the Baltics, Russia, and Other Countries of the Former Soviet Union.*

45. "The Russian Report."

46. Maxim Boycko, Andrei Schleifer, and Robert Vishny, *Privatizing Russia* (Cambridge, MA: MIT Press, 1995): p. 141.

47. Even economist Leonid Abalkin, one of the most severe critics of the Russian government's economic policies, believes that change has been major and the direction irreversible. Leonid Abalkin, "The Economic Situation in Russia," *Problems of Post-Communism* 42, no. 4 (July–August 1995): pp. 53–54.

48. Daniel Kaufmann and Aleksandr Kaliberda, "Integrating the Unofficial Economy into the Dynamics of Post-Socialist Economies: A Framework of Analysis and Evidence," in Kaminski, *Economic Transition in Russia and the New States of Eurasia,* pp. 81–120; Daniel Kaufmann, "Market Liberalization in Ukraine to Regain a Post Pillar of Reform," *Transition* 5, no. 7 (September 1994): pp. 1–6.

49. John E. Tedstrom, *Ukraine's Economy at Risk,* RAND, RM 752, O/RC, February 1996, p. 18. See also Anders Åslund, "Eurasia Letter: Ukraine's Turnaround," *Foreign Policy,* no. 100 (Fall 1995): pp. 125–43.

50. FBIS, *Daily Report, Central Eurasia* (29 March 1996), FBIS-SOV-96-062, p. 51.

51. The head of the World Bank office in Kiev, for example, has been holding economics workshops for government professionals and seminars throughout the country to discuss reform issues with influential leaders from local government, the media, academe, and business.

52. DeMelo et al., *From Plan to Market,* p. 14.

53. These are, broadly speaking, the conclusions of a major recent comparative study of the experience at all transition economies. Ibid., pp. 142–47.

54. I share the view that economic considerations were not the primary forces that have shaped politics in Russia during 1992–96. See Yitzhak M. Brudny, "Neoliberal Economic Reform and the Consolidation of Democracy in Russia: Or Why Institutions and Ideas Might Matter More than Economics," in this volume.

55. For a recent example of this, see *Economist* (13 July 1996): pp. 71–72.

56. George W. Breslauer, "Aid to Russia: What Difference Can Western Policy Make?" in *The New Russia: Troubled Transformation,* ed. Gail W. Lapidus (Boulder, CO: Westview Press, 1995): pp. 223–44.

12

External Finance, Policy Conditionalities, and Transition from Central Planning

Bartlomiej Kaminski and Zhen Kun Wang

Introduction

With the end of the Cold War and the collapse of central planning, the former Council for Mutual Economic Assistance (CMEA) region has become the focus of the assistance effort designed to support transition to market-based democracies.[1] The challenge faced by the international aid community was unique, as the transition from central planning to market economy had no historical precedent. The change of the very nature of institutions under extremely adverse domestic and international economic conditions were recognized as the essence of assistance for the transition countries.[2] Finding the right mix of assistance addressing stabilization cum liberalization and alleviating problems triggered by collapse of trade among former CMEA members and output decline was the challenge to Organization for Economic Cooperation and Development (OECD) donors as well as to multilateral institutions. The emphasis of Western donors, beginning in the early 1980s, on the quality of governance and the experience of managing debt crisis in many developing countries have offered valuable lessons to design and implement structural adjustments and institutional reforms. However, most of the reform programs in developing countries pale in comparison to the scale and intensity of the transition from central planning to markets.

The overall organizational framework of the assistance to transition economies was set up in 1989 in response to the collapse of the Communist political regime in Poland. The framework was designed to bring about close cooperation among OECD governments and multilateral institutions especially the Bretton Woods institutions—the International Monetary Fund (IMF) and the World Bank. The IMF and the World Bank have been assigned a leading role in assessing the exceptional needs of the transition countries:[3] providing policy advice and financial support for liberalizing prices and macroeconomic stabilization; developing policies on the dismantling of state monopolies and introducing new incentives systems; tax administration and banking reform; and assisting in developing legal and institutions for private sector development. In fact, they have become the major source of external finance and policy advice for many transition countries.

The question concerning the role of the IMF and the World Bank does not render itself to a straightforward analysis. These institutions are not a substitute for government. Without a government involvement and commitment to address its country's economic woes, they cannot step in. Even if they did (external assistance without substantial commitments to internal reforms), it would still lead to failure. The program implemented results from close interaction between recipient governments and the IMF or the World Bank. Moreover, the IMF and the World Bank have to operate within the limits largely set by recipient governments as well as these institutions' major shareholders. The latter, worried about the political consequences of the lack of progress in instituting reforms, often induce these organizations to proceed with assistance programs with less stringent conditionalities. On the other hand, the fear of social upheaval following the implementation of recommended policies compels governments to negotiate hard for second-best solutions. Whatever the source, economic considerations fall prey to politics, as good economics is usually bad politics. The implication is that the counterfactual for a program's design and outcome are not the best practice and maximum gains in efficiency but what would have transpired without its implementation.

It would be tempting to assess the role of the IMF and the World Bank through the lenses of deviations between actual and expected outcomes as depicted in respective programs. While this type of analysis may be important for these organizations' internal operations, it would be of little relevance for the topic under examination. The transition from central planning involves establishing a macroeconomic setting conducive to setting up market-supporting institutions and triggering economic adjustment and recovery. As long as there is a positive correlation between the progress in transition and assistance provided by the IMF and the World Bank one may draw conclusions about their positive impact. While detailed analyses might reveal stories of individual failures and successes, this would go beyond the format of this chapter.

The major question addressed in this chapter is about links between transition and IMF/World Bank assistance as captured by cross-country comparisons. With the evidence covering twenty-one countries over a period of several years, there may be enough observations to look for patterns. Yet, without a detailed country-by-country analysis, it is impossible to identify who has had a larger contribution (the government or the IMF and the World Bank) or whether some unique opportunities to move forward with reforms were either lost or delayed because of the lack of sufficient external assistance. In most cases, one will never know with certainty whether these institutions have merely responded to or inspired the reform process. But they were the main, if not the only, important external organizations that could circumvent narrow domestic interests.

The discussion is organized as follows. The section on "Progress in Transition" begins with an overview of macroeconomic stability, economic performance, and institutional advancement in transition countries. The section titled "Access to External Finance" briefly discusses the developments in external finance—that is, inflows from abroad and outflows of capital to the newly independent states. While net inflows (difference between inflows and outflows) varied across countries, they were quite substantial for most of them. Disbursements from the Bretton Woods organizations accounted for a large share of total disbursements (inflows). The section entitled "The IMF/World Bank Assistance and Transition" turns to the links between progress in transition and amounts of assistance received from the Bretton Woods institutions. At first glance, a strong positive relationship suggests that the IMF and the World Bank have influenced the pace of transition. Finally, the concluding section interprets results, arguing that conditionalities imposed on access to external assistance provide a strong incentive to implement reforms increasing national welfare rather than that of rent-seeking groups. But reforms happen only if the economic situation significantly deteriorates.

Progress in Transition: Variation in Stability, Economic Performance, and Institutional Reforms

Transition from plan to market in Central and East European Countries (CEECs) and the newly independent states extends over several years and covers a large number of countries (twenty-one countries—six CEECs and fifteen NIS). The empirical evidence seems to be large enough to make generalizations about approaches to transition, sequencing of reform measures, and their impact on economic performance. This in turn allows us to assess whether the IMF and the World Bank have supported the "right" kind of policies and imposed "transition-enhancing" conditionalities.

A stable macroeconomic setting seems to be a necessary condition to implement reforms in other domains. Inflation and uncertainty about credibility of the government commitment to macroeconomic stability do not augur well for structural adjustments as well as reforms in the areas of market-supporting institution building and private sector development. Nor do they create conditions conducive to economic recovery and growth. Thus, stabilizing the economy and freeing prices at least for tradables are regarded as the top priority for transition. Equally important and challenging, it then calls for sustaining stabilization, and developing frameworks for sound economic policies and management which are bound to take a longer time.

By historical standards, the pace at which transition economies have been successful in bringing inflation under control was astounding once their governments abandoned gradualism in favor of radical stabilization cum liberalization programs. Countries that put off fundamental macroeconomic reform—either because of regional tension (Transcaucasian newly independent states and Tajikistan) or the belief that a gradual dismantling of central controls would cause less economic hardship and disruption, or the lack of political support for more radical measures—experienced deeper output contraction and slower economic recovery and growth. The improved performance of bold reformers is particularly impressive considering the dearth of financial institutions and instruments facilitating the imposition of monetary and fiscal controls in a "normal" market economy. Using an annual inflation rate of below 50 percent as a benchmark for a credible commitment to fight hyperinflation,[4] most newly independent states have either achieved this target or are expected to achieve it in 1996. Some countries have achieved this target much earlier than others. The Baltic states were well ahead in reaching this target (Estonia and Latvia in 1993, Lithuania in 1994), followed by Armenia, Georgia, Kyrgyzstan, and Moldova. The success of Armenia and Georgia in compressing inflation is particularly noteworthy, for in 1994 these two countries were in the throes of hyperinflation: consumer prices increased by about 2,000 percent in Armenia and more than 8,000 percent in Georgia. There are now genuine signs of progress towards stabilization in almost all newly independent states.

The experience of transition countries suggests that the so-called transformational recession ends quicker if a radical program of simultaneous liberalization and stabilization is implemented and sustained. Economic turnaround in the CEECs came in the third (Poland) or fourth (Bulgaria and the former Czechoslovakia) year of liberalization and stabilization programs. This was also the case for the Baltic states, as their GNP bottomed out in 1994. Except for Moldova, no other NIS economy resumed growth in 1995, but most of them switched to a radical approach to macroeconomic stabilization only in 1994 and 1995. Yet Georgia, Kazakhstan, Kyrgyzstan, and Russia are expected to see their real output bottom out in 1996.[5]

Achieving the twin goals of sustaining stabilization and economic growth hinges critically on institutional reforms and managing the recalibration of the state. The former concerns enforcement of the rule of law, private property rights, reforming the banking sector, and establishing institutions supporting competition (easy entry), whereas the latter includes tax policy and administration, budget management, and targeted poverty programs. Interestingly, the experience of transition economies seems to suggest that the level of pretransition, market-based institutional maturity in transition countries does not have a significant impact on the pace of moving to reasonable price stability.

In contrast to macroeconomic performance, there are no simple measures that would capture the progress achieved in establishing market-based economic systems. Several attempts have been made at various organizations to develop measures portraying progress of transition and the level of market-oriented institutional maturity. The Washington-based Heritage Foundation publishes *The Index of Economic Freedom*. The London-based European Bank for Reconstruction and Development (EBRD) regularly tallies the progress in transition with the purpose of monitoring developments and assisting these countries. The World Bank's *World Development Report 1996* presents yet another measure of progress of transition.

The Heritage Foundation's index of economic freedom takes into account intensity of government intervention in such areas as trade, taxation, consumption (including government consumption), monetary policy (level of inflation), capital flows and foreign investment, banking, wage and prices, property rights, and government regulation of the economy. In addition, the extent of black market activities is included. The more government interference and the larger scope of a black market, the less economic freedom. The index is a simple average of ratings for each of ten factors with a minimum value of 1 (free) and a maximum value of 5 (maximum repression). Among 142 countries included in their analysis, Hong Kong was ranked highest (1.25) and North Korea along with Cuba and Laos lowest (5) in terms of economic freedom. Estonia ranked 26th (2.35) among all 142 sampled countries, was the most free economy among the newly independent states, followed by Latvia, which ranked 71st. All the other newly independent states included in the analysis are ranked in the bottom group of the sample in terms of economic freedom (Moldova, 94th; Lithuania and Russia, 100th; Belarus, 106th; Armenia, 117th; Georgia, 124th; Ukraine, 126th; and Azerbaijan, 134th.[6] If the index had been calculated for 1991, most newly independent states would have been, like North Korea or Cuba, at the bottom of the rankings. By this measure it may imply that almost all newly independent states have made significant strides in establishing market-based economies. However, the high ranking of Belarus relative to Georgia and Ukraine, or the equal ranking of Russia with Lithuania, raises some considerable doubts as to the reliability of scores.

The EBRD transition indicator identifies four major areas: liberalization of markets and trade, enterprise reform/restructuring, financial institutions, and legal reforms. In addition, within the first three areas several subfields are distinguished and scored. The value of each indicator is between 1 (little progress) and 4 (standards and performance typical of advanced industrial countries).[7] Thus, the index conveys information, admittedly based on subjective judgment, about the distance away from central planning. By this measure, most CEEC transition countries, along with the three Baltic states, are ranked higher than the newly independent states.

The World Bank index of liberalization is a weighted average of estimates of domestic transactions (price liberalization and abolishment of state trading monopolies), external transactions (free trade and currency convertibility), and entry of new firms (privatization and private sector development) with the weight of

0.3, 0.3, and 0.4 for each of these three components. A snapshot of a year is far too short to capture the economic impact of process of liberalization. Also, some countries started their reforms earlier than others. The World Bank's measure shows the average level of liberalization in the period 1989–95; the CEEC and newly independent states are categorized into four groups, reflecting both extent of liberalization and its longevity. The Visegrad countries were in the first group—advanced reformers; Bulgaria and Romania together with the three Baltic states were in the second group—high intermediate reformers; Russia, Kyrgyzstan, Moldova, Armenia, Georgia, Kazakhstan were in the third group—low intermediate reformers; and Uzbekistan, Belarus, Tajikistan, Ukraine, and Turkmenistan were categorized as slow reformers.[8]

There are some differences in the rankings by the EBRD and the World Bank. For the purpose of this analysis, we combine the EBRD and the World Bank rankings. We distinguish between four groups of countries in terms of the extent to which the countries in question have moved toward a market economy: advanced; intermediate; and less advanced. In terms of the EBRD transition indicator, calculated here as a simple average of scores for each of four major areas, the advanced group is above 3 out of a maximum of 4, the intermediate is between 2.35 and 2.99, less advanced is below 2.35, and the least advanced is below 1.2. Among the newly independent states only Estonia is an advanced reformer on a par with Visegrad countries. The intermediate group includes Lithuania, Latvia, Kyrgyzstan, Moldova, and Russia, as well as Bulgaria and Romania. Belarus, Ukraine, and some Asian newly independent states are among the less advanced in the transition process. Azerbaijan, Tajikistan, and Turkmenistan have experienced the slowest transition process. Here again, we must bear in mind that some countries started their reforms far earlier than others, and some made a stride in economic reform only in 1995.

Access to External Finance

An interesting question is the extent to which the external environment assisted transition economies in terms of financial flows. Have countries more advanced in transition benefited from a privileged access to international finance? Has the lack of access prevented some from introducing reforms? These are the questions addressed in this section. The analysis of this section focuses on the 1992–94 period, as complete data for 1995 are not yet available (and even when they are available for some countries, they are very preliminary). In order to set results in a comparative perspective, we shall refer to similar inflows to CEECs, but over the first three years of their respective transitions: Hungary and Poland, 1990–92; the others, 1991–93. We shall use aggregate net resource flows. Due to the importance of the IMF and technical assistance in the transition process, the aggregate net resource flows used here are different from the normal definition and include the IMF credits and technical cooperation grants. Net resource flows are the difference between total disbursements from abroad and payments to foreign creditors and indicate whether there is an inflow or outflow of resources from a country.

Unfortunately, the available data do not cover financial transactions among the newly independent states. The information on interstate finance are scarce and unreliable. As prices of energy have moved toward world levels, most newly independent states, as net energy importers, faced a very sharp deterioration in their terms of trade, whereas net energy exporters (Russia and Turkmenistan) experienced a significant improvement.[9] Except for the Baltic states, which have settled their accounts in a timely fashion since 1993, other net energy importers—especially Armenia, Belarus, Georgia, and Ukraine—were unable to finance their trade deficits. They have accumulated large external payments arrears to Russia and Turkmenistan amounting by the third quarter of 1995 to more than $3 billion. Thus, for many newly independent states flows of finance with the rest of the world do not give a full picture of the external debt position.

Net Aggregate (In)flows

Over 1992–94 the newly independent states did not finance the external world. There was no outflow of resources, but an aggregate inflow of around $40 billion. On an annual basis, these inflows, however, have been on the decline: they peaked in 1992 at $16.3 billion, fell to $13.4 billion in 1993, and further to $9.1 billion in 1994 (see Table 12.1). The fall in net resource flows to Russia—which assumed external liabilities as well as assets of the former Soviet Union—were responsible for this situation, as flows to other newly independent states increased from $2.5 billion in 1992, to $4.8 billion in 1993, and slightly declined to $4.6 billion in 1994.[10] The newly independent states together attracted only 2.2 percent of total aggregate net resource flows to developing countries in 1994. During the first three years of the transition, CEECs absorbed $20 billion of net resource flows, comparing with almost $40 billion going to the newly independent states. But either on a per capita basis or in terms of share in GNP, net flows to CEECs were higher than those to newly independent states. The difference cannot be explained by foreign direct investment (FDI) inflows. The limited administrative capacities in all newly independent states and initial social instabilities and wars in Central Asia and Transcaucasia should have made the difference in favor of CEECs much larger. One would expect many newly independent states to have little or no access to international finance during the first year of their independent existence. But this was not true. In fact, the two largest NIS economies, Russia and Ukraine, in 1992 experienced much larger net inflows than those in the subsequent two years. Overall, as measured against GNP total, external inflows to newly independent states were significant, exceeding 9 percent (an annual average of 3 percent) for Asian newly independent states

Table 12.1

Net Aggregate Resource Flows to Newly Independent States and CEECs, 1992–94

	1992	1993	1994	Total (in millions of U.S. dollars)	Total per capita (U.S. dollars)	Share of total in 1993 GNP (in percent)
Transcaucasian	54	425	573	1,051	67	10
Armenia (L)	22	164	207	393	120	18
Azerbaijan (LL)	5	11	134	150	21	3
Georgia (L)	26	250	232	508	93	16
Central Asia	213	1,710	1,510	3,432	69	6
Kazakhstan (L)	136	553	995	1,684	102	7
Kyrgyzstan (I)	3	225	181	408	95	11
Tajikistan (LL)	10	89	227	326	64	14
Turkmenistan (LL)	15	232	60	307	87	9
Uzbekistan (L)	49	611	47	707	36	4
European NIS	15,513	10,446	6,207	32,165	151	7
Belarus (L)	448	316	345	1,406	138	5
Moldova (I)	72	223	251	545	126	12
Russia (I)	13,764	8,609	4,465	26,838	182	8
Ukraine (L)	1,229	1,001	1,146	3,376	65	3
Baltic states	512	848	820	2,179	274	14
Estonia (A)	220	300	273	792	504	16
Latvia (I)	163	245	367	775	289	14
Lithuania (I)	129	303	180	612	166	13
Total NIS	16,291	13,428	9,108	38,827	135	7
Advanced (incl. CEECs)	1,853	9,104	4,784	15,740	238	10
Intermediate (CEECs excl.)	14,130	9,605	5,443	29,178	180	8
Less advanced	1,910	3,192	2,972	8,074	75	4
Least advanced	30	331	421	782	50	7
	1991	1992	1993			
Bulgaria	−46	855	534	1,343	35	2
Czech Republic	795	1,518	818	3,131	307	11
Slovakia	265	655	79	999	182	9
Hungary	89	3,052	1,404	4,545	429	13
Poland	484	3,579	2,210	6,273	164	7
Romania	29	1,199	1,805	3,033	131	11
Total CEECs	1,616	10,858	6,850	19,324	200	10
Total CEECs/NIS	17,907	24,286	15,958	58,151	152	8

Source: Calculated from data in the World Bank, *World Debt Tables* (Washington, DC: World Bank, 1996).

(except Azerbaijan, Kazakhstan, and Uzbekistan), Baltic states, and Moldova. They were the lowest for Azerbaijan, Uzbekistan, and Ukraine.

Since the variation in net resource flows within both the newly independent states and the CEECs is quite significant, any generalizations setting one group against another would be misguided. For the same reason, no firm conclusions can be drawn from linking net resource flows per head with the progress in transition. Note that advanced reformers such as Estonia, the Czech Republic, and Hungary stand out together, with net resource flows per capita exceeding $250. But so does Latvia, whereas Poland—an advanced reformer—is in a group with inflows between $150 and $249 (along with such intermediate reformers as Lithuania, Russia, and Bulgaria). Three remaining intermediate reformers—Kyrgyzstan, Moldova, and Romania—had inflows per capita below the $150 level. Across regions, net aggregate inflows per capita were the highest in the Baltic states and European newly independent states (except Ukraine). A different picture emerges when one uses the share of net resource flows in GNP. This share was higher than 12 percent (an annual average of 4 percent) not only for Estonia and intermediate reformers (the other two Baltic states and Moldova), but also for some reform laggards (Tajikistan and Turkmenistan). It can be clearly seen that none of measures—per head or as a share of GNP—is satisfactory, since the former is biased by the size of a country (a country with a small population always has a larger number per head than the one with a big population, even though the large country attracts far more inflows of resource) and the latter is distorted by the serious problem of underestimating GNP in many newly independent states.

In terms of sources, external finance to newly independent states displayed some common characteristics. First, the role of official development finance varied across newly independent states, but for all of them it was an important source of external financing (Table 12.2). And for Transcaucasian republics this was practically the only source of financing available to them in 1993–94. Over 1992–94, official development finance accounted for, on average, more than half of the total net aggregate flows to newly independent states. Moreover, excluding the Baltic states, its role tended to increase as the share of private flows in total net flows declined. This was probably due to Russia's payments to commercial banks and limited access to international financial market for many newly independent states.

Second, most flows were debt creating, although the significance of nondebt creating flows—FDI and portfolio investment—had been on the rise, with their value increasing by 60 percent between 1992 and 1994, and accounted for more than 90 percent of all net private sources. But they started from a very small base. Also, FDI remained concentrated in a small number of newly independent states: Russia, Estonia, Latvia, and Kazakhstan. Portfolio flows began in 1994, but the scale was tiny; for example, $10 million in Estonia and $273 million in Russia. Net concessional resource flows, primarily targeted at low-income Central Asian newly independent states, were flat in nominal terms in 1993–94. Their importance varied, reflecting these countries' ability to attract other resources: over 1992–94, concessional loans accounted for almost 100 percent of official assistance to Turkmenistan, 64 percent for Tajikistan, 49 percent for Latvia, and 39 percent for Kyrgyzstan.

Table 12.2

Net Aggregate Flows by Source (U.S. dollars per capita)

	Baltic States			Central Asia			European Newly Independent States			Transcaucasus		
	1992	1993	1994	1992	1993	1994	1992	1993	1994	1992	1993	1994
Aggregate net resource flows	64	107	103	4	35	31	73	49	29	3.4	27.0	36.3
Official development finance (including IMF)	45	75	47	1	25	21	28	24	15	2.1	26.7	35.7
Official grants	31	14	16	0	2	4	18	16	10	1.8	12.3	18.5
Official loans	5	34	18	1	20	13	9	8	5	0.2	14.5	13.1
Bilateral	5	6	10	1	17	8	8	2	3	0.2	4.0	7.5
Multilateral	0	27	9	0	4	5	1	5	2	0.0	10.4	5.6
IMF: Purchases (repurchases plus charges)	9	27	12	0	3	4	5	8	8	0.0	0.0	4.1
Total private flows	19	32	56	3	10	9	40	17	6	1.3	0.3	0.6
Private debt flows	4	4	−3	0	6	5	36	13	−1	1.3	0.3	0.6
Commercial banks	0	−1	0	0	0	0	−6	−1	0	1.3	0.3	0.2
Bonds	0	0	0	0	0	0	0	0	−1	0.0	0.0	0.0
Others	4	5	−2	0	6	5	42	14	6	0.0	0.0	0.4
Foreign Direct investment	15	28	58	3	4	5	4	4	1	0.0	0.0	0.0
Portfolio equity flows	0	0	1	0	0	0	0	0	0	0.0	0.0	0.0
Memo: GDP per capita, 1994			1,901			1,117			2,308			
Share of total in GDP (in %)			5.4			2.8			5.5			5.5
Memo: NET IBRD	0	10	5	0	0	4	0	0	1	0.0	0.0	
Memo: NET IDA	0	0	0	0	0	1	0	0	0	0.1	1.6	0.4
						(in terms of percent)						
Official development finance	70	70	46	26	73	69	38	49	51	61	99	98
of IMF (net)	14	25	12	0	9	13	7	16	29	0	0	11
of World Bank group	0	10	4	0	1	14	0	1	3	4	6	1
Total private flows	30	30	54	74	27	31	55	36	20	39	1	2
Foreign direct investment	24	26	56	66	11	16	6	9	21	0	0	0

Source: World Bank, *World Debt Tables* (Washington, DC: World Bank, 1996).

Third, except in the Baltic states, the role of the Bretton Woods institutions increased in all newly independent states in 1992–94. For the Baltic states, the share of the IMF/World Bank finance in total net resources flows was 14 percent in 1992, 35 percent in 1993, and fell to 16 percent in 1994. However, at the same time, private flows to these countries increased almost threefold. It indicates that these countries were able to "graduate" from reliance on official finance to becoming attractive to private finance. At the other end, Transcaucasian newly independent states did not seem to meet criteria for loans even from the IMF and the World Bank. The total external finance was very small, and the share of the IMF/World Bank finance in this small total remained low, although it rose from 4 percent in 1992 to 12 percent in 1994.

Fourth, within newly independent states, there was a significant variation in net aggregate flows per capita across regions. Baltic states and European newly independent states absorbed significantly larger amounts of external finance than much poorer Asian newly independent states. Interestingly, private flows are not responsible for this, as official development assistance to the former was considerably larger than that to the latter. By this measure, Central Asia looks like a region abandoned by the international community.

The composition of net resource flows to newly independent states differed largely from those to CEECs and developing countries. The share of official development finance was much larger (above 50 percent as compared with around 35 percent for CEECs and 35 percent for developing countries), while the share of FDI was much smaller (around 25 percent as compared with 40 percent for CEECs and 55 percent for developing countries).

Disbursements

Net aggregate resource flows take into account past decisions to draw on available credits. They provide information about the directions of financial flows, in other words—whether a country was a net "importer" or "exporter" of financial resources—whereas disbursements refer to actual amounts made available to a country by a creditor, public or private. Taking into account a short-term horizon under which most politicians seem to operate, disbursements on publicly guaranteed external commitments seem to offer a better vantage point of the use of finance to influence political outcomes in a recipient country.

The importance of access to the IMF/World Bank assistance might be more significant than data in Table 12.3 indicate. While on average around one-fifth of all disbursements to newly independent states came from the Bretton Woods institutions, since IMF/World Bank disbursements were marginal in 1992, they significantly increased in 1993–94. The process of accession to the IMF and the World Bank was exceptionally expeditious. Within ten months following the official dissolution of the Soviet Union, all newly independent states (except Azerbaijan, Armenia, and Tajikistan) became members of these organizations. In

Table 12.3

Total and IMF/World Bank Disbursements, 1992–94

	Share of IMF disbursements in total, 1992–94 (in percent)	Share of WB disbursements in total, 1992–94 (in percent)	Share of IMF/WB disbursements in 1993 GNP (in percent)	Total IMF and World Bank per capita (in U.S. dollars)
Transcaucasus	12	1	0.63	4
Armenia (L)	14	4	1.14	8
Azerbaijan (LL)	0	0	0.00	0
Georgia (L)	13	0	1.30	8
Central Asia	13	9	1.08	12
Kazakhstan (L)	23	15	1.79	28
Kyrgyzstan (I)	28	22	3.65	31
Tajikistan (LL)	0	0	0.00	0
Turkmenistan (LL)	0	0	0.00	0
Uzbekistan (L)	0	0	0.01	0
European NIS	17	3	1.14	26
Belarus (L)	10	11	0.68	19
Moldova (I)	37	22	5.53	59
Russia (I)	17	3	1.37	32
Ukraine (L)	17	5	0.40	9
Baltic States	41	12	3.46	66
Estonia (A)	31	16	1.83	56
Latvia (I)	43	12	3.67	74
Lithuania (I)	45	11	4.86	64
Total NIS	17	4	1.25	24
Advanced (incl. Visegrad)	14	10	3.47	87
Intermediate (w/o CEECs)	22	4	1.52	34
Less advanced	15	7	0.34	11
Least advanced	0	0	0.00	0
CEECs (weighted)	17	10	4.15	85
Bulgaria (I)	36	8	8.71	99
Czech Republic (A)	14	4	5.14	139
Slovakia (A)	17	4	6.76	132
Hungary (A)	12	10	6.06	203
Poland (A)	11	33	1.55	35
Romania (I)	26	8	6.25	71

Source: World Bank, *World Debt Tables* (Washington, DC: World Bank, 1996).

1992, only the Baltic states and Russia borrowed mainly from the IMF (the former $60 million and the latter $1,013 million) and very small amounts from the World Bank (Estonia and Russia $1 million each). However, at this time, the IMF and the World Bank were very much involved in CEECs.

Measures in both disbursements per capita and their share in GNP show that

IMF/World Bank financing tended to go to countries with reforms. The differences between simple averages calculated for each group are quite significant, suggesting a stronger involvement of these organizations in countries more advanced in transition. Also note that the share of the IMF/World Bank disbursements in total disbursements is the highest for intermediate reformers. This may indicate that, with the progress in transition, countries become less dependent on official and more on private capital. Assisting a country in strengthening its economic fundamentals and increasing its competitiveness to attract private capital is the main objective of the IMF/World Bank's assistance.

The IMF/World Bank Assistance and Transition

The collapse of central planning posed considerable challenges to international financial institutions. External financing declined to a trickle for many CEECs, especially those which inherited sovereign debt from the past. Except Russia, all newly independent states started the transition with a clean balance sheet—no external assets nor debts. The collapse of central planning and the Soviet Union created an institutional limbo for newly independent states and they initially had no administrative capacity to tap international markets. The rapid fall of outputs, growing fiscal deficits, and worsening external financial situations combined with uncertainties offered the newly independent states little hope of obtaining external private capital. Access to IMF/World Bank financing was the only option open to most newly independent states, especially for those which cannot generate external revenue via exporting natural resources. In contrast to many other clients of the IMF/World Bank at a similar level of development, the situation of the newly independent states was particularly dire because of their weaker institutions.

Under these circumstances, technical assistance and the design of conditionalities were crucial to external assistance to transition countries. Conditionality had to address broader issues of governance and reform of the state. These were not entirely new areas either to the IMF or to the World Bank. The IMF, which emerged as a major actor in managing debt crisis in developing countries, has accumulated considerable expertise in dealing with supply-side policies extending well beyond reliance on demand management.[11] The World Bank, which has been frustrated with a high failure rate of some of its projects in Africa, started to address institutional issues beginning in the 1980s.[12] These developments were tailor-made for former centrally planned economies: they needed a substantial amount of external help in establishing a disciplinary market framework for economic activity.

All programs financed by the IMF/World Bank programs involve policy conditionalities—that is, disbursements depend on meeting objectives mutually agreed upon with respective governments. As for the IMF, its involvement in transition countries was carried out mainly through two types of programs with a varying degree of conditionality: more stringent standby arrangements (SBAs) designed to assist in restoring macroeconomic equilibrium; and the less-stringent systemic transformation facility (STF), assistance to establish conditions conducive to launching effective policies addressing "fundamental" imbalances in the economy. Over 1990–94 borrowing by transition countries under SBAs accounted for 61 percent of the total IMF finance to transition economies; under STFs, 38 percent; and under EFFs (extended fund facilities—medium-term programs generally run for three or sometimes four years), the remaining 1 percent.

A factor facilitating the task of the IMF/World Bank was the triumph of liberal economic policies—also known as the "Washington consensus"—as the most effective way of enhancing economic welfare and a sustained economic growth. A liberal policy agenda encompasses the traditional IMF/World Bank advice of noninflationary environment, fiscal balance over time, high savings and investment, currency convertibility, economic openness, market-based pricing, and transparency in all economic policies and regulations. While initially there was some hesitancy as to the pace of breaking away with the past, which fueled inter alia an ill-conceived IMF advice to newly independent states and CEECs to reestablish their former economic links under the guise of a monetary union, around 1992–93 there was a growing convergence of opinion on the importance of swiftly addressing macroeconomic imbalances. This in turn has led to less diverse recommendations on what constitutes an effective approach to move from a planned to a market economy. Furthermore, the pressure to dismantle central planning and adopt markets rested on an internal dynamic so that the IMF/World Bank policy advice was relatively easier to swallow.[13]

Under these circumstances, a significant overlap in a number of the IMF and World Bank operations has tended to strengthen their influence on governments. First, there has been a high degree of convergence in recommendations suggested in policy dialogue, which precedes most of IMF/World Bank activities. Speaking in one voice enhances the policy message, and blocks a government from attempting to play one organization against another. Second, both organizations shared responsibility to support transition countries' liberalization and stabilization programs through technical assistance and financing. Third, stabilization in transition economies has been seen only as a component, albeit a very important one, of a broader effort to establish a competitive market economy. Fourth, as we have shown earlier, many newly independent states are highly dependent of the IMF and World Bank as sources of external finance.

There has quickly emerged a consensus among international experts that a stable macroeconomic environment is crucial to the implementation of economic reform measures and improved economic growth performance.[14] The IMF's function is to provide financial assistance to members who run into balance-of-payments difficulties, and ". . . the World Bank's first priority is to help countries restore solvency and macroeconomic stability."[15] In both cases, the assistance is conditioned on the collaborative development of a comprehensive program designed to root out the causes of macroeconomic imbalances. Money is lent to support policy reforms as long as mutually agreed upon objectives are fulfilled. The World Bank uses quick-disbursing rehabilitation loans, sector adjustment loans (SECALs), and structural adjustment loans (SALs) to support stabilization efforts, and their conditionalities cover as a rule a wide array of policy domains. Structural adjustment lending is policy-based lending offered to countries undertaking socially painful, far-reaching economic reform programs. These loans, which accounted for one-third of the World Bank's lending to newly independent states and CEECs, often parallel the IMF's assistance.

Recognizing difficulties of the newly independent states stemming in part from the collapse of the "common economic space," the IMF established the STF in April 1993 to help member states. Countries could obtain IMF financing that was subject to less-stringent requirements than those using an upper credit tranche of standby, extended arrangement, enhanced structural adjustment facilities. By the end of 1994, drawings under the STF totaled $4.9 billion: except for four newly independent states (Azerbaijan, Tajikistan, Turkmenistan, and Uzbekistan) and three CEECs (the Czech Republic, Hungary, and Poland) all other transition countries have made one or both drawings under the STF. The STF usually sets the groundwork for a full IMF Standby Agreement.

Assessments of the role of the IMF/World Bank in transition countries should focus on their contribution to the areas of liberalization and stabilization, recalibration of the state, the creation of a competitive environment in the domestic market (ease of entry for new firms and openness to imports), and viable banking. Some of these policy areas can be captured quantitatively, others—especially pertaining to institutions—can be subject only to more or less subjective judgment. As we argued earlier (in the section "Progress in Transition"), later reformers among the newly independent states began in 1994 and 1995 to catch up with the more advanced CEECs. They have made enormous progress in economic reforms. Those who were successful among these "later" reformers also used the IMF and World Bank financing facilities.[16] In fact, not a single country in Central-Eastern Europe and the newly independent states achieved stabilization cum liberalization without IMF financing, and many of them also drew on nonproject (adjustment, rehabilitation) financing provided by the World Bank. This seems to confirm a broad historical observation that ". . . almost no successful reform programs, and even fewer (if any) undertaken by democratic governments, have been able to function without sustained international support."[17] However, the above observation does not necessarily imply that each program has been well structured, designed, and delivered. This would call for a different type of analysis going beyond the scope of this chapter. This paper simply establishes the parallelism in stabilization cum liberalization efforts and the IMF/World Bank involvement, and suggests that the IMF/World Bank involvement can be regarded as a necessary condition although not a sufficient one. It does not answer the question of whether moving from a centrally planned to a market economy with stability could have been achieved earlier and with less social pain.

As for institutional change, which is at the very heart of the transition, the problem is clearly more complicated. Since the cumulative liberalization index (CLI) constructed by the World Bank measures the progress achieved in dismantling central planning by taking the duration and the intensity of reforms into account, it can be used for single-year as well as multiyear periods.[18] Using the values of CLI for individual countries as a measure of the progress achieved in the transition, we shall analyze relationships between disbursements from external sources and CLI values. We shall initially dodge the question of whether it is assistance that causes reforms or if it simply responds to them by focusing on the correlation between liberalization and official disbursements.

The question is then how to normalize disbursements in order to make them comparable across countries. The obvious choice is to use their ratio to GNP. Various well-known drawbacks of GNP estimates in transition countries, as we mentioned above, oblige us to use disbursements per capita. Differences in timing of the collapse of central planning in CEECs and newly independent states probably account for the variation in achieved progress in liberalization assessed in terms of the amount of external assistance obtained from the IMF and World Bank. CEECs started their transitions earlier and got involved in policy dialogue with the multilateral financial institutions earlier and had more time to implement reforms. To control for this difference, we shall compare the first three years after the collapse (1990–92 or 1991–93 for CEECs, and 1992–94 for NIS). Figure 12.1 juxtaposes IMF/World Bank disbursements per capita cumulatively over the first three years of the transition. Note that the value of the correlation coefficient between disbursements and liberalization for the CEECs (without Poland) is 0.99, and for the newly independent states and Poland amounts to 0.93.

It is tempting to interpret these results as suggesting some degree of preferential treatment accorded to the CEECs (excluding Poland) by the IMF and World Bank. But this is not necessarily so. The use of the IMF credits are determined by a country's quotas, which in turn affects the size of IMF's support to a country. Quotas relative to population were set for CEECs at levels exceeding those for most newly independent states. This may account for larger disbursements per capita to most of the CEECs. Further, as noted earlier, CEECs assigned priority to stabilization; except for Romania and partly Bulgaria, the other CEECs reached the stabilization stage in 1990–91 usually following a heavy involvement of the IMF. Except for the Baltic states, other newly independent states had not moved from the prestabilization stage by 1994.

While some reservations can be raised about the dependability of numerical values assigned to qualitative assessments of the progress of transition in individual countries, this analysis suggests a strong positive correlation between IMF/World Bank disbursements and progress in transition. But the extent to which the IMF and World Bank were catalysts or facilitators cannot be established on the basis of this analysis alone, however. The direction of causation— whether reforms have driven lending from the IMF and World Bank or vice

Figure 12.1 **Assistance by the IMF/WB and Progress in Economic Liberalization** (first three years of transition: NIS, 1992–94; Hungary and Poland, 1990–92; other CEECs, 1991–93)

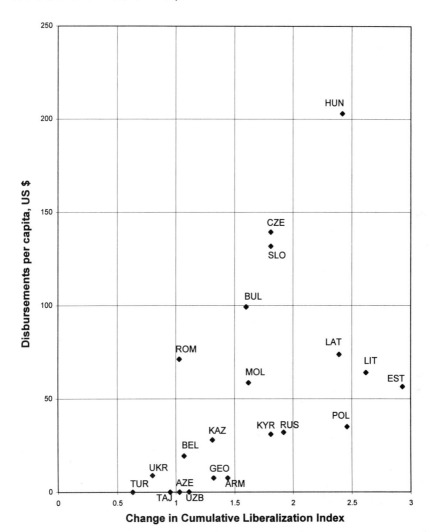

Key: ARM—Armenia; AZE—Azerbaijan; BEL—Belarus; BUL—Bulgaria; EST—Estonia; CZE—Czech Republic; GEO—Georgia; HUN—Hungary; KAZ—Kazakhstan; KYR—Kyrgyzstan; LAT—Latvia; LIT—Lithuania; MOL—Moldova; POL—Poland; ROM—Romania; RUS—Russia; SLO—Slovakia; TAJ—Tajikistan; TUR—Turkmenistan; UKR—Ukraine; UZB—Uzbekistan.

Source: World Debt Tables (Washington, DC: World Bank, 1996); World Bank, *From Plan to Market: World Development Report 1996* (Oxford: World Bank and Oxford University Press, 1996).

versa—is not clear from the above analysis. The relationship between reforms and lending should be seen in a dynamic, interactive setting. Policy dialogue between these institutions and governments to develop programs and assess meeting conditionalities for releasing funds create conditions for mutual interaction. Under these conditions, it becomes almost impossible to separate causes and effects.

Conclusions

The generic problem of interaction between economists and politicians, assuming that the former are capable of reaching consensus on policy advice, is that good economics is usually bad politics. Just as around 1992, when the economy of the first bold reformer—Poland—began to rebound, a consensus has emerged as to what policy package should be taken to put a country on the path of market-oriented transition. The implementation of any reform policy package hinges on the IMF/World Bank ability to support its policy advice with financing and the recipient governments' willingness to adopt adjustment measures. Actions by both sides are subject to some internal limitations—organizational (limited flexibility of any large organization because of budgeting and other internal procedures) or political—in recipient countries.

The issue of causation—whether reforms have driven financing from the IMF/World Bank or vice versa—does not have an easy, clear answer. Links between reforms and financing should be seen in a dynamic and interactive setting. Policy dialogue between multilateral finance institutions and recipient governments to develop reform programs and access meeting conditionalities for releasing funds create a mutual interaction. It becomes almost impossible to clearly separate causes and effects. Barry Eichengreen and Marc Uzan use a political variable to assess the impact of the Marshall Plan on developments in postwar Western Europe.[19] In a similar vein, Jeffrey Sachs develops an argument in favor of larger assistance to support Russia's reforms.[20] In this approach, assistance would serve to tip a political balance in favor of goals and programs supported by donors. The weakness of this approach as applied to transition economies resides with the notion of "tipping," as it assumes the existence of institutions responsive to public pressures and a public capable of understanding the nature of required reforms. In many transition countries, there were neither viable democratic structures nor strong support for breaking with the communist past in the aftermath of the collapse of central planning. Although political elites were clearly aware that a return to central planning was no longer a viable policy option, their interests were firmly rooted in existing economic bureaucracies and state-owned enterprises. The objective were reforms, but designed and implemented in such a way as not to weaken the position of entrenched bureaucratic interests. Under these conditions, the interest in liberal reforms could only surface when either those interests were provided for in ways compatible with these reforms or the economic situation deteriorated to the point where a major social upheaval might destabilize the political regime.

In contrast, the collapse of communism in Visegrad countries and the Baltic states witnessed the emergence of new political elites strongly determined to break with the past no matter what the short-term costs involved. They rejected gradualism (except, to some extent, in Hungary, but Hungary made significant strides in establishing a market economy even before the collapse of the communist political regime) as a method of dismantling central planning. Further, they seemed to regard external assistance as a support to implement their needed reform measures. In 1990 the Polish government viewed the IMF standby arrangement, approved in February after the Polish stabilization program, as making the program internationally credible and achieving debt reduction.[21] Initially, the idea of policy conditionalities was not used domestically to justify the implementation of reform measures. These were implemented not to please external lenders but because of the belief in their effectiveness. Hungary's prime minister Gyulu Horn recently commented on austerity measures implemented in 1996 to improve his country's macroeconomic situation: "We are not taking these tough measures in order to please the International Monetary Fund, but because we know that they are in our own interest."[22]

Notes

This is a revised version of a paper presented at the Russian Littoral Project conference, "Five Years after the Fall: The Role of the Outside World in the Transformation of the Former USSR," held at Wintergreen, VA, on 6–8 June 1996. The authors wish to thank Stijn Claeassens, Karen Dawisha, Martha de Melo, Daniel Kaufmann, Bruce Parrott, and L. Alan Winters for their comments on this paper.

1. Although our analysis focuses on the fifteen countries that emerged from the dissolution of the Soviet Union, for comparison we also include Central and East European transition countries—Bulgaria, the Czech Republic, Hungary, Poland, Romania, and Slovakia.

2. J.R. Wedel, "U.S. Aid to Central and Eastern Europe, 1990–1994: An Analysis of Aid Models and Responses," in *East-Central European Economies in Transition*, (Armonk, NY: M.E. Sharpe, 1995).

3. Countries that were not members of these institutions before the collapse of central planning (Albania, Bulgaria, and Czechoslovakia), as well as those which emerged from the dissolution of the Soviet Union, were admitted in 1990 and 1992.

4. See Michael Bruno and William Easterly, "Could Inflation Stabilization Be Expansionary?" *Transition*, vol. 6, (July–August 1995) no. 6, pp. 1–4.

5. See European Bank for Reconstruction and Development, *Transition Report Update, April 1996* (London: European Bank for Reconstruction and Development, 1996).

6. See Bryan T. Johnson and Thomas P. Sheehy, *1996 Economic Index of Freedom* (Washington, DC: Heritage Foundation, 1996).

7. European Bank for Reconstruction and Development, *Transition Report 1995: Investment and Enterprise Development* (London: European Bank for Reconstruction and Development, 1995).

8. For more information, see chapter 1 in the World Bank, *From Plan to Market:*

World Development Report 1996 (Washington, DC: World Bank and Oxford University Press, 1996).

9. David G. Tarr, "The Terms-of-Trade Effects of Moving to World Prices on Countries of the Former Soviet Union," *Journal of Comparative Economics* 18 (1994): pp. 1–24.

10. Official development finance, including official grants and loans from governments and multilateral financial institutions, fell by around 60 percent and net private flows declined by almost 90 percent as Russia's payments on the nonpublicly guaranteed debt exceeded new finance. Despite the significant increase in non–debt creating inflows (foreign direct investment and portfolio investment), this did not prevent the reduction in inflow of external capital.

11. See Harold James, *International Monetary Cooperation Since Bretton Woods* (Washington, DC: International Monetary Fund, 1995).

12. See Joan Nelson with Stephanie J. Eglinton, *Encouraging Democracy: What Role for Conditioned Aid?* Policy Essay no. 4 (Washington, DC: Overseas Development Council, 1992).

13. James, *International Monetary Cooperation Since Bretton Woods,* p. 584.

14. The resumption of growth depends on stabilizing inflation at moderate levels. The experience of transition economies shows that the growth declines were reversed only when inflation was falling. See Bruno and Easterly, "Could Inflation Stabilization Be Expansionary?" p. 5. Countries that have succeeded in stabilization and liberalized their external sector have also experienced an economic turnaround as a rule two or three years into the stabilization program.

15. Christine Wallich, "What's Right and Wrong with World Bank Involvement in Eastern Europe," *Journal of Comparative Economics* 20 (1995): pp. 57–94, quote on p. 61.

16. SBA seem to have played a major role in assisting transition economies to move from the prestabilization stage, that is, to lower inflation below 50 percent per year. Consider that all countries which had successfully moved to the stabilization stage by 1994 used SBA facility. Bulgaria and Romania recorded slippage in terms of inflation, but they, nonetheless, together with other SBA-users (except Latvia) also succeeded in entering the economic recovery stage. One may conclude that in the absence of an IMF program stabilization has not taken place. Further, among countries which are likely to reach this stage in 1995, all have been under the SBA program. These include Kyrgyzstan (1993–94), with a projected rate of inflation of around 50 percent in 1995, and Moldova (1993–95), with an estimated consumer price increase of around 25 percent. Kazakhstan, which was under SBA in 1994–95, expects to see its prices increase by 75 percent in 1995, but down from 1,858 percent in 1994. Kazakhstan used only 10 percent of its SBA credit in 1994.

17. Jeffrey Sachs, "Western Financial Assistance and Russia's Reforms," in *Making Markets: Economic Transformation in Eastern Europe and the Post-Soviet Union,* ed. S. Islam and Michael Mandelbaum (New York: Council on Foreign Relations Press, 1993), p. 154.

18. See the World Bank, *From Plan to Market: World Development Report 1996* (Oxford: World Bank and Oxford University Press, 1996).

19. Barry Eichengreen and Marc Uzan, "The Marshall Plan: Economic Effects and Implications for Eastern Europe and the Former U.S.S.R.," *Economic Policy: A European Forum,* no. 14 (April 1992): pp. 14–75.

20. Sachs, "Western Financial Assistance and Russia's Reforms," p. 157.

21. James, *International Monetary Cooperation Since Bretton Woods,* p. 571.

22. *Financial Times,* 31 October 1995, p. 3.

13

Neoliberal Economic Reform and the Consolidation of Democracy in Russia

Or Why Institutions and Ideas Might Matter More than Economics

Yitzhak M. Brudny

Six years ago, while celebrating the defeat of the August coup attempt, Boris Yeltsin proclaimed it to be a victory for Russian democracy. In 1991, Yeltsin's words were widely broadcasted, disseminated, and cheered both in Russia and the West. Yet in 1996, two distinct features of the Russian polity raised the issue of whether this statement was after all premature. The unprecedented power wielded by the office of the president and the way it was and is used and the weakness of the Western-supported liberal-democratic forces striving to consolidate Western-style political and economic structures in Russia are paralleled by a flourishing, virulently anti-Western, communist-nationalist opposition which is ideologically committed to putting an end to the Russian democratic experiment even in its present form. To elaborate, the current Russian regime could not be classified as a Western-type "representative democracy" but rather as "delegative democracy," a concept coined by Guillermo O'Donnell to describe recently emerging unconsolidated democracies in which, instead of the system of horizontal checks and balances, one finds overpowering executives, usually popularly elected presidents, whose power is constrained only by the length of their term in office. In such a system, the president strives to prevent any challenge to his powers by continuously undermining legislative, bureaucratic, and political institutions capable of doing so.[1] However, even this rather distorted model of democratic rule is being challenged by nationalist and communist forces who in the 1995 parliamentary election received a total of 52.6 percent of the vote and garnered 40.2 percent in the second round of the 1996 presidential election. Thus, in Russian democracy today, it is the anti-system parties, rather than the parties which are committed to the principles of democratic rule, which enjoy the majority in the parliament and are capable of winning a presidential election if such a ballot is called within the next two years.[2]

While each of these features is not unique to Russia and could be found in the other recently democratizing countries of Latin America, East Asia, and Eastern Europe, their combination in one country is distinctly Russian and could not be found elsewhere. The question this chapter seeks to explore is whether and to what degree this institutional and political reality is the result of the neoliberal economic reforms, launched in 1992 with the strongest encouragement of Western governments and international financial institutions such as the International Monetary Fund (IMF) and the World Bank, or whether it is a result of the noneconomic factors, be they structural, institutional, cultural, or political.[3] This question is important because of the existing situation where, on the one hand, there is a consensus (known as the so-called Washington consensus) among Western policy makers, international financial institutions, and leading academic economists that neoliberal economic reform is the only way to establish a viable market economy and therefore ought to be continued, and, on the other hand, the harsh criticism of these policies by very prominent Western and Russian political scientists (Adam Przeworski, Jerry F. Hough, James R. Millar, and Lilia Shevtsova, to name a few) as undermining Russia's fragile democracy and propelling anti-Western and antidemocratic forces to power.[4]

This chapter will argue that this debate is to a large extent misplaced since it ignores what this author considers to be the most important reasons for the contemporary Russian predicament. The delegative nature of Russian democracy is first and foremost the result of a crisis caused by the structural inability of primary Russian political institutions, the legislature, and the presidency, to cope with post-transition challenges. This structural inability, in turn, is a consequence of the timing, the sequencing, and the nature of institutional design, as well as the agency that created the institutional design.

We will reject the "economic" explanation of the strength of the antidemocratic, nationalist-communist opposition and the weakness of the liberal-democratic forces in favor of the explanation that stresses political variables. To be more precise, we will argue that the failure of liberal-democratic forces is a direct consequence of their inability to articulate a democratic and nonimperial conception of the Russian nation and the Russian nation-state and make it the foundation stone of their reform program. In the years following the collapse of communism, they allowed communists and nationalists to dominate public discourse on the matter and shape a consensus on the conception of the Russian nation and state. The ensuing electoral successes of the communist and nationalist parties and candidates were a direct consequence of the control of public discourse on this fundamental issue.

This chapter is structured in the following way: part one examines the main theories that link the consolidation of democracy with neoliberal economic reform; part two discusses why Russia became a delegative democracy; while part Three analyzes the factors strengthening the communist-nationalist opposition.

Democratic Consolidation and the Neoliberal Economic Reforms Reconsidered

Theories that link economic reforms and democratic consolidation currently dominate the literature on democratic consolidation. They represent an extension of the literature, initiated by the 1959 seminal essay by Seymour Martin Lipset, which argues that high levels of economic development are preconditions for the consolidation of democracy. In one form or another this argument was incorporated in the works of such prominent theorists of democracy and democratization as Robert Dahl, Samuel Huntington, and Adam Przeworski.[5]

All participants in the ongoing debate on the necessity of neoliberal economic reforms for the consolidation of democracy in Eastern Europe and the former Soviet Union (FSU) share one major assumption, namely that an economic reform which would lead to economic growth and higher standards of living is a critical prerequisite for the successful consolidation of democracy in these countries. They disagree, however, on what is the most desirable path of the transition to the full market economy. On one end of the spectrum stand supporters of the neoliberal economic reforms, also known as "shock therapy," which emphasize the simultaneous end of price controls on goods, services, and wages, the reduction of inflation and the stabilization of the currency through the reduction of budget deficits by means of ending subsidies for nonprofitable enterprises and industries, and a reduction in social spending. Russia's protracted economic, social, and political crisis, which followed the adoption of neoliberal reforms in January 1992, is explained by Sachs, Åslund, and other supporters of the neoliberal approach as resulting from Russia's inability to fully execute the reform plan and the absence of Western assistance and support at the crucial moments within the process.[6]

The opponents of neoliberal reforms, on the other hand, emphasize that their extremely high social and political costs would not only ultimately doom the reforms, but also undermine the fragile democracies which launch them. They are also harshly critical of Western governments and the international financial institutions for pressing these countries to adopt the neoliberal reform packages.[7]

On the issue under the consideration in this chapter, the delegative nature of Russian democracy and the strength of the communist-nationalist opposition, the supporters of the neoliberal reforms are silent. Åslund, in his book on the Russian reforms, analyzes neither the impact of the reforms on the nature of Russian democracy nor the underlying causes of the defeat of the reformers in the 1993 elections. Egor Gaidar, the architect of the Russian variant of. the neoliberal reforms, in his programmatic book and in various essays in which he defends his government policies, is also careful to avoid both issues.[8]

In sharp contrast to the advocates of the neoliberal reforms, their critics deal at length with the two issues under consideration. Przeworski, in an eloquent critique of the neoliberal policies, argues that their effect is to undermine the institutional structures of representative democracy, and he clearly suggests that the outcome is a delegative democracy-type political rule:

> Since the neoliberal "cure" is a painful one, with significant social costs, reforms tend to be initiated from above and launched by surprise, independently of public opinion and without the participation of organized political forces. Reforms tend to be enacted by fiat, or railroaded through legislatures without any changes reflecting the divergence of interests and opinions. The political style of implementation tends toward rule by decree.... In the end, the society is taught that it can vote but not choose; legislatures are given the impression that they have no role to play in the elaboration of policy; nascent political parties, trade unions, and other organizations learn that their voices do not count. The autocratic character of such "Washington-style" reforms helps to undermine representative institutions, personalize politics, and engender a climate in which politics is either reduced to fixes, or else inflated into redemption.[9]

The critics of the Russian variant of neoliberal reforms echo Przeworski's argument. Shevtsova accuses the initiators of the reforms of squandering an opportunity to consolidate democracy in Russia in the aftermath of the failed August 1991 coup by putting "economic shock therapy before democratic political change." The reforms inevitably turned Russians against democracy and its local champions because they constituted "a giant laboratory experiment ... undertaken without regard for the sociological, psychological, and political conditions of the laboratory itself—in short, without regard for the welfare of the 'animals' being experimented upon."[10]

At first glance, the Russian case appears to fit the arguments of the critics of neoliberal reform programs very well. In Russia, economic reforms produced enormous hardship for the population and this led to the dissipation of both popular and parliamentary support for the Gaidar government in 1992–93. This, in turn, triggered a confrontation between the president and the parliament over the constitutional prerogatives to carry out the reforms, and these resulted in an unresolvable constitutional crisis, the shelling of the parliament building, and the adoption of a new constitution which gave the president sweeping powers, while emasculating those of the parliament. A detailed analysis of the Russian case will be presented in the following section. At this point, it is sufficient to say that *politics* played probably a more important role than *economics* in causing the contemporary Russian predicament.

The Polish case, however, does not support the argument of the critics of the neoliberal reforms. Poland embraced neoliberal economic reforms without evolving into a delegative democracy, despite the fact that Lech Walesa certainly had ambitions to turn Poland in this direction. The crisis over economic reforms led merely to a succession of governments, but never reached the Russian levels of crisis. In Ukraine, the neoliberal reform plan did provoke a struggle between the president and the parliament, but it was settled through a compromise between two branches of government and adoption of the new constitution in late June 1996. It would appear that neoliberal economic reforms in and of themselves do not inherently undermine democracy and support the establishment a delegative-type rule.

One of the main arguments of the critics of the neoliberal reforms is that they undermine the support for democracy within the population and pave the way for the political forces advocating a variety of authoritarian solutions. This claim could be verified or rejected through the analysis of available survey data regarding Poland and Russia, the two countries which adopted the most radical versions of neoliberal economic reform. However, this data yield results which are either contradictory to this argument, as in the case of Poland, or inconclusive, as in the case of Russia. Richard Rose, in his 1994 survey of attitudes toward democracy in Eastern Europe and the former Soviet Union, found that the support for democracy in Poland stood at 69 percent, while in Hungary, which did not adopt the neoliberal economic reform program, registered a mere 51 percent. Moreover, the support for nondemocratic alternatives to democracy in Poland was very low: 6 percent supported the statement that a return to monarchy would be better than the present system of government; 11 percent supported the proposition that the army should govern the country; and 18 percent expressed their support for a return to communist rule. In a follow-up survey conducted in the fall of 1995, support for democracy in Poland increased to 76 percent (a 24 percent increase since 1991) while support for a return of communist rule declined to a mere 8 percent. In short, Rose's surveys indicate that support for democracy in Poland, despite its neoliberal reforms, is very high and growing.[11]

The available survey data, such as studies by Hahn, Gibson, Rose, and Whitefield and Evans, is inconclusive with regard to the basic political orientation of Russians. Jeffrey Hahn's conclusions, drawn from two surveys he conducted in Yaroslavl in 1990 and 1993, are that: (1) the basic political orientation of Russians with regard to democratic values and institutions is similar to that of citizens in Western democracies; and (2) there was some erosion in the commitment to democracy in the given period. He adds, however, that this erosion is not as strong as one might expect in light of the economic hardships most Russians experienced, and cautions that his findings "do not provide much support for the argument that this erosion is a result of declining economic performance." James Gibson's research yields a similar conclusion after comparing the 1990 and 1992 results of his survey of Russia and Ukraine: not only did he not find a significant decline in support for democratic values from 1990 to 1992, but also "that attitudes toward democratic institutions have been reasonably stable over time, with those favoring democracy in 1990 tending strongly to favor democracy in 1992."[12]

Richard Rose's New Russia Barometer IV survey, conducted in April 1995, supports the conclusions drawn by Hahn and Gibson. Rose's findings show that only 32 percent of Russians supported restoration of the communist rule; 39 percent supported suspension of the parliament; 43 percent supported suspension of political parties; 11 percent supported the proposition that the military should rule the country; 10 percent supported the restoration of the monarchy; and 29 percent agreed with the proposition that "a tough dictatorship is the only way out of the current situation." Thus, three studies conducted by different researchers in 1992, 1993, and 1995 came to a similar conclusion that Russians possess democratic political beliefs.[13]

Hahn's, Gibson's, and Rose's views, however, are challenged by Whitefield and Evans, who, on the basis of their summer 1993 survey, argue that commitment to market and democracy in Russia is "highly contingent on the public's evaluation of the actual performance of these principles in the transition process."[14]

While Hahn, Gibson, and Rose disassociate basic political commitments from electoral behavior, Whitefield and Evans link the two. In their view, the hardship imposed on Russians by the neoliberal reforms undermine Russian support for democracy and this, in turn leads to growing support for communist and nationalist opposition parties. This view is strongly supported by Hough, who argues that the growth of authoritarian values goes hand-in-hand with the deterioration of people's individual economic circumstances.[15]

If this argument is correct, it would not only provide an answer to one of the two main questions of this chapter, but also would make Russia fundamentally different from Western democracies where, as Lewis-Beck points out, "very few citizens are motivated to vote against the incumbent simply because they see their financial situation has deteriorated."[16]

Even if Whitefield and Evans and Hough are correct in their conclusion regarding Russian support for democratic institutions and values, their findings could be interpreted not as a condemnation of the neoliberal reforms as such but only of the unsuccessful neoliberal reforms. In other words, one can argue that only unsuccessful neoliberal reforms as was the case in Russia undermine trust in democracy. Such an argument, however, gives credence to Sachs, Åslund, and other advocates of neoliberal reform who argue that the root of Russia's economic and political woes is failure to implement the reform rather the reform itself.[17] In short, the available survey data does not conclusively link neoliberal economic reform with the erosion of democratic values. In fact, there is plenty of evidence to the contrary.

In summary, this section discussed the prevailing theories concerning the impact of the neoliberal economic reforms on the nature of Russian democracy and the degree of popular support it enjoys. We argued that there is ample empirical evidence to refute the theories which identify a negative correlation between the effect of neoliberal economic reforms and democratic consolidation. We questioned arguments postulating a causal connection between neoliberal reforms and delegative democracy. At the same time, we also found enough evidence to question the argument that economic hardship caused by neoliberal reforms leads voters to abandon democratic values and support communist and nationalist parties. In the subsequent two parts of this chapter, we will advance our own explanation of why Russia became a delegative democracy and experienced a growth in popularity of antidemocratic political forces unprecedented in Eastern Europe. In both cases, we will emphasize political factors at the expense of the economic ones.

Why and How Russia Became a Delegative Democracy

As mentioned earlier, at first glance there appears to be a very clear and strong connection between the adoption of a neoliberal economic strategy and the transformation of Russia into a delegative-type democracy. However, a counterargument could be, and indeed is, made by O'Donnell that the presidents in delegative democracies are especially likely to adopt neoliberal reform packages because of their technocratic nature. From a very different perspective, Holmes provides what might be called a "functionalist alternative" to both Przeworski and O'Donnell, arguing that the power of omnipotent presidencies in the former communist countries is a response to the necessity of carrying out economic, legal, and administrative reforms of an unprecedented magnitude. Thus, the deeper the crisis and the wider the scope of the necessary reforms, the greater the extent of presidential powers.[18]

This chapter provides another alternative to Przeworski's hypothesis. It argues that Russian presidentialism adopted the delegative style of governance not because of its adoption of a neoliberal reform package, nor out of functional necessity, nor because of the inherent nature of presidentialism. Rather, the omnipowerful Russian presidency, with its clear delegative features, was more a result of the crisis caused by the unsuitability of the political institutions created during the period of transition to the challenges of the post-communist era. In other words, we will argue that delegative democracy in Russia developed as a result of the timing, sequence, and nature of the institutional design of the post-communist political system, as well as the agency charged with creating the new institutions.[19]

The literature on the transition to and consolidation of democratic rule, while attentive to the socioeconomic preconditions and the different modes of transition, pays virtually no attention to the institutions created during the transitional period and their impact on the process of democratic consolidation.[20] At the same time, the critics of presidentialism, while emphasizing the unsuitability of the institution to newly emerging democracies, do not view the timing of the creation of the presidential institutions as critical to the ultimate outcome.[21]

The timing of the creation of the basic constitutional design of post-communist democracies is crucial since, as Lijphart points out, the initial choices of basic institutional arrangements are very difficult to change and likely to last for a very long time.[22] Poland, Hungary, and Russia are excellent examples of this reality. The preservation of the Polish presidential system was a consequence of an agreement struck by Solidarity and the Jaruzelski government during the Round Table negotiations, while the Hungarian parliamentary system is an outcome of the failure of the Communists to introduce a presidential system at the July 1989 referendum. The initial post-communist institutional design in Russia, that of an executive presidency and a two-tier assembly of the Congress of People's Deputies and the Supreme Soviet, was created during the transition by Gorbachev as a part of his reform program (the assembly) and by the referendum (the presidency). Once this system was put into place, only violence could change it.

The issue of the timing of institutional creation is closely linked to the issue of whether these institutions were created by the authoritarian regime itself, as a result of negotiations between the authoritarian regime and the democratic opposition, or by the democratic opposition following the collapse of the authoritarian regime. In most of the recent transitions in Latin America, Eastern Europe, and South Africa, post-authoritarian era institutions were created either as a result of a pact between the government and opposition or in the aftermath of the breakdown of the authoritarian regime.

In his discussion of the constitutional choices made during the transition to democracy in the former communist countries, Calomer aptly notes that "we should expect to find more institutional continuity in those cases where the communists were able to impose most or all of the institutional rules at the beginning of the reform process and where they were optimistic about their electoral chances."[23] The Russian case perfectly fits this description. Contrary to most of the cases in the recent wave of democratization, in Russia there was no pact between the government and the opposition and the downfall of the Communist regime did not trigger a change in the design or functioning of the executive and legislative institutions. Instead, as was just mentioned, these were created during the transition either by the Communist regime itself (the assembly) or by the transitional era institution created by the Communist regime (the presidency). Indeed, one of the key factors for understanding the Russian political crisis of 1992–93 is the fact that the two antagonistic political institutions—the presidency and the assembly—were created during the transitional period of 1990–1991. Another important factor was the sequence of the creation of these two institutions: they were not created simultaneously but rather sequentially, with the assembly created in the spring of 1990 and the presidency in the summer of 1991.

The design of the Russian institutional structure which emerged in the spring of 1989 was a second phase in Gorbachev's overall policy to liberalize the Soviet system while preserving the Communist Party's (hereafter, CPSU) hold on power. This was to be accomplished by making the party rule indirectly through the parliament. The new institutional design was an effort to ensure this outcome: the old structure of soviets, the institutions which unified executive and legislative powers, was kept in place but retooled to fit the new political reality. Thus, even though the principle of competitive parliamentary elections was introduced, Article 6 of the Soviet Constitution, which granted the CPSU a monopoly on political power, was kept intact.

The party was especially keen to control the key institution of the new political system—the USSR Congress of People's Deputies.[24] This was achieved through an electoral system in which 1,500 deputies were elected in competitive elections in single-member districts, while the remaining 750 were selected by a variety of political and social organizations ranging from the CPSU to the Soviet Peace Committee. The cumbersome method of candidate nomination and registration aimed to maximize the number of the Communist candidates on the ballot. Furthermore, the institutional design of the legislature, with its complicated system of indirect selection of members of the Supreme Soviet, was intended to ensure CPSU control of the Soviet parliament. This institution consisted of a two-tier structure, the 2,500-member Congress of People's Deputies and the 542-member Supreme Soviet. Most powerful was the office of the chairman, who in fact was head of both the executive and legislative branches of government. The Presidium consisted of the chairman of the Supreme Soviet, his deputies, and the heads of committees who controlled the activities of the legislature. The wide-ranging power of the chairman allowed him to manipulate and control the 2,500 deputies and thus make the Congress an obedient body. Sergeyev and Biryukov make this point very well:

> The Congress of People's Deputies was conceived and established as a purely plebiscitary body, and an easily manipulable one at that. It would allow executive power to pay lip-service to the separation of powers and maintain a representative institution that looked like a parliament while at the same time having the last word in legislation: the Congress was to be superior to the Supreme Soviet and entitled to overrule the latter's decisions. Whoever mastered the Congress would command its authority.[25]

With the single exception of not having any reserved seats for the social and political organizations, the design of the electoral system and of the Russian Congress of People's Deputies was merely a scaled-down model of the USSR institutional design. The RSFSR People's Deputies were elected in single-member districts under the same rules of nomination and registration which favored the CPSU candidates. The two-tiered legislature consisted of the 1,06-member Congress of People's Deputies and the 250-member Supreme Soviet. The legislature was headed by a chairman and Presidium with wide-ranging powers. Since Article 6 of the Soviet Constitution was abolished only a few days before the elections to the RSFSR Congress of People's Deputies, there was no time for political parties to organize for the ballot and nominate candidates. Thus, the Russian legislature, like its Soviet counterpart, was a nonparty assembly. Instead, deputies belonged to loose parliamentary caucuses, organized on the basis of ideological orientation and corporate interests.[26]

In the case of the Soviet government, the institutional design of the electoral system and of the legislature helped Gorbachev, although not without difficulties, to create a largely compliant assembly. In Russia this institutional design failed, however, to yield the desired results. The March 1990 elections produced a fragmented parliament in which the communist and democratic factions controlled 21 percent and 20 percent of the seats, respectively, while the rest of the deputies belonged either to a variety of centrist factions or were not affiliated at all.[27] This fragmentation allowed the formation of a democratic-centrist alliance which played a key role in the election of Yeltsin as chairman of RSFSR Supreme Soviet. Moreover, by passing a declaration of sovereignty, a declaration on the division of power between the federal and republican governments on the territory of the RSFSR, and a law banning state officeholders from holding positions in political parties at its first session, the new Russian parliament showed itself to be an institution determined to wrest power from both the federal government and the CPSU. In fact, the parliament shared this goal with its speaker, which explains why Yeltsin enjoyed strong parliamentary support in his first year and a half in office, during which he spent most of the time fighting Gorbachev for the right to rule Russia.

The parliamentary majority, however, was not ready to accommodate Yeltsin's desire to establish the office of a powerful president of the kind Gorbachev created between March and November 1990.[28] Yeltsin failed to convince the Third Congress of People's Deputies to establish the office of an executive presidency even though it met shortly after the March 1991 referendum which indicated that 70 percent of voting Russians supported the idea. In May 1991, when the parliament ultimately yielded to Yeltsin's demand, it was careful to craft the office in such a way to prevent Yeltsin from becoming an omnipowerful executive in the Gorbachev style. Thus, if Gorbachev's presidential prerogatives included the right of legislative initiative, the right to veto legislation, the right to impose martial law on the country as a whole or on specific regions, and the right to call referenda on key issues on the political agenda, Yeltsin, on the other hand, was denied these powers. Out of fear that Yeltsin would create a presidential party which would replace the increasingly unpopular CPSU as Russia's ruling party, the law also postulated that the president could not belong to any political party during his term in office.[29]

With the exception of the limited scope of presidential powers and the prohibition against a party affiliation for the president, the parliament's design of the new Russian institutional structure was largely modeled on that of the Soviet government circa spring 1991. In retrospect, this duplication turned out to be one of the major flaws of the Russian institutional design since the Soviet design had been specifically tailored for Gorbachev. Thus, it included a president elected by popular vote to a five-year term (Gorbachev, of course, was granted a special one-time exemption from this rule and was elected president by the USSR Congress of People's Deputies) and a vice president with no specific functions besides the stipulation that he succeeds the president in the case of the president's death, resignation, impeachment, or illness-related inability to fulfill his duties.[30] In a country with no established tradition of a vice presidential role, such a formulation invited the vice president to attempt to remove the president from office.

While some of the functions of the chairman of the Supreme Soviet were transferred to the presidency, the office was not abolished and a clear delineation of rights and responsibilities between the two offices, especially regarding orders to government ministries and agencies, was not established. Thus, while the president was given the right to issue direct orders to government ministries and agencies, the chairman of the Supreme Soviet retained the same right.[31] In this fashion, the law on the presidency effectively created two competing heads of the executive branch, the president and the chairman of the Supreme Soviet, who were bound to engage in a zero-sum game power struggle. By the same token, the issue of the subordination of the cabinet of ministers remained vague and both president and the legislature could rightfully claim control over its decisions. As Shugart points out, such a situation "has bred instability wherever it has been used."[32]

Such a system could function smoothly only as long as the parliament was an obedient institution and the offices of the chairman of the Supreme Soviet and vice president were filled by people with no political ambitions of their own and who were bound to the president through rules of party discipline and personal loyalty. However, already during the August 1991 coup attempt, in which both Vice President Yanaev and Chairman of Supreme Soviet Lukiyanov were part of the conspiracy to remove Gorbachev from office, it became clear that such an institutional design was based on assumptions about a political reality which no longer existed.

The new Russian institutional structure did not reflect the political reality from the beginning. Yeltsin did not have an obedient legislature; Aleksandr Rutskoi and Ruslan Khasbulatov, his choices for the post of vice president and chairman of the Supreme Soviet, respectively, were never his personal loyalists and were not bound by the CPSU's code of discipline. Moreover, they were typical late Soviet-era politicians: they had high political ambitions, fueled by their meteoric rise to the pinnacle of the power structure, and had little experience in the art of backroom dealing and political compromise.

The reason conflict erupted in 1992 rather than in the summer of 1991 was because the common desire of all Russian political and institutional players to seize control of Russian affairs from the CPSU, the USSR Congress of People's Deputies, and the USSR president. This explains why these actors supported

Yeltsin during the August coup, did not challenge his decree to ban the CPSU and nationalize its property, and endorsed his decision to dismantle the USSR. Thus, the very institutional design created to strengthen the Communist Party in power played a crucial role in its demise. The institution of the presidency was especially important in this respect.[33]

As soon as these goals were achieved in December 1991, conflict between the major political and institutional players was inevitable, even if Yeltsin had not adopted neoliberal economic reform strategy. Moreover, changes in the institutional design, adopted in the fall of 1991, made the impending crisis even more difficult to avoid or resolve.

Usually the period between the failure of the August coup and the launch of the neoliberal economic reform is regarded as a period during which Yeltsin missed a critical opportunity to consolidate Russian democracy. Had Yeltsin called for new elections in the fall of 1991, Russia would have likely avoided the crisis of the following years.[34] However, new elections, without a complete overhaul of the existing Russian institutional design, a task no one was prepared to undertake at the time due to the sudden collapse of the Communist regime, would probably have made the situation even worse. In fact, the decision not to call for new elections was a result of a realization by Yeltsin's advisors that new elections would more or less reproduce the results of the previous ones because of the organizational weakness of the democrats in the provinces and the entrenchment of Communists among the regional elites. Moreover, the elections would have added a new legitimacy to the legislature, which, in turn, would have significantly restricted Yeltsin's ability to act.

In order to avoid this situation, Yeltsin chose to reach a tacit agreement with the parliament at the First Congress of People's Deputies in October 1991. The result was a deal which freed his ability to act and tightened his control over the legislature while denying it the possibility of renewing its legitimacy. This agreement entailed (1) the election of Khasbulatov, at the time considered by Yeltsin to be a loyalist, to the post of chairman of the Supreme Soviet, something he had failed to achieve in July 1991; (2) support for the new course of economic reforms Yeltsin was about to launch; and (3) the granting to Yeltsin of emergency powers to issue decrees without parliamentary approval. These concessions made the scope of his prerogatives virtually equal to those of Gorbachev. In exchange for these rather significant concessions, Yeltsin agreed not to ask for Gorbachev's right to declare a state of emergency and the right to call referenda, and to postpone the adoption of the new Russian Constitution, which meant that the Congress of People's Deputies would be allowed to finish its term in office.

While this agreement made perfect political sense to all parties involved at the time, it made the Russian institutional design even less suitable for resolving potential political crises. To be precise, it created a situation which Hough aptly calls the "combination of legislative impotence and legislative omnipotence" in which, due to emergency powers it granted the president, the parliament was no longer able to shape policy, while at the same time it kept the "unlimited powers to change the constitution, and therefore, the powers of the president."[35] This situation virtually assured zero-sum game politics.

Finally, one of the key consequences of the perpetuation of the transition era institutional framework into the post-communist era was the hardening of the initial institutional mold, which, in turn, made it very difficult to create new institutional players of political significance (i.e., to increase the institutional density of the regime). Political parties were the main victims of this hardening.[36] The initial institutional design presupposed the existence of only one party, the CPSU. Its collapse made the main political institutions of the country partyless. The president, in accordance to the constitution, could not belong to any party, while the parliament lacked a representation of parties because, as we pointed out earlier, it was elected only a short time after the lifting of the ban on party competition. Thus the parties, most of which emerged in 1990–91, were only marginally represented in the Congress of People's Deputies. By the 1993 parliamentary elections, most parties had disintegrated due to the combination of a lack of resources and, more importantly, of any significant role in the system of Russian political institutions. At the same time, the parliamentary factions did not transform themselves into cohesive parliamentary parties because the Supreme Soviet was not functioning as a party-based institution, or into electoral parties because of a lack of incentives, namely scheduled national or local elections.[37]

The absence of parties as meaningful political players in a situation in which the parliament and the president were engaged in zero-sum game politics meant that the winner of this institutional struggle would emerge with virtually unlimited power. Yeltsin's victory unleashed the delegative potential of the Russian presidency, which significantly strengthened as the confrontation with the parliament intensified. Moreover, in a truly delegative manner he prevented the growth of institutional density by continuously denying the parties a role in the executive branch of the government, while limiting them to the politically weak Duma.[38]

To summarize this section, we argued that the main reason accounting for post-communist Russia's evolution into a delegative democracy was the deeply flawed design of its main political institutions. Contrary to other democratic transitions in Eastern and Central Europe where post-communist institutions were established either as a result of negotiations between the government and opposition, such Poland and Hungary, or as a consequence of the regime's collapse as in Czechoslovakia, Russian political institutions were designed by the Communist Party as a part of its own effort to stay in power. While these transitional institutions played an important role in the collapse of the Communist regime, they were bound to produce a zero-sum game political confrontation because of their inherently flawed structure. They also prevented the emergence of other important political institutions—such as parties—which could fill the void and prevent the excessive accumulation of power by the victorious institution. The presidency emerged victorious out of this zero-sum game struggle and, unchecked by strong parties, began transforming Russia into a delegative democracy with all its negative trappings.

The Roots of Strength of the Communist-Nationalist Antidemocratic Opposition

As we have argued thus far, one could hardly explain the strength of the communist and nationalist opposition primarily in terms of popular reaction to neoliberal economic reforms. Among the alternative explanations, those utilizing a structural approach popular with Russian scholars, claim that liberal-democratic forces are weak because the Russian middle class, the natural social base of these parties, is only in the early stages of its development.[39] This argument, however, ignores the fact that countries like Poland, Hungary, the Czech Republic, and the Baltic states had social structures not dissimilar to that of Russia. Yet in these countries the forces which advocate authoritarian solutions are completely marginalized.

Another alternative explanation constitutes a latter day variation of the "new class" theory. It argues that the strength of the nationalist-communist opposition is a direct consequence of the discrediting of the idea of a market economy and liberal democracy by the pragmatic wing of the nomenklatura which seized power in the aftermath of the failed August 1991 coup. Entrusted to implement the reforms, this nomenklatura distorted them beyond recognition, by using its power to enrich itself at the expense of the state. As convincing as this explanation may look at first glance, it is, after all a sophisticated variation of the conspiracy theory known as "revenge of the nomenklatura," advanced by Russian radical democrats to explain why the actual course of the reforms differed from their blueprint.[40]

In the preceding pages, we discussed the inconclusive nature of political culture explanations based on survey research. There is much greater consensus, however, among practitioners of the interpretive political culture approach, who claim that the communist and, according to some, the precommunist era legacies are not conducive to generating wide support for Western liberal-democratic ideas but rather provide fertile ground for authoritarian movements and populist demagogues. They especially point to the tremendous gap between the goals of the population, inculcated in communist-era values of a protective and paternalistic state, and the political and economic goals of the liberal-democratic elites, conditioned by Western neoliberal philosophy.[41] These theories, however, suffer from two main deficiencies: first, they seldom give any empirical evidence to support their claims; and second, these theories, as Bermeo aptly reminds us, merely repeat what was said in the late 1940s–mid-1950s about Germany and Italy, and in the 1970s about Spain and Portugal.[42]

Rather than explaining the weakness of their liberal-democratic forces in terms of the impact of the neoliberal economic reforms, the authoritarian political culture, unsuitable social structures, or the corrupt behavior of the power elite, one should look to the politics and ideas of both liberal-democrats and their communist-nationalist opponents. In particular, one should look at the democratic effort to articulate the idea of the Russian nation and the Russian nation-state.

At first glance, one can argue that Russian liberal-democrats were always weak and that the neoliberal economic reforms which they championed did not change the level of popular support in any meaningful way. In fact, even before launching these reforms, the liberal-democratic forces alone (i.e., without Yeltsin) could count on support for their candidates and causes of between 20 to 30 percent of the population.[43] Thus, the 16.5 percent of the popular vote for the liberal-democratic parties in the December 1995 parliamentary elections does not represent a significant decline of their appeal in comparison to the pre-neoliberal reform period.

This argument, however, is deceptive because it overlooks the enormous popularity the democratic movement enjoyed in the spring and summer of 1991. Democratic Russia, the most important among the democratic organizations, was a powerful social movement capable of drawing out hundreds of thousands of Russians onto the streets of Moscow and other major Russian cities. It played a crucial role in Yeltsin's victory in the presidential elections as well as in the victories of democratic candidates in the mayoral elections of Moscow and Leningrad in 1991. It was even strongly expected to become the new ruling party in the aftermath of the collapse of the CPSU. Yet by 1995 the movement was dead, while a small remnant carrying the same name failed to even qualify for the December 1995 ballot.[44]

In itself, the death of Democratic Russia was an inevitable consequence of the end of the anticommunist protest cycle which also led to the demise of such powerful social movements as Polish Solidarity, the Czech Civic Forum, the East German New Forum, and the popular fronts in the Baltic states. As Tarrow points out, at the end of the protest cycle, the initiative shifts to the elites and parties.[45] Indeed, in Eastern Europe, strong liberal parties such as the Czech Civic Democratic Party or the Polish Union of Freedom replaced social movements as the torchbearers of liberal-democratic ideas. In sharp contrast to the Eastern European parties, Gaidar's Russia's Democratic Choice and Grigory Yavlinsky's Yabloko Party, the two heirs of Democratic Russia, together drew merely 11 percent of the popular vote.

The root of this democratic malaise is not popular reaction to the neoliberal economic reform. If this were be the case, Yabloko, whose leader, Yavlinsky, opposed shock therapy from the beginning, should have done much better than 7.0 percent of the vote in the December 1995 parliamentary and 7.3 percent of the vote in the June 1996 presidential elections. In our opinion, the root of public disaffection with the liberal-democrats lies much deeper. It has to do with the

inability of the liberal-democratic elite to develop an ideology of liberal nationalism to legitimize the democratic form of government, the market economy, and
the nonimperial borders of Russia.[46]

Kolankiewicz rightly points out that the liberal idea which exclusively focuses on the construction of capitalism has little mobilizational power in the
post-communist societies since "it is difficult enough to mobilize society on the
promise of greater inequality let alone admit that it will be inherently unjust and
will consign one-third of its citizens to social redundancy."[47] The only way to do
so was to ground the movement toward market economy in a liberal-nationalist
conception of identity which, indeed, was done in Eastern Europe and the Baltics. Adoption of a democratic conception of membership, identity, and boundaries of the nation is, therefore, as crucial to democratic consolidation as the
formation of a market economy and the creation of a multiparty system.

This issue, however, was the Achilles' heel of the Russian democratic movement. It adopted a key philosophical underpinning of Western liberalism—the
concept of society as a collection of individuals pursuing their economic interests. In actual politics, this philosophical base found its manifestation in a failure
to realize the importance of issues related to state and nation building and
viewed the overthrow of communism and the rapid creation of a market economy as the panacea for all Russian ills. Liberal-democrats worked feverishly to
design blueprints for economic reforms, while largely avoiding such issues as
"who is Russian" or whether Russia should remain at the center of an empire, a
multiethnic federation, or become a nation-state. Those few, like Andrei
Sakharov and Galina Starovoitova, who did think and write on these issues did
not venture beyond advocacy of radical decentralization and the sovereignization
of the USSR and Russia.[48] Democratic Russia's opposition to Gorbachev during
the March 1991 referendum on the preservation of the Union was both a reflection of Sakharov and Starovoitova's ideas and a desire to embarrass Gorbachev
and the CPSU. Moreover, the crucial decision, made in the fall of 1991 by such
prominent liberals as Gaidar, to push for the dismantling of the USSR was not
grounded in any well thought out conception of Russian nationhood but was
merely a consequence of the determination to carry out radical economic reforms
with the least possible opposition from other Soviet republics.

Before the end of communism, Yeltsin was not different from other leaders of
the anti-communist camp. Thus, he never developed a coherent position on the
subject of the nature of Russian nationhood and statehood. His famous statement
that the republics within Russia should grab as much sovereignty as they can
swallow was not dictated by any clear view of the issues involved but was a
mere instrument in his power struggle with Gorbachev. The dismantling of the
USSR in December 1991 was also driven by the attempt to remove Gorbachev
from the political arena rather than a desire to dismantle the empire and create a
Russian nation-state.

As long as promarket and anticommunist sentiments dominated the public discourse, the weakness of the liberal-democrats was not fatal.[49] The 188 against 6 majority within the Russian parliament that ratified the Belovezh Forest Accords, which put an end to the USSR and created an independent Russian state, was symbolic of the domination of the anticommunist and nonimperial sentiments.

As economic reforms failed to live up to the expectations, republics within Russia began either to secede, like Chechnya, or to threaten to secede, like Tatarstan. The 20 million ethnic Russians who found themselves in newly independent states were often discriminated against and disenfranchised. The liberal-democrats had no conceptual and ideological tools capable of addressing these developments.

Russian nationalists and communists, who merely followed them on these issues, were quick to fill the void with their own agenda. Contrary to the democrats, the nationalists, while paying little attention to the issue of economic reform, spent enormous time and effort discussing the issues of membership, national identity, and state boundaries. Their ideas spread virtually unopposed, allowing them to set the terms of the debate. These ideas, however, were not democratic or liberal: they preached restoration of the Soviet state, and defined the Russian nation in ethnic (i.e., descent-based) rather than civic (citizenship-based) terms, which led them to demand that the Russian state intervene to defend ethnic Russians in the former Soviet republics.[50] As the economic reforms unraveled, their ideas began to penetrate into the consciousness of the political elite and general public alike. A stream of prominent radical democrats, including Yury Vlasov, Mikhail Astaf'yev (the man who gave Democratic Russia its name), Il'ya Konstantinov, and Viktor Aksiuchits, disappointed by the course of the economic reform, began moving toward the nationalist-communist platform on the nationality issue and subsequently joined the nationalist-communist opposition. The same process occurred with Rutskoi and Khasbulatov, who during their "democratic" phase played a crucial role in destroying the USSR and the Communist Party.

Moreover, many members of the democratic elite who did not switch sides formally, such as Sergei Stankevich, began incorporating key Russian nationalist ideas about state and nation into their thinking.[51] In the years 1992–93, Yeltsin did nothing to articulate a new democratic conception of the Russian nation. On one hand, he kept using the civic definition of Russian ethnicity. However, his rhetoric about defense of the rights of ethnic Russians in the former Soviet republics was legitimizing the use of the nondemocratic ethnic definition of the Russian nation.

With Yeltsin largely absent from the debate, an elite consensus emerged which spoke about the inevitability of the future restoration of the USSR, the need for the aggressive protection of ethnic Russians in the former Soviet republics, and a determination to support the Serbian side in the unfolding crisis in the Balkans. In 1991, all these views were the exclusive domain of Russian nationalists and communists.

This elite consensus began dominating both the print and electronic media and inevitably infiltrated the consciousness of the general public (especially outside major metropolitan centers), which, by the end of 1991, by and large had accepted the inevitability of the dismantling of the USSR, expressed little concern for Russians in the "near-abroad," and cared little about the plight of their Serbian brethren. The December 1995 study by Hough, Davidheiser, and Lehmann revealed that only 31 percent supported the notion of an independent Ukraine while 53 percent believed that the two countries ought to be united. The same study also revealed that 90 percent of Russians believed that their government should defend the rights of ethnic Russians in the former Soviet republics. However, the most striking of all of Hough's finding was a rise in imperial notions of identity among Russians: in 1993 only 29 percent identified the Soviet Union as their motherland, while 50 percent chose Russia; in 1995, 39 percent identified the USSR as their motherland, while the same percentage chose Russia.[52] Gaidar and other leaders of the liberal-democrats had no alternative set of ideas to counteract this creeping hegemony of the nationalist-communist views on these issues.[53] They remained convinced that the rational mind of *homo economicus* would ultimately prevail as economic reforms took root. However, this only bolstered the impression that the democrats were politicians who do not care about Russia and its "true" national interests. The failure of economic reform to improve the standard of living of the majority of Russians left the democrats with no issue they could call their own.

Vladimir Zhirinovsky's success in 1993 and the communists' success in 1995, combined with democratic defeats in the both elections, the war in Chechnya, and attempts at unification with Belarus, were all-but-natural consequences of the simplistic liberal-democratic belief that successful economic reform was the one and only foundation stone for stable democracy in Russia.[54] Losing control of the discourse on the issue of the nation proved to be a key turning point in the erosion of support for the liberal-democratic cause. Just as the 188 against 6 majority with which the Russian Supreme Soviet ratified the Belovezh Forest Accords in December 1991 was symbolic of the domination of the anti-imperial discourse, the 250 against 98 majority which abrogated these accords in March 1996 was symbolic of the domination of the new imperial discourse. Yeltsin's July 1996 victory does not change this reality since he is not an opponent of this discourse.[55]

Conclusions

In this chapter we explored the question of the degree of "responsibility" which can be attributed to neoliberal economic reforms for the delegative nature of Russian democracy and for the increased popularity of antidemocratic communist and nationalist forces. This issue is of major importance since these reforms were initiated with strong Western (especially American) support and encouragement. Thus, the affirmative answer to our question would make Western governments, international financial institutions such as the IMF, and the majority of Western mainstream economists responsible to a great extent for the inability of Russia to consolidate its fledgling democratic institutions.

We examined the argument of the critics of neoliberal economic reforms who claimed that these reforms not only undermined democracy everywhere they were introduced but also were hopelessly out of touch with political, economic, and cultural realities in Russia. On this issue our main argument is that the available empirical evidence is at best inconclusive and often contradicts the critical argument against neoliberal reforms. We showed that the degree of support for democracy remained strong in Poland despite shock therapy, and cited evidence which suggests that the degree of commitment to democratic values in Russia was not affected significantly by the introduction of the shock therapy reforms.

The argument we developed in the second part of this chapter suggests an explanation which focuses on the role of institutions. We argued that Russia became a delegative democracy because it inherited institutional structures which were designed by the Communist Party as part of its strategy to remain in power as Russia underwent liberalization, and that this development made Russia different from virtually any other recent case of democratization. To be precise, we claimed that both the executive and legislative institutions were so poorly designed that a zero-sum confrontation between and within them was inevitable. This confrontation, in turn, made impossible the emergence of other potential institutions of power, namely, political parties. Victory of the executive, combined with a lack of alternative power institutions, paved the way for omnipotent presidential rule in which the chief of the presidential bodyguards is more important politically than the speaker of the parliament.

In the final section of this chapter, we analyzed the factors that served to weaken the liberal-democratic forces and empower the anti-system nationalist and communist parties. We rejected the argument that the neoliberal economic reform was, in and of itself, the main factor influencing the increased popularity of the nationalist and communist parties. At the same time, we also rejected claims of authoritarian political culture, an unsuitable social structure, or the corrupt behavior of power elites as acceptable explanatory alternatives. Instead we argued that the decline of the liberal-democratic movement is rooted in its failure to formulate a democratic conception of the identity of the Russian nation and a nonimperial concept of the Russian state, choosing instead to focus exclusively on designing Russia's path to capitalism. Failure to ground the need for radical economic reforms in a democratic conception of the nation and state made the democrats completely unable to defend themselves when the economic reforms went awry, centrifugal forces threatened to tear Russia apart, and millions of Russians lost their status as the privileged ethnic group in the non-Russian regions. The nationalist-communist opposition used the situation of the conceptual vacuum in the discourse on nation and state and successfully promoted their nondemocratic and imperial definition of nation and state. Moreover, they succeeded in imposing these views on so many members of the political elite that one could speak about the existence of an elite consensus regarding the desirability of the restoration of the USSR, the aggressive defense of Russian ethnic minorities outside the country, and support for the Serbian side in the Balkan crisis. This consensus, in turn, penetrated to a significant extent the mass public and made democratic politicians very vulnerable to accusations of dismantling the USSR, abandoning their brothers in former Soviet republics, and kowtowing to the West in the Balkan crisis. Under these conditions, and still waiting for the benefits of economic reforms to trickle down to the majority of ordinary Russians, the liberal-democrats were doomed. We have only to hope that their defeat is a temporary one.

Notes

The author wishes to thank Professor George W. Breslauer, Professor Karen Dawisha, and Professor Bruce Parrot, as well as all the participants of the June 1996 Russian Littoral Project Conference "Five Years after the Fall: The Role of the Outside World in the Transformation of the Former USSR" who commented on the original draft of this chapter. This essay is dedicated to the memory of Professor Dankwart A. Rustow, one of the finest scholars of democratization.

1. Guillermo O'Donnell, "Delegative Democracy," *Journal of Democracy* 5, no. 1 (January 1994): pp. 55–69; Guillermo O'Donnell, "Illusions about Consolidation," *Journal of Democracy* 7, no. 2 (April 1996): pp. 34–51.

2. I borrow the term "anti-system parties" from Gunther, Puhle, and Diamandouros, who defined them as parties which are "unequivocally opposed to the existing regime;" see Richard Gunther, Hans-Jürgen Puhle, and P. Nikiforos Diamandouros, "Introduction," in *The Politics of Democratic Consolidation,* ed. Richard Gunther, P. Nikiforos Diamandouros, and Hans-Jürgen Puhle (Baltimore: Johns Hopkins University Press, 1995), p. 13.

3. I deliberately don't use the word "support" since, as Jeffrey Sachs and others have pointed out on numerous occasions, Western governments and especially the IMF failed to provide Russia with much needed economic assistance at the most crucial stages of the reforms.

4. One should also mention a minority view of those scholars who argue that simultaneous transition to the market economy (through a neoliberal or non-neoliberal path) and consolidated democracy is itself impossible because the logic of one process contradicts the logic of the other: see Jon Elster, "The Necessity and Impossibility of Simultaneous Economic and Political Reforms," in *Constitutionalism and Democracy,* ed. Douglas Greenberg et al. (New York: Oxford University Press, 1993), pp. 267–74; and Claus Offe, "Capitalism by Democratic Design? Democratic Theory Facing the Triple Transition in East Central Europe," *Social Research* 58, no. 4 (Winter 1991): pp. 865–92.

5. Seymour Martin Lipset, *Political Man,* exp. ed. (Baltimore: Johns Hopkins University Press, 1981), chap. 2; Robert A. Dahl, *Polyarchy* (New Haven, CT: Yale University Press, 1971), chap. 5; Samuel P. Huntington, *The Third Wave* (Norman: Oklahoma University Press, 1991), chap. 3; Adam Przeworski et al., *Sustainable Democracy* (New

York: Cambridge University Press, 1995), pp. 1–10. For the recent reexamination of Lipset's original argument, see Larry Diamond, "Economic Development and Democracy Reconsidered," in *Reexamining Democracy,* ed. Gary Marks and Larry Diamond (Newbury Park, CT: Sage Publications, 1992), ch. 6.

6. For arguments in support of the neoliberal economic reforms, see Jeffrey Sachs, *Poland's Jump to the Market Economy* (Cambridge, MA: MIT Press, 1993); Larry Diamond, "Democracy and Economic Reform: Tensions, Compatibilities, and Strategies for Reconciliation," in *Economic Transition in Eastern Europe and Russia,* ed. Edward P. Lazear (Stanford, CA: Hoover Institution Press, 1995), pp. 107–58. Anders Åslund, *Post-Communist Economic Revolutions* (Washington, DC: Center for Strategic and International Studies, 1992); Anders Åslund, *How Russia Became a Market Economy* (Washington, DC: Brookings Institution, 1995). For Åslund's and Sachs's criticism of Western governments and the IMF for their failure to support Russian reformers at the crucial moments, see Åslund, *How Russia Became a Market Economy,* pp. 214–18; Jeffrey Sachs, "Life in the Economic Emergency Room," in *The Political Economy of Policy Reform,* ed. John Williamson (Washington, DC: Institute for International Economics, 1994), pp. 516–23.

7. For the arguments against neoliberal economic reforms, see Adam Przeworski, *Democracy and the Market* (New York: Cambridge University Press, 1991), chap. 4; Adam Przeworski, "Economic Reforms, Public Opinion, and Political Institutions in the Eastern European Perspective," in *Economic Reforms in New Democracies,* by Luiz Carlos Bresser Pereira, José Maria Maroval, and Adam Przeworski (New York: Cambridge University Press, 1993), chap. 3; Peter Murrell, "What is Shock Therapy? What Did It Do in Poland and Russia?" *Post-Soviet Affairs* 9, no. 2 (April–June 1993): pp. 111–40; Lynn D. Nelson and Irina Y. Kuzes, *Radical Reform in Yeltsin's Russia* (Armonk, NY: M.E. Sharpe, 1995); James R. Millar, "From Utopian Socialism to Utopian Capitalism," *Problems of Post-Communism* (May/June 1995): pp. 7–14.

8. Egor Gaidar, *Gosudarstvo i evolutsiia* (Moscow: Evraziia, 1995), chap. 5; see also Egor Gaidar, "Neudobnye voprosy," *Otkrytaia politika,* no. 7 (1995): pp. 14–21. In *Poland's Jump to the Market Economy,* Jeffrey Sachs is also silent on their political impact.

9. Adam Przeworski, "The Neoliberal Fallacy," in *Capitalism, Socialism, and Democracy Revisited,* ed. Larry Diamond and Marc F. Plattner (Baltimore: Johns Hopkins University Press, 1993), p. 50.

10. Lilia Shevtsova, "The Two Sides of the New Russia," *Journal of Democracy* 6, no. 3 (July 1995): p. 64; Lilia Shevtsova, "Russia's Post-Communist Politics: Revolution or Continuity?" in *The New Russia: Troubled Transformation,* ed. Gail W. Lapidus (Boulder, CO: Westview Press, 1995), p. 28.

11. Richard Rose, "What Is the Chance for Democracy in Central and Eastern Europe?" *Studies in Public Policies,* no. 236 (1994): pp. 12, 17; Richard Rose, "Former Soviet Empire Rules out Old Regime," *Investing in Central and Eastern Europe,* supplement to *Financial Times,* 15 April 1996, p. v.

12. Jeffrey W. Hahn, "Changes in Contemporary Russian Political Culture," in *Political Culture and Civil Society in Russia and the New States of Eurasia,* ed. Vladimir Tismaneanu (Armonk, NY: M.E. Sharpe, 1995), p. 132; James L. Gibson, "The Resilience of Mass Support for Democratic Institutions and Processes in the Nascent Russian and Ukrainian Democracies," in Tismaneanu, *Political Culture and Civil Society in Russia and the New States of Eurasia,* p. 87.

13. Richard Rose, "New Russia Barometer IV: Survey Results," *Studies in Public Policy,* no. 250 (1995): pp. 45–46, 51–52. A 1996 USIA survey reported very similar findings to that of Russia Barometer IV. Thus, only 25 percent supported introduction of

dictatorship and 39 percent supported imposition of censorship in electronic media. See *USIA: Opinion Analysis* (July 19, 1996): p. 1.

14. Stephen Whitefield and Geoffrey Evans, "The Russian Election of 1993: Public Opinion and the Transition Experience," *Post-Soviet Affairs* 10, no. 1 (1994): p. 40.

15. Jerry F. Hough, "The Russian Election of 1993: Public Attitudes Toward Economic Reform and Democratization," *Post-Soviet Affairs* 10, no. 1 (1994): p. 17 (Table 7).

16. Michael S. Lewis-Beck, *Economics and Elections* (Ann Arbor: University of Michigan Press, 1988), p. 155.

17. On the issue of whether the neoliberal reforms in Russia were doomed to fail there is hardly a consensus. We already cited Shevtsova's view, which argues in the affirmative. However, Starovoitova, one of Russia's most prominent liberal-democratic politicians, in equally eloquent fashion argues that it is the inconsistency in implementing the reforms, rather than the neoliberal reforms themselves, are the cause of the economic hardship; see Galina V. Starovoitova and Eugene N. Gurenko, "Russia: A Chance for Improvement?" *Brown Journal of World Affairs* 2, no. 2 (Summer 1995): pp. 109–15.

18. O'Donnell, "Delegative Democracy," p. 60; Stephen Holmes, "The Postcommunist Presidency," *East European Constitutional Review* 3, no. 1 (Fall 1993/Winter 1994): pp. 36–39.

19. I am not denying the relative significance of noninstitutional factors such as the inability of the post-communist political elite to reach consensus over such key issues as the post-communist constitutional order, of goals and strategies of state and nation building, and the nature of the transition to the market economy, as well as the strategic choices taken by the major political players at key junctions in Russia's post-communist development. They certainly made the crisis worse. I dealt with these factors in my previous work. See Yitzhak M. Brudny, "Ruslan Khasbulatov, Aleksandr Rutskoi and Intraelite Conflict in the Post-Communist Russia, 1991–94," in *Patterns in Post-Soviet Leadership,* ed. Timothy J. Colton and Robert C. Tucker (Boulder, CO: Westview, 1995), pp. 75–101.

20. See Mainwaring's summary of democratization literature in Scott Mainwaring, "Transitions to Democracy and Democratic Consolidation," in *Issues in Democratic Consolidation,* ed. Scott Mainwaring, Guillermo O'Donnell, and J. Samuel Valenzuela (South Bend, IN: University of Notre Dame Press, 1992), pp. 294–341.

21. See, for example, Juan J. Linz and Arturo Valenzuela, eds., *The Failure of the Presidential Democracy* (Baltimore: Johns Hopkins University Press, 1994).

22. Arend Lijphart, "Democratization and Constitutional Choices in Czecho-Slovakia, Hungary, and Poland," *Journal of Theoretical Politics* 4, no. 2 (April 1992): p. 208.

23. Josep M. Colomer, "Strategies and Outcomes in Eastern Europe," *Journal of Democracy* 6, no. 2 (April 1995): p. 75.

24. On the USSR Congress of People's Deputies and the institutional devices aimed at preventing democratic candidates from winning the election to it, see Giulietto Chiesa and Douglas Taylor Northrop, *Transition to Democracy: Political Change in the Soviet Union, 1987–1991* (Hanover, NH: University Press of New England, 1993), chap. 2.

25. Viktor Sergeyev and Nikita Biryukov, *Russia's Road to Democracy* (Aldershot, UK: Edward Elgar, 1993), p. 110.

26. There were about thirty deputy groups of various types and sizes in the Russian Congress of People's Deputies. Until December 1992, deputies could belong to more than one parliamentary caucus and many did. Membership in a parliamentary faction was voluntary and the faction's leaders could not force its members to vote the "party line." Moreover, about 20 percent of the deputies did not belong to any caucus at any given time.

27. The calculation of the strength of various parliamentary factions in the Russian parliament is based upon Vladimir Pribylovskii, ed., *Politicheskie fraktsii i deputatskie gruppy Rossiiskogo parlamenta,* 2d. ed. (Moscow: Panorama, 1993).

28. On the evolution of Gorbachev's presidency, see Brenda Horrigan and Theodore Karasik, "The Rise of Presidential Power under Gorbachev," in *Executive Power and Soviet Politics: The Rise and Decline of the Soviet State,* ed. Eugene Huskey (Armonk, NY: M.E. Sharpe, 1992), pp. 106–26.

29. Valery Zorkin, who played a major role in drafting the law on the Russian presidency in his capacity as the chief legal expert of the Constitutional Committee of the Russian parliament, was very clear in his opposition to copying Gorbachev's super-presidentialism. See Valery Zorkin, "Prezident dlya suverennoi Rossii," *Rossiiskaia gazeta,* 15 March 1991, p. 2; and Valery Zorkin and Yury Ryzhov, "Prezidentskaia vlast' v Rossii," *Rossiiskaia gazeta,* 4 May 1991, pp. 1–2.

30. See *Sbornik zakonodatel'nykh aktov o Prezidente RSFSR, o vyborakh Prezidenta RSFSR* (Moscow: Verkhovyi Sovet RSFSR, 1991).

31. Ruslan Khasbulatov did not fail to use these powers. He issued sixty-six such orders in 1992, and more than 630 in the first six months of 1993. See Domenic Gualtieri, "Russia's New 'War of Laws'," *RFE/RL Research Report* 2, no. 35 (3 September 1993): pp. 14–15.

32. Matthew S. Shugart, "Of Presidents and Parliaments," *East European Constitutional Review* 2, no. 1 (Winter 1993): p. 32.

33. The Russian case thus supports Skowronek's argument, made in the context of discussion of American politics, that the institution of the presidency "functioned best when it has been directed toward dislodging established elites, destroying the institutional arrangements that support them, and clearing the way for something entirely new." See Stephen Skowronek, *The Politics Presidents Make* (Cambridge, MA: Harvard University Press, 1993), p. 27.

34. See, for example, Michael McFaul, *Post-Communist Politics* (Washington, DC: Center of Strategic and International Studies, 1993), p. 49.

35. I definitely share Hough's conclusion that "it was this institutional fact, not the alleged conservatism . . . of the Congress [of People's Deputies] that led to the deepening conflict between President and the Congress." See Jerry F. Hough, "Institutional Change and the 1993 Election Results," in *Russia's Protodemocracy in Action,* ed. Colton and Hough (Washington, DC: Brookings Institution, forthcoming).

36. On the role of parties in the process of democratic consolidation, see Geoffrey Pridham and Paul G. Lewis, eds., *Stabilising Fragile Democracies* (London: Routledge, 1996).

37. Of all the factions in the Russian Congress of People's Deputies, only one, the Agrarian Union, was able to transform itself into an electoral party and take part in the 1993 and 1995 Duma elections.

38. On Yeltsin's post-1993 presidency, see Theodore Karasik and Brenda Horrigan, "Russian Presidential Politics Today," *Demokratizatsiia* 2, no. 4 (Fall 1994): pp. 517–35.

39. See, for example, Vladimir Umov, "Rossiiskii sredny klass: Sotsial'naia real'nost' i politicheskii fantom," *Polis,* no. 4 (1993): pp. 26–40. Another version of the same argument takes a form of the Marxist thesis that post-communist Russian society has no coherent classes of the Western type because people have no consciousness of their class belonging or their "true" class interests. See, for example, Boris Kararlitsky, *The Disintegration of the Monolith* (London: Verso, 1992).

40. Anatoly M. Khazanov, *After the USSR* (Madison: University of Wisconsin Press, 1995), chap. 2. The "revenge of the nomenklatura" was first advanced by such prominent radical democrats as Iurii Afanas'ev, Marina Sal'ye, and Iurii Burtin in the spring of 1992. For the summary and criticism of this theory, see Igor Yakovenko, "Chem zaniatsia demokratam: 'vedm' goniat ili reformy dvigat?" *Gospodin narod,* no. 5 (1992): pp. 2–3.

41. See, for example, Ken Jowitt, *New World Disorder* (Berkeley: University of Cali-

fornia Press, 1992), chap. 8; George Kolankiewicz, "Elites in Search of a Political Formula," *Daedalus* 123, no. 3 (Summer 1994): pp. 143–57; George Schšplin, "Postcommunism: Problems of Democratic Construction," *Daedalus* 123, no. 3 (Summer 1994): pp. 127–42; Zygmund Bauman, "After the Patronage State: A Model in Search of Class Interests," in *The New Great Transformation?* ed. Christopher G. A. Bryant and Edmund Mokrzycki (London: Routledge, 1994), pp. 14–35. The only exception in this case is Petro. See Nicolai N. Petro, *The Rebirth of Russian Democracy* (Cambridge, MA: Harvard University Press, 1995).

42. Nancy Bermeo, "Democracy in Europe," *Daedalus* 123, no. 2 (Spring 1994): pp. 159–78.

43. As we mentioned earlier, liberal-democrats won about 20 percent of the seats in the March 1990 parliamentary elections; a year later, during the March 1991 referendum on the preservation of the Union, only 29 percent of the population voted against the ballot proposition, as democratic activists called them to do.

44. A symbolic legacy of the movement's importance is the fact that its flag became the flag of the Russian Federation after August 1991 coup attempt. On the history and politics of Democratic Russia, see Yitzhak M. Brudny, "The Dynamics of Democratic Russia, 1990–1993," *Post-Soviet Affairs* 9, no. 2 (April–June 1993): pp. 141–70.

45. On the notion of the "protest cycle," see Sidney Tarrow, *Power in Movement* (New York: Cambridge University Press, 1994), chap. 9.

46. For the definitions of the liberal and antiliberal conceptions of nationalism in Eastern Europe, see Vladimir Tismaneaunu, "Fantasies of Salvation: Varieties of Nationalism in Postcommunist Eastern Europe," in *Envisioning Eastern Europe,* ed. Michael D. Kennedy (Ann Arbor: University of Michigan Press, 1994), pp. 114–19.

47. Kolankiewicz, "Elites in Search of a Political Formula," p. 147.

48. Andrei Sakharov, "Konstitutsiia Soiuza Sovetskikh Respublik Evropy i Azii: Proekt," in *Gor'kii, Moskva, dalee vezde,* ed. Andrei Sakharov (New York: Izdatel'stvo imeni Chekhova, 1990), pp. 263–71. For a detailed discussion of Sakharov and Starovoitova's ideas, see John B. Dunlop, *The Rise of Russia and the Fall of the Soviet Empire* (Princeton, NJ: Princeton University Press, 1993), pp. 90–91, 118–20.

49. The Georgian political scientist Ghia Nodia essentially makes the same argument about the failure of liberal-democrats to come up with a consistent and nonimperial concept of the Russian state. See Ghia Nodia, "Nationalism and Democracy," *Journal of Democracy* 3, no. 4 (October 1992): p. 20.

50. For the distinction between ethnic and civic definition of nationhood and its implication for democratization, see Liah Greenfeld, *Nationalism* (Cambridge, MA: Harvard University Press, 1992), pp. 10–11.

51. Stankevich provided a programmatic statement of this emerging consensus in his famous *Nezavisimaia gazeta* essay. See Sergei Stankevich, "Derzhava v poiskakh sebia," *Nezavisimaia gazeta,* 28 March 1992, p. 4.

52. Jerry F. Hough, Evelyn Davidheiser, and Susan Goodrich Lehmann, *The 1996 Russian Presidential Election* (Washington, DC: Brookings Institution, 1996), p. 44.

53. Lustick, in his recent book *Unsettled States, Disputed Lands* (Ithaca, NY: Cornell University Press, 1993), depicts the process of how elites of dominant ethnic groups become convinced that they have to get rid of territories commonly regarded as an integral part of their state (Ireland, in the case of England; Algeria, in the case of France; and the West Bank, in the case of Israel), and how to convince the general public that it is the necessary thing to be done. In Lustick's case, it is a one-way process. The Russian example we just described, however, suggests that the elites can come to the conclusion about the necessity to get rid of the empire, convince the general public that it is a right thing to do, and then repeat the same process in reverse.

54. The Polish sociologist Jerzy Szacki suggests, in his discussion of the economic reforms in Poland, that it is typical of current liberalism in Eastern Europe to preoccupy itself exclusively with the issue of construction of capitalism. See Jerzy Szacki, *Liberalism after Communism* (Budapest: Central European University Press, 1994), esp. chap. 5.

55. Another important manifestation of the domination of the imperial discourse among Russia's political elites was the 5 December 1996 Council of the Federation resolution on the status of the Ukrainian city of Sevastopol. The resolution asserting Russian sovereignty over the city, the home port of the Russian Black Sea Fleet, was introduced by the Mayor of Moscow, Luzhkov, and passed with the overwhelming majority of 110 against 7.

14

Bringing the Rule of Law to Russia and the Newly Independent States

The Role of the West in the Transformation of the Post-Soviet Legal Systems

Robert Sharlet

Since early 1992, the successor states of the former USSR have been struggling to reinvent themselves as independent, modern countries. Law, heretofore a peripheral aspect of the Soviet system, has become the medium for the enormous state-building tasks underway throughout the region. Transforming the received Soviet legal system in the newly independent states (NIS), so that law reform can provide the scaffolding for desired political and economic reforms, as well as the substance of legal process itself, is a daunting task which has progressed to varying degrees in the different states. The United States,[1] along with several West European governments as well as international organizations, has sought to be of assistance in this difficult and complex endeavor of reforming the law and restructuring the legal systems of the newly independent states.

Much has been achieved in certain states, but a great deal remains to be accomplished. This is not the first occasion on which the United States has attempted to foster legal reform in the post–World War II period. The Alliance for Progress, initiated in the 1960s during the Kennedy administration, was the precedent for the present large-scale effort of the U.S. government (USG) to help bring about rule-of-law development in the newly independent states. The Alliance was the grand culmination of earlier American legal assistance to postwar Japan, India, and Burma which was followed, as decolonization progressed, by work in sub-Saharan Africa. The focus then was largely on implanting the American legal education model as a source for encouraging democratic development in the new postwar republics. The problem today with viewing U.S. legal assistance to Latin America as a historical precedent is that the effort was subsequently not deemed a success, and, worse, gave rise to charges of legal imperialism. Later Administration of Justice projects, essentially law enforcement programs, in the authoritarian states of Latin America did nothing to refurbish the image of American "legal missionaries" in the region.[2]

With the legacy of the legal programs of the Alliance for Progress in mind, the USG has proceeded much more modestly and cautiously in the post-Soviet states. For one thing, the USG is dealing this time with a proud former adversary and superpower. For another, we have over the decades, especially since Vietnam, tempered our messianic tendencies. In this spirit, the U.S. ambassador to Russia, Thomas Pickering, captured the mood of our involvement with the Russian Federation in a 1995 statement:

> Our goals are long term. The full fruits of our efforts will not be apparent for years, perhaps not even for decades. . . . We should not exaggerate our influence over domestic development in Russia: it is marginal at best. Russia is simply too big and complex, and the processes underway too poorly understood, for it to be otherwise.[3]

If progress in Russia, the country about which the West is best informed as well as the most progressive of the newly independent states in the sphere of legal reform, is difficult to decipher, consider the challenge of assessing change elsewhere. Possibly, our influence is marginally greater in certain other post-Soviet successors, but nonetheless Pickering's caveat informs the analysis below of the USG's legal assistance to the newly independent states.

U.S. Foreign Aid to the Newly Independent States

The end of the Cold War confronted the United States with an interesting dilemma. A psychological demobilization began, accompanied in Washington by budgetary stringency in foreign affairs and the downsizing of frontline institutions whose missions had been undercut by the outbreak of peace. At the same time, post-Soviet elites actively solicited Western assistance in their unfamiliar transitional process from authoritarianism and central planning to political democracy and a market economy. As then Secretary of State James Baker observed during a tour of several of the new states, most of their leaders had learned the vocabulary of democratization and marketization, but few understood how to proceed toward the desired future. The common currency of all such East–West discussions was money—the need for very large sums to carry out macroeconomic reform, but just as the United States and the other G-7 states had resisted Mikhail Gorbachev's outsized requests, so too did Boris Yeltsin's large numbers after 1991 fail to bring forth the decabillions sought.[4]

What to do as the Cold War entered history; should the United States leave the post-Soviet states to their fates, to possibly founder in their transitions and backslide into the recent past? National interest (hence the Nunn-Lugar program) and American messianic idealism ruled out such an option. Middle ground was sought and found at the 1993 Vancouver Summit between President Bill Clinton and Russian president Yeltsin. Yeltsin was then engulfed in serious political conflict with his parliamentary adversaries over the direction of the country, particularly the painful road to capitalism on which he had set out. His hope was that Clinton, who was sympathetic, would offer large-scale, direct economic aid—a possibility, however, ruled out in the United States by domestic political considerations and economic realities. Instead, Clinton offered unqualified rhetorical support to his colleague in his struggle with parliament, promises of large-scale multilateral direct aid and a token amount of "soft money," approximately the half billion dollars provided by the Freedom Support Act of 1992 for "technical assistance" in Russia and the newly independent states. Publicly, President Yeltsin expressed appreciation, while privately his aides at Vancouver disdained the sum as a paltry commitment to the enormous tasks of post-Soviet reform in Russia.[5]

During the summer of 1993, as Yeltsin and parliament were heading toward their final, violent collision, the U.S. Agency for International Development (AID) began announcing "Requests for Proposals" (RFPs) to open competitive bidding for technical assistance work in newly independent states. One such RFP released on 1 August, with which the author was directly involved, concerned bringing rule-of-law assistance to Russia and the newly independent states. Proposals were due in thirty days. The amount at stake for four related contracts was approximately $65 to $70 million. A number of consulting firms specializing in development, along with nongovernmental organizations (NGOs), responded to the RFP in the first round. In the so-called Best and Final Round, the competition was narrowed to three groups: ABA/CEELI and partners, Chemonics International, and a joint venture formed by ARD and Checchi. CEELI (the Central and East European Legal Initiative) had been previously established within the American Bar Association in 1989 to provide legal assistance to the newly emerging, post-communist states of the former Soviet bloc. Chemonics International is a large, global consulting firm with much experience in Third World development programs. ARD and Checchi are smaller, international consulting firms with a similar profile and many contracts under the aegis of AID for development work in Latin America, sub-Saharan Africa, and Southeast Asia.

Each group outlined a model of how rule-of-law technical assistance should be delivered to the former Soviet Union (FSU), and presented candidates expert in the region who would administer their programs. In this particular competition for delivering the soft money to the FSU, the joint venture of ARD/Checchi won three of the contracts, while Chemonics was awarded the fourth. The joint venture formed the Rule of Law Consortium (ROLC) based in Moscow, Kiev, and Washington, DC, to administer the contracts for the Russian Federation, the

Slavic area (defined as Ukraine, Belarus, and Moldova), and the FSU excluding the Baltic states as a transnational "region," with special attention to the states of the Transcaucasus. Chemonics, in turn, organized the American Legal Consortium (ALC) based in Almaty, Kazakhstan, to administer its contract for the five new post-Soviet Central Asian states. The initial life of the contracts was two years with the possibility of renewal for a third year, and an option for two additional years to be exercised at AID's discretion.

While the ROLC and ALC were staffed by specialists in the politics and law of the FSU and the post-Soviet states, AID's personnel situation in the new foreign aid environment was different. An agency founded within the U.S. State Department by the Kennedy administration as part of the New Frontier, AID drew together in a single institution much of the U.S. postwar expertise in providing foreign aid to the decolonized Third World countries. Over the years since the 1960s, AID built a staff of committed, professional development specialists (many of whom later came to the agency with Peace Corps experience), and honed its institutional skills in its missions within U.S. embassies and its numerous field stations throughout the developing world. AID's work embraced economic development, especially agriculture; local governmental infrastructures; and some legal development, primarily Administration of Justice projects. In brief, AID was a premier American frontline institution in the Cold War, doing battle pacifically with Soviet bloc and Chinese aid donors for the "hearts and minds" of the new nations.

With the waning and final end of the Cold War in the late 1980s and early 1990s, AID and other frontline U.S. Cold War agencies entered a period of crisis. AID in particular has been impacted from two directions: (1) foreign aid budgets have been progressively shrinking, inevitably necessitating the contraction of the agency's overseas operations and the downsizing of its bureaucracy; and (2) simultaneously, the shift in foreign aid priorities from the Third World to the FSU and Eastern Europe has required AID to quickly redeploy to new and unfamiliar venues.

AID missions followed the flag into old (Moscow) and new American embassies in the newly independent states (Kiev, Almaty, and Erevan). Personnel who had spent most of their careers learning the languages, customs, and mores of Third World cultures were sent north to man the new outposts of U.S. foreign aid in the FSU. Short courses in Russian, the lingua franca of the newly independent states, were possible for some of the reassigned staff at the State Department's language school in the Washington area, but knowledge of their new host country's history, culture, and the legacies, good and bad, from the Soviet period, was impossible to obtain given the imperatives of delivering aid swiftly to governments and societies passing through volatile transitions.

At best, it was learn as you go in a confusing and rapidly changing political and economic environment for AID staff in the field, and those in Washington who were tasked to oversee the delivery of foreign aid to the newly independent states. In the course of his tour, the author encountered AID personnel just off the plane from Pakistan and Ecuador as well as senior people with extensive career time in Southeast Asia and sub-Saharan Africa. To their credit, most of these individuals rose to the challenges and were quick studies. Because rule-of-law work, as well as privatization programs, became a priority for AID, lawyers were needed at headquarters and in the field and were sometimes appointed or hired with little knowledge or experience in development work or the FSU. Again, these were often smart and talented people, but not all moved upward on the learning curve at the same pace. In some instances there were problems of adjustment. "Baggage" from another career track sometimes obstructed the learning process. The author is reminded of one walk-in hire at an FSU mission and another transfer into AID from a congressional staff, both of whom subsequently moved on to other work without ever fully learning the new game. Clearly, AID has been an organization undergoing strain and transition not unlike the institutions in the new countries the agency is trying to assist.

The Agency for International Development is, of course, merely an instrument of U.S. foreign policy. In the immediate wake of the Cold War, certain invariants emerged in early U.S. policy toward the newly independent states. First, there was the preoccupation with Russia to the near exclusion of other new states in the region. This is not to deny that Russia's sheer size, international "weight," and strategic location on the borders of other weaker post-Soviet states warranted serious attention and much of the foreign aid dollar. Washington's rationale was that if we did not help Russia reform, then an unreconstructed Russia might once again become a threat to the West as well to its new neighbors in the "near abroad." This said, it was shortsighted to leave Ukraine and other countries adrift with relatively little developmental assistance from the United States in the early stages of their transitions.

Second, after the understandable denuclearization priority, the next order of business in the FSU (*read:* Russia), was the privatization of state property. Although U.S. policy proclaimed the dual goal of encouraging democracy *and* fostering market economies in the newly independent states, in fact, the emphasis was on marketization, specifically facilitating the transfer of property from the state into private hands. So long as the privatization process progressed (as it did in the Russian Federation under our initial "Russia first" policy), the USG was willing to accommodate extra-constitutional action and undemocratic behavior in Russian politics.

As a consequence of focusing on Russia and concentrating on privatization, certain advantages accrued to AID as the lead institution of the U.S. donor effort in the FSU. First, lessons were learned and experience gained in Russia that would be transferable once the turn of the other states came at the technical assistance table. Second, assisting the transfer of property (a one-time event achievable in the near term), was certainly easier to attain than the long-term, slippery task of fostering democracy. On the other hand, costs were incurred. In the short-term the United States was associated with privatization, a process which subsequently became a source of political backlash (i.e., over nomenklatura privatization), and the object of criminal inquiry (due to the involvement of organized crime in some transfers). Longer term, the political rush to privatize the economy left the then unreformed legal process far behind. Great pockets of legal and illegal wealth became a source of corruption in the legal system. The nearly unrestricted growth of organized crime in symbiosis with the emergence of market-type transactions flooded society with violence, overwhelming the capacity of the still Soviet-style police to contain it. Similarly, large-scale business crimes, heretofore unknown in Soviet times, confronted the Procuracy with investigative and prosecutional tasks for which it was not prepared. Likewise, the courts struggled to keep pace with the new types of business disputes emerging in the Russian economy, but often the implementation of judicial rulings lagged behind the needs of market participants, given the judiciary's dependence on the demoralized law enforcement machinery for compliance.

As Stephen Holmes has argued, economic reform falters without a strong supporting state, without fair, efficient, and effective "extractive, administrative, regulative and adjudicative" institutions.[6] An effective rule-of-law state in turn requires legal reform. The net result then of a weak Russian state was a diminished and declining role for legal process as new economic relations raced ahead of the ability of legal institutions to perform the necessary regulative and adjudicative functions.

Elsewhere in the newly independent states, as an unintended consequence of the USG's early obsession with Russia and its privatization process, economic reform was often slow to start. This circumstance subsequently gave AID's rule-of-law contractors an opportunity to get the process of legal modernization under way before the regulatory tasks become insuperable. In the latter instances, Elster's "impossibility theorem" came into play, reflecting the great difficulty of legislating painful economic change in societies with representative institutions. In effect, the argument goes, economic reform requires ownership and price reforms, but legislators are reluctant to vote for policies that will disemploy and impoverish large numbers of constituents.[7] A variation on the relationship of politics and economics might state that unless economic and legal reform move forward in relative tandem, the former will outstrip the latter, leading to a situation, to paraphrase a Russian legal specialist, where economic reform crushes the law.[8]

The Parameters of Rule-of-Law Assistance to Russia and the Newly Independent States

In this section, the discussion turns to the two waves of U.S. rule-of-law assistance in the East, lessons learned from the Washington foreign aid game on legal development, and the complexities of transferring Western legal concepts, especially American ideas on lawyering, to the former Soviet Union.

U.S. rule-of-law assistance to Russia and the newly independent states began in earnest following the end of the USSR. ABA/CEELI, drawing on a combination of public and private funds, led the way in the first wave of the American effort. CEELI's modus operandi involved three aspects: (1) establishing liaison offices in a number of the new states; (2) advising on legislative drafting; and (3) sending American legal personnel to the field to provide short-course training to their NIS legal brethren as well as bringing selected NIS jurists to the United States for brief periods for further consultation and discussion.

CEELI liaisons, American lawyer volunteers working nearly pro bono, were installed in Moscow, Kyiv, Minsk, Chisinau, Almaty, and elsewhere in the newly independent states, the Baltic states, and Eastern Europe. The liaison functioned as a legal advisor to the national government on a wide range of law-reform issues in the immediate wake of the Soviet breakup and the early days of the new country's independence. Much of the work involved channeling draft laws to the United States for translation and learned commentary, but liaisons also provided advice to the senior courts, existing and new bar groups, and local law schools, upon request by the aid recipients involved. Most often, though, CEELI provided advice on draft constitutions and legislation at the request of the host country. The legal draft in question would be dispatched to CEELI headquarters in Washington, DC, translated into English, and then submitted to a panel of law and political science professors for expert commentary. The commentary would then be fed back into the originating legislative process, ideally in timely fashion. Finally, CEELI sent dozens of American judges, law professors, and practicing lawyers to various NIS countries to provide short courses in trial management, bankruptcy law, and other topics requested by the host country via the CEELI liaison. Reciprocally, CEELI/Washington would bring small groups of jurists to the United States for brief visits to our legal institutions.[9]

Assessing the first wave of U.S. assistance as represented by the CEELI model for rule-of-law work in the newly independent states, certain observations are in order. In the first wave, CEELI liaisons fulfilled the function of showing the American flag on the rule-of-law front, responding to early appeals for help, and providing NIS jurists, often for the first time, an opportunity to confer regularly with a Western colleague as their countries set off on the uncharted journey of transition. On the other hand, the quality of the liaisons was uneven, the range of topics they were asked to assist on too broad and diverse even for a team of talented professionals, and thus the expectations engendered by their presence inevitably could not be fulfilled.

Similarly, the panels assembled by CEELI to evaluate draft constitutions and laws were usually comprised of leading U.S. scholars and specialists on, say, constitution drafting, commercial law, or securities legislation. Few, however, had contextual knowledge of the country and society for which the legislation was being proposed. Consequently, much of the commentary ended up being overly academic, ethnocentric, or politically unrealistic for the host country. Eventually, CEELI personnel would learn to filter out such extraneous material and present useful composite commentaries, but in the initial run, a certain amount of irrelevant commentary was passed on.

Finally, in retrospect, many of the well-intentioned short-term visitors to the newly independent states could be characterized as "parachutists" dropping into alien territory with little knowledge of the terrain or its inhabitants. As a result, much U.S. expert advice fell on deaf ears in the newly independent states. This phenomenon as well as problems referenced above and other factors (e.g., U.S. NGOs making lightning trips to the newly independent states to "shop" for projects to market for funding back in Washington and on the foundation circuit), began to cause "consultant fatigue" and provoke a political backlash to the first wave of rule-of-law assistance in parts of Russia and Ukraine. NIS jurists started to feel that American aid-donors, good intentions aside, were over-promising, underdelivering, and did not understand the environment in which they were presuming to help.

The second wave of U.S. legal assistance, launched under the Freedom Support Act, tried to learn from previous experience. The emerging new model for delivering assistance was characterized by several factors: (1) a dualistic approach pairing country specialists and technical experts; (2) a search for projects which could survive the vicissitudes of transitional politics; (3) the focus on projects that would produce cross-institutional synergism and an intra-institutional multiplier effect, in both instances to get as much mileage for the U.S. foreign aid dollar as possible; and (4) the emphasis on producing sustainability or durable institutional change.

At the same time, the evolving new approach recognized certain limits. First, there was not enough U.S. soft money to carry out all of the training/retraining of newly independent states juridical personnel, hence the need to focus on "training the trainers" or the institutional professionals responsible for the periodic upgrading of judges and others. Secondly, it soon dawned on U.S. aid donors that the task would not be easy or short-term, that nothing less than massive resocialization of senior juridical elites would be necessary. Chief Justice Yakovlev of the Higher Commercial Court of Moscow observed in Washington that his judges were smart people and could cognitively learn new skills and methodologies of adjudication, but that the problem was fundamentally a psychological one; in other words, judges were now viewing cases exemplified by private business disputes which were considered economic crimes under Soviet law.[10] Clearly, a dual approach including some kind of resocialization orientation would be necessary, but a survey of the Western literature turned up no significant and usable theoretical studies on the resocialization of legal professionals.[11]

The second wave approach has been underway since late 1993. It has involved a multistaged bureaucratic process under AID's operational procedures.

The initial step was assessment of rule of law conditions and perceived needs in each country addressed. Assessment documents proceeded from library and desk sources to field research. The latter phase required extensive interviewing of senior and mid-level elites from the various legal institutions targeted for assistance in the individual countries. The lines of inquiry included such questions as: (1) What is the current status and condition of your institution? (2) How do you perceive your institution's needs and priorities in the law reform process? and (3) What outcomes would you hope could be realized through foreign assistance and in what time frame? The results of such field inquiries were a set of collaborative proposals combining the U.S. perspective (what is possible and affordable), and the indigenous point of view (what kinds of help we need to move forward in the transition process). These joint conclusions were then incorporated into the comprehensive assessment study. Upon completion of assessment, the next phase was to develop a more detailed, operational action plan outlining specific projects to be undertaken. Each rule-of-law project, in turn, was subjected to careful vetting and close analysis of its purpose and goal, resources required, operational strategy anticipated, expected cost, and the sought-after outcomes. Once a country action plan received AID approval, memoranda of understanding, followed by contracts, were negotiated by the U.S. and NIS partners, and then drawn up and signed, allowing requisite funds to be obligated and subobligated and the technical assistance work to begin. As implementation proceeded, work plans, quarterly reports, and other aspects of monitoring and verification came into play.

By focusing schematically on the bureaucratic side of technical assistance, the process appears easier then it is because, in fact, politics are embedded at every phase. The politics of delivering U.S. foreign aid, especially to a former adversary, should not be underestimated. They are formidable and require steady attention. AID, the main conduit for U.S. aid, has been consistently buffeted from several directions in its efforts to carry out its tasks in the FSU. On the one side is the Department of State with its bigger-picture perspective and shorter-range imperatives. On the other is the Foreign Operations Subcommittee of the Senate Appropriations Committee with its oversight responsibilities for the expenditure of foreign aid funds and the pursuit of Congress's standard preoccupation with relatively quick and quantifiable results. Sometimes single-issue NGOs as well as narrowly focused diaspora groups try to work this triangulation to access funding for projects in the newly independent states which may or may not be congruent with broader strategies being pursued. The author is aware of at least one group that enlisted friends in the White House in support of its funding agenda. Other U.S. NGOs and contractors have also been known to create local allies in the field in order to compete more vigorously with each other in places like Moscow and Kyiv.

Then, like any Washington agency, AID must strive to stay out of the sights of the U.S. General Accounting Office (GAO), from inside the government, and from negative press coverage, from outside. From the field come requests (*read:* demands) for attention to the embassy's agenda, as well as the differential perceptions of needs and timing between AID missions and Washington staff. Within the beltway, AID does not enjoy a monopoly over the administration of foreign aid. Numerous other departments and agencies are involved, some with powerful friends in congressional appropriations committees.[12] In the rule-of-law field alone, AID has had to compete with the FBI, the Justice Department, and several bureaus and agencies of the Treasury Department for control over new funds for special tasks. Even in the newly independent states, AID initially did not have a clear field of vision, sometimes working on a parallel track with donor teams from European states (e.g., Germany and the Netherlands), as well as international organizations. With the support of AID, the ROLC subsequently developed a collaborative relationship with Dutch experts working in the newly independent states. More recently, in mid-1996, the author participated in an international AID coordinating conference which brought together all major rule-of-law donors in the newly independent states, including U.S., Canadian, German, Dutch, and World Bank representatives.[13] Operating thus within this universe of conflicting cross-pressures, especially with regard to the new game in the newly independent states, AID tries to carry out its mandates in a consistent and orderly way. Sometimes, however, the agency must shift from facilitator of the foreign aid process to "brakeman" as it tries to interpret confusing and frequently ambiguous signals at home and abroad.[14]

As anyone who works in the foreign aid process soon learns, money and politics prevail over reason and vision. Apropos, in response to a well-reasoned, long-range concept paper from an NGO located far from the capital, the author replied:

> Money and Politics are indivisible in the development game. Money, sometimes it appears to be there, but like a mirage moves away as you approach. Then there's the other face, Politics—the ultimate in subjectivity amenable only to intuition at best. In short, good ideas are not enough. There are limits to reason. The hidden variables must also be borne in mind; if not, they'll mock your best efforts.[15]

In brief, three unwritten rules seem to govern the foreign aid game in Washington:

1. *There is no closure*, that is, no assessment, action plan, project design, or implementation schedule is ever final; everything is amendable. This became evident to the author for the first time when he finished the eighth draft of the Ukraine Rule-of-Law Assessment in the spring of 1994. Although effectively finished, the document remained technically a draft.

2. *Neither heroes nor fools,* meaning that government officials are risk-averse and rarely will initiate or approve action that would chance greater glory or risk setback or failure. Down the middle of the road is the preferred route. This

cautious middling strategy resembles a presidential strategy in foreign policy generally dubbed "mini/max" and defined as doing the minimum necessary to sustain a policy and the maximum politically feasible.[16]

3. *Spend the money fast*, or, use it or lose it. Failure to expedite foreign aid to its intended destination is tantamount to a tragic flaw. One of the main concerns of congressional oversight committees as well as their watchdog, the GAO, is whether appropriated foreign aid funds are obligated and subobligated in timely fashion. An organization which is slow to move money given it into the pipeline runs the risk of losing its AID contract to do the work assigned.

Finally, even after all the aforementioned reefs and shoals are navigated, there still remains the problem of the reception of ideas as U.S. donors go ashore in the FSU. Dramatically different perspectives on law faced the initial aid teams which began work in the newly independent states. In Soviet jurisprudence, law performed the functions of harnessing the social energy of the individual, maximizing the power of the state over the citizen, and transforming the social and physical environment. In contrast, U.S. lawyers carried in their intellectual kit quite a different angle of vision on law. For them, law performs the functions of releasing social energy, balancing the power of social groups, and merely controlling the natural environment.[17]

Thus, the rule of law had its intellectual origins in Western political and legal philosophy which had little resonance in prerevolutionary Imperial Russia,[18] and nearly none at all during the Soviet period. The fundamental principle of a government of laws, not men or women, was derived from positivism and its derivative, legal positivism. Its corollaries, a durable due process of law to buffer citizens from the state had its roots in natural law theory, while the necessity of a supportive legal culture emerged from the historical school of jurisprudence.[19] As an example of the cultural and historical filters involved in the reception process, the Western concept of "judicial independence" has taken hold at the level of rhetoric in the newly independent states, but judicial reality remains quite different. By even the standards of a less ambitious definition such as "the [American] judiciary stands apart—not quite independent . . . but enjoying considerable autonomy,"[20] court development in Russia and the newly independent states falls far short, still bearing the imprint of the received statist legal culture. Given the difficulties of transoceanic legal transplants, U.S. donors must tread lightly, be attentive to continental norms, and work, where possible, with European colleagues in delivering rule-of-law assistance to the newly independent states.

Politics of Law Reform in Russia and the Newly Independent States

A fellow scholar of post-Soviet law has assigned to Russia, the most progressive of the newly independent states, the status of a "legal order," a concept located between Rechtsstaat or rule by law, and the rule of law, which suggests that "laws constrain governments and their leaders, as well as citizens."[21] Thus, a legal order enjoys a higher status than a Rechtsstaat, which assumes "that the state itself is the highest, if not the only, source of the law through which it operates."[22] In turn, a legal order falls short of the rule of law, which entails three premises:

> (1) A government of laws not men, (2) a durable due process of law, buffering the citizen from the power of the state, and (3) a deep-rooted, viable legal culture comprising a set of internalized attitudes, sentiments and beliefs supportive of the preceding legal institutions and process.[23]

At least six variables affect the transition from a legal order to a rule-of-law society, including power branches, legal system, institutional fragility, velocity of change, organized crime, and legal nihilism.

Power Branches

Has the struggle between the two power branches of the polity been resolved (by a presidential, parliamentary, or a hybrid model) in a new post-Soviet constitution? In Russia and other newly independent states, the answer is yes (the Transcaucasian states and Ukraine most recently ratified new constitutions). No single Western model influenced the new constitutions of the newly independent states, which are hybrids of the U.S. and French constitutions on the strong presidency, the French and German constitutions on the legislature, the German constitution on the constitutional court, and the UN and European conventions on human rights. The debilitating conflict between president and parliament in Russia's first post-Soviet republic during 1992 through early October 1993 significantly delayed the introduction of legal reforms. Law reform was deferred in Armenia and Georgia until those states completed their new constitutions in 1995. While law reform began in Ukraine in spite of the long political struggle over the shape of the new constitution, much of the elite's attention and energies had been tied down in the constitutional drafting marathon.[24]

Legal System

After 1991, absent the directive authority of the formerly ruling Communist Party, the legal systems of the newly independent states began to fly apart. Cohesion disappeared and cooperation between the various parts of the legal system declined, as their institutional leaders tried to position themselves favorably in the uncertain transition process, some by fending off criticism for the

Soviet period, others by trying to expand their jurisdiction through a kind of institutional imperialism. Turf battles broke out, a brain drain of legal talent flowed into the emerging market economy and more lucrative private law practice, while implementation of laws, decrees, and judicial decisions suffered. As a consequence, institutional energies were deflected from the tasks of law reform, which would be difficult under the best of circumstances.[25] Varying from country to country in the newly independent states, the legal systems are slowly beginning to recohere—the procuracies are regaining lost ground in the initial phase of political and legal reforms, the justice ministries (depending on the political status of the minister within the governing elite) are holding their own, while judicial reform and the quest for autonomy has slowed due to falling budgetary support.

Institutional Fragility

As the Soviet Union came apart, setting adrift many new states with, at best, weak navigational systems to guide them to an alternate future, the fate of legal institutions is particularly interesting. In the recent past, all were tightly integrated into a well-defined state schemata and depended upon appropriate higher Communist Party bodies for guidance. In the wake of December 1991, the legal system as a whole suddenly gained an unexpected degree of autonomy as the Communist Party as a ruling institution entered history, the state declined, and the new polity had not fully emerged. In the turf fighting between legal agencies which ensued, individual leaders assumed far greater authority and prominence than imaginable during the Soviet period. Institutional futures, and most certainly budgetary viability in the turbulence of transition, became dependent now on the political skills of procurator-generals, justice ministers, chief justices, and others. In the same spirit, commitment to law reform and the decision to proceed was often in the hands of these individuals. As a result, the map of the legal system began to change as one institution embraced change while another resisted. In those conditions, the incipient law reform process was often fragile, dependent as it was on one or two enlightened institutional heads. Nowhere was this phenomenon more dramatically manifested than in Ukraine, where the sudden deaths of three prominent legal reformers and power brokers, all in their mid-fifties, in the space of five months in late 1994 and early 1995 set back the process of constitutional reform.[26] Five years after the fall of the USSR, little has changed in terms of institutional fragility. Strong and politically influential jurists still tend to carry their institutions "on their backs." In Russia, Chief Justice Tumanov of the Constitutional Court continues his predecessor's tendency of identifying the court with himself, although he has shown much more political savvy than former Chief Justice Zorkin. In Armenia, a former Soviet-period procurator general who holds no public office, but is close to the president, is the main power broker propelling legal reform forward.

Velocity of Change

As change, especially economic reform, proceeded rapidly and chaotically in the post-Soviet period, new and unfamiliar demands were felt by the legal system, itself in relative disarray. The revolution in property ownership and the rise of new commercial relationships placed the courts in particular under unexpected pressure. Former Soviet judges grandfathered into the post-Soviet judiciary, and even new personnel, found it difficult to cope with the complexities of new types of business disputes. The more advanced economic reform, the greater the pressure on the legal system as in Russia. A particularly acute problem has been the inability of law enforcement to cope with organized crime, not only in Russia, but elsewhere in the newly independent states as well. The exigency has prompted sharp political reactions contravening the due-process premise of the rule of law. In Uzbekistan, draconic measures have been resorted to, while even in more reform-minded Russia and Ukraine, extraconstitutional presidential decrees have been issued empowering the police to detain organized crime suspects without charge for up to thirty days.

Organized Crime

Beginning in the more permissive conditions of the perestroika period under Mikhail Gorbachev, organized criminal activity in the newly independent states began to grow and flourish. In the new climate of private business since the end of the Soviet Union, organized crime has grown exponentially. The mobs—there are thousands of them—have invaded the emerging market economies and corrupted parts of the political systems, thus making the need for law reform more urgent. Meanwhile, crime bosses are able to suborn certain judges who, given the low salaries, are tempted by the large bribes offered.[27] Unfortunately, much of the information on organized crime outside of Russia tends to be circumstantial. For instance, Uzbekistan and Armenia are thought to be effective law and order states where the streets of the capitals are relatively safe. For what it is worth, the author can verify this perception for Erevan. However, even for Russia, the Western as well as the Russian literature tends to be either conceptual or anecdotal. An exception, a balanced social science study, appeared in Russia in the spring of 1996, indicating that the number of organized criminal gangs (three or more members) grew by a factor of sixteen from 1989 through 1994. In the same period, crimes attributed to these groups increased by 500 percent. As an example of the pervasive perception of "mafia" activity in Russia, an economics professor at Irkutsk State University asked her students to submit proposals for businesses they would like to operate in the region.

> Students responded with a variety of ideas, from travel agencies to hair salons, from butcher shops to bakeries. In the business plans, though, along with the

"cost of goods sold" and "labor costs" and "advertising expenses," nearly all the students had a simple line for "Russian mafia."[28]

Legal Nihilism

Contempt for law by both rulers and ruled alike has long been a Russian tradition, dating from the period of empire and pervading today all of the post-Soviet states without exception.[29] The Soviet period, of course, did nothing to advance the notion of justice as a fair and impartial process or the idea, familiar in democratic societies, of law and respect for it as an intrinsic value. The legacy of legal nihilism weighs heavily on the new societies, and only with time and reformed and modernized legal systems will it be likely to wither away gradually in public consciousness. Even President Yeltsin admits to the problem in his memoirs: "Everyone knows that we Russians do not like to obey all sorts of rules, laws, instructions, and directives—any kind of previously established regimentation of behavior. We are a casual sort of people and rules cut us like a knife."[30]

These factors taken together comprise a formidable complex of problems—conflict between the power branches, disarray in the legal infrastructures, weak institutionalization, the social costs of rapid change, the epidemic of organized crime, and the legacy of nihilism. While some are solvable, others will be more enduring, making evident the necessity for systemic law reform in the newly independent states along with the immense difficulties burdening the task, especially for foreign donors trying to assist the process.

Law Reform in an Open Legal Policy-Making Process: Russia as a Case Study

Perhaps nowhere in the newly independent states were the centrifugal forces within the legal system so great and the ensuing turf battles so intense as in Russia. Overarching the transition process as a whole were the dueling constitutional commissions of 1993 representing president and parliament. As the politics of power sharing subsided in 1994 under the new constitution, attention shifted within the law reform process to competition over drafting Russia's new market-oriented civil code. Here the competitors were the Private Law Research Institute and the State Legal Administration (GPU), both created under the aegis of the office of the president.[31] The year 1994 also witnessed a political struggle between the president and the upper house, the Federation Council, over the makeup of the new Constitutional Court, specifically over who was to fill the six vacant seats. After over seven months of nominations, rejections, and confirmations, the full bench was finally seated in early 1995.[32] Also in 1994, the ongoing drama of trying to enact the Federal Constitutional Law on the Ombudsman of the Russian Federation began. This important piece of reform legislation got caught up in the Chechen crisis beginning in late 1994, fell victim to the cross fire between Russian and Chechen forces, between the president and the Federal Assembly, and—through mid-1996—between rival forces on the floor of the State Duma. Starting in earnest in 1995 and continuing into early 1996, a similar turf battle was under way with diverse participants over the shape and content of Russia's pending post-Soviet Criminal Code and Code of Criminal Procedure. Complicating criminal law codification was the necessity of coordinating crime and punishment with the new civil code governing economic relations. The new Criminal Code finally passed and took effect on 1 January 1997. Russia, which has far more skilled legislative drafting experts than its neighbors because most legal drafting in the Soviet period was done in Moscow, is well ahead of NIS countries in recodification generally.

All these differences over issues of legal policy are signs of the increasing vitality of Russia's policy-making process, and particularly the increasing openness of legal policy making as the source of reform legislation and new and revitalized legal institutions. In order to provide targeted and effective rule-of-law assistance in contemporary Russia, European and American aid donors need to be aware of this post-communist policy universe and the numerous and diverse political actors and forces which vie for influence therein. For easy comprehension, the participants active in giving direction to the law reform process can be analytically classified into ten groups. In reality, many of these groups overlap in myriad ways depending on the legislative issue, be it a broad question such as judicial reform or a more technical matter like tax law. In turn, lines of conflict run both within and between various policy-making groups, again depending upon the legislative topic at hand.

Key Players

The key players include the president, the relevant parliamentary committees, the Ministry of Justice, and the GPU. The main lines of conflict over the initial drafting process for legislation on law reform run between the GPU, within the executive office of the president, and the Justice Ministry, as part of the cabinet or government. The relatively small but influential GPU, resembling more a research institute than an arm of government, has had the advantage of access to the president, while the ministry as a large bureaucracy and line agency has a decided edge in other resources.[33]

Legislative Initiative on Law Reform Issues

Legislative initiative on law reform issues is also enjoyed under the constitution by the three senior courts of the Russian Federation: the Constitutional Court, which has sole power to interpret and resolve conflicts involving constitutional issues; the Supreme Court, the highest appellate court, especially for criminal cases; and the Highest Commercial Court, which is the apex of the commercial court system with jurisdiction over business disputes.[34]

Single-Issue Law Reform Participants

Single-issue law reform participants are also involved in the legislative process, especially on bills pertaining to their corporate or corollary interests. In this category, for instance, the Procuracy was active in drafting the major reform amendments to its statute which became law in 1995, just as the Federal Security Service participated in the drafting and passage of its statute earlier in the year.[35] In the case of process-oriented versus institution-building statutes, quite a number of legal actors will participate in the policy-making effort depending upon the proposed act's relevance to their jurisdictions. In this context, the Ministry of Internal Affairs and a number of other legal agencies were involved in producing the Law on Operational-Investigative Activity of 1995.[36] Similarly, many legal actors are drawn into the complex effort of drafting and passing new codes, primarily on chapters and sections pertinent to their institutional interests.

Legal Think Tanks

Legal think tanks also come to the policy-making table with expert drafts, commentary, and amendments. Some of the most influential state think tanks include the Institute of State and Law of the Russian Academy of Sciences, Moscow State University's law faculty, other law faculties in the Russian Federation, and groups of individual legal scholars. In addition, there is a growing sector of private think tanks, some of which are headed by former government officials (e.g., the Gorbachev Foundation), while others, created "from below," reflect civil society concerns. These groups may lobby the presidential administration, the government, or the parliament on law-related issues, depending on their degree of access. For instance, the NGO think tank, Interlegal, lobbied consistently and contributed substantially to the passage of the Law on Public Associations. Other groups with more partisan orientations lobbied in the electoral legislation process during 1995, for a set of laws which created the legal frameworks for the parliamentary and presidential elections of 1995 and 1996, respectively.

Insiders and Institutional Heads

Insiders and institutional heads also, of course, weigh in heavily in legal policy making. The list is long, but prominent among them have been Sergei Pashin, until mid-1995 head of the judicial reform section of the GPU; Ruslan Orekhov, current chief of the GPU; Valentin Kovalev, minister of justice; Yuri Kalmykov, his predecessor until late 1994; Professors Alexander Yakovlev and Valery

Savitsky, respectively Yeltsin's presidential liaisons to the parliament and Constitutional Court up to 1996; the presidential legal advisers Mikhail Krasnov and Yuri Baturin; V.B. Isakov, influential chair of the principal legal policy committee in the last Duma; the changing incumbents of the Office of Procurator-General, currently Yuri Skuratov; and depending on specific issues (e.g., judicial reform), the publicly less well-known heads of such bodies as the Council for Judicial Reform, the Legal Academy, and the Council of Judges.

Policy Players External to the Legal System

Policy players external to the legal system cannot be discounted; they include knowledgeable and respected legal journalists such Yuri Feofanov of *Izvestiia,* as well as certain executive heads of republics and regions. While the former have often played a constructive role commenting on legislation in process, the latter have been active in driving the paraconstitutional process that began in early 1994 in which the center negotiates bilateral treaties and agreements on power sharing and resource control with selected subjects of the Russian Federation.[37]

Private Participants

Private participants are understandably less visible in the policy process, but, according to circumstantial evidence, probably include Russian and foreign law firms as well as public relations firms acting on behalf of clients, and possibly even mafia representatives seeking to influence the direction of certain legislative issues in the interest of their illegal business activities. In 1995–96, for example, the ongoing legislative deliberations on a natural resource production-sharing law has reportedly involved a fair amount of back-channel lobbying through private firms on behalf of American and international oil companies hoping for a favorable disposition of the issue to support their interest in oil exploration in Russia.

Foreign and International Interests

Foreign and international interests also play a discreet (and marginal) role on particular legal policy issues. Often this type of input occurs through diplomatic channels, or via Russian institutional partners in the law reform process. Foremost among this type of political actor are the Council of Europe, the Organization for Security and Cooperation in Europe (OSCE), and the United Nations Development Program (UNDP); individual national governments such as the United States, Germany, France, and the Netherlands; Western foundations that are major aid donors, such as Soros, the MacArthur Foundation, and the Ford Foundation, all of which have offices in Moscow; and various Western NGOs and contractors working on law reform with Russian institutional partners. By way of illustration, the UNDP, in conjunction with European and American partners, was an interested party in the policy-making process on the Federal Constitutional Law on the Ombudsman. UNDP was preparing to assist implementation of the expected statute until discussion of the bill was suspended as a casualty of the Chechen crisis.

In another example, the Harvard Institute for International Development, through its collaboration with the GPU, has been able to increase its influence in the Russian law reform process, while the foreign connection enhanced the GPU's ability to compete on policy inside of its own polity.

Special Interests

Special interests, as in any open policy-making process, are also involved on narrowly focused issues or particular pieces of legislation. Some examples are the Agrarian and Communist parties, which have a core interest in the drafting of the pending Land Code, particularly on the question of the acquisition and alienation of private property in land; various international energy consortia on the Law on Production Sharing, which as of mid-1996 was still under consideration; and, although not visible to the naked eye, the privatized natural gas giant Gazprom is rumored to have lobbied through its former CEO, Prime Minister Viktor Chernomyrdin, for legislative relief from tax legislation.

Russia's Voters

Finally, Russia's voters have been driving the constitutional implementation process, as well as the quest for relief (by decree or statute) on law and order, and economic issues through their significant levels of participation in the two sets of parliamentary elections, in the two rounds of the presidential election, and, presumptively, in the gubernatorial and local elections of late 1996 and early 1997.

To conclude this section, the Federal Constitutional Law on the Constitutional Court of 1994 serves as an illustration of how the various individuals, interests, and policy groups came together to reestablish the suspended Constitutional Court. As of the spring of 1994, the court bill was stalled in the Duma over the issue of relatively open or restricted access to the court. Conservative factions took the former position, proreform factions the latter. The complement of thirteen justices from the suspended court lobbied on behalf of the bill they had helped to draft, and, specifically, on the side of restrictive rules of standing. The president seemed to be in no hurry to see the relaunching of an institution which in its first incarnation (up to the fall of 1993) had caused him so much difficulty. It looked like the bill would be marooned for some time as the Duma players learned the art of compromise.

Then, in mid-June 1994, President Yeltsin issued a very severe anticrime decree. The immediate impetus was the recent assassination of a popular journalist by a mafia group. Other factors influenced his decree—in the parliamentary elections of December 1993, voters had demonstrated great concern over the crime issue; Yeltsin was anxious to be responsive, but legislation was moving through the newly elected Duma at a snail's pace, thus he launched his decree to "push" the pace of organized crime legislation; and, finally, the USG and several international organizations were beginning to express concern about the security of newly privatized property and foreign investment in crime-ridden Russia.

How did this affect the passage of the court bill? Yeltsin's decree, which empowered the police to contravene several clauses of the new constitution as well as parts of the Criminal Procedural Code, outraged nearly all factions in the Duma as well as extraparliamentary groups committed to legal reform. Absent a sitting Constitutional Court, no authority existed to review the constitutionality of Yeltsin's decree. This vacuum stimulated a vigorous lobbying process on behalf of the stalled court bill, and finally, putting aside their internal differences, the Duma indeed passed the bill with the requisite two-thirds majority with considerable dispatch.

In effect, the newly minted Russian policy-making process worked. Taken together then, the number and diversity of participants in the legal policy-making process as it impacts law reform is impressive, and speaks to the increasing institutionalization of plural interests as well as the growing dispersion of political resources as contemporary Russia continues its journey to political democracy.

The U.S. Role in Seedtime for the Rule of Law in the Newly Independent States

Russia, Ukraine, and the other newly independent states have been fully independent for five years, a very short span in the life of nations. Initially, all of the newly independent states aspired to the creation of political democracies and the building of market economies. Since the heady days of late 1991 and 1992, however, several countries have regressed politically to benign forms of executive authoritarianism, essentially to presidentialist regimes, on the assumption that the awesome tasks of state and nation building require a strong hand. Others, led by reform leader Russia, have forged ahead with varying degrees of commitment to reforms, and at different rates of speed. To mention several, Ukraine is on the cusp of gathering the political will necessary to follow Russia's path, while Georgia, still plagued by the unwanted legacies of three civil wars, and Armenia, beset by economic blockade stemming from a stalemated external war, have only recently begun the reform process.

The United States and Europe have tried to assist these and other new states in their transitions to political and economic modernity. However, in spite of rhetoric supportive of the nexus between democracy and the market, the emphasis in the West's deployment of political and financial assets in the East has been on developing market economies. This has meant priority Western attention has been given to the privatization process, the development of foreign-investor friendly ownership and tax legislation to encourage private investment, and, more recently, to the reform of criminal justice with reference in particular to containing market-oriented crime. Technical assistance on political and other legal reforms has been complementary but secondary. Political reform assistance has focused on building democratic processes, admittedly a longer term under-taking , while rule-of-law assistance has run the gamut from legislative drafting to institution building to human rights training. In most instances, rule-of-law work has been designed to be directly relevant to fostering market relations, as well as the long-term task of reforming and modernizing the legal process. Good and useful work has been done by foreign advisors on the political and legal fronts of some of the newly independent states, but at best it is still only seedtime for democracy and the rule of law in most of these societies. To be ultimately successful in their transitions, these societies must eventually organically "grow" supportive political and legal cultures. No one working on the rule-of-law front on behalf of Russia and the newly independent states has any illusions about the degree of difficulty that cultural change presents in societies shaped by centuries of authoritarianism. In recent studies of political culture in Russia, the crucial question has been posed: "will Russia internalize the challenges of modernity" or will the country backslide into "its deep political folkways"?[38] On these larger, long-term, ideational dimensions of social change, foreigners are not likely to be of much help. As Robert Dahl has observed: "Democratization depends far less on what outsiders can do than what the leaders and people within the country can and will do."[39]

Since the breakup of the USSR, the United States has consistently supported constitutional reform in the newly independent states as the necessary prelude to other political and legal reforms. U.S. constitutional lawyers and scholars, pub-licly and privately funded, have advised nearly every newly independent state— Russia and Ukraine from early in the independence period, and Armenia and Georgia most recently. The thrust of this advice has been to develop a system of separated and balanced powers, although not necessarily as a clone of the Ameri-can system; to help write judicial chapters for the constitutions friendly to greater judicial autonomy, if not independence, including sections on constitutional courts which most of the countries favored along with their supreme courts and higher commercial courts; and to offer counsel for strong chapters embracing protection of civil and human rights consistent with European and international conventions.[40]

The next priority in political reform assistance was helping the new states set up and carry out free, fair, and efficient elections. Most notable in this area has been the work of the International Foundation for Electoral Systems (IFES), an AID-sponsored NGO based in Washington, DC. IFES has assisted in the drafting and implementation of electoral legislation in several of the newly independent states, including Russia, Ukraine, and Armenia. It has also helped set up the administrative mechanisms for elections and assisted in coordinating international supervision of these elections through a system of foreign observers. Other forms of political assistance in several countries, provided by different U.S. organizations, have included executive staff training (Brookings Institution), parliamentary staff training (Congressional Research Service and the U.S.-Ukraine Foundation), and party development (National Democratic Institute and the International Republican Institute). As with election support, most of this work was accomplished under AID auspices.

U.S. support for law reform has been even more ambitious and extensive. The major aid providers working under AID have included the Rule-of-Law Consortium, Institutional Reform and the Informal Sector (IRIS), Harvard Institute of International Development (HIID), ALC, and ABA/CEELI. These organizations and their specialized subcontractors and individual consultants have addressed a wide range of reforms in the newly independent states within AID's Rule-of-Law Program. Their projects have impacted the legislative process, the legal infrastructure, and the legal process in a number of countries. Earlier U.S. drafting assistance has evolved to the point of integrating leading world specialists as consultants in the actual indigenous drafting process. This was most apparent in the passage of the three-part Russian Civil Code from 1994 to 1996, and in current civil legislation drafting under way in Ukraine and Armenia.

In addition, the ROLC took the lead in assisting the drafting of model codes by international panels of jurists from member states of the Commonwealth of Independent States (CIS). So far, this process has produced a Model Civil Code in 1994, and the CIS Model Criminal Code of 1996. The system of model codes is designed to enable the majority of the newly independent states, which do not have sufficient legislative drafting capabilities for such large projects, to adopt state-of-the-art model codes if they choose and adapt them to their national legislation. The purpose of this effort is to help expedite the rebuilding of legal process throughout the newly independent states.

The ROLC has also worked extensively with the senior personnel of the court systems of Russia, Ukraine, and Armenia, particularly the new commercial court systems and the courts of general jurisdiction. The focus has been on training the judicial trainers of these systems so they in turn will be equipped to retrain their own line judges through in-service training programs. The emphasis in the training programs has been on judging in general, and, particularly, on civil and commercial adjudication. ROLC has been assisted in this work by the National Judicial College, the Ohio Supreme Court, the Supreme Court of Vermont, and Justices Scalia, Breyer, Ginsberg, and O'Connor of the U.S. Supreme Court, along with other federal and California Supreme Court judges whose participation was organized by ROLC subcontractors the Center for Democracy and Technical Assistance to the Republic of Armenia (TARA). Topics covered included courtroom management, case management, judicial enforcement, and adjudication of new codes.

The ROLC has developed similar "train the trainer" projects with the Russian and Ukrainian procuracies, while ABA/CEELI and the U.S. Department of Justice work with line prosecutors in Russia. The ROLC has been assisted in its procuratorial work by John Jay Douglas, former dean of the National College of District Attorneys, and the American Prosecutors Research Institute. Other programs focus on seven Russian and Ukrainian law schools, helping them modernize their curricula to include commercial law and human rights law among other courses, and to improve their teaching methodologies, including moot court techniques. ROLC's subcontractors for the law schools project are the American Association of Law Schools and the National Institute for Trial Advocacy, both of which have provided leading U.S. law faculty for well-focused, short training stints in the newly independent states.

Finally, all of AID's rule-of-law providers have striven to build awareness and sensitivity to human rights in the institutions they are assisting, as well as in the codes and juridical processes they are helping to facilitate. In particular, Freedom House, which is funded by AID for a number of projects, specifically works on strengthening nascent civil societies and promoting civil rights in the newly independent states.[41]

Conclusion

The quest for law reform has gone on for nearly two centuries in Russia. Beginning with Count Speransky's unsuccessful effort to introduce a constitution in the early nineteenth century during the reign of Alexander I, and through Alexander II's legal reforms of the 1860s, Russia's search for legal modernity within an authoritarian polity continued into the Soviet period. In the early 1920s, Lenin presided over the reintroduction of law in the wake of the Bolshevik Revolution. Later, first Nikita Khrushchev and then Leonid Brezhnev directed a long and comprehensive period of legal reform from the mid-1950s to the late 1970s, culminating in the new USSR Constitution of 1977. It was left to Gorbachev, however, a lawyer like Lenin, to carry out the most radical Soviet legal reforms in the late 1980s, changes which in no small measure contributed to the destabilization and demise of the Soviet system in 1991.[42]

Contemporary post-Soviet law reform in the Russia and the newly independent states, therefore, continues a long, although discontinuous, tradition. This particular reformation period, however, includes the most ambitious goal of trying to create rule-of-law systems in place of the shards of the broken Soviet legal system. In most but not all of the newly independent states the goal is being pursued in more auspicious political environments than in past periods of Russia's legal history.

With the exception of the period following World War II when the Soviet Union exported and imposed its regime model, including the legal subsystem, on East Europe, Russia has been principally a selective borrower from foreign legal experience of ideas for reforming its own legal system. For this latest and most extensive effort at legal modernization, however, the "jury" of history will likely be out for some time on whether Russia and other successor states can develop and sustain an irreversible commitment to use law to tame long-held habits of political arbitrariness.[43]

The principal determinant of whether the rule of law has a chance to take root and flower in Russia and the newly independent states will be political will. Historically, tsarist and later communist legal reforms always foundered because neither tsars nor commissars were in the end willing to risk a systemic challenge to their hegemony. Gorbachev was the exception in a long line of reformist rulers, and his willingness to introduce political rights and legal empowerment into a closed society eventually contributed to his downfall and the end of Communist Party rule. The present question in the newly independent states is whether the post-Soviet political elites have the will and determination to continue and deepen early rule-of-law reforms. At this point in time, the most promising candidates for achieving legal modernity are Russia and Ukraine, followed much further back by Georgia and Armenia, while the prospects in several of the Central Asian states appear to be the least promising for the rule of law.

As Russia and several other states in the near abroad begin to move beyond the first, ad hoc phase of legal transformation, the reform tasks are likely to change, especially in those newly independent states where the most progress has been made. There will be a gradual shift from top-down reforms of central legal institutions to intermediate levels of authority and to civil society from below. More attention will be given to decentralization of legal capacity, devolving more extractive and regulative powers to regional and even local governments; implementation of legal action, presently the "black hole" of law reform; and to further fostering citizen and civic demand for legal remedies to social problems, or the long-term task of cultivating democratic legal cultures.

The West, which has also gone through a useful learning experience in providing technical assistance on law reform to the newly independent states, is prepared to continue to offer help in the next, more systematic phase of legal reform. Just as the targets for reform in the newly independent states are changing, so too is the ability of the West to deliver effective aid. Official Washington appears to be reviewing the rules of the foreign aid game which had hindered aid delivery to the newly independent states in the first phase. Lessons have been learned which will hopefully yield new, more streamlined procedures. Equally important, intra-agency and interagency cooperation shows signs of improving as aid budgets shrink and more efficiency is demanded by Congress. The AID's 1996 international conference, "Sustainable Legal Reform in the NIS" was dedicated, among other things, to greatly increasing collaboration and integration of American, Canadian, European, and international agency donor programs for rule-of-law assistance to the newly independent states. In the process of engaging the newly independent states on legal transformation, the West has gained insights into the complexity of the undertaking as well as humility, recognizing, as one conference participant summarized, that "the countries of the NIS will write their own legal histories."[44]

To return to the thesis of this chapter, the West has had a positive impact in the legal modernization of the newly independent states, but the potential for exogenous change is limited. The West is not going to make *the* difference, but it can make *some* difference in the newly independent states. As the author expressed it in his closing keynote address to the AID conference: "We can only assist our friends in the NIS; ultimately the task of building modern legal systems is theirs."[45]

Notes

1. The author spent two years, 1994–96, on the rule-of-law "front" in Washington, DC, and in the newly independent states of the former Soviet Union. As senior coordinator at the Rule-of-Law Consortium under the auspices of the U.S. Agency for International Development, his work involved legal and political reform in Russia, Ukraine, Armenia, and Georgia in particular. This chapter draws upon that experience, and, as such, is part memoir and part social science. However, since relationships established with post-Soviet institutions and their leading personnel are ongoing, some sections of the following discussion are of necessity circumspect. The views expressed in this chapter are solely the author's.

2. See James A. Gardener, *Legal Imperialism: American Lawyers and Foreign Aid in Latin America* (Madison: University of Wisconsin Press, 1980), chap. 13.

3. Ambassador Thomas Pickering, "Russia and America at Mid-Transition," *SAIS Review* 15, no. 1 (1995): p. 82.

4. See Peter Dombrowski's "German and American Assistance to the Post-Soviet Transition," in this volume.

5. Private communication with a member of the U.S. delegation at the Vancouver Summit.

6. Stephen Holmes, "Cultural Legacies or State Collapse? Probing the Postcommunist Dilemma," in *Post-Communism,* ed. Michael Mandelbaum (New York: Council on Foreign Relations, 1996), p. 56.

7. See John Lowenhardt, *The Reincarnation of Russia* (Durham, NC: Duke University Press, 1995), p. 32.

8. The source of the statement was Oleg Rumiantsev, then executive secretary of the Russian parliament's Constitutional Commission. The location was a working meeting in Washington, DC, attended by the author during the week of 25 January 1993.

9. "CEELI's Work in the NIS: An Overview" (Washington, DC: typescript, n.d.). In this summary of the first year and a half of work in the NIS, CEELI reported that it had established offices in six countries, sent more than three dozen Western legal specialists to work on particular projects at local request, and "performed assessments of over forty draft laws in the region."

10. Chief Justice Yakovlev made his observation at a meeting held at the Rule-of-Law Consortium, Washington, DC, during October 1994.

11. In the area of law, the literature on resocialization largely concerns the problems of resocializing prisoners so they will not become recidivists.

12. "More than 30 Federal agencies run more than 130 programs in the former Soviet Union." Steven Erlanger, "For U.S. Russia-Watchers, Bipartisan Fear Over Future," *New York Times,* 17 June 1996, p. A9.

13. "Sustainable Legal Reform in the NIS," Washington, DC, 30–31 July 1996.

14. A major source of changing signals was the off-year congressional elections of November 1994. The Republican majority in both houses signaled a shift away from the Russia-first orientation in foreign aid to the newly independent states, and increased attention to Ukraine, Armenia, and Georgia.

15. Robert Sharlet, Senior Coordinator, Rule-of-Law Consortium, Washington, DC, fax-memo to a Washington State–based NGO specializing in legal architecture, 26 October 1994.

16. See Leslie H. Gelb and Richard K. Betts, *The Irony of Vietnam: The System Worked* (Washington, DC: Brookings Institution, 1979), chap. 10.

17. See James Willard Hurst, *Law and the Conditions of Freedom in the Nineteenth-Century United States* (Madison: University of Wisconsin Press, 1964); Robert Sharlet, "Law in the Political Development of a Communist System: Conceptualizing from the Soviet Experience," in *The Behavioral Revolution and Communist Studies,* ed. Roger E. Kanet (New York: Free Press, 1971), chap. 10.

18. Western ideas did influence the theoretical legal work of the small group of Russian liberal legal philosophers in the latter half of the nineteenth century. See Andrzej Walicki, *Legal Philosophies of Russian Liberalism* (South Bend, IN: University of Notre Dame Press, 1992). The Western institution of jury trial was also imported into Imperial Russia during that period. Currently, the use of jury has been revived in post-Soviet Russia, but only on an experimental basis in approximately 10 percent of subjects of the federation. The reintroduction has been assisted by Western aid donors. For a thorough study of jury trials in Russia, past and present, see Stephen C. Thaman, "The Resurrection of Trial by Jury in Russia," *Stanford Journal of International Law* 31, no. 1 (1995): pp. 61–274.

19. See Harold J. Berman, "The Rule-of-Law and the Law-Based State with Special Reference to the Soviet Union," in *Toward the "Rule-of-Law" in Russia?* ed. Donald D. Barry (Armonk, NY: M.E. Sharpe, 1992), pp. 43–60.

20. Herbert Jacob, "Urban Trial Courts—A Different Vision," *Law and Courts* 6, no. 1 (1996): p. 5.

21. Peter H. Solomon Jr., "The Limits of Legal Order in Post-Soviet Russia," *Post-Soviet Affairs* 11, no. 2 (1995): p. 89.

22. Berman, "The Rule-of-Law and the Law-Based State with Special Reference to the Soviet Union," p. 47.

23. Robert Sharlet, "The Fate of Individual Rights in the Age of Perestroika," in Barry, *Toward the "Rule-of-Law" in Russia?,* p. 199.

24. For a study of Ukrainian constitutional drafting up to the current 1996 constitution, see Robert Sharlet, "Post-Soviet Constitutionalism: Politics and Constitution-Making in Russia and Ukraine," in *Russia and Eastern Europe After Communism,* ed. Michael Kraus and Ronald D. Liebowitz (Boulder, CO: Westview, 1996), chap. 1.

25. See Robert Sharlet, "The Politics of Law Reform in Russia, Ukraine and the newly independent states," *Rule-of-Law Consortium Newsletter,* no. 1 (1995): pp. 2–5.

26. From November 1994 to March 1995, the chief justice of the Supreme Court, the chief justice-designate of the Constitutional Court, and the chairman of a new bar association for business lawyers died. The latter two were particularly important in the political negotiations over constitution drafting.

27. The problem of organized crime in Russia and the newly independent states became a salient topic in Washington foreign aid circles with the publication of Seymour Hersh, "The Wild East," *Atlantic Monthly,* 273, no. 6 (June 1994), pp. 61–86. The most prolific and insightful scholar of crime in the East is Professor Louise Shelley. See, for example, her "Post-Soviet Organized Crime," the lead article of a special section on

"Organized Crime" in *Demokratizatsiia* 2, no. 3 (1994): pp. 341–58. For an interesting journalistic study, see also Stephen Handelman, *Comrade Criminal* (New Haven, CT: Yale University Press, 1995).

28. Gary J. Jakacky, "A Capitalist Camp in Siberia," *New York Times,* 10 March 1996, business sect., p. 14.

29. See N.I. Matuzov, "Pravovoi nigilizm I pravovi idealizm kak dve storony 'odnoi medali'," *Pravovedenie,* no. 2 (1994): pp. 3–16.

30. Boris Yeltsin, *The Struggle for Russia,* trans. Catherine A. Fitzpatrick (New York: Random House, 1995), pp. 139–40.

31. On the constitutional issues, see Robert Sharlet, "Russian Constitutional Crisis," *Post-Soviet Affairs* 9, no. 4 (1993): pp. 314–36. For a thorough study of the GPU, see Eugene Huskey, "The State-Legal Administration and the Politics of Redundancy," *Post-Soviet Affairs* 11, no. 2 (1995): pp. 115–43.

32. See Constitution of the Russian Federation, Article 83–f, and for the politics of nomination and confirmation, Herbert Hausmaninger, "Towards a 'New' Russian Constitutional Court," *Cornell International Law Journal* 28, no. 1 (1995): pp. 129–32.

33. The struggle between the GPU and the Ministry of Justice for influence over legal drafting has waxed and waned. Most recently the GPU has been downsized, while the Ministry of Justice has gained new jurisdiction.

34. See Constitution of the Russian Federation, Article 104.

35. On the Law on the Procuracy, see *Rossiiskaia gazeta,* 25 November 1995, pp. 3–5. On the new law on the FSS, see Amy Knight, *Spies Without Cloaks: The KGB's Successor* (Princeton, NJ: Princeton University Press, 1996), pp. 219–22.

36. See Knight, *Spies Without Cloaks,* pp. 168–69.

37. See Robert Sharlet, "Reinventing the Russian State: Problems of Constitutional Implementation," *John Marshall Law Review* 28, no. 4 (1995): pp. 779–81.

38. Vladimir Tismaneanu and Michael Turner, "Understanding Post-Sovietism: Between Residual Leninism and Uncertain Pluralism," in *Political Culture and Civil Society in Russia and the New States of Eurasia,* ed. Vladimir Tismaneanu (Armonk, NY: M.E. Sharpe, 1995), p. 22; Frederic J. Fleron Jr., "Post-Soviet Political Culture in Russia: An Assessment of Recent Empirical Investigations," *Europe-Asia Studies,* 48, no. 2 (1996): p. 251.

39. See Robert A. Dahl, "The Newer Democracies," in *After Authoritarianism,* ed. Daniel N. Nelson (Westport, CT: Praeger, 1995), p. 11.

40. For studies of constitutional developments in the East by American and European advisors, see *Constitution Making in Eastern Europe,* ed. A.E. Dick Howard (Baltimore: Johns Hopkins University Press, 1993). For a German perspective on the legal transition process in the newly independent states, see Rolf Knieper and Mark Boguslavskij, *Concept for Legal Counselling in Transformation States* (Eschborn, Germany: Deutsche Gesellschaft fur Technische Zusammenarbeit, 1995).

41. This section has focused primarily on the delivery of U.S. legal assistance to the newly independent states via large American organizations. Given the tasks of the initial phase of law reform—the top-down restructuring of the apex institutions of the central legal infrastructure—such large-scale donor vehicles with their extensive experience and depth of personnel have been indispensable to the U.S. effort. As foreign donor attention shifts to mid-level institutions and grassroots associations, the role of the smaller, more specialized U.S. NGO's in the West–East transfer of ideas is likely to increase. See Nancy Lubin, "U.S. Assistance to the Newly Independent States: When Good Things Come in Smaller Packages," in this volume. Top down and bottom up development are complementary, but for the United States to have reversed its initial priorities in assisting the newly independent states would have been a mistake. Just as legal modernization is

essential for enduring economic reform, an even more compelling case can be made that civil society development absent antecedent infrastructural legal reform in the newly independent states, would most likely be short-lived.

42. See Robert Sharlet, "Soviet Legal Reform in Historical Context," *Columbia Journal of Transnational Law* 28, no. 1 (1990): pp. 5–17; and Robert Sharlet, *Soviet Constitutional Crisis* (Armonk NY: M.E. Sharpe, 1992), chap. 3.

43. For a thorough analysis and rebuttal of the cultural legacy arguments against the possibility of post-Soviet democratization in the newly independent states, see Holmes, "Cultural Legacies or State Collapse?," pp. 22–76.

44. Statement by Jan van Olden, Centre for International Legal Cooperation, Leiden, The Netherlands, at the U.S. Agency for International Development conference "Sustainable Legal Reform in the NIS," Washington, DC, 30 July 1996. This thesis is reinforced in an excellent study by an Italian jurist who has participated in Western legal assistance programs in the East. See Gianmaria Ajani, "By Chance and Prestige: Legal Transplants in Russia and Eastern Europe," *American Journal of Comparative Law* 43, no. 1 (1995): pp. 93–117.

45. Robert Sharlet, "Variables of Legal Transformation in the NIS," paper presented at the U.S. Agency for International Development conference "Sustainable Legal Reform in the NIS," Washington, DC, 31 July 1996.

15

U.S. Assistance to the Newly Independent States

When Good Things Come in Smaller Packages

Nancy Lubin

At a time of great cost cutting and of reassessing U.S. assistance to the newly independent states, debates have begun to focus not only on structural or topical questions—such as whether the United States Agency for International Development (USAID) should be absorbed into the State Department; what levels of funding should be targeted for newly independent states assistance overall; how much should go to each new state of the former USSR; which sectors and programs should be emphasized; and the like—but on questions of how that assistance can be delivered most effectively.

The purpose of this chapter is to add to that debate, by focusing on the role of small projects and partnerships (typically under one million dollars, and often a fraction of that amount), in assessing what works, and how assistance monies can be spent more effectively.[1] In particular, it is intended to address a serious disconnect in the way U.S. assistance is delivered to the newly independent states. On the one hand, most observers have come to agree that smaller projects and partnerships are often among the most effective—and cost-effective—mechanisms for assistance delivery, and that the particular elements that tend to characterize them are important for any project to be effective (see section on "Key Elements" below). On the other hand, these are precisely the kinds of projects that often face the greatest obstacles in competing for funding, as government assistance continues to be channeled primarily through large consortia and contractors where these elements are often absent. Indeed, in the spring of 1995, for example—as many successful small projects were being terminated or cut back for lack of funds—several hundred million dollars in new contracts awarded to large U.S. firms brought the total of contracts and

Table 15.1

Obligations and New Contracts of Four USAID Contractors

Contractor	Obligated (as of 12/31/94)	New contracts[a] (as of 4/95)	Total (obligations and new contracts)
KPMG/Peat Marwick	$107,706,283	$27,016,447 $43,719,244	$178,441,974
Arthur Anderson	$38,048,180	$37,743,975 $30,442,164	$106,234,319
Booz-Allen and Hamilton	$35,859,400	$29,737,125 $38,363,625	$103,960,150
Chemonics	$25,812,500	$17,428,477 $44,453,813	$87,694,790
Total	$207,426,363	$268,904,870	$476,331,233

Source: U.S. Agency for International Development, *Obligation and Expenditure Report as of December 31, 1994 for USAID Programs in the NIS of the FSU* (Washington, DC: USAID, 9 February 1995).

[a]These represent only contracts awarded for Privatization and Economic Restructuring in Central and Eastern Europe and the newly independent states in March and April 1995. The breakdown of funds targeted for the newly independent states versus Central-Eastern Europe is not specified.

obligations for only four corporations to roughly half a billion dollars—not including other contracts they may have received to work exclusively in Central and Eastern Europe.[2] (see Table 15.1).

After brief background regarding the U.S. priorities, goals, and problems in assessing the impacts of U.S. assistance, this chapter examines the role of small projects and partnerships and the kinds of lessons our experience in this area may offer for assistance delivery to the newly independent states in the near future.

U.S. Assistance: The Record, Goals, and Priorities

The past few years have witnessed often heated debates over the record of U.S. assistance to the newly independent states to date, and how this assistance can be delivered most effectively. Some observers, such as Bartlomiej Kaminski, Zhen Kun Wang, and Gertrude Schroeder in this volume, argue that overall assistance to the newly independent states has been an unambiguous success. They and others believe that Western assistance has brought "spectacular progress" in a massive transfer of human capital to these new states that has been "indispensable" to their progress in economic reform.

Other observers, by contrast, such as Peter Dombrowski and Murray Feshbach in this volume, believe that the overall record of Western aid has been dismal. These and other observers believe that "donors have little to show for their efforts" and that the funding has either been misspent or gone into the hands of the mafia.[3] Many who share this view believe that overall Western assistance has been inefficient and ineffective, often inhibiting, if not foiling, America's very foreign policy, security, and commercial objectives.

Part of the problem in assessing U.S. assistance to date and determining where we go from here is the fact that there is so little consensus not only on the impacts of U.S. assistance, but on what priorities and goals U.S. aid to the newly independent states is intended to achieve in the first place. U.S. assistance is designed to meet several objectives simultaneously—such as to create a thriving market economy, instill democratic practices and ideals, support human rights, decrease the security threat, provide humanitarian aid, encourage public support for reform, and meet a host of other objectives—that often conflict or are inherently at odds with each other. This helps explain why overall U.S. strategy is often unclear, why assessments of impacts are so controversial, and why what we do with one hand is so often contradicted or negated by the other.

For example, policy makers and the public differ widely on the extent to which U.S. assistance is intended to "help" Russia and the new states, and therefore may be an appropriate lever in U.S.–NIS relations, and the extent to which it is intended to support specific U.S. interests there. Thus, while some argued, for example, that during 1995 and 1996 U.S. foreign policy, national security, and humanitarian interests should have dictated withholding assistance to Russia until they pulled out of Chechnya, others argued that other U.S. interests made it all the more imperative for the assistance program to be continued at full force.

The lack of consensus on goals and priorities also leads to differences of opinion about the impact of U.S. assistance to date and the extent to which U.S. programs may work at cross-purposes. While some assistance providers and advisors have pushed for rapid and widespread privatization at almost any cost, others criticize these programs for buttressing the very corruption, "crony capitalism," and organized crime that ultimately undermine the growth of the very stability and healthy markets that we seek. While some programs emphasize the promotion of rule of law and citizens' rights as the heart of democratic reform in these countries, others have turned a blind eye to the further consolidation of authoritarian governments and consistent human rights abuses in several of the new states in order to pursue other U.S. foreign policy or commercial interests.

And debates abound whether U.S. programs are in fact structured to help create more responsible, accountable, and effective law enforcement in the newly independent states—or whether they inadvertently are only providing the tools for an already corrupt and repressive law enforcement apparatus to become even more corrupt and repressive. Indeed, while the Clinton administration and Congress continually underscore the need for U.S. assistance to the newly independent states, many question the wisdom of providing economic assistance in the first place. Charles Krauthammer strongly questioned in the *Washington Post* whether it was really in the U.S. interest to spend taxpayer money trying to strengthen the economy of an increasingly authoritarian regime in Russia, and public opinion polls in the U.S. reflect a good deal of ambivalence towards aid to Russia among the U.S. population as a whole.[4]

Measuring Success

These problems of conflicting goals and objectives are only magnified when attempting to measure the success of any particular program or project. Attempts to quantify impacts of U.S. assistance efforts through various indicators have also highlighted the difficulties of measuring effectiveness of what is in essence a long-term process and a moving target.[5] Indeed, remarks by current and former USAID and World Bank personnel document how successful numeric indicators in project evaluation can often mask sometimes extremely poor project performance.[6]

The result in the newly independent states often has been evaluations of success and failure based on indicators that are quantifiable, but often give little sense of project content and impact. For example, measures of success have emphasized numbers of laws drafted or changed; but rarely have they addressed the extent to which these laws in fact may be implemented or applied. Other evaluations have measured the number of individuals attending a training session; but often not measured is the content of the training session itself, its relevancy for the participants, and the follow-up to ensure that lessons learned are utilized effectively or even that those trained are still employed in their field of training. And indeed, the notion of "training" itself varies dramatically from project to project: in some, it signifies weeks of intensive study and practical work on the ground; in others, it may mean attendance at a lunch.

Problems haunt other efforts to establish measurements of success. A case has been made to measure projects based on what specific goals it set for itself; but most good projects revise their goals along the way, as more information is learned and as they themselves reevaluate what works and does not. Evaluators themselves often do not have the language or country-specific knowledge to effectively interview NIS participants and aid recipients, and are often accompanied in interviews by officials of USAID and/or the project being evaluated. Moreover, projects are rarely measured in relation to each other (in other words, given the cost-effectiveness of project A, could project B have been conducted more effectively at less cost?). And even less frequently are they evaluated on the basis of their impacts on Americans: have they helped U.S. small businesses and organizations to grow and thrive? Have they led to greater business and other opportunities for U.S. citizens? Have they deepened our understanding of how these societies function, or have we simply imposed our own views?

Role of Small Projects and Partnerships

Against this background, the question of how assistance programs are shaped becomes particularly important. U.S. Freedom Support Act funds are administered through a variety of mechanisms—such as large "omnibus" contracts and "consortia," volunteer assistance programs, small grants directly to indigenous organizations, and grants to small partnerships where U.S. and NIS groups and individuals work together in designing and implementing a given project.

As mentioned above, the vast majority of U.S. government assistance funding to the newly independent states is provided through large omnibus consortia and contracts. Yet at a time when many have highlighted a number of persistent problems—such as the slow pace with which many of our programs are implemented, the degree to which program priorities may or may not be misplaced, the lack of coordination among programs, the effectiveness of oversight mechanisms, possible corruption and the like—many small-scale projects (as illustrated in the sectoral descriptions below) seem to have comprised among our most important success stories. They have been activated quickly, and their impact has been strong in a wide range of sectors. Their relatively small size often has allowed for greater focus, more comprehensive management and cost effectiveness, better oversight, more transparency, and more flexibility in all sectors and working at all levels of the government and private sector. When effectively coordinated and administered, they have had a synergistic effect that can lead to major impact in any given sector.

Among small projects, moreover, U.S./NIS *partnerships* (as opposed to direct grants to indigenous organizations) are often particularly effective. While direct grants to indigenous organizations are appropriate in many cases, in others they have proven to be premature. Many indigenous groups are not equipped to manage what would be considered small grants in the U.S.; and because of the focus on getting funding out the door, oversight and monitoring of how funds are spent by U.S. grant-giving bodies is still limited.

Partnerships also provide important U.S. technical expertise. When done properly, they create a synergistic effect in devising new approaches to problems of economic and democratic reform that neither side could do alone. They benefit the American groups that become engaged as much as the local partners, and open commercial, employment, and other economic opportunities to small U.S. businesses and nongovernmental organization (NGOs). And through their cooperative nature, they allow for a great deal more oversight and accountability regarding the way in which U.S. taxpayer money is spent.

In other words, small projects and partnerships play a particularly useful role both in filling the gaps in areas that large consortia have not addressed, and often in doing similar things only more effectively—and more cost-effectively.

Small Partnerships versus NGOs

When referring to small partnerships, two points of clarification are in order. First, most references to small projects and partnerships equate them with the role of nonprofit groups generally. But *successful small projects are not limited to NGOs or nonprofits.* Instead, the most successful projects depend more on the presence of specific elements used in project design and implementation than on the type of organization itself (in other words, whether it is tax exempt and nonprofit versus for-profit, or private versus public sector). Many for-profit companies have joined the ranks of the excellent small programs that have had major impacts in the newly independent states, while many programs conducted by U.S. private voluntary organizations (PVOs) and NGOs have been just as wasteful or counterproductive as some of the large for-profit corporations and consortia.

To date, support of small projects and partnerships has focused primarily on nonprofit organizations working with local NGOs. This focus makes it difficult to fund partnerships where, for example, a U.S. nonprofit would work in partnership with an NIS government organ, school, trade organization, or the like; and it makes it even more difficult for a small U.S. company to receive a small amount of funds to work in partnership with any of these organizations—even if their efforts would ultimately be more effective than those of their large corporate counterparts.

Second, many observers commonly associate small projects with work at the grassroots level and primarily regarding humanitarian activities. But *U.S. NGO and for-profit small projects have been key players working at all levels of government and with the newly emerging private sector in the newly independent states.* Small projects and partnerships do not only build bonds among people by conducting grassroots activities in the social and humanitarian sectors. They also directly assist presidents, ministers, and other high federal government officials in developing tax, investment, and other policies, and work with parliaments in a number of the newly independent states to develop draft legislation in areas such as privatization, mining, the role of the emerging private and nonprofit sectors, energy efficiency, public services laws, and the like.

They advise and assist local and regional governments through programs on public administration; training in taxation, budgets, and other aspects of a free market economy; environmental issues; private management of land; and a range of other programs. Likewise, small projects by for-profits and NGOs have been working in the conversion and privatization of large military and industrial enterprises, and are assisting new enterprises or entrepreneurs—through the establishment of business centers, small business lending programs, training programs, exchanges, on-site consultant services, and resident advisors—to become a solid, private business sector in a country where business has long been anathema.

And in other sectors—such as the media, nuclear proliferation and export controls, environmental policy, and energy—small projects have stimulated change at low cost to the U.S. taxpayer. The development of an infrastructure for extensive independent media throughout the newly independent states, the establishment of environmental seed grants and computer networks, export control training programs, and projects promoting energy efficiency are only a few additional examples of other sectors where the impact of small projects has been strong.

This is not to suggest that there is not room for both large and small projects. It is to say that where they overlap, smaller, more manageable entities on the ground have carried out major projects as effectively—if not more effectively— than many large-scale programs. In instances when small projects have carried out nearly identical projects as large contractors, they have done so more quickly, effectively, and at far less cost—and in every sector.

Business Development and Economic Reform

Small partnerships, for example, have contributed directly and significantly to market reforms in Russia and elsewhere in the newly independent states. With a total of roughly $250,000 of U.S. taxpayer funds, the International Tax and Investment Center (ITIC), for example, has worked closely with the governments and parliaments of Russia and Kazakhstan to create new tax and investment policies and regulations. ITIC was appointed by Vice President Asanbaev of Kazakhstan to chair a tax reform working group to advise the Ministry of Finance in developing a policy document that now serves as the foundation of tax reform in Kazakhstan. It also served as secretariat in a multinational tax reform coalition in order to draft a new tax law for Kazakhstan in July 1994, and works closely with both the public and with government ministries and parliaments to help reform one of the most problematic areas of the NIS economies.

ITIC's costs contrast markedly with those of KPMG/Peat Marwick, also working in an advisory capacity to the government of Kazakhstan, and to other contractors working in privatization and business development—where rates for overhead, fringe benefits, and general and administrative costs (G&A) alone far exceed the entire government grant paid to ITIC, and where NIS governments have suggested that their activities are not always as useful.

Likewise with loan programs and economic training. A number of small business loan programs—such as those created by Opportunity International, the CARE Small Business Assistance Corporation (CARESBAC), the Eurasia Foundation, the Center for Citizen Initiatives (CCI), and others—have been quick to start up low-cost loan programs that are now supporting a wide array of enterprises and entrepreneurs. Payback rates have been high, and these loans are helping a new entrepreneurial class to take shape. They, too, contrast markedly with some of the large enterprise funds, whose start-up was often problematic.[7]

Economics education and training is also an area where small projects have contributed a great deal. The establishment of numerous economics institutes throughout the newly independent states in conjunction with U.S. NGOs, small businesses, and universities, and the establishment of an economics "consortium" to develop large-scale training by several U.S. foundations are all filling a great need not addressed by larger consortia and contractors.

While the large and small projects are not always directly comparable, the vast difference in pace and costs suggests that the smaller partnerships are an important complement. As the smaller partnerships are currently in danger of being cut back or phased out, it suggests strongly that some of the funding directed to the larger programs could usefully be retargeted to ensure that smaller programs similar to the above are also maintained and expanded.

Rule of Law

Likewise in the areas of rule of law, where one of the most important challenges is to educate the populace to understand the importance of the rule of law and how to use the law to claim and protect their rights as citizens, this requires not only structural reform from the top down, but creating a constituency from below that can use laws that exist. Many have argued that much of our assistance in this area is based on broad, multiproject mandates, and so it lacks responsiveness, relevance, and impact. Smaller, well-targeted, low-budget, and flexible projects have worked with governments and parliamentarians to draft new laws in a range of areas, and with citizens to develop an understanding of their rights and to translate that understanding into political and legal action.

Under a small grant from USAID through ISAR,[8] for example, the joint environmental law project between the Russian NGO Ecojuris/WLED and the U.S.-based Pacific Environment and Resources Center has avoided the abstractions of seminars and conferences and worked with citizens to apply laws already on the books in real-life situations. This project has assisted groups and citizens in bringing suits all the way to the Russian Supreme Court; created the first pro bono environmental law firm in Moscow that provides legal consultation to government officials, ministries, and individuals; published a volume of environmental legislation; and has sponsored a range of meetings and workshops. In a country that long has had an extensive body of laws that have never been enforced, this is but one example of how Western assistance has helped individuals and groups learn how to use already existing laws as well as to develop new ones.

Groups such as the Natural Resources Defense Council (NRDC) and Center for Constitutionalism have been conducting similar work. The center has been praised for the legal conferences it has organized on constitutional law and human rights in regions outside of Moscow, and for its roundtables on electoral law issues. These seminars are conducted entirely in the Russian language, and organizers have had to double their limits for enrollment because of widespread demand to participate. The center also publishes a legal journal distributed to over 3,000 specialists in Russia as well as enjoying more than 3,400 subscriptions in the U.S. and Western Europe.

And programs in other sectors have also worked to develop new legislation and hold leaders accountable for implementation of new laws. With a $450,000 grant from USAID through World Learning, for example, the World Institute on Disability and a Russian partner, the All-Russian Society for the Disabled

(ARSD), submitted to President Boris Yeltsin in spring 1993 revisions and suggestions on draft legislation that would provide greater rights and protections for the disabled. Several weeks after the revisions were sent, the chairman of ARSD was invited to serve as a member of the convention that met to consider a new Russian constitution, and they continued to provide enormous input into "The Law on Social Protection of Disabled Persons in the Russian Federation."

Likewise, a $150,000 grant from World Learning to Interlegal and America's Development Foundation likewise supported efforts to assist in the development of a new "Law on Public Associations" signed by President Yeltsin in May 1995. Perhaps more important than the laws themselves, the partnership and U.S. assistance ultimately have worked to bring more individuals into the political process to coalesce around public policy issues and press for change—the essence of the development of any credible rule of law. All of these partnerships share common features in that they were able to start up fast, were able to target limited resources, and were given the breadth to shape and conduct their projects according to their own expertise and skills.

By contrast, the more than $22 million[9] USAID contract awarded to ARD/Checchi in September, 1993, and the $7.8 million contract (over three years) awarded to Chemonics to establish "stable legal and political environments"[10] in the newly independent states have been plagued by long lead times and false starts. ARD/Checchi, for example, did not hire local staff, nor did they submit to USAID an action plan (without which a contractor is prohibited from conducting activities), until a full six months into the project; it took months to open an office; and the consortium has been slow in meeting its own target dates.[11] In the past year, according to project personnel, this consortia has focused largely on training, but with little or no follow-up regarding how that training is then applied. While there have been some successes in these programs, the costs are disproportionate to impacts when measured against the practical impacts of smaller projects.[12]

Support for the Emerging NGO Sector

The same goes for the development of the social sector, especially in terms of the development of nongovernmental organizations in the newly independent states. For one of the first times in recent history, small projects and partnerships have helped to dispel among Russian and NIS citizens the long-standing notions of entitlement to social and other protections. They have helped to provide Russians who traditionally have viewed themselves as passive objects of public policy a sense of empowerment that they, too, should have a say in shaping those policies.

In 1994, for example, the Charities Aid Foundation received a grant of $95,000 to help develop the NGO sector throughout Russia. Within six months of receiving funding, the project had organized a network of seminars in six provincial regions on logistical issues involved with working as an NGO, and a

140-page manual had been produced and distributed during the seminars where turnout was high. The free legal consultations provided by CAF three days a week for NGOs were booked up several months in advance, and the roundtables they started for NGO accountants had inspired participants to create their own associations. Internships for provincial lawyers interested in the voluntary sector were also provided. CAF's staff members were all deeply involved in the local community: their chief lawyer teaches at Moscow State University once each week; and the American staff had already spent years living in Russia and working with the NGO community and were fluent in Russian.

Another contract, by contrast, was awarded simultaneously to Save the Children for $30 million also to spark the development of a "third sector." This contract—partly because of its size and broad mandate, partly because the Western staff did not have prior experience in Russia or fluency in the Russian language, partly for logistical reasons and micromanagement from USAID—spent a good deal of time finding office space, attempting to learn what NGOs exist in Russia, and creating the bureaucracy needed to run such a large program. Selection of the two regional coordinators was not completed until March 1995—six months after the project began—and the first round of grants was awarded close to one year after the start of the program.[13] Over the past year, this Save the Children consortium has begun to fund smaller projects and it reports that its more elaborate institutional structure has begun to bear fruit. But it also reports that it must now begin to dismantle the consortium structures it put in place, as USAID funding for fiscal year 1996 has been cut to $5 million dollars and additional funding is not assured beyond this year.

Health

As Murray Feshbach details in chapter 16 of this volume, U.S. assistance in the areas of health and environment has been disappointing. Feshbach mentions that key health areas—such as venereal disease, AIDS, and other infectious diseases—have received little, if any assistance; and where U.S. assistance has been provided, much of the funding has been mistargeted or wasted.

Here again, the record of small partnerships marks a dramatic contrast both in filling the gaps not covered by large consortia, and by conducting the same kinds of activities effectively and at less cost. Small projects have worked successfully in providing training, technical assistance, equipment, and resources to health organizations and professionals throughout the newly independent states in order to address some of these problems head on, and to develop a health system that meets the needs of the broader public.

With only a tiny amount of Freedom Support Act funding, for example, AIDS Infoshare Russia has been working since 1993 to provide information and create greater public awareness specifically about HIV/AIDS and sexually transmitted diseases in Russia. In conjunction with a local partner in Moscow, the AESOP

Center, AIDS Infoshare has established the first HIV/AIDS information network in Russia. The project provides an E-mail network, database, library, and bulletin devoted to HIV/AIDS issues in the former Soviet Union. They have also conducted seminars on management and development for NGOs working in the field of HIV/AIDS and have begun a project focusing on prevention among women. This project works with ten Russian organizations throughout the country providing assistance and support in implementing their own regional projects.

Likewise, Planned Parenthood of Northern New England (PPNNE), in conjunction with Management Sciences for Health and the Centre for the Formation of Sexual Culture (CFSC) in Yaroslavl, Russia, initiated the Heart to Heart Project to develop sustainable programs to educate high school students in anatomy, physiology, reproductive health, and family life in addition to offering counseling, family planning services, and classes in local schools and universities. These activities have been effective in providing information and guidance to adolescents dealing with issues related to sexuality and in initiating public dialogue on previously prohibited subjects. Members of CFSC have initiated and organized a televised "Roundtable" discussion of AIDS and discrimination among sexual minorities and representatives of city services, health providers, and other education and civil rights organizations.

Small grants from the AIHA program have likewise helped to develop this sector. As but one example, Magee Womancare International, in conjunction with the Savior's Hospital in Moscow, established the Woman and Family Center that has provided training to six childbirth educators and over 5,000 Russians since 1993; on average, the center services about 400 Russian women per week. Their Rural Outreach Program is establishing twenty-four new women's education centers, based on the model center, in different cities throughout Russia.

The partnership also established the Magee-Savior's Family Planning Clinic in June 1994 to serve as a model clinic to be replicated in eighteen cities, and opened a new birth house, based on Western standards for improved obstetric care, in September 1995. Through their centers, they also provide training to Russian health care professionals in administration, management, and technical skills, and sponsored exchange trips and conferences. As of April 1995, they had trained over one hundred Russian professionals in basic infection-control techniques and over one hundred professionals in family-centered childbirth models. Magee estimates that over fifteen thousand women and girls have benefited from health education and clinical services provided by the centers. Just as impressive, however, is the fact that these efforts have also been able to attract additional financial support from the Russian government—something quite unusual for assistance programs of this sort.

These programs are but examples of the many such partnerships that have demonstrated significant impact often with minimal funding. Almost all of these programs, however, face significant funding challenges; and as funding for partnerships is cut back, many fear that they will be terminated entirely.

Environmental Programs

Feshbach notes that environmental programs have fared no better in addressing environmental tragedies and ensuring that new environmental policies are implemented. Again, however, small projects seem to have made some of the greatest inroads in measuring and publicizing these issues, training specialists to address them directly, and putting pressure on NIS governments to encourage the implementation of sound environmental policies.

The Institute for Sustainable Communities (ISC) has worked extensively in conjunction with local NGOs and government agencies to provide training in environmental management and other areas, in community planning, and to serve as a repository and disseminator of data and information from local projects. Their programs in Ekaterinburg, Nizhnii Taigal, and other areas of the newly independent states have helped to measure pollution levels, and to implement low-cost pollution control measures. In Nizhnii Taigal, for example, ISC and its partners conducted an audit of the municipal water system that formed the basis for the U.S. Environmental Protection Agency (EPA) and its Russian counterparts to implement low-cost corrective and preventive measures to improve water quality. They have also developed environmental curricula and textbooks for the schools; implemented public awareness projects through the media in Ukraine; and organized a grant competition for nonschool-based environmental education projects.

Likewise, the extensive computer E-mail network first begun by ISAR and the Sacred Earth Network in conjunction with the Socio-Ecological Union in Moscow in 1988 with less than $300,000 in U.S. government support, has grown to over three hundred participating individuals and organizations throughout all fifteen new states of the FSU. These individuals and groups now regularly share information and expertise, develop joint efforts and partnering opportunities between NIS and U.S. environmental organizations, and plan strategies to influence environmental policy throughout the newly independent states. Indeed, it is difficult to determine whether this effort should be called a successful environmental program, or one that represents the essence of a democracy building program.

The extensive work in energy efficiency conducted by the Natural Resources Defense Council (NRDC) with governments of the new states, and NRDC's NGO capacity-building projects are also key in transforming this sector. The NRDC has also published a citizen's guide to environmental rights in Russia in English and Russian, which has been distributed to NGOs, universities, and citizens throughout the country and covers issues such as citizens' rights and obligations under the new Russian environmental protection laws, how to obtain information, and how to effectively lobby and advertise to promote environmental goals.

With a much broader mandate, by contrast, CH$_2$M Hill was awarded roughly

$37.5 million by USAID to oversee an environmental policy development and technology project. The project suffered from long delays and sometimes misguided plans in part because of its size and because it was designed and driven almost exclusively from the U.S. side.[14] The large bureaucracy created by the project was slow in staffing the operation in Russia: although the core contract was signed in September 1993, for example, the regional director did not arrive in Moscow until a full five months later, in February 1994; although the Far East project—a major component of the consortium—was approved in April 1994, on-site managers did not arrive until September and October 1994, or again, five or six months later. Local and regional NIS government officials and individuals, moreover, have said they were alienated early on when it became clear that their role was at best peripheral. And the large size of the Far East project (which involves at least sixteen subcontractors) also helps explain why it has been particularly slow getting off the ground.[15] According to USAID and Russian officials, the Far East project had "produced almost no quantifiable results as of February 1995"[16]—almost a year after it had begun. In general, despite the high price tag, the CH_2M Hill program was described by the GAO as "disappointing," and its "expected contributions to systemic reform and long-term benefits are not likely to be significant."[17]

Other Sectors

Computer networks, export control training programs, and development of an independent media are only a few examples of other sectors where the impact of small projects and partnerships generally have also been notable. The University of Georgia Center for International Trade and Security and the Monterey Institute for International Studies have established partnerships with centers in Belarus and other former Soviet republics with nuclear weapons to provide assistance to NIS policy makers and export control officials through seminars and cooperative research.

In Kiev, the most widely watched news and commentary program on Ukrainian television concentrating on economic and political reform is produced by a group of progressive Ukrainian journalists with a small grant in USAID start-up funds. Internews represents a group that, with initial small grants from private foundations, received a $1.7 million contract from USAID in 1992, followed by several additional infusions of funds from USAID in 1993, 1994, and 1995 in part to support other small projects and partnerships. Coupled with grantees from the International Media Fund, the Freedom Forum, and others, small partnerships have helped to develop a sector that is critical to the development of any functioning democracy. Also important is the extent to which funding for these organizations developed incrementally, and generally in response to programs that were focused, targeted, and with specific budgets. This has given a coherency and focus to these programs that is lacking in some of the large consortia that receive a huge budget and then must decide how to spend it.[18]

While a few of these organizations, such as Internews and CCI, have received millions of dollars in follow-up funding, others have faced severe cutbacks because the mechanisms to fund them are being retargeted, reduced, and/or phased out. A number of media, legal, and other partnerships first applying for support have been told that there is no longer funding available to support these kinds of projects, as the umbrella organizations that have traditionally funded them are being cut back or redirected to other kinds of projects. Despite the hundreds of millions of dollars in funds still to be expended in the newly independent states, it appears that small partnership projects are finding it almost impossible to be granted a level of funding similar to that which launched the above projects so successfully.

This is not to suggest that all large contracts should be replaced by small partnerships. But given the record, the wide imbalance in the way U.S. funding is divided between them could be redressed. Indeed, several large contractors have commented that it has been difficult to quickly absorb and expend contracts of upwards of $30 million, while many of the small projects are currently going out of business for lack of funds. Despite stated commitments to the contrary, the funding of small-scale projects has been minor relative to other programs, and has been close to nonexistent from other U.S. government assistance monies such as the Nunn-Lugar funds.

U.S. Policy and Funding Priorities

Since mid-to-late 1995, USAID and other donors have in fact placed greater emphasis on funding smaller programs, private voluntary organizations, and requiring some of the elements discussed below. This is reflected in the 1996 Foreign Operations Appropriations Bill Conference Report,[19] for example, and in the fact that USAID has provided more funding for small, indigenous NGOs in the newly independent states.

While these are important first steps, however, these efforts have demonstrated two drawbacks. First, increased support for small projects and volunteer organizations has not occurred primarily because of a redirection of funds from the large omnibus contracts to smaller ones; instead, their support seems to have been provided at the expense of U.S.–NIS small partnerships, whose funding is being cut back or retargeted to support local NIS groups directly.

Second, for the most part, the smaller projects that have received funding have been limited to nonprofits working at the grassroots. Partnerships that include a non-NGO partner—such as U.S. companies seeking small amounts of funding to work with NIS NGOs, or U.S. NGOs working with NIS governments, schools, or businesses—now find few possibilities for support open to them.

With well over a billion dollars of U.S. assistance funds yet to be expended in the newly independent states, it would be unrealistic to expect a large proportion of these funds to be disbursed in very small amounts. Indeed, only a small proportion of these projects already funded by USAID have been funded through direct contracts. But two other mechanisms also exist to provide funding to small projects: (1) "umbrella" mechanisms, whereby a large amount of funding is provided to an organization for the sole purpose of disbursing funds to small projects and overseeing their performance; and (2) small grants components of larger omnibus contracts and subcontracts. Despite the effectiveness particularly of umbrella mechanisms in disbursing funding quickly to small projects and partnerships, they are being dramatically cut back if not phased out altogether, while large contracts sometimes grow larger with no full financial audits conducted to date on how the funds are spent.

In general, it is difficult for many small organizations and businesses, and especially those without previous experience as a government contractor, to tap into U.S. government funding sources. Although some small grants have been made and contracts have been signed directly, most USAID contracts are for amounts far beyond what small groups can absorb. Indeed, some small projects have reported that USAID requested they greatly inflate their project budgets so that they would qualify for USAID funding.[20]

Umbrella Organizations

In order to address this problem, USAID early on created "umbrella organizations" that are designed specifically to disburse funds to small projects and provide the oversight and accountability to ensure that those monies are well spent. Typically, the umbrellas are provided annual budgets of anywhere from a few to $20 million to disburse in smaller amounts. In order to cut down on the administrative details of contracting directly with USAID, these organizations' primary function is to serve as a pass-through agent or umbrella for USAID funds, channeling grant monies to smaller organizations that otherwise would be unable to access government funds. Umbrella organizations such as the Eurasia Foundation, ISAR, and others, are widely viewed—by USAID, some congressional committees, and others—as among the more successful components of the NIS aid program.

The best of these organizations function as both "enablers" and "enforcers"— in other words, enabling smaller projects and partnerships to break into the U.S. system for providing assistance to the newly independent states and to conduct projects on the ground with local counterparts, while enforcing the requirements and standards of USAID. Umbrella organizations have been effective in increasing management efficiency, as the administrative burden of awarding and monitoring smaller grants is no longer placed on USAID, and in strengthening the "institutional capacity" of U.S. and NIS organizations alike. By focusing exclusively on disbursing funds to smaller partnerships, they are often able to facilitate the kind of rapid start-up and joint implementation of projects that is frequently missing from the larger consortia, and ensure that the grant giving focus does not get lost in a larger agenda. And by targeting their grants in particular sectors and encouraging coordination among grantees, umbrella organizations are also able to create a cohesive and coherent strategy that itself adds up to broader systemic reform.

Despite the success of these umbrella organizations in disbursing funding quickly and effectively to small projects and partnerships, the largest of them are now slated to be severely cut back or phased out. And of those remaining, the focus is shifting to funding indigenous groups in the newly independent states at the expense of the joint U.S./NIS partnerships.

World Learning, for example, was the first recipient of an umbrella cooperative agreement from USAID in 1993 to provide grants to U.S. and NIS PVO and NGO partnership projects throughout the NIS and across a variety of sectors. During the course of two years, World Learning dispersed funds to forty-six subgrantee partnerships. They also provided information on funding and partnering opportunities to indigenous and U.S. NGOs and PVOs, and had frequent workshops and seminars for all grantees to jointly discuss problems, snags, and accomplishments from which other grantees could learn. The process lent the effort a coherency and coordination among projects that would have been lacking otherwise, and earned World Learning the nickname of "NGO Central" in Moscow. Despite the broad infrastructure they set up in the NIS, the World Learning program was slated to be phased out by December 1996, and World Learning has been unable to secure follow-on funding to continue supporting their partnership projects.

The partnership grants of ISAR (the former Institute for Soviet American Relations) may face a similar fate. ISAR provides grants to grassroots environmental NGOs throughout the former Soviet Union and funds cooperative efforts between U.S. and NIS environmental NGOs. With a total of $7.2 million in USAID funds from May 1993 through May 1995, ISAR has awarded small grants of often a few hundred dollars to approximately three hundred indigenous organizations, and partnership grants of up to $70,000 to forty-three cooperative efforts in Ukraine, Central Asia, and throughout Russia. While ISAR supports projects in a variety of environmental areas, ISAR's partnership grants are limited to grassroots NGOs, which excludes the participation of schools, small businesses, or the like. And while the indigenous grants programs will continue to receive funding, the future of USAID funding to support ISAR's partnership grants currently is uncertain.

Likewise with the Counterpart consortium. A more recent addition to the USAID umbrella organizations, as of June 1995, Counterpart had received obligations of $3 million from USAID to conduct an NGO development program in the Central Asian republics. Designed to disburse close to $1 million in grants in Central Asia over three years, Counterpart provides both seed grants directly to indigenous NGOs and partnership grants. Again, however, its mandate does not address the kinds of partnerships described above: the number of U.S.–NIS partnerships that have been funded represents but a handful; the focus is exclusively on nonprofit and nongovernmental organizations; and the funding limit for partnerships is exceedingly low—at $25,000, but a fraction of the funds that allowed the types of partnership projects described above to achieve any real impact.

As of November 1995, the Eurasia Foundation had provided approximately $26.6 million in grants to over 850 projects in the NIS, consisting of U.S.–NIS partnerships and grants directly to support indigenous nongovernmental organizations; in January 1996 it celebrated the approval of its one thousandth grant. Although initially slated for a reduction in funding of nearly half in the spring of 1995, the Eurasia Foundation is likely the only umbrella organization that will remain at almost full funding for fiscal year 1996. As more and more grant-giving authority is transferred to the field offices, however, the Eurasia Foundation is increasingly providing funding to indigenous organizations in the newly independent states and is not funding new partnerships. While this is a sound planning decision for the foundation, it has contributed to the severe reduction in funding available for U.S.–NIS partnerships.

With over twenty-seven years experience in exchange programs with the former USSR, the International Research and Exchanges Board (IREX) has been working with what are now the newly independent states longer than any of the other umbrella groups. Its grants to American specialists for long- and short-term study of the region continue to develop expertise that has shaped, and will continue to shape, U.S. policy for years to come, while its training programs throughout the former USSR have worked to enhance local capabilities. The Institutional Partnerships Project links Russian and Ukrainian educational and professional associations with twenty-two counterpart institutions in the U.S. in a range of fields. Although larger than most of the partnerships referred to above, IREX believes this model works well for smaller allocations of funding, and that in the future, the size of partnerships could be reduced significantly and remain viable so that more partnerships could be funded. Currently, however, no funds remain for large or small partnerships.

A few other small umbrella organizations, such as Mercy Corps, have demonstrated a good deal of success in establishing local grant-giving programs with funds from agencies other than USAID. But here, too, funding is uncertain, and again the focus is generally on funding local organizations rather than partnership projects between U.S. and NIS counterparts.

The follow-on contracts to these efforts, moreover, have proved to be limited in number and slow in disbursing funds to smaller organizations. Partly because of its targeted program and a mix of regional as well as functional experts on its U.S. staff, within weeks of signing its contract with USAID in May 1992, for example, and with no preexisting body of information on NGOs in Russia, World Learning had begun the first round of solicitations for its first grant competition; the first grants were awarded two months later. As discussed above, by contrast, Save the Children did not expect to award any grants until around

August 1995—a full year after the original contract was signed. Save the Children personnel suggest the delay is because these grants are not the main focus of their program, which is to "train trainers" in NGO development. If so, this suggests yet further diminished financial support available for small partnership projects in the near future.

Small Grants Components and Subcontracts

Several USAID officials have said that the reason for the cutbacks in umbrella organizations is because of set asides for small grants components in large USAID-funded consortia. These allow the contractor to select competitively and award subgrants (with USAID approval) with the prime contractor ostensibly responsible for the management, oversight, and evaluation of its subgrantees.

But because they are only one component of larger consortia, these small grants components tend to become a low priority within the overall consortium: the large consortia have been much slower getting grant funding out the door, and some, if not most, of these grant programs are currently either being terminated or are seeking to transfer the grant-giving function to another organization. The small grants program of the ARD/Checchi Rule of Law Consortium, for example, was designed to provide grants between $25,000 and $100,000 for partnership projects between U.S. and indigenous organizations. Yet it took ARD/Checchi over a year even to announce the small grants competition; one and one-half years after their contract had been signed, not a single small grant had been awarded. Fifteen grant announcements were recently made for the newly independent states. ARD/Checchi personnel say that the small grants program will now likely be terminated, if it is not transferred to another entity such as the Eurasia Foundation.

A more common mechanism for transferring USAID funds to smaller organizations is through subcontracts, primarily used by larger organizations and businesses. As part of their contracts, major contractors can provide subcontracts to their consortia members to carry out specific task orders developed by USAID. When smaller projects or NGOs have been included as potential subcontractors for larger contracts and consortia, however, they are often not utilized, despite the fact that their qualifications and background materials were included in the original proposals to USAID. When utilized, the process of incorporating them has been cumbersome, and small projects that have received subcontracts compare them negatively with umbrella grants. With multiple levels of authority and oversight, subcontractors report that they often become subject to double bureaucracies on the part of both the consortia and USAID, and believe their work often becomes twisted in the effort to meet the needs of the larger consortia. Several small subcontractors commented that when funding was provided through a large contract, they lost control over most aspects of the program; were peripheral to the main project; and lost the flexibility they enjoyed with umbrella grants to design and implement projects where their expertise best could be applied to meet goals quickly.

This is not to suggest that there is no room for all of these mechanisms—large consortia, umbrella organizations, and others—to work in parallel. Indeed, it suggests the opposite. It would still take only a small proportion of U.S. assistance monies to maintain existing umbrella organizations at current performance levels to fund primarily indigenous organizations, and to fund new umbrella organizations to support joint partnerships. To address concerns that assistance be fairly distributed regionally among the former republics, and to allow for more cross-sectoral and interdisciplinary projects, it would make sense that new umbrellas be organized on a regional basis.

Key Elements

It is not only the size of projects, but a number of other factors that contribute to success and tend to be more typical of the smaller projects and partnerships. These include specific elements used in project design and implementation, such as *prior on-the-ground experience* in the region among the U.S. staff; *joint development and design* of projects with indigenous specialists; *budgets* strictly tailored to the requirements of the project and delineated before the contract is bid and awarded; strong *oversight and accountability;* a *long-term commitment;* and the flexibility to be *continuously reshaped* as circumstances require. Also important is that projects be *highly transparent* to the local populations as well as to Americans, to provide greater confidence that budgets are well spent.

These elements have enabled projects to adjust programs so that they respond to local realities, to more confidently select the most appropriate NIS partners, and to be more cost-effective than many of the major contractors. Indeed, major USAID contractors have turned to small projects for help in carrying out projects because they often do not have the same local contacts, know-how, and capabilities. Many large USAID contractors and individual businessmen and companies have often asked small projects and NGOs to help them find partners in the newly independent states, run their small grant programs, and/or to conduct different elements of the contractors' programs and training. These elements make a difference, but often they are not required of large USAID contracts.

Prior On-the-Ground Regional Expertise

Success of any program boils down to the knowledge and expertise of those who run it—particularly of the key decision-making individuals on the ground and in leadership positions. Many of the successes of smaller groups in assessing local needs, designing projects in context, and working quickly, for example, have been attributed to the presence of key staff with prior on-the-ground expertise in the former Soviet Union, and language capabilities. This is because the mission of U.S. assistance to the newly independent states is quite different from that of development assistance in other parts of the world—precisely because the newly independent states are not developing countries. Instead, they are highly developed—only poorly, or misdeveloped. The aim of U.S. assistance in the newly independent states is not to develop these new countries, but to transform entire societies twisted by more than seventy years of Soviet rule.

This challenge, therefore, requires different types of expertise than might be required in establishing the physical infrastructure for lesser developed countries. In order to shape a program that ultimately aims to transform a society, it is important to have firsthand experience with what it is one is trying to transform. It is also important to have firsthand experience in how to navigate that society, evaluate different analyses and interests, and assess impacts.

To date, many of the large-scale U.S. assistance projects have been widely criticized—by Americans and local citizens alike—for lacking and minimizing the importance of prior on-the-ground expertise. They have been criticized for leaving project design, and often implementation, to individuals who are impressive experts in their functional areas but know little about the region itself.

U.S. consortia have fielded groups, for example, to advise governments and specialists on water management, rule of law, and the like, without having a clue as to how these functions are currently carried out—in other words, who wins, who loses, the broader political and economic context in which decisions are made, the role of corruption and other vested interests, and generally, why these functions are conducted as they are. Many NIS officials have said they have simply become disillusioned with the endless stream of U.S. consultants who ask the same basic questions as the teams before them, and consistently have no context in which to interpret the answers; worse still, they resent the consultants who come with the answers, only to seek the concurrence of NIS partners that the project is optimally designed. Finally, projects without staff with prior on-the-ground expertise have spent an inordinately long time on relatively simple logistics;[21] and some have been criticized for inadvertently supporting the very corrupt, if not "mafia" structures the assistance effort is also ostensibly trying to reform.

Some observers have suggested that the inclusion of U.S. experts deeply familiar with the informal political, economic, and social dynamics of the region may not be necessary; one can rely, they argue, on "the Russians," "the Uzbeks," or "the locals." But which Russians, which Uzbeks, and which locals? In such enormously politicized and corrupt societies racked by economic hardship, it is important that expertise be included so that projects have a clearer context in which to independently interpret what they are being told. Many projects have begun to overcompensate for too much U.S. influence by requiring too little.

Despite the need, use of regional specialists is still limited. Congressional report language from summer 1994[22] calls for greater use of U.S. regional specialists. A follow-up USAID report several months later presages the slow pace with which the situation would be changed: the report suggests that the use of regional specialists was expanded primarily to provide briefings to teams of specialists with little or no knowledge of the newly independent states who would then design and implement U.S. programs there.[23] While a range of technical expertise has long been required in project proposals, regional expertise often has not. Indeed, at least one RFP (to develop grassroots NGOs in one NIS region) unambiguously stated that "prior experience in the region is not required,"[24] and the requirement for some country expertise was allegedly one reason a major contract was contested and re-competed in the spring of 1995.

The Conference Report of the Foreign Operations Appropriations Bill for fiscal year 1996 "inserts language requiring that projects in the NIS should employ in key positions individuals with prior experience in the region and relevant language skills."[25] Implementation of this amendment should be stringent, as combining technical experts with regional specialists who already have on-the-ground expertise should reduce the danger that projects might go off course in the future.

Finally, on-the-ground knowledge of the newly independent states should be applied to NIS programs in the U.S., as well. As a case in point, some training programs in the United States for NIS citizens have been roundly applauded as on target and effective. Russian, Uzbek, and other professionals have left with a greater appreciation of the challenges ahead of them, and feel they have been armed with new capabilities and the tools to address them.

But other training programs have been widely criticized for lacking a sense of the societies from which the participants are coming and a program designed accordingly. In case after case, NIS participants have voiced frustration and surprise that project staff, however well intentioned, would have designed a program with such little knowledge of the context in which its lessons would be applied. Many have commented that the training programs were patronizing or simply irrelevant. And in at least one instance, participants commented that just about everything a trainer was describing—while relevant to the United States— is illegal in the countries where the participants live. In the words of one participant: "It would have been better for someone who knows something about my country to work with the planners to adapt the materials to meet our needs. If I tried to carry out what I have learned, I would spend the rest of my life in jail."

Training of American Specialists on the Newly Independent States

Not only are specialists on the newly independent states important in the design and implementation of assistance programs today; but as U.S. assistance programs are scaled back in the months and years ahead, serious expertise on the newly independent states will increasingly be needed to evaluate our assistance efforts and better inform future policies towards the newly independent states.

Despite this need, funds for training of U.S. experts currently are being cut back dramatically. In particular, continued funding for the Russian, Eurasian, and East European Studies Program—the so-called Title VIII, program, the only federally funded program supporting basic and applied research on critical topics of economic and political reform in the newly independent states, faces serious opposition from USAID and the assistance community. Through a program of grants to American nonprofit organizations (such as the Kennan Institute for Advanced Russian Studies, the National Council for Soviet and East European Research, IREX, and others), Title VIII has provided critical support for field and collaborative research, language training, and policy-relevant contract research that informs much of our policy today. Indeed, a number of experts trained by Title VIII have served as policy analysts and advisors to federal agencies disbursing technical assistance to the newly independent states, and could not have attained their current expertise without Title VIII support. Title VIII funds, moreover, have not only supported basic research, but have helped to design banking systems in Ukraine, world-class public opinion surveys in Russia, and mechanisms for monitoring local public finance systems in key NIS regional areas, and have provided Western macroeconomic expertise to the president of Uzbekistan.

Funded at $10 million in fiscal year 1994, the Title VIII program has been steadily reduced to $7.5 million in fiscal year 1995 and $5 million in fiscal year 1996. Its fate beyond this fiscal year remains in doubt; its demise would be a serious mistake.

Joint U.S.–NIS Development of Projects

Typical of smaller projects is the inclusion of local partners in every phase of the project—from initial conception and design to implementation and evaluation. This is a lesson that could usefully be applied to all projects, and a theme that has been echoed in almost every conference on U.S. assistance.[26] Many NIS participants, as well as American observers on the scene, have noted that local input—even when solicited—is often ignored in the design phase of projects; instead, local professionals have been brought in to implement projects already designed by Americans who often have a limited understanding of the newly independent states.

Aid is a two-way process, and must be based on mutual interest and needs; if there is not a sense of stake on the part of policy makers, specialists, and the public in the newly independent states as well as the United States, projects will go nowhere. In light of the highly educated NIS population, combining expertise often has a synergistic effect, and results in ideas that are better than either side could have envisioned alone.

Oversight and Cost-Effectiveness

The gap between the oversight of small partnerships and that applied to large projects is wide. Indeed, most audits and evaluations, including those conducted by the USAID inspector general, have focused on small projects and NGOs; no omnibus contracts have had a full financial audit to date.[27] Oversight of small partnerships tends to be enormously intrusive; according to one applicant for a small grant from USAID, procedures in presenting cost estimates were so detailed—down to the requirement that they document the quality of paper they would use for fifty cent invitations to a workshop—that they almost gave up applying for the grant altogether.

Among large contractors the opposite often seems to be the case. Instead, the pressure often seems to have been great to keep costs high. Given how overhead and profits are calculated, there has often been every incentive to maximize costs and spend as quickly as possible (what contractors themselves call the "burn rate"), rather than seek to conserve. Several employees in large consortia have said that they often purchase expensive equipment, or conduct unnecessary procedures, simply to get more money out the door fast. Many say they spend much of their time trying to expand their budgets rather than contract them.

As a rule, for example, monthly rents among large contractors tend to be roughly ten times higher than those of the smaller partnerships, even when staff size and mandates are similar. The rent of an NGO conducting business development in Voronezh is currently $400 per month; the rent of the large contractor—with roughly the same size staff and mandate—is reportedly $4,000 per month. The difference in rent between the Eurasia Foundation and the large contractors and Enterprise Funds in Kiev reportedly also differ by a factor of ten—for example, from roughly $1,200 to $12,000 per month. Examples are many: in the words of one consortium employee in the newly independent states, "What are we doing here? We are throwing around so much money, and often have no idea why."

This practice is compounded by the tendency to associate the size of a project's budget with the size of its impact. But, as demonstrated above, often the two are inversely related; some of the higher cost projects have had far fewer impacts than smaller projects that are focused and well-managed.

According to several inside observers, the lack of any financial audits on large contractors in the newly independent states is because of the massive costs and man-hours this would require. Aside from the fact that it is simply not cost-effective to focus on the small projects, if a project is too big to be evaluated, is it likely too big to be well-managed and effective?

Sustainability and Benchmarks

Common challenges facing large and small projects alike are the conflicting pressures and difficulties surrounding the establishment of benchmarks and evaluation of the sustainability of projects, and the tension between long-term and short-term planning. Among larger consortia, this may have affected project performance and evaluation: the pressure to demonstrate too many results too quickly has led to unrealistic goals, unnecessary overspending, artificial benchmarks, and to a problem of local expectations raised unrealistically high. As discussed above, projects currently are often evaluated with benchmarks that are easy to quantify—such as numbers of seminars, workshops, and "trainees," or even by levels of expenditures of funds—but that have little to do with the content or genuine impact of the project. The USAID inspector general and external evaluators have also criticized USAID projects for often raising expectations with unrealistic benchmarks that could not possibly be met.[28]

But for smaller partnerships, these problems are especially problematic in a different way, largely exacerbated by the expectation that these projects be completed and sustainable within one or two years. These projects must demonstrate coherent and often wide-ranging impacts in an extremely short amount of time. And in the same amount of time that it has taken large contractors simply to get off the ground, many small projects and partnerships are forced to phase out—often just as they are starting to reap results.

These challenges have been recognized by USAID, and the tension between addressing long-term goals versus the need to demonstrate short-term impacts has been a common theme at conferences and workshops. Except for cases where it is explicitly not relevant, smaller projects as well as large should be structured to make a long-term commitment and project expenditures should be permitted to be drawn out over a longer, and more sensible, time frame. This should apply to umbrella organizations as well as to the projects they fund: for projects to be sustainable and build for the long term, the sources of funding cannot be uncertain from year to year.

Coordination of Projects and Micromanagement

Coordination of projects is another challenge that faces large and small projects alike, and where small projects provide a useful model. Many contractors and grantees alike believe they are constrained from planning and implementing projects in a timely way because of the vast number of other requirements from USAID. A number of contractors and grantees in the field have said that they spend upwards of 60 to 80 percent of their time doing paperwork for USAID; they say they have little time left to implement projects.

While some of this has been addressed in Russia, it remains a large problem in some of the non-Russian new states where assistance has been more limited but is growing. A representative from one major contractor said that after one year, USAID still had not approved the contractor's country plans, without which they are not authorized to do anything. In the words of another, "They tie our hands and make us look like fools." At the same time, USAID officials say they have been weak in coordinating and monitoring many programs because they do not have the staff or the time.

If all other project elements are required and adhered to, umbrella organizations allow USAID to free itself from micromanagement of projects to focus more on monitoring, oversight, and strategic planning. Likewise, while many large consortia are characterized by competition, the degree of cooperation and coordination among small projects and NGOs has been striking and could serve as a model for the way future projects better could be knit together.

Communications and Participation Strategies

Much of the controversy among Americans and Russians alike over U.S. aid in the newly independent states stems from the lack of information and sense of mystery surrounding U.S. activities there. Small projects tend to be more transparent, with communications and participation strategies as an integral part of their efforts. In societies of the newly independent states where access to information has been so controlled and limited, and where suspicion of Western aid is so high, availability of information (1) enables citizens in the newly independent states to better understand the nature of the problems they face; (2) gives people a sense that their own actions matter; (3) helps to break down barriers in extremely highly compartmentalized societies; (4) injects a greater sense of accountability into all projects; and (5) ultimately dispels much of the mystery and cynicism that currently surrounds U.S. assistance activities. Information strategies should be designed for all programs and targeted at all levels and regions.

Likewise, in the United States, project quarterly and annual reports, evaluations, and budgets should be available to any interested American taxpayer or organization without the necessity of filing Freedom of Information Act (FOIA) requests. The difficulties in acquiring these documents only raise public suspicion that there is something to hide.

Clearinghouse and Feedback Mechanism

In the rush to disburse large amounts of funds quickly, groups and small projects with excellent track records in the newly independent states have found it exceedingly difficult to compete for government assistance funds in the United States. Many NGOs and other small projects and organizations that are expert in working in the newly independent states are not as expert in sorting out the Washington funding bureaucracy, and have little idea where to turn, what is required, and how to meet those requirements.

For those who do receive government funding, often despite major problems in the way programs are designed and implemented, there are few, if any, effective feedback mechanisms to raise these problems constructively and encourage change.[29] Many U.S. and NIS organizations receiving aid funds have been severely critical of some assistance efforts, but have been reluctant to express constructive criticism directly to USAID or others for fear of losing future government funding. The feedback mechanisms that currently exist are comprised largely (if not entirely) of representatives of organizations that themselves receive large contracts from USAID. And turning to the inspector general's office is regarded as more antagonistic than constructive, as it tends to imply severe, if not criminal, wrongdoing.

Conclusion

Largely because of the way they are structured, small projects and partnerships have often resulted in deep and long-lasting impact in promoting U.S. strategic, foreign policy, and commercial interests. Small scale projects and partnerships—among for-profit as well as nonprofit organizations—have worked effectively with NIS ministries, parliaments, entrepreneurs, and, in general, at all levels of the government and private sectors and in a broad range of functional areas and geographic regions in the newly independent states. While these smaller projects can by no means replace the work of the large contractors and government agencies, if their role is broadened and specific standards of implementation are adopted by other contractors in delivering foreign aid, U.S. government assistance can become more balanced, comprehensive, effective on the ground, and cost-effective here at home.

As we sort out U.S. goals and priorities in the newly independent states, then, it is critical that the role of different mechanisms for delivering that aid be examined as well. For U.S. assistance depends as much on how it is packaged as on the areas of assistance themselves. At a time of such cost cutting in the United States, the cost-effectiveness of these programs is critical. And especially in the non-Russian areas where U.S. assistance is still at a nascent stage, the positive elements of our aid program as exemplified by these smaller partnerships should be maintained and expanded, and their lessons extended to every program initiated on the ground. Increasingly, despite conventional wisdom often to the contrary, it is important to recognize that as far as U.S. assistance to the newly independent states is concerned, good things often do come in smaller packages.

Notes

1. This chapter is based on a two-year study conducted by the Project on the NIS, of JNA Associates, Inc., to examine the role of small programs and partnerships in the U.S. assistance effort to the newly independent states. With the support of five private U.S. foundations, the project draws on countless site visits; interviews with roughly three hundred NGOs and small companies (both U.S. and those indigenous to the newly independent states), USAID contractors, and private foundations working in the newly independent states; examinations of close to forty independent and government audits and evaluations of projects in the newly independent states, as well as a range of annual and quarterly contractor and grantee reports and other reports; and interviews with well over fifty Russians, Kazakhs, and other indigenous specialists who are working with USAID subcontractors and grantees or are knowledgeable about U.S. assistance. The project was created in June 1994 as an independent, privately funded effort solely intended to educate Congress, the executive branch, and the public about the aid reform debate in regard to the former Soviet Union. The

author would like to thank the W. Alton Jones Foundation, the Carnegie Corporation, the Tides Foundation, and other private foundation donors for their support of this effort. For the full results of this effort, see *Aid to the Former Soviet Union: When Less Is More* (Bethesda, MD: JNA Associates, Inc., 1996), 1997 update forthcoming.

2. See, for example, list of contracts awarded in March and April 1995 for Privatization and Economic Restructuring in Central and Eastern Europe and the newly independent states and *Obligation and Expenditure Report as of December 31, 1994 for USAID Programs in the NIS of the FSU,* 9 February 1995.

3. See Murray Feshbach, "The Role of External Assistance on Environmental and Health Policies in Russia," in this volume.

4. Charles Krauthammer, "It's Their Economy, Stupid," *Washington Post,* 9 February 1996, p. A21.

5. Indicators range from the highly specific and quantitative (such as "number of partnering opportunities identified"), to broad criteria (such as "fiscal and monetary policy and regulatory reform in Ukraine," "changes in laws," or "changes in morale, motivation and attitudes through the acquisition of new knowledge and skills"). See, for example, USAID Project Summary Information, by Implementing Entity Level (Projects 110–0001, -0002, -0007, -0009, and others); and various evaluations, such as MSI Evaluations of ABA/CEELI for Democratic Pluralism Initiatives in the NIS and of National Democratic Institute for International Affairs.

6. See, for example, Paul Clements, "Impact Analysis in Development Agency Management: Current Weaknesses and Prospects for Improvement," Woodrow Wilson School of Public and International Affairs, Princeton University, September 1995. The author describes six of thirteen projects he studied in Africa as part of a comparative organizational analysis of USAID, CARE, and the World Bank.

7. The Russian American Enterprise Fund (RAEF), for example, was created in August 1993 to disburse $350 million over five years. After one year and roughly $20 million in expenditures, not a single loan had been made. In the first year that the Western NIS Enterprise Fund was in operation, it hired American staff and rented office space in Kiev, but getting the loan program itself off the ground has been slow (see below). The merger in May 1995 of the RAEF and the Fund for Large Enterprises in Russia (FLER) into the new U.S.-Russia Investment Fund was intended to address these and other serious problems.

8. Formerly the Institute for Soviet American Relations.

9. ARD/Checchi's Second Quarterly Progress Report from 1 January 1994–31 March 1994 for Contract No. CCN-0007–C-00–3166–00 for the Rule of Law Program in the Russian Federation states that for the "base period" of the contract the budget is $12,204,998. The estimated total value of the contract (with options over a five-year period, until September 1998), including all costs and fixed fees, is $22,150,005. According to the USAID Obligation and Expenditure report, as of 30 June 1995, the ARD/Checchi consortium had received over $18.7 million in obligations.

10. ARD/Checchi contract for Project No. 110–0007–C-00–3169, signed with USAID, 30 September 1993, p. 15.

11. See, for example, ARD/Checchi's Draft Second Annual Workplan, from September 1994 to September 1995, dated as of 15 March 1995, that documents the wide gap between target dates and actual project implementation.

12. For one view on the role of U.S. efforts to help establish rule of law in Central Asia, see also Barnabas Johnson, "The Role of the United States in the Erosion and Collapse of Constitutional Governance in Kazakstan," *Central Asian Monitor,* no. 6 (1995).

13. Save the Children Quarterly Activity Report for the period of 1 January 1995 to

31 March 1995 and Save the Children RFA: RUSS/LG 032495, 24 March 1995, Attachment 4: Background and Application Guidelines.

14. See, for example, *Foreign Assistance: Assessment of Selected USAID Projects in Russia,* U.S. General Accounting Office, Report No. GAO/NSIAD-95–156, August 1995. As the report notes, for example, "progress has been slow because CH_2M Hill did not fill critical staff positions in Russia in a timely manner, and it relied on staff located in the U.S. to manage the projects" (p. 40).

15. Ibid., pp. 40–42.

16. Ibid., p. 42.

17. Ibid., p. 40.

18. For the most part, these represent small projects that have been funded by USAID. Few of the partnerships that were not awarded government funds agreed to speak on the record, for fear of risking potential future support.

19. House of Representatives Report no. 104–295, *Making Appropriations for Foreign Operations, Export Financing, and Related Programs for the Fiscal Year Ending September 30, 1996, and for Other Purposes,* ordered to be printed on 26 October 1995.

20. Other factors, moreover, further inhibit small projects from tapping into government funding: required audits are often prohibitively expensive; registration with USAID (a prerequisite for NGOs applying for funding) is often too tedious and time-consuming a process for a small organization; small projects are often cut out by bidding and procurement processes geared to the large contractor; they have found it difficult to break into "networks"; and in general, they are simply too small to contribute the extensive amount of time and resources required of a smaller organization to break into the system. Current recommendations to reduce this burden, such as raising the audit level from $25,000 to $100,000, are important first steps. But much remains to be done to ensure that smaller groups in fact gain the opportunity to continue the kind of work at which they have already proven effective.

21. As but one example of the broad problem, see the 18 January 1995 CRS report by Curt Tarnoff, *The Former Soviet Union and U.S. Foreign Aid: Implementing the Assistance Program:* "Initial ignorance on the part of U.S. policymakers and aid implementors regarding conditions, players, and problems in Russia and the rest of the FSU has been a severe obstacle to rapid implementation. Contractor personnel—some with no experience of the region—seem to have had difficulty getting their bearings and establishing working projects on the ground" (p. 17).

22. The Foreign Operations, Export Financing, and Related Programs Appropriations Act, 1995, "Assistance for the New Independent States of the Former Soviet Union" (PL103–106, 108 STAT.1617), states that USAID must report on "steps being taken to include individuals and organizations with language or regional expertise in the provision of assistance to the new independent states of the FSU."

23. Report to the Committees on Appropriations of the U.S. Senate and U.S. House of Representatives on "USAID Efforts to Employ Regional Expertise in the NIS Assistance Program," 21 October 1994.

24. See, for example, the cover letter for the USAID Request for Applications to develop NGOs in Central Asia (#NIS/RCO94–05), issued July 1994, that explicitly states that "prior experience in the Central Asian Republics or with USAID is not required."

25. See U.S. House of Representatives, *Making Appropriations for Foreign Operations, Export Financing, and Related Programs,* Amendment 45, p. 44.

26. See, for example, John Harper and Janine Wedel, "Western Aid to Eastern and Central Europe: What Are We Doing Right, What Are We Doing Wrong, and How We Can Do It Better," conference report, Wilson Center, September 1995; Thomas Carothers, *Assessing Democracy Assistance: The Case of Romania* (Washington, DC: Carnegie En-

dowment, 1996); and reports and memos from conferences sponsored by USAID, the Eurasia Foundation, World Learning, and others.

27. According to the CRS report by Curt Tarnoff (*The Former Soviet Union and U.S. Foreign Aid: Implementing the Assistance Program,* 18 January 1995), of the ten IG audits and seventeen formal outside project evaluations completed by USAID, no audits of large projects (p. 36) nor project evaluations of the very large programs ("such as the privatization program," p. 41) have been done, although the report notes that evaluations are scheduled for 1995. As of December 1995, programmatic audits had been conducted that included parts of large contracts, but no full financial audits of large contractors had been conducted.

28. See, for example, Management Systems International audit of American Bar Association/CEELI Grant No. CCS-0007–G-00–2018–00, 7 April 1994, p. 2, which called for "more concrete and measurable objectives," and noted that USAID had "unrealistic expectations for the CEELI program."

29. It is striking how much unsolicited information the Project on the NIS received with the stipulation that it remain confidential out of fear that future U.S. government funding would be cut. One of the few individuals who provided constructive criticism on the record ended his fax with: "Please feel free to use whatever you want, but please don't ruin my career."

16

The Role of External Assistance on Environmental and Health Policies in Russia

Murray Feshbach

The structure of this paper on the role of outside assistance follows a format of providing essential details on issues related to environmental and health problems of the former Soviet Union (FSU), with emphasis on the Russian Federation. Only with a background of such information can the depth—or rather, lack of assistance—be discussed and evaluated. Emphasis is laid on the nuclear, air, land, water, and chemical issues, as well as population issues such as morbidity and mortality. In the end, it will be seen that insufficient priority, attention, concern, or effort has been made until very recently. Now with anticipated reductions in such funding, it may be too late to be efficacious in many areas.

State of the Environment

Issues

Nuclear/Radioactivity

For about forty years the former Soviet Union's nuclear complex was built in total disregard of environmental considerations and their possible health effects on the population. A Russian journalist described the country as being covered by a "Nuclear Plague."[1] The Soviet Union's subsequent partial dismemberment has increased the dangers of accidents and contamination, even though it has had other positive benefits.

The extent of the nuclear industry—civilian and military—is much greater than generally understood. Today there are at least 221 operating nuclear facilities, excluding civil nuclear power reactors, 99 of them located in Russia. These figures include production of plutonium and uranium processing sites as well as weapons design and production. In addition, as many as 10,000 to 20,000 organizations may be using different types of radiation sources for medicine, industry, and research with ionizing radiation sources totaling some 700,000 in Russia alone.[2]

What Happened and What Can Happen? Mainly due to a prior lack of following the most elementary rules of safety, the probability that an "accident" could happen is still high. Until recent interventions in retrofitting many civilian facilities, as well as retraining of operators and other efforts to improve safety, the denial level among Russian nuclear operators was very high; the military operation of the Russian Ministry of Atomic Energy (MinAtom) still persists in its denial pattern. In addition, until recently, there was a lack of independent and effective regulatory bodies. For instance, the State Committee for Nuclear Regulation and Safety Oversight (the Gosatomnadzor agency) not only lacks funds, but even after it gained legal authority to fully exercise its mission at military nuclear facilities in 1991, it lost this authority again in 1995. The Ministry of Defense, as well as MinAtom, did and still do place obstacles that hinder its mission.

What is needed most of all are funds in order to improve and develop nuclear safety; that is, external aid could play a decisive role, both in terms of direct funding and in technological cooperation. Much has been done in this realm, and new policies have been adopted, but much remains to be done as well. It has also come to a point where special containers as well as special train cars to transport radioactive waste from the northern nuclear submarine fleet to Mayak have been provided; but the demand is still much greater than possibly can be supplied.

Americans as well as Europeans have expressed concern for the safety of plutonium production reactors and associated reprocessing facilities at Krasnoyarsk, Tomsk, and Chelyabinsk. Not only are they over thirty-years-old, they also share design characteristics with Chernobyl-style reactors, the lack of a containment structure being the most obvious indication of design faults. The cost of shutting down Chernobyl and replacement of its lost energy-producing capacity by the year 2000 was evaluated by the Ukrainian government at $4.4 billion. Agreement was reached in April 1995 between the European Union (EU), the G-7, and President Leonid Kuchma,[3] but current plans are for provision of less than $3 billion (and even this may not be totally forthcoming).

Radioactive Waste. Russia has a reprocessing capacity of about 1,200 cubic meters a year; its needs are for at least 5,000 cubic meters per year to be properly processed.[4] The most immediate danger comes from improper storage at such sites as Murmansk-60, 130, 140, and 150, and possible explosions of the residual materials. Radioactive contamination of the environment, and therefore of the population, as a result of past and present practices is much greater than usually understood. Beyond acute radiation effects, there is the question of a lasting cumulative effect from low doses of radiation.

Among others, one can cite the example of the Chelyabinsk facilities, where radioactive waste was released uncontained into the Techa River and the immediate surroundings from the late 1940s and into Lake Karachay until the mid-1950s. At the beginning of the 1960s the Soviet Union began injecting liquid radioactive waste directly into the substrate at the Tomsk, Krasnoyarsk, and Dmitrovgrad facilities. In order to fully represent the magnitude of the effort needed, the Hanford nuclear facility in Washington state may cost over $250 billion to fully remediate its surrounding area, which contains perhaps 500 million curies of radioactive waste. At the three Russian sites near the Ob, Yenisey, and Volga Rivers, more than 1 billion curies *each* were injected at relatively low levels below the surface.[5] If they transmigrate into the rivers many people will suffer. Relative to Hanford, the total cost of remediation, including associated health costs, will be very high. Very little has been done about these three facilities to date.

Outside Russia, the most notable nuclear testing site is at Semipalatinsk in Kazakhstan. During the period of open-air testing this place remained a top-secret site. From 1949 to 1962, the Soviet military conducted more than 300 nuclear tests without informing or warning the local population about it. The consequences on the environment and the population were and are still dramatic, with effects such as congenital malformations and leukemia, to name just a few.[6]

Lagoons containing enormous amounts of radioactive waste are located on the Gulf of Finland at Sillimae, Estonia. An earthen dam only thirty meters away from the gulf, and from there, the Baltic Sea, is also an area of great concern. A ten-member team (three from Sweden, four from Finland, and three from Estonia) reported in 1993 that they found 4 million tons of uranium ore waste, 1.5 million tons of oil-shale ash, 200,000 tons of calcium fluoride, 1,200 tons of pure uranium, and 800 tons of thorium.[7] If the September 1994 storms of the Baltic Sea and the adjacent gulf are repeated, perhaps the dam will give way and the populations of ten littoral countries will be adversely affected. My recommendations to very high-level officials to minimally spray the dam with cement as a temporary "fix" have not been adopted by those with whom I have spoken in Sweden, the U.S. government, international agencies, or elsewhere, either because of a lack of funding or more probably by lack of concern. Very little except surveys and analyses have been performed by the HELCOM (Helsinki Commission) countries or others.

Nuclear Submarine Fleet. There has been dumping of liquid and solid radioactive waste into the Kara and Barents Seas and the Sea of Japan. In addition, there is much concern about accidents, as well as inadequate treatment of and storage capacity for fuel from nuclear-powered vessels. The efforts of the Bellona Foundation of Oslo, Norway, to depict and warn the world about this dangerous situation has drawn much attention. But other than the arrest of the Russian coauthor of a recent report on the situation in Zapadnaya Litsa, Captain Alexander Nikitin (Russian navy, retired), very little attention has been paid to this problem by non-Scandinavian countries. Little also has been done to ameliorate the potential explosive condition of these poor, overfull, and insecure facilities. What has been done is limited to a better, but incomplete, accounting by Gosatomnadzor of the amount and content of each facility, provision of a number of better containers for waste in the Far East, and some high-technology machinery for unloading nuclear charges from submarines.[8] Lack of funds for the Northern Fleet authorities may impel the Russians to ask for more assistance even in the closed areas involved.

Disarmament. During the Cold War the Soviet Union had accumulated a huge amount of nuclear armaments. With its ending and the signature of the START agreements dismantlement of nuclear charges became a high priority. Of particular concern are plutonium charges. Russia inherited most of the Soviet nuclear arsenal from the other republics, as well as its own. Today it does not have available financial and technological means to face such a task. Nunn-Lugar monies designed to reduce the potential threat and contribute to the dismantlement of nuclear weapons on land and sea have been diverted to other uses, and are now being cut back by U.S. budgetary constraints.

Air

Air pollution is mainly the result of the activities of gigantic industrial plants built by the Soviets. It is estimated by Dr. Aleksey Yablokov, head of the Russian Federation's Security Council Interagency Commission on Environmental Security, to be responsible for 20 to 30 percent of the overall illness rate of the population.[9] In terms of pollution rates compared with the size of the population and areas of settlement, the priority activity appears to be most needed in the northern regions of the country.[10] Since 1991 the worsening economic situation and the resulting decline in production has led to some decrease of pollutant emission into the air. In 1992, total emissions into the atmosphere was 28.2 million tons, compared to 31.8 million in 1991.[11] But levels remain high; if we prorate the emissions and production to its prior level, then current emissions would be even higher than before. As a result, whenever production will equal its prior level, the level of emissions will be even greater than earlier. Particularly significant is the emission of benzo(a)-pyrene and dioxin—known carcinogens—which are by-products of incomplete fossil fuel combustion. It would be simple to obligate city managers to burn these fuels at 1,600 degrees as we do, and not 800 degrees as they do in order to save money, and thus reduce if not eliminate these carcinogenic by-products from the air. Hopefully, this recommendation, which I gave in the spring of 1996 at a Department of State/Agency for International Development briefing, will be implemented through USAID funding.

Land

The main causes of pollution throughout the FSU are industrial and transportation accidents, breaks in pipelines, and intentional toxic waste dumping.[12] Deliberate dumping is the main source of this problem. Currently, perhaps some 106 billion tons of toxic waste are stacked in official and unofficial depots throughout Russia in conditions that threaten rivers and surrounding areas with contamination.[13] Unofficial radioactive waste deposits in Moscow city alone in 1991–92 numbered a surprising 636 sites. Even after clean-up, local authorities have found some fifty or more new ones each year since this first major inquiry. Similar investigations in St. Petersburg, Perm, Omsk, and other cities have found astonishing numbers of radioactive toxic waste sites as well.

Oil and gas producers have an extensive pipeline network which is old and poorly maintained. As a result, two major oil and gas pipeline accidents occur on average every day of the year; estimated losses range from 7 to 20 percent of total Russian output. Until recently most foreign assistance went to expanding output, rather than conservation of available supplies and improved infrastructure. Private funding for new exploration of sites is a preferred choice rather than use of scarce governmental funding.

As far as I am informed, very little assistance has gone to ameliorate arable land, and therefore the quantity and quality of the food supply to the population. Again, lack of funding by the Russian and other FSU governments deters adoption of new policies. New policies could improve a situation in which 50 percent of the arable land was eroded by wind and water, compacted by use of heavy agricultural machinery, denuded of humus, and impacted by overuse of pesticides and fertilizers. In the latter case, only the lack of funds by farms (and perhaps by individual farmers) has reduced the excess use of such materials; as a result, the food supply has become cleaner and healthier for the population. This can be seen as one of the few clear benefits of the problems engendered by the transition. Nonetheless, illness of the digestive system is still prevalent at a very high rate due to poor quality products of the domestically produced food chain. Also incriminated are dumping of poor quality, polluted, unhealthy products by foreign suppliers.

Water

In 1989 and subsequently, official Russian sources indicated that three-quarters of all surface water in the Soviet Union were polluted, and after treatment, only half was believed to be drinkable.[14] The percentage by which certain elements exceed maximum allowable concentration levels in surface waters of the Soviet Union in 1991 was staggering: copper compounds, 72 to 75 percent; phenols, 46 to 60 percent; petroleum products, 40 to 49 percent; and zinc, 34 to 36 percent.[15] Deputy Premier Aleksandr Zaveryukha declared more recently before the collegium of the Russian Water Conservancy Committee that two out of three rivers, lakes, and other open water bodies in Russia were polluted and could not be used for drinking and fish breeding.[16]

Only 30 percent of Russian villages have centralized water supply systems; it has been speculated that the extent of this crucial problem has not been explained to the highest Russian authorities. Whether or not true, efforts have been limited by both the Russians and Western aid operations. For example, U.S. efforts so far seem to be concentrated on the water situation in only two cities, Moscow and Volgograd (in addition to the overall regional Lake Baikal program of USAID).

Thus, policies in the former Soviet Union states are limited to attempts to fix the consequences rather than implementing prevention programs. The very high rates of illness due to poor water quality, from dysentery to cholera to typhoid fever to viral hepatitis, and other illnesses, also have incalculable costs. Widespread discharge of heavy metals, chemical compounds, and various other toxic materials into Russia's rivers, lakes, and seas can also become the cause of all kinds of toxic and chemical poisoning of all kinds of other environmental resources, including the water table.

Recently, a plant located on the Northern Dvina river near Arkhangel'sk decided to "clean out its pipes." They did so without notifying any regional or federal authorities. As a consequence, 16 tons of mercury—tons, not kilograms—were dumped into the river. Ingestion of mercury salts may result in severe stomach pain, vomiting, and—at high exposure—death may follow. The long-term health effects on the population is expected to be very severe and could result in liver damage and kidney failure. Thus, regardless of what environmental laws outside countries or international agencies assist the governments of the region to prepare and perhaps adopt, the microbehavior of individual plants and organizations may undermine all of these efforts.

Pollution in the Volga River is the subject of attention by the Canadian government. It cooperates with local governments in research on contaminants in the river and proposes appropriate cleanup procedures. The task remains enormous, however. The lack of budgetary or insufficient ecological funds available to the local governments means that the effort will be limited, albeit necessary.

Fresh water reserves in Lakes Ladoga, Baikal, and Onega exceed 85 percent of total Russian water supply and more than 20 percent of the world supply.[17] In 1992 and 1993, two international expeditions to research the ecology of these lakes were organized with the fiscal and scientific support of the Earthwatch Fund. The teams included Russian, English, Italian, Canadian, U.S., and South African scientists. These expeditions are useful, admirable, but only the future will see if any proposals are implemented into local policies and behavior that will improve the situation.

In Ukraine, water quality has deteriorated considerably. Among other factors contributing to the decline was a major accident at the Dikanevskiy purification plant in Kharkov in 1995. The brief but powerful flow of waters had important consequences. Samples taken at filtration stations showed a twenty- to thirty-fold increase in bacteriological pollution. The accident spread into the Rostov region and threatened the health of a large number of people.[18] While this event did not contribute to the overall large outbreak of cholera in Ukraine, it was not helpful either for the health of the population.

The Aral Sea ranks as one of the world's worst ecological catastrophes. Its consequences affect and will affect the immediate region as well as remote regions. Since 1960 it has lost more than 50 percent of its surface area. Annually, a minimum of 75 tons—and perhaps up to 150 tons—of salt, dust, and sand is lifted into the air for hundreds of kilometers. Salinity of the water has tripled to more than 30 grams per liter. This dramatic situation is the result of the deliberate diversion of the waters of the Amu-Darya and Syr-Darya Rivers away from the Aral Sea in order to develop and expand the cotton monoculture of Uzbekistan and Turkmenistan. Part of the problem today is that external intervention has to deal with four independent republics which do not always have a convergence of interests. Cotton is Uzbekistan's main hard-currency earnings, but not of all other states in the region.[19]

Until now not much actual, physical work has been done through international assistance to ameliorate the lack of water. The World Bank, perhaps belatedly, recognized the Aral Sea disaster as a priority issue. In March 1993 the presidents of Central Asia's five ex-Soviet republics agreed to contribute 1 percent of their state budgets to create a fund, the "Aralbank," that would help resolve the problem. But money has yet to be deposited. In June 1994 another conference organized by the World Bank agreed to spend $31.4 million to study the problem, but nothing tangible has been done.

The European Union created, in the framework of TACIS, a technical assistance project called WARMAP-Water Resource Management and Agricultural Production in Central Asia, which is funded at a level of ECU 4.75 million (about U.S. $5 million).[20] Its aim was to prepare measures to ameliorate the environmental problems by improving the management of water resources. How many study commissions by how many countries are required before actual efforts on location are implemented?

Chemical

Civilian and military chemicals may represent a greater threat to the health of the population than appreciated by outside governments and organizations. It is not only the seven acknowledged chemical weapon depots, but especially the very widespread pattern of chemical industrial plants, and their potentially dangerous pollution emissions, that are an important component of this issue. Other than the work of an international group which is examining the military aspect of this issue (including the participation of the Research Institute of National Defense of Sweden), I am not aware of other major activities in this regard. The delay in the adoption and then the signing of the Chemical/Biological Warfare Agreement by the U.S. government may contribute to this situation. Russian delay in the destruction of chemical and biological weapons is due not only to shortage of funds, but also to fears of local populations where the destruction is scheduled to take place (the NIMBY syndrome), and consequently to delays in construction of such facilities.

Pollution from thermal power and metallurgical plants also contributes to release of heavy metals and chemicals that destroy woods and forests in nearby regions. In addition to acid rain, fire, clear-cutting, and pest infestation are responsible for massive deforestation of the Siberian forests. The denuding of the Siberian forest has the potential to contribute more to global climate change than the assault on the Amazon basin, even though the latter has received enormous (and proper) attention. The environmental Policy and Technology Project of CH_2M Hill, sponsored by USAID, is concerned with forest management in Krasnoyarskiy Kray. An insufficient amount of attention is paid by the West to this potentially major issue. Despite the efforts of Yablokov and others to stop the rape of the forests by domestic and foreign cutters (as well as the actual and potential loss of biodiversity in the forest regions), little is done in reality.

Transboundary Issues

Worrying over the extent of Arctic pollution, and therefore its impact on Alaska due to its long-distant transport to the fishing grounds of Alaska, the U.S. Congress's Office of Technology Assessment (OTA), before its demise due to budgetary cutbacks, prepared a report on Arctic pollution at the request of Senator Ted Stevens of Alaska. While the findings did not conclude that there is an immediate and present danger, it left open the possibility that it will be a danger in the future. Again, there is some disagreement about the amount of radioactivity, especially by some of the staff of the University of Alaska at Fairbanks. Their estimates are many orders of magnitude higher than those published by the Russians and used in the OTA report. If the Fairbanks estimate is correct, then there is a much greater threat to global environmental security than deemed hitherto. Simultaneously, this also likely means that it is a greater threat to the peoples of the northern Russian Federation. The sources of the different estimates need to be determined, and then policies adopted to direct humanitarian aid to this need.

The newly created European Environment Agency (EEA) in Copenhagen devoted some of its resources for studying and proposing policies regarding the Arctic environment. It was underlined that not only individual countries must be involved but also international cooperation. Of particular concern are the consequences of the economic and industrial activities of the northwestern part of the Russian Federation upon the Arctic, which must be reconciled with environmental necessities. The most polluted area of the Arctic is the Kola Peninsula because of emissions of heavy metals and nuclear waste. As a result, infant mortality on the peninsula exceeds the average Russian level by more than a third. To date, the most integrated and structured international Arctic program is the Arctic Environmental Protection Agency (AEPA) signed in Rovaniemi, Finland in 1991 by ministers of the Scandinavian countries, the Russian Federation, the United States, and Canada. Its activities entail assessing and monitoring, prevention, and conservation, among others.[21]

Transboundary pollution particularly worries the Scandinavians. Whether it is the Norwegians and Finns worried about the health effects of serious levels of pollution emanating from the Nikel' plant or from the extensive range of nuclear facilities on the Kola Peninsula, these two governments have provided a significant amount of money and technology for environmental monitoring on the peninsula. The Swedes have contributed to extensive retrofitting and retraining of the staff at Ignalina, the RBMK-type reactor in Lithuania, but it is still considered quite dangerous. The Finns have contributed similar aid to the operators of the Sosnovy Bor atomic power plant located in the Leningrad region. The Norwegian and Russian joint explorations of the extent of radioactivity in the Kara and Barents Sea regions reflect their concern over the nuclear dumping and waste issue, as well. Norway has focused mainly on Russia, Estonia, and Lithuania, providing about $20 million worth of aid in 1995, and Sweden contributed about $10 million in 1995 for related work throughout the Baltic countries. The joint Northern Council efforts by the Scandinavians and the Russians may have positive effects in the future as their joint efforts on nuclear waste policies are actually implemented. Again, however, it is in the future tense; realities are still at a dangerous level.

Japan is worried about Russian dumping of low-level radioactive waste from its submarine base located at Vladivostok in the Sea of Japan. While the level of radioactivity actually is quite low, it has created the most concern for Japan. Although an agreement was signed for constructing a facility to store and process low-level radioactive waste on land, nothing has happened to date. Japan is concerned by the region's political and economic stability. Certain health indicators in Russia's Far East are worse than the national average, such as the infant mortality rate. Japan has recently decided to grant humanitarian assistance for 522 million yen in the form of medicine and equipment, powdered milk, and ambulances for that region.[22] Japanese humanitarian aid for the health needs of the Central Asian countries has largely gone unnoticed in the West. While again at the curative rather than preventive stage, the admission that outside aid is needed may have an effect on actual policies by the Central Asian governments; it is an important contribution as well.

Senator Murkowski of Alaska, speaking to the Senate Committee on Energy and Natural Resources in October 1993, declared that "if there is another serious nuclear accident in Russia or Eastern Europe, it could take as little as four days for radioactivity from that accident to reach Alaska."[23] He was principally referring to the Bilibino facility located on the Chukhotsk Peninsula across from Alaska. Located 1,350 miles from Anchorage, it is still in operation and is expected to expand its capacity. I am not aware of its having a containment structure, improved safety facilities, or of its retraining its staff. While this may have occurred, the explicit policies of MinAtom to expand the civilian nuclear power industry is still on the books. What is worrisome is whether specific power plants also will be sufficiently upgraded in regards to safety considerations given the shortage of funds overall.

State of Health

Issues

To Russian physicians, the health situation was so poor, and so poorly addressed by the then minister of health, ex-Colonel General Eduard Nechayev, that he was literally booed from the stage while he was delivering a speech at the All-Russian Pirogov Congress of Physicians in the fall of 1995. Several weeks thereafter he was fired. His successor, Aleksandr Tsaragorodtsev, a pediatrician, was one of the few high-level civilian survivors of the Nechayev regime. It remains to be seen what he will be able to accomplish given current severe fiscal constraints, but at least he likely will not allow an analogous situation in which for two years (1993 and 1994) there was no domestic production of human insulin at all! Many other issues need to be dealt with, but at least a beginning was made by the eviction of the minister.

Morbidity

Without going into a full description of the morbidity status of the population of the former Soviet Union, let me indicate that it continues to be appalling overall. Although some signs of improvement are becoming apparent—with and without humanitarian aid—at the same time, other illnesses are increasing at a dangerous rate. Thus, on one hand, the level of diphtheria did not reach the expected levels in 1995 that past trends indicated. At least for 1995, a turnaround occurred in the exponential increases of the past five years. This may have been due to the $50 million supply of diphtheria vaccine from the European Union. The impact of this special effort is reflected in the improvement in immunization coverage ratios. While some immunization rates still are not at the 90 to 95 percent coverage rate needed to prevent an epidemic, they are at rates much closer to this level and clearly much higher than even two years earlier. The donation of the funds for the vaccines likely were a combination of humanitarian aid and self-interest. Clearly one wants to prevent illness and deaths of children in any country, but as noted at a World Health Organization (WHO) meeting in Berlin in January 1995, a leading German epidemiologist expressed his concern about the eventual spread of diphtheria beyond the Commonwealth of Independent States (CIS) borders to Germany. Since he also indicated that only one-half of the German population had a full complement of diphtheria immunization, this alert is fully understandable. The relatively immediate utilization of the vaccines by Goskomsanepidnadzor (the State Committee for Sanitary-Epidemiological Oversight), the equivalent of our Center for Disease Control and Prevention, was very appropriate. Incidence rates in the first four months of 1996 reflect a very sharp decline relative to the level and rate of the same period in 1995.

The current need for full immunization of the population with polio vaccines has been accelerated by the news that the number of persons ill with polio increased in the Russian Federation from 3 to 17 cases per year in the previous decade to 145 cases in 1995 as information became available from Chechnya. Under the Dudayev period (1992–94), no vaccines were administered and the incidence of polio exploded. The question of its spread to other areas is pressing.

Similarly, the major increase in the number of tuberculosis cases is very worrisome and difficult to control. Tuberculosis has become rampant, not only in prisons, but also among migrants, refugees, and the homeless, whose number has increased dramatically in recent years. Moreover, the number of TB cases is underestimated, as incidence among many of the refugees and others are not captured by the medical statistics system. The levels are reaching very serious levels. Even WHO has finally come to the realization that the situation is perilous. Again I believe WHO is not only concerned for the CIS, but also for the disease spreading beyond its borders. Emerging Infectious Disease strike forces have been formed. WHO has been passive; now they are supposed to be active, that is preventive. But within the CIS, monies are still short and the TB rate in Kazakhstan, for example, is very high, as well as in Ukraine and Russia. The American level of TB increased dramatically concomitant with the rise in AIDS, especially in New York and San Francisco. TB incidence is now declining to less than 20,000 cases for the 260 million population in the United States; the Russian figure of 66,000 cases in 1995 occurred among a population of 147 million or almost 45 percent less. Drug-resistant strains of recent tuberculosis manifestations are just as worrisome, if not more so, as modern complex, fourth-generation drugs are difficult to obtain in hospitals and clinics in the former Soviet Union (especially outside Moscow and other main cities).

Very little attention has been paid until recently by governments, international organizations, and others to the likely explosion of AIDS in Russia. While it may not reach the terrible tragedy of the United States, where over 320,000 persons have died from this disease, it likely will increase dramatically. And from where will the aid be supplied to deal with this problem? Growth in venereal disease, especially syphilis among ten- to fourteen-year-old girls has exploded in the last five years; the availability and use of hard drugs has increased incredibly; and the homosexual population at risk may be much larger than previous estimates.

In addition, hospital conditions overall continue to be very bad. All of these factors lead to probable prevarication on the true number of cases of HIV and AIDS in the FSU. Since funds are not available to treat the afflicted properly, why reveal its true level? Thus, very little humanitarian aid is provided in these problem areas. Domestic policies very likely will not change in the near term.

Mortality and Life Expectancy

Humanitarian assistance to reduce mortality and simultaneously increase life expectancy has been relatively limited in quantity and quality, with perhaps one important exception. Mortality has increased across the board for males since 1987 in Russia, and since 1988 for females if measured by declines in average life expectancy at birth. If we decompose the official information available for infant mortality, it has basically increased since 1990 except for 1995, when it decreased to less than 19 deaths per 1,000 live births. Maternal mortality throughout the FSU is astonishingly high, at some seven to ten times higher than the American rate. According to WHO calculations, the maternal mortality rate in 1990 was 75 in Russia, 50 in Ukraine, and 80 in Kazakhstan, compared to 11 for North America and 11 for Northern Europe.[24] Deaths of working age males in 1993 increased by almost one-third compared with 1992, and so on and so on.

For current purposes, very few of the humanitarian assistance projects to my knowledge precisely address this problem. Perhaps the most germane of which I am aware is the point-to-point assistance provided to individual hospitals throughout the former Soviet Union by some twenty-five individual hospitals in the United States. Coordinated and managed by the American International Health Alliance (AIHA) program with funding by USAID, it may well be the most successful, relatively large-scale, health-related humanitarian assistance program of all American programs; for environmental activities, only the ISAR program (under Eliza Klose's direction) with environmental nongovernmental organizations (NGOs) in the former Soviet Union is in this class. Ecologiya (under Randy Kritkausky) provides important assistance to grassroots organizations, especially in the Baltic region. Several European countries are known to operate small-scale programs in various republics of the former Soviet Union as well. In their activities with their partners, the AIHA participating hospitals provide training for nurses as well as physicians in the latest medical procedures, sanitation, use of equipment, and other facets of this program. As a consequence, it is reported that improvements in medical practice in these facilities, and through some of their outreach, has led to a decrease in mortality in their immediate region. Whether it will be sufficient to affect the entire nation's mortality statistics remains to be seen.

The economy is affected by lower productivity due to illness, in turn caused by poor environmental and health conditions in which the working population works as well as their nonworking living conditions and behavior. As far as I am aware, no assistance has been provided to address economic questions in terms of environment and health. Rather, it is only through the FSU government's requirement of an environmental impact assessment of projects financed by foreign investors which has led to some improvements. Privatization does not incorporate social goals per se, and therefore has failed to impact the economy and society through this medium.

Policy Impacts

Domestic

Resolution of environmental and health problems is further complicated because CIS members have to deal simultaneously with a difficult economic recession and a dramatic financial crisis. In all of the countries, according to official statistics, production has not only dropped but the growth of the gross domestic product (GDP) was negative for the past three years. After seventy years of communism they are expected to make the transition to a democracy and to a market economy in a very short period of time. However, the weakness of the states, their inability to collect taxes, and the general chaos which has led to some civil wars if not wars between states, have considerably lessened their room for maneuvering on such problems as the environment and health. Moreover, the impact of past negligence continues to be felt.

What should be the priorities for humanitarian assistance? With unemployment rising, and poverty increasing at least for a large segment of the population, which should be first? I believe that the economy and society may not survive if the resolution of ecological and health problems are not sufficiently addressed by domestic and outside donors and supporters.

The newly independent states are not the only governments at fault. Western countries have tended to consider the potential effect of ecological disasters on them without taking into consideration the countries' realities. For instance, after the Chernobyl accident, the Western response was limited to demands for the *immediate* shutdown of the incriminated facilities. However, these policies were announced without taking into consideration the role of nuclear power in total energy produced and the costs that would appear with the building of fossil-fueled power plants among other things. Nuclear power represents 34.3 percent of total electric power in Ukraine, 87 percent in Lithuania, and 11.2 percent in Russia in 1994.[25] These are not unimportant shares. If MinAtom Minister Mikhaylov would have his way, the share in Russia will climb to 20 percent.

The issue is complicated. In addition to Western pressure to close dangerous nuclear facilities, there is strong pressure by the Russian military–industrial complex to expand them, as it perceives a strengthening of Russia's nuclear capacities as a way of maintaining its status as a great power. Thus, Mikhaylov strives to retain skilled staffs just in case the facilities remain open, as well as to earn hard currencies that are much needed. Russia has export capabilities, as witness their deal with Iran. Many voices in the country have denounced an alleged American conspiracy to put down Russia's nuclear potential.

In any case, Russia has yet to develop a long-term national environmental protection policy. There are some projects that are going on, but these are spread among numerous Russian ministries, departments, and large joint-stock companies such as Gazprom. We can cite the Russian Ministry on Environment, the Russian Committee on Hydroineteorology (Rosgidromet), the Russian Committee on Timber, the Russian Committee on Water, the Russian Committee on Land, the Health and Epidemiology Oversight Committee, and others, but they do not work within the framework of an integrated plan. Finally, the financial means put aside by the Russian government are very low. Ecology Minister Viktor Danilov-Danilyan himself declared that with expenses for ecology amounting to just 0.1 percent of the budget, "Russia cannot claim the title of a civilized country."[26]

External

With the collapse of the Soviet Union Western countries announced that they would provide extensive foreign aid. The recipient countries were certainly eager to receive that aid. However, for a variety of reasons, this did not occur. Much of the money promised was never disbursed, and each country had to use whatever means it had to support itself.

An often heard criticism was a total lack of coordination between country donors and between their own agencies. More money could have certainly been spent, but the real problem was on *how* it was spent. Most of the funds allocated were going directly either into the pocket of well-paid Western "overnight" consultants who knew nothing about the country, or the monies were diverted by the former nomenklatura mafia and other malefactors. Many Western programs do not take into consideration the fact that knowledge is frequently available in the recipient countries, but not the means to implement it. As a result they develop expensive seminar programs taught by people who have no clue about the real conditions in the countries or regions involved. Central Asian leaders are brought to the United States for expensive, short-term training without any particular relevance for their needs. They are then lectured down to by people who consider them as coming from Third World countries and as a result are greatly offended. The benefits of such programs are virtually nil, if not with major negative feedbacks toward future projects.

Even if some programs are set up properly no follow-up is done; as a result, their impact is very limited. The question here is to know if we are addressing short-term or long-term policies. Taking into account the magnitude of the social, health, and environmental problems in the CIS, urgent short-term policies are certainly needed but are of little long-term effect if not conceived in a broader policy framework. There is also a psychological problem where people still remember their country as a great power, yet are obliged to ask for help from what once was considered its main enemy.

The 1992 Freedom Support Act gave the USAID authority to implement significant bilateral assistance programs. As of December 1994, $539 million were expended for programs and projects in Russia.[27] The role of the USAID clearly reflects the ambiguity residing in aid offered to the FSU. It is a governmental agency, and as such is accountable to very strict rules and responsive to the perceived needs of Congress. This accountability had negative consequences in terms of flexibility and rapidity in delivering aid. A coordinator was named by President Bill Clinton in May 1993 within the U.S. Department of State with the task of putting some order in the complex and unproductive organizational structure. But conflicts between USAID and other agencies persisted over money and policies. As a result, bureaucratic "wasting" wars were carried out instead of concentrating on global strategies for U.S. assistance to the CIS.[28]

It is also true that foreign programs had to deal with the intricacies of the Russian political imbroglio. For instance, support from the Ministry of Health, with Nechayev at its head, was not noted for its forthcomingness or cooperation. On the contrary, there was even strong opposition. Nothing will be done with external help delivered by Western countries unless local authorities cooperate or at least do not oppose these activities.

Gosatomnadzor provides us with another type of problem in implementing aid and new policies. The foreign donor community understood that proper legislation was needed concerning nuclear safety problems. However, appropriate legislation has not been passed, or if passed, later rescinded as noted above. Its inspectors can even be denied access to nuclear facilities without being able to condemn such action.[29]

A storage site for materials resulting from the dismantling of nuclear submarines, above all plutonium, is now being built with U.S. cooperation in the territory of the Mayak production amalgamation in the Chelyabinsk region. Some forty tons of Russia's weapons-grade plutonium stock will be kept in that entombment. After construction of the repository is completed, the storage facility and operation will be placed under the control of the International Atomic Energy Agency (IAEA).[30] The IAEA, in conjunction with the United Nations Development Program, initiated a program to strengthen radiation protection and nuclear safety infrastructures as well as identification of the types of assistance needed in the FSU.[31] Whether the IAEA can give fully independent recommendations remains to be seen as their ties to the nuclear industry confuses outside observers about the degree of their objectivity. The European Union's funding is mostly directed to safety assistance to nuclear power reactors.

World Health Organization

Since the breakup of the Soviet Union there has been a major shift of resources by the World Health Organization toward the CIS and the countries of Central and Eastern Europe. Two-thirds of its European region's biennial budget of $46 million is now committed to the countries of central and eastern Europe.[32] According to one evaluation of this organization: "The problem is that WHO is consultant based rather than program based."[33] WHO has elaborated a plan to fight the spread of diphtheria in the CIS in association with the Red Cross and the UN Children's Fund. About $50 million was allocated in 1995. These funds helped to buy vaccines and necessary medicine for the regions most contaminated.[34] Whether this is a one-time assistance operation, or will be a long-term commitment to encourage appropriate policies in the CIS, is moot, but unlikely.

World Bank

Russia became a member of the World Bank in 1992. Since then more than ten missions have visited Russia in connection with environmental protection concerns. The lack of coordination among various governmental and nongovernmental agencies as a result of a well-determined ecological agenda led to numerous projects from the Russian part that did not fit into the Bank's agenda.[35] Nonetheless, the World Bank loaned Russia over $100 million for environmental protection. The funds will be allocated on a competitive basis among Russian enterprises. It also remains to be seen if they are able to set up such programs, if the government would be willing to help them in terms of tax policies, and so forth.

The World Bank approved a $200 million loan to support local social services in Russia. This loan will include health care, education, water supplies, and sanitation. Another $537 million loan is pending.[36] Loans should be paid back at some point in time; Russia's capability to do so may also imply that it can cope with financial requirements at home, but likely not in the near term.

European Bank for Reconstruction and Development

The European Bank for Reconstruction and Development (EBRD) has awarded a grant of ECU 75 million (or about U.S. $100 million) for short-term improvement at eight of Russia's oldest reactors. These reactors are located at three sites in Russia: four St. Petersburg RBMK-1000 units at Sosnovyy Bor; two of the four VVER-440 units at Polyarnyye Zory on the Kola Peninsula; and two of the three operating units at Novovoronezhskiy VVER-440 type 230 plant.[37] Some awards to the Baltic republics have been initiated, but only a small amount in the environmental area. Again, whether there will be policy shifts as a result is moot.

Nunn-Lugar Funding

In the course of arming themselves, the Soviet military industry developed heptyl, a liquid fuel for their ICBMs. With the signing of the START treaties the question arose of what to do with the 30,000 tons of heptyl due to be destroyed according to this agreement. The Nunn-Lugar program set aside around $30 million for the development of techniques for the safe recycling of heptyl and for the design and construction of special-purpose, self-contained, environmentally clean hydrogenation units.[38] Construction of the first unit was supposed to be initiated at the beginning of 1996. Its current status is not known. This technical assistance is equally humanitarian in that it can save many, many lives. Heptyl, or unassimilated dimethyl hydrazine, is supertoxic, carcinogenic, nerve-paralyzing, and volatile. Disposing of this dangerous material could save many people from becoming ill or dying. It has not, however, to my knowledge, caused the Russians to produce a different liquid rocket fuel, in part because they still may have another 100,000 tons of heptyl in stock available for this purpose.

Conclusion

This array of problems, activities, and unfulfilled needs may be too much for a single country or a consortium, through the medium of international organizations, to fund. We cannot expect major policy shifts based on humanitarian assistance in the near term, and even less so if there is a return to past political leadership practices. So far, we have seen some progress but the impact is very small. Regrettably, I expect the health effect of past (and present) environmental and health practices to continue to have a very negative effect on the country.

Notes

This chapter was prepared with the assistance of Julien E. Hartley, Georgetown University.

1. Murray Feshbach, *Ecological Disaster: Cleaning Up the Hidden Legacy of the Soviet Regime* (New York: Twentieth Century Fund Press, 1995), p. 20.

2. General Accounting Office, *Nuclear Safety: Concerns with Nuclear Facilities and Other Sources of Radiation in the Former Soviet Union,* Report no. GAO/RCED-96-4 (Washington, DC: U.S. GAO, November 1995), pp. 2–3.

3. James R. Schlesinger et al., *Nuclear Energy Safety Challenges in the Former Soviet Union: A Report of the CSIS Congressional Study Group and Task Force,* (Washington, DC: Center for Strategic & International Studies, 1995), p. 3.

4. "Nuclear Pollution: Radioactivity Reaches Alarming Proportions in Northern Russia," *Europe Environment,* 21 February 1995 (available on *LEXIS/NEXIS* environmental library, curnws file).

5. William J. Broad, "Poison in the Earth: A Special Report; Nuclear Roulette for Russia: Burying Uncontained Waste," *New York Times,* 21 November 1994, p. A1.

6. Murray Feshbach and Alfred Friendly Jr., *Ecocide in the USSR* (New York: Basic Books, 1992), pp. 238–39.

7. Raimo Mustonen, "Sillamae Is Not Chernobyl: The Investigative Commission's Interim Report on Sillamae Is Ready," *Rahva Hall* (Tallinn) 7 May 1993, quoted in Feshbach, *Ecological Disaster,* p. 52.

8. See Joshua Handler, *Trip Report: Greenpeace Visit to Moscow and Russian Far East July–November 1992; Russian Navy Nuclear Submarine Safety, Construction, Defense Conversion, Decommissioning, and Nuclear Waste Disposal Problems* (Washington, DC: Greenpeace, 15 February 1993).

9. Feshbach, *Ecological Disaster,* p. 67.

10. E.Yu. Bezuglaya, in *Environmental and Health Atlas of Russia,* ed. Murray Feshbach (Moscow: PAIMS Publishing House, 1995), pp. 2–15.

11. Ministerstvo okhrany okruzhaiushchei sredy i prirodnykh resursov Rossiiskoi Federatsii, *Gosudarstvennii doklad o sostoianii okruzhaiushchei prirodnoi sredy Rossiiskoi Federatsii v 1992 godu* (Moscow: Ministry of Environmental Protection 1993), p. 6.

12. Feshbach, *Ecological Disaster,* p. 68.

13. Agence France Presse, Moscow, 5 May 1994; Radio Free Europe/Radio Liberty B-Wire, 5 May 1994, quoted in Feshbach, *Ecological Disaster,* p. 68.

14. Feshbach, *Ecological Disaster,* p. 53.

15. Ministerstvo prirodopol'zovaniia i okhrany okruzhaiushchei sredy SSSR, *Natsional'nii doklad SSSR k konferentsii OON 1992 goda po okruzhaiushchei srede i razvitiiu,* draft document prepared for the Rio Summit, Moscow, 1991, p. 181, quoted in Feshbach, *Ecological Disaster,* p. 54.

16. RIA Novosti (Moscow) 1628 GMT, in English, 14 February 1995, in *JPRS-TEN-95–003–L,* 5 April 1995, p. 15.

17. L. Iu. Preobrazhenskii, N.I. Silina, et al., *Izvestiia Russkogo Geograficheskogo Obshchestva* 127.2 (1995), pp. 57–67; translated in *FBIS-UST-95–050,* 12 December 1995, p. 84.

18. Anatolii Gordeev, ITAR-TASS World Service (Moscow), 1342 GMT, 9 July 1995, translated in *FBIS-SOV-95–131,* 10 July 1995, p. 68.

19. Steve LeVine, "Aral Sea's Defenders Suspend Fight to Save It; Local Groups Shift Efforts to River Deltas," *Washington Post,* 9 September 1994, p. A31.

20. See *TACIS Newsletter,* November 1995, p. 10.

21. John R. Hansen, Rasmus Hansson, and Stefan Norris, eds., *The State of the European Arctic Environment* (Copenhagen: European Environment Agency, 1996).

22. "Japan to Give 500 Million Yen in Aid to Russian Far East," *Japan Weekly Monitor,* 10 June 1996 (available on *LEXIS-NEXIS,* World library, curnws file).

23. Schlesinger et al., p. 92.

24. World Health Organization, *Weekly Epidemiological Record* (19 April 1996).

25. Schlesinger et al., p. 22.

26. Lee Hockstader, "Tight Russian Budget Proposal Draws Sharp Criticism," *Washington Post,* 4 March 1995, p. A25.

27. General Accounting Office, *Foreign Assistance: Assessment of Selected USAID Projects in Russia,* Report no. GAO/NSIAD-95–156 (Washington, DC: U.S. GAO, August 1995).

28. General Accounting Office, *Former Soviet Union: U.S. Bilateral Program Lacks Effective Coordination,* Report no. GAO/NSIAD-95–10 (Washington, DC: U.S. GAO, February 1995).

29. Schlesinger et al., p. 31.

30. Veronika Romanenkov, ITAR-TASS (Moscow), 1531 GMT, 18 April 1996; in *FBIS-SOV-96–077,* 19 April 1996.

31. General Accounting Office, *Concerns with Nuclear Facilities and Other Sources of Radiation in the Former Soviet Union,* Report no. GAO/RCED-96–4 (Washington, DC: U.S. GAO, November 1995).

32. Fiona Godlee, "WHO in Europe: Does it Have a Role?," *British Medical Journal* 310 (1995): p. 385.

33. Dr. Jo Kreysler, medical officer for the Red Cross, quoted in Godlee, "WHO in Europe," p. 385.

34. Leonid Vorontsov, "WHO Maps Out Help Plan to Fight Diphtheria in CIS," ITAR-TASS (Moscow), 20 January 1995; (available in *LEXIS-NEXIS* World Library, curnws file).

35. *FBIS-TEN-95–103,* 8 September 1995.

36. Open Media Research Institute, *OMRI Daily Digest* 2.84 (1996).

37. "European Bank Funds Improvements for Reactors," *Nuclear News* (March 1996): p. 45.

38. Sergey Ptichkin, "Asymmetrical Poison: It Was Developed in Russia but the Americans Know How to Get Rid of It," *Rossiiskaia gazeta* (Moscow) 20 July 1995, p. 3; translated in *FBIS-TEN-95–011,* 24 July 1995, p. 55–57.

17

The Interaction Between Internal and External Agency in Post-Communist Transitions

Karen Dawisha and Michael Turner

Since 1991, the states of the former Soviet Union (FSU) have embarked upon a grand endeavor of historic proportions: to resurrect, construct, import, and invent institutions of governance, laws and constitutions, economic systems, moral and religious belief systems, societal formations, security concepts and foreign policies, historical memory and national identity. The widespread, although far from universal, yearning for the collapse of communism blinded many inside these countries and abroad to the difficulties which would be faced by this unprecedented transition. Never before had a state of such size and sway collapsed, and in its rupturing created so many new states, all of which to varying degrees were unprepared for the shattering of the Soviet colossus.

The Russian Littoral Project, of which this is the final volume, has been devoted to analyzing the domestic and foreign policies of the new states during this five-year transition period, with particular attention to the sources of these policies. Most of the volumes have focused on domestic sources, whether they be societal or elite-based. This final volume has focused specifically on the external sources of change, seeking to address both the policies pursued by international actors and their effectiveness.

It is often forgotten that not only did the collapse of the USSR create untold challenges for leaders and peoples inside these new states, but also it demolished the international political order of the past half-century. This historic upheaval has posed exceptional challenges for the leaders of major countries outside the former USSR. To adjust to radical change in world politics, they must also recast the international roles of their countries and of the international organizations which had buttressed the Cold War system.

Due partly to the breakneck rate of change since the collapse of the Soviet

Union, decision makers and citizens frequently have lacked a firm grasp of the content and evolution of their own country's interests in the region, not to mention the objectives of other major international actors with whom policies ideally should be coordinated. Intellectual elites have not always assisted in bringing clarity out of the confusion: they have remained deeply divided about the likely future course of events in Russia and its neighbors, with many of them having grown up intellectually in a bipolar era when they could rely on the Soviet Union and the United States as bipolar opposites, uncritically replacing the Soviet Union with Russia rather than seeing their own bifurcated and neat worldview collapse with the fall of communism.

Effective efforts to influence post-Soviet developments also presuppose an awareness of the conflicting objectives of Western policies toward the successor states. Different states sometimes have divergent interests toward the newly independent states (NIS), and consequently the coordination of policy toward the newly independent states is never easy and not always possible. Moreover, as the chapters by Raymond Garthoff, Michael MccGwire, George Quester, and Alvin Rubinstein all underline, frequently there are difficulties in reconciling previous definitions of national security, conceived almost exclusively in terms of the central military and nuclear balance of power between NATO and its Moscow-centered adversary the Warsaw Pact, with new definitions of national security, which added the awareness that war was less likely if the NIS and Russia in particular could be transformed from a totalitarian Communist adversary into a stable, market-oriented, democratic partner. But Western powers have not always or consistently succeeded in redefining their national interests in a way which has promoted democratization and privatization in each of the newly independent states. Rather, the stability of Russia as the only nuclear successor state to the USSR has clearly been a paramount Western interest, the safeguarding of which has often, but not always, undercut the promotion of other objectives. For example, virtually all of the U.S. government assistance to Ukraine in the first two years after independence went for the dismantling and transfer of nuclear weapons from Ukraine to Russia, not for socioeconomic or political transition in Kiev.

Despite the unevenness of assistance efforts, a variety of programs has nevertheless been pursued by many Western and non-Western governments and by international organizations, over the last five years. And while the picture is not absolutely uniform, it is possible to conclude that when the political will of state and societal actors is present, international assistance has had a major impact on shaping the policies adopted, underwriting their initial success, and promoting their consolidation. The central challenge it presented, therefore, was not in determining whether the domestic or external environment was more decisive in promoting transition, but in conceptualizing their obvious, extensive, yet highly variable interdependence. The next section will further elaborate the requirements for a state and society to be open to inputs by external actors, and will then be followed by sections considering the actual policies pursued by outside actors toward the NIS; the impact of external policies; and finally a discussion of the extent to which our whole conceptualization of the difference between weak and strong states and societies is being transformed by the post-communist transition.

The Analytical Challenge

Whether acting as academic or policy maker, living in the West or the East, it is obvious that some states are more open to the outside world than others. But within this general category of openness it is possible to distinguish between three main axes—one of agency, one of permeability, and one of mutability.

The first analytical challenge is to identify *agency:* that is, drawing the distinction between elites and society as instruments of change, as cultural carriers. Marxist-Leninist ideology and Soviet political culture distinctly emphasized the mantra that without the leading and guiding role of the Communist Party, the working class of its own accord was capable of only trade union consciousness; in other words, societal groups and organizations left to their own devices would be unable to construct socialism and a "revolution from above" would be necessary. Upon this denial of agency was built a totalitarian state which eventually, under the protective legal cover of Article Six of the Soviet Constitution, made the party and the party alone the sole agent for legitimate action.

While the general conception is that these emerging political systems continue to be dominated by political elites, that populations are used to being led by the "vanguard party" and its agents of socialization, some interesting work done during the Gorbachev era, notably by Moshe Lewin, points to the existence of a mass-based political culture in the USSR that was more than just an empty vessel waiting to be filled by the political elites, and indeed suggests that Soviet society became a partner with Gorbachev and his circle in their assault on the communist bureaucracy.[1] Thus, this view maintains that popular preferences, perceptions, and expectations found in both late Soviet and post-Soviet society can be seen as a substantial driving force for change, fed largely in the early days of independence by the desire among the population to enjoy the same human, civil, and consumer rights and comforts as enjoyed by their Western counterparts. Nevertheless, even if Lewin's argument is accepted, it is clear that the vast differences in the processes of democratization in post-communist countries to a large degree are accounted for by the varied experiences of societal exclusion from involvement in social change. The differential legacy of this "sixism," in which elites were the sole legitimate agents of change, has impeded the emergence more generally of civil society and specifically of political parties capable of responding to voter signals and appealing to voters as a constituency, as a coequal agent for transformation. The first challenge therefore in identifying how open a new state is to transformation is to analyze the extent to which both the state (seen as including both the elites and the central institutions) and the society are active agents of change.

On the second axis of *permeability,* one extreme is occupied by states that may have extensive external relations, but whose leaders construct an isolationist worldview which allows them to seal off their countries to foreign encroachment. Clearly, political and economic autarky was the cornerstone of the communist system during Stalin's years until his successors pursued peaceful coexistence, détente, and an activist policy toward progressive and radical regimes outside the Soviet bloc. While all the new states that emerged after the collapse of the USSR rushed to open relations with the outside world, the legacy of autarky has been lasting. Among elites in the new states, some are motivated by a desire to turn inward. This is seen as particularly applicable in the case of contemporary Belarus, whose President Aliaksandr Lukashenka has sought to limit his country's interaction with the outside world largely in an effort to increase his own power and stifle democracy. Also in Russia, there is a trend among some communist and nationalist elites to blame foreign governments and international financial institutions for Russia's problems.[2]

Not just elites but also societies interact with the external environment—through the lens of imbedded values, norms, and culture, and via both intermediate and state institutions, all of which act to construct a defensive shield around the society, a glaces which defuses, deflects, distorts, or redefines incoming messages from the external environment. Still at this pole of impermeability, political culture itself, imbedded as it is in a society, also reveals in the post-Soviet states an anti-Western and isolationist current which, while not a majority opinion, nevertheless is a definite factor in most of the newly independent states. Consequently, this current resists the imbedding of exogenous influences within transitional societies.

In opposition on this axis is the belief in the essential permeability of all modern advanced industrial societies. The advances in global communications, the internationalization of culture, the sway of regional and international institutions, and the emergence of a global economy can all be seen as promoting the increased transparency of state boundaries. Thus, in the case of Russia, while acknowledging that there may be temporary setbacks, many would argue, as S. Frederick Starr did in his contribution to the ninth volume in this series, that Russia will not long be able to resist integration into the world community, an integration which inevitably will weaken the pull of totalitarian and imperial ideology.[3]

On a third axis is *mutability:* that is, the extent to which societies are capable of radical, abrupt departures from existing social and cultural norms, irrespective of the will of the elites or the desire of the international system. At the core of the issue of mutability is not whether revolutions can take place, since obviously they can and have, but whether they can be sustained in the face of the deadening weight of societal stasis and reaction. At one end of the spectrum is the conviction that the legacies of the past and the cultural, economic, and social fabric of an existing society are the primary conditioning factors in any, necessarily slow, process of transformation. In the former Soviet Union, therefore, just as the

Bolshevik Revolution was seen as eventually overwhelmed by the autocratic impulses of Russian political culture, so too is it believed that the political cultural resistance to any radically new democratization effort will be strong.[4] While the differing subcultures which existed in Central Asia, the Caucasus, Ukraine, and the Baltic states will undoubtedly affect the specific nature of any given polity, in essence this school of thought maintains that the tsarist Russian and Soviet political orientations toward authoritarianism, collectivism, welfarism, intolerance, and the tendency to see even democratically elected presidents as essentially "good tsars" will continue to dominate and shape post-Soviet processes and institutions in all the new states.[5] Thus, efforts at creating liberal institutions and instilling democratic values will be undermined by preexisting social, political, and economic forces; instead, these institutions are likely to be captured, eroded, distorted, and eventually destroyed.

At the other end of the spectrum from immutability is the idea that state institutions can be designed to shape preferences and constrain choices in ways that will create new political and economic values conducive to liberalization, thereby essentially allowing for a new democratic revolution from above. Of course, Western policy is preconditioned on the conviction that not only the state but also society can act as an agent of change. Drawing upon the tradition of Talcott Parsons[6] and other modernization theorists, this approach maintains that so-called traditional societies will undergo changes in their social structures, values, and cultures as they become more "developed" and "modern." Processes such as modernization, industrialization, urbanization, advances in communications technology, increased literacy and education, the guarantee of civil liberties, intergenerational change, and transnational forces help to create and consolidate a civil society that pressures the state from below for greater political participation. In this task, external forces are capable of playing a strong role in supporting and furthering liberalization processes through aid, their role as models, and incorporating states into the international economic order.

The analytical challenge then is to conceptualize the distinctions between these variables and to examine the multiple ways in which they can and have interacted to produce, or impede, change in the former Soviet Union. The three conceptions of mutability, permeability, and agency are represented in Figure 17.1, as applied to post-Soviet societies. Clearly, an elaboration of the figure with regard to each new state would quickly reveal differences, but the figure seeks to provide a general clarification of the analytical distinction between the three concepts. Subsequent sections will return to these concepts as they deal with the role of external environment, measuring progress in the transition, and the dilemma of building states in a region with a legacy of overweening state power.

The Impact of the International Environment

It is practically a nostrum of the literature on political culture, civil society, democratization, and indeed of comparative politics itself that societal change is

Figure 17.1 **Mutability, Permeability, and Agency**

		Agency	
		Elite	Society
Mutability	Mutable	Institutional design; revolution from above	Consumer revolution; communications technology
	Immutable	Tsarist tradition; communist heritage	Good tsar; mass psychology of communism
Permeability	Permeable	Elites act to implement external norms	Communications; international business contacts
	Impermeable	Elites act in self-interest, use the West for domestic gains	Society rejects Western civilization

generated almost exclusively by domestic forces, and that attempts by international actors to influence the trajectory of a country's movement are likely at most to be marginal in their impact. Yet it is undeniably the case that the foreign aid of all states involved in promoting democratization in post-communist countries is based on a contrary assumption, namely that the external world can make an extremely decisive impact on the course of change toward or away from democracy, toward or away from a free or mixed market economy. In the work on "democratization waves," recently most associated with Samuel Huntington's *The Third Wave,*[7] the argument is made that waves are produced when several states, typically but not necessarily within the same geographic region, move toward democracy together. It is posited that these waves occur because of the tendency of democracy to be contagious and to spread by diffusion. Also, democratization gains momentum with each wave because of learning, the expansion of modern means of mass communication, increased literacy, and the emergence of more nongovernmental organizations (NGOs) in existing democratic states that are committed to the spread of democracy internationally. Thus, like a snowball, democratization gathers momentum with each wave, so that while some democratizing states may break away and revert to authoritarianism, bringing the wave to an end, nevertheless, over time, the total number of democracies will increase. Clearly, contagion, diffusion, and snowballing take place not only because of the openness of elites and societies (dual agency) in any country to the events taking place beyond their borders (permeability), and their desire to change their own country in accord with international norms (mutability), but also because of the conscious actions and policies pursued by external actors in an effort to influence the direction of development in the recipient country.

The interaction between the internal and external environment is ongoing but takes place on many more levels and with more intensity if two conditions are present: namely, that the target country is permeable, mutable, and both the elites and society regard themselves as positive dual agents of change; and that the international community has imbedded democratization as a key governing norm for the international system as a whole. Thus, during the Cold War, the Soviet Union was resistant to change primarily because permeability, mutability, and dual agency were not a feature of the domestic environment; moreover the fact that the key governing norms of the international system during the height of the Cold War were security and containment, and not the spread of democracy, removed a significant international dimension for domestic transformation. But with the collapse of the Soviet order, and the emergence of societies as agents of change, these countries both became more open to the outside world and less of a threat to the international order, thereby allowing containment and certain international security considerations to recede and democratization goals to proceed to the forefront of the international system's governing norms.

The fact of democratization's international dimension has become increasingly recognized in the literature. As Philippe Schmitter himself subsequently stated: "One of the most confident assertions in the O'Donnell–Schmitter concluding volume to the Transitions from Authoritarian Rule project was that 'domestic factors play a predominant role in the transition.'[8] Not only does this fly in the face of a substantial . . . literature that stresses the dependence, interpenetration, and even integration increasingly embedded in the contemporary world system, but it also seems to clash with some obvious facts surrounding the more recent transitions that have occurred in Eastern Europe. . . . [I]t is time to reconsider the impact of the international context upon regime change."[9]

Schmitter proposes a very interesting fourfold categorization of the ways in which the international system operates to promote change in a regime. While the argument addresses democratization in particular, in fact these four modes could also apply more generally to international sources of domestic transition. They are control, contagion, conditionality, and consent, and they can be differentiated by reference on the one hand to the coercive or voluntary nature of the action (control and conditionality being more coercive—and backed by states—than contagion and consent—which tends to be supported in Schmitter's estimation by private actors) and on the other hand in Schmitter's version to the number of actors involved in any given action (unilateral or multilateral). The distinctions drawn among these four types of agency are a definite advance over previous conceptualizations, but the dichotomy between the state and private actors, on the one hand, and multilateral and bilateral linkages, on the other, is, we believe, not useful. Obviously, states can and do engage in a wide range of nonconditional, noncoercive activities (such as international broadcasting or the provision of humanitarian assistance), just as voluntary groups can condition their assistance on certain criteria in an effort to achieve changes in the social and political structure of the recipient country (whether a country allows or does

Figure 17.2 **External Agency and Domestic Transition**

Basis for Action				
	Coercive		Voluntary	
External agency	Control	Conditionality	Contagion	Consent
State-system level	Russian military and economic influence in NIS	IMF, STF, and standby agreements; PfP/ NATO; WTO; OSCE; bilateral security, political, economic interests	*Norms:* political, economic, military, environmental regimes; states as economic/ political models	*Membership:* IMF, World Bank, WTO, OSCE, PfP/ NATO, Council of Europe, bilateral trade
Substate level	Transnational ethnic and religious groups	Media freedom; legal reform; free market; environmental standards; religious freedom	Tourism; business exchanges; academic exchanges; religious tolerance; entrepreneurship; ethnic ties	NGO activity; business exchanges; academic exchanges; religious groups

not allow abortion, for example, or whether minorities or ethnic groups will have equal access to any aid distributed). Rather, as shown in Figure 17.2, it makes more sense to distinguish between state-system (both bilateral and multilateral state actions) and substate (both bilateral and multilateral societal-level interactions) levels which allows the analyst to focus on the full range of potential actions available to both levels and their differential impacts. It also facilitates visualizing the interaction between the variables in Figure 17.1 and those in Figure 17.2, which share between them a consideration of the role of agency.

There is a wide range of international actors that are capable of influencing processes in the former Soviet Union: (1) multilateral organizations such as the International Monetary Fund (IMF), World Bank, World Trade Organization (WTO), Asian Development Bank (ABD), European Bank for Reconstruction and Development (EBRD), North Atlantic Treaty Organization (NATO), and the Organization for Security and Cooperation in Europe (OSCE); (2) numerous nongovernmental organizations active in a wide range of issue areas; and (3) sovereign states such as the United States, Germany, and others in the European Union, Japan, China, Iran, and Turkey.

Any of these actors can engage in a wide range of coercive and voluntary actions. Both control and conditionality have elements of coercion intrinsic to them. The difference between the two requires elaboration and some distinction from the categories developed by Schmitter: in this more narrow definition, control involves only those set of cases where the external agency says to the domestic agency, "If you don't do X, then I will come in and do it or force you to do it." Control implies a diminution of sovereignty. Conditionality, on the other hand, includes those actions that can be captured within the statement: "If you don't do X, then I won't do Y."

Looking first at the state-system level, there are to date no examples of *control* in relations between the newly independent states and the outside world of the kind that was seen in the case of the Gulf War, when the international community told Iraq that if it did not restore Kuwait's sovereign status by withdrawing, then the international community would restore it by forcing Iraq out. Even in the case of the ethnic conflicts that have spilled across borders, as have occurred in Nagorno-Karabagh (involving Armenia and Azerbaijan), Tajikistan (involving Tajikistan, Uzbekistan, Kyrgyzstan, Russia, and Afghanistan), Ossetia (involving Russia and Georgia), and Abkhazia (also involving Russia and Georgia), the international community has not responded with any of the control mechanisms that were employed in an attempt to deal with the conflict in the former Yugoslavia: deployment of international contingents of peacekeepers, international sponsorship of peace agreements which obligated the parties to hold free and fair elections, or the use of the International Court of Justice at the Hague to identify and punish perpetrators of crimes against humanity. While peacekeeping observers from the Organization for Security and Cooperation in Europe are present in some NIS conflicts, none of the elements of control is present.

Still at the state-system level, if one examines relations not between the newly independent states and the outside world, but within the newly independent states, the situation is somewhat different. Russia as an external actor in Eurasia is in a position to exercise enormous control. Russian behavior in Tajikistan during the civil war in 1991–92 was one such example of control in which Russian troops stationed there were directly involved in aiding one group of elites to displace another. Similarly, when Chechen fighters fled to Azerbaijan, Russia warned Baku not to provide supplies and a safe haven to them. When Azerbaijan continued, Russia effectively sealed the border and imposed a blockade on Azerbaijan's border with Russia, powerfully demonstrating Moscow's ability to exercise control. Russia also used its relative economic and financial power to control events in other newly independent states, including in the direction of reform. In the summer of 1993, for example, when some of the other newly independent states refused to take fiscal measures to limit spending and control inflation, Russia announced a currency reform, which effectively forced these states to introduce their own stabilization programs and thereby reduce the inflationary pressure on Russia's own economy.

At the nonstate level, it is obviously very difficult for societal groups in the external environment to engage in activities designed to control the behavior of societal groups, much less states. Certain examples lend themselves to scrutiny, however: because of the greater transparency of borders, ethnic, and religious groups in the external environment are freer to help transform those NIS societies which are permeable and mutable but where the state is resistant. For example, in Uzbekistan, external Islamic organizations assisted in the establishment of religious schools sometimes against the wishes of state authorities. In Tajikistan, Iranian fundamentalist groups assisted in the establishment of the Islamic Renaissance Party before the victory of Russian-backed troops led to its banning. In Armenia, the nationalist Dashnak Party, which pressured the state to pursue a more militant line in support of Armenian compatriots in Nagorno-Karabagh, received significant support from like-minded groups in the Armenian diaspora. However, external groups did not control the event, but were able to exercise influence and provide these groups with direct support, sometimes against the wishes of the established government.

Turning to *conditionality,* Schmitter's identification of it as the most rapidly expanding subtext for the exercise of international influence is very appropriate. With the emergence of so many newly independent states, all of which highly value their sovereignty, the exercise of control is very difficult. Conditionality, however, allows the recipient to maintain independence, while accepting the prenegotiated consequences of failing to act in the way the donor expects. At the level of the international system, with its multilateral and international organizations and its individual states, interaction with the newly independent states has proceeded primarily via conditionality.

The newly independent states have actively sought membership in multilateral institutions such as the IMF, the World Bank, the WTO, the OSCE, and NATO's Partnership for Peace (PfP) program, and the material benefits to which membership within these institutions provides access. Perhaps the most important multilateral institutions active in the post-Soviet states have been the IMF and the World Bank. Most states joined the IMF and the World Bank by the end of 1992 (with Armenia and Tajikistan following in 1993 and Azerbaijan in 1994) and have received substantial assistance in macroeconomic stabilization and liberalization and in the building of market-friendly institutions. However, this assistance has been conditioned on the signing of Macroeconomic Stabilizing (Standby) Agreements and Structural Transformation (STF) Agreements with the IMF which set out the terms for the receipt of IMF credits. These terms have included liberalization of prices and economic activity, macroeconomic stabilization, national currency convertibility, privatization, structural reform, and debt management.

In addition to setting conditions for the receipt of assistance, another form of conditionality arises when international or multilateral organizations establish criteria for membership. Membership has the multiple effects of structuring state interactions, conditioning or constraining state behavior, as well as instilling the norms, standards, and behavior accepted by the international community. States seeking membership in the WTO, for example, must first demonstrate that their economies are operating on a free-market basis and that they are committed to open and unrestricted international trade, thereby reducing the ability of a member-state to use trade as a political weapon. The OSCE, which is made up of fifty-three Western European states, the United States, Canada, and the post-communist states, has established verification and enforcement procedures that oblige member-states to submit to a process of mediation (with admittedly only recommendatory powers) if the elected governments of member-states are overthrown.

Turning from multilateral to bilateral state interactions with the newly independent states, it is clear that a number of individual states have been extraordinarily involved and a number have set conditions, including the United States, Germany, Japan, China, Turkey, and Iran. All of them have attached conditions to their assistance, although those conditions are often structured very differently and are frequently at odds with each other. In the economic realm, as Gertrude Schroeder underlines in her chapter, the interaction between the newly independent states and the established market economies—via the technical aid, advice, and dialogue over economic institutions; the interaction and investment within the private and business sectors; and the learning that resulted from these processes—has been as important as the conditions set by state-to-state agreements in promoting change. Bilaterally, the overall conditions imposed by Western governments have been designed to bolster and reinforce multilateral conditions, although the American insistence that any purchases made with aid dollars be made from American manufacturers, and German insistence that aid monies be spent on building housing for redeployed Red Army troops (discussed more broadly in the chapters by Peter Dombrowski and Angela Stent) so as to speed their withdrawal from Germany are two examples of the interaction between the donors' interests in NIS transition and the role of domestic considerations in shaping specific donor policies.

In particular, states have a greater tendency than multilateral agencies to set noneconomic conditions to their aid: for example, American aid to Russia became bound up in concerns that Russia would undermine U.S. positions on Bosnia, the Middle East, arms sales, or NATO enlargement. By so doing, the long-term goal of democratic and economic transition can be jeopardized, as the chapters by Raymond L. Garthoff and Alvin Z. Rubinstein both stressed, by short-term considerations of realpolitik. Japan is the only other state which has had an extensive interest in developing relations with the newly independent states and which has used conditionality; here, however, Japan has shown itself less interested in transition than in the return of the disputed Northern Islands. Although Japan has participated in the development of small-scale local investment projects in Sakhalin and the Maritime Provinces, as Gilbert Rozman showed in his chapter, extensive economic involvement and sustained large-scale investment and aid aimed at Russia has been handicapped by the Northern Islands issue and is conditional upon the resolution of this political dispute.

At the nonstate level, it is clear that nongovernmental organizations (some of which can themselves be international in scope) in general have not set universal and tightly structured conditions of the kind imposed by the multilateral organizations. In addition, the breadth of the agenda across which NGOs act makes it unlikely that strict conditionality would succeed across societal subsectors as diverse as rule of law, institutional development, economic reform, religious revivalism, humanitarian assistance, health care, environmental activism, free press development, educational reform, and so on. Nevertheless, individual groups lend support which in fact is highly conditional: religious organizations, including Catholics, Jews, Protestants, and Muslims, have established community centers and religious schools on the condition that local authorities guarantee their right to operate freely. Because so many NGOs in the West are subcontractors implementing World Bank, European, or American government-funded programs, in fact the same conditions set at the state-system level often operate at the societal level: no NGO receiving money from Western sources, for example, is going to establish links with groups in the newly independent states that reject an opening to the West and favor a return to a centrally planned economy. Such a state of "trickle down conditionality" has the potential for accelerating the speed with which those newly independent states and societies committed to openness, permeability, and mutability can reach their own transition objectives.

Turning from the coercive actions (control and conditionality) to the voluntary behavior of external agencies, we find that these are divided into two subcategories: contagion and consent. Recapping Schmitter, contagion is the "diffusion of experience through neutral, i.e. non-coercive and often unintentional, channels from one country to another,"[10] while consent is "a complex set of interactions between international processes and domestic groups that generates new democratic norms and expectations from below."[11] It is clearly the case that a single action can contain within it elements of both coercion and voluntarism. Thus, international institutions that make commitment to democracy a condition of membership nevertheless are joined voluntarily and without redress by applicants.

Contagion, involving the diffusion of experience, typically produces the unintentional transmission of values, standards, and behaviors, and is greatly facilitated not only by proximity, mutual exchange, and participation, but also by societal permeability and mutability. At the level of the international system, participation in multilateral organizations helps to anchor these states and to instill international norms, principles, and behaviors. For example, membership within the IMF and World Bank has generated acceptance of market principles and institutional reform. Accession to OSCE has promoted the spreading of international mediation as a norm in conflict management.

Turning to bilateral state interactions, it is clear that a number of states have influenced the political-economic processes via demonstration effect. It is obviously the case that a primary reason for the very collapse of the Soviet system was the widespread wish to emulate the lifestyles and gain the democratic freedoms prevalent in Western countries. This attraction led, at the state level, to the adoption of French, Swedish, German, and U.S. institutional designs as models by various newly independent states.

If the Western model is so contagious, why haven't Western democratic practices become more widespread? Part of the reason rests with higher than expected resistance within these states to translating institutional design into practice, of which more is dealt with below, and part of the reason rests with the fact that the West is not the only model available to these states. Certainly not all competitors to the West will necessarily contribute to a favorable political-economic transformation and acceptance of international norms. Turkey has been active in Central Asia and the Caucasus. Its commitment to a Turkic national identity has contributed to a developing sense of nationness among the states in this region, but Turkey's own internal debate about its identity as a multiethnic, secular, democratic, and Westward-oriented country casts into doubt the extent to which it exerts a positive influence in the region. Due to its proximity, Islamic ties, and Persian language, Iran is able to compete not only with the West but also with Turkey as a rival model in the Central Asian and Caucasus region, even though the narrow reach of the Persian connection (the Persian language is shared only with ethnic Tajiks), Iran's hostility toward Azeri nationalism within its own borders, and the increasingly secular, West-ward orientation of the Central Asian states have all worked to limit Iran's appeal. Other potential influences are newly industrializing countries (NICs) like South Korea, Singapore, Taiwan, and China. These states offer examples of dramatic economic development based on authoritarianism, a mode that may be attractive to elites more interested in economic growth than political reform. Lastly, Russia also must be considered an external actor whose own experience is widely disseminated via the continuing influence of Russian television, ongoing contacts among Russophone elites, and institutional links within the context of the Commonwealth of Independent States. Multiple channels also allow multiple messages, however, so that those newly independent states interested in reform can draw succor from the success of privatization in Russia while strong rulers in Belarus, Central Asia, and Azerbaijan are able to look to a revived Russian state to legitimize their own authoritarianism and resist substantial reform in their own states.

At the substate level, exchanges and interaction between NGOs, tourists, students, businessmen, scientists, religious groups, political parties, and official government representatives have the primary effect of generating learning, understanding, and the transferral of values in many diverse areas, like environmental norms, entrepreneurial mind-sets, legal practices, and so on. Such exchanges fulfill the dual function of promoting nonascribed identities and civil awareness within these countries and at the same time weakening the mobilizational potential of narrow nationalism by providing a tangible benefit to international contacts.

Turning lastly to *consent*, the post-Soviet states have lined up to join such state-level multilateral institutions as the IMF, World Bank, WTO, OSCE, Council of Europe, and NATO's Partnership for Peace program. To some extent this is indicative of self-interest among these states, but is also an indication of their willingness to participate in organizations that increase transparency and permeability. It is obviously the case that many states (not only the newly independent states) participate in many international organizations without any real intention of complying with their norms—that is, consent without contagion. Russia, for example, is an active member of the Helsinki Commission, the Baltic Sea littoral environmental regime, and is an active participant in its meetings; but more than the other NIS participants, Russia has not been in compliance with environmental standards set by the commission. Yet the objective of international organizations like Helcom is to create an environment in which, over time, compliance is achieved via contagion.[12] The task of international actors, then, is to incorporate the newly independent states in international networks and generate incentives that will reinforce consent and adherence to international norms.

In terms of bilateral state interaction, the NIS have also made conscious choices to develop political and economic relations with the United States, Europe, South Korea, China, and numerous other states outside the former Soviet Union. Thus, for example, the average share of each new state's trade with the other new states (interrepublic trade) declined 25 percent between 1991 and 1994. This compares well with an average decline of roughly 50 percent for the Central European states for the same period, with the Baltic states slightly outperforming the Central Europeans in terms of reorientation.[13]

The substate level of interaction may be the most important determining factor in the ability of external actors to influence the transformations that are under way. Though there are conditional aspects to the international and transnational linkages between nonstate actors, these are predominantly voluntary interactive relationships. NGOs, religious groups, political parties, and individuals such as businessmen, students, scientists, and official representatives of foreign governments offer advice, information, and programs on such reform issues as electoral reform, legislative rules and procedures, political party development, legal reform, entrepreneurship, environmental standards, and humanitarian assistance. A further example of consensual change can be seen in the increasing numbers of students from the newly independent states who study such topics as journalism, business, and law in Western academic institutions or in Western-sponsored programs in their own universities. The transferral of international norms at the subnational level is a fundamental mechanism to create compliance within these states because, if exchange were limited only to the state-system level, it is likely that institutions would be created that would not be supported by the population. As norms become fundamentally accepted at the subnational level, the ability of societies to act as agents, as interest groups that form the foundation of Western democracies, increases as well.

Assessing Impact

In the introduction to this volume, George W. Breslauer was quite right to focus attention on the fact that in assessing the influence of external variables, "the 'dependent variable' (that which is being influenced) is bound to vary greatly among the states.... Hence, the first question to ask about the impact of the outside world is: 'Impact on what?' " This section seeks to tie together the previous consideration of the activities of external actors with an assessment of their differential impact across the economic, political, and social realms in the various countries. Judging success is easier in some areas than others. Aggregate data on inflation rates, for example, can be set alongside data about the introduction of externally conditioned economic measures, and a strong argument can be built about the correlation between IMF-imposed conditionality and the quickness of economic transition. In the political and social realm, it is more difficult to establish the causal relationship between an external policy and an internal impact, particularly as regards long-term political and societal transformation. Nevertheless, keeping in mind the issues raised about permeability, mutability, and agency (Figure 17.1) as affecting the receptivity of any polity toward external influence and underlining that this influence, whether exercised by control, conditionality, contagion, or consent (Figure 17.2), comes not only from state but also from nonstate actors, it is possible to at least make some broad observations about associations, while necessarily remaining cautious about overdrawing conclusions.

Economic Conditions

The post-Soviet states face a complex set of problems and obstacles derived from the centrally planned economic system of the former Soviet Union: (1) economies isolated from the outside world and oriented toward the military-industrial complex and inefficient forms of agriculture; (2) specialized economies which served the functionally specific needs of the central Soviet state and lacked diversity; (3) technologically backward capital equipment and labor intensive industries; (4) subsidized enterprises and populations protected by a paternalistic state from economic insecurity and competition; (5) near universal state ownership of property; (6) an absence of market-based financial accounting or regulatory principles; and (7) an entrenched and corrupt state and party bureaucracy which enjoyed the benefits of controlling the economy without having to run any of the risks of ownership. As a result, a large number of economic problems had emerged, including hidden inflation, huge budget deficits, declining production, distorted prices, large foreign debts, and consumer shortages.

Since the collapse of the system, Western states and international organizations have consistently emphasized that the best way to overcome these problems is to introduce a market economy using a mix of policies aimed at stabilization, liberalization, and privatization of the economy. Stabilization involves the creation of credible, convertible currencies. Privatization involves the transfer into the private sector of all or nearly all state property, including enterprises, housing, and land. Liberalization entails the introduction of measures that free prices and lift restrictions on economic activity and foreign trade. And as Gertrude Schroeder, Bartlomiej Kaminski, Anders Åslund, and others have argued in this volume, in the eighth volume of the Russian Littoral Project series, and elsewhere, the rewards in terms of the revival of growth, investment, and foreign trade have come soonest to those countries that have quickly implemented a uniform package of stabilization, privatization, and liberalization measures—so-called shock therapy.[14]

According to data presented in this volume, all fifteen successor states have made considerable progress toward market economy reforms over the last five years despite being overburdened by economic, political, and social crises. The progress has not been uniform across the region by any means, however. The Baltic states and then Russia have remained the most advanced reformers. This progress, however, does not mean that the transition is complete or that these reforms will necessarily be sustained and consolidated over time. There is still much to be done in the area of privatization, especially in Belarus, Moldova, Ukraine, and the Central Asian republics. In addition, these countries still lag behind in terms of consolidating a second generation of reforms focusing on financial, accounting, and pension systems, public finances, and the paternalistic legacy left by the former Soviet Union. Though private commercial banks and exchanges have expanded in Russia and the Baltics, many are precariously weak and fragile. Throughout the newly independent states, states have been slow to improve prudential controls and bank supervision and as a result the banking sector has continued to lack public trust.

Every post-Soviet state has had difficulty in the *stabilization* of its economy and has suffered hyperinflation. After the initial wave of price liberalization in 1992, inflation rates skyrocketed to levels near or over 1,000 percent in ten of the fifteen new states (as indicated in Table 17.1). The Baltic states and Moldova did manage to reduce their inflation rates dramatically starting in 1993, followed by Kyrgyzstan, Russia, Uzbekistan, and Ukraine in 1994, but the other post-Soviet states—specifically Armenia, Azerbaijan, Belarus, and Kazakhstan—continued to suffer four-digit inflation rates. Tajikistan and Turkmenistan continued to suffer from inflation in excess of 300 percent per annum in 1995. The reasons for this hyperinflation in all these countries rested largely in the slowness in freeing prices, irresponsible fiscal policies, budget deficits, and continued subsidization of unproductive state enterprises. Additionally, ethnic conflicts and civil strife in Armenia, Azerbaijan, Georgia, Moldova, Russia, and Tajikistan exacerbated the difficulty of bringing the economy under control. By the end of 1996, however, virtually every state had achieved a remarkable turnaround and had made spectacular progress in stabilizing inflation rates. Except for Tajikistan,

Table 17.1

Annual Inflation Rates in Russia and the Newly Independent States, 1991–95

State	1991	1992	1993	1994	1995
Armenia	274	828	1,450	15,555	28.8
Azerbaijan	105	1,174	1,080	1,742	66.0
Belarus	94	970	1,192	2,583	138.0
Estonia	210	1,069	85	50	25.2
Georgia	N/A	N/A	N/A	N/A	31.2
Kazakhstan	91	1,162	1,659	2,310	48.0
Kyrgyzstan	82	1,555	1,208	315	27.6
Latvia	172	958	100	38	21.6
Lithuania	224	1,162	400	59	37.6
Moldova	90	1,255	788	331	21.6
Russia	152	1,350	930	218	87.6
Tajikistan	N/A	N/A	N/A	N/A	381.6
Turkmenistan	N/A	N/A	N/A	N/A	304.8
Ukraine	91	1,445	6,288	850	109.2
Uzbekistan	105	530	880	792	82.8

Source: World Bank data as presented in Daniel Kaufmann, "Reforms, Lack Thereof and Economic Dynamics in the Transition from Plan to Market in the FSU," unpublished statistical tables compiled by the author and distributed at the Wintergreen conference, June 1996.

Turkmenistan, Belarus, and Ukraine, every other state had lowered their inflation rates to below 100 percent in 1995, with ten of the fifteen new states lowering their inflation rates further to approximately 3 percent per month in 1996.

Privatization has met with mixed results. Whereas states like Armenia, Estonia, Latvia, Lithuania, and Russia have made substantial progress especially in privatizing small-scale state firms, privatization of large state enterprises remains slow throughout the region. The predominant problem is foot-dragging by entrenched bureaucracies and industrial interests who continue to pressure governments for subsidies and security from economic competition. Privatization of firms has made especially little headway in Azerbaijan, Belarus, and Georgia, and is virtually nonexistent in the Central Asia republics.

On the question of privatizing state housing, the picture is somewhat brighter, particularly in Armenia, Georgia, Lithuania, Moldova, and, to some extent, Russia (where one-third of the eligible housing has been privatized). However, housing reform remains slow in Latvia, Ukraine, and Belarus, and severely limited in Azerbaijan and Central Asia.[15]

The third aspect of privatization involves the privatization of agricultural land and the break up of the huge state and collective farms. Considerable progress has been made in Armenia, Lithuania, Latvia, and Russia (where 66 percent of targeted agricultural land has been privatized); however, it has been slowed in

Estonia because of restitution issues. Land reform has also been limited in Azerbaijan, Belarus, Moldova, Ukraine, and the Central Asian states.

The most successful aspect of economic transformation has been the *liberalization* of prices and economic activity. Russia decontrolled prices for most goods and services other than oil, natural gas, and energy sources in 1992 with every other state following suit between 1992 and 1994. The cumulative liberalization index (CLI) constructed by the World Bank and discussed by Kaminski and Zhen in chapter 12 measures the progress achieved in dismantling central planning by taking the duration and intensity of reforms into account. Using the CLI, it is clear that as of mid-1996 the countries which have experienced the most progress in liberalization were, in descending order, the Baltics, Russia, Kyrgyzstan, Moldova, Armenia, Georgia, Kazakhstan, Uzbekistan, Belarus, Azerbaijan, Tajikistan, Ukraine, and Turkmenistan. When judging how far these economies have gone in comparison with the Central European post-communist states, only Romania and Albania scored worse on the CLI than any of the NIS states: in other words, only the Baltic states scored better than any of the Central European states (Albania and Romania) in the liberalization of the economy in the first three years of the transition.

This assessment of positive advances in the liberalization of economic activity is reinforced when analyzing the levels of government expenditures as a percentage of gross domestic product (GDP). Throughout the region, government and public expenditures as a percentage of GDP declined, indicating an increasing market orientation. As seen in Figure 17.3, the level of government expenditures as a percentage of GDP decreased in Russia from 65 percent in 1992 to 45 percent in 1994; the Baltics decreased from 35 percent in 1992 to 32 percent in 1994; and Kazakhstan decreased from 32 percent in 1992 to 25 percent in 1994. Ukraine presents a more negative picture, with government expenditures as a percentage of GDP only marginally declining from 55 percent in 1992 but remaining high at 52 percent in 1994.[16] Spending priorities also shifted between categories depending on the level of commitment to economic transitions. As presented in Figure 17.3, state subsidies to enterprises, industry, agriculture, construction, and consumers declined in the Baltics, Kazakhstan, and Russia. Ukraine, on the other hand, actually increased its level of subsidies (up to 17 percent of GDP).

In addressing the impact of external actors in achieving the economic transition that has taken place, it is arguable that the ability to measure many of these variables more or less accurately gives social scientists a unique opportunity to assess the causal relationship between external policies and domestic transition. Indeed, the work that has been done does suggest a positive correlation between aid disbursements and progress in transition. Specifically, the data presented by Kaminski and Zhen (in Figure 12.1) showed a positive correlation between World Bank/IMF disbursements and the CLI over time, operating for all post-communist states. It is reasonable to assume that all aid disbursements might

Figure 17.3 **Government Expenditure by Category in Selected Transition Economies**

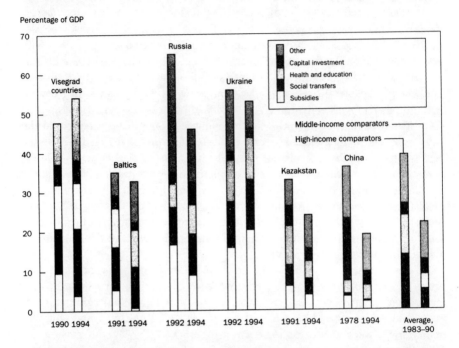

Source: World Bank, *From Plan to Market: World Development Report 1996* (Washington, DC: World Bank, 1996), p. 116.

Note: Data include central and local government plus extrabudgetary expenditures (quasi-fiscal and state enterprise expenditures are excluded). Visegrad countries are Poland, Czech Republic, and Hungary. Baltics are Latvia, Lithuania, and Estonia. For the high-income comparators (Australia, Canada, Germany, Israel, Luxembourg, United Kingdom, and United States) and the middle-income comparators (Argentina, Chile, Malaysia, Panama, Republic of Korea, Swaziland, Turkey, and Zimbabwe), data are weighted averages, and the bottom segment represents subsidies plus social transfers.

have a similar effect, but clearly this would only be the case if the conditions for transforming the economy imposed by the IMF are used by all aid donors. This is not always the case, since some aid donors like China, Iran, and Turkey conceivably have different objectives in Eurasia than the West on some issues, and even Western donors relax conditionality under certain circumstances. Thus, Armenia was not subject to the same stabilization and liberalization criteria to receive its aid (by far the largest per capita of the newly independent states) because its supporters abroad were able to make the case that urgent aid was needed to support the nation's very existence in a time of war and crisis (Azerbaijan, Georgia, and Tajikistan, nations also subject to civil and ethnic conflict, were not, however, similarly favored by international organizations).

Equally, because the international community wanted to support Boris Yeltsin's reelection bid against the Communists in the 1996 elections, the IMF released in March 1996 a SDR 6.9 billion (equivalent to over $10 billion) extended fund facility arrangement for Russia (the largest EFF in IMF history), even though Russia had not lived up to the agreement to increase state capacity and revenue collection capability. Yet few would argue with the contention that macroeconomic stabilization is a lesser goal than the very survival of a fledgling democracy: indeed, the IMF's own executive board's guidelines on conditionality stress that "the IMF pay due regard to members' domestic social and political objectives, as well as economic priorities and circumstances; and permit flexibility in determining the number and content of performance criteria."[17] Arguably, therefore, the correlation between disbursements and CLI might be even stronger in the short-term if it were not for the willingness of international organizations and nation-states to forgive, relax, ignore, or renegotiate conditions for the purpose of achieving noneconomic aims, the subject of discussion below.

Political Conditions

A crucial measure of progress toward democratization emphasized in the transition literature is Samuel P. Huntington's "two-turnover test." A political elite or party loses an election and peacefully surrenders power to an opposition group. The new group in power then loses a successive election and also surrenders power peacefully.[18] This willingness by two separate groups of elites to transfer power indicates the commitment of elites to democratic norms and processes.

The focus on turnover is not an entirely adequate measure of progress, however, because while there has been enormous progress in institutional development, in some cases there has been little real turnover in the political leadership. Throughout the former Soviet Union, top communists and communist-era functionaries continue to remain in power and hold important positions. The Russian, Ukrainian, and Belarusian parliaments have been dominated by Communists and revived communist parties throughout the transition period. Presidents Gaidar Aliev of Azerbaijan, Nursultan Nazarbaev of Kazakhstan, Saparmurad Niiazov of Turkmenistan, and Islam Karimov of Uzbekistan were all first secretaries of their respective republican Communist parties; Eduard Shevardnadze of Georgia was his republic's KGB chief; and Emomali Rakhmonov of Tajikistan was speaker of parliament and a Central Committee member. All remain the dominant force in their countries today. In Lithuania, the 1992 parliamentary elections returned the Lithuanian Communist Party—now reformed, transformed, and re-named the Lithuanian Democratic Labor Party (LDDP)—to power under the leadership of former party secretary Algirdas Brazauskas, who was later elected president in February 1993. A similar trend occurred in Moldova, where former communists have also been able to resurrect themselves: Andrei Sangheli, former Central Committee secretary of the CPSU, was elected president; Petru

Lucinschi, a former first secretary of the Central Committee of the Moldavian Communist Party and member of the Politburo Central Committee of the CPSU, became the chairman of the Moldovan parliament; and the communist-successor Democratic Agrarian Party won a majority of seats in the 1994 parliamentary elections.

These states then have made little progress in replacing old elites with new ones. Former party functionaries continue to dominate both the economic and political spheres. However, this begs two essential questions: first, does it really matter if Communists remain in, or return to, power? Second, how should external actors react to this pattern?

In addressing the first question, it must be understood that all communists cannot be classified together in one group, that there are gradations and variations among the communist parties in the post-Soviet states. Yet many of the communist parties and former Communist elites in these countries—highlighted by Russia, Ukraine, and Belarus—are indeed opposed to extensive reform and do present a significant danger of authoritarian retrenchment of various stripes. In Russia, the array of successor communist parties range from proponents of neo-Stalinism to the arguably semireformed Communist Party of the Russian Federation. Former communist elites like Lukashenka, Aliev, Niiazov, and Karimov have shown themselves to be resistant to democratic reform, but they are not necessarily communists. Rather, they threaten democratization because of their inclination to mix national populism with authoritarian styles that have been inherited from the Soviet political culture.

On the other hand, the communist comebacks in Lithuania and Moldova have been made by transformed communist parties similar to those in Eastern Europe. The Lithuanian Democratic Labor Party and the Moldovan Democratic Agrarian Party have recognized the importance and necessity of reform. Even Nazarbaev, despite his regression towards presidential rule, cannot be considered a recalcitrant communist hard-liner. These experiences indicate the ability of these elites and political parties to internalize democratic values.

How then should the international environment react to communist rule? A return of communism in Russia or other post-Soviet states will likely transform their images in the psychological mind-set of international actors, reducing the willingness of these actors to extend aid. International actors would then have the choice of either becoming more engaged in attempts to transform the psychological environment in these states or risk reinforcing the existing one by not acting.

Thus, strictly adhering to Huntington's "two-turnover test" as a measure of progress and focusing on the staying power of the old elite and communist nomenclature miss a crucial aspect of the transformation. Whereas these states have not had a dual turnover, what is more crucial to the democratization process and must not be overlooked when measuring progress is the guarantee of contested multiparty parliamentary and presidential elections. For example, Lithuania has had two sets of parliamentary elections (October 1991 and October 1993, with a third set in October 1996) which have resulted in transferrals of power from the Communist Party to Sajudis and back to the reformed Communist Party. Russia, despite the tense conditions and inability of certain radical political parties to participate in the December 1993 parliamentary elections, has had two sets of parliamentary elections and one presidential election since the collapse of the USSR. Armenia, Belarus, Estonia, Georgia, Kazakhstan, Kyrgyzstan, Latvia, and Ukraine also have evolving multiparty systems even if some do face political pressures from the regimes in power. Other states have a much worse record: Turkmenistan's Niiazov has refused official recognition of opposition parties; Uzbekistan's Karimov has openly repressed political opponents, especially since 1992; and Tajikistan has banned opposition political parties. It is possible then to see a significant variation developing among the newly independent states, with the Baltic states at one end of the spectrum and Turkmenistan and Tajikistan at the other.

A fundamental dimension of the democratic transformations has also been defining institutional power relationships between branches of government. Virtually every post-Soviet state has experienced struggles between the executive and legislative institutions for political dominance. With few exceptions, the political style prevalent in these countries is presidentialism and bureaucratism. Aliev, Lukashenka, Nazarbaev, Niiazov, and Islamov are powerful, dominant presidents who have little tolerance for parliamentary opposition, rendering them largely rubber stamp institutions.

This is not to say, however, that parliaments do not matter. Though presidentialism is the rule in post-Soviet politics, Russian president Boris Yeltsin would not have turned tanks on the parliament in October 1993 if the Duma had not mattered. Parliaments and presidents in Russia, Ukraine, Belarus, Georgia, and Moldova often coexist in a state of "dual legitimacy." These parliaments retain some semblance of legitimacy and represent a venue for elected political elites, political movements, and parties which possess their own constituencies and social bases. Until constitutionally defined systems of normal checks and balances characteristic of Western democracies replace the tenuous presidential-parliamentary power struggles, the tendencies toward strong, semiauthoritarian presidential rule will continue.

The key is to put in place constitutions and institutions such as independent judiciaries that are capable of sustaining the rule of law. Constitutions, constitutionalism, and the rule of law are vital to the democratization process in that they define institutional power relationships, provide accountability, buttress multiparty systems, and guarantee civil rights and freedoms—thus mitigating the potential for authoritarian-minded presidencies. Every post-Soviet state has ratified a new constitution (see Table 17.2). These are indeed often imperfect documents and are sometimes vehicles put in place to justify strong presidential rule; however, their value lies in the symbolic break from the Soviet past and the standards which they provide.

Table 17.2

Ratified Post-Communist Constitutions

State	Date of Constitution's Adoption
Armenia	July 1995
Azerbaijan	August 1991
Belarus	March 1994
Estonia	June 1992
Georgia	February 1996
Kazakhstan	January 1993
Kyrgyzstan	May 1993
Latvia	February 1992
Lithuania	October 1992
Moldova	August 1994
Russia	December 1993
Tajikistan	November 1994
Turkmenistan	May 1992
Ukraine	June 1996
Uzbekistan	December 1992

Legal reform, as Robert Sharlet points out in his chapter, has been problematic in the post-Soviet states. The most obvious reason is that reform priorities within these new states have focused on economic, not institutional, reform. Reforms focusing on court systems, legal processes, civil liberties, and criminal codes have been slow to materialize, often leaving Soviet-era criminal codes still in place and inoperable. Ironically, the legal framework that could sustain and support economic reform is weak, exacerbating such problems as corruption and crime. International assistance aimed at legal reform has correspondingly had a limited impact despite a large number of nongovernmental organizations active in promoting law reform. These NGOs have suffered from the same basic problems that other external actors have faced—the lack of background knowledge of local histories, languages, and cultures. The key problem, though, as mentioned above, is that aid has followed domestic reform priorities, meaning that legal reform assistance has gone more toward sustaining economic transformation.

Social Conditions: Mass-Based Support for Democracy

Most transitions are "revolutions from above" in that political elites are the initiators of reform processes and their acceptance of democratic norms is vital for the sustainability of reform. Thus, there is a strong emphasis on the role of elites in the transition process. The new sets of norms and institutions accompanying "revolutions from above," however, must take root in a receptive society and its political culture. The question is whether the post-Soviet political cultures are both malleable and permeable to outside influences. There are fundamental differences among these societies, but they do suffer from a common condition; they are largely hybrids that mix democratic procedures, norms, institutions, and values with residues of both the pre-Leninist and Leninist political cultures.[19]

There are a large number of studies that have attempted to gauge the level of widespread, mass-based support for democratic institutions and values in the post-Soviet states. Focusing on Russia, Ukraine, and the Baltics, they indicate significant levels of support for majority rights, independent and pluralistic media protected by the law, competitive elections, multiparty systems, participation, and the protection of civil liberties and political freedoms.[20] If these trends were to continue, then this would be a good indication of the essential permeability and malleability of these societies.

Many studies, however, question the level and depth of support for democratic values. Whereas there has been widespread abstract support for the process and goals of democratization, there has also been a tendency to hold democracy responsible for falling living standards and failing institutions. Poor economic performance has resulted in unemployment, the collapse of the social safety net, increased labor migration and social dislocation, impoverishment of all but a narrow band of nouveau riche, corruption, crime, and a generalized exacerbation of social, class, and ethnic tensions—conditions that some in these societies have tended to equate with democracy. Apathy and disillusionment has already resulted in growing disenchantment with institutions in Russia.[21] The worst-case scenario drawn from this condition would then be the reemergence of orientations supportive of semiauthoritarian solutions that emphasize law and order which would indeed endanger the democratic transformations.

These societies are also characterized by questionable levels of tolerance toward minorities and expressions of difference. For democracy to develop, societies must be open to free expression and activism even by groups that articulate radically different viewpoints. According to James Gibson, a range of 24 to 43 percent of respondents in Russia and Ukraine thought that free speech should be curtailed if it becomes disruptive, threatening, extremist, or even just different. Furthermore, 65 to 85 percent of respondents felt that disliked groups should be banned or silenced.[22]

Post-Soviet elites have shown similar tendencies in their efforts at nation building. Citizenship and language laws giving preference to native Estonians threaten to alienate the Russian minority population. Policies designed to build an ethnocentric Georgian nation-state are partially responsible for the interethnic conflicts between Georgians and both Abkhazians and South Ossetians. Both of these are examples of what Dominique Arel identifies as the "nationalizing temptation," in which post-Soviet elites seek to build a unitary national community based on narrow ethnic terms rather than broad, inclusive terms.[23]

Liberalizing trends seem weakest in Central Asia and the Caucasus. Civil societies are weak and fragile in the face of authoritarian elites who have consolidated their authority and limit pluralism and political party development. Liberalized political activity based on party-based systems and recognition of the importance of pluralist media and intermediate organizations does exist in Kazakhstan, Kyrgyzstan, Armenia, and Georgia; however, the political cultures of these societies in general have not been characterized from the outset by responsive, accountable institutions or open public discourse. The societies in Central Asia and the Caucasus were traditional societies at the time the Bolsheviks took over and were characterized as heavily influenced by considerations of fealty to custom, clan, religion, ethnicity, and family. What the Bolsheviks achieved in these societies was the forced tying of these traditions to a centralizing and modernizing state. Once this was achieved, of course, these traditions were distorted, repressed, or destroyed altogether. Thus, post-Soviet states in Central Asia and the Caucasus and to a lesser extent elsewhere, rather than struggling to exist in a milieu of strong societies, actually find themselves capable of acting as active agents in either the reconstruction of pluralistic societies or in the resuppression of societal agency. Whereas political power has always involved balancing ties between a single ruler and other social groups, Central Asian societies have had structures emphasizing state control and the supremacy of the elite class. This is a hybrid of the variant seen in postcolonial Third World countries, where to use Joel Migdal's very interesting analysis, strong societies effectively stymied the ability of weak states to gain control.[24] In the newly independent states, these societies had been destroyed or deformed by the imposition of Soviet rule, so that the temptation at first flush of independence was to try to rediscover and remythologize ancient and broken traditions, sometimes in quite deformed ways.[25] Nowhere except in the Baltics and western Ukraine did weak post-Soviet states confront strong societies. Without exception, including the Baltic states, all societies were demoralized, distorted, and infected by the Soviet experience; and none of these societies has been in a position to cast off the Soviet legacy without a period of significant recovery and strengthening.[26]

Overall, we must be cautious in our evaluations of the progress of assimilating democratic norms. The widespread economic problems associated with the transition that have prompted a yearning for order and stability and have weakened the appeal of democratic political forces should not necessarily be mistaken as a mentality hostile to democracy. At the same time, the visible support for liberal democratic principles cannot presume their sustainability. It is here that external interactions, including intersocietal support directly funded by states and massively increased interactions resulting from border transparency (tourism, broadcasting, cultural exchange, etc.) have the potential to act as a contagion by facilitating social learning and instilling such norms as the rule of law, free speech, and tolerance.

The central argument here has been that internal and external agency are of equal and vital importance in the transformation that is under way in the successor states of the Soviet Union. Serious reform cannot succeed without a commitment both by domestic governments and by societies that are open and permeable. External actors do play a significant role in supporting and furthering reform, and that role proceeds not only by setting conditions, but also by engaging in dialogue, gaining voluntary consent to change, and by acting as a model.

Notes

1. Moshe Lewin, *The Gorbachev Phenomenon: An Historical Interpretation* (Berkeley: University of California Press, 1991).

2. This argument is made by Yitzhak Brudny in his chapter in this volume. Also see Stephen White, Richard Rose, and Ian McAllister, *How Russia Votes* (Chatham, NJ: Chatham House Publishers, 1996), chap. 12.

3. S. Frederick Starr, "The Fate of Empire in Post-Tsarist Russia and in the Post-Soviet Era," in *The End of Empire? The Transformation of the USSR in Comparative Perspective,* ed. Karen Dawisha and Bruce Parrott (Armonk, NY: M.E. Sharpe, 1996).

4. Richard Pipes, "Imperial Russian Foreign Policy," *Times Literary Supplement,* no. 4755 (20 May 1994): pp. 3–5; Peter Reddaway, "The Role of Popular Discontent," *National Interest* 31 (Spring 1993): pp. 57–63; Peter Reddaway, "Russia on the Brink," *New York Review of Books* 40, no. 3 (28 January 1993): pp. 30–36; and Peter Reddaway, "Yeltsin and Russia: Two Views," *New York Review of Books* 40, no. 8 (22 April 1993): pp. 16–19.

5. Stephen White, "The USSR: Patterns of Autocracy and Industrialism," in *Political Culture and Political Change in Communist Societies,* ed. Archie Brown and Jack Gray (London: MacMillan Press, 1979).

6. Talcott Parsons, "Evolutionary Universals in Society," *American Sociological Review* 29 (June 1964): pp. 338–57.

7. Samuel Huntington, *The Third Wave: Democratization in the Twentieth Century,* (Norman: University of Oklahoma Press, 1991). Also see Geoffrey Pridham, ed., *Encouraging Democracy: The International Context of Regime Change in Southern Europe* (Leicester, UK: Leicester University Press, 1991).

8. Guillermo O'Donnell and Philippe C. Schmitter, *Transitions from Authoritarian Rule: Tentative Conclusions about Uncertain Democracies* (Baltimore: Johns Hopkins University Press, 1986), p. 19.

9. Philippe C. Schmitter, "The Influence of the International Context upon the Choice of National Institutions and Policies in Neo-Democracies," in *The International Dimensions of Democratization,* ed. Laurence Whitehead (Oxford, U.K.: Oxford University Press, 1996), p. 27.

10. Ibid., p. 31.

11. Ibid.

12. Stacy Vandeveer, "The State, Transnational Norms and International Organizations: Environmental Cooperation Around the Baltic," paper presented at the annual meeting of the American Political Science Association, Chicago, IL, 21 August–3 September 1995.

13. See Table 4 on "Export Reorientation of ECA Transition Economies," in *Foreign Trade in the Transition: The International Environment and Domestic Policy* (Washington, DC: World Bank, 1996), p. 24.

14. In addition to the chapters by Gertrude Schroeder and Bartlomiej Kaminski and Zhen Kun Wang in this volume, see Bartlomiej Kaminski, ed., *Economic Transition in Russia and the New States of Eurasia* (Armonk, NY: M.E. Sharpe, 1996); Anders Åslund, *How Russia Became a Market Economy* (Washington, DC: Brookings Institution, 1995).

15. Information on privatization is drawn from Gertrude Schroeder's chapter in this volume.

16. World Bank, *From Plan to Market: World Development Report 1996* (New York: Oxford University Press, 1996), pp.115–17.

17. "IMF Financing is Tied to Strong Remedial Policies," *IMF Survey,* September 1996, p. 11.

18. Huntington, *The Third Wave,* pp. 266–67.

19. See Vladimir Tismaneanu and Michael Turner, "Understanding Post-Leninism: Between Residual Leninism and Uncertain Pluralism," in *Political Culture and Civil Society in Russia and the New States of Eurasia,* ed. Vladimir Tismaneanu (Armonk, NY: M.E. Sharpe, 1995), p. 7.

20. See James L. Gibson, "The Resilience of Mass Support for Democratic Institutions and Processes in the Nascent Russian and Ukrainian Democracies," Jeffrey W. Hahn, "Changes in Contemporary Russian Political Culture," and Cynthia S. Kaplan, "Political Culture in Estonia: The Impact of Two Traditions on Political Development," all in Tismaneanu, *Political Culture and Civil Society in Russia and the New States of Eurasia;* see also William M. Reisinger, Arthur H. Miller, and Vicki Hesli, "Political Behavior Among Post-Soviet Republics," paper presented at the American Association for the Advancement of Slavic Studies, Washington, DC, 26–29 October 1995, p. 29. They find that political participation is generally high in terms of voting, but few citizens in Lithuania, Russia, and Ukraine belong to voluntary civil associations. It must also be noted that much of the information found in these studies is from 1990 and 1992, making their conclusions provisional.

21. According to public opinion research carried out by the United States Information Agency in 1994, the percentage of respondents having little to no confidence in the State Duma was 71 percent, the Council of Ministers 71 percent, the judicial system 67 percent, and local government 61 percent; see "Russians Disenchanted with Leaders and Institutions," *USIA Opinion Analysis,* M-40–95, 7 March 1995, pp. 2–4. A nationwide sampling of over 4,000 Russians in July 1995 found that 63 percent of the respondents felt that elected officials in Moscow were just interested in helping themselves. See White, Rose, and McAllister, *How Russia Votes,* p. 188.

22. Gibson, "The Resilience of Mass Support for Democratic Institutions and Processes, pp. 64–77.

23. See Dominique Arel, "Ukraine: The Temptation of the Nationalizing State," in Tismaneanu, *Political Culture and Civil Society in Russia and the New States of Eurasia.*

24. Joel S. Migdal, *Strong Societies and Weak States: State-Society Relations and State Capabilities in the Third World* (Princeton, NJ: Princeton University Press, 1988).

25. These themes of the rediscovery and invention of historical myths, national identities, and religious roots—and the impact of these journeys in each country on emerging polities—were the subject of the first three volumes of the Russian Littoral Project: *The Legacy of History in Russia and the New States of Eurasia,* ed. S. Frederick Starr (Armonk, NY: M.E. Sharpe, 1995); *National Identity and Ethnicity in Russia and the New States of Eurasia,* ed. Roman Szporluk (Armonk, NY: M.E. Sharpe, 1995); *The Politics of Religion in Russia and the New States of Eurasia,* ed. Michael Bourdeaux (Armonk, NY: M.E. Sharpe, 1995).

26. See Roger D. Kangas, "State Building and Civil Society in Central Asia," and Patricia M. Carley, "The Legacy of the Soviet Political System and the Prospects for Developing Civil Society in Central Asia," in Tismaneanu, *Political Culture and Civil Society in Russia and the New States of Eurasia.*

Appendix: Project Participants

List of Workshop Participants, 6–8 June 1996
*Five Years After the Fall: The Role of the Outside World in the
Transformation of the Former USSR*

Jonathan Aves, University of Sussex
George Breslauer, University of California at Berkeley
Yitzhak Brudny, Yale University
Adeed Dawisha, George Mason University
Karen Dawisha, University of Maryland
Peter Dombrowski, Iowa State University
Janine Draschner, Russian Littoral Project
Anne Dronnier, Idiom Linguistics
John Dunlop, Hoover Institution
Stewart Edelstein, University of Maryland
Murray Feshbach, Georgetown University
Raymond Garthoff, The Brookings Institution
Giorgi Gogsadze, Centre for Democratic Development and Conflict Resolution
Steve Grant, U.S. Information Agency
Virginia Haufler, University of Maryland
Bakhtior Islamov, Macroeconomic Project
Bartlomiej Kaminski, University of Maryland
Kemal Karpat, University of Wisconsin
Mark Katz, George Mason University
Daniel Kaufmann, Harvard University
Andrei Kortunov, Russian Science Foundation
Andrew Kuchins, MacArthur Foundation
Wayne Limberg, Department of State
Nancy Lubin, JNA Associates, Inc.

Ambassador Jack Matlock, Columbia University
Rebecca Matlock, Columbia University
Michael MccGwire, Cambridge University
Marie Mendras, Centre d'Études et de Recherches Internationales
Branko Milanovic, The World Bank
Bruce Parrott, School of Advanced International Studies
    Vyacheslau Paznyak, International Institute for Policy Studies
Margaret Pearson, University of Maryland
Dennis Pirages, University of Maryland
Ilya Prizel, School of Advanced International Studies
Aline Quester, Center for Naval Analyses
George Quester, University of Maryland
Gilbert Rozman, Princeton University
Alvin Z. Rubinstein, University of Pennsylvania
Nikolai Rudensky, Institute for the Economy in Transition
Miranda Schreurs, University of Maryland
Gertrude Schroeder, University of Virginia
Robert Sharlet, Union College
Mary Sladek
Angela Stent, Georgetown University
Stephen Szabo, School of Advanced International Studies
Vladimir Tismaneanu, University of Maryland
Michael Turner, University of Maryland
Yuri Urbanovich, University of Virginia
Peeter Vares, Institute of International and Social Studies
Celeste Wallander, Harvard University
Adam Wasserman, Central Intelligence Agency
Jonathan Wilkenfeld, University of Maryland
Trevor Wysong, University of Maryland

Index to Volume 10

Cumulative Subject Index
(Tables of Contents)

Cumulative Geographic Index

Cumulative List of Participants

The following people have participated in the series of Russian Littoral Project conferences and workshops upon which the ten volumes of the International Politics of Eurasia series is based:

Abdujabar Abduvakthitov, Meros Academy, Tashkent
Ermias Abebe, University of Maryland
Dan Abele, Woodrow Wilson Center
Rakhat Achylova, Bishkek University
Irina Akimushkina, Russian People's Friendship Treaty
Vasilii Aksionov, George Mason University
Olga Alexandrova, Federal Institute for Russian, East European, and International Studies
Kadir Alimov, University of World Economy and Diplomacy, Tashkent
Roy Allison, Royal Institute of International Affairs
Rafal Antczak, Center for Social and Economic Research, Warsaw
Ibrahim Arafat, Cairo University
Andrei Artamonov, Embassy of Russia
Jonathan Aves, University of Sussex
Kathleen Avvakumovits, School of Advanced International Studies
Nicholas Babiak, The Washington Group
Charles Ball, Stanford University
Igor Barsegian, Institute of Philosophy and Law, Erevan
Mykola Basyluk
Mark Beissinger, University of Wisconsin
Serhii Bilokin, Institute of History, Kiev
The Honorable Oleh Bilorus, Ambassador of Ukraine
Britta Bjornlund, School of Advanced International Studies
Sally Blair, U.S. Institute of Peace
Stephen Blank, U.S. Army War College
Will Blunt, Boston University
Bohdan Bociurkiw, Carleton College
Samargul Borbieva, Embassy of Kyrgyzstan
Andrei Bouchkin, Institute of World Economy and International Studies
Rev. Canon Michael Bourdeaux, Keston Research, Oxford

Wayne Bowman, U.S. Information Agency
Hilary Brandt, University of Maryland
George Breslauer, University of California at Berkeley
Jeffrey Brooks, The Johns Hopkins University
Bess Brown, Radio Free Europe/Radio Liberty Research Institute
Betty Brown, University of Maryland
Yitzhak Brudny, Yale University
Abraham Brumberg, Chevy Chase, Maryland
Laurie MacDonald Brumberg, American Bar Association
Oleg Bukharin, Moscow Institute of Physics and Technology
Liazat Buranbayeva, Export-Import Bank of Kazakhstan
Boris Burkinsky, Academy of Sciences of Ukraine
Barbara Butterton, Institute on Global Conflict and Cooperation
Patricia Carley, U.S. Institute of Peace
Cliff Chanin, The Rockefeller Foundation
Fr. Vsevolod Chaplin, Moscow Patriarchate
Anita Chapman, Washington Baha'i Community
Jeffrey Checkel, University of Pittsburgh
Galina Cherednichenko, Odessa State Economics University
Martha Chomiak, National Endowment for the Humanities
Peter Clement, Central Intelligence Agency
David Coder, National Endowment for the Humanities
Steve Coffey, U.S. Department of State
Simon Commander, The World Bank
Heather Conley, U.S. Department of State
Julian Cooper, University of Birmingham
Phil Costopolous, Journal for Democracy
John Crosson, School of Advanced International Studies
Kenneth Cummings, University of Maryland
Kenneth Currie, U.S. Army War College
Marek Dabrowski, Center for Social and Economic Research, Warsaw
Khadisa Dairova, Embassy of Kazakhstan
Catherine Dale, U.S. Institute of Peace
Roland Dannreuther, International Institute for Strategic Studies
John Danylyk, U.S. Department of State
Christopher Davis, Oxford University
Ron Davis, U.S. Department of State
Toby Davis, U.S. Department of State
Adeed Dawisha, George Mason University
Karen Dawisha, University of Maryland
Rev. Stan De Boe, St. John De Matha Monastery
Dorothy Delahanty, U.S. Department of State
Renee de Nevers, International Institute for Strategic Studies and Hoover Institution
Robert Destro, Catholic University
Dieter Dettke, The Friedrich Ebert Stiftung
Nadia Diuk, National Endowment for the Humanities
Orest Diychak, U.S. Department of State
Richard Dobson, U.S. Information Agency
Tracy Dolan, School of Advanced International Studies
Peter Dombrowski, Iowa State University
Janine Draschner, Russian Littoral Project

Mary Ann Drinan, Palomar College
Patrick Drinan, University of San Diego
Anne Dronnier, Idiom Linguistics
Nora Dudwick, The Kennan Institute
John Dunlop, Hoover Institution
Robert Edelman, University of California at San Diego
Stewart Edelstein, University of Maryland
Massoud Eghbarieh, University of Maryland
Arun Elhance, Social Science Research Council
Ulughbek Eshankhojayov, Embassy of Uzbekistan
Charles Fairbanks, School of Advanced International Studies
Murray Feshbach, Georgetown University
John Finerty, Commission on Security and Cooperation in Europe
Carole Fink, Ohio State University
Rosemarie Forsythe, National Security Council
Clifford Foust, University of Maryland
Martyna Fox, U.S. Department of State
Marcus Franda, University of Maryland
Mykola Fransuzhenko, Voice of America
Lawrence Freedman, Department of War Studies, King's College
Robert Freedman, Baltimore Hebrew University
Leonid Friedman, Moscow State University
Sherman Garnett, Carnegie Endowment for International Peace
Raymond Garthoff, The Brookings Institution
Valerie Gartseff, Voice of America
Philip Gillette, Old Dominion University
Heather Giordanella, Central Connecticut State University
John Glad, University of Maryland
Paul Goble, Carnegie Endowment for International Peace
Robert Goeckel, State University of New York at Geneseo
Giorgi Gogsadze, Centre for Democratic Development and Conflict Resolution
David Goldfrank, Georgetown University
Olexander Gorin, Kiev University
Nubar Goudsouzian, School of Advanced International Studies
Thomas Graham, U.S. Department of State
Steven Grant, U.S. Information Agency
Patrick Gray, Institute of Religion and Democracy
Victor Gray, University of Maryland
Hrach Gregorian, U.S. Institute of Peace
Fr. Dmitrii Gregorieff, Orthodox Church in America
Sergei Gretsky, Advisor, Muslim Spiritual Board, Tajikistan
Richard Grimes, Central Intelligence Agency
Eerik Gross, Embassy of Estonia
Steve Guenther, School of Advanced International Studies
Jon Gundersen, U.S. Department of State
Alec Guroff, Center for Strategic and International Studies
Greg Guroff, Center for Post-Soviet Studies
Larisa Gutsu, National College of Commerce, Chisinau
Vladimir Gutsu, Ministry of Privatization, Moldova
Lubomyr Hajda, Harvard Ukrainian Research Center
Kathleen Hancock, University of California at San Diego

John P. Hardt, Congressional Research Service
Dadahan Hasanov, Islamic Democratic Party for Turkestan
Griffin Hathaway, University of Maryland
Virginia Haufler, University of Maryland
Peter Hauslohner, formerly U.S. Department of State
Martin Heisler, University of Maryland
Anne Herr, U.S. Department of State
Nancy Hewitt, U.S. Department of State
Elaine Holoboth, Department of War Studies, King's College
Yurij Holowinsky
Shireen Hunter, Center for Strategic and International Studies
Robert Hutchings, Woodrow Wilson Center
Mahir Ibrahimov, Embassy of Azerbaijan
Irina Isakova, Institute of USA and Canada
Timus Isataev, International Monetary Fund
Bakhtior Islamov, Macroeconomic Project
Jon Jacobson, University of California at Irvine
Philip Johnston, School of Advanced International Studies
Abram Kagan, University of Maryland
Frederick Kagan
Miles Kahler, University of California at San Diego
Aleksander Kaliberda, The World Bank, Kiev
The Honorable Ojars Kalnins, Ambassador of Latvia
Bartlomiej Kaminski, University of Maryland
Cynthia Kaplan, University of California at Santa Barbara
Olga Karazhas, American University
Kemal Karpat, University of Wisconsin
Oumirseric Kasenov, Kazakhstan Institute for Strategic Studies
Mark Katz, George Mason University
Edy Kaufman, University of Maryland
Daniel Kaufmann, Harvard University
Catherine Kelleher, The Brookings Institution
Davlat Khudonazarev, Kennan Institute
Judith Kipper, The Brookings Institution
Jutta Klapisch, Friedrich Ebert Stiftung
Israel Kleiner, Voice of America
Amy Knight, Congressional Research Service
Mark Koenig, University of Maryland
Patricia Kolb, M.E. Sharpe, Inc.
Mikhail Korchemkin, East European Gas Analysis, Inc.
Viktor Korovin, Academy of Sciences of Ukraine
Andrei Kortunov, Russian Science Foundation
Fr. Ted Kravchuk, Ukrainian Catholic National Shrine
Major General Nicholas Krawciw, U.S. Army, ret.
Dmitriy Kreshenko, Odessa State University
Andrew Kuchins, MacArthur Foundation
Valeri Kuchinsky, Embassy of Ukraine
Nikolai Kulinich, Ukrainian Institute of International Relations
Erjan Kurbanov, Moscow State University
Rafik Kurbanov, Institute of Philosophy, Moscow
Fyodor Kushnirsky, Temple University

Taras Kuzio, School of Slavonic and East European Studies, University of London
Yevgeny Kuznetsov, Institute of Economic Forecasting, Moscow
Michael LaCivita, Catholic Near East Magazine
David Lake, University of California at San Diego
Lee LaMora, Jamestown Foundation
Gail Lapidus, Stanford University
Irena Lasota, Institute for Democracy in Eastern Europe
Murat Laumulin, Ministry of Foreign Affairs, Kazakhstan
Kim Lawton, News Network International
Eve Lebo, Central Intelligence Agency
Jack Lebo
John Lepingwell, Radio Free Europe/Radio Liberty Research Institute
Larisa Leshchenko, Central European University
Laura Libanati, American Enterprise Foundation
Wayne Limberg, U.S. Department of State
Valentina Limonchenko, U.S. Information Agency
George Liska, School of Advanced International Studies
Fr. Taras Lonchyna, Ukrainian Catholic Church
The Honorable Stasys Lozoraitis, Ambassador of Lithuania
Nancy Lubin, JNA Associates, Inc.
Petr Lunak, School of Advanced International Studies
Jane Madden, The World Bank
George Majeska, University of Maryland
Michael Mandelbaum, School of Advanced International Studies
Serif Mardin, The American University
Malgorzata Markiewicz, National Bank of Poland
Vasyl Markus, Loyola University and Encyclopedia of Ukraine
Jim Martin, U.S. Department of State
The Honorable Sergei Martynov, Charge d'Affaires, Embassy of Belarus
Sergei Martynovsky, Ukrainian State Academy of Communications
Ambassador Jack Matlock, Columbia University
Rebecca Matlock, Columbia University
Dan Matuszewski, IREX
Stanislav Matveyev, Odessa State Economics University
Ali Mazrui, State University of New York at Binghamton
Michael MccGwire, Cambridge University
Paul McDonough, School of Advanced International Studies
Mary McIntosh, U.S. Information Agency
Nancy Meech, School of Advanced International Studies
Melissa Meeker, Center for Strategic and International Studies
Walter Melnik, University of Maryland
Natalia Melnyczuk, U.S. Institute of Peace
Zoya Mendjuk, Congress of Russian-Americans
Marie Mendras, Centre d'Études et de Recherches Internationales
Sergei Mikoyan, Institute of Peace, Moscow
Branko Milanovic, The World Bank
James Millar, George Washington University
Steven Miller, Harvard University
George Mirsky, Institute of World Economy and International Relations
Piotr Mishchenko, United Nations
Jayhun Molla-zade, Embassy of Azerbaijan

Steven Muller, School of Advanced International Studies
David Mussington, International Institute for Strategic Studies
Kendall Myers, Foreign Service Institute
Yuri Mylko, U.S. Department of State
Michael Nacht, University of Maryland
David Naile, Central Asia Monitor
Anatolii Naimin, Kennan Institute
Galina Naimin, St. John the Baptist, Russian Orthodox Church
Rusi Nasar, Central Asia Associates
Seyyed Hossein Nasr, George Washington University
Vali Nasr, University of San Diego
Craig Nation, The Johns Hopkins University Bologna Center
Tom Navratil, U.S. Department of State
Susan Nelson, U.S. Department of State
Natalia Novgrodskaya, Institute of Far Eastern Studies
Michael Oakes, Helsinki Committee
Piotr Ogrodzinski, Ministry of Foreign Affairs, Poland
Daniel Olsen, St. John the Baptist, Russian Orthodox Church
Nurbek Omuraliev, Institute of Philosophy, Bishkek
Mark Orzikh, Odessa State University
Elizabeth O'Shea, Central Intelligence Agency
Elena Osokina, The Kennan Institute
Gueorgiu Otyrba, Abkhazia State University
Soli Ozel, School of Advanced International Studies
Sergei Panchekhin, Embassy of Russia
Bruce Parrott, School of Advanced International Studies
Fiona Paton, Department of War Studies, King's College
Vyacheslau Paznyak, Centre for Strategic Initiatives, Minsk
Margaret Pearson, University of Maryland
Marta Peryma, U.S. Information Agency
Phillip Petersen, The Potomac Foundation
Linda Petrou, University of Maryland
Wolfgang Pfeiler, Ernst Mortiz Arndt University
Dennis Pirages, University of Maryland
Diana Pisheva, University of Delaware
Fr. Hryhory Podaurec, St. Andrew's Orthodox Church
Dimitry Ponomareff, Department of Defense
Vasilii Pospelov, Embassy of Russia
Maria Potapov, St. John the Baptist, Russian Orthodox Church
Mark Potapov, St. John the Baptist, Russian Orthodox Church
William Potter, Monterey Institute of International Studies
Jerry Powers, U.S. Catholic Conference
Alex Pravda, Oxford University
Algimantas Prazauskas, Institute of Oriental Studies, Moscow
Serik Primbetov, Interstate Council of Kazakhstan, Kyrgyzstan, and Uzbekistan
Ilya Prizel, School of Advanced International Studies
Aleksandr Prokopenko, Vice-Mayor of Odessa
Aline Quester, Center for Naval Analyses
George Quester, University of Maryland
Christine Quickenden, University of Maryland
Kevin Quigley, Pew Charitable Trusts

Bohdan Radejko, The Washington Group
Vladimir Rakhmanin, Embassy of Russia
George Reardon-Anderson, Georgetown University
Marion Recktenwald, University of Maryland
Peter Reddaway, The George Washington University
Kjetil Ribe, Department of War Studies, King's College
Alvin Richman, U.S. Information Agency
Fr. Ron Roberson, St. Paul's College
Philip Roeder, University of California at San Diego
Sergei Romanenko, Institute of Slavonic and Balkan Studies, Moscow
Richard Rosecrance, University of California at Los Angeles
Robert Rotberg, Harvard University
Eric Rothberg, Central Intelligence Agency
Anatolii Rozanov, Belarusian State University
Gilbert Rozman, Princeton University
Eric Ruben
Trudy Rubin, The Philadelphia Enquirer
Alvin Rubinstein, University of Pennsylvania
Blair Ruble, Kennan Institute
Nikolai Rudensky, Institute for Economy in Transition, Moscow
Richard Rudolph, University of Minnesota
Elena Ruseva, Odessa State Economics University
David Russell, The Kennan Institute
Dankwart Rustow, City University of New York
Elena Sadovskaya, University of Maryland
Igor Safonov, International Information Academy
Sayed Said, International Institute of Islamic Thought
George Sajewych, Window on America
Barri Sanders, University of Maryland
Mark Saroyan, Harvard University
Maroud Sattarov, Tashkent State Economics University
Anna Scherbakova, Monterey Institute for International Studies
Gertrude Schroeder, University of Virginia
Miranda Schreurs, University of Maryland
Lee Schwartz, U.S. Department of State
Martin Schwartz, Central Intelligence Agency
Janice Sebring, Central Intelligence Agency
Alexandra Service, St. John the Baptist, Russian Orthodox Church
Cevdet Seyhan, Voice of America
Tatiana Shakleina, Institute of USA and Canada Studies, Moscow
Nasir Shanseb, Democracy International
Robert Sharlet, Union College
Maxim Shashenkov, Oxford University
Gary Shenk, School of Advanced International Studies
Natalia Shevchenko, St. John the Baptist, Russian Orthodox Church
Lilia Shevtsova, The Kennan Institute
Avi Shlaim, Oxford University
Rouben Shugarian, Embassy of Armenia
Nikolai Shutov, Odessa City Council
Miraj Siddiqi, Metro International
Yuri Sigov, '*Vek*' Moscow Weekly

Aida Simonia, Institute of Oriental Studies, Moscow
Nodari Simonia, Institute of World Economy and International Studies
Mary Singer, Central Intelligence Agency
Nikolai Sirotkin, Voice of America
Mikhail Sivertsev, Institute of USA and Canada Studies, Moscow
Mary Sladek, National Science Foundation
Sonya Sluzar, U.S. Department of State
Amy Smith, Kennan Institute
Christopher Smith, Pew Charitable Trusts
Robert Snyder, Christian Science Organization
Anatolii Solianik, International Center for Policy Studies, Kiev
John Sontag, U.S. Department of State
David Speedie, The Carnegie Corporation
Hendrik Spruyt, Columbia University
S. Frederick Starr, The Aspen Institute
Peter Stavrakis, The Kennan Institute
Jim Steiner, U.S. Department of State
Angela Stent, Georgetown University
Elena Suhir, The World Bank
Yurii Suhir, The World Bank
Ronald Suny, University of Chicago
Evgen Sverstiuk, *Nasha Vera*, Kiev
Marilyn Swezey, Holy Archangels Broadcasting Center
Stephen Szabo, School of Advanced International Studies
Darius Szwarcewicz, School of Advanced International Studies
Roman Szporluk, Harvard University
Rasim Tajuddin, Khazar University, Baku
Nadia Tangour, U.S. Department of State
Lowry Taylor, U.S. Department of State
Thomas Thornton, Georgetown University
Vladimir Tismaneanu, University of Maryland
Andrew Torre, School of Advanced International Studies
Andrei Tsygankov, George Washington University
Misha Tsypkin, Naval Post-Graduate School, Monterey
Astrid Tuminez, Carnegie Corporation
Michael Turner, University of Maryland
Vadim Udalov, Embassy of Russia
Anthony Ugolnik, Franklin and Marshall College
Joan Barth Urban, Catholic University
Yuri Urbanovich, University of Virginia
Ruth Urell, Amnesty International
Ekaterina Usova, Institute for Oriental Studies, Moscow
Stacy VanDeveer, University of Maryland
Lauren Van Metre, Center for Naval Analyses
Peeter Vares, Institute of International and Social Studies
Phillippe Voiry, School of Advanced International Studies
Vladimir Volkov, Institute of Slavic and Balkan Studies, Moscow
Jim Voorhees, Congressional Research Service
Aleksei Voskressensky, Institute of Far Eastern Studies, Moscow
Martin Walker, The Guardian
Celeste Wallander, Harvard University

Solomon Wank, Franklin and Marshall College
Sheila Ward, School of Advanced International Studies
Adam Wasserman, U.S. Department of State
Fr. Alexander Webster, Romanian Episcopate, OCA
Fred Wehling, University of California at San Diego
Carola Weil, University of Maryland
Jonathan Wilkenfeld, University of Maryland
David Wilkinson, University of California at Los Angeles
Elizabeth Wishnick, U.S. Information Agency
Sharon Wolchik, George Washington University
Susan Woodward, The Brookings Institution
Trevor Wysong, University of Maryland
Alexander Yakunin
Fr. Gleb Yakunin, Russian Parliament
Vladimir Yanin, Embassy of Russia
Oleg Yaroshin, Catholic University
Mary Yntema, School of Advanced International Studies
Volodymyr Zabihailo, Embassy of Ukraine
Tom Zamostny, U.S. Department of State
Jan Zaprudnik, Belarusan Institute of Science and Arts
Lena Zezulin, Slevin and Hart
Madeline Zilfi, University of Maryland
Marc Zlotnik, National Intelligence Council
Vladislav Zubok, Institute of USA and Canada Studies, Moscow
Vladimir Zviglyanich, George Washington University
Karmit Zysman, International Azerbaijan Research and Development Institute